The University of Law
incorporating The College of Law

THE OXFORD INTERNATIONAL LAW LIBRARY

THE OXFORD INTERNATIONAL LAW LIBRARY

General Editor: SIR FRANK BERMAN KCMG QC

This series features works on substantial topics in international law which provide authoritative statements of the chosen areas. Taken together they map out the whole of international law in a set of scholarly reference works and treatises intended to be of use to scholars, practitioners, and students.

The Law of Investment Treaties

Second Edition

JESWALD W. SALACUSE

OXFORD
UNIVERSITY PRESS

OXFORD
UNIVERSITY PRESS

Great Clarendon Street, Oxford, OX2 6DP,
United Kingdom

Oxford University Press is a department of the University of Oxford.
It furthers the University's objective of excellence in research, scholarship,
and education by publishing worldwide. Oxford is a registered trade mark of
Oxford University Press in the UK and in certain other countries

© Jeswald W. Salacuse 2015

The moral rights of the author have been asserted

First Edition published in 2010
Second Edition published in 2015

Impression: 1

Published in the United States of America by Oxford University Press
198 Madison Avenue, New York, NY 10016, United States of America

British Library Cataloguing in Publication Data
Data available

Library of Congress Control Number: 2015931228

ISBN 978–0–19–870397–6

Printed and bound by
CPI Group (UK) Ltd, Croydon, CR0 4YY

For Donna, Bill, Maria, Mike, Glen, Jack,
Anna, Olivia, and Miles

Preface to the Second Edition

The nations of the world have made approximately 3,300 investment treaties since the end of World War II. Investment treaty-making continues unabated as new agreements emerge almost monthly from diplomatic negotiations. The rapid growth in investment treaties has led to a burgeoning number of international arbitration decisions that have applied and interpreted treaty provisions in disputes between investors and states concerning their respective rights. One result of this flurry of treaties and arbitral decisions has been the creation of a new branch of international law—the law of investment treaties. This new law has been both a consequence and a cause of the increasing economic globalization and vast growth in capital movements that have characterized the last half of the twentieth century and the beginning of the twenty-first. Investment treaties have become important factors that corporate executives, lawyers, bankers, and government officials must consider in planning, executing, and managing foreign investments.

The purpose of this book is to examine the law of international investment treaties, particularly with respect to its origins, structure, content, and effects. As a new body of law, it presents many problems that have yet to be resolved and many questions with answers that are at best tentative. It is truly a law in full evolution. At the same time, it also grapples with ancient problems that date from the time that the first investor ventured abroad to undertake activities in the territory of a foreign sovereign.

The first edition of this book was published in 2010. Since that time, the law of international investment treaties has both experienced considerable growth and generated considerable controversy. Its growth has been manifested primarily in the increased number of treaties negotiated and arbitral decisions rendered. The treaties concluded in the last five years, while building on the concepts employed in earlier international agreements, have also included new elements shaped by prior experience in actually applying treaty texts to the complex world of international investment. The many arbitral decisions issued in the last half decade refined earlier interpretations of treaty provisions and at the same time have demonstrated a tendency to handle larger and larger cases and to grant injured investors increasing amounts of damages, culminating in July 2014 with awards in the Yukos cases under the Energy Charter Treaty of over US$50 billion, surely a historic record for any arbitration.

The controversy in the field has primarily revolved around the investor–state dispute settlement process, which has thus far involved at least ninety-eight states as respondents. Governments and sympathetic international organizations have questioned its high costs, its large awards, the legitimacy and fairness of its procedures, and its alleged curtailment of state sovereignty and governments' right to regulate. In reaction, many governments, international institutions, and non-governmental organizations have pressed for reform, and a few states have gone so far as to withdraw from investment treaties and from the International Centre for Settlement of Investment Disputes (ICSID), the principal investor–state dispute settlement institution. Despite the controversy, at the beginning of 2015, some eighty-eight countries were nonetheless actively engaged in negotiating at least seven broad regional and interregional trade and investment arrangements based on investment treaties and investor–state dispute settlement processes. The second edition of *The Law of Investment Treaties* has sought to capture all of these developments. As a result, each chapter has been expanded. Moreover, the book has added a new Chapter 16 on the consequences of treaty violations and the determination of damages in investor–state disputes.

In preparing the second edition of the book, I received invaluable assistance from Mitchell Moranis, Claudio Guler, and Aditya Sarkar to whom I express thanks. I have worked in the field of investment treaty law for nearly forty years as teacher, scholar, legal consultant, investment company director, and arbitrator. During that time, I have benefited from instructive conversations with countless lawyers, government officials, scholars, arbitrators, and international experts in many disciplines on the complexities of international investment and the law. They are too numerous to list here by name but I am deeply grateful to all of them for helping me understand this rapidly evolving branch of international law.

Jeswald W. Salacuse
Henry J Braker Professor of Law
The Fletcher School of Law and Diplomacy
Tufts University

Medford, Massachusetts
5 November 2014

Contents—Summary

Contents

List of Abbreviations

ACIA	ASEAN Comprehensive Investment Agreement
ADR	alternative dispute resolution
ASEAN	Association of Southeast Asian Nations
BIT	bilateral investment treaty
CAFTA-DR	Dominican Republic–Central America–United States Free Trade Agreement
CETA	Canada–EU Comprehensive Economic and Trade Agreement
CISS	Comprehensive Import Supervision Services
COMESA	Common Market for Eastern and Southern Africa
CRF	Clean Report of Findings
DCF	discounted cash flow
DFI	direct foreign investment
EAC	East African Community
ECJ	European Court of Justice
ECT	Energy Charter Treaty
EISIL	Electronic Information System for International Law
EPA	economic partnership agreement
FCN	friendship, commerce, and navigation (treaty)
FDI	foreign direct investment
FIC	Foreign Investment Commission (Chile)
FIPA	Foreign Investment Protection Agreement
FTA	free trade agreement
FTC	Free Trade Commission (NAFTA)
GAOR	General Assembly Official Records (UN)
GATS	General Agreement on Trade in Services (WTO)
GATT	General Agreement on Tariffs and Trade (WTO)
IBRD	International Bank for Reconstruction and Development
ICC	International Chamber of Commerce
ICJ	International Court of Justice
ICMA	International Capital Market Association
ICSID	International Centre for Settlement of Investment Disputes
IFC	International Finance Corporation
IIA	international investment agreement
IPPA	Investment Promotion and Protection Agreement
ITO	International Trade Organization
MAI	Multilateral Agreement on Investment
Mercosur	Common Market of the Southern Cone (Argentina, Brazil, Paraguay, Uruguay and Venezuela)
MFN	most-favoured-nation (clause)
MIGA	Multilateral Investment Guarantee Agency
MNC	multinational corporation
MNE	multinational enterprise
NAAEC	North American Agreement on Environmental Cooperation

NAFTA	North American Free Trade Agreement
NGO	non-governmental organization
NIEO	New International Economic Order
OECD	Organization for Economic Cooperation and Development
OIC	Organization of Islamic Cooperation (formerly Organization of the Islamic Conference)
IMF	International Monetary Fund
OPIC	Overseas Private Insurance Corporation
PSI	Pre-Shipment Inspection
RCEP	Regional Comprehensive Economic Partnership (of ASEAN countries)
SCE	state-controlled entity
SADC	Southern African Development Community
SLD	Softwood Lumber Division (Canadian government agency)
SOE	state-owned enterprise
SWF	sovereign wealth fund
TEU	Treaty on European Union
TFEU	Treaty on the Functioning of the European Union
TNC	transnational corporation
TPP	Trans-Pacific Partnership
TRIM	trade-related investment measure
TRIMs	Agreement on Trade-Related Investment Measures
TTIP	EU–United States Transatlantic Trade and Investment Partnership
UNCITRAL	United Nations Commission on International Trade Law
UNCTAD	United Nations Conference on Trade and Development
UNCTC	United Nations Centre on Transnational Corporations
UNGA	United Nations General Assembly
UNRIAA	Reports of International Arbitral Awards (UN)
VCLT	Vienna Convention on the Law of Treaties
WTO	World Trade Organization

Table of Cases

Table of Conventions, Treaties, and Agreements

DRAFT AGREEMENTS

1

A Global Regime for Investment

1.1 Introduction to Investment Treaties

Since the end of World War II, the nations of the world have been engaged in building a global regime for investment through the negotiation of investment treaties. Investment treaties, often referred to as 'international investment agreements' (IIAs), are essentially instruments of international law by which states (1) make commitments to other states with respect to the treatment they will accord to investors and investments from those other states, and (2) agree to some mechanism for enforcement of those commitments. A fundamental purpose of investment treaties, as indicated by their titles, is to protect and promote investment.[1]

International investment treaties consist principally of three types: (1) bilateral investment treaties, commonly known as 'BITs'; (2) bilateral economic agreements with investment provisions; and (3) other investment-related agreements involving more than two states. At the beginning of 2014, the total number of all investment treaties, according to the United Nations Conference on Trade and Development (UNCTAD), was 3,236, consisting of 2,902 BITs and 334 other types of international investment agreements.[2] Approximately 180 countries had signed at least one of them.[3]

BITs, as their name indicates, exclusively govern investment relations between two signatory states. The degree to which individual countries have participated in concluding BITs has varied. For example, 41 per cent of all BITs concluded as of 2014 were between a developing and a developed country (ie 'north-south agreements'), while only 9 per cent were between developed countries (ie 'north-north agreements').[4] Agreements among developing

---

[1] eg Treaty Concerning the Reciprocal Encouragement and Protection of Investment (United States–Armenia) (23 September 1992) S Treaty Doc No 1993103-11; Treaty Concerning the Promotion and Reciprocal Protection of Investments (Germany–Poland) (10 November 1989) (1990) 29 ILM 333; Agreement for the Promotion and Protection of Investments (Indonesia–United Kingdom) (27 April 1976), Treaty Series No 62. US bilateral investment treaties (BITs) tend to refer to the 'encouragement of investment', rather than the 'promotion of investment'. Based on an analysis of BIT provisions, it appears that the two terms, encouragement and promotion, have the same meaning.
[2] UNCTAD, *World Investment Report 2014* (2014) 114.
[3] For a listing of countries that have signed BITs and other investment agreements, see ibid 222–5.
[4] ibid 123.

countries ('south-south agreements') accounted for 27 per cent of the total. And while Germany, by the beginning of 2014, led the world in the number of signed investment treaties, having concluded 134 BITs and sixty-two other international investment agreements making a total of 196, with China having signed 130 BITs and seventeen other IIAs,[5] certain other states, like Somalia and North Korea, had signed very few. Moreover, even if a state signs an international investment agreement, its governing authorities may refuse to ratify it or subject ratification to long delays. Brazil, for example, signed fourteen BITs during the 1990s but as of the beginning of 2014 had failed to ratify any of them.[6]

In addition to BITs, which concern investment only, various other bilateral agreements of an economic nature also contain investment provisions. Among the most important of these are modern free trade agreements, such as those pursued by the United States,[7] and economic partnership and cooperation treaties, like those advanced by Japan,[8] which contain chapters on investment that replicate many of the provisions in BITs. As of 2014, 334 such agreements were in existence. In addition, one must also consider earlier bilateral commercial and trade agreements, such as the Treaties of Friendship, Commerce, and Navigation negotiated by the United States with numerous countries, which often include provisions that affect foreign investments and can become the basis for international litigation to protect investor interests.[9]

Investment treaties as a group include more than strictly bilateral agreements. Numerous treaties with more than two state parties set down important enforceable international rules concerning foreign investment. These include the North American Free Trade Agreement (NAFTA),[10] a treaty among the United States, Canada, and Mexico, in which one chapter, Chapter 11, is itself an investment treaty, and the Energy Charter Treaty (ECT),[11] a multilateral convention among fifty-one countries, setting down rules for trade and investment in the energy sector. Also included in the group of multilateral treaties are various regional international arrangements such as the Unified Agreement for the Investment of Arab

---

[5] ibid 223–5.

[6] See YZ Haftel and A Thompson, 'Delayed Ratification: The Domestic Fate of Bilateral Investment Treaties' (2013) 67 Int'l Org 355, 357.

[7] eg United States–Colombia Trade Promotion Agreement (signed 22 November 2006), US Trade Representative website, at <http://www.ustr.gov/trade-agreements> accessed 1 September 2009.

[8] M Yasushi, 'Economic Partnership Agreements and Japanese Strategy' (2006) 6(3) Gaiko Forum 53; see also S Yanase, 'Bilateral Investment Treaties of Japan and Resolution of Investment Disputes with Respect to Foreign Direct Investment' in AJ van den Berg (ed), *International Commercial Arbitration* (Kluwer Law International, 2003) 426.

[9] eg *Case concerning Elletronica Sicula spa (ELSI), (United States of America v Italy)* [1989] ICJ 15 (applying the 1948 Treaty of Friendship, Commerce and Navigation between Italy and the US); see also *Case concerning Oil Platforms (Islamic Republic of Iran v United States of America)* [2003] ICJ Rep 161 (applying 1955 Treaty of Amity, Economic Relations and Consular Rights between the US and Iran).

[10] North American Free Trade Agreement (United States–Canada–Mexico) (17 December 1992) (1993) 32 ILM 289.

[11] European Energy Charter Treaty (opened for signature 1 February 1995) (1995) 34 ILM 360.

Capital in the Arab States,[12] the Association of Southeast Asia Nations' (ASEAN) Comprehensive Investment Agreement,[13] and the Dominican Republic-Central America-United States Free Trade Agreement (CAFTA-DR),[14] often referred to simply as 'CAFTA', a grouping of the United States and six central American states, which includes an investment chapter similar to that of the NAFTA. In addition, it is worth mentioning that the Treaty on the Functioning of the European Union,[15] which governs the most economically important regional grouping in the world, also contains important provisions concerning investment within the European Union.

As a result of the surge in treaty-making undertaken by states since the end of World War II, the total number of treaties with meaningful provisions relating to foreign investment as of the beginning of 2014 probably exceeded 3,300. That number is certain to grow as states continue to negotiate significant numbers of investment treaties each year.[16] An important support mechanism for this emerging international investment regime has been and will continue to be the International Centre for Settlement of Investment Disputes (ICSID), which was formally established in 1966 as an affiliate of the World Bank to resolve disputes between host countries and foreign private investors.[17] Although ICSID did not hear its first case until 1972, it has become an important institution for international investment dispute resolution.[18] It is through the dispute resolution process that substantive treaty commitments towards

[12] 'Unified Agreement for the Investment of Arab Capital in the Arab States' in *Economic Documents* (Tunis: League of Arab States) No 3, UNCTAD website (original language: Arabic), at <http://investmentpolicyhub.unctad.org/Download/TreatyFile/2394> accessed 9 September 2014.

[13] ASEAN Comprehensive Investment Agreement, signed 26 February 2009, entered into force 29 March 2012. This Agreement terminated and replaced the previous investment agreements among the ASEAN states, notably the Agreement for the Promotion and Protection of Investments of 1987. ASEAN website, at <http://www.asean.org/images/2012/Economic/AIA/Agreement/ASEAN%20Comprehensive%20Investment%20Agreement%20(ACIA)%202012.pdf> accessed 9 September 2014.

[14] For text of CAFTA-DR, see the website of the US Trade Representative at <http://www.ustr.gov/trade-agreements/free-trade-agreements/cafta-dr-dominican-republic-central-america-fta/final-text> accessed 9 January 2015.

[15] European Union: Consolidated Version of the Treaty on the Functioning of the European Union [2012] OJ C329/49, available at <http://eur-lex.europa.eu/legal-content/EN/TXT/?uri=CELEX:12012E/TXT> accessed 9 January 2015. See particularly, Title IV, Free Movement of Persons, Services and Capital.

[16] eg UNCTAD has determined that in 2014, 44 new international investment treaties were signed and that many states were actively engaged in the negotiation of 'megaregional agreements', defined as 'broad economic agreements among a group of countries that together have significant economic weight and in which investment is only one of several subjects'. 'Megaregional agreements' include the Trans-Pacific Partnership (TPP), the EU–United States Transatlantic Trade and Investment Partnership (TTIP), and the Canada–EU Comprehensive Economic and Trade Agreement (CETA). UNCTAD, *World Investment Report 2014* (2014) 118.

[17] Convention on the Settlement of Investment Disputes between States and the Nationals of Other States (18 March 1965) 17 UST 1270; 575 UNTS 159.

[18] 'List of Concluded Cases', International Centre for Settlement of Investment Disputes website, at <http://icsid.worldbank.org/ICSID/FrontServlet?requestType=GenCaseDtlsRH&actionVal= ListConcluded> accessed 18 August 2014 (listing concluded cases in chronological order).

investments and investors from other treaty countries are given meaning and made a reality.

1.2 The Significance of Investment Treaties

The six decades since the end of World War II have thus witnessed a widespread *treatification*[19] of international investment law. Today, unlike the situation that prevailed before World War II, foreign investors in many parts of the world are protected primarily by international treaties, rather than by customary international law alone. For all practical purposes, treaties have become the fundamental source of international law in the area of foreign investment.[20] Indeed, in 2003, an arbitral tribunal that included a former president of the International Court of Justice suggested that the 2,000 BITs then in existence had shaped the customary international law with respect to the rights of investors.[21]

This shift from customary international law to treaty law in the domain of international investment has been anything but theoretical. For one thing, it has imposed a discipline on host country treatment of foreign investors. In those cases in which host governments have failed to abide by their commitments to investors, governments have found themselves involved in international arbitration proceedings (some 568 known cases involving ninety-eight countries, in both the developing and the developed world, at the beginning of 2014),[22] and in many cases arbitral tribunals have held them liable to pay substantial damages awards to injured investors.[23] The decisions in those investor–state arbitrations are becoming an increasingly important source of international jurisprudence on the respective rights of foreign investors and the states in which they invest.

---

[19] The word 'treatification', while not recognized by any standard English dictionaries, has been used on rare occasions. The origin of this derivation of the word 'treatify' may perhaps be found in the 1908 Nobel lecture of the Peace Prize Laureate Frederik Bajer, who urged that a treaty be established to govern the canals between the North and Baltic seas, stating, 'there is a need to "treatify", if I may coin this expression, the waterways—the French call them "canaux interocéaniques"—which connect the two seas'. 'The Organization of the Peace Movement', available at <http://www.nobelprize.org> accessed 14 September 2014. JW Salacuse, 'The Treatification of International Investment Law' (2007) 13 Law and Business Review of the Americas 55.

[20] P Juillard, 'L'Evolution des sources du droit des investissements' (1994) 250 *Receuil des Cours* 74.

[21] *Mondev Int'l Ltd v United States*, Case No ARB(AF)/99/2 [2003] (NAFTA Ch 11 Arb Trib [11 October 2002]) 42 ILM 85, ¶ 125.

[22] UNCTAD, *World Investment Report 2014* (2014) 1254.

[23] One early notable example is the case of *CME Czech Republic BV v The Czech Republic*, UNCITRAL (14 March 2003) UNCITRAL Final Award, arbitration under the Netherlands–Czech Republic BIT, which resulted in an award and payment of $355 million to an injured investor in 2003, one of the largest awards ever made in an arbitration proceeding up to that time; P Green, 'Czech Republic Pays $355 Million to Media Concern' (16 May 2003) *New York Times*, available at <http://www.nytimes.com/2003/05/16/business/czech-republic-pays-355-million-to-media-concern.html> accessed 14 September 2014. More recent awards have approached US$1 billion. See eg *Mohamed Abdulmohsen Al-Kharafi & Sons Co v Libya and ors*, CRCICA Final Arbitral Award (22 March 2013).

In summary, international investment treaties are playing and will continue to play a growing role in international business and economic relations. An intensified knowledge of investment treaties is therefore vital for government officials who negotiate, interpret, and apply them, as well as for those who manage relations with actual and prospective foreign investors in their territories. Many officials and their governments have learned at significant cost that international investment treaties are not just 'expressions of good will' but are binding instruments of international law that impose enforceable legal obligations on host country governments.

Similarly, international business executives, bankers, and their lawyers must take account of relevant investment treaty provisions in planning, executing, and managing foreign investment projects. International investment treaties have become, and will remain, vital elements in evaluating political risk in any country in which investors hope to operate. And when, as a result of changes in circumstance or policy, conflict arises between investors and host countries, international investment treaties usually play a significant role in their resolution. The treaty enforcement provision whereby individual investors are given the right to initiate arbitration against host countries has led to the development of an increasingly important area of legal practice. Law firms and practising lawyers need to understand, interpret, and apply international investment treaties in order to effectively advise clients and represent them before arbitral tribunals, and in some cases, national courts. Thus, international investment agreements have a growing significance for the conduct of international business, finance, and legal practice.

But beyond the application of specific treaties to individual investors, one may well ask: What is the significance as a whole of all of this treaty-making over the last six decades? Just what does it all add up to? On the one hand, certain scholars have said that each of these approximately 3,300 treaties are *lex specialis* that do nothing more than define specific rules for regulating investments between individual pairs of countries that are parties to the treaties.[24] According to this view, the whole is merely the sum of its parts. On the other hand, in view of the strong similarity among treaties and the common concepts, language, structure, and processes they employ, other scholars have argued that given the large number of countries involved in the movement to negotiate international investment agreements these treaties constitute customary international law.[25] This debate is not new. Indeed, virtually since the beginning of the investment treaty movement, scholars have debated the extent to which such treaties constitute or form customary international law with respect to foreign investment. One argument is that investment treaties 'establish and accept and thus enlarge the force of traditional

---

[24] eg M Sornarajah, *The International Law on Foreign Investment* (3rd edn, Cambridge University Press, 2010) 176–7.
[25] A Lowenfeld, 'Investment Agreements and International Law' (2003) 42 Col J Transnat'l L 12; SM Schwebel, 'The Influence of Bilateral Investment Treaties on Customary International Law' (2004) Proceedings of the 98th Annual Meeting of the American Society of International Law 27–30.

conceptions' of the law of state responsibility for foreign investment.[26] Others have countered that, despite their prevalence, investment treaties have effect only between the parties to them and are not sufficiently uniform to establish custom accepted by the international community.[27]

1.3 A Regime for International Investment

Without resolving the debate as to whether or not investment treaties constitute customary international law, one may conceptualize the mass of investment treaties made over the last sixty years in yet another way. Borrowing from international relations theory, one can think of the existing body of investment treaties as constituting a *regime*.[28] An international regime is essentially a system of governance in a particular area of international relations.[29] Focusing on the elements of a regime, a leading scholar of international relations has defined an international regime as 'principles, norms, rules and decision-making procedures around which actors' expectations converge in a given area of international relations'.[30] International regimes, according to two other scholars, 'constrain and regularize the behavior of participants, affect which issues among protagonists are on and off the agenda, determine which activities are legitimized or condemned, and influence where, when, and how conflicts are resolved'.[31] Thus, one may argue that international investment treaties as a group represent a convergence of expectations by states as to how host governments will behave towards investments from other regime members. The norms and rules embodied in investment treaties are intended to constrain and regularize such behaviour in order to fulfil those expectations.

One of the ways in which international law becomes a reality, in the sense of actually affecting the behaviour of both states and private parties, is through the creation of international regimes. For nearly three decades, international relations scholars have worked to develop a theory of regimes to explain the phenomenon of cooperation among states in an otherwise anarchic world.[32] Although regime theory as a body of scholarly endeavour has been the almost exclusive province

---

[26] FA Mann, 'British Treaties for the Promotion and Protection of Investments' (1982) 52 BYIL 241, 249.

[27] B Kishoiyian, 'The Utility of Bilateral Investment Treaties in the Formulation of Customary International Law' (1994) 14 Nw J Int'l L & Bus 327, 329. See also Sornarajah (n 24 above) 177.

[28] JW Salacuse, 'The Emerging Global Regime for Investment,' (2010) 51 Harv Int'l LJ 427.

[29] *Webster's Third New International Dictionary* defines the word regime as 'a method of ruling or management' and 'a form of government'. *Webster's Third New International Dictionary* 1911 (3rd edn, G & C Merriam Co, 1981).

[30] SD Krasner, 'Structural Causes and Regime Consequences: Regimes as Intervening Variables' in SD Krasner (ed), *International Regimes* (Cornell University Press, 1983) 2.

[31] DJ Puchala and RF Hopkins, 'International Regimes: Lessons for Inductive Analysis' in Krasner (n 30 above) 62.

[32] See eg R Crawford, *Regime Theory in the Post-Cold War World: Rethinking Neoliberal Approaches to International Relations* (Dartmouth, 1996); A Hasenclever et al, *Theories of International Regimes* (Cambridge University Press, 1997); SD Krasner (ed), *International Regimes* (Cornell University

of political scientists rather than international lawyers, some of its insights and frameworks may be useful in explaining how and why international investment law works the way it does.

Although each of the 3,300 investment treaties is legally separate and distinct, thus binding only the states that have concluded it, investment treaties as a group are remarkably similar with respect to structure, purpose, and principles. In addition, the language used in expressing these principles is often identical, so that it is not uncommon, for example, to find that both counsel and arbitrators will refer to arbitral decisions in cases interpreting one type of investment treaty, such as the investment chapter of NAFTA, to interpret a similar provision in a totally separate and unrelated treaty, like a BIT between Chile and Malaysia.[33] It is for this reason, among others, that one may view these agreements, despite individual differences in text, as constituting a single international regime for investment.

Two principal theoretical explanations have been advanced as to why states form regimes. For some scholars associated with the realist school, regimes are a means by which a hegemonic state asserts power in order to advance its own interests and thereby attain and preserve relative gains over other countries.[34] According to this view, often referred to as the theory of hegemonic stability, a regime cannot exist without a hegemon.[35] An initial problem with applying this theory to explain the existence of the investment regime is that it is difficult to identify the specific hegemon that has advanced and maintained the investment treaty system. Normally, a hegemon is a particular, dominant country, such as the United States, a country that, in the words of one scholar, 'is powerful enough to maintain the essential rules governing interstate relations and willing to do so'.[36] As will be seen in Chapter 4, which examines the history of investment treaties, no particular country has acted as a hegemon in its development and maintenance in order to advance its own particular interests and gain an advantage over all other countries. On the contrary, many capital-exporting countries, through their individual and largely uncoordinated actions, have been active in its creation.

One could argue, of course, that capital-exporting countries have acted as a collective hegemon to create and maintain the investment regime and thereby maintain their global economic advantage, particularly in relation to developing, capital-importing nations. However, given the number and diversity of capital-exporting states, designating them as a 'hegemon' would distort the usual meaning of that term, which traditionally has referred to a single state. On the other hand, the rhetoric of certain developing country leaders, particularly in Latin America, who have viewed the spread of bilateral treaties as a threat to their

---

Press, 1983); V Rittberger (ed), *Regime Theory and International Relations* (Cornell University Press, 1993).

[33] See eg *MTD v Chile*, ICSID Case No ARB/01/7 (25 May 2004) ¶¶ 3, 22, 110–111.

[34] See eg Crawford (n 32 above).

[35] RO Keohane, *After Hegemony: Cooperation and Discord in a World of Political Economy* (Princeton University Press, 1984) 32–9.

[36] ibid 34–5.

countries' sovereignty, suggests that they do indeed view capital-exporting countries as a collective hegemon that has put in place a system of international investment rules designed to preserve their dominance in the global economy vis-à-vis developing countries.[37] For these leaders and many of their followers, the investment treaty regime is a clear manifestation of an effort at hegemonic stability.

The debate over whether the investment regime is an act of hegemonic stability or an act of cooperation to advance the interests of all regime participants may grow sharper in the future. The ultimate resolution of that debate may have significant consequences for the legitimacy of the regime in the eyes of the world.

A second explanation for the creation of an investment regime is that countries build regimes because they believe that such a cooperative arrangement will advance their individual interests. Regimes, according to this explanation, are instances of international cooperation in an otherwise anarchic world of independent sovereign states.[38] States form international regimes in order to deal with problems in a manner that advances their interests. Their stated aim in building a global investment regime has been to facilitate the flow of capital and related technology among states so as to promote economic development and prosperity,[39] often by solving the problem of foreign investment insecurity due to the risk of adverse actions by governments in host countries.[40] The basic building block for this emerging international investment regime has been the investment treaty.

According to the second theory, nations create and join regimes out of a desire to reduce the relative costs of desired transactions. Thus, capital-importing states have been led to sign investment treaties in the belief that the treaty commitments they make to protect foreign investment will reduce the perceived risks associated with investing in their territories and thereby lower their costs of obtaining needed foreign capital and technology. Capital-exporting countries, for their part, have

---

[37] See eg '"Capitalism Needs to Go," Says Hugo Chavez', 3 April 2009, available at <http://ourlatinamerica.blogspot.com/2009/04/capitalism-needs-to-go-says-hugo-chavez.html> accessed 14 September 2014; G Parra-Berna, 'Multilateral Banks Pose Problem for Latin America, Correa Says', BLOOMBERG, 20 December 2006, available at <http://www.bloomberg.com/apps/news?pid=20601086&sid=aqxeFXqL9vpQ&refer=latin_america> accessed 14 September 2014.

[38] RO Keohane, *International Institutions and State Power: Essays in International Relations Theory* (Westview Press, 1989) 132.

[39] Investment treaty preambles, which state the contracting parties' goals, often provide that the aim of the treaty is to promote 'economic cooperation' between the concerned states. See eg the preamble to the BIT between France and Argentina, which begins: 'Desiring to develop economic cooperation between the two States and to create favourable conditions for French investments in Argentina and Argentine investments in France...' Accord entre le Gouvernement de la République française et le Gouvernement de la République Argentine sur l'encouragement et la protection réciproques des investissements [Agreement between the Argentine Republic and the Republic of France for the Promotion and Reciprocal Protection of Investments], Argentina–France, 3 July 1991, 1728 UNTS 282, translated in 1728 UNTS 298. Similarly, the preamble to the BIT between Argentina and Spain expresses that the states are: 'Desiring to intensify economic cooperation for the economic benefit of both countries.' Acuerdo para la promoción y protección recíprocas de inversiones entre el Reino de España y la República Argentina [Agreement on the Promotion and Reciprocal Protection of Investments between the Kingdom of Spain and the Argentine Republic], Argentina–Spain, 3 October 1991, 1699 UNTS 188, translated in 1699 UNTS 202.

[40] See AT Guzman, 'Why LDCs Sign Treaties That Hurt Them: Explaining the Popularity of Bilateral Investment Treaties' (1998) 38 Va J Int'l L 639.

joined the regime in the hope of reducing the foreign investment transaction costs associated with adverse actions by host country governments, such as expropriation without compensation and negative governmental interference with enterprises owned by their nationals.[41] In a similar vein, international regimes, while lowering the costs of transactions that are considered legitimate, also raise the costs of those that are deemed illegitimate. Thus, the investment regime, through its dispute resolution mechanisms and particularly investor–state arbitration, secures compliance with regime norms and rules by imposing costly payments in the form of damage awards on regime members who engage in actions that violate regime norms and rules.[42] The use of regime theory as a lens through which to examine the mass of investment treaties negotiated over the last sixty years would seem to have several potential advantages. First, it offers an analytical framework to understand and capture the essential, common elements of the approximately 3,300 legally separate and distinct treaties and to understand the systemic nature of what states have created through the treaty-making process. Second, it may enable observers and scholars to gain a better understanding of the dynamics of the relationships established by these treaties among states and between states and foreign investors. Examining the accumulated treaties through the lens of traditional treaty analysis alone, on the other hand, often yields a static picture that does not fully reflect the dynamism and fluidity of the system that such treaties have created. Traditional treaty analysis tends to concentrate on investor rights under individual treaties rather than on the international relationships that treaties have created among states. Third, regime theory may make more visible the political nature and dimensions of these treaties, for political issues are often at the heart of investment relationships between states and are also deeply imbedded in investor–state disputes, regardless of their applicable legal superstructures. An exclusively legal analysis of treaty provisions and investor–state disputes often overlooks this important dimension. And finally, one might also suggest that while lawyers and arbitrators do not normally use the term 'regime' in referring to investment treaties, they implicitly treat investment treaties as constituting a regime in that they regularly refer to prior decisions applying one treaty in order to interpret a wholly separate treaty.[43] Regime analysis may make explicit what has heretofore been implicit.

---

[41] KJ Vandevelde, 'A Brief History of International Investment Agreements' in KP Sauvant and LE Sachs (eds), *The Effect of Treaties on Foreign Direct Investment: Bilateral Investment Treaties, Double Taxation Treaties, and Investment Flows* (OUP, 2009) 3, 13. The average number of nationalizations of foreign investor property per year rose steadily from 1960, the year when many former colonies became independent, when such measures averaged slightly more than 15, until 1975, when they reached over 50, resulting in significant losses to foreign investors. UNCTAD, *International Investment Agreements: Key Issues*, 7, UN Doc UNCTAD/ITE/IIT/2004/10 (2004). It is no coincidence that the movement to negotiate BITs, discussed earlier, took root during this period as a means to avoid such costs in the future.

[42] See generally UNCTAD, *Investor–State Disputes Arising From Investment Treaties: A Review*, UNCTAD/ITE/IIT/2005/4 (1 February 2005).

[43] See eg *MTD v Chile*, ICSID Case No ARB/01/7 (25 May 2004) 3, 22, ¶¶ 110–111.

1.4 The Application of Regime Theory to Investment Treaties

(a) Regime elements

Following the 'consensus definition' quoted earlier, a regime consists of four elements: (1) principles; (2) norms; (3) rules; and (4) decision-making processes.[44] Each of these elements is examined later in connection with the regime created by investment treaties.

(b) Regime principles

The first element of a regime is principles. By principles, regime theorists mean something different from what lawyers and legal scholars usually understand by that term. Within the context of international regimes, principles may be defined as 'beliefs of fact, causation, and rectitude'.[45] Regimes are based on a belief by their participants that cooperation in a particular area will lead to some desired outcome. Thus, for example, one may say that a regime for the prevention of nuclear proliferation is based on the principle that the proliferation of nuclear arms increases the likelihood of nuclear war and that a regime to control proliferation will achieve the desired outcome of reducing that likelihood.[46] What then are the principles upon which the international investment regime is based? An examination of investment treaty texts indicates a set of more or less common principles that reflect the beliefs of the participating states negotiating them.

A first principle is the belief that increased investment between and among contracting states will increase their prosperity, economic development, and business activity, and will lead to heightened economic cooperation among them.[47] Thus, the treaties' ultimate goal, as envisioned by their contracting states, is not just to increase the flow of capital and to protect individual investors.

A second principle is that favourable conditions in host states will, all other things being equal, lead to increased investment. The reference to 'favourable conditions' does not merely mean the natural state of things; it refers in particular to conditions that can be affected by host government actions and recognizes that such actions can either encourage or discourage investment. Thus, the title of virtually all investment treaties states that the agreement is to 'promote' or 'encourage' investment, and the targets of that promotion are investors of the other contracting party.

---

[44] Hasenclever et al (n 32 above) 9.   [45] Krasner (n 30 above) 2.

[46] H Muller, 'The Internationalization of Principles, Norms, and Rules by Governments: The Case of Security Regimes' in Rittberger (n 32 above) 361–8. See also Hasenclever et al (n 32 above) 9.

[47] eg the preamble to the 1995 BIT between Mongolia and Singapore states: 'RECOGNIZING that the encouragement and reciprocal protection of such investments will be conducive to stimulating business initiative and increasing prosperity in both States…'.

A third principle of the investment regime is that the law and administrative decisions of host states can influence investment by giving increased predictability to rules under which investors make their investments and conduct their activities. Underlying this principle, one may cite the work of the great German sociologist Max Weber, who sought to understand why capitalism arose in Europe. He concluded that one of the reasons was the nature of European law, which allowed what he called the 'calculability' of transactions. Weber emphasizes the role that law plays in raising the probability that actions will take place. Calculability, according to Weber, encourages investment transactions. For Weber three conditions were necessary for law to be calculable: (1) the legal text must lend itself to prediction; (2) the administration and application of the legal text must not be arbitrary; and (3) contracts must be enforced.[48] Similarly, the goal of investment treaties has been to increase the calculability of foreign investment transactions.

A fourth principle underlying the treaty regime is that the means to promote investment is to guarantee its protection. The promise of investment protection results in investment promotion. Thus, the titles of nearly all investment treaties state that their purpose is not only to promote investment but to protect it. The connection between promotion and protection lies in investor concepts of risk and predictability.

The general premise of investment treaties is that investment promotion is to be achieved by the host country's creation of a stable legal environment that favours foreign investment. The basic working assumption upon which investment treaties rest is that clear and enforceable rules that protect foreign investors reduce investment risk, and a reduction in risk, all other things being equal, promotes investment. Investment treaties, on the other hand, do not generally bind a capital-exporting country to encourage its nationals and companies to invest in the territory of a treaty partner.

The risk for any foreign investor is that once the investment is made, the host state may change the rules. A sudden, unexpected change in the rules is a principal form of political risk, perhaps its very essence. In order to encourage investment within their territories, host states make various kinds of commitments to investors, including investment agreements, development contracts, public service concessions, and tax stabilization agreements, to mention only a few. Such agreements contain important commitments upon which investors rely in deciding to invest their capital in the host country. The continuing respect by the host government of such commitments is usually crucial for the profitability of the investment, and sometimes for its very survival. Since these arrangements are governed by the law of the host country and subject to the actions of its institutions, their continued stability faces the risk that the host government will unilaterally modify or terminate them at some later time, a phenomenon that has in fact taken place on numerous occasions. Such obligations made by host states to foreign investors are, in the oft-quoted words of the late Professor Raymond Vernon of

---

[48] R Swedberg, 'Max Weber's Contribution to the Economic Sociology of Law' (2006) 2 Annu Rev Law Soc Sci 61.

the Harvard Business School, 'obsolescing bargains' between the investor and the host country.[49] The cause of their obsolescence has much to do with the decline in bargaining power of the investor during the life of the investment. At the time that an investor is proposing an investment to a country, the investor has a certain amount of bargaining power with the host government to secure favourable treatment and conditions for its investment; however, once the investor makes the investment and thereby places its capital under the sovereignty of the host state, its bargaining power diminishes and the commitments received risk becoming obsolete in the eyes of the host government.

The fifth principle of the investment regime is that international rules with effective enforcement mechanisms will deal with the problem of the obsolescing bargain by restraining the actions of the host government towards foreign investment in its territory. Rules and enforcement mechanisms are seen as a basic means to protect investment.

Thus, one may summarize the structure of the principles underlying the investment treaty regime as follows:

1. Increased international investment fosters economic development and prosperity.
2. Favourable conditions in host countries lead to increased investment.
3. Appropriate host country laws and institutions create favourable conditions for investment by increasing the predictability of economic transactions.
4. Increasing the predictability ('calculability' in Weber's terms) of transactions has the effect of reducing perceived risk and therefore promoting investment.
5. Enforceable international rules that restrain host country governmental actions protect and therefore promote investment.

(c) Regime norms

Norms are the second element of a regime. Norms in regime theory are defined as 'standards of behaviour defined in terms of rights and obligations'. Investment treaties specify standards of 'treatment' (a term of art in all investment treaties) that host states are obliged to accord to investors and investments from their treaty partners.

In order to protect foreign investors against the political risk resulting from placing their assets under host country jurisdiction, investment treaties include obligations with respect to the 'treatment' that host countries must give to investors and their investments. Although the treaties do not usually define the meaning of 'treatment', that word in its ordinary dictionary sense includes the 'actions

---

[49] R Vernon, *Sovereignty at Bay: The Multinational Spread of U.S. Enterprise* (Basic Books, 1971) 46.

and behaviour that one person takes towards another person'. By entering into an investment treaty, a state makes promises about the actions and behaviours—that is, the treatment—it will give to investments and investors of its treaty partners in the future.[50] The treaty provisions on investor and investment treatment are intended to restrain host country government behaviour and to impose a discipline on governmental actions. They seek to achieve this goal by defining a *standard* to which host countries' governments must conform in their treatment of investors and investments. State actions that fail to meet the defined standard constitute treaty violations that engage the offending state's international responsibility and render it potentially liable to pay compensation for the injury it has caused.

The standards of treatment—that is, the norms of the regime—are remarkably similar in language and concept across investment treaties. Thus, host states are to respect the norms of 'fair and equitable treatment', 'full protection and security', 'most-favoured-nation treatment', 'national treatment', and 'non-discriminatory treatment' with respect to protected investors and their investments. At the same time, it should be emphasized that treatment standards in treaties are almost always expressed in general and even vague terms so as to render difficult the task of applying them to concrete, complex fact situations of the type that usually arise in investment disputes. Indeed, for many lawyers accustomed to interpreting domestic legislation, they are breathtaking in their generality, vagueness, and lack of specificity. The application of these vague norms in investment treaties has been the work of investor–state arbitration tribunals, primary decision-making bodies of the international investment regime.

(d) Regime rules

Rules are the third element of a regime. For purposes of regime theory, rules are defined as 'specific prescriptions or proscriptions for actions'. The difference between a 'norm' and a 'rule' is not always clear. But one finds rules, in the form of prescriptions for action, in the investment regime in two places. First, the treaty texts contain many specific prescriptions for action. Thus, in addition to norms, the treaties express rules about such matters as expropriation, monetary transfers, and compensation of injured investors because of war, revolution, and civil strife. The second set of rules lies in the decisions of arbitral tribunals, which apply the regime norms to specific fact situations. For example, according to many investment tribunals, fair and equitable treatment means that the host government must respect 'the legitimate expectations' that it has created in the investor.

---

[50] In the ICSID case of *Suez, Sociedad General de Aguas de Barcelona SA, and Vivendi Universal SA v The Argentine Republic*, ICSID Case No ARB/O3/19, (Decision on Jurisdiction) (3 August 2006) ¶ 55, the tribunal defined 'treatment' as follows: 'The word "treatment" is not defined in the treaty text. However, the ordinary meaning of that term within the context of investment includes the rights and privileges granted and the obligations and burdens imposed by a Contracting State on investments made by investors covered by the treaty.'

Indeed, one cannot fully know or understand the rules of the investment regime without studying the decisions of the arbitral tribunals that have applied often vague treaty terms to concrete fact situations. Thus, one may conclude that the deliberate use by contracting states of vague and general norms in investment treaties, coupled with the well-known tendency of lawyers and arbitrators to be guided by previous arbitral decisions, has the effect of creating an implicit system of delegated rule-making within the investment regime. From this perspective, arbitrators do not merely settle disputes; they also make rules for the regime.

(e) Regime decision-making

The fourth and final regime element is decision-making procedures, which are defined as 'prevailing practices for making and implementing collective choice'. The international regime for investment has no centralized governing council with the power to administer and apply its rules or the authority to make and implement collective choice. In that respect, it is unlike the European Union, the World Trade Organization (WTO), or the United Nations. Decision-making processes and authority are decentralized and diffused throughout the regime by individual treaties. Investment treaties provide for decision-making in basically four ways: (1) by consultation between the state parties to the treaty; (2) by arbitration between state parties in cases where they are unable to resolve conflicts through consultation and negotiation; (3) by consultations and negotiations between the investor and the state; and (4) by investor–state arbitration.

In the early days of the investment treaty movement, once states had signed a BIT they seemed to have engaged in little state-to-state consultation about its application. In more recent times, such consultation has taken place with increasing frequency and some treaties have even given it institutional form. One example is the North American Free Trade Agreement (NAFTA), which created a Free Trade Commission with the power to make binding interpretations of NAFTA provisions that NAFTA tribunals must follow in making their decisions.[51]

The last mentioned decision-making procedure, investor–state arbitration, is the most important of the four, particularly from the point of view of frequency of use. It is a unique feature of the regime for two reasons. First, there are few instances in the international system where international law gives private persons and companies the right to compel a sovereign state to appear before a tribunal and defend its sovereign actions, ostensibly taken to protect the public interest. The WTO, for example, has dispute resolution processes, but states, and states alone, are participants in those processes. Thus, the global investment regime has to a large extent granted a private right of action to investors and has thereby also privatized the decision-making process to a large extent, since arbitrators are

---

[51] North American Free Trade Agreement (United States–Canada–Mexico) (17 December 1992) (1993) 32 ILM 289, Arts 2001–2002. The Commission has exercised this power on occasion. See NAFTA Free Trade Commission, 'Notes of Interpretation of Certain Chapter 11 Provisions', 31 July 2001.

private persons compensated by the disputants, not officials of governments or international organizations. Second, it is within the investor–state arbitrations that the most important decisions about the regime are decided. The decisions of arbitral tribunals in the approximately 568 investor–state disputes that have arisen under investment treaties have not only resolved a vast array of investor–state conflicts but have also shaped the rules and norms of the regime. Their number will continue to grow in the years ahead.

Why have states chosen this essentially private method for implementing collective choice? No doubt capital-exporting countries believed that granting investors a private right of action for violation of regime rules would be an effective way of assuring that regime rules were respected. But investor–state arbitration as a decision-making procedure has another advantage for home countries: it is a way for capital-exporting governments to reduce governmental transaction costs arising out of the investments made by their nationals. Under the previous systems, governments had to deal with their nationals seeking diplomatic protection and other forms of interventions with host country governments. That method potentially entailed significant diplomatic, political, and economic costs, since it might impact on and complicate important multifaceted relationships between the investor's home country and the host country. Investor–state arbitration relieves home countries of those costs. In effect, it allows them to say to their nationals and companies aggrieved by host government acts: 'You have your own remedy in the treaty. Use it if you wish. Go away and don't bother us.'

1.5 A Different Kind of Regime

While the approximately 3,300 investment treaties would seem to meet the definition of an international regime, one must acknowledge that this emerging regime for international investment has significant differences from other international regimes. Three of the most important are: (1) the regime has largely been constructed bilaterally, rather than multilaterally; (2) it gives broad scope to private and decentralized decision-making; and (3) no multilateral international organization supports the investment regime.

(a) Bilateral construction

First, the investment regime has been constructed largely through bilateral negotiations, rather than multilateral ones. Most other international regimes, like the WTO, the International Criminal Court, the international human rights regime, and the nuclear non-proliferation regime, have been the product of multilateral, indeed global, negotiations.

An interesting question is *why* the nations of the world have been willing to conclude BITs in growing numbers over the last fifty years but have generally resisted global agreements on investment. There is both a technical and a political explanation for this result. The technical explanation is that a bilateral treaty must accommodate the interests of only two parties and is therefore far less complicated to negotiate than a multilateral, global treaty, which must accommodate the interests of many countries.[52] The political explanation is that, given the asymmetric nature of bilateral negotiations between a strong, developed country and a usually much weaker developing country, the bilateral setting allows the developed country to use its power more effectively than does a multilateral setting, where that power may be much diluted. For example, in multilateral settings, developing countries have the opportunity to form blocking coalitions with like-minded states to enhance their power in the negotiations, something that is impossible in bilateral negotiations. On the other hand, the prospects of investment capital from specific developed countries, along with other political and economic benefits arising from a definite bilateral relationship, may make a developing country more willing to enter into a BIT with a specific developed country than it would a multilateral agreement where those benefits may seem more tenuous and theoretical. Moreover, whereas developed countries would be willing to enter into bilateral treaties with developing countries for investment liberalization, knowing full well that few if any enterprises from the developing country would ever invest in the developed state, they have been unwilling to enter into treaties that would grant such liberalization to investors from other developed states, who could become strong competitors to the host countries' own enterprises.[53]

Viewed from a different perspective, it is possible to conclude that the approximately 2,900 BITs, although bilateral in form, have not really been negotiated on a strictly bilateral basis. One might say that they have been the product of 'serial multilateralism', instead of the traditional 'conference multilateralism', which has produced most of the world's international regimes. That is to say, capital-exporting states, which have driven the treaty-making process, have done so on the basis of prepared models or prototypes, which they then proceeded to negotiate with individual countries, showing little willingness to deviate significantly from the model that they had prepared. Thus, from the outset those capital-exporting states contemplated engaging in a multilateral process of negotiating with other states one at a time.

The similarity in models used by capital-exporting states has, of course, led to a similarity in the treaties actually concluded. What explains the similarity of the models that states have used to negotiate BITs? Do they represent a grand conspiracy among capital-exporting states? Certainly there has been communication among capital-exporting states over the years as they have developed and

---

[52] For a discussion of the differences between bilateral and multilateral negotiations, see FO Hampson, *Multilateral Negotiations: Lessons from Arms Control, Trade, and the Environment* (JHU Press, 1995) 1–51, 345–60; IW Zartman (ed), *International Multilateral Negotiation: Approaches to the Management of Complexity* (Jossey-Bass, 1994) 1–10, 213–22.

[53] Such a problem arose during the negotiation of the failed OECD Multilateral Agreement on Investment, conducted between 1995 and 1998. See G Kelley, 'Multilateral Investment Treaties: A Balanced Approach to Multinational Corporations' (2001) 39 Col J Transnat'l L 483, 494–8.

refined their models. But an even more important factor has helped to shape the investment treaty regime: the epistemic community of international lawyers and scholars. Epistemic communities are defined as 'networks of professionals with recognized expertise and competence in a particular domain and an authoritative claim to policy relevant knowledge within that domain or issue area'.[54] Epistemic communities are vital to regime creation and maintenance because, according to one scholar, they 'are crucial channels through which new ideas circulate from societies to government as well as from country to country'.[55] Since the movement to negotiate investment treaties began, the epistemic community of international lawyers, scholars, jurists, and arbitrators has through advising, writing, advocacy, and judicial and arbitral decisions shaped the regime. They are now the principal actors for maintaining and operating it.

(b) Privatized and decentralized decision-making

A second important difference from other international regimes is the strong roles that non-state actors play in formulating, elaborating, and applying the rules of the regime. In effect, the investment regime 'privatizes' decision-making, whereas in other regimes, such as the WTO, decision-making remains firmly in the hands of member states.

In most other regimes, states and their representatives are entrusted with the crucial function of elaborating and defining the rules of the regime. Thus, for example, state representatives may meet periodically to negotiate new rules, and institutions under the control of states may be entrusted with the task of applying those rules to specific cases. A similar model of decision-making does not prevail in the international investment regime. Instead, it has delegated decision-making to private persons—arbitrators, who are not representatives of states, and whose mission, unlike that of diplomats, is not to pursue state policy. Indeed, arbitral rules of conduct require them to decide and act 'independently', which means that they may not be influenced by states, governments, the parties, or anybody else for that matter. Other private parties—lawyers and law firms representing investors and states—also play an important role in the decision-making process. Through their advocacy, they strongly influence both the process of decision-making and its end result. Thus, to a significant extent, regime elaboration and operation are largely in the hands of private parties who are not accountable to the states that have created the regime.

In theory, of course, arbitrators only decide disputes. They have no authority to make rules, and their decisions do not formally constitute legal precedent. But in practice, the approximately 560 decisions that have emanated from tribunals are consistently cited by lawyers and other tribunals and have a powerful influence on the making of future regime decisions.

---

[54] P Haas, 'Introduction: Epistemic Communities and International Policy Coordination' (1992) 46 Int'l Org 1, 3.
[55] ibid 27.

Despite the decentralized and privatized decision-making processes of the regime, the resulting decisions by arbitral tribunals demonstrate a surprisingly high degree of uniformity and consistency. Three factors seem to explain this phenomenon. First, the norms and rules applied by tribunals are significantly similar, if not identical, among investment treaties. Second, arbitrators are conscious of and influenced by the decisions of other investor–state tribunals. Although they are not bound by the decisions of other tribunals, arbitrators, to a greater or lesser extent, are concerned that arbitral decisions create a consistent jurisprudence of international investment law. Third, arbitrators are very much a part of an international epistemic community with similar training and, in many cases, comparable professional backgrounds.[56]

(c) Lack of a multilateral international organization

Normally, an international regime is supported by a multilateral international organization.[57] For example, the global trade regime rests upon the WTO, a robust international organization, which as of March 2013 consisted of 159 member states, a staff of 639 persons, and a budget of 197,203,900 Swiss Francs (approximately US$165 million).[58] It has a broad mandate to oversee the implementation of multilateral trade agreements and to serve as a forum for consultation and negotiations among states with respect to international trade.[59] The international investment regime has nothing similar. Individual international organizations—such as ICSID, which only facilitates the resolution of investor–state disputes; the ECT organization and secretariat, which only concern trade and investment in the energy sector; and the North American Free Trade Commission, which only deals with the application of NAFTA—serve to support parts of the regime but do not do so in a comprehensive fashion similar to that of the WTO. Nonetheless, the very existence of the international investment regime indicates that a multilateral international organization is not a necessary condition for the creation of a regime. On the other hand, the absence of such an organization—with its associated resources, knowledge, and structures—may impede the future development of the regime and reduce its ability to withstand challenges.

---

[56] As of 31 December 2009, a total of 1,004 appointments of arbitrators and conciliators had been made in the 305 cases registered with ICSID since its inception. (It should be noted that several individuals were appointed in more than one ICSID case.) Although they represented 72 different nationalities, 43% (435) of the arbitrators and conciliators were nationals of only five countries: US (120), France (106), UK (94), Canada (75), and Switzerland (70). Ten nationalities accounted for 607 appointments (60.45% of the total), of which only Mexicans (32 appointments) were from a developing country. ICSID, *The ICSID Caseload—Statistics* (Issue 2010–11) 7, 8, 17 (2010), available at <http://icsid.worldbank.org/ICSID/FrontServlet?requestType=ICSIDDocRH&actionVal=ShowDocument&CaseLoadStatistics=true&language=English> accessed 12 September 2014.

[57] Hasenclever et al (n 32 above) 2.

[58] WTO, *Annual Report 2013*, 135, available at <http://www.wto.org/english/res_e/booksp_e/anrep_e/anrep13_chap8_e.pdf> accessed 9 January 2015..

[59] Marrakesh Agreement Establishing the World Trade Organization, 15 April 1994, 1867 UNTS 154 (1994).

1.6 Regime Challenges and Prospects

Regime theorists recognize that regimes are not permanent. The fact that at a particular moment in time the parties' expectations may have 'converged' around a given
set of principles, norms, rules, and decision-making procedures in the investment
area of international relations to form a regime does not mean that those expectations
have converged permanently. Thus, despite the fact that the international investment
regime is founded on 3,300 treaties solemnly concluded by some 180 different states,
one cannot assume that it will endure. The endurance of a regime depends on two
factors: regime effectiveness and regime robustness.[60] Regime effectiveness requires
the continued willingness and ability of its members to abide by its rules and to pursue its objectives and purposes. Regime robustness refers to the ability of the regime
to withstand external threats and challenges. The effectiveness and robustness of the
international investment regime is by no means assured. It faces four salient challenges: two are internal to the regime and two are external.

1. The investment regime has been founded on the assumption that it will
   increase international investment, which in turn will lead to increased
   prosperity and economic development. Much research has questioned
   whether investment treaties have in fact increased investment flows to poor
   countries.[61] If the regime is ultimately judged not to have achieved its fundamental objective of promoting investment, then the justification for its
   continued existence becomes problematic.

2. While public opinion generally seems to accept the norms and rules of the
   regime, its decision-making processes, particularly investor–state arbitration, have been seriously called into question. Host governments and elements of civil society have challenged the decision-making process on many
   grounds: that it is not transparent, that it does not account for the disparity
   in the economic situations of the regime members, that arbitrators are not
   truly independent, that they have an investor bias, and that their decisions
   infringe on the legitimate exercise of sovereignty by host states.[62] For these
   alleged reasons, Bolivia in 2007[63] and Ecuador in 2010[64] formally withdrew

---

[60] Hasenclever et al (n 32 above) 2.

[61] eg M Hallward-Driemeier, 'Do Bilateral Investment Treaties Attract FDI? Only a Bit...and
They Could Bite', World Bank, Working Paper No 3121 (June 2003); JW Salacuse and N Sullivan,
'Do BITs Really Work? An Evaluation of Bilateral Investment Treaties and Their Grand Bargain'
(2005) 46 Harv Int'l LJ 66.

[62] eg JA Van Duzer, 'Enhancing the Procedural Legitimacy of Investor–State Arbitration
through Transparency and Amicus Curiae Participation' (2007) 52 McGill Law Review 681; SD
Franck, 'The Legitimacy Crisis in Investment Treaty Arbitration: Privatizing International Law
through Inconsistent Decisions' (2005) 73 Fordham Int'l L R 1521; M Sornarajah, 'A Coming
Crisis: Expansionary Trends in Investment Treaty Arbitration' in K Sauvant (ed), *Appeals
Mechanisms in International Investment Disputes* (OUP, 2008) 39.

[63] ICSID News Release of 16 May 2007.

[64] ICSID News Release of 9 July 2009, announcing Ecuador's denunciation of the ICSID treaty
with effect from 7 January 2010.

from ICSID, an important pillar of the regime. These factors have also led Venezuela to terminate its BIT with the Netherlands,[65] Ecuador to denounce nine of its BITs and announce its intention to renegotiate the remainder,[66] Bolivia in 2012 to terminate its BIT with the United States,[67] South Africa to begin terminating its BITs as they reach their initial date of expiration,[68] and Indonesia in 2014 to declare its intention to terminate all 67 of its BITs.[69] More generally, governments have chafed at the constraints that treaty provisions impose on their exercises of national sovereignty, particularly on their ability to enact laws and regulations in the public interest that may negatively affect investor interests. It is for these reasons, for example, that the Russian Federation, one of the original members of the ECT in 1994, decided to terminate its provisional application in July 2009,[70] thereby removing itself from the Treaty's mandatory investor–state dispute settlement provisions, among other provisions.

3. The Washington Consensus—the shared belief in many countries from the late 1980s until the end of the 1990s that increased investment, open economies, privatization, and economic deregulation would result in increased global prosperity and economic development[71]—was a powerful force for the spread of investment treaties and the development of the regime that they created.[72]

---

[65] UNCTAD, *Recent Developments in International Investment Agreements (2007–June 2008)*, 2 IIA MONITOR 6 (2008), available at <http://www.unctad.org/en/docs/webdiaeia20081_en.pdf> accessed 9 January 2015.

[66] ibid.

[67] 'Notice of Termination of United States-Bolivia Bilateral Investment Treaty' *The Federal Register*, 23 May 2012, available at <https://www.federalregister.gov/articles/2012/05/23/2012-12494/notice-of-termination-of-united-states-bolivia-bilateral-investment-treaty> accessed 9 January 2015.

[68] 'South Africa begins Withdrawing from EU Member Bits', IISD, News in Brief, 30 October 2012, available at <http://www.iisd.org/itn/2012/10/30/news-in-brief-9/> accessed 9 January 2015.

[69] 'Indonesia to Terminate More Than 60 Bilateral Investment Treaties,' *Asia Pacific*, 16 March 2014, available at <http://www.ft.com/cms/s/0/3755c1b2-b4e2-11e3-af92-00144feabdc0.html#axzz34ZPTTWA7> accessed 9 January 2015.

[70] Government of the Russian Federation, Decree No 1005-r: On Russia's Intention Not to Become a Member of the Energy Charter Treaty (30 July 2009) (approving a *note verbale* notifying the Portuguese Republic, the depository of the Energy Charter Treaty, that it does not intend to become a party to the Treaty and that 'it did not apply provisionally any provision of the Treaty to the extent that such a provision was inconsistent with the Constitution, laws or regulations of the Russian Federation').

[71] The term 'Washington Consensus' is said to have been coined by economist John Williamson in 1989. It consisted of 10 broad reforms: (1) fiscal discipline; (2) reordering public spending priorities away from politically powerful groups, such as the military, and towards basic services and infrastructure; (3) tax reform; (4) financial liberalization; (5) competitive, stable exchange rates; (6) trade liberalization; (7) reduction in barriers to foreign investment; (8) privatization of state enterprises; (9) deregulation; and (10) property rights reform. S Flanders, 'A New Washington Consensus', *The Financial Times*, 14 March 1997, 2. See also JW Salacuse, 'From Developing Countries to Emerging Markets: A New Role for Law in the Third World' (1999) 33 Int'l Lawyer 875.

[72] See UNCTAD, *World Investment Report 2013* (2013) 101, affirming that the years 1994–98 witnessed the most rapid growth of signed investment treaties in their history, with nearly 1,000 investment treaties concluded during that period and an average of four per week signed in the three-year period 1994–96. During the period 2010–12, by contrast, international investment agreements were concluded on average at a rate of one per week.

Many parts of the world have lost faith in the ability of the Washington Consensus to bring prosperity, and therefore they are looking for alternative ways of achieving economic development.[73] The shattering of the Washington Consensus may constitute the loss of an important conceptual support for a global investment regime based on treaties.

4. Serious regional and global economic crises, like the one that struck Argentina in 2001 and much of the developed world in 2008, pose important external threats to the international investment regime. Countries under great stress, faced with potential social and political upheaval as a result of rapidly declining standards of living, often seek radical solutions and are impatient with international investment rules that may restrict their latitude of action. For example, during times of economic crisis, they may be unwilling to grant national treatment to foreign investors, to avoid changing regulations in the name of 'fair and equitable treatment', and to refrain from seizing vital national resources held by foreigners just because they have made treaty promises not to expropriate.

These threats are real and they have the potential power to undermine the regime that has been painstakingly constructed over the last sixty years. The regime's future will require wise management and flexible leadership if it is to withstand the challenges.

1.7 Conclusion: A Sticky Regime?

The actions of Ecuador, Bolivia, Venezuela, South Africa, Indonesia, and Russia in withdrawing, at least to a limited degree, from the international investment regime, along with unofficial expressions of dissatisfaction in other countries, raise a question as to whether their initiatives are the beginning of an effort to change the nature of the regime or to dismantle it entirely, or whether they are merely aberrations that will have no effect on regime robustness. Before predicting the end of the international investment regime and hearing such criticisms as 'clarion calls to roll back the foreign investment regime',[74] one should recognize certain factors that will foster its stability and continued growth.

First, it should be noted that it is not an easy matter for a state to withdraw completely from the investment treaty regime with no negative consequences. For one thing, a country's withdrawal from or denunciation of an investment treaty, whose purpose, after all, is to reduce political risk to investors, may be seen by the international investment community as a negative signal, and may result in a slowing of the flow of foreign capital and technology needed by that country

---

[73] eg M Hudson and J Sommers, 'The End of the Washington Consensus', Counterpunch, 12–14 December 2008.

[74] A Kaushal, 'Revisiting History: How the Past Matters for the Present Backlash Against the Foreign Investment Regime' (2009) 50 Harv Int'l LJ 491, 495.

or in significantly raising their cost. Capital-importing countries sign investment treaties in order to promote investment by reducing their level of political risk as perceived by investors. Therefore, to withdraw from an investment treaty would seem to have the effect of increasing perceived political risk and thereby impeding foreign investment. Moreover, because capital-importing states are often in competition with one another for foreign investment, and because they have signed investment treaties in order to gain an advantage in that competition, they may also fear that opting out of investment treaties will place them at a competitive disadvantage.

A second important factor is that virtually all treaties contain provisions that inhibit their denunciation once approved by the contracting states. Foreign investments are generally long-term transactions. To give foreign investors assurance of a predictable and stable legal framework, investment treaties: (1) establish an initial period for which the treaty will be in force without providing for a right to terminate the treaty during that period; and (2) specify how long the treaty will continue following the expiration of its initial period or its termination. Investment treaties generally provide that they shall be in force for ten or fifteen years. Upon the expiration of this initial period, the treaty may continue either for a fixed additional period or until it is terminated by one of the parties. As a rule, a treaty may be terminated by the parties only after the end of the initial period or after the submission of advance written notice; however, the termination of a treaty does not usually result in the immediate denial of treaty protection for investments made while it was in effect. Most treaty termination provisions contain a 'continuing-effects clause' or 'survival clause' stipulating that investments made, acquired, or approved prior to the date of the termination of the treaty will be protected by the treaty's provisions for a further period of ten, fifteen, or twenty years. Thus, for example, in 2009, a tribunal hearing claims against Russia under the ECT in the much publicized Yukos expropriation cases held that Russia's termination of the Treaty's provisional application did not affect the continuing protection (including investor–state arbitration) under its provisions for another twenty years of investments made before the withdrawal of provisional application.[75] The investment regime therefore appears to have a 'sticky'

---

[75] *Hulley Enterprises Ltd (Cyprus) v The Russian Federation*, PCA AA 226 (Interim Award on Jurisdiction and Admissibility) (30 November 2009) ¶ 339; *Yukos Universal Ltd (Isle of Man) v the Russian Federation*, PCA AA 227 (Interim Award on Jurisdiction and Admissibility) (30 November 2009) ¶ 339; *Veteran Petroleum Ltd (Cyprus) v the Russian Federation*, PCA AA 228 (Interim Award on Jurisdiction and Admissibility) (30 November 2009) ¶ 339. Stating at ¶ 339:

> Furthermore, pursuant to Article 45(3)(b) of the Treaty, investment-related obligations, including the obligation to arbitrate investment-related disputes under Part V of the Treaty, remain in force for a period of 20 years following the effective date of termination of provisional application. In the case of the Russian Federation, this means that any investments made in Russia prior to 19 October 2009 will continue to benefit from the Treaty's protections for a period of 20 years—*i.e.*, until 19 October 2029. As a result, the Tribunal finds that the provisional application of the ECT, including the continuing provisional application of Article 26 in this case, does provide a basis for the Tribunal's jurisdiction over the merits of this claim.

quality which causes a country that has denounced the treaty nonetheless to give treaty treatment to an investor that had made its investment while the treaty was in force, thus requiring a country to continue to adhere to treaty norms, rules, and decision-making processes with respect to covered investments.

Third, rather than abandon the investment treaty movement entirely, many states in their more recent treaties have included new provisions to deal with some of the criticisms levelled at earlier treaty texts. Thus, the new treaties give host governments more latitude to regulate investor conduct in the interests of protecting important national concerns such as public health, the environment, and national security. This ability to adapt treaty provisions to new realities has given the investment regime a dynamic quality.

Finally, despite criticism of investment treaties, countries continue to negotiate them. Moreover, as the developed world emerges from a serious economic and financial crisis at the end of the first decade of the twenty-first century, nation states have energetically launched campaigns to negotiate 'mega-regional economic groupings', which are 'broad economic agreements among a group of countries that together have significant economic weight and in which investment is only one of several subjects'.[76] They include the contemplated Trans-Pacific Partnership (TPP), the EU–United States Transatlantic Trade and Investment Partnership (TTIP), and the Canada–EU Comprehensive Economic and Trade Agreement (CETA), among others. Following other regional economic treaties, the new agreements on which these groups will be based will include investment chapters the provisions of which will in all probability mirror those of earlier agreements, such as the NAFTA. The successful conclusion of these mega-negotiations will give added momentum and permanence to the international investment regime and the treaties on which it is based. Faced with being excluded from these groupings, countries that have previously terminated their participation in investment treaties may reconsider the wisdom of their attempted withdrawal from the international investment regime.

1.8 The Aim and Scope of This Book

The basic building block of this emerging regime for investment has been the international investment treaty. The aim of this book is to examine investment treaties of all varieties in a comprehensive and integrated fashion. Although over 3,300 individual investment treaties exist as distinct instruments of international law, this book examines them as a single phenomenon.

Several reasons justify an integrated and comprehensive approach to the study of investment treaties. First, the movement to conclude investment treaties, both bilateral and multilateral, has been driven by many common factors. These include the perceived inadequacy of pre-existing international law in the area of

---

[76] See n 16 above.

investment and the desire of investors and their home countries to gain increased protection from political risk. Second, the content of specific investment treaties has been shaped and informed by earlier treaties. For example, the experience of negotiating BITs influenced the content and approach of the investment chapters in the North American Free Trade Agreement and the Energy Charter Treaty. Third, as a result, investment treaties, while not identical, demonstrate as a whole a remarkable similarity in terminology, structure, legal concepts, and approach. At the same time, because the applicable investment law is founded on treaties, it has distinct features that differentiate it from the customary international law of investment. Fourth, because of the similarities in language and content among investment treaties, both lawyers and arbitration tribunals are increasingly citing provisions from arbitral interpretations of investment treaties that do not strictly apply in the cases they are facing. For example, in arbitration cases involving a specific BIT, arbitrators and lawyers may cite relevant NAFTA treaty provisions and arbitral cases, and NAFTA arbitral tribunals and counsel may refer to BITs and arbitral decisions interpreting them. And fifth, because investment treaties have become an increasingly common phenomenon, individuals planning and executing international investments need to understand them better and take due account of them.

In approaching its subject, *The Law of Investment Treaties* will begin by examining the phenomenon of international investment, its significance, the forces that drive it, and its attendant risks (Chapter 2). The book will then consider the history of international investment law (Chapter 3), with particular emphasis on the factors that gave rise to the development of investment treaties. It will also discuss the movement to negotiate such treaties as it has emerged and grown since the end of World War II (Chapter 4). That discussion will consider the aims and purposes of investment treaties, as well as the process by which such treaties come into existence. Generally, all investment treaties have two basic purposes: to promote foreign investment and to protect it. Most investment treaties pursue these objectives by establishing rules about the host country's treatment of foreign investment and by providing processes for enforcing these rules. These rules restrain the host government's ability to deal with foreign investors and investments. In cases of dispute, the enforcement process provides an international mechanism outside the jurisdiction of the host country.

Although the precise provisions of investment treaties are not uniform, and some treaties restrict host country governmental action more than others, virtually all investment treaties address the same issues and employ similar concepts and terminology. One of the consequences of the investment treaty movement has been to define in some detail what an investment treaty should be, thereby creating an agreed-upon legal framework for the protection of foreign investment, notwithstanding variations among individual treaties concerning specific provisions. The book will next give the reader an overview of the general structure of an investment treaty (Chapter 5) and will then consider the sources and methods that may be used in the study and interpretation of investment treaties (Chapter 6).

Succeeding chapters will consider the basic issues covered by investment treaties, namely: their scope of application, particularly with regard to the investments and the investors covered by the treaty (Chapter 7); investment promotion, admission, and establishment (Chapter 8); and the general standards of treatment to be accorded to covered investors and investments, such as 'fair and equitable treatment', 'national treatment', 'most-favoured-nation treatment', 'full protection and security', and 'the standards of international law' (Chapter 9). Thereafter, the book will discuss special treatment standards, including those related to monetary transfers (Chapter 10); investor–state obligations (Chapter 11); protection against expropriation, nationalization, and dispossession (Chapter 12); and various other standards of treatment (Chapter 13). It will conclude with a consideration of treaty provisions on exceptions, modifications, and terminations (Chapter 14); the various dispute settlement mechanisms provided by investment treaties (Chapter 15); and the consequences for states and investors of the breach by host states of their treaty commitments to protected investments, particularly the issues of compensation and damages resulting from treaty breaches (Chapter 16).

2

The Nature and Significance
of International Investment

2.1 Introduction

All international investment treaties focus on two subjects: (1) investments, particularly international or 'foreign investments'; and (2) investors, especially international or 'foreign investors'. An understanding of both of these phenomena is fundamental to understanding the growing role and significance of investment treaties in international economic life. The purpose of this chapter is to explain the nature and significance of international investments and investors.

2.2 The Meaning of Investment

The meaning of the term 'investment' at its most basic level is the commitment of resources by a physical or legal person to a specific purpose in order to earn a profit or to gain a return. Etymologically, the word 'invest' is derived from the Latin *investire*, which means 'to clothe'.[1] An investor is in effect 'clothing' an enterprise with capital through the process of investment. In economic terms, investment, a form of savings, is the opposite of consumption. Investment is fundamental to economic growth and to the provision of needed goods and services in any society.

The term 'investment' is generally used in two senses. One sense is the *process* by which a person or legal entity makes an investment. Thus, the act of purchasing a hundred shares of stock on an exchange or buying a shop in which to sell goods is an investment. The second meaning refers to the *asset* acquired as a result of investing. Thus, the shares purchased by the shareholder and the shop acquired by the shopkeeper are both considered investments. Discussions of investment and foreign investment sometimes emphasize its process dimensions

---

[1] *The Oxford English Dictionary* defines 'to invest' as 'to employ (money) in the purchase of anything from which a profit is expected'. *The Oxford English Dictionary* (2nd edn, 1989) vol 8, p 46. *Webster's Third New International Dictionary of the English Language, Unabridged* defines the term as 'to commit money for a long period in order to gain a return'. *Webster's Third New International Dictionary of the English Language, Unabridged* (3rd edn, 1981) 1189.

and sometimes its asset dimensions.[2] As we shall see, the term 'investment' is a basic concept used in any investment treaty, and it is therefore important to understand its ramifications. Most such treaties, as shown in Chapter 7, adopt an asset-based, rather than a process-based, definition of investment. It is also important to recognize at the outset that lawyers, arbitrators, economists, financiers, and business executives may define investment in different ways. As a result, a transaction that an entrepreneur may consider as an 'investment' may not qualify as such under relevant legislation or treaties. For example, in one case that arose in Congo in 1999, the country's armed forces closed down a thriving law firm established by an American in Kinshasa, thereby effecting a total deprivation of the American's enterprise. When the American lawyer sought to bring a claim against the Congolese government before an international tribunal under the United States–Congo BIT, the arbitrators rejected his claim on the grounds that his firm did not constitute an 'investment' under the treaty.[3]

2.3 Forms of Investment

Investments can take many forms. Indeed, the great diversity of individual investment forms seems to be limited only by the creativity of investors seeking to meet their interests and those of the enterprise in which they are investing. As a result, new types and forms of investments are continually developing to meet new economic situations and achieve evolving financial objectives. An understanding of these diverse forms is important because the form an investment takes may influence the legal rights to which it and the investor are entitled under domestic legislation and international treaties. Three attributes of any investment form are particularly important: (1) the property and contractual rights resulting from the investment; (2) the control attributes of the investment; and (3) the enterprise form in which the investment is made.

---

[2] eg the *Encyclopedia of Public International Law* in defining foreign investment as 'a transfer of funds or materials from one country (called capital exporting country) to another country (called host country) in return for a direct or indirect participation in the profits of that enterprise' focuses on the process of making the investment. *Encyclopedia of Public International Law* (North-Holland, 1985) vol 8, p 246. On the other hand, E Graham and P Krugman, in their *Foreign Investment in the United States*, focus primarily on the result of that process when they define foreign investment in the following terms: 'Foreign direct investment is formally defined as ownership of assets by foreign residents for purpose of controlling the use of those assets.' E Graham and P Krugman, *Foreign Investment in the United States* (2nd edn, Institute for International Economics, 1991) 7.

[3] JD Mortenson, 'The Meaning of "Investment": ICSID's *Travaux* and the Domain of International Investment Law' (2010) 51 Harv Int'l LJ 257. See also *Mihaly International Corp v The Democratic Socialist Republic of Sri Lanka* (ICSID Case no ARB/00/02) (2002) 17 ICSID Rev—FILJ 142, in which the tribunal determined that expenses incurred in the preparation of an investment project that never materialized did not constitute an 'investment' either under the ICSID Convention or the United States–Sri Lanka BIT and that therefore the tribunal had no jurisdiction over the claim.

(a) **Property and contractual rights resulting from investments**

Legally, when an investor makes an investment in an enterprise, the investor gains certain specified property and contractual rights in the investment as a result. Generally speaking, an investor's rights with respect to an investment fall into two basic categories: *equity* or *debt*. An equity investment, like shares of stock in a company or a fixed asset like a shop, gives the investor an ownership interest. As an ownership interest, equity in company shares or a fixed asset entitles the investor to share in the profits (if any) of the enterprise, to participate to a greater or lesser extent in its management, and to hold that property interest until that investor transfers its interest to another person. On the other hand, an investment in the form of debt, like a loan or a bond, gives the investor a claim to be repaid, entitles the investor to fixed payments of principal and interest at specified times according to the investment agreement, and normally provides for a maturity date on which the investor's claim will end. In most legal systems, debt has priority over equity in the event of the enterprise's bankruptcy and liquidation, which means that holders of debt are paid before holders of equity from whatever enterprise assets remain.

Whether an investment in a given enterprise takes the form of debt or equity and the specific nature of the rights and liabilities attached to a particular equity or debt investment will depend on a host of variables. These include the prevailing law, projected interest rates, the financial goals and intentions of the parties involved in the enterprise, evaluations of the risks to be encountered, the projected revenues of the enterprise, and many other factors. In most instances, investments in specific enterprises will consist of a mixture of equity and debt, and that mixture is referred to by financial analysts as the enterprise's *capital structure*.[4]

An important element of the capital structure of any enterprise is its debt-to-equity ratio. In many investment projects, the amount of debt invested may far exceed the amount of equity. For instance, in 1995 the capital structure of the first phase of the Dabhol Power Company, then the largest foreign investment undertaken in India, amounted to US$932 million, which consisted of US$289 million in equity contributed by the three project partners and US$643 million in debt provided by a variety of foreign and domestic banks and financial institutions. The debt–equity ratio of the Dabhol Power Company was therefore more than 2 to 1.[5]

In most industries, it is generally believed that the higher the debt–equity ratio, the greater the risk faced by the enterprise. This is because the greater the amount of debt assumed by an enterprise, the greater its burden to make regular debt servicing payments to its creditors in order to meet its fixed obligation as required by its loan agreements. The failure to make such required payments because of insufficient earnings will entitle its creditors to take various legally authorized

---

[4] F Modigliani and MH Miller, 'The Cost of Capital, Corporation Finance and the Theory of Investment' (1958) 48 Amer Econ Rev 261.

[5] For background, see RP Teisch and WA Stoever, 'Enron in India: Lessons From a Renegotiation' (1991) 35 Mid-Atlantic J Bus 51.

remedies, including forcing the enterprise into bankruptcy or some form of judicial reorganization. The precise debt–equity ratio in a specific enterprise usually depends on the relative cost of debt and equity to the investors seeking to establish the enterprise, as well as the legal or regulatory requirements of the specific industries or countries. Indeed, the usual investment to establish or rehabilitate an enterprise rarely takes the form of a contribution of equity or debt alone but often also involves a host of other complex legal arrangements, including loans (both short-term and long-term), credit arrangements to finance equipment purchases, loan guaranties, licensing agreements, management contracts, and long-term sales and supply arrangements. Moreover, in addition to the more common forms of equity and debt, there are hybrid investments, such as preferred shares and convertible debentures, which possess some of the characteristics of both debt and equity securities.[6]

(b) Control attributes of the investment

A second important question concerning an investment relates to the extent of the investor's legal rights to control the underlying enterprise or assets in which the investment is made. 'Control' in this context means the ability of the investor to determine the actions and policies of that enterprise. An investor may have an ownership interest in an enterprise from which it gains certain financial benefits but still may not be able to control it because that ownership interest is not large enough. Thus, to take an extreme example, an investor who purchases a hundred shares of Microsoft Corporation or Barclays plc gains an equity interest in those enterprises but that interest is not large enough to allow the investor to determine the policies and actions of either company. On the other hand, if two companies form a joint venture to manufacture software and each elects members of the venture's board of directors, they each have an equity interest that allows them to participate in the control of the enterprise. Thus, it is by having rights to select members of an enterprise's governing board that an investor is able to influence the actions and policies of that enterprise.

Whether or not an investor has control of the enterprise in which it invests is a matter of importance both for the investor and for the government of the country in which the enterprise is located. For the investor, control not only enables the investor to determine the actions and policies of the enterprise, and therefore to pursue actions that will bring benefits to the investor, but also allows individual investors to protect themselves from the potentially negative and self-serving actions of other investors, creditors, and managers. Since governments are also concerned about the actions of enterprises taken on their territories, they too are often vitally interested in who controls those enterprises. For example, if foreign

---

[6] EF Brigham and MC Ehrhardt, *Financial Management: Theory and Practice* (14th edn, South Western, 2014) 13–18.

persons seek to buy a controlling interest in certain enterprises, local law may require prior government approval or even forbid such foreign control altogether.

The issue of enterprise control requires a second categorization of investment forms that distinguishes *direct investment* from *portfolio investment*. A direct investment establishes or purchases some form of permanent enterprise or facility, such as a factory, mine, plantation, hotel, or power station, in whose control and management the investor will participate. A portfolio investment is one which gives the investor no right to participate in the control and management of the underlying enterprise. Whether an investor has such control, and whether the investment therefore qualifies as direct or portfolio investment, will depend, of course, on the specifics of the investment. For statistical purposes, governments and international organizations classify an equity investment of 10 per cent or more as a direct investment.[7] An investment that gives the investor less than a 10 per cent voting interest is considered a portfolio investment.

The International Monetary Fund distinguishes between direct and portfolio investments in similar terms. It provides that a direct investment consists of either equity capital or retained earning between 'affiliated enterprises'. One enterprise is affiliated with another enterprise if the former has a voting interest of 10 per cent or more in the latter.[8] The key difference between these two categories of investment is the right of the investor to exert control over the investment. Thus, as a general rule, a direct investment is an equity interest in an enterprise that gives the investor 10 per cent or more voting power.

(c) Enterprise form

Yet a third way of categorizing investments relates to the legal form of the enterprise in which the investment is made. An enterprise is usually enclosed within a particular legal form of enterprise organization. Here, a fundamental distinction is whether the enterprise or asset is owned directly by the investor or owned by

---

[7] eg US Dept of Commerce, *Statistical Abstract of the United States 2011* (130th edn, 2011) 789–91. See also International Investment Survey Act of 1976, 22 USC § 3102(10).

[8] The International Monetary Fund defines direct investment as follows:

> a direct investment enterprise is defined in this Manual as an incorporated or unincorporated enterprise in which a direct investor, who is resident in another economy, owns 10 percent or more of the ordinary shares or voting power (for an incorporated enterprise) or the equivalent (for an unincorporated enterprise). Direct investment enterprises comprise those entities that are subsidiaries (a nonresident investor owns more than 50 percent), associates (an investor owns 50 percent or less) and branches (wholly or jointly owned unincorporated enterprises) either directly or indirectly owned by the direct investor. Subsidiaries in this connotation also may be identified as majority owned affiliates. Foreign-controlled enterprises include subsidiaries and branches, but associates may be included or excluded by individual countries according to their qualitative assessments of foreign control. Also, a public enterprise may in some instances be a direct investment enterprise, as defined in this paragraph.

International Monetary Fund, *IMF Balance of Payments Manual* (5th edn, 2010) ¶ 362, available at <https://www.imf.org/external/pubs/ft/bopman/bopman.pdf> accessed on 19 September 2014.

a separate legal entity in which the investor has an equity interest. If the asset is owned directly by the investor, it is considered a *branch* of the investor. On the other hand, the asset or enterprise might be owned by a separate legal entity all of whose shares are in turn owned by the investor. In this case, the investment would take the form of a *subsidiary* of the investor. For example, a refrigerator manufacturer that wants to establish a factory to produce air conditioners might make the factory a branch of its existing operations or alternatively create a separate subsidiary to own the factory and produce the air conditioners. The decision on whether to make an international investment in the form of a branch or a subsidiary involves numerous factors. For example, from the point of view of the investor, a branch may make the efficient management of a foreign investment easier than would a subsidiary. On the other hand, a subsidiary in the form of a separate company or corporation enjoying limited liability will protect the parent company from liabilities incurred by the subsidiary.[9] The choice of whether to make a foreign investment in the form of a branch or a subsidiary is not always a matter to be decided by the investor alone. Host country laws may require that any direct investment take the form of a subsidiary organized under and subject to host country company laws and regulations.

Whether an enterprise is a branch or a subsidiary can have significant legal consequences for the investor and the operation of the enterprise. When the enterprise has a separate entity, other investors may take part through the contribution of capital. In such cases, the investment, instead of being a wholly-owned subsidiary, will take the form of a joint venture or consortium. If the investment receives capital from numerous shareholders who do not participate actively in the business of the enterprise, the enterprise may take the form of a publicly traded corporation. Depending on the legal system of the country concerned, the law may provide a variety of enterprise forms such as a sole proprietorship, partnership, limited partnership, closely held corporation, or publicly traded corporation. Each form has different legal attributes and is subject to different legal requirements. And if a state invests in an enterprise, that enterprise may take the form of a government corporation subject to laws and rules separate from those governing private companies.

2.4 The Nature of Investors

Investment treaties govern not only investments but also investors: the persons and organizations that make investments. There are many kinds and types of investors. Depending on the nature of their owners, one can divide them into four basic categories: (1) private investors; (2) state investors; (3) international organizations; and (4) mixed enterprises.

---

[9] See J Fiechter et al, 'Subsidiaries or Branches: Does One Size Fit All', IMF Staff Discussion Note, SDN 11/04, 7 March 2011, available at <http://www.imf.org/external/pubs/ft/sdn/2011/sdn1104.pdf> accessed 18 September 2014.

(a) Private investors

The first category consists of private investors, physical and legal persons who are not part of any government or state apparatus. Among private investors, the most important are those that take the form of corporations or companies.

It has been said that '[t]he most important organization in the world is the company: the basis of the prosperity in the West and the best hope for the rest of the world'.[10] Companies and corporations are the world's most significant depositories of assets and technology and a primary force for wealth creation and allocation. Although companies and corporations are generally created under the domestic law of a particular country,[11] they share many common features and have all been designed to encourage investment. For example:

1. Companies and corporations are legal entities that exist separate and distinct from their investors and shareholders. Thus, they are said to have 'legal personality'. As a result, they may hold, acquire, and transfer property in their own names, make contracts, sue and be sued in their individual capacity, and engage in legal transactions just as physical persons can.

2. Shareholders in companies and corporations enjoy 'limited liability'. That is, they are not liable for the debts and obligations of the company in which they have invested—a factor that encourages investment by reducing investor risk. Since investors in the shares of corporations risk only their initial investment and are not personally liable for the debts and obligations incurred by the corporation itself, they are generally more willing to make investments than they would be if they were liable for such corporate obligations as well.

3. As entities existing apart from their investors, companies and corporations usually have an unlimited life under most domestic legal systems. This factor gives stability to enterprises in corporate form, since their existence is unaffected by the entry and departure of individual managers or investors.

4. The corporate structure allows centralized control and management by a few managers of the assets and operations of potentially diverse, vast, and widely dispersed enterprises. A company's usual organizational structure provides that the shareholders, based on the voting rights of the shares they own, elect a board of directors that is legally responsible for the management of the company. This structure facilitates the development of easily controlled groups of corporations, often located in many different countries. Indeed the much discussed 'multinational corporation' is legally not a single

---

[10] J Mickelwait and A Wooldridge, *The Company: A Short History of a Revolutionary Idea* (Modern Library, 2003) xv.

[11] Certain international organizations, such as the World Bank and the various regional development banks, that adopt the corporate form, are created by treaty. See generally, Articles of Agreement, International Bank for Reconstruction and Development, available at <http://web.worldbank.org/WBSITE/EXTERNAL/EXTABOUTUS/0,,contentMDK:20049557~menuPK:63000601~pagePK:34542~piPK:36600~theSitePK:29708,00.html> accessed 20 September 2014.

corporation but many corporations and companies linked together by share ownership and contractual rights.

5. The domestic law of the country concerned usually allows ownership interest in the form of shares of stock to be transferred from one investor to another without affecting the legal structure of the underlying enterprise. This factor encourages investment by giving liquidity to investments in companies and allows for the easy entry and exit of shareholders.

The vast majority of the world's corporations are private corporations, since their ownership and control are in the hands of private individuals and organizations. Nevertheless, they are each creatures of national law and are subject to the differing laws and regulations of the countries of their creation and their operation.

(b) State investors

A second large and important category of investors consists of governments and governmental entities, known variously as 'state-owned enterprises' (SOEs), 'government corporations', or 'state-controlled entities' (SCEs). Virtually all governments, to a greater or lesser extent, invest in enterprises designed to provide services or goods to the inhabitants of their countries. Thus, states may establish corporations to provide air and maritime transportation, telecommunications, mining, and steel production, to mention just a few. Such state entities are usually subject to a separate legal regime that is distinct from that governing private companies and corporations. Traditionally, governments created them to serve the local economy; however, more recently they have begun to act as significant international investors.

State entities may choose to invest at home or abroad for myriad financial or political reasons. The extent to which a government becomes an investor depends on a variety of factors, including the existence or lack of private investors in a particular economic field or sector, the quality and cost of needed goods and services provided by such private enterprise, the existing political situation, and the prevailing ideology in that country. Indeed, in many countries whether private enterprise or government should invest in a particular economic sector is an important public policy question having strong ideological and political implications. For instance, since 2004, China's strategy of state intervention through private investment in Africa has raised questions over the geopolitical impact of the scale of such investments.[12]

The question of who invests in what is not a purely economic one. The identity of who owns and controls a country's enterprises has important political implications because assets and enterprises endow their owners with political power. As

---

[12] D Brautigam, 'Africa's Eastern Promise: What the West Can Learn From Chinese Investment in Africa' (January 2010) Foreign Affairs 5.

a result, the subject of investment by foreigners, as will be seen, has significant ideological and political overtones in most countries.

The prevailing ideology in a country may significantly influence the respective roles accorded to private and state investors. For example, countries with a strong socialist orientation may choose to reserve to the state important areas of economic activity, such as the production of electricity, the provision of air and land transportation, and the pursuit of mineral development, and to exclude private enterprise from these economic sectors. A government's nationalist ideology may exclude foreigners from investing in economic sectors considered vital to preserving a country's sovereignty, economic independence, or national security. One of the consequences of the end of communism in eastern Europe and the former Soviet Union and the elimination of socialism in many other countries was 'privatization', or the transfer of state enterprises and assets to private hands and the reduction of barriers to private investment throughout the economy.[13]

Today, despite the end of communism and the widespread and massive privatization of state assets throughout the world, governments remain important investors both domestically and internationally and often prohibit private investment in specific sectors and industries. In the field of international investment, one may distinguish between state-owned multinational corporations whose purpose is to undertake and conduct business activities in specific economic sectors, usually through direct foreign investments, and sovereign wealth funds (SWFs) whose purpose is to invest a state's monetary reserves in order to gain a return to finance state activities, often through portfolio investments.

(c) International organizations

A third important category of investors consists of international institutions and organizations created and owned by states. These international institutions and organizations have international legal personalities and are subject to international law, primarily the treaties that created them. The World Bank, its affiliates (such as the International Finance Corporation), and regional development banks (such as the Asian Development Bank and the InterAmerican Development Bank) are all international institutions whose purpose is to invest funds secured from states and from private capital markets in order to promote economic development.[14]

---

[13] JW Salacuse, 'From Developing Countries to Emerging Markets: A New Role for Law in the Third World' (1999) 33 Int'l Lawyer 875.

[14] RD Fraser, *The World Financial System* (1st edn, Longman, 1987) 363–450. See also statements about the mission of selected international financial institutions at <http://www.worldbank.org/en/about/what-we-do> accessed 22 April 2015 (for the World Bank); <http://www.ifc.org/wps/wcm/connect/corp_ext_content/ifc_external_corporate_site/home> accessed 19 September 2014 (for International Financial Corporation); <http://www.adb.org/site/business-opportunities/mission> accessed 19 September 2014 (for Asian Development Bank); and <http://www.iadb.org/en/topics/transparency/support-for-countries/mission-vision-and-values,1178.html> accessed 22 April 2015 (for Inter-American Development Bank).

They invest billions of dollars each year through both loans and equity participations in order simultaneously to support economic development and earn a return on their invested capital. One distinguishing characteristic of loans from international organizations is that they often impose severe conditions on the governmental policies of debtor countries, a process known as 'conditionality'.[15]

(d) Mixed enterprises

Frequently, the various types of investors mentioned earlier invest together in particular enterprises. For example, it is common for private companies to form joint ventures with state corporations to undertake productive enterprises, such as the manufacture of machines or the operation of an airline. In some countries, such mixed enterprises may be subject to a distinct legal regime. Often, an international organization such as the World Bank or the International Finance Corporation is included as a party. Thus, a large infrastructure project such as an electrical generation and transmission system or a telecommunications network may involve a state corporation, a private company, and an international organization as investors within a single legal entity.

2.5 The Role of Return and Risk

With the possible exception of certain subsidized government enterprises, investors are concerned primarily about two factors in making and managing their investments: return and risk. Indeed, one can say that return and risk are the driving factors behind all investment decisions. The reason investors invest is to gain a return, to make a profit. The ways in which an investor will gain a return from a particular investment will depend on the nature of the enterprise and the investment made in it. Investors may gain a return through sharing in the profits of the enterprise, through the receipt of interest paid on debt obligations, through capital gains made on the sale of an investment to a third party, as well as by a variety of other transactions, such as technology transfers and management contracts, associated with the investment.

At the same time, all investors are also concerned about the risks affecting their proposed investments. One may define risk as the probability that expected returns from an investment will not be realized. Investors evaluate potential investments not in terms of the absolute returns to be expected from a particular investment but on the basis of the expected returns measured against the projected levels of risk. In the calculation of most investors, a greater risk requires a higher rate of return to justify an investment.

---

[15] eg S Koerberle et al (eds), *Conditionality Revisited* (World Bank, 2005); K Elborgh-Woytek and M Lewis, 'Privatization in Ukraine: Challenges of Assessment and Coverage in Fund Conditionality', IMF Policy Discussion Paper (2002) available at <https://www.imf.org/external/pubs/ft/pdp/2002/pdp07.pdf> accessed 19 September 2014.

Investors analyse risk in various ways, but a basic distinction made by most investors is between commercial risk and political risk. Commercial risks are those possible negative effects derived from ordinary commercial activities affecting the enterprise. For example, market sales may be less than expected, management may be inefficient, or the enterprise's technology may prove more costly or less effective than planned. Political risks are negative events that derive from political actions, such as the expropriation of an enterprise by the government, the establishment of price controls by a regulatory authority, or riots that damage investment assets. A fundamental purpose of investment treaties is to provide foreign investors and their investments with a level of protection against political risk.

All investors, private, state, and international, seek to structure and operate their investments in ways that will enhance their returns and minimize their risks. To achieve this result, they use a variety of devices, including contracts, legislative provisions, and, as will be seen later in this volume, international treaties. From the point of view of the investor, the primary utility of an investment treaty is that it reduces the political risks of investing in a foreign country. Similarly, countries and communities seeking to attract or encourage investment will try to find ways to increase returns to potential investors, perhaps by building roads or granting tax exemptions, or to reduce risk, possibly by lessening governmental corruption or guaranteeing to purchase the product produced by the investment. In general, actions that increase return or reduce risk encourage investment. Conversely, actions that threaten returns or increase risk discourage investment. Thus, from the point of view of many states, a primary utility of an investment treaty is to promote investment from another signatory country. Reflecting these two goals, the title of most investment treaties states that they are 'agreements to protect and promote investment'.

2.6 The Nature of International Investment

Historically, investors and entrepreneurs have sought economic gain not only in their home countries but in other countries as well. Originally, the primary mechanism for seeking such gains was through foreign trade. Trade eventually led to early forms of international investment. Indeed, such international investment was originally focused on financing trade with other countries. Thus, for example, during the Renaissance, individual merchants formed limited partnerships or *commenda* with a ship's owners or sea captains to finance the shipment of goods or trade in goods with other countries.[16] Later, in connection with trade, merchants might acquire buildings or property within foreign countries to create trading establishments. For example, in AD 991, the Byzantine Emperors Basil II and Constantine VIII, in a document known in Latin as a *chrysobul*, granted

---

[16] J McCusker (ed), *History of World Trade since 1450* (Macmillan Reference, 2006) vol 2, pp 557–8.

the merchants of Venice the right to trade in the ports and other places of the Byzantine Empire without paying customs duties, as well as the right to a quarter in Constantinople, known as an *embolum*, for dwelling and trading.[17] The acquisition and development of such a trading and dwelling quarter in Constantinople was a form of direct foreign investment by the Venice merchants. In time, investors would undertake investments in other countries for other purposes, including acquiring natural resources and conducting manufacturing.

In most cases, an international investment is *international* because it has two defining attributes: (1) the person or entity undertaking the investment is not a citizen, or at least not a resident, of the country in which the investment is made; and (2) the investment process includes the transfer of funds or capital from a foreign country to the country of investment, which results in a continuing legal relationship between the investor and the foreign enterprise. Thus, most 'foreign investments' in a particular country are made by a foreign corporation or foreign individual and involve the transfer of money or capital from one country to another. For example, a corporation with headquarters in France wishing to establish a factory in Malaysia that manufactures refrigerators or computers would establish a wholly-owned subsidiary in Malaysia and transfer to that subsidiary the necessary capital and technology to build and operate the factory. In that situation, France would be considered the 'home country' of the investor and Malaysia would be considered the 'host country'.

On the other hand, while the previous description is the basic model for many direct foreign investment transactions, an investor of foreign nationality or residence and a physical transfer of capital from one country to another may not necessarily be present in all international investment transactions. For example, a foreign company could undertake an investment by mobilizing capital within a host country by borrowing from local banks or raising funds on the local capital market.

On the other hand, indigenous entrepreneurs may mobilize capital from abroad for investment in their home countries. For example, they might borrow from foreign banks or issue corporate bonds abroad. Does either of the transactions just described qualify as 'international' or 'foreign' investment? The answer depends upon who is characterizing the transaction and for what purpose. Economists and economic institutions may use one definition of foreign investment to gather statistics or analyse financial trends, but lawyers, regulatory authorities, and arbitration tribunals might use another when applying laws and treaties. Without engaging in a detailed discussion of this issue, it is worth noting that the definitions of foreign investor and foreign investment are important starting points

---

[17] P Fischer, 'Some Recent Trends and Developments in the Law of Foreign Investment' in K-H Boeckstiegel et al (eds), *Völkerrecht, Recht der internationalen Organisationen, Weltwirtschafatsrecht: Festschrift für Ignaz Seidl-Hohenveldern* (Carl Heymanns Verlag, 1988) 97. See also 'Concessions Granted to the Merchants of Venice, by the Byzantine Emperors Basilius and Costantinus, Executed in March 991' in P Fischer, *A Collection of International Concessions and Related Instruments* (Oceana Publications, 1976) vol 1, pp 15–18.

in analysing the coverage of foreign investment treaties and foreign investment legislation, a subject discussed in Chapter 7.

While foreign investment is often associated with international trade or has trade as its objective, investment transactions and trade transactions are conceptually distinct. For one thing, the typical trade transaction is basically an exchange of goods or services for money. Once that exchange is made, the transaction is complete and usually no further legal relationship exists between buyer and seller. Investment transactions, on the other hand, are of a longer duration and once made result in a continuing legal relationship between the investor and the enterprise in which the investor has invested. Foreign investment also results in a continuing relationship between the investor and the foreign country where the investment occurred because the investor's capital is now subject to the sovereignty of that country. Because an asset owned by the investor is subject to the jurisdiction of a foreign sovereign, the investor and its investment is subject to that sovereign's future actions. To the extent that those future actions have a negative impact on the investment, the investor and its investment are subject to the political risk emanating from that country. Normal trade transactions do not result in similar continuing relationships and so are not subject to the same kinds of political risks as foreign investment transactions.

While they are conceptually distinct, trade and investment are nonetheless often interrelated. Many foreign investments are undertaken to facilitate and foster trade. For example, the French company mentioned earlier may have established a subsidiary to manufacture refrigerators in Malaysia specifically in order to take account of lower production costs and gain the ability to sell its product throughout Asia. Because of the close connection between investment and trade activities, the World Trade Organization (WTO) has adopted various rules through binding treaties that govern investments that have an impact on trade. One such treaty, to be discussed later in this volume, is the Agreement on Trade-Related Investment Measures (TRIMs).[18]

2.7 Forms of International Investment

Like purely domestic investment, foreign investment can take a variety of forms. The following are some of the most common.

(a) Foreign direct investment

Foreign direct investment (FDI), sometimes also called direct foreign investment (DFI), is an equity or ownership investment of more than 10 per cent by

---

[18] 'Uruguay Round Agreement on Trade-Related Investment Measures' in *The Results of the Uruguay Round of Multilateral Trade Negotiations: The Legal Texts* (1994) 163 (TRIMs Agreement). Also available at the WTO website <http://www.wto.org/english/docs_e/legal_e/18-trims.pdf> accessed 18 September 2014.

an investor in one country (known as 'the home country' or 'capital-export-ing country') in an enterprise located in another country (the 'host country' or 'capital-importing country').[19] FDI is a vitally important feature of modern economic life. In 2013, UNCTAD estimated that the total stock of FDI in the world was US$25.5 trillion, of which US$16 trillion was invested in developed economies, US$9.4 trillion in developing countries, and US$940 billion in 'tran-sition economies', a group composed of South-East Europe, the Commonwealth of Independent States, and Georgia.[20] The total FDI invested in that year was US$1.45 trillion, of which US$566 billion (39%) went to developed countries, US$788 billion (54%) went to developing countries, and the remainder, US$108 billion, went to transition economies. 2013 was the first year in which invest-ment to developing countries exceeded the amount invested in developed econo-mies. By comparison, in 2007, total FDIs reached a record amount of US$1.833 trillion.[21] Of that amount, US$1.248 trillion was invested in developed coun-tries, approximately US$500 billion was invested in developing countries, and US$86 billion was invested in South-East Europe and the Commonwealth of Independent States.[22]

FDI has the effect of giving investors in one country ownership rights in and control over economic assets in another country. As a result, FDI is a powerful force for integrating national economies and fostering the phenomenon of glo-balization. As governments and populations in host countries become concerned about the influence of foreigners on domestic politics, local economies, national security, and indigenous culture as a result of their direct investments, these same factors give FDI important political overtones. In this regard, it is important to recognize that FDI in most instances involves more than the transfer of money or assets from one country to another. Its purpose is to create productive capacity. To achieve that goal, the foreign direct investor usually must also transfer know-how, skills, and management capability along with money, capital, and technology. Thus, in most cases, an FDI, like the one to create a factory to manufacture air conditioners, consists of a package of money, equipment, human skills, technol-ogy, and know-how.

(b) Foreign portfolio investment

A foreign portfolio investment is an investment by a resident of one country in a company based in another country with shares equaling less than 10 per cent of the overall voting power. Here, too, the fundamental distinction between FDI and foreign portfolio investment lies not in the form of the investment (ie shares)

---

[19] Cohen states: 'Quantitatively, the nearly universally accepted definition of FDI is ownership of at least 10 percent of common (voting) stock of a business enterprise operating in a country other than one in which the investing company is headquartered.' SD Cohen, *Multinational Corporations and Foreign Direct Investment: Avoiding Simplicity, Embracing Complexity* (OUP, 2007) 38. For the definition used by the IMF, see also n 8 above.

[20] UNCTAD, *World Investment Report 2014* (2014) 208–12.

[21] UNCTAD, *World Investment Report 2008* (2008) 2.   [22] ibid 8–9.

but in the amount of control transferred. A DFI is large enough to enable the investor to participate in control of the enterprise, while a portfolio investment is not large enough to give such control.

The purchase of shares of one country's companies by another country's persons has also grown significantly in recent years. The total value of portfolio investments of this type amounts to trillions of US dollars, and that total seems to be growing rapidly.[23] A variety of factors have driven this phenomenon, including the development of stock markets in many countries, the emergence of technologies to facilitate cross-border portfolio investment, the removal or reduction of legal restriction on the investment by foreigners in local companies, and improved knowledge and information about foreign stock markets and foreign companies. Another factor has been the recognition by institutional investors throughout the world that exposure to foreign markets is an important element in increasing the returns earned by such institutions as mutual funds, pension funds, and endowment funds.

(c) International loans

Loans by banks and other financial institutions based in one country to enterprises located in another country constitute yet another form of foreign investment. In many cases, in order to spread the risk, especially large loans are provided not by a single financial institution but by a syndicate of several banks located in different countries. International loans are also not only made between unrelated entities; corporations often make them to their subsidiaries and affiliates as a means of financing the latter's operations. In some cases, loans are often a substitute for an equity investment.

(d) International bonds

Both governments and corporations raise some of the needed capital for their activities by issuing bonds, notes, and other negotiable instruments to investors in other countries. Once issued, such bonds, notes, and other negotiable instruments are often traded among investors on capital markets. The value of new international bonds issued during 2013 was equivalent to US$3,966.2 billion.[24]

---

[23] eg foreign holdings of US securities as of 30 June 2013 were measured at US$14,410 billion, of which US$13,532 billion were holdings of US long-term securities (original term-to-maturity in excess of one year) and US$878 billion were holdings of US short-term securities. As of 30 June 2012, total foreign holdings amounted to US$12,451 billion. US Department of the Treasury, 'Report on Foreign Portfolio Holdings of U.S. Securities as of June 30, 2013' (April 2014), available at <http://www.treasury.gov/ticdata/Publish/shla2013r.pdf> accessed 19 September 2014.

US holdings of foreign securities as of 31 December 2012 totalled US$7,941 billion, of which holdings of foreign equities amounted to US$5,312 billion and holdings of foreign debt US$2,630 billion. US Department of the Treasury, 'Report on U.S. Portfolio Holdings of Foreign Securities as of December 31, 2012' (October 2013), available at <http://www.treasury.gov/ticdata/Publish/shc2012r.pdf> accessed 19 September 2014.

[24] The International Capital Market Association (ICMA) has found that the total of new international bond market issues for the first half of 2014 is US$2,447.8 billion. This figure shows a 13%

Normally, such loans are denominated in dollars, euros, yen, and other readily convertible international currencies. However, with the development of local credit markets, foreign investors are increasingly investing in bonds and notes of foreign issuers denominated in other local currencies that are less easily convertible.

(e) Suppliers' and others' credits

Companies in one country will often sell goods on credit to a company in another country. In many situations, that credit is supported by a guarantee from a financial or governmental institution. Such credit is also a type of investment by the supplier and often accrues interest until the amount of the purchase is fully paid. In such a transaction, unlike a loan or the purchase of a bond from a foreign issuer, no money crosses borders. Nevertheless, it is an investment because the supplier has committed capital in the form of goods to the transaction, and it expects a return in the form of repayment of the purchase price, plus an agreed amount of interest, for financing the sale.

(f) Other contractual arrangements

A variety of other contractual arrangements, particularly long-term arrangements between persons in different countries, may also qualify as investments to the extent that they require one party to commit capital or money to a venture with the expectation of receiving a return at a later time. Thus, concession contracts between persons and entities based in different countries to run public services, mineral exploration and development agreements, construction contracts, land purchase agreements, and innumerable other contractual devices may all be considered international investments.

International investment transactions and forms have been growing rapidly in size, frequency, and variety in recent decades as a result of the economic imperatives of globalization. The continuing drive for economic efficiency will propel this trend in the decades ahead. Globalization is both a cause and a result of the movement to conclude international investment treaties among nations.

The forms of international investment indicated earlier are by no means an exclusive list. They are offered as illustrations of the principal ways in which international or foreign investments are made. In response to business and economic necessity, and the creativity of business and financial entrepreneurs, new forms will no doubt arise in the future. Foreseeing this, investment treaties have generally avoided giving an exclusive listing of covered investments and have instead opted to provide an open-ended definition to allow for the future evolution of investment transactions. Nonetheless, as will also be seen, definitions of international

---

increase in the value of new issuance compared with the figure for the first half of 2013. Total market size in terms of outstanding international bonds stood at over US$22 trillion as at 30 June 2014. For more information, see the ICMA website, at <http://icmagroup.org/resources/market-data/Market-Data-Dealogic/#8> accessed 19 September 2014.

investment are important in applying treaties. A transaction will be protected by a treaty if it meets the treaty's definition of investment. It will not be protected if it fails to meet that definition.

2.8 The Nature of International Investors

Who exactly are international investors? Simply put, an international investor is a physical or legal person in one country who invests funds or capital in another country in an investment transaction, such as those listed earlier. That bland definition masks the great diversity of individuals and organizations engaged in international investment and the broad variations in their economic objectives and activities. One of the principal types of foreign investor is the 'multinational corporation' (MNC), also known as the 'multinational enterprise' (MNE) and the 'transnational corporation' (TNC). Basically, an MNC is an enterprise that owns or has control over income-producing facilities in at least two countries.[25] Applying that definition, the United Nations Conference on Trade and Development (UNCTAD) estimated that in 2006 there were 77,000 multinational corporations with 770,000 affiliates in the world.[26] That definition covers an extremely wide variety of enterprises, from global companies like Shell or General Motors with hundreds of subsidiaries around the world to small specialized enterprises with a single subsidiary in another country. MNCs are by no means found exclusively in developed countries. Increasingly, emerging market countries like China, India, and certain Arabian Gulf states are developing their own MNEs, which are becoming active investors around the globe. In addition, important MNEs are owned or controlled by states. In 2013, UNCTAD estimated that there were at least 550 state-owned MNCs, from both developed and developing countries, with more than 15,000 foreign affiliates and foreign assets valued at over US$2 trillion. In that year alone, FDI by state-controlled MNCs was more than US$160 billion. At that level, although their number constitutes less than 1 per cent of the MNCs in the world, they accounted for over 11 per cent of global FDI flows.[27]

MNCs include a wide variety of business enterprises pursuing a diverse set of objectives. One way of trying to understand MNCs is by the objectives they pursue. Companies invest abroad for different reasons. Some, which might be called 'market seekers', invest in order to find and develop new markets for their products. Others, like petroleum or mineral companies, invest in order to find and obtain raw materials. They might therefore be called 'raw-material seekers'. Still others searching to reduce costs and improve efficiency of production by finding

---

[25] 'The nearly universally accepted definition of multinational corporation is one that owns outright, controls, or has direct managerial influence in income-generating, value-added facilities in at least two countries.' Cohen (n 19 above) 39.

[26] See UNCTAD, *World Investment Report 2008* (2008) 9–10.

[27] UNCTAD, *World Investment Report 2014* (2014) ix.

lower cost factors of production, like cheap labour or low-cost energy, might be called 'efficiency seekers'. Some companies, particularly in high technology areas, invest abroad in order to obtain knowledge and might therefore be called 'knowledge seekers'. And yet others acquire or establish new operations in countries that are considered unlikely to expropriate or interfere with private enterprise, and might be called 'political safety seekers'.[28]

Regardless of their aim, for many years MNCs have been the subject of intense study and commentary by both scholars and the public and have engendered strong and opposing views. For some people, MNCs are important engines of economic development. For others, they are exploiters of labour and destroyers of the environment.[29] For some, their potential for economic development needs to be released from the strictures of onerous government policies and laws. For others, their potential for self-enrichment at the expense of national sovereignty, human rights, and the environment needs to be controlled by strict legislation and international agreements. As a result, the role of MNCs is central in international development, and they are important subjects of all international investment treaties.

New types of MNEs seem to be evolving constantly. Traditionally, multinational corporate investors have been engaged in manufacturing and production activities, but non-manufacturing firms have also become important direct investors. Thus, private equity firms are now actively engaged in DFI in foreign enterprises. Their goal is to take control of those enterprises, reorganize them to make them more efficient, and then sell them.

But multinational direct investors are by no means the entire universe of international investors. Banks and financial firms that extend loans and credits to governments, companies, and individuals in other countries are also foreign investors. These banks and firms control significant amounts of capital and devote considerable funds to international investments. Institutional investors, such as pension, endowment, and mutual funds, are increasingly devoting their resources to both debt and equity investments in foreign countries to enhance their returns and manage their risks through diversification. And as a result of the development of capital markets around the world, improved communications, and more readily available financial information on a global scale, individual portfolio investors are also increasingly seeking to invest their funds in shares, credit instruments, and bonds issued by entities outside their home countries.

An increasingly important manifestation of governments as investors is the sovereign wealth fund. SWFs are state agencies holding a portion of a country's foreign currency reserves. Established by such countries as Kuwait, Norway, Singapore, and China with the goal of maximizing returns, they are authorized to

---

[28] D Eiteman, A Stonehill, and M Moffett, *Multinational Business Finance* (12th edn, Prentice Hall, 2014) 9. Eiteman and Stonehill have thus categorized investors into five types: market seekers, raw-material seekers, production-efficiency seekers, knowledge seekers, and political safety seekers.

[29] For a discussion of the history of MNCs and the various views concerning their role in the international economy, see generally Cohen (n 19 above).

invest their assets in foreign investments of varying degrees of risk. Their investment capital is derived from their countries' growing foreign currency reserves resulting from revenues from their commodity exports and expanding international trade. In addition to formally established SWFs, other important sources of state funds for investment abroad are central bank reserves, public pension funds, and state-owned enterprises and development funds.[30] In 2013, UNCTAD estimated that there were seventy-three recognized SWFs, 60 per cent of which had been established since 2000, and that they managed US$5.3 trillion in assets.[31] Other sovereign investment vehicles held an additional US$6.8 trillion.[32] Because of their potential economic power and the fact that they are controlled by governments with various political aims, the activities of these sovereign investors have raised concern in host countries and prompted calls for increased transparency and regulation of their activities.[33]

As a result of globalization, growing numbers of individuals and organizations invest abroad and are therefore in a general sense to be considered 'foreign investors'. Thus, the universe of potential foreign investors consists of literally millions of individuals, companies, and organizations, and that number continues to expand steadily. Each of these millions of individuals, companies, and organizations and their trillions of dollars of capital may potentially be affected by international investment treaties.

2.9 State Interests in International Investment

An international investment is not only a transaction between a foreign investor and the enterprise in which an investment is made, it is also an act of international relations between sovereign states. While investors' primary interest is protecting their investments from risk and maximizing their returns, national governments and the international community have other, broader interests that need to be considered and accounted for in developing an international regime for investment. Since it is governments, not individuals or corporations, that negotiate investment treaties, they will normally seek to pursue their interests through the treaty-making process. As a result, officials, executives, and lawyers engaged in making and managing foreign investments must take account of these interests in order to understand and interpret investment legislation and treaties appropriately.

---

[30] R Kimmitt, 'Public Footprints in Private Markets: Sovereign Wealth Funds and the World Economy' (January/February 2008) Foreign Affairs 119.

[31] UNCTAD, *World Investment Report 2013* (2013) 10.

[32] TheCityUK, *Sovereign Wealth Funds* (April 2011) 1.

[33] E Truman, *Sovereign Wealth Funds: Threat or Salvation?* (Peterson Institute for International Economics, 2010), available at <http://bookstore.piie.com/book-store/4983.html> accessed 15 September 2014. See also M Sornarajah, 'Sovereign Wealth Funds and the Existing Structure of the Regulation of Investments' (2011) 1 Asian J Int'l L 267; YCL Lee, 'The Governance of Contemporary Sovereign Wealth Funds' (2010) 6 Hast Bus LJ 197.

National governments are concerned with achieving prosperity, economic development, and security, and improving the general welfare of their people. To the extent that international investment in their territory facilitates the achievement of those goals, national governments will foster and encourage foreign investment. To the extent that a government perceives the goals of foreign investors as contrary to its aims, its response will be less favourable. Indeed, it is in that circumstance of perceived conflicting interests and goals that investor–state disputes arise.

States view foreign investment as a form of international economic cooperation. As seen by states, its purpose is not just to assure legal rights to investors but to achieve broader societal goals that individual investors often forget or ignore. Investment treaties are a mechanism to concretize and advance the economic cooperation between states that advances their individual economic development and prosperity. States often make their intentions clear in that regard in the preambles to their international investment agreements. Thus, they express such goals as '[d]esiring to develop economic cooperation between the two States',[34] 'anxious to give formal expression to this new desire for a European-wide and global cooperation based on mutual respect and confidence',[35] and 'wishing to strengthen their partnership and promote mutually advantageous economic relations'.[36] In the end, it is important to remember that international investment treaties are not just instruments to grant rights to investors. They are above all instruments of international economic relations among states. Government officials, corporate executives, and lawyers must approach them not just within the framework of narrow investor interests but within the broader framework of international economic cooperation.

[34] Agreement between the Argentine Republic and the Republic of France for the Promotion and Reciprocal Protection of Investments (signed 3 July 1991, entered into force 3 March 1993) 1728 UNTS 298.

[35] European Energy Charter Treaty (opened for signature 1 February 1995) (1995) 34 ILM 360 preamble.

[36] United States–Morocco Free Trade Agreement (signed 15 June 2004, entered into force 1 January 2006) preamble, available at <http://www.ustr.gov/trade-agreements/free-trade-agreements/morocco-fta/final-text> accessed 20 September 2014.

3

The Foundations
of International Investment Law

3.1 Background of the Investment Treaty Movement

The movement to negotiate the approximately 3,300 investment treaties that have reshaped international investment law did not arise suddenly and miraculously the way Athena sprang from the head of Zeus. The movement finds its origins in nations' diverse economic interests and the state of international investment law of an earlier time. Those interests and that law shaped and influenced the growth of investment treaties. It is necessary to understand that background not only to comprehend how and why investment treaties have become important instruments of international economic relations but also to interpret and apply the treaty provisions themselves. Moreover, where treaty provisions are silent on particular issues of international investment law, reference must be made to traditional non-treaty principles of international law. The purpose of this chapter is to examine the state of international investment law that exists in the absence of an applicable treaty, as that law remains an important foundation for the international law governing investments.

3.2 State and Investor Interests Shaping International
Investment Law

One of the purposes of law is to protect the legitimate interests of persons, groups, and states and to provide a mechanism for resolving disputes when those interests are in conflict. In any international investment transaction, there are three primary parties in interest: the investor, the host country in which the investment is made, and the home country of the investor. Each party ordinarily uses laws and legal devices to advance its perceived interests.[1] Let us examine briefly the interests of the three key participants in the investment process and then consider how those interests have shaped the law.

---

[1] See generally JW Salacuse, *The Three Laws of International Investment: National, Contractual and International Frameworks for Foreign Capital* (OUP, 2013).

(a) Host country interests

Since an international investment results in placing a foreign person's assets under the sovereignty of another country, that country (the host state) ordinarily considers itself to have sole authority over the investment and the activities of the investor in its territory. In its view, the host country's law is the primary, if not the exclusive, source of rules applicable to international investments and international investors in its territory.

The host country (sometimes referred to as the 'capital-importing country') may have a variety of interests in the investment process. Like foreign investors, host country governments view foreign investments in terms of their costs and their benefits, their risks and their rewards. For example, a host country may perceive the benefits of foreign investment as including the creation of new jobs for its nationals, the transfer of new technology and skills to its territory, the creation of improved linkages between the host country and world markets, the development of its natural resources, the strengthening of local industries and means of production, the improvement of its balance of payments—especially when the investment project will yield export earnings—and increased taxes and other revenue resulting from the activities of the foreign investor's enterprise.

Similarly, most host countries are not unmindful of the potential costs of foreign investment. These costs may include damaging competitive effects on local industries, possible interference in the domestic political process, security risks posed by the foreign ownership of strategic industries and companies, and the introduction of potentially injurious technologies and practices to the local environment, indigenous cultures, and the health and safety of its other inhabitants.

Few host countries, therefore, view foreign investment as an unmixed blessing. Most recognize that it has benefits and costs. As a result, through a variety of devices, a host country government will ordinarily attempt to maximize its perceived benefits and minimize its perceived costs, while still seeking to attract capital from abroad to a greater or lesser extent. Indeed, this is the primary objective of the investment legislation and regulatory schemes of most countries throughout the world.[2]

Moreover, a host country's interest in and approach to international investment may change over time. The government of a host state may actively seek foreign capital to achieve national objectives one year, and another government, for ideological or practical reasons, may decide to restrict, curtail, or even seize these very same foreign investments a year later. Thus, promises made to investors through laws and contracts may be changed or cancelled entirely when, acting in what it considers the national interest, a host government repeals those laws and abrogates or demands changes to those contracts.[3]

---

[2] JW Salacuse, 'Host Country Regulation and Promotion of Joint Venture and Foreign Investment' in DN Goldsweig and RH Cummings (eds), *International Joint Ventures: A Practical Approach to Working with Foreign Investors in the U.S. and Abroad: A Case Study with Sample Documents* (2nd edn, American Bar Association, 1990) 107–36.

[3] eg D Smith and L Wells, *Negotiating Third World Mineral Agreements: Promises as Prologue* (Ballinger Pub Co, 1975); JW Salacuse, 'Renegotiating International Project Agreements' (2001) 24 Ford Int'l LJ 1319.

(b) Investor interests

The basic interest of any investor is to maximize the returns from its investment and to protect itself from risks to those returns and the investment itself. While a foreign investor has no power to make laws and regulations, it can often invoke existing laws and regulations and construct legal devices to maximize its returns and minimize its risks. Thus, investors make contracts and agreements with agencies in host country governments in order to obtain special privileges and benefits that they would not otherwise have—a dynamic that seems to have existed since the advent of foreign investment.[4] For example, foreign investors may request tax exemptions, customs duties privileges, access to natural resources, and even subsidies from host governments in order to encourage them to make an investment.

Such special treatment is not limited to poor developing countries. State and local governments in the United States, for example, grant incentives to foreign investors worth nearly US$50 billion each year.[5] If a proposed investment is large enough and important enough, virtually any country, wealthy or poor, will offer incentives to induce the investor to make the investment. Such agreements between investors and host governments become part of the legal framework of the investment and may even be legally enforceable against the granting government. Indeed, it is not an exaggeration to say that concession contracts (allowing foreign investors to operate public services), natural resource agreements, industrial development contracts, stabilization agreements, and infrastructure construction contracts are all intended to be part of the 'law of the investment'.[6] Moreover, powerful investors with especially desirable investment projects may even induce a host government to adopt regulations and legislation designed to favour their particular interests.

(c) Investor home country interests

An investor's home country may have a variety of interests at stake in investments undertaken by its nationals and companies in other countries. On the positive side, foreign investments by nationals may lead to increased trade with countries in which they invest, secure needed natural resources, lead to a repatriation of profits to the home country from the investor's foreign operations, and strengthen economic and political relations between the two countries. To the extent that the home country's government views foreign investment by their nationals as being

---

[4] eg 'Concessions Granted to the Merchants of Venice, by the Byzantine Emperors Basilius and Costantinus, Executed in March 991' in P Fischer, *A Collection of International Concessions and Related Instruments* (Oceana Publications, 1976) vol 1, pp 15–18.

[5] KP Thomas, *Investment Incentives and the Global Competition for Capital* (Palgrave Macmillan, 2011) 102.

[6] Note that the French Civil Code, Art 1134 declares: 'Agreements legally entered into have the force of law for those who have made them' ('Les conventions légalement formées tiennent lieu de loi a ceux qui les ont faites.').

in the national interest, it is likely to want to facilitate the investment process and assure the protection of those nationals and their investments abroad. As we shall see, one way that home countries have pursued this interest is by concluding investment treaties with host states.

On the other hand, home country governments may also view foreign investments by their nationals as a mixed blessing. They may be concerned that the outward flow of capital could be used more fruitfully at home, or worried about the negative economic impact of industries moving overseas, closed local factories, and discharged workers. In addition, they may fear the loss of tax revenues as a result of foreign investment by their nationals. For strategic reasons, a home country may want to avoid allowing the investment process to strengthen a country it considers an adversary. Accordingly, home countries may seek to limit or curtail investments by their nationals in countries with which they are in conflict—particularly in strategic sectors.[7] More generally, large investments by nationals in other countries can ultimately complicate diplomatic relations. For example, their investors may allege that a foreign government has not treated them fairly or properly. In those situations, an investment by a country's nationals in another country can become the basis for a diplomatic conflict. In response to these concerns and interests, home countries may use their legislative and regulatory powers to foster certain foreign investments by their nationals and curtail others.

(d) Conflicts of interest and their settlement

The potential for conflict among the three parties is ever present. In most instances, conflicts arising out of a foreign investment result in disputes between the investor, on the one hand, and the host country government, on the other. The home country of the investor may become engaged in those conflicts at the request of its national. In such conflicts, the host country often considers the dispute to be subject to host country law and host country legal and judicial processes. Thus, if a host country expropriates an investment owned by a foreign national, it normally considers the question of the legality of the seizure and the amount of compensation due, if any, to be a matter exclusively for its own national law and its own national courts. Host governments tend to see foreign laws and foreign courts as irrelevant to any issues of disagreement with foreign investors and may view any potential interference as an outright challenge to national sovereignty.

Aggrieved foreign investors are often sceptical about the impartiality and quality of justice that they will receive in host country courts and agencies. They often fear that such courts will be subject to the influence of the host government or will be prejudiced against the investor. On the other hand, if the aggrieved

---

[7] eg The Iran and Libya Sanctions Act of 1996, 50 USC § 1701, Pub L No 104–172.

investor should try to seek redress in the courts of its home country, not only would the host country be likely to challenge the jurisdiction of such courts, but the home country court may decide of its own accord that it has no jurisdiction on the grounds of sovereign immunity, the act of state doctrine, or for some other reason.[8]

In view of the perceived limitations of national law and legal processes to resolve investment disputes, investors, with the support of their home countries, have sought to find additional protection in international law and international legal processes, as well as in foreign law. For example, an investor may specifically agree with the host country government prior to an investment that the law applicable to its investment will be international law, general principles of law, or the law of a specified foreign country.[9] Even if there is no such specific agreement, if a court or international tribunal finds that the host country's law includes international law, it may conclude that international law governs the investment.[10] In order to enforce such agreements, the investor and the host government may agree to submit any dispute arising out of the investment to an international arbitration tribunal outside the jurisdiction of the host country. Without such an agreement, an arbitration tribunal would have no jurisdiction over either the parties or their dispute.

Similarly, a home country that believes that its nationals have not been treated fairly or properly may have recourse to international law in pursuing claims against the host country. While the home country could not invoke the assistance of an international court or tribunal without a pre-existing agreement with the host country, it could rely on international law in making representations to the offending host country through diplomatic channels, a process known as 'diplomatic protection'. Consequently, to fully understand the legal framework that may apply to international investment and international investors, one needs to examine the applicable international law.

---

[8] See eg *Banco Nacional de Cuba v Sabbatino*, 376 US 398, 425 (1964), in which the US Supreme Court stated: 'The courts of one independent government will not sit in judgment upon the validity of the acts of another done within its own territory, even when such government seizes and sells the property of an American citizen within its boundaries.'

[9] See eg the Convention on the Settlement of Investment Disputes between States and Nationals of Other States (ICSID Convention) of 18 March 1965, Art 42(1) which provides: 'The Tribunal shall decide a dispute in accordance with such rules of law as may be agreed by the parties. In the absence of such agreement, the Tribunal shall apply the law of the Contracting State party to the dispute (including its rules on conflict of laws) and such rules of international law as may be applicable.' Convention on the Settlement of Investment Disputes between States and Nationals of Other States (18 March 1965), 17 UST 1270; 575 UNTS 159.

[10] See eg *Southern Pacific Properties (Middle East) Ltd [SPP(ME)] v Arab Republic of Egypt* ICC Award No YD/AS No 3493 (11 March 1983); (1983) 22 ILM 752, ¶ 49, in which the tribunal found that 'International law principles such as "Pacta Sunt Servanda" and "Just compensation for expropriatory measures" can be deemed as part of Egyptian law.'

3.3 The Sources of International Law

(a) In general

International law has traditionally been conceived as the law governing relations among states.[11] Strictly speaking, in former times, international law did not apply to individuals and private organizations. In the contemporary era, however, international law has given a growing role to non-state actors. One authoritative definition provides:

International law ... consists of the rules and principles of general application dealing with the conduct of states and of international organizations and with their relations *inter se*, as well as with some of their relations with persons, whether natural or juridical.[12]

As will be seen, international investment law is the area of international law in particular that has given an increasing role to legal and physical persons.

The world is organized on the basis of sovereign and equal states and has no supranational legislature or court with authority to make rules governing such states. As a result, the rules of international law are those that have been accepted as such by the international community. Where is one to find those rules? What are the sources of international law?

The most generally accepted statement of the sources of international law is found in Article 38(1) of the Statute of the International Court of Justice (ICJ), which provides:

1. The Court, whose function is to decide in accordance with international law such disputes as are submitted to it, shall apply:
   a. international conventions, whether general or particular, establishing rules expressly recognized by the contesting states;
   b. international custom, as evidence of a general practice accepted as law;
   c. the general principles of law recognized by civilized nations;
   d. subject to the provisions of Article 59, judicial decisions and the teachings of the most highly qualified publicists of the various nations, as subsidiary means for the determination of rules of law.[13]

According to this provision, there are three fundamental sources of international law: (1) international conventions; (2) international custom; and (3) general principles of law recognized by states. The basic norm that underlies all three of

---

[11] 'International law governs relations between independent States. The rules of law binding upon States therefore emanate from their own free will as expressed in conventions or by usages generally accepted as expressing principles of law and established in order to regulate relations between these co-existing independent communities or with a view to the achievement of common aims.' *The Case of the SS Lotus* (*France v Turkey*) (1927) PCIJ Series A, No 10; 2 Hudson, World Ct Rep 20.

[12] The American Law Institute, *Restatement of the Law, The Foreign Relations Law of the United States* (3rd edn, 1987) vol 1, § 101, at 22.

[13] Statute of the International Court of Justice (26 June 1945) 33 UNTS 993; 59 Stat 1055, Art 38(1).

these sources of law is state consent. States are sovereign, which means that a state has complete and absolute power and authority over its affairs, its existence, and its territory; however, a state may consent to yield sovereignty to another power. That consent may be manifested in a state's agreements and its practices.

In addition to these three sources of law, one may refer to two other sources of legal information, 'judicial decisions' and the 'teaching of highly qualified publicists' as subsidiary means to determine applicable rules of international law. Judicial decisions and the teachings of publicists are not in themselves autonomous sources of international law. They are supplemental or secondary sources, which are used by courts, tribunals, governments, and others to establish what a specific rule of international law is.[14] As these three basic international sources of law (in particularized form), as explicated by the two subsidiary sources, constitute the foundations of international investment law, let us examine each briefly.

(b) International conventions

International conventions are binding agreements between or among states. International conventions have a variety of designations in their titles: treaty, agreement, protocol, pact, convention, and covenant, among others. Thus, in the field of investment law, important international sources of law include the North American Free Trade *Agreement*,[15] the Energy Charter *Treaty*,[16] and the *Convention* on the Settlement of Investment Disputes between States and Nationals of Other States.[17] Despite their differences in name, each of these three documents has the same binding effect on the states that have consented to them. The particular name given to an international agreement has no consequence as to its legal force or the binding effect it has on its parties.[18]

The basic international law governing treaties and their interpretation and application is the Vienna Convention on the Law of Treaties (VCLT).[19] Like contracts, treaties bind only the state parties which have consented to them. If a state's internal law is inconsistent with its obligations under the treaty, that state may not invoke that internal law as a justification for not performing its obligations under the treaty.[20] Thus, for example, if a state has entered into a treaty in which it promises not to expropriate property without payment of full compensation, it may not in an international proceeding use a domestic law that authorizes the taking of property without compensation as an excuse for failing to live up to its

---

[14] J Crawford, *Brownlie's Principles of Public International Law* (8th edn, OUP, 2012) 37, 42.
[15] North American Free Trade Agreement (signed 17 December 1992) (1993) 32 ILM 289, 605 (NAFTA).
[16] Energy Charter Treaty (17 December 1994) (1995) 34 ILM 360 (ECT).
[17] ICSID Convention (n 9 above).
[18] Crawford (n 14 above) 30–1; A Aust, *Modern Treaty Law and Practice* (Cambridge University Press, 2000) 15.
[19] Vienna Convention on the Law of Treaties (opened for signature 23 May 1969) 1155 UNTS 331; UN Doc A/Conf.39/27; (1969) 8 ILM 679; 63 AJIL 875 (1969) (VCLT).
[20] ibid Art 27; Aust (n 18 above) 144.

treaty obligations. On the other hand, states that are not signatories to an international agreement or treaty are usually not bound by its terms. But, if a treaty gains wide enough acceptance among states, it will be deemed to constitute international customary law and will have binding effect even on non-signatories.[21]

Article 38 of the ICJ Statute cites international conventions first in its listing of the sources of international law, but it does not specifically state that they will have precedence over the other two sources, that is, customary international and general principles of law.[22] It is generally agreed that should a custom of international law conflict with a treaty provision, the treaty provision will prevail unless the custom is determined to fall under Article 53 of the VCLT, which describes 'peremptory norm[s] of general international law', sometimes referred to as *jus cogens*. A peremptory norm of international law is one that is 'accepted and recognized by the international community of States as a whole as a norm from which no derogation is permitted and which can be modified only by a subsequent norm of general international law having the same character'.[23]

Just as national legislation and regulation have increasingly supplanted custom and common law to become the legal foundation of domestic economies, international treaties have increasingly become the foundation for international economic relations. As will be seen, this shift has been particularly clear in the area of international investment, and the reasons for it will be explained in more detail in Chapter 4. At the same time, the existence of a treaty does not mean that the other sources of international law, namely custom and general principles of law, are not relevant or applicable. Often treaties incorporate concepts whose full meaning cannot be understood without reference to customary international law. Moreover, treaties may specifically declare that the other sources of international law are to supplement the treaty if its provisions are silent about a particular issue or problem. Thus, for example, if an investment treaty declares that an investor

---

[21] McNair, *Law of Treaties* (Clarendon Press, 1961) 5, 124, 749–52; RR Baxter, 'Treaties and Custom' (1970) 129 *Recueil des Cours* 25, 101; RR Baxter, 'Multilateral Treaties as Evidence of Customary International Law' (1965) 41 BYIL 275.

[22] Crawford, in *Brownlie's Principles of Public International Law*, notes:

> [Article 38] makes no reference to 'sources' and, on close inspection, cannot be regarded as a straightforward enumeration of the sources. The first question is whether paragraph 1 creates a hierarchy of sources. There is no express hierarchy, but the draftsmen stipulated an order and in one draft the word 'successively' appeared. In practice sub-paragraphs (a) and (b) are the most important: we can explain the priority of (a) by the fact that this refers to a source of obligations which will ordinarily prevail as being more specific.

Crawford (n 14 above) 5. Lauterpacht has a similar view:

> The rights and duties of States are determined in the first instance, by their agreement as expressed in treaties—just as the case of individuals their rights are specifically determined by any contract which is binding upon them. When a controversy arises between two or more States with regard to a matter regulated by a treaty, it is natural that the parties should invoke and the adjudicating agency should apply, in the first instance, the provisions of the treaty in question.

H Lauterpacht, *International Law: Collected Papers* (Cambridge University Press, 1970) 86–7.

[23] VCLT, Art 53.

is to be given 'full protection in accordance with international law', an arbitration tribunal would have to refer to customary international law to determine the extent of protection provided.[24] More generally, virtually all investment treaties specifically provide that international arbitration tribunals—in deciding investor state disputes—are to apply, in addition to the treaty text, 'the applicable rules of international law',[25] a term that encompasses all of international law derived from all its sources. As will be seen in Chapter 16, tribunals must refer to customary international law in determining the consequences of and the compensation for investment treaty violations.

(c) International custom

International custom is a second source of international law under Article 38 of the ICJ Statute. International custom is defined simply as 'a general practice accepted as law'. Thus, a customary rule of international law must meet two criteria: (1) it must be a general practice of states; and (2) states must engage in that practice out of a sense of legal obligation.[26] With respect to the first criterion, the practice of states consists of the actions states undertake to carry out government business. These can include policy pronouncements, statements at international conferences, diplomatic communications and correspondence with other states, national legislation, decisions of domestic courts, and other actions taken by governments in respect of international matters.[27] To satisfy this first criterion, the practice, according to the ICJ, must be 'both extensive and virtually uniform'.[28] The practice need not be particularly long-standing to be a custom, for as the Court has also stated, 'the passage of only a short period of time is not necessarily, or of itself, a bar to the formation of a new rule of customary international law'.[29]

Just because states act in a particular way does not mean that such actions automatically constitute customary international law. States must act in a particular way out of a sense of legal obligation. This is the second requirement under Article 38, the requirement of *opinio juris sive necessitatis*, that state practice should 'occur[ ]

---

[24] eg NAFTA, Art 1131 empowers the Free Trade Commission of NAFTA to make binding interpretations of NAFTA provisions on investment arbitration tribunals. In the exercise of that power, the Commission issued an interpretation holding that NAFTA, Art 1105(1) 'prescribes the customary international law minimum standard of treatment of aliens as the minimum standard of treatment to be afforded investments of investors of another Party' and that 'the concepts of "fair and equitable treatment" and "full protection and security" do not require treatment in addition to or beyond that which is required by the customary international law minimum standard of treatment of aliens'. NAFTA Free Trade Commission, 'NAFTA Commission Notes of Interpretation of Certain Chapter 11 Provisions' (31 July 2001).

[25] eg Agreement between the Government of the Republic of Korea and the Government of Japan on the Liberalization, Promotion, and Protection of Investment (22 March 2002), Art 14(2); ASEAN Comprehensive Agreement (2009), Art 40(1).

[26] The American Law Institute (n 12 above) vol 1, § 102(2), at 24.

[27] ibid § 102, comment b, at 25. See also Crawford (n 14 above) 24.

[28] *North Sea Continental Shelf* (*FRG v Den; FRG v Neth*) [1969] ICJ Rep 3, 43.

[29] ibid.

in such a way as to show a general recognition that a rule of legal obligation is involved'.[30]

These two requirements for international customary law can make it difficult to establish a particular rule of customary law even under the best of conditions. Where there is significant disagreement among states or significant differences in practice, finding a rule of customary international law may be next to impossible. As will be seen, the field of international investment law has generated significant disagreement among nations as to the nature and content of applicable international rules. As a result, in many forums the very existence of customary international investment law has been questioned, if not challenged outright, over the years.

(d) General principles of law

The third and final source of international law is the 'general principles of law recognized by civilized nations'.[31] This source of law refers to the legal principles that are common to the world's major legal systems.[32] These 'general principles' are often seen as a source to help fill in gaps where no applicable treaty provision or international custom exists. While certain general principles, such as *pacta sunt servanda*, have emerged to become custom, tribunals will generally be hesitant to find such a general principle, unless it is clear that there is broad acceptance in the world's legal systems.[33]

(e) Subsidiary sources

Article 38(1)(d) of the ICJ Statute states that the Court may apply 'judicial decisions' and 'the teachings of the most highly qualified publicists of the various nations' as 'subsidiary means for the determination of rules of law'. It is clear that 'judicial decisions' and the 'teachings of publicists' are not themselves sources of international law but merely means for ascertaining the content of the three specified sources of law. The usual dictionary definition of 'subsidiary' is 'functioning in the provision of aid or support';[34] therefore a 'subsidiary means' is something that aids or supports the determination of rules of international law.

---

[30] ibid.

[31] On their status as a source of law, Brownlie observes: 'This source is listed after treaty and custom, both of which depend more immediately on state consent.' Crawford (n 14 above) 34.

[32] O Schachter distinguishes five categories of general principles that have been invoked and applied in international law discourse and cases. O Schachter, *International Law in Theory and Practice* (Martinus Nijhoff, 1991) 50. Crawford notes: '[T]he Oppenheim's view is preferable: "The intention is to authorize the Court to apply the general principles of municipal jurisprudence, in particular of private law, in so far as they are applicable to relations of States."' Crawford (n 14 above) 34.

[33] Schachter (n 32 above) 50–5.

[34] *Webster's Third New International Dictionary of the English Language, Unabridged* (3rd edn, 1981) vol III, p 2279.

A further question concerns the precise meaning to be given to these two specified subsidiary means. The ICJ Statute does not define the term 'judicial decisions' or limit it to the decisions of any particular type of judicial body. Thus, the decisions of domestic courts as well as those of international tribunals would be included within the term. Similarly, since the term 'judicial' may be defined as 'the function of judging',[35] one may interpret a 'judicial decision' as one that emanates from the process of judging. Thus, the decisions of arbitrators would be included within the definition of 'judicial decision' for purposes of interpreting Article 38(1)(d) of the ICJ Statute. International practice supports this interpretation. In fact, the pleadings by advocates before international tribunals and the decisions of the tribunals themselves are filled with references to decisions by courts, arbitration tribunals, and similar bodies throughout the world.

While the term 'publicist' may have other meanings in ordinary parlance, it has only one meaning in the international domain: 'an expert in international law'.[36] The 'teachings of... publicists' referred to in Article 38(1)(d) of the ICJ Statute may take many forms, including books, articles, lectures, legal opinions, and testimony before official and academic bodies. Moreover, they may include the collective, as well as the individual, work of international law experts, such as the decisions of the International Law Commission and professional bodies such as the American Law Institute. For example, the Draft Articles on Responsibility of States for Internationally Wrongful Acts, issued by the International Law Commission,[37] is widely cited by advocates and arbitrators in treaty-based investor–state arbitrations as stating principles of customary international law applicable to such cases.

3.4 Customary International Law and General Principles of Law Governing International Investment

(a) Introduction

Investment treaties, as will be seen, have evolved and are interpreted against a background of customary international law and general principles of law relating to foreign investment. As a result, in order to understand the history of investment treaties and in order to interpret current treaty provisions, it is necessary to refer to the history of customary international law as well as to its current status. The purpose of this section is to provide that background.

At the outset, it must be acknowledged that this area of international law has been fraught with disagreement among states, particularly between developed, capital-exporting states, on the one hand, and developing, capital-importing

---

[35] ibid vol II, p 1223.   [36] ibid vol II, p 1836.

[37] United Nations, *Draft Articles on Responsibility of States for Internationally Wrongful Acts, with Commentaries*, 2001 (2008), adopted by the International Law Commission at its fifty-third session, in 2001, and submitted to the General Assembly as part of the Commission's Report covering that session, available at <http://legal.un.org/ilc/texts/instruments/english/commentaries/9_6_2001.pdf> accessed 11 January 2015.

states, on the other. Doctrines and rules that seemed settled in earlier times, particularly during the era of colonialism, have been challenged as the territories formerly under colonial rule emerged as fully independent and sovereign states after the end of World War II. In that earlier era, the effort to develop principles of customary international law respecting the rights of investors abroad evolved out of the law of state responsibility for injury to aliens and alien property.[38] The basic questions asked by this area of international law are: (1) What is the legal standard that states must respect in their treatment of aliens living and working in their territories? (2) What means are available for aliens and their home governments to ensure that host countries live up to those standards? (3) How specifically do those standards and means of enforcement apply to investment activities of aliens in host countries? We consider each of these questions in turn.

(b) Standards of treatment owed to aliens by host states

There is a fundamental, recurring issue in international law and international relations: What is the standard of treatment that a host country government owes to aliens residing and working in its territory? One possible answer is that a host government need not treat aliens any better than its own nationals. This view incorporates the *principle of equality*. This principle draws its justification from the fact that as an equal, sovereign state in the international system a host country is not subject to any legislative authority other than its own. Moreover, a foreigner who voluntarily takes up residence in a host country must accept that he or she is subject to host country law and is assumed to understand the risks that such a situation entails. In a famous exchange of correspondence between US Secretary of State Cordell Hull and Mexican Foreign Minister Eduardo Hay concerning the expropriation of agricultural land in Mexico that was owned by US citizens but that equally affected Mexican owners, the Mexican Foreign Minister argued the principle of equality quite forcefully: 'the foreigner who voluntarily moves to a country which is not his own, in search of a personal benefit, accepts in advance, together with the advantages he is going to enjoy, the risks to which he may find himself exposed. It would be unjust that he should aspire to a privileged position'.[39]

An opposing view, which evolved in the nineteenth century among European countries and the United States, was that a host state has an obligation under international law to observe *an international minimum standard* that provides for a minimum set of principles which states, regardless of their domestic legislation and practices, must respect with regard to the treatment of aliens and their property. This doctrine takes into account the possibility that the standards prevailing in a given state may be so low that, even if nationals and aliens are treated alike, the norms of international law may be violated.[40]

---

[38] See generally R Lillich (ed), *The International Law of State Responsibility for Injuries to Aliens* (University of Virginia Press, 1983).

[39] 'Official Documents' (1938) 32 AJIL Supp 181, 188.

[40] 'The prevailing rule [is] that such national treatment is not always sufficient, and that there is an international standard of justice that a state must observe in the treatment of aliens, even if the

An authoritative statement of the international minimum standard was made by US Secretary of State Elihu Root in 1910:

There is a standard of justice, very simple, very fundamental, and of such general accept-ance by all civilized countries as to form a part of the international law of the world. The condition upon which every country is entitled to measure the justice due from it to an alien by the justice which it accords to its own citizens is that its system of law and administration shall conform to this general standard. If any country's system of law and administration does not conform to that standard, although the people of that country may be content or compelled to live under it, no other country can be compelled to accept it as furnishing a satisfactory measure of treatment to its citizens.[41]

On the question of the treatment of aliens by host states, including foreign investors, there is thus a fundamental tension between the equality principle and the minimum international standard principle. This tension has in varying degrees pervaded the evolution and content of international investment law over the years. While the partisans of each view often justify their positions by ref-erence to abstract notions of justice, the fundamental interests of nations have also shaped the debate and influenced positions on the question. Countries that had expanding foreign economic interests have quite naturally sought to protect those interests by advancing the principle of a minimum international standard of protection. Countries that had few foreign interests and saw themselves as the target of other countries' expansionist activities quite naturally asserted the equal-ity principle as a means to protect themselves and to assure their full sovereignty over foreign economic actors in their territory.

During the nineteenth and the first half of the twentieth centuries, with the expansion of western economic powers, the spread of European colonialism, and American influence in Latin America and Asia, the principle of a minimum inter-national standard became dominant, at least among western states. For example, Lauterpacht, in the fifth edition of *Oppenheim, International Law*, stated:

It is a well-established principle that a State cannot invoke its municipal legislation as a reason for avoiding its international obligation. For essentially the same reason a State, when charged with a breach of its international obligations with regard to the treatment of aliens, cannot validly plead that according to its Municipal Law and practice the act com-plained of does not involve discrimination against aliens as compared with nationals. *This applies in particular to the question of treatment of the persons of aliens. It has been repeatedly laid down that there exists in this matter a minimum standard of civilization, and that a State which fails to measure up to that standard incurs international liability.* (emphasis added)[42]

Despite this affirmation of a minimum standard of international law, legal scholars and government officials in the countries subject to the intervention of

---

state does not observe it in the treatment of its own nationals, and even if the standard is inconsist-ent with its own law.' The American Law Institute, *Restatement (Second) of Foreign Relations Law* (1965) § 165, comment (a), at 502.

[41] E Root, 'The Basis of Protection to Citizens Residing Abroad' (1910) 4 AJIL 517, 521–2.

[42] H Lauterpacht, *Oppenheim, International Law* (5th edn, Cambridge University Press, 1937) 283.

European and American influence continued to assert that customary international law did not recognize such a standard. Probably the most important formulation of this position was that of the Argentine jurist and foreign minister Carlos Calvo (1824–1906), whose 'Calvo doctrine' was adopted throughout Latin America at a time when many countries felt threatened by US domination. Calvo argued that a sovereign independent state was entitled by reason of the principle of sovereign equality to complete freedom from interference by other states in any form, whether by diplomacy or by force. Therefore, according to the Calvo doctrine, when an alien suffers an alleged injury his or her only remedies are local ones. In the absence of a denial of justice, which Calvo defined narrowly, diplomatic protection is unavailable to an injured alien. Calvo argued that aliens and nationals are entitled in principle to equal treatment, but once equality of treatment is granted, the host state has fulfilled its obligations regardless of whether the alien or his or her state is dissatisfied with the treatment received. Thus, Latin America's response to the international minimum standard was the doctrine of national treatment.[43] European governments, the United States, and many international forums and tribunals tended to dismiss this approach as not representing customary international law. Nevertheless, as will be seen later in this chapter, individual Latin American countries took significant measures to implement the Calvo doctrine through the inclusion of 'Calvo clauses' in their constitutions, legislation, and contracts with foreign companies.

(c) The application and enforcement of a minimum standard

The debate between the minimum standard and national treatment principles was by no means a purely theoretical one. It had its application in diplomatic relations between nations and in various forums of international adjudication in the nineteenth and twentieth centuries.

Investors, for example, had little effective means to press claims directly against offending host governments based on the international minimum standard of treatment. Customary international law did not give individuals or companies the right to press such claims directly against an offending host government nor did it provide them with any other enforcement mechanism. Rather, investors had to rely on their home governments to give them 'diplomatic protection'.

The interest of investor home governments in protecting their nationals abroad was not just to satisfy powerful domestic constituencies but also to advance

---

[43] R Lillich, *The Human Rights of Aliens in Contemporary International Law* (Manchester University Press, 1984) 16–17; SKB Asante, 'International Law and Investments' in M Bedjaoui (ed), *International Law: Achievements and Prospects* (UNESCO, 1991) 670. Crawford, in *Brownlie's Public International Law*, observes: 'The controversy surrounding the national and international standards has not been finally resolved, and this is not surprising as the two viewpoints reflect conflicting economic and political interests.' Crawford (n 14 above) 614. The most complete exposition of the Calvo doctrine by the jurist himself is C Calvo, *Le Droit international théorique et pratique* (5th edn, 1896) vols 1–6. See also A Freeman, 'Recent Aspects of the Calvo Doctrine and the Challenge to International Law' (1946) 40 AJIL 121.

important economic and political interests abroad. Their investors were one means of achieving that goal. Aliens have always been subject to discrimination and abuse in foreign countries. What right under international law did their home governments have to protect them? Drawing on the work of the eighteenth-century Swiss philosopher, diplomat, and jurist Emerich de Vattell (1714–67), who declared '[w]hoever ill-treats a citizen injures the state, which must protect that citizen',[44] countries developed the concept of the diplomatic protection of aliens. Thus, under international law a host country that injured an alien was simultaneously injuring the state of that national and that state had the right to protect itself from such injurious acts.[45]

Home country governments therefore took the position that international law gave them a right to pursue claims against foreign countries that illegally injured their nationals. The violation of the minimum standard of treatment was considered to be such an injury under international law and, provided that the alien had exhausted local remedies, could give rise to international action on behalf of the injured alien by his or her home state. The doctrine of diplomatic protection, in turn, provided a procedural vehicle for a home state to seek redress in cases where a foreign state allegedly violated the international minimum standard in its treatment of home country nationals.[46] During the nineteenth and early twentieth centuries, in the era of 'gunboat diplomacy', states sometimes also sought redress through military interventions when nationals suffered injuries in foreign countries.[47] In most cases, they used diplomatic or international judicial means to press their claims. The legal basis for such actions was explained by the Permanent Court of International Justice in the *Mavromatis* case:

---

[44] E de Vattel, *The Law of Nations*, C Fenwick (tr) (1919) Book II, Ch 6, at 136.

[45] RB Lillich, 'The Current Status of the Law of State Responsibility for Injuries to Aliens' in Lillich (n 38 above) 1.

[46] 'In precise language, diplomatic protection can be defined as a procedure for giving effect to State responsibility involving breaches of international law arising out of legal injuries to the person or property of the citizen of a State. With the expansion of economic and commercial intercourse between nations, diplomatic protection evolved into a rule of customary international law.' J Cuthbert, *Nationality and Diplomatic Protection* (AW Sijthoff, 1969) 1.

[47] Lillich acknowledges criticism of the abuse of diplomatic protection, noting:

> The history is full of examples of the use of military force on a massive scale to redress alleged wrongs which, in retrospect, seem quite minor. Probably the most notorious such incident involved a British military action against Greece in 1850, what is known as the Don Pacifico incident.... This affair was a particularly egregious one for a number of reasons, the most important perhaps being that the alien had not exhausted his local remedies, as the traditional international law rule that had developed by the mid-19th century required.... The most common arena for the fulsome application of the doctrine of diplomatic protection [during the nineteenth century] was Latin America, where there were numerous forcible interventions by the various European powers, as well as by the United States.... [T]he most noteworthy of these incidents was the blockading of Venezuela by the combined forces of Germany, Italy, and Great Britain in 1902–03 on behalf of various persons with claims against the Venezuelan government.

Lillich (n 43 above) 14–15, 24.

It is an elementary principle of international law that a State is entitled to protect its subjects, when injured by acts contrary to international law committed by another State, from whom they have been unable to obtain satisfaction through the ordinary channels. By taking up the case of one of its subjects and by resorting to diplomatic action or international judicial proceedings on his behalf, a State is in reality asserting its own rights—its right to ensure, in the person of its subjects, respect for the rules of international law.... Once a State has taken up the case on behalf of one of its subjects before an international tribunal, in the eyes of the latter the State is sole claimant.[48]

The concept of 'diplomatic protection of aliens' by their home states did not receive universal acclaim. As one might imagine, certain states, notably those in Latin America, viewed the concept as another tool by which the United States and European powers could undermine their national sovereignty. As noted earlier in this chapter, the Calvo doctrine represented an opposing view, holding that in pressing a claim against a host government a foreigner had no right to seek the diplomatic protection of its government and that customary international law did not allow a home country to extend diplomatic protection to its nationals living and working in another sovereign state.[49]

Governments of injured aliens nonetheless sought redress through diplomatic representations for injuries suffered by their nationals in host countries. A famous example of such a representation was the exchange of diplomatic correspondence, referred to earlier in this chapter, between Mexico and the United States concerning the expropriation of agricultural land owned by Americans in Mexico. In its note of 3 August 1938, the Mexican government, through its minister of foreign affairs, not only contested the right of the United States to demand compensation for the agricultural lands expropriated by Mexico but also argued that the United States had no right *at all* to intervene on their behalf.[50] In support of his position, the Mexican minister of foreign affairs invoked Article 9 of the Convention on the Rights and Duties of States, which was signed at Montevideo in 1933. This Convention gives complete jurisdiction to states over inhabitants within their national territory, meaning that 'nationals and foreigners are under the same protection of the law and the national authorities, and foreigners may not claim rights other than or more extensive than those of nationals'.[51] US Secretary of State Cordell Hull in his reply asserted that 'when aliens are admitted into a country the country is obligated to accord them that degree of protection of life and property consistent with the standards of justice recognized by the law of nations'.[52] He denied that this was a claim of special privilege in contravention of

---

[48] *Case Concerning Mavromatis Palestine Concessions* (1924) PCIJ Series A, No 2, at 2. See also A Bagge, 'Intervention on the Ground of Damage Caused to Nationals, with Particular Reference to Exhaustion of Local Remedies and the Rights of Shareholders' (1958) 34 BYIL 162.

[49] Lillich (n 45 above) 2–6; Lillich (n 43 above) 16–17.

[50] cf with the citation in E Borchard, 'The "Minimum Standard" of the Treatment of Aliens' (1939–40) 38 Mich L Rev 445, 446.

[51] ibid.   [52] cf Borchard (n 50 above) 446, citing (1938) 32 AJIL Supp 198.

the Montevideo Treaty and maintained that confiscation could not be excused by the 'inapplicable doctrine of equality'.[53]

During the nineteenth and twentieth centuries, various international tribunals applied the minimum international standard to protect aliens in foreign countries and to recognize the right of home countries to extend diplomatic protection to their nationals injured abroad. For example, in 1926 the Permanent Court of International Justice, in the famous *Chorzów* case, recognized 'the limits set by generally accepted principles of international law' regarding the treatment of aliens, and stated that 'the only measures prohibited are those which generally accepted international law does not sanction in respect of foreigners'.[54]

A number of arbitral awards also recognized the duty of a state to conform to international standards of justice even when there may be a conflict with domestic law. In the *Hopkins* case before the United States–Mexico General Claims Commission of 1923 the tribunal concluded:

it not infrequently happens that under the rules of international law applied to controversies of an international aspect a nation is required to accord aliens broader and more liberal treatment than it accords to its own citizens under municipal laws. The reports of decisions made by arbitral tribunals long prior to the Treaty of 1923 contain many such instances. There is no ground to object that this amounts to a discrimination by a nation. It is not a question of discrimination but a difference in their respective rights and remedies. The citizens of a nation may enjoy many rights which are withheld from aliens, and, conversely, under international law aliens may enjoy rights and remedies which the nation does not accord to its own citizens.[55]

Other claim cases reached similar conclusions, finding that the test, broadly speaking, is whether aliens are treated in accordance with 'the ordinary standards of civilization'[56] and whether the 'international minimum standard has been extended

---

[53] ibid. Another example of diplomatic protection was the *Tinoco Case* in 1923, in which Great Britain asserted claims of a British company and the Royal Bank of Canada, both of which had allegedly made contracts with the government of Costa Rica during the regime of Frederico Tinoco, who had come to power as a result of a coup in January 1917. Within two years Tinoco was forced from power, elections were held, and a Constitutional Congress began to function. In 1922, the Constitutional Congress adopted legislation invalidating all contracts made by the executive power during the Tinoco regime. The effect of this action was to invalidate an oil concession granted to the British company and loan obligations to the Royal Bank of Canada. Since the shareholders in both entities were British subjects, the government of Great Britain vigorously brought a claim against Costa Rica, which, under significant pressure, agreed to arbitrate the British claims and to accept the US Chief Justice William Howard Taft, the former American president, as sole arbitrator. *Tinoco Case (Great Britain v Costa Rica)* 1 R Int'l Arb Awards 369, 375–85 (1923), available at (1924) 18 AJIL 147.

[54] The American Law Institute, *Restatement of the Law, The Foreign Relations Law of the United States* (1965) § 165, reporters' note 1, at 505, citing the *Case Concerning Certain German Interests in Polish Upper Silesia* (1926) PCIJ Rep Series A, No 7, at 22.

[55] *Hopkins (US) v Mexico* (21 March 1926) I Opinions of Commissioners, General Claims Commission (US and Mexico, 1923) 42, 50–1 (1927).

[56] *Roberts (US) v Mexico* (2 November 1926) I Opinions of Commissioners, General Claims Commission (US and Mexico, 1923) 100, 105 (1927).

to cover the instances of discrimination against aliens, denial of justice and injuries to aliens' economic interests (eg expropriation)'.[57]

Despite the pronouncements of diplomats and international tribunals, foreign investors considered diplomatic protection to be far from a complete protection for their property and activities in host countries. For one thing, the existence of diplomatic protection depended entirely on the willingness of the investor's home country to extend it in any given situation. Home country governments were not then, and are not now, required to take up or 'espouse' a claim against an offending host state, no matter how egregious its conduct might have been. The decision to take a claim up or not, and to pursue it with vigour or not, is completely within the discretion of the home government.

Second, once the home country government has espoused the claim, it effectively 'owns' it. It controls how the claim will be made, what settlement if any to accept, and whether any portion of that settlement should be paid to its aggrieved national. Thus, for example, the home country might settle or abandon a claim for injury to its nationals if it judged that this is justified by other factors in its relations with the host country, such as security or broader economic concerns. In such a situation, the injured investor is left with no redress either against the offending host country or its unsympathetic home country.

A further complication involved a home country's ability to extend diplomatic protection to nationals who are shareholders in foreign corporations. In the famous *Barcelona Traction* case,[58] Belgium sued Spain in the ICJ on behalf of injured Belgian shareholders of a Canadian corporation, Barcelona Traction. Barcelona Traction was supplying electricity to that Spanish city when it was expropriated by the government of Spain. The Court ruled that Belgium had no right to make a claim on behalf of the Belgian shareholders, since the primary party injured by the expropriation was the Canadian corporation, not the Belgian shareholders. Although this decision has been strongly criticized over the years,[59] it remains difficult for shareholders of one nationality to press claims for injuries to a corporation that was incorporated in a country other than that of their nationality—an obstacle that is particularly problematic, since investors commonly purchase shares in companies and corporations organized or with headquarters in other countries.

And finally, once the era of gunboat diplomacy ended, the process of diplomatic protection of aliens and foreign investors in many cases did not necessarily result in a meaningful remedy. Often, nothing more than an exchange of oral or written statements took place between the two states, and the injured investor received no compensation. The investor's home state could bring the matter to an international tribunal only if the offending state agreed to submit the case

---

[57] The American Law Institute, *Restatement of the Law, The Foreign Relations Law of the United States* (1965) citing 'France v Great Britain (1931)' (1933) 27 AJIL 153, 160. See also A Freeman, *The International Responsibility of States for Denial of Justice* (Longmans Green and Co, 1938) 502 et seq.

[58] *Barcelona Traction, Light and Power Co Ltd (Belgium v Spain)* [1970] ICJ Rep 3, (1970) 64 AJIL 653.

[59] eg RB Lillich, 'Two Perspectives on the Barcelona Traction Case' (1971) 65 AJIL 522–32.

to that tribunal, whose jurisdiction always depended on the consent of the states concerned. Thus, diplomatic protection proved to be a very uncertain and often ephemeral remedy for injured international investors.

3.5 Customary International Law on Expropriation and Breach of State Contracts

(a) In general

Traditionally, foreign investors in host countries have had two primary concerns: (1) the protection of their investments from expropriation or other unjustified interference by host governments with their property rights; and (2) the assurance that host country governments will respect the contracts and other commitments they have made with investors. During the nineteenth and twentieth centuries, when western states dominated the international system, their governments sought to develop customary international law to deal with both problems.

With respect to expropriation, international law has always recognized the state's power of eminent domain to take property—at least for public purposes and on payment of compensation. Indeed, this power, which is derived from the sovereignty of the state over all things within its boundaries, is an essential attribute of state sovereignty. In fact, a state may not validly bind itself not to exercise it. The justification for this principle is that a state's fundamental purpose is to safeguard the public interest of its citizens and, if such interest will be properly safeguarded by nationalization, the state must be free to pursue that course of action.[60]

At the same time, western governments and jurists appeared to agree that even though a government taking of foreign property may be legal under host country law, such a taking was also subject to certain minimum standards of international customary law. One example of such a standard was that customary international law permitted expropriation of an alien's assets provided it was for a public purpose, was non-discriminatory, and was accompanied by compensation to the injured alien.[61] In the 1903 *Upton* case, the Mixed Claims Commission held that 'the right of the State... to appropriate private property for public use is unquestioned, but always with the corresponding obligation to make just compensation to the owner thereof'.[62] In the *De Sabla* case, the United States–Panama General Claims Commission held: 'It is axiomatic that acts of a government in depriving an alien of his property without compensation impose international responsibility.'[63] And in one of the leading pre-World War II cases on the subject, the

---

[60] I Delupis, *Finance and Protection of Investments in Developing Countries* (Gower, 1973) 31.

[61] CF Amerasinghe, *State Responsibility for Injuries to Aliens* (Clarendon Press, 1967) 124–5.

[62] *United States–Venezuela Mixed Claims Commission* (1903) 174.

[63] (1934) 28 AJIL 602, 611–12.

Permanent Court of International Justice in the *Chorzów Factory* case,[64] which involved the expropriation by Poland of German-owned industrial property in Upper Silesia, declared that in the event of expropriation the expropriating state had the obligation to pay the 'just price of what was expropriated'. This meant 'the value of the undertaking at the moment of dispossession, plus interest to the day of payment'.

The traditional western position with respect to expropriation is perhaps best summed up in § 712 of the *Restatement (Third) of the Foreign Relations Law of the United States*, which provides:

A state is responsible under international law for injury resulting from:
(1) a taking by the state of the property of a national of another state that
    (a) is not for a public purpose; or
    (b) is discriminatory; or
    (c) is not accompanied by provision for just compensation.

A consideration of this principle requires a discussion of the meaning of its constituent elements.

(b) Taking under international law

In any case of an alleged interference by the host country with a foreign investment, one must first of all determine whether such interference constitutes a 'taking' under international law that would thereby give rise to the application of international legal principles of expropriation. In years past, such a determination was not difficult to make, since the host country government, in effecting an expropriation or nationalization, would specifically transfer title of the foreign investor's assets to the government or a public agency. Such instances were

---

[64] *Factory at Chorzów (Germany v Poland)* (Indemnity), (Judgment of 13 September 1928) PCIJ Series A, No 17, at 47. In an often cited passage in this case, the Court attempted to distinguish internationally illegal acts of expropriation from legal acts, and described the remedy appropriate in each of the cases:

> The essential principle contained in the actual notion of an illegal act—a principle which seems to be established by international practice and in particular by the decisions of arbitral tribunals—is that reparation must, as far as possible, wipe out all consequences of the illegal act and reestablish the situation which would, in all probability, have existed if that act had not been committed. Restitution in kind, or, if that is not possible, payment of a sum corresponding to the value which a restitution in kind would bear [must be made].

In contrast, lawful expropriation, the PCIJ held, did not require restitution but only payment of 'the just price of what was expropriated', measured as 'the value of the undertaking at the moment of dispossession, plus interest to the day of payment'. This distinction between illegal and lawful expropriation would have significant practical effect in the evolution of customary international law on expropriation.

As will be seen in Ch 12, section 12.10, however, the tribunal in *ADC Affiliate Ltd and ADC & ADMC Management Ltd v Republic of Hungary*, ICSID Case No ARB/03/16 (Award) (2 October 2006), (Cyprus–Hungary BIT), applied this distinction in determining the applicable compensation standard in an expropriation that it found to be illegal.

clearly an exercise of the power of eminent domain. In recent years, however, governments have engaged in more subtle means of interference—often through the arbitrary or discriminatory exercise of their police power—by imposing onerous regulations and taxation upon the investor or the investment project. This approach, sometimes referred to as 'creeping expropriation' or 'regulatory taking', may gradually achieve the same result that a formal act of expropriation achieves immediately. Thus, through the imposition of discriminatory taxes or various forms of regulation, the host country government may induce the investor either to abandon the investment entirely or to transfer it to the host country government at a bargain price.[65]

While western views of international law hold such use of state regulatory power to be a taking in certain situations,[66] they also recognize that a state is not responsible for losses resulting from the bona fide exercise of regulatory or taxation authority. So long as such action is not exercised discriminatorily, that authority is commonly accepted as part of a state's police powers.[67] Determining whether a specific governmental regulation is an ordinary exercise of police power or is instead a disguised form of expropriation is not an easy matter, since the precise boundary between the two situations is not always clear. For example, the commentary to the ALI *Restatement (Third)* asserts that regulatory action that is 'confiscatory' or 'unreasonably interferes with' a foreign national's use of his property is to be considered a taking. These concepts, of course, are subject to a variety of interpretations. In the Reporters' Notes, the *Restatement (Third)* further contends that the distinction between a taking requiring compensation and a lawful exercise of police power not requiring compensation 'is similar to that drawn in United States jurisprudence for purposes of the Fifth and Fourteenth Amendments to the Constitution in determining whether there has been a taking requiring compensation'.[68]

In determining the nature of a regulatory action, one might also consider the government's intent. A determination of such intent could be established, for example, if the government issued a series of discriminatory regulations making continued profitable operation impossible, purchased the property from the investor at a low price, and then later rescinded the regulations.

A government can also effect a taking under international law if it nullifies important contractual relationships with the investor. Cancelling a concession agreement or investment contract with an investor could constitute a taking, since the contractual right to operate a concession or carry out an investment project is

---

[65] See generally D Vagts, 'Coercion and Foreign Investment Rearrangements' (1978) 72 AJIL 17; B Weston, '"Constructive Takings" under International Law: A Modest Foray into the Problem of "Creeping Expropriation"' (1975) 16 Va J Int'l L 103.

[66] eg *Restatement (Third) of the Foreign Relations Law of the United States*, § 712, comment g, at 200 states: 'A state is responsible for an expropriation of property when it subjects alien property to taxation, regulation, or other action that is confiscatory or that prevents, unreasonably interferes with, or unduly delays, effective enjoyment of an alien's property or its removal from the state's territory.' The American Law Institute, *Restatement of the Law, The Foreign Relations Law of the United States* (3rd edn, 1987) vol 2.

[67] ibid.   [68] ibid, vol 2, § 712, at 211.

a valuable property right. Moreover, if a host country, in order to raise revenues, imposes a levy upon a mining concession in violation of an agreement, that levy might constitute a taking even if the investor continues to control the mining investment.[69]

A taking can also occur where a government, instead of asserting property rights in foreign-owned property, merely seizes control of an investment. For example, a government might appoint a new manager to administer a property or operate the investor's business. Provided the deprivation of the investor's right of control is not merely ephemeral, this might also qualify as a taking.[70]

(c) Public purpose

The traditional rules of international law require that the taking be for a public purpose; however, this requirement has not figured prominently in international claims in recent years. For one thing, the concept is extremely broad and is not subject to precise definition. Indeed, it can be argued that virtually any expropriation by a government is done for a public purpose, such as developing the national economy, executing development plans, or protecting foreign currency reserves. On the other hand, a mere assertion by an expropriating government that the expropriation was for a public purpose or 'in the public interest', without specifying the nature of that public purpose or interest, would seem not to be sufficient to establish the existence of the public purpose requirement to justify the legality of the government taking.[71] The principal problem for investors challenging an expropriation for lack of the requisite public purpose is that there is to be no effective means under customary international law for reviewing whether or not a particular expropriation is for a public purpose.[72]

---

[69] See *Revere Copper and Brass, Inc v Overseas Private Investment Corp (OPIC)* (1978) 17 ILM 1321, particularly the majority and minority opinions as to whether the Jamaican government's repudiation of its agreement with the investor on taxation prevented the investor from exercising effective control of its investment.

[70] GH Aldrich, 'What Constitutes a Compensable Taking of Property? The Decisions of the Iran–United States Claims Tribunal' (1994) 88 AJIL 585.

[71] See eg *ADC Affiliate Ltd and ADC & AMDC Management Ltd v The Republic of Hungary*, ICSID Case No ARB/03/16 (Award) (2 October 2006), (Cyprus–Hungary BIT), in which the tribunal rejected Hungary's assertion that its expropriatory action was in the country's 'strategic interest' without specifying the particular nature of that interest. The Cyprus–Hungary BIT, Art 4, stipulated that for an expropriation to be legal under the treaty the measures must be taken 'in the public interest and with due process of law'. The tribunal stated at paragraph 432:

> In the Tribunal's opinion, a treaty requirement for '*public interest*' requires some genuine interest of the public. If mere reference to '*public interest*' can magically put such interest into existence and therefore satisfy this requirement, then this requirement would be rendered meaningless since the Tribunal can imagine no situation where this requirement would not have been met.

[72] See generally M Sornarajah, *The International Law on Foreign Investment* (3rd edn, Cambridge University Press, 2010) 407–9.

(d) Discrimination

Although traditionally international law has prohibited discriminatory taking, the application of this principal also poses considerable difficulties. Often, the investor stands in a class by itself within the host country because nationals or other foreigners do not own comparable investments. Consequently, it is difficult to establish whether or not an act of expropriation directed against a foreign investor is discriminatory in nature. For example, if a foreign consortium owns the only mine in a small developing country, it is difficult to show that the nationalization of that mine was discriminatory. Unlawful discrimination requires the government of the host country to make arbitrary or unreasonable distinctions among investors. It may well be that the reasons for the expropriation bear a reasonable relationship to the security interests or economic policy of the host government. As a practical matter, injured investors will only claim discrimination or lack of public purpose if the host country government does not provide adequate compensation.

(e) Compensation

In contemporary international economic life, the essential objective of an injured investor is to secure adequate compensation for its expropriated investment. Even though the taking may not have been for a public purpose, and even though it may have been grossly discriminatory, no investor has a realistic hope—through legal, diplomatic, or other means—of obtaining restitution of the nationalized property, unless, of course, a radical change of regime takes place in the country of expropriation. Indeed, even if the expropriation has been discriminatory and not for a public purpose, most investors would not raise a claim if they received adequate compensation.

Generally speaking, almost all of the nations in the world today would claim to recognize the principle that a state which has expropriated the property of a foreign investor has the obligation to pay compensation to that investor. However, all nations do not agree on the appropriate standard of compensation for expropriation or on its application in specific cases. One traditional formulation of the appropriate standard is the 'Hull formula', which was derived from the correspondence, previously referred to, between US Secretary of State Cordell Hull and Mexican Minister of Foreign Affairs Eduardo Hay. In that correspondence, Hull declared that the property of aliens was protected by an international standard under which expropriation was subject to limitations, which required that there be 'prompt, adequate and effective compensation'.[73] In its international relations, the US government has consistently maintained that the standard to be applied in cases of expropriation is the 'prompt, adequate, and effective standard of compensation'.[74] As will be seen, the United

---

[73] 'Official Documents' (1938) 32 AJIL Supp 181, 193.
[74] E McDowall, *Digest of U.S. Practice in International Law* (US Government Printing Office, 1975) 488; *Digest of U.S. Practice in International Law* (US Government Printing Office, 1978) 1226–7.

States and various European countries have at times incorporated the Hull formula into their investment treaties.

Many western countries and several international tribunals, while recognizing a host state's international obligation to pay compensation when alien property is taken or injured by a state, have not employed the Hull formula, but instead have used different terms that seem to be its functional equivalent.[75] In the *De Sabla* case, for example, the tribunal found that the claimant was entitled to the 'full value' of property that had been adjudicated to third parties.[76] In *Delagoa Bay*, the tribunal stated:

Even if the present case should be regarded as one of legal expropriation, the fact remains that the effect was to dispossess private persons from their rights and privileges of a private nature conferred upon them by the concession, and that...the State, which is the author of such dispossession, is bound to make full reparation for the injuries done by it.[77]

In the *Selwyn* case, relied upon by US Secretary of State Hull to justify the 'prompt, adequate, and effective compensation' standard, the umpire stated:

The fundamental ground of this claim as presented is that the claimant was deprived of valuable rights, of moneys, properties, property and rights of property by an act of the Government which he was powerless to prevent and for which he claims reimbursement. This act of the Government may have proceeded from the highest reasons of public policy and with the largest regard for the state and its interests; but when from the necessity or policy of the Government it appropriates or destroys the property or property rights of an alien it is held to make full and adequate recompense therefor.[78]

---

[75] O Schachter, 'Compensation for Expropriation' (1984) 78 AJIL 121. Schachter, at 124, also observed:

> The argument that the 'prompt, adequate and effective' formula is 'traditional' international law finds little support in state practice or authoritative treatises and monographs. For example, Judge Charles De Visscher, a past President of the International Court of Justice, concluded that state practice in cases of nationalization on a broad scale has substantially qualified the right to full and prompt indemnification for the taking of alien property. He observed that 'nationalization hardly ever permits more than partial compensation calculated less by the extent of damage than by the capacity and good will of the nationalizing State.' Rousseau points out that the 'prompt, adequate and effective' formula has not won general acceptance in cases or state practice. Oppenheim, as edited by Sir Hersch Lauterpacht, states an important qualification to the duty to compensate 'in cases in which fundamental changes in the political system and economic structure of the State or far-reaching social reforms entail interference, on a large scale, with private property.' In such cases, Lauterpacht concluded, a solution must be sought in the grant of 'partial compensation.' Similar views were reflected in the resolution and discussions of the Institut de Droit International in 1950 as well as in detailed studies by Western European jurists.

[76] (1934) 28 AJIL 602, 611–12. This passage is also cited in Report of BL Hunt, 'American and Panamanian General Claims Arbitration' (1934) 447.

[77] *Delagoa Bay and East African Railway Co (US and Great Britain v Portugal)* (1900) in A Moore, *Digest and History of the International Arbitrations* (US Government Printing Office, 1908) vol 2, p 1875.

[78] 'Official Documents' (1938) 32 AJIL Supp 193.

In the *Norwegian Claims* case, the Permanent Court of Arbitration held that the claimants were entitled to 'just compensation...under the municipal law of the United States, as well as under the international law'.[79] One commentator noted:

Some sixty international claims tribunals sat between the early nineteenth century and the Second World War, many dealing with claims arising out of takings of alien property. Although their reasoning is sometimes obscure, none held that the appropriate measure of compensation was less than the full value of the property taken, and many specifically affirmed the need for full compensation.[80]

As far as rules regarding determination of the precise amount of compensation to be paid in specific cases are concerned, other commentators observed that 'it is extremely difficult, if not entirely impossible, to set out systematically the criteria which seem to have been observed in practice'.[81] Although the Permanent Court of International Justice in the *Chorzów Factory* case set down, albeit indirectly, the criterion of the 'value of the undertaking at the moment of dispossession, plus interest to the day of payment',[82] this formula has not been followed in the same way in all cases.[83]

Following more general usage, the *Restatement (Third) of the Foreign Relations Law of the United States*, unlike its predecessor, does not use the formulation 'prompt, adequate, and effective compensation'. Rather, it simply provides for the payment of 'just compensation'. For compensation to be just, 'it must, in the absence of exceptional circumstances, be in an amount equivalent to the value of the property taken and be paid at the time of taking, or within a reasonable time thereafter with interest from the date of taking, and in a form economically usable by the foreign national'.[84] The *Restatement*'s view would seem to represent the current position of most western states on the standard of compensation due to investors for the illegal acts of host states under international law. More recently, that view is reflected in Article 31(2) of the Draft Articles on Responsibility of States for Internationally Wrongful Acts,[85] which provides that a state responsible for an internationally wrongful act is 'under an obligation to make full reparation for the injury caused by [its] internationally wrongful act'.

(f) Breaches of state contracts

Under traditional principles of customary international law, a state that is a party to a contract with a foreign national may be liable for its repudiation or breach in certain instances. According to the *Restatement (Third) of the Foreign Relations*

[79] *Norwegian Claims* case (1922) in *The Hague Reports* (1932) vol 2, p 69.

[80] PM Norton, 'A Law of the Future of a Law of the Past? Modern Tribunals and the International Law of Expropriation' (1991) 85 AJIL 474, 477.

[81] FV Garcia-Amador, LB Sohn, and RR Baxter, *Recent Codification of the Law of State Responsibility for Injuries to Aliens* (Oceana Publications, 1974) 55.

[82] *Factory at Chórzow* (n 64 above) 47.   [83] Garcia-Amador et al (n 81 above) 55.

[84] The American Law Institute, *Restatement of the Law, The Foreign Relations Law of the United States* (3rd edn, 1987) vol 2, § 712, pp 198–9.

[85] *Draft Articles* (note 37 above).

Law of the United States, a state is liable: (a) if the repudiation or breach is discriminatory or motivated by non-commercial considerations and compensation is not paid; or (b) if the foreign national is not given an adequate forum to hear his or her claim or is not compensated. On the other hand, if a state repudiates or breaches a commercial contract with a foreign national for commercial reasons, for example, where performance becomes uneconomical, international law will not be applicable. In such cases, where the state is acting as any private contractor might, the state is only liable under the law applicable to the contract.[86] Nonetheless, breaches of concession agreements, development contracts, and investment contracts may be akin to an expropriation, since through such a breach the investor is effectively deprived of its investment.[87]

As a general rule, contracts between a state and a foreign private investor are governed by the law of that state.[88] At the same time, the parties to that contract may agree to a choice of law clause expressly stipulating that the contractual relationship shall be governed, either wholly or in certain particulars, by a legal system or specified legal rules other than the municipal law of the contracting state, including the principles of international law. Often in major contracts involving large projects or long-term concessions, in order to gain added protection against unjustified cancellation by the host country government, the foreign investor will include a clause stating that the contract is to be governed by general principles of international law or general principles of law common to the world's legal systems.[89] The purpose of this type of clause is to 'internationalize' the contract and thus protect it from attempts by the state party to cancel or modify it without the consent of the investor. In order to give additional assurance of the enforceability of their contract, the parties might also agree to settle any dispute arising under the agreement by international arbitration rather than in the courts of the host country.

---

[86] The American Law Institute, *Restatement of the Law, The Foreign Relations Law of the United States* (3rd edn, 1987) vol 2, § 712, p 212, reporters' n 8.

[87] It is for this reason that the Multilateral Investment Guarantee Agency (MIGA) includes as one of its covered, non-commercial risks 'any repudiation or breach by the host government of a contract when the investor has no access to a competent forum, faces unreasonable procedural delays, or is unable to enforce decisions made in its favor'. Convention Establishing the Multilateral Investment Guarantee Agency (11 October 1985) 24 ILM 1598, 1605 (The MIGA Convention), Art 11(a).

[88] G Schwarzenberger, *Foreign Investments and International Law* (Praeger, 1969) 5–7.

[89] eg a 1954 consortium agreement between Iran and various foreign investors provided:

> In view of the diverse nationalities of the parties to this Agreement, it shall be governed and interpreted and applied in accordance with principles of law common to Iran and the several nations in which the other parties of this Agreement are incorporated, and in the absence of such common principles, then by and in accordance with principles of law recognized by civilized nations in general, including such of those principles as may have been applied by international tribunals.

JC Hurewitz, *Diplomacy in the Near and Middle East, A Documentary Record: 1914–1945* (Macmillan Press, 1956) vol 2, p 48. This provision is also cited in Garcia-Amador et al (n 81 above) 62.

By analogizing between treaties among states and contracts between a state and an alien, various jurists and tribunals have argued that the principle of *pacta sunt servanda* is applicable to such contracts as a matter of international law. The basis of this view lies in the contracts' international character and also the fact that failure to apply the principle would place the validity and effectiveness of obligations made to aliens at the mercy of the unilateral decisions of the host country government. Moreover, it has also been argued that the principle of *pacta sunt servanda* is applicable as one of 'the general principles of law recognized by civilized nations'. Thus, once a state has entered into an international agreement with an investor, such state must abide by that agreement. Various tribunals have confirmed that the principle of *pacta sunt servanda* underlies contracts entered into by states and foreign investors.[90] The Permanent Court of International Justice, in the *Chorzów* case, also confirmed that a lawfully concluded public contract is a property or 'vested' right in the technical sense.[91] Contractual rights, like any other property rights, are protected by international law against confiscation by the state party to the contract. According to the traditional view of international law prevailing in western countries, a state that breaks its obligations of non-interference with a public contract violates both the minimum standards of international law and the general principles of law recognized by civilized nations.

3.6 Challenges to Western Views on International Investment Law

(a) Background

Not all countries meekly accepted the western position on the customary international law governing foreign investments. Indeed, there were numerous challenges to western views, and those challenges had an impact on the investment treaty movement that emerged after World War II. The three most notable challenges were: (1) the Soviet challenge; (2) the Latin American challenge; and (3) the post-colonial challenge. Each of these challenges is considered briefly.

---

[90] eg in the *Sapphire* case the tribunal stated: 'It is a fundamental principle of law, which is constantly being proclaimed by international courts, that contractual undertakings must be respected. The rule of *pacta sunt servanda* is the basis of every contractual relationship.' *Sapphire International Petroleum Ltd (Sapphire) v National Iranian Oil Co* (1953) 35 ILR 136, 181. In *TOPCO*, sole arbitrator Dupuy reiterated that 'the maxim *pacta sunt servanda* should be viewed as a fundamental principle of international law'. *Texaco Overseas Petroleum Co and California Asiatic Oil Co (TOPCO) v Government of the Libyan Arab Republic* (1978) 17 ILM 1.

[91] *Case Concerning Certain German Interests in Polish Upper Silesia* (1926) PCIJ Rep Series A, No 7, at 21–2, 42.

(b) The Soviet challenge

The October Revolution of 1917 in Russia and the subsequent establishment of the Dictatorship of the Proletariat resulted in the confiscation of foreign private property on a vast scale.[92] The new Soviet government refused to make restitution or pay compensation for the seized foreign property. In response, the western governments of nationals affected by the seizures lodged vigorous protests with the Soviet government. For example, on 13 February 1918, the US Ambassador protested in the name of fourteen Allied powers and sixteen neutrals, stating: 'In order to avoid any misunderstandings in the future, the representatives at Petrograd of all the foreign powers declare that they view the decrees relating to the repudiation of the Russian state loans, the confiscation of property and other similar measures as null and void insofar as their nationals are concerned.'[93]

At the Brussels Conference on Russia of October 1921, the delegates passed a resolution stating what they perceived as a well-established principle of international law on the question of expropriation: 'The forcible expropriations and nationalizations without any compensation or remuneration of property in which foreigners are interested is totally at variance with the practice of civilised states. Where such expropriation has taken place, a claim arises for compensation against the Government of the country.'[94]

In the 1920s, the Soviet Union, still unrecognized by the major powers and with an economy in ruins, launched its New Economic Policy and actively sought to obtain international recognition and economic assistance. As part of this effort, it expressed a readiness to consider foreign claims arising out of the expropriations that followed the Russian Revolution.[95] However, the offer was conditioned on a satisfactory settlement of the Soviet Union's own claims against the western countries that had militarily intervened in Soviet territory after the October Revolution. Throughout this period, the Soviet Union refused to recognize the duty of a state, as a principle of customary international law, to make restitution or pay compensation for foreign property it had seized.[96]

---

[92] The Decree of 26 October 1917, adopted by the Second All-Russian Congress of Soviets, abolished private property in land without compensation. The Decrees of 14 December 1917 and 26 January 1918, socialized the banks 'in order to liberate the workers and peasants and the whole population from the exploitation of the capitalist banks' and provided that the assets of the former private banks were to be confiscated. By June 1920 most industry had been socialized in the USSR. S Friedman, *Expropriation in International Law* (Stevens, 1953) 17–23; BA Wortley, *Expropriation in Public International Law* (Cambridge University Press, 1959) vol 1, 61–2; Legislative Reference Service, Library of Congress for the Committee on Foreign Affairs, 88th Congress, 1st Session, Report on Expropriation of American-Owned Property by Foreign Governments in the Twentieth Century (19 July 1963) 8–10.

[93] Friedman (n 92 above) 18, quoting Correspondence between His Majesty's Government and the French Government respecting the Anglo-Russian Trade Agreement, 1921.

[94] Wortley (n 92 above) 9.

[95] Friedman (n 92 above) 19, citing Correspondence between the British and Russian Governments concerning Russia's Foreign Indebtedness (1921) 114 British and Foreign State Papers 380.

[96] Friedman (n 92 above) 19; Report on Expropriation of American-Owned Property (n 92 above) 9.

After the failure of the 1922 Cannes and Hague conferences seeking a possible multilateral settlement of the various claims and counter-claims between Soviet Russia and western countries, individual western governments, desiring access to the large Russian market, began to conclude bilateral agreements with the Soviet government. The result of these efforts was generally little compensation compared to investors' actual losses. In 1924, for example, the British concluded a treaty in which they agreed in principle to Russian counter-claims based on the British intervention that occurred after the Russian Revolution and recognized the possibility of setting them off against claims by British nationals arising out of Soviet confiscations. The British also promised a financial loan, while the Soviet Union, in its turn, undertook to open negotiations for these purposes with interested parties in the United Kingdom. A separate agreement was reached between the Soviet government and one of the nationalized British enterprises, Lena Goldfields Limited, whereby the enterprise renounced its claims in return for the concession of its former properties.[97] A subsequent change in Soviet policy led to a revocation of the concession and, ultimately, to one of the first investor–state arbitrations, the *Lena Goldfields* case.[98]

A similar development took place between the United States and the USSR. In an exchange of communications by which the United States recognized the Soviet government on 16 November 1933, the government of the Soviet Union released and assigned to the US government all amounts due to the Soviet government from American nationals.[99] This agreement, known as the Litvinov Assignment, formed the basis of a fund out of which some of the claims against Russia made by American nationals for confiscation of their property could be paid. Although the Litvinov Assignment was only intended to be a temporary measure preceding a final settlement of the claims and counterclaims, subsequent negotiations between the two governments on an overall settlement proved unsuccessful. As of the early 1960s, only a portion of the claims of American nationals had been paid from the Litvinov Assignment funds. Those that were paid were distributed by the Foreign Claims Settlement Commission under title III of the International Claims Settlement Act of 1949.[100]

---

[97] Friedman (n 92 above) 21.

[98] In accordance with the concession agreement, the company holding the concession instituted arbitration proceedings against the USSR. The *Lena Goldfields* arbitral award of 1930 decided in favour of the company after the abrupt withdrawal of the Soviet government from the arbitral proceedings. It was not until 1934, when the Anglo-Soviet Trade agreement was signed, that the Soviet Union, after protracted diplomatic negotiations, gave the company transferable but non-interest-bearing notes payable over 20 years. This sum (£3 million) was considerably less than the arbitration award (£13 million); however, even this compensation arrangement was repudiated by the USSR in 1940. Wortley (n 92 above) 62. The circumstances surrounding the *Lena Goldfields* case have prompted one commentator to note: 'Historically, the *Lena* case remains a baleful monument to the absolute power of a State.' VV Veeder, 'The Lena Goldfields Arbitration: The Historical Roots of the Three Ideas' (1988) 47(4) ICLQ 747.

[99] 'Exchange of Communications between the President of the United States and the President of the All Union General Executive Committee' (1934) 28 AJIL Supp 1–20.

[100] Report on Expropriation of American-Owned Property (n 92 above) 9.

Reviewing the history of efforts to secure compensation from the Soviet Union for foreign property seized by the Soviet government, one commentator concluded: 'One after another, States ceased to press their claims arising out of the Soviet socialization measures. They even went so far as actually renouncing these claims, either expressly as in the case of Germany, or tacitly as in the case of the United States.'[101]

Thus, by its actions and inactions, the Soviet Union, one of the world's great powers, expressed its clear opposition to the traditional western position on expropriation and the enforcement of state contracts under international law.

(c) The Latin American challenge

Latin American countries also challenged the western view of the customary international law of investment, primarily through their efforts to implement the Calvo doctrine. One common method was to include 'Calvo clauses' in their constitutions. These clauses purported to make all property within their territories subject only to domestic law. For example, the Constitution of Peru provided:

Property, whoever may be the owner, is governed exclusively by the laws of the Republic and is subject to the taxes, charges and limitations established in the laws themselves. The same provisions regarding property apply to aliens as well as [nationals], except that in no case may said aliens make use of their exceptional position or resort to diplomatic appeals.[102]

A similar provision was incorporated into the Bolivian Constitution: 'Foreign subjects and enterprises are, in respect to property, in the same position as Bolivians, and can in no case plead an exceptional situation or appeal through diplomatic channels unless in case of denial of justice.'[103]

Another approach was to implement the Calvo doctrine through legislation. Thus, for example, in 1938, Article 26 of a 1938 law of Ecuador provided that 'the foreigners, by the act of coming to the country, subjected themselves to the local laws without any exception and may in no case, nor for any reason, avail themselves of their status as foreigners against laws, jurisdiction and police'. Furthermore, Article 30 of the law subjected the contractual rights of foreigners 'to exclusive jurisdiction of the national judges and courts', while Article 31 flatly stated that 'the renunciation of diplomatic claims will be an implicit and essential condition of all contracts concluded by foreigners with the state' and 'foreigners who have been employed or carried out a commission subjecting them to the Ecuadorian laws and authorities may not claim indemnification through diplomatic channels'.[104]

---

[101] Friedman (n 92 above) 23.
[102] R Fitzgibbon, *Constitutions of the Americas* (University of Chicago Press, 1948) 670, citing the 1933 Constitution of Peru, Art 31.
[103] ibid Art 35.
[104] DR Shea, *The Calvo Clause: A Problem of Inter-American and International Law and Diplomacy* (OUP, 1955) 26, quoting (1938) 32 AJIL Supp.

A third approach to implementing the Calvo doctrine was to include 'Calvo clauses' in contracts with foreign companies by which the companies agreed to pursue claims only in local courts and to relinquish the right to diplomatic protection in any dispute arising out of the contractual relationship.[105] In such cases, the enforceability of the Calvo clause gained additional force because the foreign company had specifically agreed to it.[106]

The widespread use of the Calvo clause in Latin America raised the question of whether such use was compatible with international law. Some opponents argued that the right to protect investors under international law belonged to the investors' states of nationality and so only those states, not the investors, could waive the right to diplomatic protection.

The issue of the Calvo clause's compatibility with international law was considered in the decision of the United States–Mexican Claims Commission in the *North American Dredging Company* case,[107] which is regarded as the leading case on the subject.[108] The Commission stated that, for the clause to be declared void, one would have to prove that a generally accepted rule of international law exists that condemns the Calvo clause and that denies 'an individual the right to relinquish to any extent, large or small, and under any circumstances or conditions, the protection of the government to which he owes allegiance'. After declaring that no such rule exists, the Commission held that because of its Calvo clause contractual commitment, 'the present claimant is precluded from presenting to its Government any claim relative to the interpretation or fulfillment of this contract'.

---

[105] An example of a Calvo clause is found in the contract between Mexico and the North American Dredging Company of Texas, later subject to an international law claim, which reads as follows:

> The Contractor and all persons, who as employees or in any other capacity may be engaged in the execution of the work under this contract either directly or indirectly, shall be considered as Mexicans in all matters, within the Republic of Mexico, concerning the execution of such work and the fulfillment of this contract. They shall not claim, nor shall they have, with regard to the interests and the business connected with this contract, any other rights or means to enforce the same than those granted by the laws of the Republic to Mexicans, nor shall they enjoy any other rights than those established in favor of Mexicans. They are consequently deprived of any rights as aliens, and under no conditions shall the intervention of foreign diplomatic agents be permitted, in any matter related to this contract.

Shea (n 104 above) 29, quoting *United States (North American Dredging Co) v United Mexican States*, Opinions of Commissioners, I at 21–2.

[106] Shea (n 104 above) 28. The commentator asserts that the Calvo clause differs from the Calvo doctrine in one very important respect: the enforcement of the latter was a unilateral act, whereas in the case of the former the individual has consented of his own free will to surrender the right of recourse to his government in case of contractual controversies or disputes.

[107] *North American Dredging Co of Texas (United States v United Mexican States)* (31 March 1926), reproduced in (1926) 20 AJIL 800.

[108] UNGA, 'Diplomatic Protection', Report of the International Law Commission Fifty-fourth Session (29 April to 7 June and 22 July to 16 August 2002) GAOR 57th Session Supp No 10 (A/57/10) Ch V, ¶ 253, at 160. The Special Rapporteur noted, in particular: '[In the case] it had been shown that the Calvo clause was compatible with international law in general and with the right to diplomatic protection in particular, although the decision in that case had been subjected to serious criticism by jurists.'

The claimant, because it violated its contractual renunciation, 'has not put itself in a position where it may rightfully present this claim to the Government of the United States for its interposition'. The Commission, in enunciating this rule, asserted:

Under Article 18 of the contract [the Calvo clause]...the present claimant is precluded from presenting to its government any claim relative to the interpretation or fulfillment of this contract....As the claimant voluntarily entered into a legal contract binding itself not to call as to this contract upon its Government to intervene on its behalf, and as all of its claim relates to this contract, and as therefore it can not present its claim to its Government for interposition or espousal before this Commission, the second ground to the motion to dismiss is sustained.[109]

Summarizing the international jurisprudence dealing with the Calvo clause from the *Dredging* decision of 1926 through to the 1950s (a period when the clause gained significant use), one commentator observed that in five out of seven cases international tribunals applied the rule to bar claims that would have been otherwise admissible in the absence of the renunciatory provision (among them are the *International Fisheries Company*,[110] *Mexican Union Railway*,[111] *Interoceanic Railway*,[112] and *Veracruz Railways*[113] cases). Two cases held that the Calvo clause did not bar claims: in the *MacNeill*[114] case the clause's wording was found to be so vague that the intent of the parties was not clear to the Commission, and in *El Oro Mining and Railway Company*[115] the case was based on claims of a flagrant denial of justice.[116]

In 2002, the International Law Commission issued its Third Report on Diplomatic Protection to the UN General Assembly. The Special Rapporteur on Diplomatic Protection referred to several considerations concerning the Calvo clause's purpose and scope. First, the Calvo clause was of limited effect in that it did not constitute a complete bar to diplomatic intervention. It applied only to disputes relating to the contract between the alien and host state containing the clause, but it did not apply to breaches of international law. Second, the Calvo clause confirmed the importance of the rule requiring the exhaustion of local remedies. Some writers had suggested that the clause was nothing more than a reaffirmation of that rule, but most saw it as extending beyond that principle. Third, international law placed no bar on the right of an alien to waive his right to request his state of nationality to exercise diplomatic protection by contract. Fourth, an alien could not waive rights that under international law belonged to his government through a Calvo clause. Fifth, the waiver in a Calvo clause

---

[109] Shea (n 104 above) 263, citing Opinions of Commissioners, vol 1, pp 30–3.
[110] *International Fisheries Co (USA) v United Mexican States* (1931) 4 Reports of International Arbitral Awards (United Nations) 691 (hereinafter UNRIAA).
[111] *Mexican Union Rly (Great Britain) v United Mexican States* (1930) 5 UNRIAA 115.
[112] *Interoceanic Rly Co of Mexico Ltd (Great Britain) v United Mexican States* (1930) 5 UNRIAA 135.
[113] *Veracruz Rlys Ltd (Great Britain) v United Mexican States* (1931) 5 UNRIAA 221.
[114] *Douglas G Collie MacNeill (Great Britain) v United Mexican States* (1931) 5 UNRIAA 135.
[115] *El Oro Mining and Rly Co (Great Britain) v United Mexican States* (1930) 5 UNRIAA 191.
[116] Shea (n 104 above) 255–6.

extended only to disputes arising out of contract or out of a breach of contract. The waivers did not cover disputes that constitute a breach of international law and, in particular, did not extend to breaches that represented a denial of justice.[117]

(d) The post-colonial challenge

In the aftermath of decolonization in the post-World War II era, the legitimacy and content of traditional principles of the law regarding states' international responsibility for injuries to investors came under increased attack from the newly emerging states. Developing countries challenged its legitimacy by arguing that customary international law had been shaped exclusively by western countries and that developing countries, being under colonial or imperialist domination at that time, played no part in its formation and evolution. One commentator aptly summarized their position with respect to the international law on this point:

The law of responsibility...is not founded on any universal principles of law or morality. Its sole foundation is custom, which is binding only among states where it either grew up or came to be adopted. It is thus hardly possible to maintain that it is still part of universal international law. Whatever the basis of obligation of international law in the past, when the international community was restricted to only a few states...the birth of a new world community has brought about a radical change which makes the traditional basis of obligation outmoded.[118]

Developing countries also viewed the content of traditional international law—with its emphasis on the protection of foreign investment—as playing an important role in their economic underdevelopment and continued dependence on western countries. In short, they saw international law as an obstacle to their economic advancement. International law, as shaped by their former colonial masters, elevated the protection of foreign-owned property and contracts over the right to nationalize ownership of property on their territories and prioritized the commercial and economic freedom of foreigners over the right of the state to regulate economic activities in its own territory.[119]

To deal with this problem, developing countries sought to use their numerical superiority in the United Nations to shape the international law of state responsibility to foreign investors in a way that was more in keeping with their interests. An early effort in this respect was the 1962 UN General Assembly Resolution 1803 on Permanent Sovereignty over Natural Resources.

Establishing sovereignty over the natural resources in their territories was a prime concern for developing countries. They therefore sought to secure international recognition of their right to nationalize and re-establish sovereignty over the natural resources contained in their territories, without regard to the necessity

---

[117] UNGA, 'Diplomatic Protection' (n 108 above) ¶ 256, at 162.
[118] SN Guha Roy, 'Is the Law of Responsibility of States for Injuries to Aliens a Part of Universal International Law?' (1961) 55 AJIL 863.
[119] T Wälde, 'Requiem for the "New International Economic Order"' in G Hafner et al (eds), *Festschrift für Ignaz Seidl-Hohenveldern* (Kluwer, 1998) 761.

or adequacy of compensation. Developed nations, for their part, were willing to recognize such a right only if the developing nations abided by established rules of international law providing for the payment of adequate compensation.[120]

In fact, investors' home countries had good reason to emphasize the importance of adequate compensation. From 1960 to mid-1974, some sixty-two different developing countries engaged in 875 nationalizations or takeovers of foreign enterprises. The majority of the cases (591) took place in ten states.[121] As a result, disputes about the existence and nature of obligations to pay compensation for the expropriation of alien property under international law increased dramatically.[122]

Beginning from the 1960s and continuing through the 1970s, developing countries attempted to revise the established principles regarding compensation and to bring about what they termed the 'New International Economic Order' (NIEO). They did this through a series of UN General Assembly resolutions dealing with the issue of permanent sovereignty over natural resources and the economic rights and duties of states.

In 1962, the UN General Assembly adopted Resolution 1803 (XVII), which contained the Declaration on Permanent Sovereignty over Natural Resources. It provided in part:

3. In cases where authorization is granted, the capital imported and the earnings on that capital shall be governed by the terms thereof, by the national legislation in force, and by international law. The profits derived must be shared in the proportions freely agreed upon, in each case, between the investors and the recipient State, due care being taken to ensure that there is no impairment, for any reason, of that State's sovereignty over its natural wealth and resources.

4. Nationalization, expropriation or requisitioning shall be based on grounds or reasons of public utility, security or the national interest which are recognized as overriding purely individual or private interests, both domestic and foreign. In such cases the owner shall be paid appropriate compensation, in accordance with the rules in force in the State taking such measures in the exercise of its sovereignty and in accordance with international law. In any case where the question of compensation gives rise to a controversy, the national jurisdiction of the State taking such measures shall be exhausted. However, upon agreement by sovereign States and other parties concerned, settlement of the dispute should be made through arbitration or international adjudication....

8. Foreign investment agreements freely entered into by or between sovereign States shall be observed in good faith.[123]

---

[120] M Mugharby, *Permanent Sovereignty over Oil Resources* (OUP, 1966) 15.

[121] UNGA, 'Permanent Sovereignty over Natural Resources', UN Doc A/9716 (20 September 1974) annex at 2, table 1.

[122] Writing in 1964, Justice Harlan of the US Supreme Court concluded:

There are few if any issues in international law today on which opinion seems to be so divided as to the limitations on a State's power to expropriate the property of aliens.... The disagreement as to relevant international law standards reflects an even more basic divergence between the national interests of capital importing and exporting nations and between the social ideologies of those countries that favor state control of a considerable portion of the means of production and those that adhere to a free enterprise system.

Banco Nacional de Cuba v Sabbatino, 376 US 398, 428–9 (1964).

[123] UNGA Res 1803 (XVII) (14 December 1962) UN Doc A/RES/1803 (XVII) (1962).

Some observers interpreted the Declaration as not being too radical a departure from the traditional international customary law understood by western nations.[124] The Declaration incorporated by reference the international law requirement that foreign capital not be subject to discriminatory treatment and it affirmed the binding character of foreign investment agreements. Although the stipulation that compensation need only be 'appropriate' was ambiguous, the legislative history was said to support the US interpretation that 'appropriate compensation' meant 'prompt, adequate, and effective compensation'.[125] Adopted by a vote of 87 to 2 with 12 abstentions, the Declaration has been viewed as the last consensus on the issue of expropriation under international law.[126]

In the 1970s, developing countries became more assertive in their efforts to reshape the customary international law affecting foreign investments. Under their impetus, the UN General Assembly, in 1973, adopted Resolution 3171, which affirmed:

3. ... the application of the principle of nationalization carried out by States, as an expression of their sovereignty in order to safeguard their natural resources, implies that each State is entitled to determine the amount of possible compensation and the mode of payment, and that any disputes which might arise should be settled in accordance with the national legislation of each State carrying out such measures.[127]

The Resolution omitted language concerning the guarantee of compensation for foreign investors and also references to international law. This left the host state with wide discretion in determining what, if any, compensation was due through its municipal law without regard to the objective standards under international law.

In the following year, developing countries pushed the UN General Assembly to adopt resolutions departing even further from the traditional western positions on the international law governing foreign investments. In May 1974, the General Assembly adopted Resolution 3201 containing the Declaration on the Establishment of a New International Economic Order.[128] Resolution 3201 declared the right of each state to exercise control over and exploit its natural resources, 'including the right to nationalization or transfer of ownership to its nationals'.[129] It was followed on 12 December 1974 by Resolution 3281 containing

---

[124] SM Schwebel, 'The Story of the United Nations Declaration on Permanent Sovereignty over Natural Resources' (1963) 49 ABAJ 463, 469.

[125] ibid 463, 469. Steven Schwebel, later to become a judge of the ICJ, wrote at the time:

Cast in the form of a declaration, which in United Nations usage is meant to give a resolution a particular weight, it represents a consensus of the economically developed and less developed countries. The fact that that consensus includes positive recognition of the obligation to pay compensation where property is taken, to observe investment agreements and agreements to arbitrate and to abide by other requirements of international law should contribute to the enhancement of the international investment climate.

[126] P Norton, 'A Law of the Future or a Law of the Past? Modern Tribunals and the International Law of Expropriation' (1991) 85 AJIL 474, 479.

[127] UNGA Res 3171 (XXVIII) (17 December 1973) UN Doc A/RES/9030 (XVIII) (1973).

[128] UNGA Res 3201 (S-VI) (1 May 1974) UN Doc A/RES/3201 (S-VI) (1974), reprinted in (1974) 13 ILM 715.

[129] ibid ¶ 6.

the Charter of Economic Rights and Duties of States.[130] Resolution 3281 was adopted by a vote of 120 to 6, with 10 abstentions (the states voting 'against' included Belgium, Denmark, the German Federal Republic, Luxembourg, the United Kingdom, and the United States).[131] This Resolution reiterated the urgent need 'to establish generally accepted norms to govern international economic relations systematically'. It also recognized that 'it is not feasible to establish generally accepted norms to govern international economic relations systematically' and 'to establish a just order and a stable world as long as a charter to protect the rights of all countries and in particular the developing states is not formulated'. It further noted that the Charter was designed as 'the first step in the codification and development' of the norms for 'the development of international economic relations on a just and equitable basis'.

The most contentious provisions in the Charter were contained in Article 2 on private foreign investment. Article 2(2) of the Charter provided that each state has the right:

(a) To regulate and exercise authority over foreign investment within its national jurisdiction in accordance with its laws and regulations and in conformity with its national objectives and priorities. No State shall be compelled to grant preferential treatment to foreign investment;

...

(c) To nationalize, expropriate or transfer ownership of foreign property, in which case appropriate compensation should be paid by the State adopting such measures, taking into account its relevant laws and regulations and all circumstances that the State considers pertinent. In any case where the question of compensation gives rise to a controversy, it shall be settled under the domestic law of the nationalizing State and by its tribunals, unless it is freely and mutually agreed by all States concerned that other peaceful means be sought on the basis of the sovereign equality of States and in accordance with the principle of free choice of means.

During the debate on the Charter, Canada and the United States underlined the fundamental differences between the Charter's supporters and the minority of states that voted against it or abstained. The Canadian representative, arguing against Article 2, stated:

Even among States which, like Canada, hold the view that there are principles of customary international law which are relevant to the treatment of foreign investments, there is disagreement about the precise content of those principles. Where the old law is unjust or ineffective, it must be changed to reflect the present economic interdependence of States and the need for the development of the developing countries, which are the two most important facts of economic life in our generation. It had been the hope that this charter would command the consensus necessary to enable it to contribute to the codification and progressive development of law in this area; unhappily, this is not the case.[132]

---

[130] UNGA Res 3281 (XXIX) (12 December 1974) UN Doc A/RES/3281 (XXIX) (1974) reprinted in (1975) 14 ILM 251.

[131] GAOR, Twenty-ninth Session, annexes, agenda item 48, at 31.

[132] Cited in G White, 'A New International Economic Order?' (1975–6) 16 Va J Int'l L 323, 334–5.

The United States joined Canada in criticizing the Charter as unbalanced: 'Many of the provisions on which agreement had been lacking were fundamental and were unacceptable in their present form. They included the treatment of foreign investment in terms which did not fully take into account respect for agreements and international obligations.'[133]

Two basic reasons prevented developed countries from accepting the Charter. First, the document was an attempt to assert principles of international law, or at least *opinio juris*, without specific reference to established international legal doctrine and practice. Second, the Charter failed to formulate and articulate propositions that would give predictability to international economic transactions. The developed states, therefore, had no assurance that their economic relations with the developing states would be subject to a predictable or stable legal regime,[134] which was a fundamental requirement for their nationals to undertake international investments.

Commentators argued that Article 2 of the Charter departed dramatically from the existing international law in several important respects. Critics claimed that its most fundamental weakness was its general failure to state clearly that the economic rights and duties of states are subject to international law, or, at a bare minimum, that international law is a relevant consideration. In dealing with the compensation of an alien whose property has been seized, Article 2(2)(c) provided only that 'appropriate compensation should be paid by the State adopting such measures, taking into account its relevant laws and regulations and all circumstances that the State considers pertinent'.

In analysing its text, critics noted that Article 2 is prefaced with the precatory 'should' rather than the mandatory 'shall'. Thus, they argued that if there is an obligation, it is solely to grant whatever compensation a host state subjectively believes 'appropriate', with consideration given only to local law and circumstances and not necessarily to international law, which may not be 'pertinent'. They also pointed to the fact that the text contains no requirement that a taking must be for a public purpose and that Article 2 is also silent on the traditional principle that any taking of alien property by a state must not be discriminatory. They found this to be particularly strange because the Charter stipulates that 'no state shall be compelled to grant preferential treatment to foreign investment', which is the natural corollary of non-discrimination. The Charter also denied the inviolability of contracts by boldly proclaiming without limitation that 'every state has and shall freely exercise full permanent sovereignty, including possession, use and disposal, over all its wealth, natural resources and economic activities'.[135]

---

[133] ibid 335.   [134] ibid.
[135] CN Bower and JB Tepe, 'The Charter of Economic Rights and Duties of States: A Reflection or Rejection of International Law?' (1975) 9 Int'l Lawyer 295, 304–7. But cf EJ de Arechaga, 'Application of the Rules of State Responsibility to the Nationalization of Foreign-Owned Property' in K Hosena (ed), *Legal Aspects of the New International Economic Order* (F Pinter, 1980) 225–7.

The Charter also departed significantly from traditional international law with respect to the settlement of disputes between aggrieved investors and host countries. First, instead of exhausting local remedies and then proceeding to arbitration and international adjudication, cases were to be decided nationally (in the host country) or possibly by other peaceful means. Second, any agreement to utilize other peaceful means was required to be between 'states concerned' rather than 'upon agreement by sovereign states and other parties', which effectively excluded private companies as parties. Developed countries exerted strong pressure to include the following language from the 1962 Resolution in Article 2: 'foreign investment agreements freely entered into by' or construed the phrase 'international obligation' to apply only to agreements between states, not between governments and foreign investors.[136]

The adoption of the Charter provoked a vehement debate not only regarding its content but also its legal nature and effect on existing international law. The original intent of the Charter's sponsors was for it to be a legally binding document. However, as the divergence of opinion between the developing and developed nations became apparent, the latter grew increasingly opposed to creating legally binding obligations in the Charter.[137] The question of the legal nature of the Charter was left to the General Assembly, but it never reached any determination on the matter, leaving developing countries free to try to bring the document into line with their preferences.[138]

Commentators' views on the legal effect of the Charter varied greatly. Some emphasized the norm-making power of the Charter, equating the instrument to 'a constitution' that served the dual purpose of codifying existing customary law and progressively developing new rules to address the current and future needs of international society.[139] Others asserted that the Charter expressed both traditional principles of international law that were binding on all states and also new principles that were a stage in the progressive development of international law, but possessed no more weight than an unratified treaty.[140] Still others, primarily from developed

---

[136] RF Meagher, *An International Redistribution of Wealth and Power: A Study of the Charter of Economic Rights and Duties of States* (Pergamon Press, 1975) 53–4. Meagher summarized the thrust of the Charter as follows:

> there has been an expansion of the concept of permanent sovereignty; nationalization is now an unqualified right; transnational corporations have become a special category of institutions subject to particular rules; the standards for compensation are determined by national laws based upon what the nationalizing state considers pertinent; and disputes over compensation are to be decided by national tribunals utilizing national laws, unless states agree on other peaceful means.

ibid 54.
[137] UN Doc, TD/B/AC.12/4, at 2. See also Bower and Tepe (n 135 above) 295, 300.
[138] Meagher (n 136 above) 89.
[139] ibid 90, citing J Castaneda, 'La Charte des Droits et Devoirs Economique des Etats' (1974) XX *Annuaire Français de Droit International* 39.
[140] Meagher (n 136 above) 90, citing G Feuer, 'Reflexions sur La Charte des Droits et Devoirs Economique des Etats' (April/June 1975) *Revue Generale de Droit International Public* 274.

countries, emphasized the General Assembly's lack of law-making authority[141] and concluded that the Charter 'is not a legally binding instrument'.[142]

The *TOPCO* arbitration[143] considered the legal validity of the various UN resolutions on the New International Economic Order and the possible existence of a custom resulting from them. Sole Arbitrator Dupuy, by looking at the circumstances under which the resolutions were adopted and analysing the principles that they stated, concluded that only Resolution 1803 (XVII) of 1962 reflected the state of existing customary international law.[144] He further stated that 'Article 2 of this Charter [ie the Charter of Economic Rights and Duties of States] must be analyzed as a political rather than as a legal declaration concerned with the ideological strategy of development and, as such, supported only by non-industrialized States'.[145] Moreover, as will be seen, state practice among developing countries, particularly their subsequent willingness to consent to investment treaties giving strong protection to investor interests, demonstrated that customary international law had not evolved in the direction developing countries had hoped in the 1970s.[146]

Regardless of its legal effect, the Charter of Economic Rights and Duties of States, even though it did not create international law, was a clear challenge to the traditional western view of international law.[147] That challenge, to a greater or lesser extent, served to undermine the solidity of the traditional international legal framework for foreign investment and led both investors and their home

---

[141] '[A]part from its control over the budget, all the General Assembly can do is to discuss and recommend and initiate studies and consider reports from other bodies. It cannot act on behalf of all members, as the Security Council does, and its decisions are not directions telling the member states what they are or are not to do.' JL Brierly, *The Law of Nations* (OUP, 1963) 110.

[142] Bower and Tepe (n 135 above) 295, 301.

[143] *Texaco Overseas Petroleum Co and California Asiatic Oil Co (TOPCO) v Government of the Libyan Arab Republic* (Award on the Merits) (1977) 17 ILM 1 (1978); 53 ILR 389 (1977).

[144] ibid ¶ 87.   [145] ibid.

[146] See eg BH Weston, 'The New International Economic Order and the Deprivation of Foreign Proprietary Wealth: Some Reflections upon the Contemporary International Law Debate' in RB Lillich (ed), *International Law of State Responsibility for Injuries to Aliens* (University of Virginia Press, 1983) 106, stating:

> Because the UN majority did not actually assume they were creating law in the binding or codificatory sense when they adopted the NIEO Charter, because a substantial and critical segment of the international economic community refused to endorse the Charter as written, and, most importantly, because State practice since the Charter's creation and adoption demonstrates a continued adherence to the customary international law principle of compensation (at least as interpreted since World War II), it is appropriate—necessary—to conclude that Article 2(2)(c) is not presently an authoritative statement of existing international law, i.e., not *lex lata*.

See also Crawford (n 14 above) 626.

[147] O Schachter, 'The Evolving International Law of Development' (1976) 15 Col J Transnat'l L 1, 4 stating:

> These declarations and charters are not neutral principles. They are, by and large, challenges to the existing order and their leading motif is the demand for a wider distribution of wealth. Moreover, their adoption by large majorities through parliamentary and conference voting procedures is seen as an attempt to impose obligatory norms on dissenting minorities and to change radically the way in which international law is created.

countries to search for means to strengthen it in order to protect their economic interests in a new era.

3.7 Deficiencies of Customary International Law on Investment

As can be seen from the preceding sections of this chapter, foreign investment gained momentum as an increasingly important international economic activity in the period after World War II when new states joined the international community. Foreign investors and their home governments seeking the protection of international investment law in this period encountered an ephemeral structure consisting of scattered treaty provisions, a few questionable customs, and contested general principles of law. The resulting legal structure was seriously deficient in several respects. First, the applicable international law failed to take into account contemporary investment practices and to address important issues of concern to foreign investors.[148] For example, customary international law had virtually nothing to say about the right of foreign investors to make monetary transfers from a host country or to bring foreign managers into the host country to manage their investments. Second, the principles that did exist were often vague and subject to varying interpretations. Thus, although there was strong evidence that customary international law required the payment of compensation upon nationalization of an investor's property, no specific principles had crystallized as to how that compensation was to be calculated.

Third, the existing framework prompted disagreement between industrialized countries and newly decolonized developing nations. For example, as we have seen, capital-exporting states claimed that international law imposed an obligation on host countries to accord foreign investors a minimum standard of protection and required that states expropriating the property of foreign investors needed to provide compensation. Many developing countries, believing that the existing international rules served only to maintain their poverty, rejected this view and, beginning in the 1970s, demanded that their particular needs and circumstances be taken into account.[149] Their position on foreign investment was

---

[148] In 1970, the ICJ, in the *Barcelona Traction* case, found it 'surprising' that the evolution of international investment law had not gone further and that no generally accepted rules had yet crystallized in the light of the growth of foreign investments and the expansion of international activities by corporations in the previous half-century. *Barcelona Traction, Light and Power Co Ltd (Belgium v Spain)* [1970] ICJ Rep 3, 46–7 (5 February). As recently as 2010, a leading commentator on international investment law stated: 'There are few customs in this sense in the field of foreign investment.' M Sornarajah, *The International Law on Foreign Investment* (3rd edn, Cambridge University Press, 2010) 82.

[149] Inspired by the success of the oil-producing countries in raising petroleum prices in 1973–4, developing countries had hoped that by building a numerically strong coalition among themselves, they would be able to bring about desired change in various international forums. As a result of the debt crisis in the early 1980s, the internal economic restructuring demanded by international financial institutions, such as the International Monetary Fund (IMF) and the World Bank, and the abandonment of command economy models by developing countries, the movement for a 'New

incorporated into Article 2 of the 1974 UN Charter of Economic Rights and Duties of States, which was adopted by the UN General Assembly.

Finally, existing international law offered foreign investors no effective enforcement mechanism to pursue claims against host countries that seized their investments or refused to respect their contractual obligations. As a result, investors had no assurance that investment contracts and arrangements made with host country governments would not be subject to unilateral change at some later time. Although an affiliate of the World Bank, the International Centre for Settlement of Investment Disputes (ICSID), was formally established in 1966 to resolve disputes between host countries and foreign private investors,[150] it required the specific consent of the parties to exercise jurisdiction over an investor–state dispute. As a result, the Centre did not hear its first case until 1972.[151] Injured foreign investors who were unable to negotiate a satisfactory settlement, secure an arbitration agreement with a host government, or find satisfaction in the local courts had few options other than to seek espousal of their claims by their home country governments. By its very nature, this process was more political than legal and, in any event, yielded results that were always uncertain and invariably slow.

In summary then, as global economic expansion began to accelerate in the years following World War II, the existing international law on foreign investment was for most investors incomplete, vague, contested, and without an effective enforcement mechanism. Because of these defects, investors and their home governments needed to find another means to protect their investments abroad from the injurious actions of host country governments. That means would lie in negotiating investment treaties.

International Economic Order' lost steam and was virtually dead by 1990. Wälde (n 119 above) 771. See generally J Hart, *The New International Economic Order* (Macmillan Press, 1983); JN Bhagwati (ed), *The New International Economic Order: The North-South Debate* (MIT Press, 1977).

[150] The ICSID Convention (n 9 above).
[151] ICSID, 'List of Concluded Cases', available at <https://icsid.worldbank.org/apps/ICSIDWEB/cases/Pages/AdvancedSearch.aspx?cs=CD28> accessed 12 January 2015 (listing concluded cases in chronological order).

4

A History of International Investment Treaties

4.1 Introduction: The Treatification
of International Investment Law

As a result of the perceived deficiencies of the customary international law applicable to foreign investments discussed in the preceding chapter, international investors in the mid-twentieth century had no assurance that investment arrangements and contracts made with host country governments would not be subject to unilateral change by those governments at some later time. In fact, they did experience expropriations and forced renegotiation of contracts on many occasions. As a result, foreign investments at that time, particularly in developing countries, seemed to be, in the oft-quoted words of Professor Raymond Vernon, 'obsolescing bargains' between the investor and the host country.[1] Years earlier, in his exploration of the role of contract in the social order, noted American legal scholar Karl Llewellyn captured more graphically this same tension between negotiated agreements and subsequent reality when he likened it to a Greek tragedy: 'Life struggling against form....'[2] In the post-colonial era of nationalizations and contract renegotiations, the economic facts of life in host countries struggled against the form of various legal commitments made to foreign investors. In that struggle, life usually seemed to triumph over form.

To change the dynamics of this struggle so as to protect the interests of their companies and investors, capital-exporting countries began a process of negotiating international investment treaties that, to the extent possible, would be: (1) complete; (2) clear and specific; (3) uncontestable; and (4) enforceable. These treaty efforts took place at both the bilateral and multilateral levels, which, though separate, tended to inform and reinforce each other. As a result of this process, a widespread *treatification*[3] of international investment law took

---

[1] R Vernon, *Sovereignty at Bay: The Multinational Spread of U.S. Enterprises* (Basic Books, 1971) 46.

[2] 'One turns from the contemplation of the work of contract as from the experience of Greek tragedy. Life struggling against form...' KN Llewellyn, 'What Price Contract? An Essay in Perspective' (1931) 40 Yale LJ 704, 751.

[3] The word 'treatification', while not recognized by any standard English dictionaries, has been used on rare occasions previously. The origin of this derivation of the word 'treatify' may perhaps be found in the 1908 Nobel lecture of the Peace Prize Laureate Frederik Bajer, who urged that a treaty be established to govern the canals between the North and Baltic seas, stating, '[T]here is a need to "treatify", if I may coin this expression, the waterways—the French call them "canaux

place in a relatively short time. By the beginning of the second decade of the twenty-first century, unlike the situation in the immediate post-World War II era, foreign investors in many parts of the world were protected primarily by international treaties rather than by customary international law alone. For all practical purposes, treaties have become the fundamental source of international law in the area of foreign investment.[4] This shift has been anything but theoretical. For one thing, it has imposed a discipline on host country treatment of foreign investors by obliging them to grant covered investors full protection and security, fair and equitable treatment, national treatment, most-favoured-nation treatment, full rights to make international monetary transfers, and protection against arbitrary treatment and expropriation without adequate compensation. In those cases where host governments have failed to abide by their foreign investment commitments aggrieved investors have invoked their treaty rights to sue those governments in arbitration, a phenomenon that has become increasingly common in the new century. As beneficiaries of resulting arbitral awards, many of which were substantial, investors had the power to seek enforcement in national courts throughout the world under treaties such as the ICSID Convention[5] and the New York Convention.[6] Today, as a result, it increasingly seems that in the international investment domain legal form is winning out in its struggle with life.

The aim of this chapter is to examine the history, purposes, and consequences of the investment treatification process. Subsequent chapters will analyse the structure and content of investment treaties and how their provisions have been applied to protect, advance, and accommodate the diverse interests of international investors, capital-exporting countries, and host states.

4.2 Historical Background of the Treatification Process

The modern investment treaty is the product of a historical process that has passed through several phases. Let us briefly examine each phase.

(a) The early beginnings

Since the very inception of international investment, foreign investors have sought assurances from the sovereigns in whose territory they invest that their interests would be protected from negative actions by the sovereign and

---

interocéaniques"—which connect the two seas.' Available at <<http://nobelprize.org/nobel_prizes/peace/laureates/1908/bajer-lecture.html> accessed 5 October 2014.

　[4] P Juillard, 'L'Evolution des sources du droit des investissements' (1994) 250 *Recueil des Cours* 74.
　[5] Convention on the Settlement of Investment Disputes between States and Nationals of Other States (18 March 1965) 575 UNTS 159; 17 UST 1270 (ICSID Convention).
　[6] Convention on the Recognition and Enforcement of Foreign Arbitral Awards (concluded 10 June 1958) 330 UNTS 3; 21 UST 2517.

local individuals. Investors have even requested that the sovereign grant them privileges and benefits that nationals themselves did not enjoy. Often these assurances and grants of privilege would be embodied in a document that the sovereign issued or agreed to. In the era before the formation of states that conducted foreign relations, traders and investors often formed themselves into associations and negotiated directly with foreign sovereigns to obtain such assurances and grants. For example, in AD 991 the Byzantine Emperors Basil II and Constantine VIII, in a document known in Latin as a *chrysobul*, granted to the merchants of Venice the rights to trade in the ports and other places of the Byzantine Empire without paying customs duties, as well as the right to a quarter in Constantinople, known as an *embolum*, for dwelling and trading.[7] Various other sovereigns also granted concessions and franchises to individuals or groups of traders and investors. Similar developments were taking place at the same time across western, northern, and eastern Europe. For example, King Henry II of England issued a grant, dated AD 1157, guaranteeing protection to German merchants from Cologne and to their establishment in London.[8]

Although these documents were called 'grants' or 'concessions' and not agreements and usually took the form of a unilateral act by the sovereign, they were also usually the product of some degree of negotiation between the sovereign or his representatives and the foreign traders who were their beneficiaries. Sovereigns were motivated to grant protection and privileges to foreign traders out of a desire to secure certain advantages for themselves, such as the promotion of foreign trade or the improvement of relations with groups in foreign territories. Thus, the basis of these early grants and concessions was reciprocity of benefits. This rationalization was articulated, for example, by King Erik of Norway in AD 1296 when he granted the Hamburg merchants extensive privileges for the purpose of *ad meliorandum terram nostram cum mercaturis* ('for the amelioration of our territories through trade').[9]

While the instruments issued by sovereigns during this period are most directly analogous to modern international concession contracts granted to foreign companies, one can also view these grants and concessions, in their enunciation of certain standards of investor treatment, as the distant ancestors of modern investment treaties.

---

[7] P Fischer, 'Some Recent Trends and Developments in the Law of Foreign Investment' in K-H Boeckstiegel et al (eds), *Völkerrecht, Recht der internationalen Organisationen, Weltwirtschafatsrecht: Festschrift für Ignaz Seidl-Hohenveldern* (Carl Heymanns Verlag, 1988) 97. See also 'Concessions granted to the Merchants of Venice, by the Byzantine Emperors Basilius and Constantinus, Executed in March 991' in P Fisher, *A Collection of International Concessions and Related Instruments* (Oceana Publications, 1976) vol 1, pp 15–18.

[8] Fischer (1988) (n 7 above) 97. Hansa societies worked to acquire special trade privileges for their members. For example, in 1157 the merchants of the Cologne (Köln) Hansa persuaded Henry II of England to grant them special trading privileges and market rights, which freed them from all London tolls and allowed them to trade at fairs throughout England.

[9] Fischer (1976) (n 7 above) vol 1, p xix.

(b) The emergence of a treaty framework for investment protection in the seventeenth and eighteenth centuries

As Europe emerged from the Middle Ages and began to form nation-states, the sovereigns of those states acted in various ways to protect and advance the interests of their nationals in other countries.[10] Towards this end, they would often negotiate with foreign countries to obtain commercial and trading rights for their nationals. The product of such negotiations was usually a written agreement between the two sovereigns. This historical period witnessed an increase in the reliance on treaties between two sovereigns as an important means of regulating trans-border economic activity. The result was a welter of bilateral agreements among the states and principalities of Europe, which, over time, began to demarcate principles of protection for aliens and their property that would later be echoed in modern-day investment treaties. Specifically, in varying degrees one can find the following principles of treatment in these early international agreements: (1) protection and security of aliens and their property;[11] (2) special means of protection for asset recovery and monetary transfers; (3) most-favoured-nation treatment[12] (which requires equality of treatment with other foreigners); (4) national treatment (which prohibits unfavourable discrimination in favour of nationals); and (5) guarantees of access to justice and safeguards against its denial.[13] Thus, during this period one can say that the sovereigns of Europe laid a foundation for what would later become the framework for the international investment treaty. And, like modern investment treaties between states, the subjects of the sovereigns concerned were not themselves parties to these agreements—they were mere beneficiaries.[14]

During this period, treaties were not only used to establish mutual economic relationships among nations but were also employed as instruments of economic domination. One of the most important treaties in this respect was between the King of France and the Ottoman Sultan in 1536, providing for reciprocal trading and navigation rights between the two monarchs' subjects.[15] Although

[10] R Lillich, *Human Rights of Aliens in Contemporary International Law* (Manchester University Press, 1984) 8–11.

[11] eg the Peace Treaty between Spain and the Netherlands of 1648 provided that the assets of the merchants were not to be seized, not even on account of war, except by judicial process to satisfy debts, other obligations, and contracts. Several treaties between European nations accepted the principles of freedom and security of aliens' person and property, with the exception of those made by Russia, which granted that treatment to merchants only. Because of such provisions, these treaties were called 'an international bill of rights'. H Neufeld, *The International Protection of Private Creditors from the Treaties of Westphalia to the Congress of Vienna (1648–1815)* (Sijthoff, 1971) 98.

[12] One of the earliest bilateral treaties to have employed the term 'the most-favoured-nation' appears to be have been the Trade Treaty of Nijmwegen (also spelt as Nijmegen or Nimwegen) of 1679 between Sweden and Holland. Since the Treaties of Utrecht of 1713, the term has had regular usage in the treaties of European nations. ibid 29, 110.

[13] ibid.   [14] Lillich (n 10 above) 2–3.

[15] See generally, H Maurits van den Boogert and K Fleet (eds), *The Ottoman Capitulations: Text and Context* (Istituto per 'Oriente CA Nallino, 2003). In 1536, Francis I of France and Süleyman I of Turkey signed a *capitulation treaty* that became the model for later treaties with other powers. It allowed the establishment of French merchants in Turkey, granted them individual and religious liberty, and provided that consuls appointed by the French king should judge the civil and criminal affairs of French subjects in Turkey according to French law, with the right of appeal to officers of

this agreement and others like it purported to be based on principles of equality and mutuality, they in fact favoured European nationals, not Ottoman subjects, because of the Europeans' superior economic and technological power. These treaties were the basis of what became known as the capitulary system. Individual treaty chapters (*capitula* in Latin) granted foreign traders a variety of privileges, including exemptions from customs duties, the right to be governed by their home country law, freedom from the jurisdiction of local courts, and the right to sue and be sued exclusively in special consular courts. In many places, these treaties became the basis of a fully-fledged extraterritorial system of privilege and immunity that applied not only to all European nationals but also to a select group of Ottoman subjects.[16]

These capitulations were an institutionalized symbol of the inferiority and subservience of local institutions and individuals to European power, and they facilitated the domination of much of the non-western world by western states. Treaties having a similar effect were negotiated in many areas, including the Middle East and Asia.[17] Thus, the international economic treaty became an important instrument for spreading European economic power and influence. For people in the non-western world, however, these treaties were an instrument of economic exploitation. In time, with the end of colonialism and the emergence of newly sovereign states in many parts of the non-western world, the capitulary system would end. However, the memory of these experiences would die much less quickly and would influence some groups in these countries to resist investment treaties in

---

the sultan for assistance in carrying out their decisions. During the eighteenth century nearly every European power obtained capitulations in Turkey, and in the nineteenth century such newly established countries as the US, Belgium, and Greece followed suit. *The New Encyclopaedia Britannica* (15th edn, 2002) vol 2, p 832.

[16] B Lewis, *The Emergence of Modern Turkey* (OUP, 1968) 455.

[17] The capitulation system spread widely in the 17th, 18th, and early 19th centuries, when traders from the West extended western influence by a process of infiltration rather than by annexation. 'Unequal treaties' soon developed, and such treaties as the Sino-British supplementary treaty (1843) and its later amendments established a system of provincial courts and a British supreme court in China to try all cases involving British subjects while granting no corresponding rights to Chinese residents in Britain. The evils to which the system gave rise were exemplified particularly in Turkey and China. The fact that a foreign consul had jurisdiction in all matters concerning foreign nationals led to encroachments on Turkish sovereignty, and it was even possible for foreign governments to levy duties on goods sold in Turkish ports, eg the 2% duty established on Venetian goods by the treaty of Adrianople in 1454. Foreign powers were also able to set up banks, post offices, and commercial houses on Turkish soil that were exempt from Turkish taxes and were able to compete with local firms. In both Turkey and China, the existence of capitulations led to the development of a class of persons immune from local jurisdiction— protégés of a foreign power, who, because they were employed by foreigners, claimed partial immunity from their own laws and were particularly useful as pawns in diplomatic intrigue. In China, especially, it was possible for fugitives from Chinese justice to seek sanctuary with foreigners. Inevitably, foreigners misused their privileges; their own law was sometimes badly administered, their courts tended to favour their own nationals at the expense of the natives of the countries in which they were living (particularly in China, where there were no mixed courts), and the way was opened for bribery and corruption. In the Chinese treaty ports, a multiplicity of territorial settlements and concessions, practically exempt from local jurisdiction, led inevitably to administrative confusion; each foreign legation had its own, sometimes conflicting, rights. *The New Encyclopaedia Britannica* (15th edn, 2002) vol 2, pp 832–3.

the modern era.[18] Nonetheless, the historical foundations of the investment treaties that proliferated in the twentieth and twenty-first centuries and became an important basis for much contemporary international investment law may be traced to these early trading agreements.

(c) Further developments in the eighteenth, nineteenth, and early twentieth centuries

Most foreign investment in the eighteenth, nineteenth, and early twentieth centuries was made in the context of colonial expansion. Because imperial powers imposed their political and military power on colonized territories and controlled the actions of colonial and protectorate governments and their legal systems, the European countries felt no need for commercial and investment treaties.[19] A blend of diplomacy and force[20] was relied on to prevent adverse interference with the investments and commercial activities of European nationals in their countries' colonies and protectorates.

Beginning in the eighteenth century, western countries began to conclude commercial treaties among themselves on a basis of greater equality than those negotiated with non-western nations.[21] The purpose of these agreements was to facilitate trade, rather than investment. For example, from its foundation at the end of the eighteenth century, the United States made large numbers of agreements known as treaties of friendship, commerce, and navigation (often called FCN treaties),[22] and their geographical spread reflected the expansion of US foreign trade.[23] Although these treaties were intended to facilitate trade and shipping, some contained provisions affecting the ability of one country's nationals to own property or do business in the territory of the other country. European countries made similar treaties, although they did not use the same designation.[24]

---

[18] JW Salacuse, 'Foreign Investment and Legislative Exemptions in Egypt: Needed Stimulus or New Capitulations?' in LD Michalak and JW Salacuse (eds), *Social Legislation in the Contemporary Middle East* (Berkeley, 1986) 241–61.

[19] On the general history of international law on foreign investments, see M Sornarajah, *The International Law on Foreign Investment* (3rd edn, Cambridge University Press, 2010) 18–30.

[20] See generally G Schwarzenberger, *Foreign Investments and International Law* (Praeger, 1969) 22–4; A Bagge, 'Intervention on the Ground of Damage Caused to Nationals, with Particular Reference to Exhaustion of Local Remedies and the Rights of Shareholders' in *Selected Readings on Protection by Law of Private Foreign Investments by International and Comparative Law Center* (1964).

[21] Lillich (n 10 above) 18–21.

[22] R Wilson, *United States Commercial Treaties and International Law* (Hauser Press, 1960); K Vandevelde, *United States Investment Treaties: Policy and Practice* (Kluwer Law and Taxation, 1992); R Wilson, 'Property-Protection Provisions in United States Commercial Treaties' (1951) 45 AJIL 83; H Walker, 'Modern Treaties of Friendship, Commerce and Navigation' (1957–8) 42 Minn L Rev 805.

[23] Thus, the US first made bilateral commercial treaties with western Europe, then with Latin America, later with Asia, and still later with Africa. K Vandervelde, 'The Bilateral Investment Treaty Program of the United States' (1988) 2 Corn Int'l LJ 201, 203–6.

[24] Before the adoption of the bilateral investment treaty programmes, European nations relied predominantly on agreements regarding establishment, trade/commerce, and double-taxation avoidance. For references to such agreements, see KW Hancock, *Survey of British Commonwealth Affairs,*

Many of the concepts and terms used in these agreements would find their way into the investment treaties concluded in the twentieth and twenty-first centuries.

Emerging countries at that time, such as the United States, felt the need to develop a new international legal instrument that would serve two important purposes: (1) establish a comprehensive legal framework for developing good relations with stronger powers to assure national security and further commerce; and (2) create new commercial relations with other emerging nations. The solution to this problem was to create a broad treaty covering friendly relations, establishment, commerce, and navigation. This was the origin of the 'friendship, commerce, and navigation treaty' of which the United States became a leading exponent.[25] The FCN treaties evolved to play an important role in the articulation and implementation of US policy concerning standards of treatment and the protection of foreign investment.[26] Their provisions evolved over time to respond to the needs and business practices of US commercial interests, and the political and legal environment affecting investment activities.[27]

The first Treaty of Amity and Commerce, concluded by the United States with France in 1778, established bilateral trade on a most-favoured-nation basis and provided for the protection of vessels, crews, passengers, and cargoes;[28] however, it did not include any general property protection provisions.[29] The early FCN treaties were principally trade-oriented agreements. Investment protection did not play an important role in their provisions, though the treaties did include the obligation to protect the property of nationals of the other party in its territory. The standard was an 'absolute' one because it did not depend upon the level of protection afforded to the property of nationals of other countries, typically guaranteeing 'special protection' or 'full and perfect protection' to the covered property.[30]

In addition to broad terms of property protection clauses, these early treaties developed specific provisions covering commercial property and persons engaged in commerce. For example, an 1815 treaty between the United States and Great Britain restricted protection to 'merchants and traders' and promised 'the most complete protection and security for their commerce'. The 1903 US–Ethiopia FCN treaty assures 'security of those engaged in business and of their property' in order to facilitate bilateral commercial relations.[31] Implicit in all of the provisions

---

vol 2: Problems of Economic Policy (OUP, 1940) 278; J Alenfeld, *Die Investionsförderungsverträge der Bundesrepublik Deutschland* (Atheneum-Verlag, 1971) 2–21; M Banz, *Völkerrechtlicher Eigentumsschutz durch Investitionsschutzabkommen* (Duncker & Humblot, 1987) 3–17; M Kamyar, 'Ownership of Oil and Gas Resources in the Caspian Sea' (2000) 94 AJIL 1, 179–89.

[25] K Vandevelde observes that the earliest FCNs were first concluded with important European powers that became major US trading partners, and then were employed as the principal legal basis for establishing commercial relations with newly emerged Latin American republics, and later with other nations in Asia and Africa. Vandevelde (n 22 above) 5.

[26] In 1776 the US Congress approved the Plan for Treaties that provided guidance to American negotiators for concluding the country's first treaties of amity and commerce. See generally Wilson (1960) (n 22 above) 1–26.

[27] See generally Vandevelde (n 22 above).   [28] ibid 14.

[29] A Benton, 'The Protection of Property Rights in Commercial Treaties of the US' (1965) 25 *Zeitschrift für ausländisches öffentliches Recht und Völkerrecht* 50, 52.

[30] Vandevelde (n 22 above) 15.   [31] Benton (n 29 above) 55.

is the idea that the persons and property of foreigners are entitled to a minimum of respect and protection. Similarly, and regardless of the fact that domestic law might offer a lower level of protection, host governments might not take such property by arbitrary executive decree and were subject to FCN provisions that must be applied according to a broad rule of reason.[32] Thus, a fundamental objective of the treaty-making process was to secure minimum international standards of treatment for investors and investments abroad.

The early FCN treaties also granted foreign nationals the right of equal access to domestic courts and later began to include most-favoured-nation[33] and national treatment provisions covering other activities potentially related to investment. FCN treaties of this era also began to include provisions dealing explicitly with the problem of expropriation. Typical provisions prohibited the seizures of 'vessels, cargoes, merchandise and effects' of the other party's nationals without payment of 'equitable and sufficient compensation' or 'sufficient indemnification'. Later, this protection was extended to cover 'property' generally. These FCN treaties also prohibited the confiscation of debts or other property during hostilities.[34] Towards the end of the nineteenth century, FCN treaties extended the scope of protection in an important new domain when they began to address restrictions on earnings repatriation. After World War I, these principles became the foundation for more explicit and effective investment provisions.

(d) From World War I until World War II

After World War I, US FCN treaties increasingly dealt with investment abroad by focusing on the treatment of US nationals and companies regarding the establishment of businesses, the protection of American property from arbitrary and discriminatory governmental actions, expropriation, the processes for settling disputes, and the protection of intellectual property. Nonetheless, during this time US direct foreign investment was not significant and European investment, with certain exceptions, still favoured their colonial and dependent territories. In such areas, European governments judged that special agreements to protect their nationals' investments were not needed.

Immediately after World War I, under the leadership of the Secretary of State Charles Evans Hughes, the United States broadened and revitalized its commercial treaty programme and focused particularly on the expansion of US foreign trade. One of the results of the effort was the development of a new FCN treaty model containing a uniform clause for investment protection the provisions of which, though clothed in new language, were analogous to those initiated in the

---

[32] For a detailed discussion of property protection provisions, see Wilson (1960) (n 22 above) 105–12.

[33] One of the earliest MFN provisions appeared in a US–France FCN; it dealt with the 'enjoyment of all rights, liberties, privileges, immunities, and exemptions in trade, navigation, and commerce'. Benton (n 29 above) 55.

[34] Vandevelde (n 22 above) 16.

nineteenth century. The new FCN treaties distinguished between absolute and relative standards of treatment. The absolute treatment standard required each party to provide 'the most constant protection and security' as well as 'protection required by international law'. The relative standard guaranteed national and most-favoured-nation treatment with respect to the right to 'engage in scientific, religious, philanthropic, manufacturing and commercial work' by a national of one party in the territory of the other party, thus broadening the list of protected activities to include non-commercial enterprises. To address the problem of expropriation, the new FCN model introduced a refinement assuring that the property of the other party's national 'shall not be taken without due process of law and without payment of just compensation'.[35] Although these inter-war FCN agreements in many respects provided for a heightened standard of protection compared to the pre-World War I treaties, they nevertheless failed to provide protection to property owned by corporations, a matter to be addressed only in the post-World War II period.

(e) The immediate aftermath of World War II

In the immediate aftermath of World War II, the nations of the world laid the foundations for a set of new institutions that they hoped would lead to global economic expansion and prosperity. One of the envisioned goals was the facilitation of the international flow of capital and investment. The new institutions, all of which were based on international treaties, included the International Bank for Reconstruction and Development (IBRD), one of the stated purposes of which was 'to promote private foreign investment',[36] the International Monetary Fund (IMF),[37] and the General Agreement on Tariffs and Trade (GATT),[38] which set the foundation for a multilateral trading system that nearly fifty years later would evolve into the World Trade Organization (WTO).[39]

Just as the nations of the world in the immediate post-war era attempted to create a multilateral framework for trade and currency, so too did they attempt to establish a similar framework for investment. This effort took the form of the Havana Charter of 1948,[40] which would have allowed the International Trade

---

[35] Vandevelde (n 22 above) 17; Benton (n 29 above) 57–9.

[36] Articles of Agreement of the International Bank for Reconstruction and Development (formulated at the Bretton Woods Conference 1–22 July 1944) (opened for signature at Washington 27 December 1945, entered into force 27 December 1945) 2 UNTS 134; 60 Stat 1440; TIAS 1502; 3 Bevans 1390.

[37] Articles of Agreement of the International Monetary Fund (formulated at the Bretton Woods Conference 1–22 July 1944) (opened for signature at Washington 27 December 1945, entered into force 27 December, 1945) (1944) 2 UNTS 39; 60 Stat 1401; TIAS 1501; 3 Bevans 1351.

[38] General Agreement on Tariffs and Trade (30 October 1947) 55 UNTS 194; 61 Stat A-11; TIAS 1700 (GATT).

[39] General Agreement on Tariffs and Trade 1994 (15 April 1994), Marrakesh Agreement Establishing the World Trade Organization, Annex 1A, The Legal Texts: The Results of the Uruguay Round of Multilateral Trade Negotiations 17 (1999) 1867 UNTS 187; (1994) 33 ILM 1153.

[40] Havana Charter for an International Trade Organization (24 March 1948) UN Doc E/Conf 2/78.

Organization (ITO) to promulgate rules on international investment as well as trade.[41] Notwithstanding its focus on international trade, however, an important objective of the Charter was to encourage economic development, especially in developing countries, and to foster 'the international flow of capital for productive investment'. Consequently, the Havana Charter contained a number of provisions concerning foreign investment and the relationship between host states and foreign investors.[42] For example, Article 11(2)(a) of the Charter would have authorized the ITO, *inter alia*, to make recommendations for and promote bilateral or multilateral agreements on measures designed *to assure just and equitable treatment* for the skills, capital, enterprise, arts, and technology brought from one member country to another. This was done in order to avoid international double taxation and stimulate foreign private investments. Article 11(2)(c) of the Charter also envisioned that the ITO would formulate and promote the adoption of a general agreement or statement of principles regarding the conduct, practices, and treatment of foreign investment. In Article 12(2) of the Charter, participating states were *to provide reasonable opportunities* for investments acceptable to them and *adequate security* for existing and future investments and to give *due regard to the desirability of avoiding discrimination* as between foreign investments.[43]

Capital-exporting countries and investors considered that the Havana Charter's investment-related provisions did not create an effective investment protection regime. For instance, the reference in Article 11(2) to 'just and equitable' treatment did not place a legal obligation on host countries but merely authorized the ITO to recommend that this standard be included in future agreements. This provision was viewed as simply an exhortation with respect to future governmental actions.[44] The vague language of Article 12(2) provided only a qualified protection against discriminatory treatment and expropriation; therefore capital-exporting states judged it insufficient to meet the challenges that began to arise during the decolonization period. Because of these concerns, coupled with other broader trade issues, the capital-exporting nations opted not to ratify the Havana Charter.[45]

Due partly to opposition from the western business community, the Havana Charter failed to be ratified by a sufficient number of participating states and, as a result, never became a reality.

---

[41] W Diebold, Jr, 'The End of ITO' (1952) 9(16) Princeton Essays in International Finance, cited in TS Shenkin, 'Trade-Related Investment Measures in Bilateral Investment Treaties and the GATT: Moving toward a Multilateral Investment Treaty' (1994) 55 U Pitts L Rev 541, 555.

[42] United Nations Conference on Trade and Development: Fair and Equitable Treatment (1999) UNCTAD/ITE/IIT/11 (vol 3) 24 (UNCTAD).

[43] Havana Charter for an International Trade Organization (24 March 1948), UN Doc E/Conf 2/78), available at <<http://www.wto.org/english/docs_e/legal_e/havana_e.pdf> accessed 5 October 2014.

[44] See generally United Nations Conference on Trade and Development: Fair and Equitable Treatment (1999) UNCTAD/ITE/IIT/11 (vol 3) 24–5.

[45] See generally 'United Nations Conference on Trade and Development' in *International Investment Instruments: A Compendium* (1996) vol 1, p 3.

Despite this early failure to create a global treaty on investment, in the following years capital-exporting nations continued to make international rules through treaties that facilitated and protected the investments of their nationals and companies abroad in other forums. These efforts took place at both the bilateral and multilateral levels, which, though separate, tended to inform and reinforce one another through the next sixty years.

(f) The later post-World War II years

(i) Bilateral efforts

The post-World War II years witnessed a great expansion in foreign investment, led initially by the United States, then joined by Europe, later by Japan, and still later by other parts of the world. Responding to this growth in US foreign investment after World War II, the US government undertook a programme to conclude a network of bilateral treaties of friendship, commerce, and navigation which, in addition to other commercial matters, specifically sought to facilitate and protect US direct foreign investments abroad.[46] Indeed, because of the diminished importance of bilateral commercial treaties as a means to promote trade in the post-war era of multilateral trade rules, the United States increasingly viewed FCN treaties as the preferred method for investment protection.[47] Starting with the existing FCN framework, the United States added various new provisions that were basically of two types: (1) those dealing with the protection of the investment property itself; and (2) those dealing with subjects other than property, but which nevertheless were vital in determining the legal and economic status of foreign-owned property. The provisions under the first category dealt with (a) taking of property; (b) protection and security of property; (c) equitable treatment; (d) unreasonable and discriminatory measures; and (e) public ownership.[48] The provisions under the second category concerned most-favoured-nation and national treatment and expanded those standards to cover new investment activities and intellectual property. This second category also included dispute settlement clauses.[49]

The post-World War II US FCN treaties contained a number of innovations that would later shape the investment treaty practice of other nations. One important innovation of the revised FCN treaties was the application of traditional FCN treaty benefits to corporate activities, including those of local subsidiaries.[50] Even more important, for the first time in US treaty practice, FCN treaties

---

[46] For a concise overview of the history of US bilateral investment treaties, see the US Supreme Court decision in *Sumitomo Shoji America v Avagliano*, 457 US 176 (1982). See also JW Salacuse, 'BIT by BIT: The Growth of Bilateral Investment Treaties and Their Impact on Foreign Investment in Developing Countries' (1990) 24 Int'l Lawyer 655, 656–61.

[47] Vandevelde (n 22 above) 17; Benton (n 29 above) 60.

[48] Benton (n 29 above) 60–7.   [49] ibid 67–72.

[50] KS Gudgeon, 'United States Bilateral Investment Treaties: Comments on their Origin, Purposes, and General Treatment Standards' (1986) 4 Int'l Tax & Bus Lawyer 105, 108.

contained a clause providing a legal remedy for the resolution of conflicts between the contracting parties concerning the interpretation and application of treaty provisions[51] by agreeing to submit to the jurisdiction of the International Court of Justice (ICJ) for the settlement of all such disputes.[52] Moreover the FCN treaties also encouraged the settlement of private controversies through commercial arbitration by including a clause providing for judicial enforcement of arbitration awards.[53] A dispute between the United States and Italy over Italy's treatment of an American subsidiary in Sicily under the 1948 United States–Italy FCN Treaty would in fact result in a decision by the ICJ in 1989.[54] In addition, the FCN treaties of this period specifically incorporated the 'Hull formula' by requiring 'prompt, adequate, and effective compensation' for the expropriation of the property of nationals and companies of the other party. This provision was intended to expand the previous requirement of 'just compensation' significantly and thereby reinforce protection guarantees.[55] In an effort to protect investors from host country exchange controls, the FCN treaties also constrained the rights of state parties to impose restrictions on currency transfers.[56] Another distinctive feature of the FCNs of this era was their basic purpose of establishing binding principles for the treatment of foreign nationals and their property. Unlike earlier FCN agreements, they did not contain schedules of customs duties,[57] a basic feature of those early treaties the principal focus of which was international trade.

Although the United States signed approximately twenty-three such treaties between 1946 and 1966,[58] the effort soon lost momentum as developing countries, increasingly sceptical of the benefits of foreign investment, demonstrated a growing reluctance to make the types of guarantees requested by the US government to protect investments abroad made by their nationals and companies.

(ii) Multilateral efforts

At the same time, despite the defeat of the Havana Charter, official and non-governmental efforts were made to prepare multilateral conventions governing foreign investment exclusively. These endeavours included the International Chamber of Commerce's International Code of Fair Treatment of Foreign

---

[51] Vandevelde (n 22 above) 19. Another decided innovation occurred in the Article concerning the settlement of any dispute between the parties as to interpretation or application of an FCN. The disputes that the parties do not satisfactorily settle by diplomacy 'shall be submitted to the International Court of Justice unless the parties shall agree to settlement by some other pacific means'. R Wilson, 'Postwar Commercial Treaties of the US' (1949) 43 AJIL 262, 275.

[52] Benton (n 29 above) 72.   [53] ibid.

[54] *Elettronica Sicula SpA (ELSI) (US v Italy)* (Judgment) (20 July 1989) [1989] ICJ Rep 15. A subsequent ICJ case based on an FCN treaty was *Case Concerning Oil Platforms (Islamic Republic of Iran v United States of America)* (Judgment) (6 November 2003) [2003] ICJ Rep 161, in which Iran sought compensation under the 1955 Treaty of Amity, Economic Relations, and Consular Rights between Iran and the US for the destruction in 1987 and 1988 by US warships of three offshore oil platforms owned by the National Iran Oil Company.

[55] Vandevelde (n 22 above) 19.   [56] ibid.   [57] Wilson (n 51 above) 277.

[58] Shenkin (n 41 above) 555. See also K Kunzer, 'Developing a Model Bilateral Investment Treaty' (1983) 15 L & Pol Int'l Bus 273, 276.

Investment (1949),[59] the Draft International Convention for the Mutual Protection of Private Property Rights in Foreign Countries (1957),[60] a private effort known as the Abs-Shawcross Convention, and the OECD Draft Convention on the Protection of Foreign Property (1967), among others.[61] Although none of these proposals was ever adopted, they did inform and influence the development of the bilateral investment treaty movement that was to come.[62]

One multilateral effort in the mid-twentieth century that did have great significant, lasting impact was the creation by six European states (Belgium, France, Germany, Italy, Luxembourg, and the Netherlands) of the European Economic Community in 1957 by agreeing to the Treaty of Rome.[63] Over the next half century, through a series of subsequent treaties and treaty amendments, their creation would evolve into the European Union (EU), which by 2014 consisted of twenty-eight states. As a result of the Treaty of Lisbon,[64] signed in 2007 and which became effective in 2009, the European Union is founded upon two treaties, the Treaty on European Union (TEU) and the Treaty on the Functioning of the European Union (TFEU),[65] both of which bind all member states. This treaty structure, and in particular the TFEU, contains important provisions relating to intra-European investment and investment relations between the Union and its member states, on the one hand, and non-member states, on the other. Thus, in part, the TFEU may be seen as an investment treaty designed to promote and protect the flow of capital among EU members.

One of the basic purposes of the European Union is to create an internal market among its member states, an internal market which, according to the TFEU, 'shall comprise an area without internal frontiers in which the free movement of goods, persons, services and capital is ensured in accordance with the provisions of the Treaties'.[66] Various specific treaty provisions seek to achieve this result with

[59] For text, see United Nations Conference on Trade and Development, *International Investment Instruments: A Compendium* (1996) vol 3, pp 273–8.

[60] 'Proposed Convention to Protect Private Foreign Investment: The Introduction' (1960) 9 J Pub L 115.

[61] For the text of the OECD Draft Convention on the Protection of Foreign Property, see (1968) 7 ILM 117. For a survey of the various multilateral efforts to prepare treaties on foreign investment, see F Tschofen, 'Multilateral Approaches to the Treatment of Foreign Investment' (1992) 7 ICSID Rev—FILJ 384, 385–6.

[62] TW Wälde, 'Introductory Note, European Energy Conference: Final Act, Energy Charter Treaty, Decisions, and Energy Charter Protocol on Energy Efficiency and Related Environmental Aspects' (1995) 34 ILM 360, 360 (noting the strong influence of BITs on the trade provisions of a multilateral energy treaty); P Juillard, 'Le Réseau français des conventions bilatérales d'investissement: A la recherche d'un droit perdu?' (1987) 13 *Droit et Pratique du Commerce Internationale* 9, 16 (noting that France based its model BIT on the 1967 Organization for Economic Cooperation and Development (OECD) Draft Convention on the Protection of Foreign Property).

[63] Treaty Establishing the European Economic Community, 25 March 1957, 298 UNTS 11.

[64] Treaty of Lisbon Amending the Treaty on European Union and the Treaty Establishing the European Community, 13 December 2007, [2007] OJ C306/1.

[65] Consolidated Versions of the Treaty on European Union and the Treaty on the Functioning of the European Union [2010] OJ C83/1. Treaty of European Union, Art 1 states: 'The Union shall be founded on the present Treaty and on the Treaty on the Functioning of the European Union (hereinafter referred to as 'the Treaties'). Those two Treaties shall have the same legal value. The Union shall replace and succeed the European Community.'

[66] TFEU, Art 26(2).

respect to the movement of capital. For example, Articles 49, 54, and 55 of the TFEU grant all member-state firms and nationals the right of establishment in all EU member countries and guarantee that such firms will receive national treatment. Moreover, under Articles 63 to 66 of the TFEU, investors from EU member states have the right to transfer capital and earnings freely, and are guaranteed national treatment on expropriation. Indeed, Article 63 of the EU Treaty specifically prohibits restrictions on the movement of capital and payments between member states and between member states and third countries. Any alleged violation of treaty rights can be adjudicated by the Court of Justice of the European Union (ECJ), which has jurisdiction to hear cases related to violations of treaty rights directly and to overturn national legislation, regulations, and court decisions inconsistent with EU treaties. In addition to enforcing treaty provisions within the EU, the ECJ's jurisprudence has influenced tribunals in investor–state arbitrations in the interpretation of other investment treaties. The EU Treaties authorize the European Commission, the European Union's executive arm, to reduce barriers to investment both among EU members and from third countries, a task that the Commission has pursued quite energetically, both through regulatory actions and the initiation of cases before the ECJ. Finally, as a result of the Treaty of Lisbon, EU institutions also gained authority over the foreign investment relations of its members with third states and to negotiate investment treaties with non-member states on behalf of the Union.[67]

(g) The development of the bilateral investment treaty and the creation of the International Centre for Settlement of Investment Disputes

A new and important phase in the historical development of investment treaties began on the eve of the 1960s. At this point, individual European countries began to negotiate bilateral treaties that were unlike previous bilateral commercial agreements but that were similar in many ways to the multilateral efforts mentioned previously. These new treaties dealt exclusively with foreign investment and sought to create an international legal framework to govern investments by the nationals of one country in the territory of another. The modern bilateral investment treaty (BIT) was thus born.

Germany, which had lost all of its foreign investments as a result of its defeat in World War II, took the lead in this new phase of investment treaty-making. Beginning with the first such agreement with Pakistan in 1959, Germany proceeded to negotiate similar investment treaties with countries throughout the developing world. Eventually, Germany would become one of the nations with the greatest number of BITs, having concluded 134 such treaties, in addition to sixty-two other international investment agreements, by the end of 2013.[68] At

---

[67] See generally A Reinisch, 'The EU on the Investment Path—*Quo Vadis* Europe? The Future of EU BITs and other Investment Agreements' (2013) 12 Santa Clara J Int'l L 111.
[68] UNCTAD, *World Investment Report 2014* (2014) 223.

the same time, various European countries that were in the process of liquidating their colonial empires felt a need to safeguard the existing investments of their nationals in the newly independent territories and also to facilitate future investments. Therefore, the former colonial powers also began to develop bilateral treaty programmes,[69] concluding BITs not only with their former colonies but also with other developing countries. Moreover, not only did former colonial powers like the United Kingdom, Belgium, France, and the Netherlands actively negotiate BITs, but European countries that had no colonies, such as Switzerland, Austria, and Italy, joined the BIT movement in relatively short order.[70] By 1980, European countries had concluded approximately 150 BITs with a broad array of developing countries.[71]

As will be seen in subsequent chapters, the European BITs incorporated many of the principles that had been elaborated in earlier bilateral commercial agreements, as well as in the various unsuccessful multilateral efforts. To implement their bilateral treaty programmes, each capital-exporting state would develop a model or prototype treaty that it would use in negotiations with other countries. The models developed by the European states bore significant similarities.[72] Generally, the BITs guaranteed investors of one treaty partner in the territory of another treaty partner various standards of protection, including protection from expropriation without just compensation, and the right to make monetary transfers.

One of the BIT movement's most important innovations was the treaty provision allowing aggrieved investors to bring claims directly against host governments in international arbitration for BIT violations. This process, known as investor–state arbitration, became a powerful enforcement tool to assure host country respect for treaty standards. Prior to this time, unless an investor had concluded a separate agreement with a host government calling for arbitration, an aggrieved investor could only rely on its home country to press claims against the

---

[69] FA Mann, 'British Treaties for the Promotion and Protection of Investments' (1981) 52 BYIL 241; P Juillard, 'Les Conventions bilatérales d'investissements conclues par la France' (1979) 106 *Journal du Droit International* 274; J Karl, 'The Promotion and Protection of German Foreign Investment Abroad' (1996) 11 ICSID Rev—FILJ 1; M Bos, 'The Protection of Foreign Investments in Dutch Court and Treaty Practice' (1980) 3 Int'l L in the Netherlands 221; W Van de Voorde, 'Belgian Bilateral Investment Treaties as a Means for Promoting and Protecting Foreign Investment' (1991) 44 Studia Diplomatica 87; Y Matsui, 'Japan's International Legal Policy for the Protection of Foreign Investment' (1989) 32 Japanese Annual of Int'l L 1.

[70] M-Ch Kraft, 'Les Accords bilatéraux sur la protection des investissements conclus par la Suisse' in D Dicke (ed), *Foreign Investment in the Present and a New International Economic Order* (Westview Press, 1987) 72–95; N Huu-tru, 'Le Réseau suisse d'accords bilatéraux d'encouragement et de protection des investissements' (1988) 92 *Revue Générale de Droit International Public* 577; OM Maschke, 'Investitionsschutzabkommen: Neue vertragliche Wege im Dienste der Österreichischen Wirt-schaft' (1986) 37 *Österreichische Zeitschrift für Öffentliches Recht und Völkerrecht* 201.

[71] International Chamber of Commerce, *Bilateral Investment Treaties for International Investment* (1980).

[72] The similarity is attributed to the fact that some European countries seemed to have emulated the German BIT model. 'Reforming the International Legal Order: German Legal Comments' in T Oppermann and E-U Petersman (eds), *Tübinger Schriften zum internationalen und europäischen Recht*, Band I (Duncker & Humblot, 1987) 37.

host government. As indicated in Chapter 3, a home government was not obliged to press such claims, and if it chose to do so, it became the owner of that claim. This gave the home government the full and exclusive power to decide how to press it, whether and how to settle it, and what should be done with any settlement payments.

An important institutional support for the enforcement of BIT provisions was the creation of the International Centre for Settlement of Investment Disputes (ICSID) in 1966. In the early 1960s, the World Bank directed its attention to the problem of resolving disputes between foreign investors and host governments because it believed that the lack of a fair and effective means of investment dispute settlement was impeding the flow of capital necessary for the economic development of less developed countries.[73] The concern of investors that host countries would not respect their commitments was an important element of political risk and created an unfavourable investment climate. The Bank came to believe the problem of unfavourable investment climates in many poor countries might be addressed *procedurally* by creating international machinery that would be voluntarily available for the conciliation and arbitration of investment disputes.[74] In other words, the establishment of an adequate method of investor–state dispute settlement was seen as a way to improve a country's investment climate and thus to encourage foreign private capital flows to developing countries.

The World Bank therefore proposed the adoption of an international convention that would create a new international institution: the International Centre for Settlement of Investment Disputes. ICSID was to provide conciliation and arbitration facilities for investment disputes between foreign investors and host country governments. The Convention on the Settlement of Disputes between States and Nationals of Other States[75] was concluded in 1965, initially adopted by thirty states,[76] and entered into force on 14 October 1966. It sought to foster a climate of mutual confidence between capital-importing and capital-exporting states by providing basic rules to protect the legitimate interests of governments and foreign investors alike in the resolution of investor–state disputes. Both capital-exporting and capital-importing states were to be members of the Centre and participate in its governance.[77] After the adoption of the Convention, countries began to consent to ICSID jurisdiction in the BITs

---

[73] Paper Prepared by the General Counsel of the World Bank and Transmitted to the Members of the Committee of the Whole, SID/63-2 (18 February 1963) 3 in ICSID, *History of the ICSID Convention* (1968) vol 2, part I, at 73.

[74] Note by the President of the Executive Directors, R 61-128 (28 December 1961) in ICSID, *History of the ICSID Convention* (1968) vol 2, part I, at 4–6.

[75] ICSID Convention (n 5 above).

[76] List of Contracting States and other Signatories of the Convention (as of 11 April 2014), available at <https://icsid.worldbank.org/apps/ICSIDWEB/icsiddocs/Documents/List%20of%20 Contracting%20States%20and%20Other%20Signatories%20of%20the%20Convention%20-%20 Apr%202014.pdf> accessed 24 March 2015.

[77] Report of the World Bank Executive Directors on the ICSID Convention, Doc ICSID/2 in ICSID, *History of the ICSID Convention* (1968) vol 2, part II, at 1072–4.

they negotiated. The first BIT to include an ICSID clause was the Netherlands–Indonesia treaty signed in 1968, nearly ten years after the conclusion of the first BIT.[78] Increasingly, it has become standard practice for BITs to make a reference to ICSID for the settlement of disputes arising under their provisions, as well as to other international arbitral processes. In addition, the membership of ICSID grew steadily over the years and by June 2014 included 150 states.[79] Owing to the great number of BITs and the incorporated references to ICSID arbitration within them, some commentators claim ICSID is the natural forum for the resolution of investor–state disputes.[80] At the same time, many, if not most BITs also offer ad hoc arbitration under United Nations Commission on International Trade Law.(UNCITRAL) Rules as an alternative method of resolving investor–state disputes.

Although ICSID was formally established in 1965,[81] it did not hear its first case until 1972.[82] Despite this somewhat delayed start, ICSID was destined to become an important institution for international investment dispute resolution.[83] By the end of 2013, for example, it had administered more than 430 investor–state cases, out of 568 total known cases,[84] involving more than ninety-five states.[85] Of that number, 285 ICSID cases had resulted in final decisions.[86] From the point of view of the investor, a mechanism in international law had at last been created to deal with investors' historic inability to pursue and enforce international legal provisions against host states. While in general terms the ICSID Convention can be considered an 'investment treaty', it is beyond the scope of this book, since it governs the procedure for dispute settlement, rather than the substantive standards for the treatment of investment and investors.[87]

---

[78] ICSID clauses were added to several other early treaties, by reference to the Convention in subsequent protocols. See eg Netherlands–Cote d'Ivoire BIT of 1965 and the Protocol thereto of 1971. R Dolzer and M Stevens, *Bilateral Investment Treaties* (Martinus Nijhoff, 1995) 130.

[79] See <https://icsid.worldbank.org/apps/ICSIDWEB/icsiddocs/Documents/List%20of%20 Contracting%20States%20and%20Other%20Signatories%20of%20the%20Convention%20-%20 Apr%202014.pdf> accessed 24 March 2015. As of April 2014, of 159 states that signed the Convention on the Settlement of Investment Disputes between States and Nationals of Other States, 150 states had deposited their instruments of ratification and attained the status of contracting state (see n 76 above). Three member states have denounced the Convention and withdrawn from ICSID: Bolivia in 2007, Ecuador in 2010, and Venezuela in 2012.

[80] BM Cremades, 'Arbitration in Investment Treaties: Public Offer of Arbitration in Investment-Protection Treaties' in R Briner and K-H Böckstiegel (eds), *Law of International Business and Dispute Settlement in the 21st Century: Liber amicorum Karl-Heinz Böckstiegel* (Carl Heymanns Verlag, 2002) 158.

[81] ICSID Convention (n 5 above).

[82] ICSID, List of Concluded Cases, available at <https://icsid.worldbank.org/apps/ICSIDWEB/ cases/Pages/AdvancedSearch.aspx?cs=CD28> accessed 12 January 2015 (listing concluded cases in chronological order).

[83] ibid.   [84] UNCTAD, *World Investment Report 2014* (2014) 124.

[85] ICSID, *ICSID 2013 Annual Report* (2013) 5.

[86] ICSID, List of Concluded Cases (n 82 above).

[87] For a thorough analysis of the ICSID Convention and ICSID arbitration rules, see C Schreuer, *The ICSID Convention: A Commentary* (2nd edn, Cambridge University Press, 2009).

(h) The gathering momentum of the BIT movement

The reason for the greater success of the European BIT programmes as compared with earlier US efforts is not completely clear, but the answer may lie in the fact that the European countries were less demanding with respect to guarantees on such matters as free conversion of local currency, abolition of performance requirements, and protection against expropriation. Moreover, specific foreign aid relationships between some European countries and the European Community, on the one hand, and individual developing countries, on the other, may have predisposed the developing countries to look more favourably on concluding BITs with European states.[88]

Nonetheless, spurred in part by the experience of the Europeans, the United States launched its own BIT programme in 1981.[89] By September 2014, the United States had signed forty-six BITs with developing countries and emerging markets.[90] As non-western countries began to export capital, they too negotiated BITs to create a legal framework for their nationals' investments in specific countries. Thus, by 1997, Japan had signed four BITs, and Kuwait had signed twenty-two.[91]

With the end of the Communist era and the abandonment of command economies in many parts of the world, the late 1980s witnessed a new phase in the history of the BIT movement. The emerging economies of Eastern and Central Europe, as well as some Latin American, African, and Asian countries that had previously been hostile to foreign investment, now actively sought foreign capital to finance their development. This dramatic transformation entailed sweeping changes in law and policy.[92] Reflecting this policy shift, countries with emerging markets entered into BITs with industrialized states in order to receive capital and technology to advance their development and did so at an accelerating pace. Whereas some 309 BITs had been concluded by the end of 1988,[93] more than

---

[88] A donor state's foreign aid to developing countries is a function of numerous factors, including strategic, commercial, political, and humanitarian considerations. P Hjertholm and H White, 'Foreign Aid in Historical Perspective: Background and Trends' in F Tarp (ed) *Foreign Aid and Development: Lessons Learnt and Directions for the Future* (Routledge, 2000) 99–100. As a result, it is difficult to know precisely the impact of a donor country's aid policies on its BIT negotiations with a specific aid recipient. From the point of view of a recipient country, one indicator of the quality of aid is the percentage that is 'untied', ie not required to be spent on acquiring goods and services from the donor country. It is interesting to note that European countries whose aid was the least 'tied' were among the countries that had concluded the largest number of BITs in 1981. In that year, when the percentage of untied aid given by the US was only 33%; Germany, with untied aid of 74%, had signed 49 BITs; Switzerland, with untied aid of 50%, had signed 33 BITs; the Netherlands, with untied aid of 57%, had signed 16 BITs; and Sweden, with untied aid of 84%, had signed 8 BITs. UNCTAD, *Bilateral Investment Treaties in the Mid-1990s* (1998) 159–217.

[89] Vandevelde (n 22 above) 29–45; PB Gann, 'The U.S. Bilateral Investment Treaty Program' (1985) 21 Stan J Int'l L 373; Gudgeon (n 50 above) 107–11; JW Salacuse (n 46 above) 655–75.

[90] For a listing of all US BITs currently in force, see the website of the US Department of State, at <http://www.state.gov/e/eb/ifd/bit/117402.htm> accessed 4 October 2014.

[91] UNCTAD, *Bilateral Investment Treaties in the Mid-1990s* (1998) 185–6.

[92] JW Salacuse, 'From Developing Countries to Emerging Markets: A Changing Role for Law in the Third World' (1999) 33 Int'l Lawyer 875, 875–7.

[93] AJ Pappas, 'References on Bilateral Investment Treaties' (1989) 4 ICSID Rev—FILJ 189, 194–203.

2,608 BITs were concluded by 2008.[94] This dramatic change in so short a time period represents a substantial feat of international law-making. In 2001 alone, a total of ninety-seven countries concluded some 158 BITs, a numerical record for any single year since the BIT movement began in 1959.[95] The cumulative result of this effort has been the creation of an increasingly dense BIT network of 2,902 BITs, in addition to some 334 other international investment agreements with similar provisions, for a total of 3,236 treaties linking over 180 different countries by the year 2014.[96]

Meanwhile, the number of BITs involving two developing countries, what one may call 'south-south' BITs, began to increase steadily. By the end of 2005, the number of 'south-south' BITs had grown to 644, representing 26 per cent of BITs overall. Non-western countries with large FDI outflows, such as China, Malaysia, and the Republic of Korea, have been among those with the highest number of BITs. As of 2014, the leading developing country among BIT signatories was China, with 130 BITs, followed by Egypt, with 100, many of which were signed with other developing economies.[97]

While BITs are usually made between capital-exporting states and developing countries, on occasion two developing countries or two industrialized countries have formed such agreements, often referred to as 'north-north' treaties. Examples of the former include BITs between Thailand and China and between Egypt and Morocco.[98] The most notable example of the latter is the 1988 agreement between the United States and Canada which created a free trade area.[99] This agreement included a special chapter that in effect functioned as a BIT and closely paralleled BITs that the United States had negotiated with other countries.[100] By 1994, the agreement evolved into the North American Free Trade Agreement (NAFTA) between Canada, Mexico, and the United States.[101] For all intents and purposes, NAFTA's section on investment, Chapter 11, constitutes a BIT among the three countries. BITs have become a global phenomenon, not limited to efforts by developed countries to obtain protection for their nationals in developing countries. As of 2014, UNCTAD estimated that among all BITs, 41 per cent were north-south, 27 per cent were south-south, 9 per cent were north-north, and 27 per cent were between 'countries in transition' (a group defined as Southeast Europe and the Commonwealth of Independent States) and other parts of the world.[102]

---

[94] UNCTAD, *World Investment Report 2008* (2008) 14.

[95] UNCTAD, *World Investment Report 2002: Transnational Corporations & Export Competitiveness* (2002) 8.

[96] UNCTAD, *World Investment Report 2014* (2014) 114.   [97] ibid 222–5.

[98] Agreement for the Promotion and Protection of Investments (PRC–Thailand) (12 March 1985), available at <<http://investmentpolicyhub.unctad.org/Download/TreatyFile/786> accessed 5 October 2014; Agreement regarding the Encouragement and Protection of Investment (Egypt–Morocco) (14 May 1997) available in Arabic at <http://investmentpolicyhub.unctad.org/Download/TreatyFile/1093> accessed 12 January 2015.

[99] Free Trade Agreement (US–Canada) (2 January 1988), (1988) 27 ILM 281.

[100] ibid 373–80.

[101] North American Free Trade Agreement (US–Canada–Mexico) (17 December 1992), (1993) 32 ILM 289 (NAFTA).

[102] UNCTAD, *World Investment Report 2014* (2014) 123.

(i) The development of multilateral regional and sectoral investment agreements

The 1980s and 1990s also witnessed a new phase in the evolution of investment treaties: the development of regional investment agreements the purpose of which was to promote and protect investments among countries within a geographical area. Up to that point, the most famous and most successful of such endeavours was the European Union, discussed earlier, which had been launched in the late 1950s and had become increasingly integrated and enlarged in the following years. With varying degrees of success, other regions, often under the auspices or with the support of regional international organizations such as the League of Arab States or the Association of Southeast Asian Nations, also sought to develop regional international investment treaties. The principal regional arrangements are examined briefly.

(i) Arab States Investment Agreement

One of the earliest of such regional multilateral investment treaties was the *Unified Agreement for the Investment of Arab Capital in the Arab States*,[103] which was signed on 26 November 1980 in Amman, Jordan, during the Eleventh Arab Summit Conference, and entered into force on 7 September 1981.[104] The Middle East is characterized by countries such as Kuwait, Saudi Arabia, and the United Arab Emirates, which have accumulated significant capital reserves as a result of their oil revenues, and others, like Egypt, the Sudan, and Syria, which have a significant need for investment funds.[105] One of the purposes of the Unified Agreement for the Investment of Arab Capital in the Arab States is to encourage nationals of the wealthy Arab states to invest in the region's poorer countries. Towards this end, the Agreement seeks to protect 'Arab investors' from injurious actions that might be taken by the governments of foreign states that have ratified it and in which they have invested. An 'Arab investor' is defined by Article 1(7) as 'an Arab citizen who owns Arab capital which he invests in the territory of a State Party of which he is not a national'. An 'Arab citizen' according to Article 1(4) is 'an individual or body corporate having the nationality of a State Party, providing that no part of the capital of such body corporate belongs either directly or indirectly to non-Arab citizens'.

Like other investment treaties, the Agreement sets down various standards of treatment that a host state owes to the investments of Arab investors. Thus under Article 6, the capital of Arab investors is to be given the same treatment as capital

---

[103] League of Arab States (1982). 'Unified Agreement for the Investment of Arab Capital in the Arab States', Economic Documents, No 3 (Tunis: League of Arab States).

[104] The agreement has been ratified by all member states of the League except Algeria and the Comoros. The text of the 'Unified Agreement for the Investment of Arab Capital in the Arab States' is available in (2004) 1(4) Transnat'l Disp Man.

[105] J Salacuse, 'Arab Capital and Trilateral Ventures in the Middle East: Is Three a Crowd?' in M Kerr and A Yassine (eds), *Rich and Poor States in the Middle East* (Westview Press, 1982) 129–63.

owned by citizens of the host state. In addition, it allows Arab investors to transfer their capital and earnings and also protects Arab investments from expropriation and confiscation by the host country government. Expropriation for a 'public benefit' is permitted, 'provided that this is done on a non-discriminatory basis in return for fair compensation and according to general legal provisions regulating the seizure of property for the purposes of the public benefit'.[106] On the other hand, the Agreement does not offer protective standards as high as those usually found in BITs. For example, it contains no specific guarantees of full protection and security or of fair and equitable treatment. Nor does it provide strong enforcement by guaranteeing the right to dispute settlement under ICSID's auspices. It does, however, provide for a rather elaborate investor–state dispute settlement. It states that until the Arab Court of Justice is established and its jurisdiction is determined, investment disputes under the Agreement will be settled by an Arab Investment Court; however, the Court's jurisdiction is subordinate to other forms of dispute settlement, specifically conciliation and international arbitration to which the investor and the state party may have agreed. Since the adoption of the Agreement, certain investor–state disputes have been decided under its provisions,[107] including one in 2013 which resulted in an arbitral award of US$935 million in favour of a Kuwaiti investor against the government of Libya, arising out of the cancellation of a hotel and resort development on the Mediterranean coast.[108]

(ii) Islamic States Investment Agreement

The Organization of Islamic Cooperation (OIC) (formerly known as the Organization of the Islamic Conference) was founded in 1969 for the purpose of strengthening solidarity and cooperation among Islamic States. As of 2014, it had a membership of fifty-seven states spread over four continents, making it the second largest intergovernmental organization after the United Nations. The present charter[109] of the OIC was adopted in 2008 and requires that a state have a Muslim majority to be eligible for membership.[110]

Article 1(9) of the Charter provides that one of the Organization's purposes is to 'strengthen intra-Islamic economic and trade cooperation; in order achieve economic integration leading to the establishment of an Islamic Common Market'. In pursuit of that goal, in 1981, a year after its Arab members had approved the Unified Investment Agreement of the Arab States, the OIC adopted the Agreement for the Promotion, Protection, and Guarantee of Investments Among

---

[106] Unified Agreement, Art 9(2).

[107] WB Hamida, 'The First Arab Investment Court Decision' (2006) 7 JWIT 699, 702.

[108] *Mohamed Abdulmohsen Al Kharafi & Sons Co v Libya* (Award) (22 March 2013), available at <http://italaw.com/cases/documents/2199> accessed 5 October 2014. See D Rosert, 'Libya Order to Pay US$935 to Kuwaiti Company for Canceled Investment Project' Investment Treaty News (IISD), 19 January 2014.

[109] Charter of the Organization of the Islamic Conference, adopted at Dakar, Senegal 14 March 2008, available at <http://www.oic-oci.org/is11/english/Charter-en.pdf> accessed 5 October 2014.

[110] Charter of the OIC, Art 3(2).

Member States of the Organization of the Islamic Conference.[111] The Agreement became effective in 1988 when it secured ratification by ten states. As of 2014, thirty-three states had signed the Agreement and twenty-five had ratified it.

In comparison to most BITs and multilateral investment treaties, the OIC's Agreement provides rather weak investment protection. Although the Agreement protects covered investment from expropriation and affords them most-favoured-nation treatment, it does not guarantee them fair and equitable treatment, full protection and security, or national treatment, provisions that are commonly found in most BITs. Moreover, its provisions on dispute settlement are vague and seem to leave open the question of whether injured investors have any right at all to invoke investor–state arbitration against an offending state. It was perhaps for these reasons that arbitration under its provisions did not arise until 2012, nearly a quarter of a century after the Agreement came into effect. In that year, an arbitral tribunal functioning under UNCITRAL Rules determined, in a case brought by a Saudi national against Indonesia relating to the governmental seizure of a bank in which the Saudi held shares, that states bound by the Agreement had made a standing offer to protected investors to arbitrate claims arising under the Agreement and that investor–state arbitration was therefore authorized.[112]

(iii) ASEAN Comprehensive Investment Agreement

The Association of Southeast Asian Nations (ASEAN) was established in 1967 by five Asian states—Indonesia, Malaysia, the Philippines, Singapore, and Thailand.[113] One of its basic purposes, according to its founding Declaration, was to 'accelerate the economic growth, social progress and cultural development in the region through joint endeavours in the spirit of equality and partnership in order to strengthen the foundation for a prosperous and peaceful community of South-East Asian Nations…'. In subsequent years, ASEAN would become increasingly institutionalized and its membership would expand to include Brunei Darussalam (1984), Viet Nam (1995), Lao PDR (1997), Myanmar (1997), and Cambodia (1999). In order to give the organization greater institutional and legal form and to advance regional integration, the ten nations of ASEAN adopted a formal constitution, the Charter of the Association of Southeast Asian Nations, which entered into effect in December 2008.[114] Among other things,

---

[111] Available at <http://www.oic-oci.org/english/convenion/Agreement%20for%20Invest%20in%20OIC%20%20En.pdf> accessed 5 October 2014.

[112] *Hesham Taalat M Al-Warraq v The Republic of Indonesia* (Award on Respondent's Preliminary Objections to Jurisdiction and Admissibility of Claims) (21 June 2012).

[113] The ASEAN Declaration (Bangkok Declaration), 8 August 1967, 1331 UNTS 243, available at <http://www.asean.org/news/item/the-asean-declaration-bangkok-declaration> accessed 5 October 2014.

[114] Available at <http://www.asean.org/archive/publications/ASEAN-Charter.pdf> accessed 5 October 2014.

the Charter formally recognized ASEAN as an intergovernmental organization with legal personality.[115]

From its foundation, ASEAN has sought to advance regional economic development and integration. Towards this end, it has endeavoured to facilitate the flow of capital and investment among its members. Its Charter makes this clear by stating that one of ASEAN's fundamental purposes is 'to create a single market and production base which is stable, prosperous, highly competitive and economically integrated with effective facilitation for trade and investment in which there is free flow of goods, services and investment'.[116] One of the mechanisms it has employed to achieve this goal is the investment treaty.

The creation of a strong regional investment treaty among the ASEAN states has been a progressive step-by-step process. The first step took place in 1987 when the governments of Brunei Darussalam, Indonesia, Malaysia, the Philippines, Singapore, and Thailand concluded the ASEAN Agreement for the Promotion and Protection of Investments (15 December 1987).[117] Similar to many BITs, this treaty provided a higher level of protection for other ASEAN investors than that found in either the Arab or Islamic states investment agreements mentioned earlier. For example, each country undertook an obligation to ensure full protection to investments made by investors of other member nations and not to impair by unjustified or discriminatory measures the management, maintenance, use, enjoyment, extension, disposition, or liquidation of such investments. All investments made by investors of a member were to be accorded fair and equitable treatment in the territory of other treaty members. The investor's treatment can be no less favourable than that granted to an investor from a most favoured nation.

Investments made by nationals or companies of a member country were not to be subject to expropriation or nationalization or any equivalent measure, except for public use or in the public interest, under due process of law, on a non-discriminatory basis and upon payment of adequate compensation. The compensation should amount to the market value of the investment that prevailed immediately before the measure of dispossession became public knowledge, and it should be freely transferable in usable currencies from the host country. The compensation is to be determined and paid without undue delay. The national or company affected has the right to a prompt review of the amount by a judicial body or some other independent authority.

The treaty provided for various dispute settlement options to be decided upon by mutual agreement of the parties, including: (a) (ICSID); (b) arbitration under UNCITRAL rules; (c) the Regional Arbitration Centre at Kuala Lumpur; or (d) any other regional centre for arbitration in ASEAN. The first arbitral decision under the treaty was rendered in 2003.[118]

---

[115] ASEAN Charter, Art 3. S Chesterton, 'Does ASEAN Exist? The Association of Southeast Asian Nations as an International Legal Person' (2008) 12 Sing YBIL 199.

[116] ASEAN Charter, Art 1(5).

[117] The ASEAN Agreement for the Promotion and Protection of Investments of 1987 (1988) 27 ILM 612, available at <http://www.asean.org/communities/asean-economic-community/item/the-1 987-asean-agreement-for-the-promotion-and-protection-of-investments> accessed 5 October 2014.

[118] *Chi Oo Trading Pte Ltd v Government of the Union of Myanmar*, ASEAN Case No ARB/01/1 (Award) (31 March 2003), (2003) 42 ILM 3, 540.

ASEAN took a second major step when, in 1998, the ASEAN members adopted the Framework Agreement on the ASEAN Investment Area[119] to reduce barriers to investment within the entire ASEAN region, while specifically affirming their 1987 Investment Agreement. The Framework Agreement appears to have had limited success in that regard.[120] Finally, in order to lay the legal foundation for the ASEAN Economic Community envisioned by the ASEAN Charter, and in particular to facilitate the free flow of capital required by such an Economic Community, in 2010 the ten ASEAN states signed the Comprehensive Investment Agreement (ACIA),[121] which after ratification by all ten states came into effect on 1 March 2012. The basic purpose of the ACIA is to replace the 1987 Investment Agreement and the 1998 Framework Agreement, mentioned previously, and consolidate them 'into a comprehensive investment agreement which is forward-looking, with improved features and provisions, comparable to international best practices in order to increase intra-ASEAN investments and to enhance ASEAN's competitiveness in attracting inward investments into ASEAN'.[122] The 'international best practices' which were taken into account in drafting the ACIA are those found in the 2004 Model US BIT, NAFTA, the OECD Guidelines for Multinational Corporations, and the then Draft Free Trade Agreements between ASEAN and China, Korea, and Australia/New Zealand.[123] The ACIA is thus not only a consolidation of its two predecessor treaties but also provides more comprehensive investor protection and lays the foundation for increased liberalization of investments within the ASEAN region. Indeed the stated objectives of the ACIA, according to Article 1, are: (a) the progressive liberalization of investment regimes of Member States; (b) the provision of enhanced protection to investors of all Member States and to their investments; (c) improvement of transparency and predictability of rules, regulations, and procedures conducive to increased investment among Member States; (d) the promotion of the region as an integrated investment area; and (e) cooperation to create favourable conditions for investment by investors of a Member State in the territory of the other Member States. The ACIA also authorizes the ASEAN Investment Area Council, a ministerial body with representation from all ten ASEAN states, to oversee the implementation of the Agreement.[124]

---

[119] Framework Agreement on the ASEAN Investment Area, 7 October 1998, available at <http://www.asean.org/images/2012/Economic/AIA/other_document/Framework%20Agreement%20on%20the%20ASEAN%20Investment%20Area.pdf> accessed 12 January 2015.

[120] M. Sornarajah, 'Review of Asian Views on Foreign Investment Law' in V Bath and L Nottage (eds), *Investment Law and Dispute Resolution Law and Practice in Asia* (Routledge, 2011) 242–8.

[121] 2009 ASEAN Comprehensive Investment Agreement, signed by the Economic Ministers at the 14th ASEAN Summit in Cha-am, Thailand, on 26 February 2009, available at <http://www.asean.org/images/2012/Economic/AIA/other_document/Framework%20Agreement%20on%20the%20ASEAN%20Investment%20Area.pdf> accessed 5 October 2014.

[122] ACIA Preamble. ACIA, Art 47 provides that upon its entry into force the 1987 and 1998 investment agreements are terminated.

[123] ASEAN, 'Highlights of the ASEAN Comprehensive Investment Agreement' (ACIA), 26 August 2008, available at <http://www.asean.org/resources/publications/asean-publications/item/asean-comprehensive-investment-agreement> accessed 5 October 2014.

[124] ACIA, Art 42.

ASEAN has not only sought actively to advance the economic integration of the ASEAN region through the progressive negotiation of investment treaties among its members, but in the first decade of the twenty-first century in its strengthened institutional form as an intergovernmental organization has also undertaken to negotiate trade and investment agreements on behalf of its membership with other countries. Thus, it has concluded the ASEAN–Australia–New Zealand Agreement (AANZFTA)[125] and the ASEAN-China Economic Cooperation Agreement,[126] both of which contain investment provisions. In addition, as of 2014 it was engaged in negotiating similar agreements with Japan and Korea.[127]

(iv) Mercosur investment treaties

Yet another regional treaty effort took place within Latin America among the countries of the Common Market of the Southern Cone ('Mercosur'), a customs union and trade bloc comprising Argentina, Brazil, Paraguay, Uruguay, and Venezuela, established in 1991 by the Treaty of Asunción.[128] The Mercosur members concluded two regional investment treaties in 1994 as protocols to the Treaty of Asunción. The first, the Protocol of Colonia for the Promotion and Reciprocal Protection of Investments in Mercosur, is intended to serve as the region's main investment legal regime.[129] As such, it defines the rights enjoyed by persons from a member state who make investments in other member states.

Mercosur's second regional investment treaty—the Protocol of Buenos Aires for the Promotion and Reciprocal Protection of Investments Coming from Non-Mercosur State Parties—serves as a baseline agreement, outlining the 'general legal principles to be applied by each of the State Parties to investments coming from non-Mercosur states...so as not to create differentiated conditions that would distort the flow of investments'.[130] Despite their relatively broad investor protection provisions, the Colonia and Buenos Aires Protocols were not in force

---

[125] Agreement establishing the ASEAN–Australia–New Zealand Free Trade Area, Cha-am, Phetchaburi, Thailand, 27 February 2009, entered into force 1 January 2010, [2010] ATS 1, Ch 11.

[126] Agreement on Investment of the Framework Agreement on Comprehensive Economic Cooperation between the People's Republic of China and the Association of Southeast Asian Nations, Bangkok, 15 August 2009, available at <http://fta.mofcom.gov.cn/inforimages/200908/20090817113007764.pdf> accessed 5 October 2014.

[127] V Bath and L Nottage, 'The ASEAN Comprehensive Investment Agreement and "ASEAN Plus"—The Australia-New Zealand Free Trade Area (AANZFTA) and the PRC-ASEAN Investment Agreement', Legal Studes Research Paper No 13/60, Sidney Law School, University of Sidney, September 2013, available at <http://papers.ssrn.com/sol3/papers.cfm?abstract_id=2331714> accessed 5 October 2014.

[128] Treaty Establishing a Common Market between the Argentine Republic, the Federal Republic of Brazil, the Republic of Paraguay, and the Eastern Republic of Uruguay (signed 26 March 1991, entered into force 19 November 1991), (1991) 30 ILM 1041.

[129] Protocol of Colonia for the Promotion and Reciprocal Protection of Investments in Mercosur (17 January 1994) MERCOSUR/CMC/DEC No 11/93 (Colonia Protocol).

[130] Protocol of Buenos Aires for the Promotion and Reciprocal Protection of Investments Coming from Non-Mercosur State Parties (5 August 1994) MERCOSUR/CMC/DEC No 11/94 at preamble (Buenos Aires Protocol), available at <http://www.sice.oas.org/trade/mrcsrs/decisions/dec1194e.asp> accessed 5 October 2016.

as of 2014. Both treaties require ratification by the four Mercosur member countries.[131] However, the first had been ratified only by Argentina and Uruguay and the second only by Argentina, Paraguay, and Uruguay.

(v) COMESA Treaty

A fifth regional treaty was concluded within Africa: The Common Market for Eastern and Southern Africa (COMESA).[132] COMESA is one of the largest trading blocs in Africa. Encompassing 374 million people,[133] it is a preferential trading area with nineteen members that stretches from Libya to Zimbabwe.[134] COMESA replaced a preferential trade area that had existed since 1981.[135] By 2000, COMESA aimed for the removal of all internal tariffs through a free trade area, and by 2004, a common external tariff was meant to be created. By 2005, the goals set for the year 2000 had only been partially achieved.[136]

In 2007, member states agreed to impose a common external tariff, which is a vital step to creating a customs union. Having reservations about liberalized trade, Angola, Ethiopia, and Uganda declined to adopt the measure.[137] COMESA representatives have met with their European counterparts to discuss a new economic partnership agreement.[138] In 2008, COMESA agreed to expand the free trade zone to include the East African Community and the Southern Africa Development Community.

While COMESA's primary focus is the development of intra-regional trade, the COMESA Treaty also contains provisions on investment that may have significance for foreign investment in the future. One of the Treaty's declared aims is 'to create an enabling environment for foreign, cross border, and domestic investment',[139] and it also states: '[t]he member states shall permit the free flow of capital within the Common Market'.[140] Moreover, it calls for member states to adopt various standards, including fair and equitable treatment, refraining from expropriating investment, and guaranteeing monetary transfers by investors, the purpose of which is the protection and promotion of investment.[141] These projected

---

[131] Colonia Protocol (n 129 above) Art 11(1); Buenos Aires Protocol (n 130 above) Art 4.

[132] Treaty Establishing the Common Market for Eastern and Southern Africa (5 November 1993), (1994) 33 ILM 1067.

[133] S Flatto, 'Too Much of a Good Thing?: Reassessing the Proliferation of African Regional Agreements' (2007) 30 Suffolk Transnational Law Review 407, 415.

[134] Current members include: Burundi, Comoros, Democratic Republic of Congo, Djibouti, Egypt, Eritrea, Ethiopia, Kenya, Libya, Madagascar, Malawi, Mauritius, Rwanda, the Seychelles, Sudan, Swaziland, Uganda, Zambia, and Zimbabwe. Former members include: Angola, Lesotho, Mozambique, Tanzania, and Namibia.

[135] M Oduor, 'Resolving Trade Disputes in Africa: Choosing between Multilateralism and Regionalism: The Case of COMESA and the WTO' (2005) 13 Tul J Int'l Comp L 177, 189.

[136] ibid 189–90.

[137] YMA Abebe et al, 'International Legal Developments in Review: 2007 Regional and Comparative Law' (2008) 42 Int'l Lawyer 863, 875.

[138] ibid.   [139] COMESA Treaty, Art 3(3).   [140] COMESA Treaty, Art 81.

[141] COMESA Treaty, Arts 159–162.

standards have, however, yet to become a legal reality throughout the COMESA region.

(vi) North American Free Trade Agreement

Certainly the most famous and successful of the regional arrangements concluded at the end of the twentieth century was the North American Free Trade Agreement (NAFTA), signed by the United States, Canada, and Mexico on 17 December 1992.[142] NAFTA put in place the legal structure for one of the largest free trade areas in the world, with over 360 million consumers and $6 trillion in annual output. Despite the omission of the word 'investment' from its title, NAFTA governs both trade and investment among its three member states. In effect, Chapter 11 of NAFTA, entitled 'Investment', constitutes an investment treaty among the three countries and its text has clearly been influenced by the provisions of earlier BITs.

In order to facilitate the flow of capital within the NAFTA area, Chapter 11 seeks: (1) to reduce or remove barriers to investment in one country by investors of another member country; (2) to create a secure investment climate by specifying clear rules concerning the treatment to which NAFTA investors and their investments are entitled; and (3) to provide a fair means for the settlement of disputes between a NAFTA investor and the host country. Section A of the chapter contains provisions on the establishment and treatment of investment, and section B governs investor–state dispute settlement.

Key NAFTA investment provisions in facilitating the flow of capital and the making of investments are found in Articles 1102, 1103, and 1104 which guarantee that investors and investments will receive national treatment or most-favoured-nation treatment, whichever is the more favourable, with respect to the 'establishment, acquisition, expansion, management, conduct, operation and sale or other disposition of investments'. Article 1106 of NAFTA prohibits a host country from imposing any specified performance requirements on an investment undertaken not only by an investor of a NAFTA country (including investors of the host country) but of other foreign investors in connection with the establishment, acquisition, expansion, management, conduct, or operation of any investment.

Other important provisions in NAFTA require each member country to permit all monetary transfers by an investor relating to an investment of another NAFTA country to be made freely, without delay, and in freely usable currency at the market exchange rate prevailing on the date of transfer. NAFTA also prohibits member states from directly or indirectly nationalizing or expropriating an investment of an investor from another NAFTA party or taking a measure tantamount to nationalization or expropriation except for a public purpose,

---

[142] North American Free Trade Agreement between the Government of the United States of America, the Government of Canada and the Government of the United Mexican States (17 December 1992), (1993) 32 ILM 289 (NAFTA).

on a non-discriminatory basis, and upon payment of just compensation.[143] In addition, the NAFTA chapter on investment requires each country to accord investments from other member countries the minimum treatment required by international law, including fair and equitable treatment and full protection and security. NAFTA also gives an aggrieved individual the right to bring a claim in arbitration against a state that has violated NAFTA treatment standards. In the years since NAFTA was launched, it has been the subject of a significant number of investor–state arbitrations in which investors have brought claims against each of the three member states.

(vii) *The Energy Charter Treaty*

Another important multilateral treaty affecting international investment is the Energy Charter Treaty (ECT),[144] which was opened for signature in Lisbon on 17 December 1994 and had gained fifty-four members by 2014, including the European Union and Euratom. The ECT has a sector, rather than a regional, focus. It aims to create a legal framework that will encourage the development of a secure international energy supply through liberalized trade and investment among member states. The treaty arose out of the idea, emerging with the end of Communism, that western countries were in need of stable, efficient sources of energy while the states of the former Soviet Union, because of their natural resource endowment, had great energy potential whose development required the capital and technology held by the west; consequently, cooperation in the international energy sector could bring benefits to all sides. The ECT became effective in 1998.

Part III of the ECT, entitled 'Investment Promotion and Protection', is in effect an investment treaty, and it clearly has been profoundly influenced by the language of the various European and American BITs in its structure, content, and drafting.[145] One of the unique features of the treaty, which distinguishes it from other international investment agreements, is that it is a sector agreement, meaning that it only applies to investments in a particular economic sector. According to Article 1, the ECT's scope is limited to investments associated with economic activities concerning the exploration, extraction, refining, production,

---

[143] T Levy, 'NAFTA's Provision for Compensation in the Event of Expropriation: A Reassessment of the Prompt, Adequate and Effective Standard' (1995) 31 Stan J Int'l L 423–53.

[144] The text of the ECT may be found in The Final Act of the European Energy Charter Conference (12 December 1994) AF/EECH en 1, reprinted at (1995) 34 ILM 373. For an extensive discussion of the provisions of the Energy Charter Treaty, see TW Wälde (ed), *The Energy Charter Treaty: An East-West Gateway for Investment and Trade* (Kluwer Law International, 1996).

[145] The Legal Counsel of the International Energy Agency, a principal adviser to the European Energy Charter Conference, has stated that the investment provisions of the ECT 'resemble provisions in bilateral investment treaties although their drafting has not been based on any single negotiating party's treaty practice'. Legal Counsel of the IEA, *The Energy Charter Treaty: A Description of Its Provisions* (1994) 15. For a comparison of the ECT's investment provisions with the BITs, see JW Salacuse, 'The Energy Charter Treaty and Bilateral Investment Treaty Regimes' in Wälde (n 144 above) 321–48.

storage, land transport, transmission, distribution, trade, marketing, or sale of energy materials and products. On the other hand, its substantive provisions on the protection and treatment of investments and investors, as well as their enforcement through investor–state arbitration, are very similar to what one might find in a western BIT with a developing country. The resemblance is not accidental. Virtually all of the states participating in the Conference that wrote the treaty had previously signed at least one BIT, and many had concluded several.

Like most BITs and regional investment agreements, the ECT provides for two basic forms of dispute settlement: (1) Article 26 provides for investor–state arbitration in disputes between investors and host states for alleged injuries to investment due to breaches of the treaty; and (2) Article 27 sets down procedures for the settlement of disputes between member states over the interpretation or application of treaty provisions. Investors have invoked the investor–state dispute provisions on numerous occasions since the treaty's inception. The Energy Charter Secretariat estimates that aggrieved investors had lodged fifty-eight international arbitration cases by mid-2014, many of which have resulted in awards against member states.[146]

(viii) Dominican Republic–Central America–United States Free Trade Agreement

In an effort to build an eventual free trade area for North and South America and the Caribbean and thereby expand on the work of NAFTA, the United States concluded an agreement with the Dominican Republic and five Central American states, Costa Rica, El Salvador, Honduras, Nicaragua, and Guatemala, in 2004. Signed on 5 August 2004, it is known as the Dominican Republic–Central America–United States Free Trade Agreement (CAFTA-DR), sometimes simply referred to as 'CAFTA'. After contentious debate, the US Congress approved the CAFTA-DR Agreement in July 2005, and the President signed the implementing legislation on 2 August 2005.[147] The agreement was implemented on a rolling basis: El Salvador was the first to ratify on 1 March 2006, and Costa Rica the last, on 1 January 2009. The Agreement went into effect fully among all seven signatories on 1 January 2009. According to its preamble, one of the objectives of CAFTA-DR is '...to contribute to hemispheric integration and to provide impetus toward establishing the Free Trade Area of the Americas'.[148] Although

---

[146] For a listing and summary of such cases with links to available awards, see <http://www.encharter.org/index.php?id=213&L=0L50A> accessed 6 October 2014.

[147] Dominican Republic–Central America–United States Free Trade Agreement Implementation Act 2005 (PL 109-53, 119 Stat 462). See generally, JR Hornbeck, 'The Dominican Republic-Central America-United States Free Trade Agreement' (CAFTA-DR) (Congressional Research Service 2008).

[148] The full text of the Agreement may be found on the website of the US Trade Representative, at <<http://www.ustr.gov>. See also, VHW Wang, 'Investor Protection or Environmental Protection? "Green" Development Under CAFTA' (2007) 32 Col J Envir L 251; MB Baker, 'No Country Left Behind: The Exporting of US Legal Norms Under the Guise of Economic Integration' (2005) 19 Emory Int'l LJ 1346.

CAFTA-DR, like the North American Free Trade Agreement (NAFTA), does not refer to investment in its title, it is similar to NAFTA in that it covers both trade and investment. Indeed, CAFTA-DR's investment chapter borrows heavily from Chapter 11 of NAFTA, as well as from the US Model BIT. CAFTA contains twenty-two chapters and annexes detailing, *inter alia*, country-specific tariff schedules and rules of origin.

Chapter 10 of CAFTA-DR, which contains the investment provisions, is highly similar to the investment provisions in prior US agreements, particularly NAFTA. As such, it safe to assume that US views and interests were critical in shaping Chapter 10 and that the influence of the other six parties seems limited primarily to the reservations and certain limitations in the party-specific annexes, particularly those with respect to sectors in which national treatment is not required for foreign investors. Like Chapter 11 of NAFTA, Chapter 10 of CAFTA-DR on investment is divided into three sections. Section A contains the substantive investment protections. Section B sets down the rules for investor–state dispute settlement. Section C contains definitions of key terms employed in Chapter 10. The provisions on investment largely follow the structure and content of NAFTA. As in most other investment treaties, CAFTA's main protections are national treatment (Article 10.3), Most-Favored Nation Treatment (Article 10.4), minimum standard of treatment (Article 10.5, encompassing 'fair and equitable treatment'[149] and 'full protection and security'),[150] and protection against expropriation (Article 10.7). The treaty prohibits certain performance requirements (Article 10.9), and allows states to maintain non-conforming measures that pre-date CAFTA (Article 10.13). It also allows member states to deny the benefits of the treaty to investors of non-parties with which those CAFTA states do not have diplomatic relations. CAFTA, like other modern investment treaties, also provides for investor–state arbitration for the settlement of disputes arising under its provisions.[151]

(j) The evolution of BIT provisions into free trade agreements

NAFTA and the ECT also signalled the development of another trend in investment treaty-making: the incorporation of investment treaty provisions into free trade agreements (FTAs). Following NAFTA, the United States proceeded to make a number of FTAs, all of which included a separate chapter that was virtually indistinguishable from a BIT.[152] Such agreements were concluded, for

---

[149] CAFTA-DR, Ch 10, Art 10.5(a).   [150] CAFTA-DR, Ch 10, Art 10.5(b).

[151] See Investor–State Dispute Resolution Under DR-CAFTA, available at <http://www.whitecase.com/idq/fall_2007/ia2/> accessed 6 October 2014. For one of the first investor–state cases to arise under its provisions, see *Railroad Development Corp v Guatemala*, ICSID Case No Arb/07/23 (Award) (29 June 2012). See also *CAFTA-DR Investor-State Arbitrations*, available at <http://www.state.gov/s/l/c33165.htm> accessed 24 March 2015.

[152] For the text of the various FTAs concluded by the US, see the website of the US Trade Representative at <<http://www.ustr.gov/trade-agreements> accessed 6 October 2014.

example, with Israel,[153] Jordan,[154] Bahrain,[155] Chile,[156] and Singapore.[157] Japan would adopt a similar approach in the promotion of its economic partnership agreements (EPAs),[158] which also contain chapters on investment and provide for investor–state arbitration as a means of enforcement. Other Asian countries have followed suit, so that by the year 2014 there were 324 such combined trade and investment agreements and many others were in the process of negotiation.[159] Thus, it appears that the investment treaty, which arose out of trade agreements, is returning to its origins.

Although conceptually distinct, international investment and international trade are functionally connected in that most enterprises invest in order to trade. It is through trade in the products and services they produce that most direct foreign investments ultimately secure profits for their investors. Thus, oil companies invest in petroleum exploration in order to find oil that they may sell to the international market. Agro-industrial firms invest abroad in large-scale land developments in order to sell the products they grow. Tourism companies invest in hotels in tropical countries in order to sell their services to tourists from countries in colder climes. Multinational firms engage in vast amounts of intra-firm trade as they invest abroad to create global supply chains that maximize manufacturing efficiencies by locating production facilities among different countries depending on the advantages they offer and then exporting the components thus produced back to the investor's home country for final assembly. Such multinational investors are not only concerned to protect their investments in those countries but they also want to be certain that they will be able to export goods and services back to their home country with minimum cost. Modern FTAs with investment chapters provide both of these valuable functions. From the point of view of host countries, the prospect of the economic benefits of increased international exports of goods and services produced in their territories has been a powerful incentive to agree to high standards of foreign investor protection that they might otherwise have been hesitant to accept. Whereas traditional investment treaties had imposed legal obligations only on host countries to protect covered foreign investments, FTAs impose obligations on both host and home countries. They oblige

[153] Agreement on the Establishment of a Free Trade Area (signed 22 April 1985, entered into force 19 August 1985). US Dept of State, Treaties in Force: A List of Treaties and Other International Agreements of the United States in Force on January 1, 2007, available at <<http://www.state.gov/e/eb/tpp/bta/fta/fta/index.htm> accessed 6 October 2014.

[154] Agreement on the Establishment of a Free Trade Area (signed 24 October 2000, entered into force 17 December 2001). US Dept of State, Treaties in Force (n 153 above).

[155] Agreement on the Establishment of a Free Trade Area (signed 14 September 2004, entered into force 1 August 2006). US Dept of State, Treaties in Force (n 153 above).

[156] US–Chile Free Trade Agreement (signed 6 June 2003, entered into force 1 January 2004). US Dept of State, Treaties in Force (n 153 above).

[157] US–Singapore Free Trade Agreement (signed 6 May 2003, entered into force 1 January 2004). US Dept of State, Treaties in Force (n 153 above).

[158] M Yasushi, 'Economic Partnership Agreements and Japanese Strategy' (2006) 6(3) Gaiko Forum 53.

[159] UNCTAD, *World Investment Report 2014* (2014) 114.

host countries to protect covered investments and they require home countries to accept the importation of goods produced in their treaty partner's territory.

The connection between trade and investment was also formally recognized by GATT, which would later become the WTO, during its Uruguay Round of negotiations between 1986 and 1994.[160] One of the products of that negotiation, to which all WTO members must now adhere, is the Agreement on Trade-Related Investment Measures (TRIMs).[161] This Agreement forbids the imposition of measures that are inconsistent with Article III of GATT on national treatment[162] and its Article XI on the elimination of quantitative restrictions.[163] Its purpose is to prevent WTO members from imposing local content and trade balancing requirements as a condition for the creation or operation of foreign investment projects. One WTO dispute settlement case has applied the Agreement to invalidate Indonesian measures used to favour the development of a 'national car' enterprise.[164] In addition, the WTO's General Agreement on Trade in Services[165] also includes provisions affecting investment related to services.

(k) Efforts at a global treaty on investment

While negotiations over the years have led to a substantial number of investment treaties, the results of these efforts have been limited in geographical scope, being either bilateral or regional, or in the case of the ECT, restricted to a particular sector. Given the success of their efforts at international rule-making, it was natural for capital-exporting countries to contemplate the negotiation of a global treaty on investment;[166] however, thus far, concrete results in this domain have been virtually non-existent. Two initiatives at the end of the twentieth century are worthy of note, in addition to those that took place immediately after World War II.

The first of these began in April 1991 when the Development Committee, which is a Joint Ministerial Committee of the Boards of Governors of the IMF and the World Bank, requested that the Multilateral Investment Guarantee Agency (MIGA) prepare a 'legal framework' to promote foreign direct investment. The resulting *Guidelines on the Treatment of Foreign Investment*,[167] which had a long

---

[160] General Agreement on Tariffs and Trade: Multilateral Trade Negotiations Final Act Embodying the Results of the Uruguay Round of Trade Negotiations (15 April 1994), (1994) 33 ILM 1125.

[161] Agreement on Trade-Related Investment Measures (15 April 1994) 1868 UNTS 186 (TRIMs).

[162] General Agreement on Tariffs and Trade (30 October 1947) 55 UNTS 194; 61 Stat A-11; TIAS 1700 (GATT).

[163] ibid Art XI.

[164] *Indonesia—Certain Measures Affecting the Automobile Industry* WT/DS54/15 of 7 December 1998, available at <<http://www.wto.org/english/tratop_e/dispu_e/cases_e/ds54_e.htm> accessed 5 October 2014.

[165] General Agreement on Trade in Services (15 April 1994) UNTS 183; (1994) 33 ILM 1167 (GATS).

[166] JW Salacuse, 'Towards a New Treaty Framework for Direct Foreign Investment' (1985) 50 Journal of Air Law and Commerce 969.

[167] World Bank, 'Report to the Development Committee and Guidelines on the Treatment of Foreign Direct Investment' (1992) 31 ILM 1363.

gestation period in the World Bank Group (mainly at the IBRD, MIGA, and IFC) and was based upon extensive consideration of important legal instruments in the field, such as BITs, was then considered at an international conference held under the auspices of the Bank Group and the French Ministry of Finance in July 1992. It was later resubmitted to the Development Committee, which gave its approval in September 1992. Because of their source and the careful process by which they were developed, the *Guidelines*, although not law, have enjoyed considerable influence and credibility.[168] The *Guidelines* set out a general framework for the treatment of foreign investors by host states and cover areas of concern to investors, such as the admission of foreign investment, standards of treatment and transfer of capital and net revenues, expropriation and its compensation, and the settlement of disputes.[169] The basic goal of the *Guidelines* is to set down a global framework.

The second notable initiative to establish global rules on investment took place within the Organization for Economic Cooperation and Development (OECD). In September 1995, negotiations to establish a Multilateral Agreement on Investment (MAI) began at the OECD with the goal of completing a draft treaty in time for the 1997 ministerial meeting. The OECD mandate called for 'a broad multilateral framework for international investment with high standards of liberalization of investment and investment protection and with effective dispute settlement procedures'.[170] Thus, the dual objectives of investment liberalization and investment protection, which had directed developed countries' BIT efforts, also appeared in the search for a workable Multilateral Agreement on Investment.

In developing a treaty framework, the MAI negotiators drew heavily on NAFTA and the BITs. For example, the draft MAI structure addressed the same issues as those earlier treaties. While a structure for the MAI was agreed upon relatively quickly, the precise content of the rules to govern that structure were not. The negotiating states achieved consensus fairly quickly on the issues of investment protection and dispute resolution. Following the BITS, the states seem to have agreed on strong dispute settlement procedures and on post-investment national or most-favoured-nation treatment, whichever was the most favourable. They also agreed on extensive rights to monetary transfers and to require prompt, adequate, and effective compensation in cases of expropriation.

It was on the question of investment liberalization that significant disagreements surfaced—disagreements that often brought the United States into conflict with European countries. All the principal negotiating states had substantial investments abroad and so had a common interest in seeing that those investments received maximum protection. Moreover, the developed OECD members

---

[168] SJ Rubin, 'Introductory Note for International Legal Materials' (1992) 31 ILM 1363.

[169] IFI Shihata, 'Introductory Note of September 25, 1992' in *Legal Framework for the Treatment of Foreign Investment: Volume II* (1992) 31 ILM 1367.

[170] OECD, 'Multilateral Agreement on Investment: The Original Mandate', available at <<http://www.oecd.org/daf/mai/intro.htm> accessed 6 October 2014. See also G Kelly, 'Multilateral Investment Treaties: A Balanced Approach to Multinational Corporations' (2001) 39 Col J Transnat'l L 483.

had already established strong systems of investment protection within their own borders. On the other hand, the OECD states each had different economic interests with respect to investment liberalization, particularly with regard to foreign investments that might be undertaken in their territories. Each had different procedures governing investments and different local industries that they wished to protect from competition by foreign investors. The negotiators were unable to find common ground with respect to investment liberalization.

Beyond disagreement among OECD members, other parties raised their voices to contest the MAI negotiations. First, developing countries, led by India, opposed the MAI and any attempt to create new rules of international law to protect and liberalize foreign investment. They saw the prospect of a global treaty on investment as a threat to their national sovereignty and economic independence. They therefore challenged the legitimacy of a forum that did not allow developing countries to participate fully in the negotiating process. Second, a broad coalition of non-governmental organizations (NGOs), based largely in developed countries, arose to challenge both the process and content of the MAI negotiations. In 1997, the NGOs obtained a draft of the MAI. Discovering that negotiators had consulted business interests but not other elements of civil society, the NGOs mounted an effective worldwide protest through the internet. The NGOs argued that the drafting process was flawed because the OECD chose to conduct secret negotiations with business interests at the expense of labour unions, environmentalists, human rights organizations, and others. Seeing the MAI as yet another instrument that would advance globalization at the expense of local groups and interests, anti-globalization forces soon joined the protest.

As the public within OECD countries became aware of the contested MAI negotiations, various American and European politicians and groups took opposing stands on the issue and their governments became more cautious in pressing for conclusion of the treaty. In early 1998, as the talks seemed to slow down, the negotiators decided to take a six-month hiatus and reconvene in October. In the meantime, the French government commissioned a study, to be known as the Lalumière report, on the MAI negotiations. The report supported the need to protect foreign investment and to liberalize investment rules, but it criticized the structure and content of the MAI draft and argued that the OECD was not the right forum for negotiating a major international agreement of the scope and impact of the proposed MAI. It concluded that negotiations should not continue on the existing basis. Less than a week before the MAI negotiations were to resume, French Prime Minister Lionel Jospin announced that France would no longer participate in the MAI talks. Citing the Lalumière report, Jospin argued that the MAI would allow private interests to erode state sovereignty and that the effort needed a new framework encompassing all countries, including the developing nations. The right forum, Jospin argued, was not the OECD but 'quite naturally that of the WTO'.[171] On 3 December 1998, after unsuccessfully trying

---

[171] N Bray, 'Politics and Policy: France Remains Obstacle to Global Investment Plan' *Wall Street Journal in Europe*, 15 October 1998, 2.

to restart negotiations without France, the OECD announced officially that the MAI negotiations were closed.

Looking back at the effort to negotiate the MAI, one may say that it failed for several reasons. First, the OECD was the wrong forum in which to negotiate a treaty meant to have a global scope and which would potentially impact so many non-OECD countries. Second, the process that the OECD constructed was flawed. Secrecy is important in many negotiations; transparency is important in others. In the MAI negotiation, the OECD achieved the worst of both worlds: secrecy with leaks. It gave the public the impression that the OECD was actually a cabal bent on foisting corporate interests on the world. NGOs, in particular, skillfully exploited the failings of the negotiating process. Third, the timing was wrong. Many countries at the time were suffering from 'economic treaty fatigue'. They had recently negotiated far-reaching economic treaties, including the WTO, NAFTA, and the European single market, and were still experiencing a painful adjustment. Countries needed time to implement these existing rules before taking on yet another set of new economic rules. Recognizing this fact, the US government, for example, did not attach great importance to the negotiations and did not make a major effort on their behalf. It assigned lower level officials to the negotiations, and President Clinton never put his own personal political prestige and effort behind the MAI, as he had done to secure the ratification of NAFTA and the Uruguay Round agreements. Fourth, the negotiators were unable to find a grand bargain that would sustain the MAI treaty structure. The old BIT bargain of 'investment protection for investment promotion' was not a sound basis for the MAI. Most OECD countries already had strong protective investment regimes and were therefore unwilling to grant investment liberalization for something they already had. They judged that the MAI's cost to their domestic industries was too high a price to pay. Fifth, NGOs, while technically not part of negotiations, had recently become an important factor in many multilateral negotiations. The NGOs had skillfully developed new techniques to influence negotiations, but the OECD had no experience in dealing with them and, as a result, was out-manoeuvred.

Although the OECD effort failed and a global treaty on investment does not yet exist, efforts towards that goal may yet be rekindled in the future, possibly through the WTO.[172] In any event, the lessons learned in the MAI experiment

---

[172] After considerable struggle, the members of the WTO meeting at Doha in November 2001 agreed to include the subject of foreign investment on the agenda of its next round of trade talks, known commonly as the Doha Round. With respect to investment, the work plan for the round approved at the Ministerial meeting in November 2001 recognized 'the case for a multilateral framework to secure transparent, stable and predictable conditions for long-term cross border investment, particularly foreign direct investment that will contribute to the expansion of trade'. Ministerial Declaration (adopted 14 November 2001) ¶ 20, World Trade Organization Ministerial Conference (9–14 November 2001). This was, however, dropped from the Doha Round pursuant to the 'July 2004 Package' which decided that 'no work towards negotiations on any of these issues will take place within the WTO during the Doha Round.' See 'Decision adopted by the General Council on 1 August 2004' (2 August 2004) WT/L/579, available at <http://www.wto.org/english/tratop_e/dda_e/draft_text_gc_dg_31july04_e.htm#invest_comp_gpa> accessed 12 January 2014.

may ultimately prove instructive in formulating a process that will result in a similar global agreement. It may also be necessary to broaden the scope of such global investment treaty to include provisions that will impose obligations on investor behaviour while carrying out activities in a host country.[173]

(l) The trend towards regional and inter-regional trade and investment treaties

Perhaps in part because of the failure to achieve a global treaty on investment and the inability of the WTO's Doha Round of international trade negotiations, begun in 2001, to produce concrete results, the second decade of the twenty-first century has witnessed the growth in regional investment agreements, plus a new development in the evolution of investment treaties: the negotiation of inter-regional trade and investment treaties. The new regional investment treaties include the China–Japan–Republic of Korea Investment Agreement,[174] the Central America–Mexico Free Trade Agreement,[175] and the various investment treaties, mentioned previously, negotiated by ASEAN on behalf of its members with other countries in the Pacific. One question raised by the new regional treaties is their effect on existing BITs between countries signing the regional agreements. Generally, most regional agreements allow the continuation of relevant BITs, thus creating parallel systems of investment protection.[176]

A potentially far-reaching development is the negotiation of investment agreement among countries in different regions that together have a significant economic importance. UNCTAD has called these proposed agreements 'mega-regional agreements'[177] but some might also be called 'mega-interregional treaties' because they involve countries from more than one region. One may identify seven separate negotiations which together involve eighty-eight countries, accounting for a substantial portion of the world's population and GDP. As of 2014, the seven negotiations are: (1) the Canada–EU Comprehensive Economic and Trade Agreement (CETA); (2) the Tripartite Agreement among the Common Market for Eastern and Central Africa (COMESA), the East African Community (EAC), and the Southern African Development Community (SADC); (3) the EU–Japan Free Trade Agreement; (4) the 'Pacer

---

[173] For discussion of this approach, see J Salacuse, 'Towards a Global Treaty on Foreign Investment: The Search for a Grand Bargain' in N Horn and S Kröll (eds), *Arbitrating Foreign Investment Disputes: Procedural and Substantive Issues* (Kluwer Law International 2004) and J Salacuse (n 166 above) 1007–10. See also G Kelly, 'Multilateral Investment Treaties: A Balanced Approach to Multinational Corporations' (2001) 39 Col J Transnat'l L 483, who argues that international human rights law should be applied to foreign investors in return for their right to invest.

[174] Agreement Among the Government of Japan, the Government of the Republic of Korea, and the Government of the People's Republic of China for the Promotion, Facilitation and Protection of Investment (13 May 2012).

[175] Tratado de Libre Comercio entre México y Costa Rica, El Salvador, Guatemala, Honduras y Nicaragua (5 December 2011).

[176] UNCTAD, *World Investment Report 2013* (2013) 106.

[177] UNCTAD, *World Investment Report 2014* (2014) 118.

Plus' negotiations among Australia, New Zealand, and the Pacific Islands Forum developing countries; (5) the Regional Comprehensive Economic Partnership (RCEP) involving the ASEAN countries, Australia, Japan, China, India, Korea, and New Zealand; (6) the Trans-Pacific Partnership (TPP) involving Australia, Brunai Darussalam, Canada, Chile, Japan, Malaysia, Mexico, New Zealand, Peru, Singapore, the United States, and Vietnam; and (7) the EU–United States Transatlantic Trade and Investment Partnership (TTIP).[178] These negotiations have the potential to affect international economic activity on a global scale. For example, if successful, it is estimated that the EU–United States negotiations alone would have an impact on 45 per cent of global GDP.[179] As of the middle of 2014, none of these negotiations had resulted in final treaty texts, let alone ratified binding international agreements. All, however, are virtually certain to include investment chapters, and those chapters will in all likelihood incorporate and build upon the concepts, rules, processes, and terminology developed by the treatification process launched in the years following World War II. On the other hand, a significant new development is the important role played by regional organizations in investment treaty negotiations, a role that had previously been played by states alone. Thus, for example, in the European Union, as a result of the Treaty of Lisbon, foreign investment is now constitutionally a union, rather than a member state function.[180] EU institutions, not the governments of individual states, are responsible for conducting and approving investment treaty negotiations and they are leading the negotiations for the mega-regional organizations mentioned previously. However, pursuant to an EU Regulation adopted in December 2012, existing BITs between an EU member state and a non-member state are to remain in force until a treaty between the European Union and such other state enters into force.[181]

(m) Conclusion

Since World War II, the nations of the world have been actively engaged in creating an international law based on treaties, both bilateral and multilateral, in order to remedy the defects perceived by capital-exporting states and their investors in customary international investment law. The process of treatification has proceeded rapidly and will almost certainly continue as countries create an increasingly dense treaty network, despite certain stresses and strains that it has experienced as a few countries have sought to disengage from the regime by denouncing some investment treaties and other countries have sought to renegotiate certain treaty

---

[178] ibid 118–22.   [179] ibid 120.
[180] Treaty on the Functioning of the European Union, Consolidated Version of the Treaty on the Functioning of the European Union, 26 May 2012, [2012] OJ C326/47, Arts 206 and 207. See generally Reinisch (n 67 above).
[181] Regulation (EU) 2019/2012 of 12 December 2012 establishing transitional arrangements for bilateral investment agreements between Member States and third countries [2012] OJ L351/40, Art 3.

provisions.[182] That network has had a growing impact on international investments and on the behaviour of host states towards investments and investors. Its impact seems bound to increase in the future.

4.3 The Objectives of the Movement to Negotiate Investment Treaties

Having reviewed the history of the development of investment treaties, a history that has largely been driven by capital-exporting countries and their nationals and companies, one may well ask: What was the objective of this international law-making during the last half of the twentieth century and the beginning of the twenty-first? An understanding of these objectives is an important element in interpreting the treaty texts and successfully applying them to specific situations. It is to be recalled that Article 31(1) of the Vienna Convention on the Law of Treaties (VCLT)[183] provides: 'A treaty shall be interpreted in good faith in accordance with the ordinary meaning to be given to the terms of the treaty in their context and in light of *its object and purpose*' (emphasis added).

The objects and purposes of investment treaties are often specifically stated in the body of the treaty, its preamble, or related documents. Although specific objectives may vary from treaty to treaty, as a group, contemporary investment treaties appear to share remarkably similar goals. In reviewing investment treaties and their surrounding circumstances, one can identify three orders of objectives: (1) primary objectives; (2) subsidiary objectives; and (3) long-term objectives. The following sections will examine each of these three.

4.4 Primary Objectives of Investment Treaties

Nearly all investment treaties pursue two primary objectives: (1) investment protection; and (2) investment promotion. Thus, most BITs bear the title 'Treaty Concerning the Promotion and Protection of Investment', or some variation thereof.[184]

---

[182] See Ch 1, section 1.6.

[183] Vienna Convention on the Law of Treaties (22 May 1969) 1155 UNTS 331; (1969) 8 ILM 679; 63 AJIL 875; UN Doc A/Conf.39/27 (1969) (VCLT).

[184] Treaty Concerning the Reciprocal Encouragement and Protection of Investment (US–Armenia) (23 September 1992), S Treaty Doc No 103-11 (1993); Treaty Concerning the Promotion and Reciprocal Protection of Investments (Federal Republic of Germany–Poland) (10 November 1989), (1990) 29 ILM 333; Agreement for the Promotion and Protection of Investments (Indonesia–UK) (27 April 1976), Treaty Series No 62. Similarly, the Energy Charter Treaty, Part III is entitled 'Investment Promotion and Protection'.

(a) Investment protection

The primary motives behind the rapid expansion of international investment treaties were the desire of investors from capital-exporting states to invest safely and securely abroad and the need to create a stable international legal framework to facilitate and protect those investments. Such protection has been aimed at investment risks posed by injurious acts and omissions by host governments themselves and also injurious acts and omissions by other persons in the host country. Without an applicable investment treaty, international investors would be forced to rely on host country law alone for protection, a reliance that entails a variety of risks to their investments. Host governments can easily change their own domestic law after a foreign investment is made, and host country officials may not always act fairly or impartially towards foreign investors and their enterprises. Moreover, host country officials may fail to take action to protect foreign investors and their investments from injurious actions by other persons. Investor recourse to local courts for protection may prove to be of little value in the face of prejudice against foreigners or governmental interference in the judicial process.[185] Indeed, these fears were realized in the 1960s and 1970s when numerous instances of interference and expropriation of foreign investments by host country governments occurred. The number of expropriations of foreign-owned property grew steadily each year from 1960 and reached its peak in the mid-1970s.[186]

The lack of consensus on the customary international law applicable to foreign investments, discussed in Chapter 3, created further uncertainty in the minds of investors about the degree of protection they could expect under international law. To decrease their uncertainty and counter the threat of adverse national law and regulation, the home countries of these investors attempted to conclude a series of treaties that would provide clear rules and effective enforcement mechanisms, at least with regard to their treaty partners. Their primary goal was therefore the *protection* of investments made by their nationals and companies in foreign countries.

(b) Investment promotion

A second primary objective of investment treaties is the promotion or encouragement of investment. This objective is based on the assumption that increased investment will further a country's economic development and prosperity, and that foreign sources of capital and technology can usefully contribute to a country's economic advancement.

---

[185] UNCTAD, *Bilateral Investment Treaties in the Mid-1990s* (1998) 114–18. The UN identified 875 distinct acts of governmental taking of foreign property in 62 countries during the period between 1960 and 1974. D Piper, 'New Directions in the Protection of American-Owned Property Abroad' (1979) 4 Int'l Trade LJ 315, 330.

[186] This question assumes that the developing country is not expecting other benefits from its developed country treaty partner, such as increased foreign aid or enhanced security guarantees, which are extraneous to a BIT relationship.

Concluding and maintaining a treaty requires a bargain from which both parties believe they derive benefits. An investment treaty between two developed states, both of whose nationals expect to invest in the territory of the other, would be based on the notion of reciprocity and mutual protection. That is, a host state is induced to grant protection to investors from another country to be assured that the other state will grant similar protection to investors from the host state. However, this bargain would not seem to apply to a treaty between a developed, capital-exporting state and a developing, capital-importing country whose nationals are unlikely to invest abroad. One might therefore ask: Why would developing countries enter into such agreements? Why would they constrain their sovereignty by entering into treaties that specifically limit their ability to take necessary legislative and administrative actions to advance and protect what they perceive as their national interests?[187]

The answer to this question is that many countries sign investment treaties to *promote* foreign investment, thereby increasing the amount of capital and associated technology that flows to their territories. The basic assumption in this respect is that treaties with clear and enforceable rules to protect and facilitate foreign investment reduce risk and that such reduction in risks, all things being equal, encourages investment. In the 1980s and 1990s, as other forms of financial assistance became less available from commercial banks and official aid institutions, developing countries increasingly felt the need to promote private foreign investment in order to foster economic development. Investment treaties were seen as one means of pursuing a broader campaign of investment promotion and so developing nations signed them in increasing numbers.[188] Thus, an investment agreement between a developed and a developing country is founded on a grand bargain: a *promise* of protection of capital in return for the *prospect* of more capital in the future.[189]

Developing countries have sometimes entered into investment treaty negotiations with the expectation that the capital-exporting country would take affirmative measures to encourage its nationals to invest in the developing country—an expectation no doubt fostered by the word 'encouragement' appearing in the titles

---

[187] UNCTAD, *Bilateral Investment Treaties in the Mid-1990s* (1998) 85.

[188] JW Salacuse and NP Sullivan, 'Do BITs Really Work? An Evaluation of Bilateral Investment Treaties and Their Grand Bargain' (2005) 46 Harv Int'l LJ 67; J Salacuse, 'Toward a Global Treaty on Foreign Investment: The Search for a Grand Bargain' in N Horn and S Kröll (eds), *Arbitrating Foreign Investment Disputes: Procedural and Substantive Legal Issues* (Kluwer Law International, 2004) 51.

[189] The Deputy US Trade Representative stated the US goals in negotiating BITs as follows: The BIT program's basic aims are to:

> (1) protect U.S. investment abroad in those countries where U.S. investors' rights are not protected through existing agreements;
> (2) encourage adoption in foreign countries of market-oriented domestic policies that treat private investment fairly; and
> (3) support the development of international law standards consistent with these objectives.

J Lang, *Keynote Address* (1998) 31 Corn Int'l LJ 455, 457.

of most draft treaties. Capital-exporting states, however, have generally refused to agree to any provision obliging them to encourage or induce their nationals to invest in the foreign state. On the contrary, many BITs have terms that encourage or oblige the *host* country to create favourable investment conditions in *its* territory.

It should also be noted that some investment treaties have sought to *facilitate* the entry and operation of investments by inducing host countries to remove various impediments in their regulatory systems. This has clearly been the goal of the Treaty on the Functioning of the European Union, and particularly Article 49 of that treaty, which grants investors from any EU member state a right of establishment, that is, the right to set up business in any other EU member state. Other measures designed to create a single European market for the movement of capital have also supported this goal. The North American Free Trade Agreement pursued a similar purpose, as is clear from the fact that in Article 102(1)(b), one of its stated purposes is 'to increase substantially investment opportunities in the territories of the Parties'.

4.5 Secondary Objectives of Investment Treaties

Countries often have various secondary objectives in concluding investment treaties. The specific secondary objective pursued by a particular country may vary according to its economic situation, policy goals, ideology, or the state of its international relations. Sometimes such objectives are not stated in the treaty and sometimes government officials may not even be willing to acknowledge them publicly. Among some of the more common secondary goals for concluding investment treaties are the following.

(a) Market liberalization

In negotiating BITs with developing countries, some capital-exporting states have sought to use the investment treaty as a means to encourage or induce investment and market liberalization within their negotiating partners.[190] Moreover, in the view of certain developed countries, BITs can have the effect of liberalizing developing countries' whole economies by facilitating the entry of investment and creating conditions favouring their operation. In the process of reforming their economies to foster private enterprise, some developing countries have concluded that creating favourable conditions for foreign investment can be integral to their success.[191] Although the BITs themselves do not specifically enunciate the goal

---

[190] See generally Salacuse (n 92 above) 875–7.
[191] See eg Investment Treaty with Albania (US–Albania) (11 January 1995), S Treaty Doc No 104–19 (1995). In the message from the President of the United States transmitting the Treaty between the Government of the United States of America and the Government of the Republic of Albania Concerning the Encouragement and Reciprocal Protection of Investment with Annex and Protocol Signed at Washington on 11 January 1995, President Clinton stated: 'The bilateral

of investment and market liberalization, it is clear those goals are in the minds of developed country negotiators and are sometimes reflected in background documents.[192] This is also a stated goal of certain regional entities and organizations such as the European Union and ASEAN.[193]

It should be noted that investment promotion, a fundamental objective of developing countries, and investment and market liberalization, a subsidiary aim of developed countries, are separate and distinct goals. Within the context of BITs, for example, host country investment promotion means attracting investment projects that the host country determines are in *its* best interests. Investment liberalization, on the other hand, is a favourite term of capital-exporting countries that generally means creating a climate in which investors may undertake investments they judge to be in *their* interests. For example, a host country government might seek to promote investments in its electronics industry if it judged doing so would develop its economy in ways not yet present in the country. At the same time, that country may desire to impede investment in the retail industry if that industry is already served by politically powerful local entrepreneurs who fear foreign competition. In such a situation the developing country, through its treaty relationships and internal legislation, would be following a policy of investment promotion but not of investment liberalization.

(b) Relationship building

Some developing countries have also been led to sign BITs with developed capital-exporting countries to strengthen their relationship with those countries and obtain the benefits and favours, such as increased trade or foreign aid, that such strengthened relationships may yield. Thus, even though a developing country may not be certain of increased investment flows from its developed-country treaty partner after signing an investment treaty, it may well expect that the treaty will result in closer ties that will lead to increased trade, foreign aid, security assistance, technology transfers, or other benefits. For example, when a left-of-centre government came to power in Uruguay in 2005 after a previous government had signed but not yet ratified a BIT with the United States, the new government

---

investment treaty (BIT) with Albania will protect U.S. investment and assist the Republic of Albania in its efforts to develop its economy by creating conditions more favorable for U.S. private investment and thus strengthen the development of its private sector.'

[192] Investment protection and investment liberalization are also distinct concepts. Investment liberalization refers to facilitating the entry and operation of foreign investments in the host country. Investment protection refers to protecting the investment, once it has entered the country, from actions by governments and others that would interfere with investor property rights and the functioning of the investment in general. For example, in launching negotiations for a Multilateral Agreement on Investment in September 1995, the OECD mandate called for 'a broad multilateral framework for international investment with high standards of liberalisation of investment regimes and investment protection'. OECD, Multilateral Agreement on Investment: Launch of the Negotiations: 1995 CMIT/CIME Report and Mandate, available at <<http://www.oecd.org/daf/mai/intro.htm> accessed 6 October 2014.

[193] See eg the ASEAN Comprehensive Investment Agreement, Art 1(a) which states as a treaty objective 'the progressive liberalization of the investment regimes of member states'.

renegotiated but ultimately ratified the BIT. The Uruguayan government justified its action on the grounds that ratifying the BIT would protect and strengthen its important export markets in the United States. To the extent that investment treaty provisions are embedded in FTAs, such as those advanced by the United States and Japan, the prospect of improved trade relations as an inducement to agree to investment treaty provisions is quite explicit.

(c) Domestic investment encouragement

Related to the objective of economic liberalization is the goal of encouraging domestic entrepreneurs, who may be sceptical of their government's intentions towards private capital, to undertake productive investments. An investment treaty therefore serves as a 'signalling device' to the domestic private sector that the government's intentions towards private capital, both foreign and domestic, are benign in view of the international commitments it has made in the treaty to protect the capital of foreigners.

(d) Improved governance and a strengthened rule of law

Another secondary purpose for some developing countries in signing investment treaties is to remedy the deficiencies in their own governance institutions and enforcement of the rule of law. Investment treaties thus become international substitutes for domestic institutions.[194] The theory underlying this rationale is that developing country authorities and institutions that have prevented themselves from acting in an arbitrary and abusive fashion towards foreign investors by signing a treaty will also be led to avoid arbitrary and abusive actions towards their own nationals. Over time those authorities and institutions may demonstrate improved governance and a heightened respect for the rule of law. Thus, as the Minister of Finance of Uruguay privately explained to a journalist at the time his country ratified its BIT with the United States: 'We are not signing this treaty for *them* [ie the United States], we are signing it for *us*.'

4.6 Long-Term Goals of Investment Treaties

Lawyers, arbitrators, government officials, and corporate executives sometimes view investment treaties solely as being about foreign investment and foreign investors. That view may lead to distortions in understanding and interpreting investment treaty texts. Investment treaties are basically instruments of international relations, and the parties to them—sovereign states, not investors—undertake them in order to further certain long-term goals that may go well beyond the

---

[194] T Ginsburg, 'International Substitutes for Domestic Institutions: Bilateral Investment Treaties and Governance' (2005) 25 Int'l Rev L & Econ 107–23.

domain of investment. For investors, investment treaties are quite naturally about investments, but for a state that is a party to them they may be about 'economic cooperation', 'economic development', or 'mutual prosperity'. A careful reading of investment treaty preambles reveals these long-term objectives. For example, the Preamble to the BIT between France and Argentina[195] asserts the parties' purpose as '[d]esiring to intensify economic cooperation for the economic benefit of both countries' and the Preamble to an investment agreement between the Netherlands and the then Czechoslovakia[196] states the parties' aims as '[d]esiring to extend and intensify the economic relations between them' and to 'stimulate the flow of capital and technology and the economic development of the Contracting Parties'. It is important to place treaty texts within the context of their stated long-term objectives in order to interpret and understand their provisions fully. The importance of this is emphasized by Article 31(1) of the VCLT which requires that such context be taken into account in interpreting a treaty. The arbitral tribunal in the case of *Saluka Investments BV v The Czech Republic* adopted precisely this approach in interpreting the term 'fair and equitable treatment' to take into account the stated long-term objectives as expressed in the Preamble to the previously-quoted Netherlands–Czech and Slovak BIT:

This is a more subtle and balanced statement of the Treaty's aims than is sometimes appreciated. The protection of foreign investments is not the sole aim of the Treaty, but rather a necessary element alongside the overall aim of encouraging foreign investment and extending and intensifying the parties' economic relations. That in turn calls for a balanced approach to the interpretation of the Treaty's substantive provisions for the protection of investments, since an interpretation which exaggerates the protection to be accorded to foreign investments may serve to dissuade host States from admitting foreign investments and so undermine the overall aim of extending and intensifying the parties' mutual economic relations.[197]

4.7 The Treaty Negotiation Process

Investment treaties do not simply spring into being. They are usually the product of long and hard negotiation between the countries concerned. Those negotiations explain why textual differences occur among investment treaties. It is therefore worthwhile to consider briefly the processes by which investment treaties come into existence. In doing so, one must distinguish the negotiation of BITs from those treaties involving more than two countries.

---

[195] Accord entre le Gouvernement de la République Française et le Gouvernement de la République Argentine sur l'encouragement et la protection réciproques des investissements (Agreement between the Argentine Republic and the Republic of France for the Promotion and Reciprocal Protection of Investments) (signed 3 July 1991, entered into force 3 March 1993) 1728 UNTS 298.

[196] Agreement on Encouragement and Reciprocal Protection of Investments between the Kingdom of The Netherlands and the Czech and Slovak Federal Republic (signed 29 April 1991).

[197] *Saluka Investment BV v The Czech Republic*, UNCITRAL (Partial Award) (17 March 2006) ¶ 300.

(a) Bilateral negotiation processes

Having determined the need for treaty protection for their investors abroad, capital-exporting countries did not immediately proceed to negotiate BITs or FTAs with developing nations. They first devoted considerable time and effort to the preparation of what they called a 'model treaty', 'prototype treaty', or 'draft treaty', to serve as the basis for negotiations with individual developing countries. Preparing the draft treaty usually took significant time and involved intensive consultation with various organizations, including relevant government agencies and representatives from the private sector. For example, preparation of the US model treaty took nearly four years.[198] For capital-exporting states, which without exception have been the ones to initiate negotiations, model or prototype treaties have been the basic and essential elements in their attempts to conclude BITs or FTAs. Individual countries have published or otherwise made their prototype or model texts available to the public. For example, the latest model US BIT, the 2012 US Model Bilateral Investment Treaty, can be found at the website of the Office of the US Trade Representative,[199] and the 2004 Canadian prototype, known as a Foreign Investment and Promotion Agreement, may also be found online.[200] The texts of many of these models have evolved over time. Thus, the model used by the United States at the beginning of the twentieth-first century was not the same as the model that it developed to launch its BIT programme in the 1980s.

The model treaty serves several purposes. First, its preparation is an occasion for capital-exporting states to study the entire question of investment protection, to consult with interested governmental and private sector organizations, and to formulate a national position on the question. The government emerges from this process with a firm idea of the kind of treaty that would be acceptable to various domestic constituencies, knowledge that is essential if a negotiated treaty is to secure the approval and ratification of home country authorities. Second, since the capital-exporting countries wish to negotiate BITs or FTAs with many developing countries, the prototype is an efficient means of communicating to those countries concretely what type of treaty the capital-exporting state seeks. Third, to the extent possible, a capital-exporting state usually wants relative uniformity in its BITs and FTAs with developing countries. Starting all negotiations with the same draft treaty is a way to attain that goal. An additional motivation for the preparation of a prototype is that it gives the capital-exporting state a negotiating advantage, as the party which controls the draft usually controls the negotiation. By preparing a draft BIT or FTA that will become the basis of discussion, the capital-exporting country has, in effect, determined the agenda of the negotiation and has established the conceptual framework within which bargaining will take

---

[198] Vandevelde (n 23 above) 210.

[199] Available at <http://www.ustr.gov/sites/default/files/BIT%20text%20for%20ACIEP%20 Meeting.pdf> accessed 6 October 2014.

[200] Available at <http://ita.law.uvic.ca/documents/Canadian2004-FIPA-model-en.pdf> accessed 6 October 2014.

place. The developing country, at least at the outset, is often placed in a position of merely reacting to the draft.[201] After completing the preparation of the prototype, a capital-exporting state often informally makes contact with a developing country to determine its level of interest in concluding a BIT or FTA. When selecting countries to approach for an indication of interest, a developed country considers a variety of factors, including the state of friendly diplomatic relations between the two countries, the extent to which its nationals have already invested in the developing country, whether their nationals can be expected to invest in the host country in the future, and finally, the extent to which the potential host country's existing economic policies are conducive to foreign private investment.

If a developing country decides to enter into BIT or FTA negotiations with a capital-exporting state, it too must engage in a consultative process among various government agencies and representatives of its private sector to formulate a negotiating position. Often this consultative process is accomplished by creating a team of representatives to carry on the negotiations. Inevitably, the views of individual negotiating team members may differ on many questions with respect to the proposed BIT or FTA. For example, officials of the Central Bank normally oppose treaty obligations that increase demands on the country's foreign exchange reserves. Others with a different viewpoint, such as representatives of the government's investment promotion agency, stress the importance of securing new investment for the country and accordingly often urge quick acceptance of the proposed BIT or FTA with as few changes as possible.

A BIT or FTA purports to create a symmetrical legal relationship between the two states, in that it provides that either party may invest under the same conditions in the territory of the other. In reality, an asymmetry exists between the parties to many BITs and FTAs, since one state will often be the source and the other the recipient of most investment flows. This asymmetry affects the dynamics of the BIT negotiation. Recognizing that the BIT essentially defines the developing country's obligations towards investment from the developed country, the developing country tends to negotiate obligations that are more general than specific, vague rather than precise, and subject to exceptions rather than absolute requirements. On the other hand, capital-exporting countries seek guarantees of protection that are precise and all-encompassing. Thus, for example, a capital-exporting country will want the treaty in all cases to guarantee investors the right to transfer revenues and capital out of an investment. In contrast, a developing country will try to negotiate exceptions in appropriate situations, so that the transfer obligation will not apply, say, if the country is suffering from balance of payment difficulties. Generally, however, negotiations that result in an agreement do not depart significantly from the capital-exporting state's model.

---

[201] For a discussion of this negotiating problem, see J Salacuse, *The Global Negotiator* (Palgrave Macmillan, 2003) 39–42.

(b) Multilateral negotiation processes

The process for negotiating a multilateral investment treaty is usually more complex and lengthy than the process for negotiating a bilateral treaty. This complexity arises from the number of parties at the negotiating table, which usually takes the form of a diplomatic conference. The use of a multilateral forum means that the interests and resulting issues that have to be accommodated are more numerous than in a bilateral setting. Moreover, the existence of more than two parties in the negotiation enables the parties to form blocs and coalitions to increase their influence, a factor that further complicates and lengthens the multilateral process. Then too, a multilateral negotiation usually attracts significant public attention and may invite the intervention of NGOs and other elements of civil society, and they too may increase the difficulty of arriving at an agreement.[202]

These procedural obstacles, along with more substantive issues discussed in Chapter 1,[203] may explain why the nations of the world have yet to conclude a multilateral treaty on investment.

4.8 The Consequences of Investment Treaties

If an important goal of the investment treaty movement has been investment protection and promotion, and a secondary goal has been economic liberalization, one may well ask whether the approximately 3,300 investment treaties negotiated over the past six decades have achieved these goals. To what extent have investment treaties actually protected, liberalized, and promoted foreign investment? The answer to this question is important. The continued vitality of the investment treaty movement and the prospects for creating a global, multilateral legal structure for foreign investment similar to that which exists for international trade will be influenced by how the concerned countries view the benefits and costs of their existing investment treaties.

(a) Investment protection

It is difficult, if not impossible, to find a methodology that will measure the degree of protectiveness that investment treaties provide. One crude measure is the number of actual arbitration cases that have been brought against host countries. During the last three decades, one of the most significant developments in contemporary international investment law has been the growth of investor–state arbitration to settle investment disputes. According to the *World Investment Report 2014*, during

---

[202] For discussion of a multilateral treaty process that successfully resulted in the creation of the Energy Charter Treaty, see J Doré, 'Negotiating the Energy Charter Treaty' in Wälde (n 144 above) 137–53. For a description of the OECD's failed process to negotiate the Multilateral Investment Agreement, see C Devereaux, RZ Lawrence, and MD Watkins, *Studies in US Trade Negotiation* (Washington, DC: Institute for International Economics, 2006) 135–86.

[203] See Ch 1, section 1.6.

the period between 1987 and 2013 a total of 568 investor–state treaty arbitrations were brought, virtually all of which involved private investors as claimants and states as respondents.[204] In the realm of international investment, investor–state arbitration has become increasingly common, and arbitral awards interpreting and applying investment treaty provisions have become increasingly numerous. For international law firms, investor–state arbitration—once an arcane field of interest to only a few scholars and specialists—has become an established and lucrative area of practice.

The potential costs to a host country for violating their commitments under an investment treaty are great and would seem to serve as a significant deterrent against violating investment treaty commitments. For one thing, the amount of money at stake in investor–state disputes is large, sometimes reaching into hundreds of millions, even billions, of dollars. As a result, in most treaty-based investor–state disputes, a host country faces the risk of having to pay a substantial arbitration award that, in relation to the country's budget and financial resources, may prove onerous. Whereas the average award in an ordinary international commercial arbitration is less than a million dollars, an award in an investor–state arbitration is usually many times that.[205] In fact, significant arbitral awards have been rendered against several states.[206] Moreover, the costs of defending an investor–state arbitration can be burdensome, especially for a developing country. In addition to indirect costs, such as the time of government officials devoted to preparing and participating in the case, the direct costs usually consist of two elements: (1) the expenses of legal representation; and (2) a share of the costs of administering the arbitration. The precise amount of such costs will vary depending on the complexity of the case, the amount in dispute, and the extent of time needed to resolve it. In a highly complicated and lengthy case, the costs of legal representation in an arbitration proceeding can be extremely heavy. For example, in *CME v Czech Republic*, the Czech Republic reportedly spent US$10 million on its legal defence.[207] A more typical investor–state case is perhaps *International Thunderbird Gaming Corporation v United Mexican States*, a NAFTA case decided under UNCITRAL rules in January 2006. There, the total cost of the proceeding was US$3,170,692, including US$405,620 in arbitrators' fees, US$99,632 in various administrative expenses, US$1,502,065 in Mexico's legal representation costs, and US$1,163,375 in Thunderbird's costs of representation.[208]

---

[204] *World Investment Report 2014* (n 68 above) 124.

[205] N Rubins, 'The Allocation of Costs and Attorney's Fees in Investor–State Arbitration' (2003) 18 ICSID Rev—FILJ 109, 125 (observing that whereas 58% of commercial arbitration claims brought to the ICC in 1999 were for less than US$1 million, the average claim for ICSID cases in 1997 was US$10 million).

[206] eg arbitral tribunals rendered awards of US$353 million against the Czech Republic, US$71 million against Ecuador, US$824 million against Slovakia, and US$133.2 million against Argentina.

[207] International Institute for Sustainable Development, 'Czech Republic Hit with Massive Compensation Bill in Investment Treaty Dispute', *Investment Law and Policy Weekly News Bulletin*, 21 March 2003.

[208] *Int'l Thunderbird Gaming Corp v United Mexican States* (26 January 2006), NAFTA Ch 11 Arb Trib Arbitral Award 68, 72.

The statistics on investor–state arbitration may understate the protective quality of investment treaties. Faced with the potential costs of investor–state arbitration, host countries may well be led to settle disputes rather than litigate them. Many disputes between foreign investors and host countries are resolved through negotiation. Indeed, nearly all investment treaties provide that in the event of a dispute between an investor and the host country, the parties are to engage in consultations and negotiations, often for a specified period of time (six months in many cases), before the investor may seek other remedies. As a result, it is safe to say that virtually all such disputes go through a period of negotiation before reaching settlement or advancing to the stage of formal investor–state arbitration. Because of the confidentiality usually surrounding such settlements, accurate, comprehensive statistics on negotiated settlements of investor–state conflicts are not available. Still, one would suppose that over the last eighteen years such settlements have vastly outnumbered the estimated 568 investor–state arbitrations that have been lodged.

After reviewing the nature and scope of investment treaty provisions, the strength of related enforcement mechanisms, and the actual cases brought against host countries by aggrieved investors, one may conclude that investment treaties have achieved their goal of fostering investment protection. While that protection is not absolute (no legal device provides absolute protection), investors and investments covered by a treaty seem to enjoy a higher degree of protection from political risks than those which are not.

(b) Investment promotion

In the light of the many variables that influence investment decisions, it is probably impossible to pinpoint the precise effect of an investment treaty on an individual's decision to invest in a given country.[209] Local economic conditions and government policies are probably more important than investment treaties in influencing the investment decision. Indeed, industrialized countries probably sign investment treaties only with those developing countries whose policies and laws are sufficiently protective of, and favourable to, foreign investment.[210] Thus, the investment treaty is often a codification, and not a source, of pro-foreign investment policies. On the other hand, by entering into a treaty, an instrument of international law, a signatory country is raising those policies to the level of international law and thereby limiting its ability to change policies easily. Investment treaties therefore have the effect of stabilizing a county's investment policy and its legal and contractual commitments with individual foreign investors.[211]

Evidence demonstrating that investment treaties have promoted the flow of significant amounts of capital to developing countries is not entirely convincing and has been the subject of debate. Various studies have concluded that investment

---

[209] K Vandevelde, 'Investment Liberalization and Economic Development: The Role of Bilateral Investment Treaties' (1998) 36 Col J Transnat'l L 501, 524–25.
[210] ibid 523.   [211] ibid 522–55.

treaties do not in fact result in increased investment flows,[212] that only some encourage capital flows,[213] that they have a very limited impact on economic liberalization,[214] and that they may actually lead to reductions in governance quality.[215] On the other hand, one can also find evidence to the contrary.[216] Given the diversity of their political and economic situations, individual developing countries have no doubt become treaty signatories for one or more of the reasons cited earlier. Some countries have probably been more influenced by some goals than others. While scholars have imputed one reason or another to developing countries for participating in the investment treaty movement, they have usually done so without undertaking specific empirical research into the motives that drove a particular developing country to sign a particular treaty. Opponents of investment treaties have argued not only that developing countries have not attained the benefits they sought but also that the costs to developing countries have been too high. Those costs lie primarily in the restrictions on actions that governments feel compelled to take to protect and strengthen their countries' environmental, labour, and other standards to improve the lives of their populations. Governments that have taken actions negatively affecting investor interests have found themselves involved in growing numbers of expensive investor–state arbitrations.

More generally, the discussion about the costs and benefits of investment treaties seems to have overlooked an important question: What is the effect of investment treaties upon a country's cost of capital? Every country must pay a cost for the foreign capital it receives whether this is in the form of debt or equity. The cost that a country must pay for its capital from foreign sources is affected by many factors, one of the most significant of which is investors' perception of the country's political risk. The greater a country's political risk, the higher its cost of capital. If, by signing investment treaties, a country lowers its cost of capital, it may save significant amounts of money. Consequently, in determining whether investment treaties bring net benefits to a country those savings must be weighed against any resulting costs. Thus far, no empirical research has given a definitive answer to this question.

[212] See eg M Hallward-Driemeier, 'Do Bilateral Investment Treaties Attract DFI? Only a BIT...and They Could Bite', World Bank Working Paper No 3121 (June 2003).

[213] Salacuse and Sullivan (n 188 above) 67–130, concluding with regard to US BITs that there is a strong correlation between the existence of a US BIT with a developing county and increased capital flows to the developing country concerned but indicating that the evidence is much less strong with respect to BITs concluded with other OECD countries.

[214] Vandevelde (n 209 above).   [215] Ginsburg (n 194 above) 107–23.

[216] SE Graham, 'FDI in the World Economy', IMF Working Paper wp/95/59, Washington, DC (2005); E Graham and E Wada, 'Foreign Direct Investment in China: Effects on Growth and Economic Performance' in P Drysdale (ed), *Achieving High Growth: Experience of Transitional Economies in East Asia* (OUP, 2001); EJ Borensztein, 'How Does Foreign Direct Investment Affect Economic Growth?' (1998) 45 J Int'l Econ 115; R Lensink and O Morissey, 'Foreign Direct Investment: Flows, Volatility and Growth', Paper presented at the Development Economic Study Group Conference, University of Nottingham (April 2005) 5–7.

(c) Economic liberalization

The ideal of economic liberalism holds that the market, not governmental laws and regulations, should determine economic decisions.[217] Beginning in the post-World War II period, virtually all developing countries rejected the liberal economic model and relied on their governments to bring about national economic development.[218] As a result, their systems were characterized by: (1) state planning and public ordering of their economies and societies; (2) reliance on state enterprises as economic actors; (3) restriction and regulation of the private sector; and (4) governmental limitation and control of international economic transactions, especially foreign investment.[219] By the mid-1980s, this approach to development began to lose its hold on the minds and actions of policy-makers, aid agencies, and international financial institutions. Developing countries increasingly privatized their state enterprises, engaged in deregulation, and opened their economies.[220] In short, they embarked on a process of economic liberalization. As indicated earlier in this chapter, one of the goals of many countries in negotiating investment treaties, particularly the United States, was to encourage their economic liberalization.

An evaluation of the extent to which investment treaties have achieved the goal of market and investment liberalization depends on one's definition of liberalization. Two definitional approaches to liberalization present themselves. The first, which could be called the 'absolutist approach', seeks to determine how well the actual situation meets the liberal economic model; the second, which could be referred to as 'the relativist approach', aims primarily to determine the extent to which a country has moved away from the pre-existing command economy system towards the liberal model.

(i) An absolutist evaluation of liberalization

With respect to foreign investment, applying an absolutist approach to economic liberalization would mean that foreign investors would not be subject to legal or regulatory constraints whenever undertaking investments in the country concerned. In fact, probably no country, either in the developed or the developing world, has taken the absolutist position.[221] Further, investment treaties have not denied countries the right to control the entry of foreign investment.

---

[217] IBRD, 'World Development Report: The State in a Changing World' (1997).

[218] JW Salacuse, 'From Developing Countries to Emerging Markets: A New Role for Law in the Third World' (1999) 33 Int'l Lawyer 877–80.

[219] ibid 882–6.

[220] Even the US, which strongly supports the liberal economic model, restricts or limits the ability of foreigners to invest in certain areas, including commercial aviation, telecommunications, and maritime industries. Moreover, several states restrict the ability of foreigners to own real estate. RH Cummings, 'United States Regulation of Foreign Joint Ventures and Investment' in DN Goldsweig and RH Cummings (eds), *International Joint Ventures: A Practical Approach to Working with Foreign Investors in the U.S. and Abroad* (American Bar Association, 1990) 137, 139.

[221] See eg Agreement for the Promotion and Protection of Investments (India–UK) (14 March 1994), (1995) 34 ILM 935, 940 Art 3(1).

Many investment treaties make a distinction between the treatment to be accorded an investor in making an investment (pre-establishment) and the treatment to be given after the investment is made (post-establishment). With respect to the former, treaties generally contain a provision to the effect that 'each Contracting Party shall encourage and create favourable conditions for investors of the other Contracting party to make investments in its territory'.[222] Despite the inclusion of such provisions, no investment treaty requires a host country to admit any and all investments proposed by an investor from the other treaty country. Most countries have special laws governing the entry of foreign capital,[223] and investment treaties generally provide that host countries may admit investment in accordance with their own laws.[224] In effect, no treaty ever guarantees investors of a contracting state access to the markets of other contracting states.[225] A common provision is that a host country 'shall admit investments in conformity with its laws'.[226] Consequently, one must conclude that the investment treaty movement generally has not been effective in attaining the goal of absolute investment liberalization, if by that term one means completely opening a country to investment from a treaty partner.[227] This is unsurprising when one considers that no treaty has expressly adopted such an objective. Investment and market liberalization are better characterized as the hoped for consequences of a developed country when it enters a treaty. From an absolutist point of view, while the use of investment treaties 'affirm[s] liberal economic theory' and supports the adoption

[222] See generally JW Salacuse, 'Host Country Regulation and Promotion of Joint Ventures and Foreign Investment' in Goldsweig and Cummings (n 220 above) 107–36 (explaining how host countries regulate joint ventures and the effect of such regulation on their operation and formation) and JW Salacuse, 'Direct Foreign Investment and the Law in Developing Countries' (2000) 15 ICSID Rev—FILJ 382.

[223] See eg Agreement for the Promotion and Reciprocal Protection of Investments, (Hungary–UK) (9 March 1987), 1990 UKTS 44 (Cm 1103) Art 2.1; reprinted in (1989) 4 ICSID Rev—FILJ 159, 160 ('Each Contracting Party...subject to its right to exercise powers conferred by its laws, shall admit...capital [of the other contracting party]').

[224] Vandevelde (n 209 above) 511.

[225] See eg Investment Agreements in the Western Hemisphere: A Compendium (14 October 1999) ('The most representative clause reads as follows: Each Contracting Party shall promote, in its territory, investments of investors of the other Contracting Party and shall admit such investments in accordance with its laws and regulations'), available at <http://www.ftaa-alca.org/ngroups/ngin/publications/english99/compinv1.asp> accessed 2 April 2009.

[226] Professor Vandevelde has concluded:

> BITs are very limited tools for liberalization. Access provisions are subordinate to local law; nondiscrimination provisions apply only post establishment of investment and are subject to exceptions; security is afforded against certain types of state interference, but generally not against private interference; dispute provisions apply only to public, not private, disputes; and transparency provisions are rare.

Vandevelde (n 209 above) 514.

[227] K Vandevelde, 'The Political Economy of a Bilateral Investment Treaty' (1998) 92 AJIL 621, 633. According to Vandevelde, a liberal economic model of a BIT would do a better job reflecting 'investment neutrality' (ie state non-intervention in cross-border investment flows) and 'market facilitation' (enabling the state to correct market failures) (ibid 633–5). As they stand now, however, BITs are more about 'protecting the interests of home state investors and preserving the political prerogatives of the host state' than they are about improving economic efficiency (ibid 634).

of liberalizing policies, the treaties are not actually designed to create a liberal investment regime. In fact, investment treaties are driven more by motives of economic nationalism than they are economic liberalism.[228] Indeed, according to one observer, '[t]he interventionist measures permitted by the BITs are antithetical to economic liberalism'.[229]

(ii) A relativist evaluation of liberalization

Viewing the significant changes in many developing countries over the last twenty years as they have sought to transform themselves into emerging markets,[230] it is clear that their economies have experienced significant liberalization, even if they have not attained the liberal ideal. Their laws and regulations governing FDI, in particular, have been liberalized as a general phenomenon. For example, a study by the United Nations Conference on Trade and Development (UNCTAD) found that during the period between 1991 and 2002, '1551 (95%) out of 1641 changes introduced by 165 countries in their FDI laws were in the direction of greater liberalization'.[231] At this point, it is difficult to determine the precise role that investment treaties played in this liberalization process. A study seeking to correlate the timing and number of investment treaties signed by individual countries with the timing and number of their liberalizing reforms would shed some important light on this question. In general terms, it is interesting to note that during the period measured by the UNCTAD study, investment treaties, particularly BITs, experienced their most significant expansion in number and geographical coverage.[232]

The link between investment treaties and liberalization may be both direct and indirect. The direct link may be found in some treaty provisions that have a liberalizing effect. For example, in the negotiation of some BITs, capital-exporting states, with varying degrees of success, have sought to protect their nationals and companies from unfavourable discrimination by securing treatment that is no less favourable than the treatment given to investments made by host country nationals or nationals of a third country.

---

[228] ibid 634.

[229] JW Salacuse, 'From Developing Countries to Emerging Markets: A New Role for Law in the Third World' (1999) 33 Int'l Lawyer 875–90.

[230] UNCTAD, *Latest Developments in Investor–State Dispute Settlement* (2005) 20 UN Doc UNCTAD/WEB/ITE/IIT/2005/2, available at <http://www.unctad.org/en/docs//webiteiit20052_en.pdf> 20, accessed 17 Janaury 2015; see also IBRD, 'World Development Report 2005: A Better Investment Climate for Everyone' (2004) 111–12.

[231] UNCTAD, *Bilateral Investment Treaties in the Mid-1990s* (1998) 159–217.

[232] Egypt is an excellent example of this phenomenon. During the time of President Gamal Abdel Nasser, the country was virtually closed to foreign investment. After his death, the Sadat government took a first tentative step towards liberalization by seeking only Arab capital in 1971 and then foreign investment in 1974. Gradually, both policy and law evolved to the point where Egypt was encouraging all private investment, both foreign and domestic. JW Salacuse, 'Back to Contract: Implications of Peace and Openness for Egypt's Legal System' (1980) 28 Amer J Comp L 315. See also JW Salacuse, 'Foreign Investment and Legislative Exemptions in Egypt: Needed Stimulus or New Capitulations?' in L Michalak and JW Salacuse (eds), *Social Legislation in the Contemporary Middle East* (University of California Press, 1986) 241.

Investment treaties may also have an indirect positive effect on the liberalization of host country economies. Under certain circumstances, the introduction of foreign direct investment can contribute to that liberalization. The demonstrated economic success of particular foreign enterprises, the competitive pressures caused by their presence, a governmental desire to attract even more foreign direct investment, and the demands by national entrepreneurs to secure equal treatment to that given to foreigners all may create strong pressures for change in host country regulatory systems.[233] So, to the extent that investment treaties have encouraged foreign investment in developing countries, they have also contributed indirectly and modestly to economic liberalization.

Economic liberalization is a complex process that cannot be brought about by a magic bullet. It requires a host of sound policies, laws, and institutions across a wide domain of human activity. An investment treaty is just one policy instrument among many others that may facilitate the process.

(d) Conclusion

The nature and sources of international investment law have undergone a significant transformation in a relatively short time. The creation of an increasingly dense network of international investment treaties therefore represents a further step in the development of international economic law and the creation of a global regime for investment.

One important consequence of treatification is that it has increased the importance of international investment law in economic relations to a level that it never enjoyed before. Prior to treatification, international investment law was basically an arcane subject that interested only a few academic international lawyers. It had little practical effect. Today, it has become of immense practical concern to a much wider audience, including the practising bar, environmentalists, NGOs, multinational companies, and governments, both industrialized and developing, who sometimes question the consequences of what they have created over the last five decades. As a result, unlike the situation that prevailed in the mid-twentieth century, government officials, international executives, lawyers, and financiers must increasingly take investment treaties into account in planning, negotiating, undertaking, and managing international investment transactions.

---

[233] On the discussion about complexities of developing a liberal investment climate, see generally *World Development Report 2005: A Better Investment Climate for Everyone* (2004).

5

The General Structure of Investment Treaties

5.1 A Structural Overview

An investment treaty is an international agreement embodied in one or more written documents by which two or more states agree to certain legal rules to govern investments undertaken by nationals of one treaty party in the territory of another treaty party.[1] A treaty is an instrument of international law that binds the contracting states. Although the specific provisions of individual investment treaties are not uniform and some investment treaties restrict host country governmental action more than others, virtually all investment treaties address the same issues and follow a similar structure. Despite variations in language from treaty to treaty, the investment treaty movement discussed in Chapter 4 has resulted in a comprehensive understanding of what an investment treaty should contain, the development of common legal concepts and rules, and the creation of an agreed-upon legal framework for the protection of foreign investment. If the more than 3,300 individual investment treaties negotiated over the last six decades constitute a single, integrated global regime for investment, it is because of the strong commonality among them.

An investment treaty usually consists of a single document. However, the parties may use an exchange of letters or separate protocols to explain, modify, or elaborate on certain treaty provisions. For example, an investment treaty may provide that it applies to 'companies controlled by nationals of the other state Party', and a subsequent exchange of letters between the countries' foreign ministers or ambassadors may define in detail the meaning of 'control'.[2] Such documents are considered an integral part of the treaty and have the same binding effect as the treaty text. They are often published as an annex to the treaty in the contracting states' official publications.

---

[1] The Vienna Convention on the Law of Treaties, Art 1(1)(a) states: '"treaty" means an international agreement concluded between States in written form and governed by international law, whether embodied in a single instrument or in two or more related instruments and whatever its particular designation'. Vienna Convention on the Law of Treaties (23 May 1969) 1155 UNTS 331 (VCLT).

[2] See eg the letters annexed to the Agreement between the Government of the French Republic and the Government of the Republic of Argentina on the Reciprocal Encouragement and Protection of Investment (3 July 1991).

The basic structure of most modern investment treaties encompasses ten topics:

1. Treaty Title and Statement of Purpose
2. Definitions and Scope of Application
3. Conditions for the Entry of Foreign Investment and Investors
4. General Standards of Treatment of Foreign Investments and Investors
5. Monetary Transfers
6. Expropriation and Dispossession
7. Operational and Other Conditions
8. Losses from Armed Conflict or Internal Disorder
9. Treaty Exceptions, Modifications, and Terminations
10. Dispute Settlement

This chapter briefly examines the content of these topics in order to provide a general understanding of investment treaty structure. Subsequent chapters will discuss treaty provisions on each topic in depth and, to the extent possible, consider how courts, arbitration tribunals, and governments have interpreted and applied them.

5.2 Treaty Title and Statement of Purpose

All investment treaties have a title and preamble. The title usually states the general aim of the treaty and, if it is a bilateral agreement, identifies the parties to it, for example 'Agreement between the Government of the United Kingdom of Great Britain and Northern Ireland and the Government of the Republic of Albania for the Promotion and Protection of Investments'.[3] The title of a multilateral investment treaty usually states its nature but not the names of the parties to it, for example 'The Energy Charter Treaty'.[4] As noted previously, the precise designation or title given to a treaty does not affect its status as a binding international agreement.

Directly after the title, an investment treaty normally contains a preamble in which the parties state the aims and purposes of the treaty. While neither the title nor the preamble impose legal obligations, they may be relevant to the interpretation of a treaty's substantive provisions. Article 31(1) of the Vienna Convention on the Law of Treaties (VCLT)[5] provides that '[a] treaty shall be interpreted in good faith in accordance with the ordinary meaning to be given to the terms of the treaty in their context and in light of *its object and purpose*' (emphasis added).

---

[3] Agreement between the Government of the United Kingdom of Great Britain and Northern Ireland and the Government of the Republic of Albania for the Promotion and Protection of Investments (30 March 1994).

[4] The Energy Charter Treaty (17 December 1994), (1995) 34 ILM 360 (ECT).

[5] VCLT (n 1 above).

Accordingly, an important source for determining a treaty's objects and purposes is its title and preamble.[6]

5.3 Scope of Application of Investment Treaties

The key elements in any investment treaty are its provisions defining the treaty's terms and its scope of application, that is, the persons, organizations, and investments that may benefit from the treaty. Persons, organizations, or investments that fall outside a treaty's terms or scope of application are not entitled to the benefit of its provisions. Thus, if a particular enterprise in a host country lies within the definition of 'investment' in an investment treaty, that enterprise may take advantage of the treaty's privileges and benefits, as well as its enforcement mechanism. If not, then it may not take advantage of the treaty.

Definitions of treaty terms and rules on scope of application are generally found at the beginning of the treaty in sections defining 'investors', 'companies', 'nationals', 'investments', and 'territory'.[7] As a result of entering into an investment treaty, a contracting state owes obligations only to the investors of contracting states who make investments in its territory. Conversely, a contracting state has no obligation to persons or investments that do not come within the definitions of these terms as defined in the treaty document.

In defining the nature of covered investments, most investment treaties take four basic considerations into account: (1) the form of the investment; (2) the area of the investment's economic activity; (3) the time when the investment is made; and (4) the investor's connection with the other contracting state.

---

[6] In the ICSID case of *LG&E Energy*, for example, the tribunal in considering the context within which Argentina and the US included the fair and equitable treatment standard, and its object and purpose, observed in ¶ 124:

> in the Preamble of the Treaty that the two countries agreed that 'fair and equitable treatment of investment is desirable in order to maintain a stable framework for investment and maximum effective use of economic resources.' In entering the Bilateral Treaty as a whole, the parties desired to 'promote greater economic cooperation' and 'stimulate the flow of private capital and the economic development of the parties.' In light of these stated objectives, this Tribunal must conclude that stability of the legal and business framework is an essential element of fair and equitable treatment in this case, provided that they do not pose any danger for the existence of the host State itself'.

LG&E Energy Corp v Argentine Republic, ICSID Case No ARB/02/1 (Decision on Liability) (3 October 2006).

[7] See eg Agreement between Japan and the Socialist Republic of Vietnam for the Liberalization, Promotion and Protection of Investment (14 November 2003), Art 1 (defining 'investor', 'investments', and 'Area'); Treaty between the Czech and Slovak Federal Republic and the United States of America Concerning the Reciprocal Encouragement and Protection of Investment (22 October 1991), Art 1(a)–(b) (defining 'investment' and 'company of a Party'); and the Treaty between the United States of America and the Republic of Turkey Concerning the Reciprocal Encouragement and Protection of Investments (3 December 1985), Art 1(a), (c), (e) (defining 'company', 'Investment', and 'national').

Chapter 7 will explore these terms in considerable detail. Most investment treaties define the concept of investment broadly so as to include various investment forms: tangible and intangible assets, property, and rights. This approach gives the term 'investment' a broad, non-exclusive definition and recognizes that investment forms are constantly evolving in response to the creativity of investors and the rapidly changing world of international finance. The effect is to provide a potentially expanding umbrella of protection to investors and investments.

Another issue faced in investment treaty negotiation is whether investments made prior to the treaty will benefit from its provisions. Developing countries have sometimes sought to limit a treaty's application to future investment only or at least to those investments made in the relatively recent past.[8] Viewing the treaty primarily as an investment promotion mechanism, they claim to see little purpose in granting additional protections to investments already made in the host country. Moreover, they argue that their governments might not have approved such investments if they had realized an investment treaty would later expand the investor's rights and privileges.[9] Capital-exporting states, on the other hand, have generally sought to protect all investments made by their nationals and companies, regardless of when they were made.

Most investment treaties also seek to provide continued protection to investors even after a host country has terminated or withdrawn from the treaty.[10] These continuing effects provisions protect investors who have made investments based on the expectation of treaty protection. The usual period of continued protection is between fifteen and twenty years.

Defining which investors can benefit from the treaty is an important issue, since the goal of the contracting state is to secure benefits for its own nationals, companies, and investors, rather than those of other countries. The problem is essentially one of determining what links need to exist between an investor and a party to a treaty for the investor to benefit from the treaty's provisions. In the case of physical persons, the task is not difficult, since virtually all investment treaties rely on a status that is generally easily determined, such as nationality or citizenship. For investors that are companies or other legal entities, the problem of determining an appropriate link with a contracting state becomes more

---

[8] See eg Agreement between the Government of the United Kingdom of Great Britain and Northern Ireland and the Government of the Republic of Indonesia for the Promotion and Protection of Investments (27 April 1976), Art 2(3) ('The rights and obligations of both Contracting Parties with respect to investments made before 10 January 1967 shall be in no way affected by the provisions of this Agreement').

[9] UNCTAD, *Bilateral Investment Treaties in the Mid-1990s* (1998) 42. See also, UNCTAD, *Bilateral Investment Treaties 1995–2006: Trends in Investment Rulemaking* (2007), available at <http://unctad.org/en/docs/iteiia20065_en.pdf> accessed 12 January 2015.

[10] See eg Agreement between Japan and the People's Republic of Bangladesh Concerning the Promotion and Protection of Investment (10 November 1998), Art 14.3 ('In respect of investments and returns acquired prior to the date of termination of the present Agreement, the provisions of Articles 1 to 13 shall continue to be effective for a further period of fifteen years from the date of termination of the present Agreement').

complex. Such legal forms may be created and owned by persons who have no real connection with the countries that are parties to the treaty. In particular, three types of cases raise problems in this respect: (1) companies organized in a treaty country by nationals of a non-treaty country; (2) companies organized in a non-treaty country by nationals of a treaty country; and (3) companies in which nationals of a non-treaty country hold a substantial interest. For a company to be covered by the treaty, most bilateral investment treaties (BITs) require that a treaty partner at least be one of the following: (1) the country of the company's incorporation;[11] (2) the country of the company's seat, registered office, or principal place of business;[12] or (3) the country whose nationals have control over, or a substantial interest in, the company making the investment.[13] Sometimes these requirements are combined so that an investing company must satisfy two or more to qualify for coverage under a particular investment treaty.[14]

---

[11] See eg Treaty between the United States of America and the Democratic Socialist Republic of Sri Lanka Concerning the Encouragement and Reciprocal Protection of Investment (20 September 1991), Art 1(b) ('"company" of a Party means any kind of corporation, company, association, partnership or other organization, legally constituted under the laws and regulations of a Party or a political subdivision thereof'). BITs concluded by Denmark, the Netherlands, the UK, and the US are frequently of this type. See UNCTAD (1998) (n 9 above) 38–40.

[12] See eg Treaty between the Federal Republic of Germany and the Kingdom of Swaziland Concerning the Encouragement and Reciprocal Protection of Investments (5 April 1990), Art 1(4)(a):

> The term 'companies' means...in respect of the Federal Republic of Germany: any juridical person as well as any commercial or other company or association with or without legal personality having its seat in the German area of application of this Treaty, irrespective of whether or not its activities are directed at profit.

BITs concluded by Belgium, Germany, and Sweden are frequently of this type. UNCTAD (1998) (n 9 above) 40.

[13] See eg Agreement on Encouragement and Reciprocal Protection of Investments between the Government of the Kingdom of the Netherlands and the Government of the Republic of Lithuania (26 January 1994), Art 1(b)(iii):

> The term 'investor' shall comprise with regard to either contracting party:...(iii) legal persons not constituted under the law of that Contracting Party but controlled, directly or indirectly, by natural persons as defined in (i) [of the Contracting Party's nationality] or by legal persons as defined in (ii) [legal persons constituted under the law of the Contracting Party] above, who invest in the territory of either Contracting Party.

'Ownership or control', as these provisions are called, is used in BITs concluded by the Netherlands, Sweden, and Switzerland. UNCTAD (1998) (n 9 above) 39.

[14] In addition, some treaties include a separate provision allowing states to deny the benefits of the treaty to an investor that is owned by or controlled from a third party state. For example, the China–Japan–Korea Trilateral Investment Agreement states:

> A Contracting Party may deny the benefits of this Agreement to an investor of another Contracting Party that is an enterprise of the latter Contracting Party and to its investments if the enterprise is owned or controlled by an investor of a non-Contracting Party or of the denying Contracting Party, and the enterprise has no substantial business activities in the territory of the latter Contracting Party.

Agreement among the Government of Japan, the Government of the Republic of Korea and the Government of the People's Republic of China for the Promotion, Facilitation and Protection of Investment (13 May 2012), Art 22(2).

5.4 Conditions for the Entry
of Foreign Investment and Investors

Virtually all investment treaties deal with the entry or establishment of investments emanating from treaty partners. A few treaties, like the Treaty on the Functioning of the European Union,[15] grant investors from other contracting states the right of establishment in those states. Most investment treaties, however, allow each member state some control over the extent of investments in their territories by investors from treaty partners. Related to the issue of the entry or establishment of investment is the ability of the host country to impose conditions on that entry. One type of condition that host countries often impose on the making and operation of foreign investments is a 'performance requirement' or 'trade-related investment measure' (TRIM). Such conditions may require an investment project, as a condition of entry, to export a certain proportion of its production, restrict its imports to a certain level, or purchase a minimum quantity of local goods and services. The World Trade Organization (WTO) has sought to curtail this practice through its Agreement on Trade Related Investment Measures. Although most investment treaties have not dealt with the question of performance requirements,[16] the United States, with some success, has sought to protect its investors from them through its BIT negotiations,[17] as well as through the North American Free Trade Agreement.

5.5 General Standards of Treatment
of Foreign Investments and Investors

The totality of obligations that a host country owes a foreign investor or investment is generally referred to as the *treatment* owed to the investor or the investment. The word 'treatment' has thus become a term of art in investment treaties and investor–state arbitration. Investment treaties stipulate the standard of treatment a host country must accord to a foreign investment in two respects. They define certain *general* standards of treatment and also state *specific* standards for

[15] Consolidated Version of the Treaty on the Functioning of the European Union, May 9, 2008, [2008] OJ C115/47, Art 49.

[16] SH Nikièma, *Performance Requirements in Investment Treatieis* (IISD November 2014) 7, available at <https://www.iisd.org/sites/default/files/publications/best-practices-performance-requirements-investment-treaties-en.pdf> accessed 24 March 2015. However, see the 2009 ASEAN Comprehensive Investment Agreement, Art 7, entitled 'Prohibition of Performance Requirements', which expressly incorporates the WTO Agreement on TRIMS into the ASEAN Agreement. 2009 ASEAN Comprehensive Investment Agreement, signed by the Economic Ministers at the 14th ASEAN Summit in Cha-am, Thailand, on 26 February 2009, available at <http://www.asean.org/images/2012/Economic/AIA/Agreement/ASEAN%20Comprehensive%20Investment%20Agreement%20(ACIA)%202012.pdf> accessed 17 October 2014.

[17] See eg Treaty between the Government of the United States of America and the Government of the Republic of Albania Concerning the Encouragement and Reciprocal Protection of Investment (11 January 1995), Art VI (prohibiting four specified types of performance requirements).

particular matters such as monetary transfers, the seizure of investment property, the employment of foreign personnel, and the resolution of disputes with the host government. In addition, some general standards, such as guarantees of full protection and security or fair and equitable treatment, are absolute in nature. Others, such as national treatment or most-favoured-nation treatment, are considered contingent or relative because their application depends on the treatment accorded by the state to other investors.

One may identify six general standards of treatment: (a) fair and equitable treatment; (b) full protection and security; (c) protection from unreasonable or discriminatory measures; (d) treatment no less than that accorded by international law; (e) the requirement to respect obligations made to investors and investments; and (f) national and/or most-favoured-nation treatment. An individual investment treaty may provide for some or all of these treatment standards. Each treatment standard is considered briefly later but will be explored in greater depth in subsequent chapters.

(a) Fair and equitable treatment

One of the most common standards of treatment found in investment treaties is an obligation that the host country accord foreign investment 'fair and equitable treatment'.[18] A common statement in international law, the phrase has been the subject of much commentary and state practice.[19] Nonetheless, its precise meaning in specific situations has been open to varying interpretations. A vague and ambiguous expression on its face, the term 'fair and equitable' is not defined in investment treaties even though virtually all such treaties include it as a mandatory standard of treatment. It has been interpreted in a large number of arbitral awards and has been extensively analysed by scholars. Indeed, it is invoked so often in contemporary investor–state arbitration that one observer has labelled it 'an almost ubiquitous presence' in investment litigation.[20]

(b) Full protection and security

Another general standard of treatment found in most investment treaties is the obligation of the host country to accord 'full protection and security' or 'constant protection and security' to investments made by nationals and companies of its treaty partners. Here too, the precise meaning of the term may be open to widely varying interpretations in different situations. Consequently, courts, including the International Court of Justice, and arbitration tribunals have struggled to

---

[18] MI Khalil, 'Treatment of Foreign Investment in Bilateral Investment Treaties' (1992) 7 ICSID Rev—FILJ 339, 351.

[19] UNCTC, *Bilateral Investment Treaties* (1998) 41–5.

[20] R Dolzer, 'Fair and Equitable Treatment: A Key Standard in Investment Treaties' (2005) 39 Int'l Lawyer 87.

determine the proper scope of its protection. Cases interpreting this treaty standard have held that it does not make the host country responsible for all injuries that befall the investment.[21] Thus, although the host country is not a guarantor, it is liable when it fails to show due diligence in protecting the investor from harm. One definition of due diligence that was cited favourably by an ICSID arbitral tribunal is 'reasonable measures of prevention which a well-administered government could be expected to exercise under similar circumstances'.[22] Consequently, the failure by a host government to take reasonable measures to protect the investment against threats, such as attacks by brigands or violence by police and security officers, renders that government liable to compensate an investor for resulting injuries.

(c) Unreasonable or discriminatory measures

Many investment treaties provide protection promising that 'no Contracting Party shall in any way impair by unreasonable or discriminatory measures the management, maintenance, use, enjoyment or disposal' of an investment.[23] The specific application of this provision to the individual case depends on the facts involved; however, it is worth noting that the term 'unreasonable' may give host countries significant grounds to defend actions taken against foreign investors.

(d) International law

Many investment treaties provide that in no case should foreign investments be given less favourable treatment than that required by international law. Thus, this provision constitutes the minimum international standard of treatment discussed in Chapter 3. The application of this principle in individual cases is subject to a variety of interpretations, particularly on issues where there is significant dispute among developing countries. One example is the efforts made by developing countries to secure a New International Economic Order (NIEO), discussed in Chapter 4. A further question is whether the reference to 'international law' is

---

[21] cf *Asian Agricultural Products Ltd v Sri Lanka*, ICSID Case No ARB/87/3 (Final Award) (27 June 1990) ¶¶ 49–50 (interpreting the words 'full protection and security' in the UK–Sri Lanka BIT as not creating a 'strict liability' standard) and *Elettronica Sicula SpA (US v Italy)* [1989] ICJ Rep 15 (20 July) (interpreting the words 'constant protection and security' in the US–Italy Treaty of Friendship, Commerce and Navigation).

[22] *Asian Agricultural Products Ltd v Sri Lanka*, ICSID Case No ARB/87/3 (Final Award) (27 June 1990) ¶ 77 (citing AV Freeman, *Responsibility of States for Unlawful Acts of Their Armed Forces* (Martinus Nijhoff, 1957) 15–16).

[23] See eg Treaty between the United States of America and the Republic of Turkey Concerning the Reciprocal Encouragement and Protection of Investments (3 December 1985), Art 2(3) ('Neither Party shall in any way impair by arbitrary or discriminatory measures the management, operation, maintenance, use, enjoyment, acquisition, expansion, or disposal of investments').

limited only to customary international law or if it includes treaty provisions and general principles on investments.

(e) State obligations

To the extent that a contracting party has entered into obligations with an investor or investment, many investment treaties require a signatory state to respect those obligations. Such provisions are commonly known as 'umbrella clauses' and are discussed in Chapter 11. These provisions seek to counter the claim advanced by developing countries during the era of the NIEO that host countries should be able unilaterally to revise contracts that they have made with foreign investors. It may also mean that, as a result of such a provision in an investment treaty, the state has an obligation under international law to respect contracts between foreign investors and host governments that are otherwise normally subject only to host country law.[24]

(f) National and/or most-favoured-nation treatment

In addition to these general standards, many investment treaties contain relative standards, particularly with respect to non-discrimination in relation to both foreign and national investors. They thus provide for *national treatment*, which requires that a host country treat an investor, or an investment, no less favourably than it treats its own national investors or investments made by its own nationals. Treaties may also provide for *most-favoured-nation treatment*, which means that a host country may not treat an investor or investment from an investment treaty party less favourably than investors or investments from any other country. National treatment allows protected foreign investors to take advantage of any benefits that a host country grants to its own nationals. Some developing countries, recognizing the disparity in financial and technological resources between their national enterprises and those of foreign companies, have resisted or sought to limit the scope of the national treatment guarantee in investment treaties. In particular, they have tried to avoid giving foreign investors benefits and subsidies designed to strengthen national industries.[25]

Most-favoured-nation treatment, on the other hand, has the effect of granting to protected foreign investors any benefit or advantage granted by the host country to investors from any third country. It thus enables such investors to take advantage of the higher standards of investor protection that may be contained in other investment treaties to which the host country is a party.

Certain investment treaties, like those negotiated by the United States, combine both of these standards and require host countries to grant investors national treatment or most-favoured-nation treatment, *whichever is more favourable.*

---

[24] UNCTAD (1998) (n 9 above) 56–7.   [25] ibid 64–5.

5.6 Monetary Transfers

For any foreign investment project, the ability to repatriate income and capital, to pay foreign obligations in another currency, and to purchase raw materials and spare parts from abroad is crucial to a project's success. For this reason, in investment treaty negotiations, capital-exporting states have pressed for unrestricted freedom for their investors to undertake these monetary operations. Such operations are collectively referred to as 'transfers'.[26] Like the word 'treatment', 'transfer' has also become a term of art in investment treaties and basically means 'monetary transfers'. The monetary transfer provisions of most investment treaties deal with five basic issues: (1) the general nature of the investor's rights to make monetary transfers; (2) the types of payments that are covered by the right to make transfers; (3) the currency with which the payment may be made; (4) the applicable exchange rate; and (5) the time within which the host country must allow the investor to make transfers. Chapter 10 discusses these issues in detail.

Developing countries facing chronic balance-of-payments difficulties and needing to conserve foreign exchange to pay for essential goods and services are often unable or unwilling to grant foreign investors an unrestricted right to make such monetary transfers. Moreover, many developing countries have exchange-control laws to regulate the conversion and transfer of currency abroad.[27] As a result of this fundamental conflict in goals, negotiations of treaty provisions on monetary transfers are sometimes difficult to conclude. Capital-exporting countries seek broad, unrestricted guarantees on monetary transfers while developing countries press for limited guarantees subject to a variety of exceptions.

5.7 Expropriation and Dispossession

One of the primary functions of any investment treaty is to protect foreign investments against nationalization, expropriation, and other forms of interference with property rights by host country governmental authorities. Despite opposition by some developing nations in multilateral forums, virtually all investment treaties adopt some variation of the traditional western view of international law that a state may not expropriate an alien's property except: (1) for a public purpose; (2) in a non-discriminatory manner; (3) upon payment of just compensation; and, in most instances, (4) with provision for some form of judicial review. As will be seen in Chapter 12, the various elements of the traditional rule have taken different formulations in different treaties, some more and some less protective of investor interests. Perhaps the greatest variations in treaty provisions and the most difficult negotiations arise with respect to standards of compensation. Nonetheless many,

---

[26] Khalil (n 18 above) 360.
[27] JW Salacuse, *The Three Laws of International Investment: National, Contractual, and International Frameworks for Foreign Capital* (OUP, 2013) 75–88.

if not most, investment treaties have adopted the traditional rule or its equivalent, often expressed in the so-called 'Hull Formula',[28] that compensation must be 'prompt, adequate, and effective'.[29] They then proceed to define the meaning of each of these words in the particular circumstances.[30]

5.8 Operational and Other Conditions

Investment treaties sometimes provide treatment standards with respect to certain operational conditions, such as the investor's right to enter the country, employ foreign nationals, and be free of performance requirements. One of the most important conditions, of course, is the ability of the investor's employees to enter the host country freely and manage and operate the investment. Most investment treaties do not grant the investor an automatic right to enter and stay in a host country. German BITs, for example, provide that each contracting party will give 'sympathetic consideration' to applications for entry.[31] Similarly, US BITs give 'nationals' of contracting parties the right to enter for purposes of establishing or operating investments subject to the laws of the host state.[32]

5.9 Losses from Armed Conflict or Internal Disorder

Many investment treaties also deal with investment losses due to armed conflict or internal disorder within the host country. They do not, however, normally establish an absolute right to compensation in such cases. Instead, treaties promise that foreign investors will be treated in the same manner as nationals of the host country with respect to compensation.[33] Some also provide for most-favoured-nation treatment on this question. The ICSID case of *Asian Agricultural Products Ltd v Sri Lanka*[34] is one of the few cases that has considered this provision in detail with regard to a dispute between an injured investor and a host country government. The tribunal concluded that in addition to any specific compensatory

---

[28] GH Hackworth, *Digest of International Law* (Government Printing Office, 1942) 655–64.

[29] See eg UNCTAD (1998) (n 9 above) 69.

[30] See eg Agreement between the Government of Costa Rica and the United Kingdom of Great Britain and Northern Ireland on the Promotion and Reciprocal Protection of Investments (7 September 1982), Art 5.

[31] Treaty between the Kingdom of Thailand and the Federal Republic of Germany concerning the Encouragement and Reciprocal Protection of Investments (24 June 2002), Art 2(5).

[32] See eg Treaty between the United States of America and the Democratic Socialist Republic of Sri Lanka Concerning the Encouragement and Reciprocal Protection of Investment (20 September 1991), Art 2(3).

[33] See eg Agreement between the Government of the United Kingdom of Great Britain and Northern Ireland and the Government of Ukraine for the Promotion and Reciprocal Protection of Investments (10 February 1993), Art 5.

[34] *Asian Agricultural Products Ltd v Sri Lanka*, ICSID Case No ARB/87/3 (Final Award) (27 June 1990).

actions taken for the benefit of other investors the treaty provision in question would make any promised higher standard available to an injured investor. Such a different standard could come, for example, from another BIT granted to investors from other countries.[35]

5.10 Treaty Exceptions, Modifications, and Terminations

Because of the great diversity of national policies and situations, it is natural that in negotiating investment treaties individual states seek to introduce exceptions to their investment treaties' obligations in order to take into account national policies and situations. Thus, most investment treaties have provisions that carve out exceptions to the general standards of treatment that they seek to apply to investments between the two countries. Investors considering a particular investment should understand the scope and force of such treaty exceptions.

No treaty is ever permanent and unchanging. Thus, most international agreements, including investment treaties, contain provisions describing the process for terminating a treaty and in a few instances for modifying treaty provisions.

5.11 Dispute Settlement

The issues discussed earlier form the basic architecture of most investment treaties. In theory at least, the scope of protection seems broad in that these issues govern most, if not all, of the foreign investor's principal areas of concern regarding the political risks associated with a foreign investment. A fundamental, practical question, of course, is whether countries actually respect their treaty commitments and, if not, whether an injured investor has effective legal redress against a host country's treaty violations. For foreign investors and their governments, one of the great deficiencies of customary international law has been its lack of effective and binding mechanisms to resolve investment disputes. One aim of the investment treaty movement has been to remedy this situation.

Most investment treaties, as will be seen in Chapter 15, provide for two distinct dispute settlement mechanisms: one for disputes between the two contracting states and another for disputes between a host country and an aggrieved foreign investor. With respect to the former, contemporary investment treaties usually stipulate that in the event of a dispute over the interpretation or application of the treaty, the states concerned will first seek to resolve their differences through negotiation and then, if that fails, through ad hoc arbitration.

With respect to the latter, the trend among more recent investment treaties is to provide a separate international arbitration procedure, often under the auspices of ICSID, for disputes between aggrieved foreign investors and host country

---

[35] Ibid ¶ 43.

governments. By agreeing to an investment treaty, a state often simultaneously gives the consent needed to establish the jurisdiction of ICSID or another arbitral forum for any future dispute between one contracting state and a national of another contracting state. Although the investor must first try to resolve the conflict through negotiation and may also have to exhaust remedies available locally, the investor ultimately has the power to invoke compulsory arbitration in order to secure a binding award.[36]

Granting a private party the right to bring an action against a sovereign state in an international tribunal regarding an investment dispute is a revolutionary innovation that now seems largely taken for granted. Yet its uniqueness and power should not be overlooked. The field of international trade law, for example, contains no similar procedure. Violations of trade law, even though they strike at the economic interests of private parties, are resolved directly and solely by states. The WTO does not give a remedy to private persons injured by trade law violations.[37] It should also be noted that modern investment treaties grant aggrieved investors the right to prosecute their claims independently, without regard to the concerns and interests of their home country governments. It is this mechanism that gives important, practical significance to an investment treaty, and which truly enables investment treaties to afford protection to foreign investment. As a result of this treaty mechanism, foreign investors are bringing increasing numbers of arbitration claims when they believe host countries have denied them protection under a treaty.

The ultimate aim of aggrieved investors who bring claims against states for treaty violations is not just a scholarly adjudication of their rights but compensation for the injuries they have sustained. In general, as will be seen in Chapter 16, investment treaties are much less specific on the complicated subjects of the consequences of and the compensation for treaty violations than they are on the processes of dispute settlement. Nonetheless, relying on customary international law, arbitral tribunals have rendered substantial monetary awards in favour of injured investors and against host countries for treaty violations, and it appears that host countries have generally paid them. One effect of such awards is to cause host countries to take their treaty responsibilities seriously. Investment treaty provisions, their enforcement mechanisms, and the fact that arbitral tribunals hold host countries accountable, each exert an external discipline upon governments' behaviour in their relations with foreign investors. Together, this results in a relatively effective system of foreign investment protection. It is also to be noted that decisions of arbitral tribunals, although unfortunately not always made public, tend to be lengthy, reasoned, and scholarly decisions that form part of the jurisprudence of this emerging international investment law and also solidify and give force to investment treaty provisions.

[36] See eg Agreement between Japan and the Socialist Republic of Vietnam for the Liberalization, Promotion and Protection of Investment (14 November 2003), Art 13.

[37] See eg GT Schleyer, 'Power to the People: Allowing Private Parties to Raise Claims before the WTO Dispute Resolution System' (1997) 65 Ford Int'l L Rev 2275, 2277.

5.12 Conclusion

Although the more than 3,300 investment treaties concluded since the mid-twentieth century tend to cover the same issues, they differ in how they treat those issues. Some are more protective than others. For example, the BITs negotiated by the United States generally exhibit higher standards of protection than the BITs of many other countries.[38] Nonetheless, despite divergence among individual treaties, as a group investment treaties demonstrate many commonalities, including their coverage of similar issues and their use of equivalent or comparable legal concepts and vocabulary. It is these commonalities, despite individual differences, that are contributing to the creation of a global regime for international investment.

---

[38] P Juillard, 'L'Evolution des sources du droit des investissements' (1994) 250 *Recueil des Cours* 74, 211 (asserting that the level of protection achieved by US BITs is superior to the level of protection achieved by European BITs).

6

The Interpretation of Investment Treaties

6.1 The Task of Interpretation

Investment treaties take a written form and usually, though not always, consist of a single instrument.[1] For investment treaties to become a reality, however, and actually influence the behaviour of governments and investors, they must be interpreted and applied by government officials, lawyers, corporate executives, and arbitrators.[2] Government officials interpret them in order to decide whether actions and policies affecting investors meet treaty commitments. Corporate executives and their counsel interpret them in planning investment projects and in negotiating with host governments about past and future treatment. And arbitrators interpret them to settle disputes between investors and states.

Treaty interpretation is never easy, but the task of interpreting investment treaties is rendered particularly difficult by two factors: first, the generality and vagueness of many of the terms used in their texts, such as 'fair and equitable treatment', 'full protection and security', and 'expropriation and measures tantamount to expropriation', which are rarely defined in the treaty text itself and which reasonable persons may interpret differently. The second difficulty is the factual and legal complexity of the investment transactions and relationships to which investment treaties are applied. As a result of these complexities, arbitral tribunals and lawyers must devote significant effort and time to give meaning to words that at first glance appear simple but usually are not. Further, these definitions must be painstakingly applied to determine whether actions taken by governments in their complex dealings with investors over lengthy periods of time comply with or violate treaty standards.

The purpose of this chapter is to examine some of the issues that arise in the interpretation of investment treaties and to provide guidance on treaty interpretation.

---

[1] The Vienna Convention on the Law of Treaties, Art 1(a) defines a 'treaty' as 'an international agreement concluded between States in written form and governed by international law, whether embodied in a single instrument or in two or more related instruments and whatever its particular designation'. Vienna Convention on the Law of Treaties (23 May 1969) 1155 UNTS 331 (VCLT).

[2] For an extensive discussion of investment treaty interpretation, see generally Trinh Hai Yen, *The Interpretation of Investment Treaties* (Martinus Nijhoff, 2014).

6.2 Rules of Interpretation

The basic rules of investment treaty interpretation are found in Articles 31, 32, and 33 of the Vienna Convention on the Law of Treaties (VCLT). Article 31 sets down the general rules of interpretation, Article 32 guides the use of supplementary means of interpretation when a treaty text is ambiguous or obscure, and Article 33 applies to the interpretation of treaties that are authenticated in two or more languages, a situation which affects most investment treaties.

Arbitral tribunals faced with the task of interpreting investment treaty provisions invariably begin by invoking Article 31(1) of the VCLT. Article 31(1), which sets out the basic rule of treaty interpretation, provides that '[a] treaty shall be interpreted in good faith in accordance with the ordinary meaning to be given to the terms of the treaty in their context and in light of its object and purpose'. This provision points to four essential elements in the interpretation of a treaty: (1) the treaty text; (2) the ordinary meaning of the terms; (3) the context of the treaty terms; and (4) the treaty's object and purpose. The following sections of this chapter examine each of these elements.

6.3 The Treaty Text

(a) Sources of investment treaty texts

Essential to the process of treaty interpretation is the existence of an authentic treaty text to interpret. The texts of investment treaties are found in three types of sources: (i) government sources; (ii) international organization sources; and (iii) unofficial and non-governmental sources. Each is examined in turn.

(i) Government sources

Governments of states nearly always publish in an official publication the authoritative texts of treaties to which they have agreed. Depending upon the laws of the particular country concerned, the publication will usually be the official and definitive source of laws, legal instruments, and treaties. Normally, such publications appear regularly in the country concerned, although the frequency of publication may vary depending on the amount of legislation and treaties needing to be published. The publications have differing names, including 'official gazette', 'official journal', or 'official bulletin'. Thus, in Austria the publication is known as *Bundesgesetzblatt*, in Bahrain and many Arabic-speaking countries as *Al-Jaridah al-Rasmiyah*, in Chile and many Spanish-speaking countries as *Diario Oficial*, in France and in many French-speaking countries as *Journal Officiel de la République*, in Korea as

Kwanbo, and in Japan as *Kampo*.[3] Despite the variation in title, these governmental publications all serve the same function: they are official sources of treaty texts.

Certain countries adopt a different approach to treaty publication. They publish the agreements they conclude with other countries in treaty series. For example, the United States publishes *United States Treaties and Other International Agreements* (cited as UST) (Washington, DC: USGPO, 1950–), which is the cumulative collection of *Treaties and Other International Acts Series* (cited as TIAS) (Washington, DC: USGPO, 1946–) and the current official collection of US treaties and agreements. TIAS is the first US official publication of new treaties and agreements—slip treaties—and is later bound in UST. It combines and continues the numbering of the Treaty Series and Executive Agreement Series. The United Kingdom publishes *Treaty Series* (cited as TS) (London: HMSO, 1892–) and formerly published treaties in a series called *British and Foreign State Papers* (London: HMSO, 1812). Among other countries that publish a treaty series are Australia (*Australian Treaty Series* (ATS)), Canada (*Canada Treaty Series* (CTS)), and the Netherlands (*Tractatenblad* (Trb 'year', 'nr', eg Trb 1994, 12)). This list is not exhaustive. When conducting research, one must inquire into the existence and availability of a treaty series in the country in question.

Many states also maintain government websites that publish either the full text of treaties, indexes to treaties, or both. For example, Australia maintains the *Australian Treaties Library*,[4] a website that contains the full text of Australia's multilateral and bilateral treaties and their current status. The website is updated by the Department of Foreign Affairs and Trade. The *Verdragenbank*, published by the Netherlands Ministry of Foreign Affairs, contains information on treaties published in the official treaty series *Tractatenblad* as well as on treaties for which the Netherlands is the depositary.[5] The UK's Foreign and Commonwealth Office maintains an official website with links to the full texts of treaties involving the United Kingdom on a searchable database.[6] The database of Switzerland's Federal Department of Foreign Affairs contains information on all the international treaties that are either in force or signed by Switzerland, together with information on other important treaties and non-binding instruments.[7] In the United States, a useful website for treaty texts is one maintained by the US Department of State Office of the Assistant Legal Adviser for Treaty Affairs. This website serves as the principal US government repository for US treaties and other international agreements.[8] The text of treaties,[9] published

---

[3] JE Roberts (ed), *A Guide to Official Gazettes and their Contents* (Washington, DC: Law Library, Library of Congress, 1985).

[4] See <http://www.austlii.edu.au/au/other/dfat/> accessed 16 October 2014.

[5] See <https://verdragenbank.overheid.nl/> accessed 16 October 2014.

[6] See <https://www.gov.uk/government/publications> accessed 16 October 2014.

[7] See <https://www.eda.admin.ch/eda/en/fdfa/foreign-policy/international-law/internationale-vertraege.html> accessed 16 October 2014.

[8] See <http://www.state.gov/s/l/treaty/> accessed 16 October 2014.

[9] The US legal system distinguishes between international treaties and agreements. The former are concluded in accordance with US Constitution, Art II, § 2 which gives the President the power 'by and with the *advice and consent* of the *Senate* to *make treaties*, provided *two-thirds of the Senators present concur*'. Art VI states that the Constitution and 'the laws of the United States which shall be made in pursuance thereof; and all treaties made, or which shall be made, under the authority of the United States, shall be the supreme law of the land'. The latter type consists of two kinds of

as Senate Treaty Documents, may be accessed through the Library of Congress' THOMAS website.[10]

Some other governmental websites include: Belgium's *Treaties*,[11] Canada's *Treaty Information*,[12] France's *Base Pacte*,[13] and India's Ministry of External Affairs *Bilateral/Multilateral Documents*.[14]

As with the official printed treaty series, the availability of official websites containing investment treaty texts and their legal status should be researched in each case: ministries of foreign affairs or trade and commerce may be a good starting point for the search.

(ii) International organization sources

Certain international organizations are also depositories of investment treaty texts. These include the United Nations, the United Nations Conference on Trade and Development (UNCTAD), the International Centre for Settlement of Investment Disputes (ICSID), and the Organization of American States (OAS), among others. Each is examined in turn.

The United Nations The United Nations Treaty Collection (UNTS) is a collection of treaties and international agreements concluded since 1946. Treaties are registered or filed with the UN Secretariat and then recorded and published pursuant to Article 102 of the Charter.[15] The UNTS includes the texts of treaties in their authentic language(s), along with translations into English and French, as appropriate. The collection currently contains over 50,000 treaties and a similar number of related subsequent actions. The United Nations Treaty Collection, which has been published in hard copy in over 2,100 volumes, also continues to be the largest single collection of treaties on the internet.[16]

United Nations Conference on Trade and Development (UNCTAD) UNCTAD provides many resources for accessing international investment agreements.

---

agreements: *executive-congressional agreements*, entered by the President in accordance with legislation enacted by Congress, and *presidential agreements*, entered by the President in reliance on his constitutional powers.

[10] See <http://thomas.loc.gov/home/treaties/trhelp.htm> accessed 16 October 2014.
[11] See <http://diplomatie.belgium.be/en/treaties/> accessed 16 October 2014.
[12] See <http://www.treaty-accord.gc.ca/index.aspx> accessed 16 October 2014.
[13] See <http://basedoc.diplomatie.gouv.fr/Traites/Accords_Traites.php> accessed 16 October 2014.
[14] See <http://www.mea.gov.in/bilateral-documents.htm?53/Bilateral/Multilateral_Documents> accessed 16 October2014.
[15] The UN Charter, Art 102 states:

> (1) Every treaty and every international agreement entered into by any Member of the United Nations after the present Charter comes into force shall as soon as possible be registered with the Secretariat and published by it.
> (2) No party to any such treaty or international agreement which has not been registered in accordance with the provisions of paragraph 1 of this Article may invoke that treaty or agreement before any organ of the United Nations.

[16] See <https://treaties.un.org/>accessed 16 October 2014.

UNCTAD's website 'Investment Policy Hub' is an extremely valuable and accessible source for the texts of investment treaties signed by a selected country or the text of a specific treaty between two countries until the end of 2014. The database is searchable by keywords, country/region, categories (multilateral, regional, bilateral, non-governmental, and prototype instruments), and date.[17] Details of the bilateral investment treaties (BITs) signed by most countries are also provided through an interactive resource.[18]

International Centre for Settlement of Investment Disputes (ICSID) Since the early 1970s, ICSID, an affiliate of the World Bank, has collected and published the texts of BITs. Most have been included in a multi-volume collection of investment treaties entitled *Investment Promotion and Protection Treaties*, compiled by the International Centre for Settlement of Investment Disputes (London; New York: Oceana Publications, c 1983–). Lists of BITs were also published in 1989 and 1992 in the ICSID Review—Foreign Investment Law Journal. In addition, ICSID maintains a webpage that provides a chronological list of BITs concluded up to the end of 2007, and an alphabetical list of signatories that indicates the treaties which a given state has concluded. The data contained in both lists, which include signature and (where applicable) entry into force dates, are based on information provided to ICSID by foreign governments.[19]

Organization of American States (OAS) The website supported by the OAS contains complete information of every trade[20] and investment-related[21] bilateral or multilateral legal instrument concluded by a member state of the OAS.

Energy Charter Treaty The Energy Charter Secretariat, located in Brussels, Belgium, maintains a website containing the text of the 1994 Energy Charter Treaty (ECT) and its related documents.[22]

(iii) Unofficial and non-governmental sources of investment treaty texts

One can also consider a variety of unofficial and non-governmental sources to locate investment treaty texts. These include: (1) the Electronic Information System for International Law (EISIL), which was developed and maintained by the American Society of International Law (ASIL) and contains specific references to BITs and other international investment agreements;[23] and (2) Investment Treaty Arbitration (ITA). ITA maintains a useful website

---

[17] See <http://investmentpolicyhub.unctad.org/IIA> accessed 16 October 2014.
[18] ibid.
[19] The ICSID website no longer provides up-to-date information on bilateral investment treaties.
[20] See <http://www.sice.oas.org/agreements_e.asp> accessed 16 October 2014.
[21] See <http://www.sice.oas.org/investment/bitindex_e.asp> accessed 16 October 2014.
[22] See <http://www.encharter.org/> accessed 21 July 2014.
[23] See <http://www.eisil.org/index.php?sid=346890273&cat=483&t=sub_pages> accessed 16 October 2014.

providing access to all publicly available investment treaty awards, information, and resources relating to investment treaties and investment treaty arbitration, and useful links to resources on BITs, Free Trade/Sectoral Agreements with Investment Protections, and Model BITs.[24] Also, (3) InvestmentClaims. com, an online resource providing access to all relevant foreign investment law instruments and jurisprudence, includes references to international investment agreements;[25] and (4) NAFTAClaims.com provides information about NAFTA investor–state dispute settlement and contains copies of important NAFTA legal documents.[26]

(b) The language of treaty texts

While the basic source for interpreting an investment treaty is the text of the treaty itself, often the treaty is embodied in two or more separate texts, each in the official language or languages of the parties to the treaty. Almost invariably, when parties to a treaty have different official languages, the official text of the treaty is in those different languages. Moreover, the treaty text itself normally states that the treaty is done in the specified languages and that the different texts are 'equally authentic'.[27] Under Article 33 of the VCLT, '[w]hen a treaty has been authenticated in two or more languages, the text is equally authoritative in each language, unless the treaty provides or the parties agree that, in case of divergence, a particular text shall prevail'. It further provides in Article 33(3) that '[t]he terms of the treaty are presumed to have the same meaning in each authentic text'.

Despite the skill and efforts of translators, one occasionally finds differences between the versions of specific treaty provisions, a factor that greatly complicates treaty interpretation and application. As a guide for resolving such conflicts, Article 33(4) of the VCLT stipulates:

Except where a particular text prevails in accordance with paragraph 1, when a comparison of the authentic texts discloses a difference of meaning which the application of articles 31 and 32 does not remove, the meaning which best reconciles the texts, having regard to the object and purpose of the treaty, shall be adopted.

The case of *Berschader v Russia* provides an example of such an interpretational problem and its resolution.[28] In that case, an investment arbitration tribunal had

---

[24] See <http://italaw.com/> accessed 16 October 2014.
[25] See <http://oxia.ouplaw.com/home/ic> accessed 16 October 2014.
[26] See <http://www.naftaclaims.com/> accessed 16 October 2014.
[27] eg North American Free Trade Agreement, Art 2206 states: 'The English, French and Spanish texts of this Agreement are equally authentic.'
[28] *Vladamir Berschader and Moïse Berschander v Russia*, SCC Case No 080/2004 (Award) (21 April 2006). See also *Elettronica Sicula SpA (ELSI) (United States v Italy)*, (Judgment) (20 July 1989) [1989] ICJ Rep 1, 57–60, in which the International Court of Justice, in interpreting the Treaty of Friendship, Commerce and Navigation between Italy and the United States, was faced with the question of whether the word 'taken' in Art V(2) of the English language text meant the same thing as *'espropriati'* in the Italian version.

to interpret the Russia–Belgium BIT written in the Russian and French languages, each of which was equally authentic by the terms of the treaty. In order to establish its jurisdiction over the dispute, the tribunal had to determine whether the claimant's financial contribution to the construction of a building for the Russian Supreme Court was an 'investment' under the BIT. The Russian language version, in Article 1.2 of the BIT, employed the term *kapitalovlozhenie* as the noun form of the word 'investment' and the term *vlozhit* as the verb form 'to invest'. The French text used the words *investissement* and *investir*. Russia argued that the meaning of *kapitalovlozhenie* was restricted to capital investments contributed to the charter capital of a joint venture and that, although such interpretation was narrower in scope than the French term '*investissement*', the tribunal should adopt a narrower interpretation to best carry out the object and purposes of the BIT, as required by Article 33 of the VCLT.

The tribunal found that such a narrow interpretation could not be supported and dismissed Russia's arguments on several grounds. First, the tribunal found that Russian–English legal and economic dictionaries translated the term *kapitalovlozhenie* as *investment*. Second, it took note of BITs concluded by Russia in which the contracting parties agreed that the Russian and English were equally authentic languages and in which the term *kapitalovlozhenie* was translated as *investment*. Based on this analysis, the tribunal concluded that 'while those terms may sometimes be used in the Russian language in the more limited sense of "contributions to the charter capital of a joint venture," they are in fact also frequently used in a broader sense corresponding exactly to the English terms "investment" and "invest"'.[29] Furthermore, the tribunal also took note of the French version of the Russia–Belgium BIT, which according to that treaty's Protocol is equally authoritative as the Russian version. Since the French text uses the words *investissement* and *investir*, the tribunal concluded that the ordinary meaning of the words is identical to that of the English words *investment* and *to invest*.[30]

6.4 'Ordinary Meaning' of Treaty Terms

The first principle stated in Article 31(1) of the VCLT is that 'a treaty shall be interpreted in good faith in accordance with the *ordinary meaning* to be given to the terms of the treaty'.[31] Accordingly, the first step in interpretation is to establish the ordinary meaning of an investment treaty provision. To accomplish this, those engaged in the task of interpretation ordinarily refer to recognized dictionaries. For example, in the ICSID case of *MTD v Chile*, the tribunal interpreted the 'fair

---

[29] *Vladamir Berschader* (n 28 above) ¶ 109.
[30] ibid ¶ 110.
[31] See eg the *Admissions* case, [1950] ICJ Rep 8; J Crawford, *Brownlie's Principles of Public International Law* (8th edn, OUP, 2012) 379.

and equitable' standard of treatment by looking to a dictionary to determine the ordinary meaning of the terms 'fair' and 'equitable'.[32]

Difficult interpretational problems are rarely settled conclusively by this first step. For example, in interpreting the words 'fair and equitable treatment' in a BIT, the tribunal in *Saluka Investment BV (Netherlands) v The Czech Republic* observed that the '"ordinary meaning" of "fair and equitable treatment" can only be defined by terms of almost equal vagueness'.[33] After referring to the interpretational approaches of previous tribunals, the tribunal in *Saluka* concluded with respect to ordinary meaning:

> In MTD, the tribunal stated that: 'In their ordinary meaning, the terms 'fair' and 'equitable'... mean 'just', 'evenhanded', 'unbiased', 'legitimate'. On the basis of *such and similar definitions, one cannot say much more than the tribunal did in S.D. Myers* by stating that an infringement of the standard requires 'treatment in such an unjust or arbitrary manner that the treatment rises to the level that is unacceptable from the international perspective.' This is probably *as far as one can get by looking at the 'ordinary meaning' of the terms* of Article 3.1 of the Treaty (emphasis added).[34]

Thus, an inquiry into 'the ordinary meaning' of a treaty term may not always yield conclusive results. In such a case, one would have to rely on other principles of treaty interpretation to determine the meaning of a treaty term.

6.5 'Context' of Treaty Terms and 'Object and Purpose' of the Treaty

According to Article 31(1) of the VCLT, the ordinary meaning of the terms of the treaty is to be given 'in their context' and 'in the light of [the treaty's] object and purposes'. Thus, the interpretation of an investment treaty requires a determination of the 'context' of the treaty terms and the treaty's object and purpose. Article 31(2) provides that the context of the terms of a treaty consists of the treaty text, including the preamble and annexes, any agreement relating to the treaty made by the parties in connection with the conclusion of the treaty, and any instrument made by one or more parties in connection with the conclusion of the treaty that was accepted by the other parties as an instrument related to the treaty. Thus, diplomatic correspondence between two states with respect to a BIT could be considered part of the context of the treaty terms and, therefore, useful for interpretation.

---

[32] In their ordinary meaning, the terms 'fair' and 'equitable' used in Art 3(1)62 of the BIT mean 'just', 'even-handed', 'unbiased', and 'legitimate'. *MTD Equity Sdn Bhd & MTD Chile SA v Chile*, ICSID Case No ARB/01/7 (Award) (25 May 2004) ¶ 113.

[33] *Saluka Investments BV (The Netherlands) v The Czech Republic*, UNCITRAL (Partial Award) (17 March 2006) ¶ 297.

[34] ibid.

Investment arbitration tribunals often refer to the context of a treaty term and to the object and purpose of an investment treaty to interpret a specific treaty provision. For example, in considering the context within which Argentina and the United States included the fair and equitable treatment standard in their BIT, and its object and purpose, the *LG&E* tribunal[35] referred to the Preamble to the BIT. In the Preamble, the two countries agreed that 'fair and equitable treatment of investment is desirable in order to maintain a stable framework for investment and maximum effective use of economic resources'.[36] As a result, the tribunal concluded:

> In entering the Bilateral Treaty as a whole, the parties desired to 'promote greater economic cooperation' and 'stimulate the flow of private capital and the economic development of the parties'. In light of these stated objectives, this Tribunal must conclude that stability of the legal and business framework is an essential element of fair and equitable treatment in this case, provided that they do not pose any danger for the existence of the host State itself.[37]

In *Saluka*, the tribunal made a clear distinction between the context of the treaty terms and the object and purposes of the treaty itself. It also distinguished the immediate context, which included the language used in the treaty regarding the level of treatment each state was to accord to investors from other states, from the 'broader context', which included the other provisions of the treaty.[38] In determining the treaty's object and purpose, the *Saluka* tribunal looked to the title of and preamble to the treaty and found its purpose was not only to protect investment but, more generally, to promote investment and intensify economic relations between the two states. This finding led the tribunal to take a balanced approach in interpreting the term 'fair and equitable' treatment. The tribunal chose this approach because 'an interpretation which exaggerates the protection to be accorded to foreign investments may serve to dissuade host States from admitting foreign investments and so undermine the overall aim of extending and intensifying the parties' mutual economic relations'.[39]

Thus, an examination of the context of the terms and the object and purpose of a treaty itself may assist in the interpretation of a treaty term when its ordinary meaning is elusive. At the same time, as the tribunal in *Plama v Bulgaria* noted, one should be mindful of the warning of Sir Ian Sinclair that 'the risk that the placing of undue emphasis on the "object and purpose" of a treaty will encourage teleological methods of interpretation [which], in some of its more extreme forms, will even deny the relevance of the intentions of the parties'.[40]

---

[35] *LG&E Energy Corp et al v The Argentine Republic*, ICSID Case No ARB/02/1 (Decision on Liability) (26 September 2006).

[36] ibid ¶ 124.   [37] ibid.

[38] *Saluka Investments BV (The Netherlands) v The Czech Republic*, UNCITRAL (Partial Award) (17 March 2006) ¶ 298.

[39] ibid ¶ 300.

[40] I Sinclair, *The Vienna Convention on the Law of Treaties* (2nd edn, Manchester University Press, 1984) 130; *Plama Consortium Ltd v Bulgaria*, ICSID Case No ARB/03/24 (Decision on Jurisdiction) (8 February 2005) ¶ 193 (Energy Charter Treaty).

6.6 'Subsequent Agreement' and 'Subsequent Practice'

In addition to context, Article 31(3) of the VCLT requires that the interpretation of a treaty term take into account subsequent agreements between the parties regarding the interpretation and application of the treaty as well as any 'subsequent practice in the application of the treaty which establishes the agreement of the parties regarding its interpretation'.

Since the contracting parties may agree on the interpretation of an investment treaty's terms in subsequent agreements and practice, investment arbitration tribunals and others engaged in treaty interpretation should refer to such agreements in interpreting such treaty terms. This is especially pertinent in the context of NAFTA's Chapter 11 arbitrations. Under Article 1131(2) of NAFTA, the NAFTA Free Trade Commission (FTC) has the authority to issue interpretations of NAFTA provisions that are binding on NAFTA-based arbitration tribunals.[41] As of January 2009, the FTC had issued several statements concerning the interpretation of some Chapter 11 provisions,[42] non-disputing party participation,[43] and notice of intent to submit a claim to arbitration.[44] It is worth noting the distinction in legal character between the FTC's Statement on Interpretation

---

[41] The text of NAFTA, Art 1131(2) reads:

2. If the Commission submits to the Tribunal an agreed interpretation, the *interpretation shall be binding* on the Tribunal. If the Commission fails to submit an agreed interpretation or fails to submit an agreed interpretation within such 60 day period, the Tribunal shall decide the issue of interpretation of the exception. (emphasis added)

The North American Free Trade Agreement of 1992, (1993) 32 ILM 289, 605.

[42] The Statement of Interpretation of Certain Chapter 11 Provisions of 31 July 2001 addressed two important issues: access to documents and the scope of minimum standard of treatment. In addressing the former issue, the FTC took the view that nothing in NAFTA imposes a general duty of confidentiality on the disputing parties to a Chapter 11 arbitration. Further, subject to the application of Art 1137(4), nothing in NAFTA precludes the parties from providing public access to documents submitted to, or issued by, a Chapter 11 tribunal. In addressing the latter issue, the FTC adopted the interpretation that (1) NAFTA, Art 1105(1) requires that the customary international law minimum standard of treatment of aliens also be the minimum standard of treatment afforded to the investments of another party; (2) the concepts of 'fair and equitable treatment' and 'full protection and security' do not require treatment in addition to or beyond what is required by the customary international law minimum standard for the treatment of aliens; and (3) a determination that there has been a breach of another provision of NAFTA, or of a separate international agreement, does not establish that there has been a breach of Art 1105(1). Statement on Interpretation of Certain Chapter 11 Provisions, 31 July 2001.

[43] The Commission's Recommendation on Non-Disputing Party Participation made clear that no NAFTA provision limits a Chapter 11 tribunal's discretion to accept written submissions from a non-disputing party. It also recommended that tribunals adopt the procedures agreed by NAFTA parties with respect to such submissions. Recommendation on Non-disputing Party Participation, 7 October 2004.

[44] The FTC determined that the approved form for notices of intent to submit a claim to arbitration, if properly completed, would satisfy the requirements of NAFTA, Art 1119 and clarify the basis of a claim. The FTC also recommended that disputing investors use it. Recommendation on the Format of Notices of Intent, 7 October 2004.

of Certain Chapter 11 Provisions and the Statements of the NAFTA Free Trade Commission on the operation of Chapter 11. The former was adopted 'in order to *clarify* and *reaffirm* the *meaning* of certain of Chapter 11 provisions',[45] whereas the latter was adopted 'in order to enhance the transparency and efficiency of Chapter 11 and *provide guidance* to investors and to Tribunals constituted under Section B of the Chapter'.[46] This distinction is especially important in the light of Article 31(3)(a) of the VCLT, since the Statement on Interpretation of Certain Chapter 11 Provisions may be construed to constitute a subsequent agreement between the parties regarding the proper interpretation of Article 1105 and thus under the VCLT must be taken into account in interpreting a treaty's terms. On the other hand, the Statements of the NAFTA Free Trade Commission on the operation of Chapter 11 represent mere 'recommendations' and thus lack binding character.[47]

6.7 'Relevant Rules of International Law Applicable between the Parties'

Article 31(3)(c) of the VCLT requires that, along with the context, subsequent agreements, and practice, treaty interpretation will also take into account any relevant rules of international law applicable to the relations between the parties. The importance of this provision is that it permits reference to other sources of international law for guidance in interpreting an unclear or deliberately ambiguous term. An example of such a situation is the ICSID case of *LG&E v Argentina*,[48] where the tribunal had to decide claims arising out of what was

---

[45] Statement on Interpretation of Certain Chapter 11 Provisions, 31 July 2001 (emphasis added).

[46] Statements of the NAFTA Free Trade Commission on the Operation of Chapter 11 (emphasis added).

[47] The FTC's Statement on Interpretation of Certain Chapter 11 Provisions has elicited strong criticism regarding both its nature (whether it was 'an amendment' and the FTC had thus overstepped its powers under NAFTA or whether it was 'a subsequent agreement' and the FTC thus acted within the treaty's limits) and its content (whether the words 'international law' in NAFTA, Art 1105 meant only 'customary international law') on the part of commentators and international tribunals. Subsequent decisions followed the FTC interpretation. For more details, see T Weiler, 'NAFTA Article 1105 and the Free Trade Commission; Just Sour Grapes, or Something More Serious?' (2001) 29 Int'l Bus Lawyer 491, 496; P Dumberry, 'The Quest to Define "Fair and Equitable Treatment" for Investors under International Law: The Case of the NAFTA Chapter 11 Pope and Talbot Awards' (2002) 3 JWIT 657, 674–6; C Schreuer, 'Fair and Equitable Treatment in Arbitral Practice' (2005) 6 JWIT 357, 362; T Westcott, 'Recent Practice on Fair and Equitable Treatment' (2007) 8 JWIT 413; *Second opinion* of Christopher Greenwood of 16 August 2001, ¶ 77 in *Loewen Group, Inc and Raymond L Loewen v United States*, ICSID Case No ARB(AF)/98/3; *Second opinion* of Robert Jennings of 18 September 2001, Part I in *Methanex v United States*, UNCITRAL (NAFTA); *Pope & Talbot Inc v The Government of Canada*, UNCITRAL (Award on Damages) (31 May 2002) (NAFTA) ¶ 47; *Mondev Int'l Ltd v United States* ICSID Case No ARB(AF)/99/2 (Award) (11 October 2002) (NAFTA) ¶¶ 120–122.

[48] *LG&E Energy Corp et al v The Argentine Republic*, ICSID Case No ARB/02/1 (Decision on Liability) (26 September 2006).

asserted to be an indirect expropriation. The tribunal noted that in order to find an indirect expropriation it first had to define the concept, a task that was complicated by the fact that '[g]enerally, bilateral treaties do not define what constitutes an expropriation—they just make an express reference to "expropriation" and add the language "any other action that has equivalent effects"'.[49] The US–Argentina BIT, the treaty that the tribunal had to apply, followed a similar pattern: 'Likewise, Article IV of the [US–Argentina] Bilateral Treaty does not define the term "expropriation" and does not establish which measures, actions or conduct would constitute acts "tantamount to expropriation."'[50] To interpret the BIT, the tribunal therefore found it necessary to look to international law, provisions of other BITs,[51] decisions of other international investment tribunals,[52] and writings of publicists.[53] Its reference to such sources of international law allowed the tribunal to define indirect expropriation and to determine that the respondent's actions did not fall within the scope of the US–Argentina BIT's expropriation clause, which protected against 'any action that has the equivalent effects' of expropriation.

In order to interpret the NAFTA provisions in *SD Myers, Inc v Canada*,[54] the tribunal found it necessary 'to review the other international agreements to which the Parties adhere'.[55] Accordingly, it analysed the Canada–USA Transboundary Agreement on Hazardous Waste (Transboundary Agreement) and the North American Agreement on Environmental Cooperation (NAAEC) to assist in determining the scope of a state's freedom under NAFTA to regulate the cross-border movement of toxic wastes. The tribunal found guidance in Article 11 of the Transboundary Agreement, which 'does not give a party...absolute freedom to exclude the import or export of hazardous waste simply by enacting whatever national laws it chooses'.[56] It also pointed out that the NAAEC and the international agreements affirmed in the NAAEC suggested that specific provisions of NAFTA should be interpreted in the light of the general principle that 'where a state can achieve its chosen level of environmental protection through a variety of equally effective and reasonable means, it is obliged to adopt the alternative that is most consistent with open trade'.[57] Although the tribunal acknowledged the possible relevance of the 1989 Basel Convention on the Control of Transboundary Movements of Hazardous Waste and Their Disposal, it refrained from applying it because at the time of the dispute the United States, unlike Canada, was not a party to that treaty.[58] The tribunal's reference to the applicable treaties

---

[49] ibid ¶ 185.   [50] ibid.   [51] ibid ¶ 188.   [52] ibid ¶¶ 191–195.
[53] ibid ¶ 196.
[54] *SD Myers, Inc v Canada*, UNCITRAL (First Partial Award) (13 November 2000).
[55] ibid ¶ 204.   [56] ibid ¶ 208.   [57] ibid ¶¶ 220–221.
[58] Still the tribunal made this observation:

> Even if the Basel Convention were to have been ratified by the NAFTA Parties, it should not be presumed that CANADA would have been able to use it to justify the breach of a specific NAFTA provision because...*where a party has a choice among equally effective and reasonably available alternatives for complying...with a Basel Convention obligation, it is obliged to choose the alternative that is...least inconsistent...with the NAFTA*. If one

between the United States and Canada was a key factor in its interpretation of Article 1102 of NAFTA and its subsequent finding that Canada's regulatory measures were in breach of its obligations.

At the same time, the application of Article 31(3)(c) of the VCLT to the interpretation of investment treaties requires a careful and balanced approach in order to avoid unjustifiably including the same rules of international customary law that the contracting states sought to avoid by making a treaty. States have often decided to conclude an investment treaty either for substantive reasons, such as giving investors higher standards of protection than that afforded by customary international law, or for procedural reasons, such as avoiding the methodological problems associated with establishing the customary international norm's constitutive elements—'general practice' and *opinio juris sive necessitatis*—which is often a contentious process.

On the other hand, in some cases contracting states may specifically intend to link an investment treaty's substantive provisions with the rules of international customary law. For example, paragraph 1 of Article 5 of the US–Uruguay BIT of 2005 provides that each contracting party will grant covered investments treatment consonant with customary international law, including fair and equitable treatment and full protection and security.[59] Paragraph 2 of that Article clarifies that 'paragraph 1 prescribes the customary international law minimum standard of treatment of aliens as *the minimum standard of treatment* to be afforded to covered investments' and that '"full protection and security" requires each Party to provide the level of police protection required under *customary international law*'.[60] Such language clearly demonstrates the intent of the parties to incorporate the requirements of international customary law into the interpretation of the terms 'the minimum standard of treatment' and 'full protection and security' as it existed at the time of the conclusion of that treaty and as it has evolved over time.[61]

In general, then, the application of Article 31(3)(c) of the VCLT to the interpretation of investment treaties should proceed carefully and with due regard to the intentions of the contracting states.

---

such alternative were to involve no inconsistency with the Basel Convention, clearly this should be followed.

ibid ¶ 215.

[59] Treaty Between the United States of America and the Oriental Republic of Uruguay Concerning the Encouragement and Reciprocal Protection of Investment (4 November 2005), Art 5(1).

[60] ibid Art 5(2) (emphasis added).

[61] See eg ¶¶ 107–8, 124 of *Mondev*, where Mexico and Canada were found to have expressly accepted the point that the 'minimum standard of treatment' adopted in NAFTA, Art 1105 'existed

6.8 Special Meanings Intended by the Parties

Article 31(4) of the VCLT provides that a special meaning shall be given to a treaty term if it can be established that such was the contracting parties' intention. Thus, for example, the tribunal in *Parkerings-Compagniet AS v Lithuania*[62] had to decide whether 'fair and *reasonable* treatment' had the same meaning as 'fair and equitable treatment', and whether the former holds the respondent state to a stricter standard of conduct than the more commonly found fair and equitable treatment standard. The tribunal concluded:

The standard of 'fair and equitable treatment' has been interpreted broadly by Tribunals and, as a result, a difference of interpretation between the terms 'fair' and 'reasonable' is insignificant. The Claimant did not show any evidence which could demonstrate that, when signing the BIT, the Republic of Lithuania and the Kingdom of Norway intended to give a different protection to their investors than the protection granted by the 'fair and equitable' standard.[63]

One may therefore infer from this statement that the proponent of the special meaning has the burden of proving that the contracting parties intended the asserted special meaning.

6.9 Supplementary Means of Interpretation

Article 32 of the VCLT allows recourse to supplementary means of interpretation, including the preparatory work of the treaty and the circumstances of its conclusion, in order to confirm the meaning resulting from application of article 31, or to determine the meaning when the interpretation according to article 31: '(a) leaves the meaning ambiguous or obscure, or (b) leads to a result which is manifestly absurd or obscure'.

An illustration of recourse to supplementary material in treaty interpretation is found in *Plama Consortium Limited v Bulgaria*,[64] in which the claimant, a Cypriot company, sought to establish ICSID jurisdiction on the basis of the ECT and the 1987 BIT between Cyprus and Bulgaria. The tribunal affirmed ICSID jurisdiction under the ECT and also considered whether it had jurisdiction under the Bulgaria–Cyprus BIT. This BIT contained a very limited international dispute settlement offer that, in essence, provided that only the measure of compensation for expropriation could be submitted to an UNCITRAL arbitration. It contained

in 1994,...had developed to that time...[and] has evolved and can evolve'. *Mondev International Ltd v United States*, ICSID Case No ARB(AF)/99/2 (Award) (11 October 2002).

[62] *Parkerings-Compagniet AS v Lithuania*, ICSID Case No ARB/05/8 (Award) (11 September 2007).

[63] ibid ¶ 277.

[64] *Plama Consortium Ltd v Bulgaria*, ICSID Case No ARB/03/24 (Decision on Jurisdiction) (8 February 2005).

no offer of ICSID arbitration. The BIT did, however, have a most-favoured-nation clause. Since other BITs concluded by Bulgaria provided for ICSID arbitration, the claimant relied upon the most-favoured-nation clause to take advantage of the ICSID dispute settlement mechanism included in the other BITs. The investor argued that: (1) the claimant *Plama Consortium Limited* qualified as an investor under the Bulgaria–Cyprus BIT; (2) the Bulgaria–Cyprus BIT contained an MFN provision; (3) the MFN provision in the Bulgaria–Cyprus BIT applied to all aspects of investor 'treatment'; and (4) 'treatment' covers settlement of disputed provisions in other BITs to which Bulgaria is a contracting party. As a result, the tribunal had to decide whether the term 'treatment' in the MFN provision of the BIT included or excluded dispute settlement provisions contained in other BITs to which Bulgaria was a contracting party.

The tribunal found that neither the ordinary meaning of the term 'treatment', nor its context, nor the object and purpose of the treaty provided legally sufficient guidance to conclude that the contracting states to the Bulgaria–Cyprus BIT intended the MFN provision to incorporate agreements to arbitrate in other treaties to which Bulgaria was a contracting party.[65] Nor did it find any guidance in the provisions of paragraphs 2, 3, and 4 of Article 31 of the VCLT, since there were no facts or circumstances that indicated their application to the issues at hand.[66] Lacking both specific textual support in the treaty and related documents on which to base a conclusion regarding the scope of the MFN clause, the tribunal turned to the negotiating history of the Bulgaria–Cyprus BIT. There, the tribunal found a sufficient basis to infer that the contracting parties did not consider the MFN provision to extend to dispute settlement provisions in other BITs.[67] Although the parties were unable to produce actual preparatory work for the BIT, as authorized in Article 32 of the VCLT, the tribunal did find assistance in two facts relating to Bulgaria's general negotiating behaviour. First, in 1998, after the end of communism, Bulgaria and Cyprus specifically sought to negotiate a revision to the dispute settlement provisions of the 1987 BIT. The negotiations failed. The *Plama* tribunal 'inferred from these negotiations that the Contracting Parties to the BIT themselves did not consider that the MFN provision extends to dispute settlement provisions in other BITs'.[68] Second, at the time Bulgaria concluded the BIT with Cyprus, 'Bulgaria was under a communist regime that favored bilateral investment treaties with limited protections for foreign investors and with very limited dispute resolution provisions'.[69] Thus, when faced with an inconclusive textual basis for interpreting the investment treaty, the tribunal resorted to facts outside the treaty and to its negotiating history as supplementary means of interpretation to determine the contracting parties' intention at the time they concluded their BIT in 1987.

Despite the more than 3,300 investment treaties that have been negotiated over the last six decades, for various reasons obtaining useful negotiating history

---

[65] ibid ¶¶ 189–193.   [66] ibid ¶ 194.   [67] ibid ¶ 195.
[68] ibid ¶ 195.   [69] ibid ¶ 196.

to assist in interpreting a treaty can be difficult, if not impossible. The recorded negotiating history and preparatory work may be scant or lost, or contracting states may be unwilling to provide the record to litigants, since such material, once released, may be used against the state that released it.[70]

One important preparatory document that is often publicly available, as was discussed in Chapter 4, at section 4.7 is the 'model' or 'prototype' treaty prepared by many capital-exporting countries to conduct BIT negotiations. While no arbitration cases seem to have referred to such prototypes of models yet, these documents may be used to interpret or illuminate the meaning of provisions in the BITs for which they were used. In studying investment treaties, a model BIT may not only provide a historical perspective but could also conceivably be used to interpret unclear treaty text. Under Article 32 of the VCLT, if the meaning of the text is ambiguous or obscure, recourse may be had to 'the preparatory work of the treaty' to interpret its text. Model or prototype treaties would certainly constitute 'preparatory work' within the meaning of that Article.

6.10 Arbitration and Judicial Decisions

International law contains no doctrine of binding precedent making the decisions of an international judicial or arbitral body in one case binding upon international judicial or arbitral bodies deciding similar, future cases.[71] Article 59 of the Statute of the International Court of Justice specifically states that '[t]he decision of the Court has no binding force except between the parties and in respect of that particular case'.[72] Similarly, Article 1136(1) of NAFTA, in virtually identical language, makes clear that decisions of investment arbitral tribunals under Chapter 11 do not constitute binding precedent for the future. The treaty states: 'An award made by a Tribunal shall have no binding force except between the disputing parties and in respect of the particular case.'[73] Neither the

---

[70]　eg in *Pope & Talbot*, Canada initially refused to reveal the *travaux préparatoires* that led to the adoption of NAFTA, Art 1105. The tribunal criticized that action:

> having the documents would have made [the tribunal's] earlier interpretations of Article 1105 less difficult and more focused on the issues before it. In this sense, the failure of Canada to provide the documents when requested ... was unfortunate. Forcing the Tribunal to chase after the documents as it did is not acceptable.

Pope & Talbot Inc v The Government of Canada, UNCITRAL (Award on Damages) (31 May 2002) ¶ 39. When Canada finally acceded only partially to the tribunal's request, the tribunal observed '[i]t is almost certain that the documents provided ... are not all that exists, yet no effort was made by Canada to let the Tribunal know what, if anything, has been withheld'. ibid ¶ 41. Accordingly, the tribunal concluded that '[t]his incident's injury to the [NAFTA] Chapter 11 process will surely linger'. ibid ¶ 42.

[71]　G Kaufmann-Kohler, 'Arbitral Precedent: Dream, Necessity or Excuse?' (2007) 23 Arbitration Int'l 357.

[72]　Statute of the International Court of Justice (1945), 3 Bevans 1179; 59 Stat 1031; TS 993; (1945) 39 AJIL Supp 215 (ICJ Statute).

[73]　The North American Free Trade Agreement of 1992, (1993) 32 ILM 289, 605 (NAFTA).

ICSID Convention nor individual investment treaties contain a similarly specific prohibition, but they do not expressly recognize that investment arbitration awards constitute precedent.[74]

On the other hand, Article 38(d) of the ICJ Statute, in defining the sources of international law, recognizes 'judicial decisions and the teachings of the most highly qualified publicists of the various nations as subsidiary means for the determination of rules of law'.[75] An initial question is whether arbitral decisions constitute 'judicial decisions' within the meaning of Article 38(1). On the one hand, if one adopts a formal and structural definition, it is possible to argue that since arbitral decisions do not emanate from a formally constituted 'court', they are not 'judicial decisions'. On the other hand, if one makes a functional interpretation and defines 'judicial decision' as one 'relating to judgment and the administration of justice', then arbitral decisions do qualify as 'judicial decisions'.[76] In fact, in applying international law, international courts and tribunals, as well as governments and litigants, do refer to previous judicial decisions and arbitral decisions to determine the applicable rules of international law. In international investment arbitration, in particular, counsel for the parties regularly cite prior cases in support of their positions, and tribunals, while reaffirming that they are not bound by previous arbitral decisions and awards, nonetheless regularly refer to earlier awards and decisions in interpreting investment treaty provisions and deciding investment disputes. Various factors have supported this trend. First, the vague and general language of many investment treaties and the fact that treaties employ common legal concepts and phrases naturally lead lawyers and tribunals to refer to decisions in other cases to determine how such provisions should be interpreted. Second, the recognized goal of international investment law is to establish a predictable, stable legal framework for investments, which causes tribunals to pay attention to previous decisions on similar issues. Third, tribunals, like courts, are motivated by the underlying moral consideration that 'like cases should be decided alike', unless a strong reason exists to distinguish the current case from previous ones.

The growth in investor–state arbitration in recent years has led to a significant expansion in the jurisprudence of investment treaties. The commonality of

---

[74] The ICSID Convention, Art 53(1) states: 'The award shall be binding on the parties.' Schreuer suggests that this provision may be interpreted as 'excluding the applicability of the principle of binding precedent to successive ICSID cases'. He also notes that there is nothing in the preparatory work of the Convention suggesting that the doctrine of precedent should be applied to ICSID arbitration. C Schreuer, 'A Doctrine of Precedent?' in P Muchlinksi et al, *The Oxford Handbook of International Investment Law* (OUP, 2008) 1190.

[75] ICJ Statute (n 72 above). See Ch 3, section 3.3(e).

[76] *The Oxford Dictionary of English* defines 'judicial' as 'of, by, or appropriate to a law court or judge; relating to the administration of justice'. See *The Oxford Dictionary of English*, (3rd edn, OUP 2010), available at <http://www.oxforddictionaries.com/us/definition/american_english/judicial> accessed 4 October 2014.

language and provisions among investment treaties makes an understanding of judicial and arbitration decisions important to the interpretation and application of investment treaties. The sources for locating such decisions include: ICSID's website,[77] the Permanent Court of International Arbitration's website,[78] InvestmentClaims.com,[79] Investment Treaty Arbitration (website edited by Professor Andrew Newcombe),[80] Investor–State Law Guide,[81] and NAFTA Claims.[82] The NAFTA Chapter 11 awards and briefs can also be retrieved from governmental websites of the United States,[83] Canada,[84] and Mexico.[85] On the other hand, principles of confidentiality, which to a greater or lesser extent apply to all investor–state arbitrations, may prevent the publication of important arbitral decisions and related documents in specific cases. Thus, unfortunately, unlike most well-administered national judicial systems, it is likely that some important arbitral decisions interpreting key treaty provisions are kept private and so are not part of investment treaty jurisprudence because the parties to the dispute or their counsel sought this result.[86]

6.11 Scholarly Commentary on Investment Treaties

The writing of scholars and practitioners is another source of assistance in interpreting investment treaties. As noted previously, Article 38 of the ICJ Statute specifies the use of 'teachings of the most highly qualified publicists of the various nations as subsidiary means for the determination of rules of law'. The word 'publicist' has several meanings today, but its traditional definition is 'an expert in international law'.[87] Their 'teachings' refers to more than classroom lectures, also including their books, articles, monographs and testimony on international law. In short, 'teachings' refers to any medium by which experts on international law comment on their specialization. Both counsel and tribunals in investor–state arbitrations

---

[77] See <https://icsid.worldbank.org/apps/ICSIDWEB/cases/Pages/ViewRecentUpdates.aspx?view=RECREGISTERED> accessed 16 October 2014.

[78] See <http://www.pca-cpa.org> accessed 16 October 2014.

[79] See <http://oxia.ouplaw.com/home/ic> accessed 16 October 2014.

[80] See <http://italaw.com/> accessed 16 October 2014.

[81] The guide lets users search for arbitral decisions by specific topics, see how tribunals have referenced earlier decisions, and see how tribunals have interpreted specific treaty articles. See <http://www.investorstatelawguide.com/> accessed 16 October 2014.

[82] See <http://www.naftaclaims.com> accessed 16 October 2014.

[83] See <http://www.state.gov/s/l/c3433.htm> accessed 16 October 2014.

[84] See <http://www.international.gc.ca/international/index.aspx?lang=eng> accessed 16 October 2014.

[85] See <http://www.economia.gob.mx/?NLanguage=en&P=5500> accessed 16 October 2014.

[86] Even ICSID, which is the most open of the arbitral institutions, is prevented by ICSID Convention, Art 48(5) from publishing awards without the consent of the parties.

[87] eg *The Oxford Dictionary of English* defines publicist to mean, in addition, 'a person responsible for publicizing a product, person, or company' or a 'journalist, especially one concerned with current affairs'. *The Oxford Dictionary of English* (n 76 above).

routinely refer to such works in analysing the meaning of treaty terms in specific cases. The amount of such doctrinal literature on international investment law is vast and growing quickly. Useful bibliographies include ICSID's Bibliography on Bilateral Investment Treaties and International Investment Law[88] and the Peace Palace Library's Research Guide on Foreign Direct Investment.[89]

---

[88] See <http://www.oxforddictionaries.com/us/definition/american_english/judicial> accessed 16 October 2014.

[89] See <http://www.peacepalacelibrary.nl/research-guides/economic-and-financial-law/foreign-direct-investment/> accessed 16 October 2014.

7

Scope of Application of Investment Treaties

7.1 The Significance of a Treaty's Scope of Application

Any international regime must have rules to determine which persons and actions are governed by the regime. A fundamental question that all governments, investors, and arbitrators must answer in the application of an investment treaty is therefore whether the treaty applies to the particular persons, organizations, transactions, or assets seeking to benefit from its provisions. If it does apply, then those persons, organizations, transactions, and assets may be entitled to the privileges and protections of the treaty. If it does not so apply, then those persons, organizations, transactions, and assets are not protected and may not claim treaty benefits.

The scope of an investment treaty's application has at least two important legal ramifications. First, a contracting state owes obligations under the treaty only to investors and investments that fall within the treaty's scope of application or treaty definitions. Second, the treaty's definitions and scope of application affect the jurisdiction of any international arbitral tribunal adjudicating a dispute brought under its provisions. Therefore, whether a company or person constitutes an 'investor' or whether an asset or transaction constitutes an 'investment' under the applicable treaty are important jurisdictional questions in investment treaty arbitrations and must be answered at the threshold of a case. A common, initial defensive move by governments in investor–state arbitrations is to argue that the treaty does not apply to the complaining investor or its investment and that, therefore, the arbitration tribunal has no jurisdiction to hear the dispute. Because of the large and growing number of cases dealing with such jurisdictional questions, the body of arbitral jurisprudence interpreting and applying the treaty definitions of 'investments' and 'investor' is substantial and expanding. It should be noted, however, that in ICSID arbitrations the underlying investment must meet the definitional requirements of *both* the applicable investment treaty and Article 25 of the ICSID Convention, which provides that a tribunal will have jurisdiction over 'any legal dispute arising directly out of an investment'. It is possible for a particular asset to qualify as an investment under a treaty but not under the Convention; consequently, in order to establish jurisdiction in a particular case an ICSID tribunal must find that the investment upon which the claim is based meets the definition of investment under the treaty and under the Convention.[1]

---

[1] In *Salini Costruttori SpA & Italstrade SpA v the Kingdom of Morocco*, ICSID Case No ARB/00/4 (Decision on Jurisdiction) (23 July 2001), (2001) 42 ILM 609, the tribunal stated

Unlike nearly all investment treaties, however, the Convention does not define the term 'investment'. This omission has provoked speculation as to whether certain cases will fail to meet ICSID jurisdictional requirements if they do not constitute an 'investment' under Article 25 even though they qualify under the applicable investment treaty.[2]

As a result of these factors, government officials, lawyers, arbitrators, and anyone seeking to understand an investment treaty must closely examine the treaty provisions to determine the persons, organizations, transactions, and assets to which it applies. The key provisions in answering these questions are usually located at the beginning of the treaty text, primarily in the treaty's definitional articles,[3] which define important terms such as 'investments', 'investors', 'companies', 'nationals', and 'territory'.[4] In some cases, a treaty may also include a separate article entitled 'scope of application'. A person, organization, transaction, or asset that falls outside of one of the treaty's terms or the scope of the treaty's application is not entitled to benefit from its provisions.

Key questions that must always be answered in the application of an investment treaty are whether the alleged investment meets the definition of 'investment' under the treaty and whether the legal or physical person owning the investment meets the legal definition of 'investor'. This chapter examines these two questions. At the outset, however, it should be stressed that while investment treaties exhibit strong similarities in definitions and definitional approaches, significant textual differences can also be found since contracting states always have control in defining the scope of the treaty.[5] Consequently, those interpreting investment treaties

---

at ¶ 44: 'The Arbitral Tribunal, therefore, is of the opinion that its jurisdiction depends on the existence of an investment within the meaning of the Bilateral Treaty, as well as that of the Convention, in accordance with the case law.'

[2] eg F Yala, 'The Notion of "Investment" in ICSID Case Law: A Drifting Jurisdictional Requirement?' (2005) 22(2) J Int'l Arb 105; M Waibel, 'Opening Pandora's Box: Sovereign Bonds in International Arbitration' (2007) 101 AJIL 711. See generally, CH Schreuer, *The ICSID Convention—A Commentary* (2nd edn, Cambridge University Press, 2009).

[3] Note, however, that definitions in some treaties are found at the end of the text. See eg NAFTA, Chapter 11 which includes definitions at the end of the Chapter in Art 1139.

[4] See eg Agreement between Japan and the Socialist Republic of Vietnam for the Liberalization, Promotion and Protection of Investment (14 November 2003), Art 1 (defining 'investor', 'investments', and 'Area'); Treaty between the United States of America and the Czech and Slovak Federal Republic Concerning the Reciprocal Encouragement and Protection of Investment (22 October 1991), Art 1(a)–(b) (defining 'investment' and 'company of a Party'); Treaty between the United States of America and the Republic of Turkey Concerning the Reciprocal Encouragement and Protection of Investments (3 December 1985), Arts 1(a), (c), (e) (defining 'company', 'Investment', and 'national').

[5] See *Romak SA v Republic of Uzbekistan*, PCA Case No AA280 (Award) (26 November 2009) ¶ 205:

contracting States are free to deem any kind of asset or economic transaction to constitute an investment as subject to treaty protection. Contracting States can even go as far as stipulating that a 'pure' one-off sales contract constitutes an investment, even if such a transaction would not normally be covered by the ordinary meaning of the term 'investment.' However, in such cases, the wording of the instrument in question must leave no room for doubt that the intention of the contracting States was to accord to the term 'investment' an extraordinary and counterintuitive meaning.

to determine the extent of their coverage must focus carefully on the language of the definitional sections of the specific treaty in question.

7.2 'Investments' Covered by Investment Treaties

As discussed in Chapter 2, the term 'investment' in ordinary parlance can refer to the *process* or *transaction* by which an investment is made or to the *asset* acquired as a result of that process or transaction. Generally speaking, investment treaties define an investment as an asset, rather than a process or transaction by which an asset is acquired. Thus, they tend to employ *asset-based definitions* of investments.[6] Such definitions tend to be broad in scope. For example, Article I(g) of the Canada–Costa Rica BIT provides that '"invest-ment" means any kind of asset owned or controlled either directly or, indi-rectly...by an investor of one Contracting Party in the territory of the other Contracting Party'.[7] In order to come within this and similar asset-based, treaty definitions, an investment must first of all be an asset. An initial prob-lem in applying this provision is that treaties, like the Canada–Costa Rica BIT, employing an asset-based definition of investment, rarely define the term 'asset'. One must therefore look to dictionaries to determine its ordinary mean-ing. The word 'asset' in most dictionaries is defined as 'anything of value' or a 'valuable item that is owned'. Thus, it can be seen that the concept of 'asset' is very broad indeed.

At the same time, one can identify three different approaches to employing an asset-based definition in investment treaties: (1) a broad asset-based defini-tion with a non-exhaustive list of investment forms; (2) a broad asset-based defi-nition specifying substantive investment characteristics as well as investment forms; and (3) an asset-based definition with an exhaustive list of investment forms.[8]

In addition, as will be seen, even if an investment meets the asset-based definition of a treaty, that asset may nonetheless not be covered by the treaty if it does not meet certain specified legal, geographical, temporal, or other requirements.

---

[6] UNCTAD, *Bilateral Investment Treaties 1995–2006: Trends in Investment Rulemaking* (2007) 7.

[7] Agreement between the Government of Canada and the Government of the Republic of Costa Rica for the Promotion and Protection of Investments (18 March 1998). See *Alasdair Ross Anderson et al v Republic of Costa Rica*, ICSID Case No ARB(AF)/07/3l (Award) (19 May 2010), applying this provision of the Canada–Costa Rica BIT.

[8] See generally UNCTAD, *Bilateral Investment Treaties 1995–2006: Trends in Investment Rulemaking* (2007) 7–12; N Rubins, 'The Notion of "Investment" in International Investment Arbitration' in N Horn and S Kröll (eds), *Arbitrating Foreign Investment Disputes* (Ringgold Inc, 2004) 283–324; R Dolzer, 'The Notion of Investment in Recent Practice' in S Charnovitz, D Steger, and P van den Bossche (eds), *Law in the Service of Human Dignity. Essays in Honor of Florentino Feliciano* (Cambridge University Press, 2005) 261–75.

7.3 Broad Asset-Based Definitions of Investments with an Illustrative List of Investment Forms

Most modern investment treaties provide for a very broad asset-based definition of investment.[9] This definition recognizes the fact that investment forms are constantly evolving in response to the creativity of investors and the rapidly changing world of international finance, so a broad definition is necessary to cover the wide and potentially expanding spectrum of investments. The effect of this approach is to provide an expanding umbrella of protection to investors and investments. Treaties achieve this result by employing a formula in which the term 'investment' is defined as 'every kind of asset' and is followed by a *non-exhaustive* list of asset categories that usually includes: (1) movable and immovable property and any related property rights; (2) various types of interests in companies or any other form of participation in a company, business enterprise, or joint venture; (3) claims to money and claims under a contract having a financial value; (4) intellectual property rights; and (5) business concessions.[10] One of the purposes of this broad language is to make clear that both tangible and intangible assets are protected and to clarify that the treaty's protection of investments does not depend on the particular form an investment takes. Thus, for example, while it has been claimed that customary international law does not protect portfolio investments and patents,[11] virtually all investment treaties affirm that shares and participations are 'investments' and so are subject to treaty protection. Most also provide protection to patents and other forms of intellectual property.

---

[9] UNCTAD, *Bilateral Investment Treaties 1995–2006: Trends in Investment Rulemaking* (2007) 7–12. See also *Fedax NV v Venezuela*, ICSID Case No ARB/96/3 (Decision of the Tribunal on Objections to Jurisdiction) (11 July 1997), in which the tribunal stated at ¶ 34: 'A broad definition of investment...is not at all an exceptional situation. On the contrary, most contemporary bilateral treaties of this kind refer to "every kind of asset" or to "all assets"'. The tribunal also found that '[a] similar trend can be found in the context of major multilateral instruments' (ibid ¶ 35).

[10] Such an approach can be seen in the Germany–Bosnia and Herzegovina BIT, Art 1(1) which states:

> the term 'investment' comprises *every kind of asset, in particular, though not exclusively* :
>
> (a) movable and immovable property as well as any other rights *in rem*, such as mortgages, liens and pledges;
> (b) shares of companies and other kinds of interest in companies;
> (c) claims to money which has been used to create an economic value or claims to any performance having an economic value;
> (d) intellectual property rights, in particular copyrights, patents, utility-model patents, industrial designs, trade-marks, trade-names, trade and business secrets, technical processes, know-how, and good will;
> (e) business concessions under public law, including concessions to search for, extract and exploit natural resources. (emphasis added)

Treaty between the Federal Republic of Germany and Bosnia and Herzegovina concerning the Encouragement and Reciprocal Protection of Investments (18 October 2001).

[11] M Sornarajah, *The International Law on Foreign Investment* (3rd edn, Cambridge University Press 2010) 8, 12 (without citing supporting authority for the statement).

In interpreting a similar provision, one tribunal[12] noted that '[t]he specific categories of investment included in the definition are included as examples rather than with the purpose of excluding those not listed'.[13] The tribunal also emphasized that '[t]he drafters were careful to use the words "not exclusively" before listing the categories of "particularly" included investments'.[14] Since one of the investment categories in that dispute consisted of 'shares, rights of participation in companies and other types of participation in companies', the tribunal found that the plain meaning of the term 'investment' in the Germany–Argentina BIT included shares held by a German shareholder.[15]

The tribunals in *Abaclat v Argentina*[16] and *Ambiente Ufficio v Argentina*[17] had to interpret a similar definition in the Argentina–Italy BIT in order to determine whether sovereign bonds and security entitlements held in those bonds were protected investments. In both cases, questions arose about the translation of the treaty from Italian and Spanish into English. The tribunal in *Abaclat* found that the BIT defined 'investment' as 'any conferment or asset invested', which 'includes, without limitation:... (c) obligations, private or public titles or any other right to performances or services having economic value, including capitalized revenues'.[18] It concluded that the term 'obligations' covered bonds and the term 'titles' covered securities.[19] The claimants in *Ambiente Ufficio* argued that 'obligaciones' and 'obbligazioni' should be translated as 'bonds', while the respondent argued it should be translated as 'obligations'.[20] The tribunal in *Ambiente Ufficio* concluded that whichever translation it adopted, the BIT covered the bonds and security entitlements at issue.[21]

The tribunals also had to determine 'whether the connection between the security entitlements and the bonds could be seen as so remote as to consider that the dispute is not "directly" related to an investment, since the dispute related primarily to the rights arising from Claimants' security entitlements'.[22] Argentina argued that the tribunal should distinguish between 'bonds' and 'security entitlements', whereas the claimants argued that both comprised the single economic operation of bond issuances. Both tribunals found that the bonds and security entitlements formed 'part of one and the same economic operation and they make only sense together'.[23] The tribunal in *Ambiente Ufficio* added:

To seek to split up bonds and security entitlements into different, only loosely and indirectly connected operations would ignore the economic realities, and the very function, of the bond issuing process. In particular, it would disregard the fact that it is the bond

---

[12] *Siemens v Argentina*, ICSID Case No ARB/02/8 (Decision on Jurisdiction) (3 August 2004).
[13] ibid ¶ 137.   [14] ibid.   [15] ibid.
[16] *Abaclat and Ors v Argentine Republic (Case formerly known as Giovanna a Beccara and Ors)*, ICSID Case No ARB/07/5 (Decision on Jurisdiction and Admissibility) (4 August 2011).
[17] *Ambiente Ufficio SPA and Ors v Argentine Republic (Case formerly known as Giordano Alpi and Ors)*, ICSID Case No ARB/08/9 (Decision on Jurisdiction and Admissibility) (8 February 2013).
[18] *Abaclat* (n 16 above) ¶ 352.   [19] ibid ¶¶ 355–357.
[20] *Ambiente Ufficio* (n 17 above) ¶ 489.   [21] ibid ¶ 490.
[22] *Abaclat* (n 16 above) ¶ 358.
[23] ibid ¶ 359; quoted in *Ambiente Ufficio* (n 17 above) ¶ 423.

issuing State itself that departs from the assumption, and counts on the fact, that persons will purchase shares of the bonds on the secondary market, in the form of security entitlements, since otherwise the bond could not have been successfully issued in the first place.[24]

While the language of the Argentina–Italy BIT allowed the tribunal to find that it had jurisdiction, such claims could not have been brought under the UK–Colombia BIT, which provides a broad asset-based definition of 'investment' with an illustrative list, but states that 'investment' does not include 'public debt operations',[25] a term which would include sovereign bonds issued by a state or state entity.

Some treaties may expand the definition of 'investment' even further. For example, a BIT between the Belgo-Luxembourg Economic Union and Egypt provides in Article III(1) that:

The term 'investments' means any kind of assets and any direct or indirect contribution in cash, in kind or in services, invested or reinvested in any sector of economic activity...and includes in particular, though not exclusively moveable and immoveable property, shares, debts, intellectual property, and business concessions, among others.[26]

The tribunal's interpretation of this provision in *Jan de Nul NV and Dredging International NV v Arab Republic of Egypt*[27] illustrates how a broad definition of 'investment' may alter a treaty's scope of application. In that case, the tribunal had to decide whether the activities related to the dredging of the Suez Canal constituted an investment under the treaty. Based on common usage of the term 'investment', one might conclude that dredging activity could be considered to be only the provision of a service and not an investment. However, noting that the applicable BIT defined 'investment' to include 'any direct or indirect contribution in cash, in kind, or in services, invested or reinvested in any sector of economic activity', the tribunal found that the activities in question constituted a contribution in services and that, accordingly, they were an investment under the treaty.[28]

Many international investment agreements, including the Energy Charter Treaty (ECT),[29] accompany their definition of the term 'investment' with a clause stating that any alteration in the form in which the assets are invested will not affect their classification as investment.[30] The purpose of such a clause is to ensure

---

[24] *Ambiente Ufficio* (n 17 above) ¶ 425.

[25] Bilateral Agreement for the Promotion and Protection of Investments between the Government of the United Kingdom of Great Britain and Northern Ireland and the Republic of Colombia (17 March 2010), Art 1(2)(b)(i). In Art 1(2)(d) the BIT also requires that investments have certain substantive characteristics, specifically the commitment of capital and the assumption of risk. See the discussion in section 7.4 below.

[26] Agreement between the Belgo-Luxembourg Economic Union and the Arab Republic of Egypt on the Reciprocal Promotion and Protection of Investments (28 February 1999).

[27] *Jan de Nul NV and Dredging International NV v Arab Republic of Egypt*, ICSID Case No ARB/04/13 (Decision on Jurisdiction) (16 June 2006).

[28] ibid ¶¶ 105–106.

[29] ECT, Art 1(6): 'A change in the form in which investments are invested does not affect their character as investments.'

[30] See eg Agreement between the Government of the United Kingdom and Northern Ireland and the Government of the Republic of Croatia for the Promotion and Protection of Investments

that the treaty covers reinvestment of the proceeds of the initial investment to the same extent as it applies to the original assets. At the same time, any limitations imposed by the government on the original investment, for example that it be limited to a certain economic sector, will equally apply to the reinvestment.

Based on the preceding paragraphs, one may conclude that by extending the treaty's application to 'any kind of assets' the definitions are designed to protect as wide a range of investment forms as possible. The non-exhaustive lists of investment categories that refer to 'any kind of assets' exist only for illustrative purposes and to guide interpreters with respect to what investment forms may be recognized under the applicable treaty. Accordingly, even if an alleged investment does not fall within any of the specified categories, it may still enjoy protection under the treaty if it qualifies as 'an asset'. In addition, broad categories such as 'claims to money', 'right to performance or services having economic value', and 'other types of participation' would seem to broaden the scope of what one would traditionally consider to be an 'asset'. Though tribunals have not addressed the issue, it is plausible that rights arising under a franchise agreement or management contract[31] could qualify as an 'asset' within the meaning of an investment agreement.

On the other hand, even if a treaty uses a broad asset-based approach to defining investment, it may still state definitional limitations by specifying particular assets that are *not* to be covered. For example, the NAFTA definition of 'investment' in Article 1139 is broad, but specifies certain limits. It provides that 'investment' does not mean, among other things, '(i) claims to money that arise solely from...commercial contracts for the sale of goods or services by a national or enterprise in the territory of a Party to an enterprise in the territory of another Party, or...(ii) the extension of credit in connection with a commercial transaction, such as trade financing'. Thus, NAFTA is clearly seeking to exclude purely commercial transactions from the coverage of Chapter 11, which is intended to protect investments.

7.4 Broad Asset-Based Definitions Specifying Substantive Investment Characteristics as well as Illustrative Forms

Some investment treaties, while adopting a broad asset-based approach to defining investment and providing a non-exhaustive list of investment forms, also require that such forms have certain substantive investment characteristics. Thus, they define investment as 'an asset that has the characteristics of an investment'

(11 March 1997); Treaty between the Federal Republic of Germany and Bosnia and Herzegovina Concerning the Encouragement and Reciprocal Protection of Investments (18 October 2001); Agreement between the Government of the Republic of Azerbaijan and the Government of the Republic of Finland on the Promotion and Protection of Investments (26 February 2003).

[31] See *Saur International SA v Argentine Republic*, ICSID Case No ARB/04/4 (Award, in French) (22 May 2014) ¶ 329, in which Argentina did not contest and the tribunal accepted that a technical assistance contract was an 'investment' under both the Argentina–France BIT and the ICSID Convention.

and include a non-exhaustive list of the forms that such an investment may take. For example, Article 1 of the 2005 US–Uruguay BIT provides that '"investment" means *every asset that an investor owns or controls, directly or indirectly, that has the characteristics of an investment, including such characteristics as the commitment of capital or other resources, the expectation of gain or profit, or the assumption of risk'* (emphasis added).[32]

Article 1 then proceeds to list the various forms that an investment may take, including:

(a) an enterprise; (b) shares, stock, and other forms of equity participation in an enterprise; (c) bonds, debentures, other debt instruments, and loans; (d) futures, options, and other derivatives; (e) turnkey, construction, management, production, concession, revenue-sharing, and other similar contracts; (f) intellectual property rights; (g) licenses, authorizations, permits, and similar rights conferred pursuant to domestic law; and (h) other tangible or intangible, movable or immovable property, and related property rights, such as leases, mortgages, liens, and pledges.

This definition clearly demonstrates the contracting parties' intention to limit the BIT's scope of application to those assets having investment characteristics such as: (1) a commitment of capital or other resources; (2) the expectation of gain or profit; or (3) the assumption of risk. The treaty's reference to these characteristics is designed to distinguish investments from transactions of an ordinary, short-term character (for example the sale of a good or a service or a short-term financial transaction) in order to exclude the latter from the treaty's protection.[33] The motivation behind this limitation is the belief of certain governments that while long-term economic transactions with the characteristics of 'investments' contribute to host countries' economic development, which after all is one of the primary goals in concluding investment treaties, short-term financial transactions do not. Indeed, some governments believe that short-term transactions contribute to undesirable speculation, instability, and volatility in domestic markets. Through the treaty process, these countries seek to encourage asset flows that they consider constructive and discourage those they consider unconstructive.[34]

The 2009 ASEAN Comprehensive Investment Agreement adopts a similar approach. Article 4 of the Agreement gives the term 'investment' a broad asset-based definition with a non-exclusive list of examples; however, a footnote to that Article states: 'Where an asset lacks the characteristics of an investment, that asset is not an investment regardless of the form it may take. The characteristics of

---

[32] Treaty between the United States of America and the Oriental Republic of Uruguay Concerning the Encouragement and Reciprocal Protection of Investment (4 November 2005); see also 2012 US Model BIT, Art 1; Agreement among the Government of Japan, the Government of the Republic of Korea and the Government of the People's Republic of China for the Promotion, Facilitation and Protection of Investment (13 May 2012), Art 1(1).

[33] eg in the ICSID case of *Joy Mining Machinery*, the tribunal concluded that since the contract whose breach gave rise to claims under the Egypt–UK BIT had the characteristics of a normal sales contract, it did not qualify as an investment within the meaning of that treaty. *Joy Mining Machinery Ltd v Egypt*, ICSID Case No ARB/03/11 (Award on Jurisdiction) (6 August 2004) ¶¶ 55–63.

[34] Rubins (n 8 above) 286–7.

an investment include the commitment of capital, the expectation of gain or profit or the assumption of risk.'[35]

In view of the fluidity and evolving nature of investment transactions, the task of drawing a precise boundary between desirable investments granted treaty protection and other forms of economic transaction is not easy. One method of providing greater precision to this delineation is by including in the treaty explanatory notes concerning the interpretation of the term 'investment'. For example, Article 1 of the 2005 US–Uruguay BIT, clarifies that some forms of debt, such as bonds, debentures, and long-term notes, are more likely to have the characteristics of an investment; however, other forms of debt, such as bank accounts that do not have a commercial purpose and are not related to an investment in the territory where the bank account is located, and are not an attempt to make such an investment, are less likely to have such characteristics.[36] Another note in the same treaty makes clear that claims to immediately due payments resulting from the sale of goods or services do not qualify as investments. Yet another stipulates:

Whether a particular type of license, authorization, permit, or similar instrument (including a concession, to the extent that it has the nature of such an instrument) has the characteristics of an investment depends on such factors as the nature and extent of the rights that the holder has under the law of the contracting party. Among the licenses, authorizations, permits, and similar instruments that do not have the characteristics of an investment are those that do not create any rights protected under domestic law. For greater certainty, the foregoing is without prejudice to whether any asset associated with the license, authorization, permit, or similar instrument has the characteristics of an investment.[37]

The notes also make clear that 'investment' does not include an order or judgment entered in a judicial or administrative action.[38]

Therefore, under this approach only assets that have certain desired substantive characteristics of an investment fall within the definition of 'investment' and are protected by the applicable treaty. Moreover, the fact that a treaty text references a non-exhaustive list of investment characteristics implies that other traditional characteristics of investment[39] may also have to be satisfied for an asset to be covered by the treaty. On the other hand, the effectiveness of such limitation depends on the interpretations attached to them. For example, although the three investment characteristics of commitment of capital, expectation of profit, and assumption of risk are often used in investment treaties in an effort to limit the scope of

---

[35] 2009 ASEAN Comprehensive Investment Agreement, signed by the Economic Ministers at the 14th ASEAN Summit in Cha-am, Thailand, on 26 February 2009, available at <http://agreement.asean.org/media/download/20140119035519.pdf> accessed 17 October 2014.

[36] Treaty between the United States of America and the Oriental Republic of Uruguay Concerning the Encouragement and Reciprocal Protection of Investment (4 November 2005), Art 1.

[37] ibid.   [38] ibid.

[39] The question of the characteristics that an asset must have to establish ICSID jurisdiction is separate from what characteristics, if any, are required under an investment treaty. For a list of characteristics drawn from ICSID jurisprudence that are common in investment operations, see Schreuer (n 2 above).

investments covered, those three characteristics may be interpreted so broadly as to include almost any business transaction from a thirty-day promissory note to a bank account.

7.5 Asset-Based Definitions with an Exhaustive List of Investment Forms

In contrast to the approaches already mentioned, some treaties define the term 'investment' by providing an exhaustive list of the assets that are covered by the treaty and those that are not. Such listings are not merely illustrative or suggestive; they are intended to be definitive.[40]

---

[40] This approach is illustrated in the 2006 Canada–Peru BIT, Art 1, which states:

Investment means:

    (I) an enterprise;

    (II) an equity security of an enterprise;

    (III) a debt security of an enterprise
        (i) where the enterprise is an affiliate of the investor, or
        (ii) where the original maturity of the debt security is at least three years;

    (IV) a loan to an enterprise
        (i) where the enterprise is an affiliate of the investor, or
        (ii) where the original maturity of the loan is at least three years;

    (V) (i) notwithstanding subparagraphs (III) and (IV) above, a loan to or debt security issued by a financial institution is an investment only where the loan or debt security is treated as regulatory capital by the Party in whose territory the financial institution is located, and
        (ii) a loan granted by or debt security owned by a financial institution, other than a loan to or debt security of a financial institution referred to in (i), is not an investment;
      for greater certainty:
        (iii) a loan to, or debt security issued by, a Party or a state enterprise thereof is not an investment; and
        (iv) a loan granted by or debt security owned by a cross-border financial service provider, other than a loan to or debt security issued by a financial institution, is an investment if such loan or debt security meets the criteria for investments set out elsewhere in this Article;

    (VI) an interest in an enterprise that entitles the owner to share in income or profits of the enterprise;

    (VII) an interest in an enterprise that entitles the owner to share in the assets of that enterprise on dissolution, other than a debt security or a loan excluded from subparagraphs (III) (IV) or (V);

    (VIII) real estate or other property, tangible or intangible, acquired in the expectation or used for the purpose of economic benefit or other business purposes; and

    (IX) interests arising from the commitment of capital or other resources in the territory of a Party to economic activity in such territory, such as under
        (i) contracts involving the presence of an investor's property in the territory of the Party, including turnkey or construction contracts, or concessions, or
        (ii) contracts where remuneration depends substantially on the production, revenues or profits of an enterprise; but investment does not mean,

    (X) claims to money that arise solely from
        (i) commercial contracts for the sale of goods or services by a national or enterprise in the territory of a Party to an enterprise in the territory of the other Party, or

Although such definitions limit the investments covered to only the listed forms, usually they are still broad enough to include all the major investment forms currently employed by investors. Meanwhile, the clarifications and exclusions ensure that any assets lacking the traditional characteristics required by the treaty parties will not be protected. An UNCTAD study has observed that among newer treaties this approach constitutes an emerging trend.[41] The origins of this trend may be found in the decisions of tribunals applying treaties to transactions that the contracting states did not intend to protect.

7.6 Limitations on Definitions of 'Investment'

Regardless of whether a treaty defines 'investment' broadly or narrowly, assets that fall within a treaty's definition nonetheless may have to meet additional qualifications or requirements in order to come within that treaty's scope of application and protection. Such additional qualifications may require that an investment be made (a) in accordance with the laws and regulations of the host state; (b) in the territory of a host state; (c) before and/or after the date of entry into force of the BIT; (d) in certain sectors of the economy; or (e) in projects classified as 'approved' by appropriate governmental authorities. The nature and application of each of these limiting conditions is now examined.

(a) Legal requirements

The practice in most, but not all investment treaties,[42] of conditioning coverage of an investment on its compliance with local laws is an attempt to achieve a very important public purpose—ensuring that foreign investors observe host states' laws and regulations. This requirement also reflects the well-known legal maxim: 'No one should benefit from his own wrong.' For example, Article 1(1) of the Austria–Saudi Arabia BIT defines 'investment' to mean 'every kind of asset,

---

  (ii) the extension of credit in connection with a commercial transaction, such as
    trade financing, other than a loan covered by subparagraphs (IV) or (V); and
 (XI) any other claims for money, that do not involve the kinds of interests set out in
    sub-paragraphs (I) through (IX).

 Agreement between Canada and the Republic of Peru for the Promotion and Protection of Investments (14 November 2006); see also Agreement Between the Government of Canada and the Government of the Republic of Benin for the Promotion and Reciprocal Protection of Investments (9 January 2013), Art 1.

 [41] UNCTAD, *Bilateral Investment Treaties 1995–2006: Trends in Investment Rulemaking* (2007) 7–12.

 [42] eg the ECT contains no such requirement, a fact noted by the tribunal in *Anatolie Stati, Gabriel Stati, Ascom Group SA and Terra Raf Trans Traiding Ltd v Republic of Kazakhstan*, SCC Case No V116/2010 (Award) (19 December 2013) ¶ 812 ('the Tribunal notes that the ECT contains no requirement in this regard. Indeed, if the contracting states had intended there to be such a requirement, they could have written it into the text of the Treaty').

owned or controlled by an investor of a Contracting Party in the territory of the other Contracting Party *according to its legislation* and in particular, but not exclusively, includes...' (emphasis added).[43] Thus, under this definition an investment will enjoy treaty protection only if a claimant establishes that its investment has been owned and controlled in accordance with the host state's legislation. Conversely, a host government, and ultimately a tribunal, may deny treaty protection of an investment that is found not to be in compliance with host state national law.

Three arbitration cases illustrate some of the issues involved in applying this type of provision. In *Salini Construtorri SpA and Italstrade SpA v Morocco*,[44] the claimants relied on the broad definition of investment in the Italy–Morocco BIT, which included 'rights to any contractual benefit having an economic value' and 'any rights of an economic nature conferred by law or by contract' to argue that the contract in question gave them a right to economic value and that a breach of the treaty entitled them to damages. Morocco, however, responded that those categories of investments, when analysed in conjunction with the language 'invested in accordance with the laws and regulations of the party', should lead to the conclusion that 'it is Moroccan law [not the Italy–Morocco BIT] that should define the notion of investment'.[45] Accordingly, Morocco argued that because the transaction in question was characterized as a contract for services and not as a contract for investment under Moroccan law, the complaint did not allege violations of the BIT but only a contractual breach governed by Moroccan domestic law. The tribunal rejected this argument, concluding that '[i]n focusing on "*the categories of investment assets...in accordance with the* laws and regulations of the aforementioned party," this provision refers to the validity of the investment and not to its definition' (emphasis added).[46] More specifically, the tribunal stressed that such language 'seeks to prevent the Bilateral Investment Treaty from protecting investments that should not be protected, particularly because they would be illegal'.[47] The tribunal found that the contract was legally valid in Morocco and that it constituted an investment under the Morocco–Italy BIT.

In *Tokios Tokelés v Ukraine*,[48] the Ukrainian government argued that the claimant's investments were not made in accordance with Ukrainian law as required by Article 1(1) of the Ukraine–Lithuania BIT. The Ukrainian government based its argument on the grounds that 'the full name under which the Claimant registered its subsidiary...is improper, because "subsidiary enterprise" but not "subsidiary *private* enterprise" is a recognized legal form under Ukrainian law'. Ukraine also asserted that 'it has identified errors in the documents provided by the Claimant related to asset procurement and transfer, including, in some cases, the absence

---

[43] Agreement between The Kingdom of Saudi Arabia and The Republic of Austria concerning the Encouragement and Reciprocal Protection of Investments (30 June 2001).
[44] *Salini Construtorri SpA and Italstrade SpA v Morocco*, ICSID Case No ARB/00/4 (Decision on Jurisdiction) (23 July 2001) 42 ILM 609.
[45] ibid ¶ 38.   [46] ibid ¶ 46.   [47] ibid.
[48] *Tokios Tokelés v Ukraine*, ICSID Case No ARB/02/18 (Decision on Jurisdiction) (29 April 2004).

of a necessary signature or notarization'.[49] In responding to these allegations, the tribunal noted that Ukraine did not allege that the claimant's investments were illegal per se. Moreover, it found that Ukrainian authorities registered the claimant's subsidiary as a valid enterprise and had also subsequently registered each of the claimant's investments. Although Ukraine claimed that some of the registered investments' underlying documents contained various defects, some of which related to matters of Ukrainian law, the tribunal concluded: 'Even if we were able to confirm the Respondent's allegations, which would require a searching examination of minute details of administrative procedures in Ukrainian law, to exclude an investment on the basis of such minor errors would be inconsistent with the object and purpose of the Treaty [...which is to protect investments]'.[50] The fact that Ukraine registered each of the claimant's investments was sufficient evidence for the tribunal to conclude that the 'investment' in question was made in accordance with Ukrainian laws and regulations.

Finally, in *Alasdair Ross Anderson et al v Republic of Costa Rica*,[51] the claimants, a group of 137 Canadian nationals, had deposited funds between 1996 and 2002 along with some 6,200 persons, with Luis Enrique Villalobos and his brother Osvaldo, money changers in San Jose, Costa Rica, with the promise of high interest on a monthly basis. Although the Villalobos brothers were licensed money changers, the Central Bank had not authorized them to receive deposits, such transactions constituting illegal financial intermediation under the Central Bank Law. In effect, the two brothers were operating a 'Ponzi scheme'. As a result, the investors lost nearly all the money they had deposited. The Canadian investors brought a claim against the government of Costa Rica under the Canada–Costa Rica BIT,[52] but Costa-Rica challenged jurisdiction on various grounds, including that the deposits were not within the scope of the BIT which states in Article I(g): '"investment" means any kind of asset owned or controlled either directly, or indirectly through an enterprise or natural person of a third State, by an investor of one Contracting Party in the territory of the other Contracting Party in accordance with the latter's laws...'. Costa Rica argued that the Ponzi scheme was illegal under Costa Rican law and that therefore the claimants' deposits with the two brothers were not 'investments' under the BIT since they were not made in accordance with Costa Rican law. The tribunal found that the deposits by the claimants with the Villalobos brothers were assets since they resulted in a legal obligation to pay principal and interest therefore constituted a thing of value.[53] However, it ultimately concluded that since the Ponzi scheme operated by the Villalobos brothers violated Costa Rican law, the obligations held by the claimants were not owned or controlled in accordance with the law of Costa Rica as required by the BIT, stating:

---

[49] ibid ¶ 83.   [50] ibid ¶ 86.

[51] *Alasdair Ross Anderson et al v Republic of Costa Rica*, ICSID Case No ARB(AF)/07/3l (Award) (19 May 2010).

[52] Agreement between the Government of the Republic of Costa Rica and the Government of Canada for the Protection and Promotion of Investment (18 March 1998).

[53] *Alasdair Ross Anderson et al v Costa Rica* (n 51 above) ¶ 49.

The entire transaction between the Villalobos brothers and each Claimant was illegal because it violated the Organic Law of the Central Bank. If the transaction by which the Villalobos acquired the deposit was illegal, it follows that the acquisition by each Claimant of the asset resulting from that transaction was also not in accordance with the law of Costa Rica.[54]

The tribunal denied jurisdiction in the case.

It is to be noted that the requirement that investments be in accordance with law raises a possible defence in investor–state arbitration, for example, where an investment has been made through corruption or illegal payments by the investor to governmental authorities, a situation that unfortunately occurs with some frequency. In *Inceysa Vallisoletana SL v Republic of El Salvador*, El Salvador claimed that the investor made investments through fraud and misrepresentation. Since the investments had not been established 'in accordance with law' as required by the BIT, El Salvador argued that the claimant should be deprived of the protections of the treaty. In the light of these facts, the tribunal dismissed the claims of the Spanish company Inceysa Vallisoletana SL for lack of jurisdiction, since the treaty conditioned the tribunal's jurisdiction on investments being made 'in accordance with law'. It also noted that any contrary finding would run counter to the general principle, inherent in the notion of the international public order, that parties should not benefit from their own wrongdoing.[55] A similar result came about in the ICSID case of *World Duty Free v The Republic of Kenya* in which undisputed evidence was introduced during the proceedings that the claimant had secured its investment in question by paying a bribe to the then head of state. As a result, the tribunal held that the claimants' claims should be dismissed immediately and in their entirety.[56] In *Metal-Tech v Uzbekistan*, the tribunal also found that corruption was established to an extent sufficient to violate Uzbekistan law in connection with the claimant's investment. Therefore, it concluded the investment in question was not 'implemented in accordance with the laws' of Uzbekistan and declined jurisdiction.[57]

In general, the inclusion of the qualification 'in accordance with the laws and regulations of the host State' in the definition of 'investment' refers to the validity of the investment and is designed to prevent the treaty from protecting investments that were not made in compliance with the host state's national legislation. It should be noted that such provisions place an absolute obligation on the investor to make its investment in accordance with the host country law. The fact that an investor made a 'reasonable effort' or 'exercised due diligence' to assure the

---

[54] ibid ¶ 55.

[55] Summary of Award by counsel for El Salvador, *Inceysa Vallisoletana SL v Republic of El Salvador*, ICSID Case No ARB/03/26 (Award) (2 August 2006).

[56] For a summary of this case, see Chatham House, 'World Duty Free v. The Republic of Kenya: A Unique Precedent?', available at <http://star.worldbank.org/corruption-cases/sites/corruption-cases/files/documents/arw/Moi_World_Duty_Free_Chatham_House_Mar_28_2007.pdf> accessed 17 October 2014. See also J W Yackee, 'Investment Treaties & Investor Corruption: An Emerging Defense for Host States?' (2012) 52 Va J Int'l L 723.

[57] Chatham House, 'World Duty Free' (n 56 above) ¶¶ 372–373.

legality of its investment would not be sufficient to meet the obligation imposed by such treaty language.[58]

(b) Territorial requirements

Investment treaties often specifically limit their application to investments made within the territory of the respective contracting parties. The rationale behind this practice is to ensure that the host state obtains the benefits from the operation of foreign investments within its territory, whether such benefits consist of obtaining new technologies, developing important economic sectors, creating new jobs, or collecting additional tax revenues. Such a condition may be included either in the definition of the term 'investment' or in the provision on the treaty's scope of application. The former approach is illustrated in Article 1 of the Canada–Peru BIT, which provides: '"Covered investment" means, with respect to a Party, *an investment in its territory of an investor of the other Party* existing on the date of entry into force of this Agreement, as well as investments made or acquired thereafter' (emphasis added).[59] The latter approach is illustrated in Article II of the Switzerland–Philippines BIT, which provides: 'The present agreement applies to investments in the territory of the one Contracting Party made in accordance with its laws and regulations by investors of the other Contracting Party, whether prior to or after the entry into force of the Agreement'.[60] Thus, according to such provisions treaty protection extends to an investment only if it is made in the territory of the host State.

The challenges of determining whether an investment was made in the territory of the treaty state and thus qualifies as a covered investment are illustrated in a number of arbitral cases. In *Fedax NV v Venezuela*,[61] Venezuela argued that Fedax did not qualify as an investor because, only being the holder of promissory notes, it had not made any 'investment' in the territory of the host state. In response to this argument, the tribunal recognized that 'it is true that in some kinds of investments, such as the acquisition of interests in immovable property, companies and the like, a transfer of funds or value will be made into the territory of the host country' but it stressed that 'this does not necessarily happen in a number of other types of investments, particularly those of a financial nature'.[62]

---

[58] See *Alasdair Ross Anderson et al v Costa Rica* (n 51 above) ¶ 58.

[59] Agreement between Canada and the Republic of Peru for the Promotion and Protection of Investments (14 November 2006).

[60] The French text of Art II reads:

Champ d'application

Le présent Accord est applicable aux investissements *effectués sur le territoire d'une Partie contractante*, conformément à ses lois et règlements, par des investisseurs de l'autre Partie contractante, avant ou après son entrée en vigueur. (emphasis added).

Accord entre la Confédération suisse et la République des Philippines concernant la promotion et la protection réciproque des investissements (31 March 1997).

[61] *Fedax NV v Venezuela*, ICSID Case No ARB/96/3 (Award on Jurisdiction) (11 July 1997).

[62] On this point the tribunal observed:

It is a standard feature of many international financial transactions that the funds involved are not physically transferred to the territory of the beneficiary, but put at its

The test in such circumstances, according to the tribunal, is whether the available funds are used by the beneficiary of the credit to finance its various governmental needs.[63] Since it was not disputed that through its promissory notes Venezuela had received credit that was put to work for its financial needs, those promissory notes were determined to be invested in the territory of Venezuela within the meaning of the treaty.[64]

The issue of whether an investment was made in the territory of a treaty party also arose in three cases by the same claimants involving similar transactions, one against Pakistan, one against the Philippines, and one against Paraguay.[65] In *SGS Société Générale de Surveillance SA v Islamic Republic of Pakistan*[66] and *SGS Société Générale de Surveillance SA v Republic of the Philippines*,[67] the disputes arose out of the alleged wrongful termination of contracts under which SGS, a Swiss group, was to provide 'pre-shipment inspection services', including comprehensive import supervision of goods before shipment to the Philippines and Pakistan. In *SGS Société Générale de Surveillance SA v Republic of Paraguay*,[68] SGS brought a claim for unpaid invoices for the same services. Because of the nature of the services to be rendered, the SGS activity was carried out in the territories of exporting countries. In all three cases the respondent states objected to the tribunal's jurisdiction by arguing that SGS's investments were not made in the territory of the host states and so were not covered by the applicable BITs, which included the territoriality investment requirement. As a result, they argued, the dispute did not arise out of an investment. In determining whether SGS made an 'investment'

disposal elsewhere. In fact, many loans and credits do not leave the country of origin at all, but are available to suppliers or other entities. The same is true of many important offshore financial operations relating to exports and other kinds of business. And, of course promissory notes are frequently employed in such arrangements.

ibid ¶ 41.

[63] ibid.

[64] This approach has been adopted in subsequent cases. See *Abaclat and Ors (Case formerly known as Giovanna a Beccara and Ors) v Argentine Republic*, ICSID Case No ARB/07/5 (Decision on Jurisdiction and Admissibility) (4 August 2011) ¶¶ 373–378 (security entitlements on sovereign bonds fulfilled territorial requirement because funds were ultimately made available to Argentina and financed its economic development); *Deutsche Bank AG v Democratic Socialist Republic of Sri Lanka*, ICSID Case No ARB/09/2 (Award) (31 October 2012) ¶¶ 288–292 (hedging agreement to protect Sri Lanka against rising oil prices fulfilled territorial requirement because funds were made available to Sri Lanka, were linked to an activity taking place in Sri Lanka, and served to finance its economy); *Ambiente Ufficio SPA and Ors (Case formerly known as Giordano Alpi and Ors) v Argentine Republic*, ICSID Case No ARB/08/9 (Decision on Jurisdiction and Admissibility) (8 February 2013) ¶¶ 498–509 (security entitlements on sovereign bonds fulfilled territorial requirement because bonds aimed to raise money for budgetary needs of Argentina and further its development).

[65] See also *Bureau Veritas, Inspection, Valuation, Assessment, and Control, BIVAC BV v The Republic of Paraguay*, ICSID Case No ARB/07/9 (Decision of the Tribunal on Objections to Jurisdiction) (29 May 2009) ¶¶ 74–105.

[66] *SGS Société Générale de Surveillance SA v Islamic Republic of Pakistan*, ICSID Case No ARB/01/13 (Decision on Jurisdiction) (6 August 2003).

[67] *SGS Société Générale de Surveillance SA v Republic of the Philippines*, ICSID Case No ARB/02/6 (Decision on Jurisdiction) (29 January 2004).

[68] *SGS Société Générale de Surveillance SA v The Republic of Paraguay*, ICSID Case No ARB/07/29 (Decision on Jurisdiction) (12 February 2010).

'in the territory of Pakistan', the tribunal noted that the Pre-Shipment Inspection (PSI) Agreement defined SGS's commitments in such a way as to ensure that SGS, if it were to comply with them, had to make certain expenditures within Pakistan. It observed that '[w]hile the expenditures may be relatively small (Pakistan's Reply estimated them as amounting to approximately US$800,000, while SGS's estimate put them at US$1.5 million), they involved the injection of funds into the territory of Pakistan for the carrying out of SGS's engagements under the PSI Agreement'.[69] The tribunal also found relevant the fact that the claimant adduced evidence of expenditures to establish and operate liaison offices in Pakistan to perform its obligations under the PSI Agreement,[70] and that Pakistan itself recognized that the PSI Agreement involved the delegation of some of the state's customs powers to the private party in order to increase the customs revenue of that state.[71] Therefore, the tribunal held that the expenditures made by SGS pursuant to the PSI Agreement constituted an investment within the meaning of the BIT and, moreover, that the ICSID Convention's requirement that there be a legal dispute arising directly out of an 'investment' was satisfied.[72]

In the SGS arbitration against the Philippines, a different tribunal arrived at the same conclusion. The tribunal stressed the clear language of the territorial limitation and stated:

In accordance with normal principles of treaty interpretation, investments made outside the territory of the Respondent State, however beneficial to it, would not be covered by the BIT. For example the construction of an embassy in a third State, or the provision of security services to such an embassy, would not involve investments in the territory of the State whose embassy it was, and would not be protected by the BIT.[73]

In its analysis of the facts of the dispute, the tribunal found that under the Comprehensive Import Supervision Services (CISS) Agreement between SGS and the Philipines, SGS was to provide services, inside and outside the Philippines, to improve and integrate the import services and associated customs revenue-gathering of the Philippines. It gave particular attention to the fact that the purpose of the agreement was the creation in the Philippines of a reliable inspection certificate (Clean Report of Findings (CRF)) on the basis of which import clearance could be expedited and the appropriate duty charged. SGS's inspections abroad were not carried out for their own sake but to provide an inspection certificate in the Philippines that governmental authorities could rely on in allowing the entry of goods to the customs territory of the Philippines and in assessing and collecting the resulting customs revenue. Although the certificate was not a legal instrument, it was nonetheless valuable evidence and its provision was central to SGS's operations. Further, those operations were organized through SGS's Manila Liaison Office, which under Article 5 of the CISS Agreement SGS was obliged to 'continue and maintain...until the date upon which this Agreement ceases to be effective or its implementation is interrupted or indefinitely suspended'.

---

[69] *SGS v Pakistan* (n 66 above) ¶ 136.   [70] ibid ¶ 137.   [71] ibid ¶ 139.
[72] ibid ¶ 140.   [73] *SGS v Philippines* (n 67 above) ¶ 99.

The liaison office was of substantial size, employing a significant number of people, and played an important role in providing the required service.[74] These elements taken together enabled the tribunal to find that SGS had made an investment in the Philippines within the meaning of the BIT; however, it implied that its position might have been different if SGS had provided the certificates and issued its reports abroad, for example to a Philippines trade mission in each exporting country.

In *SGS v Paraguay*, the respondent argued that the preponderance of SGS's services took place outside Paraguay and that SGS's specific claims concerned non-payment for services performed abroad and not acts and omissions affecting its activities in Paraguay.[75] The tribunal rejected the respondent's distinction, stating:

this Tribunal does not consider it consistent with the facts presented to subdivide Claimant's activities into services provided abroad and services provided in Paraguay, and to then attribute Claimant's claims solely to the former category. SGS's inspections abroad were not carried out for separate purposes, but rather in order to enable it to provide, in Paraguay, a final Inspection Certificate on which the Paraguayan authorities relied to enter goods into the customs territory of Paraguay and to assess and collect the resulting customs revenue.[76]

The tribunal added that even if it were possible to separate the services between those provided abroad and those provided in Paraguay, there would be no way to attribute Paraguay's non-payment to only those services provided abroad.[77] The tribunal concluded its analysis by noting that its decision was consistent with those in *SGS v Philippines* and *SGS v Pakistan*.

NAFTA, unlike many BITs, contains no explicit territorial requirement in the definitions of 'investor' or 'investment'. However, Article 1101 of Chapter Eleven's scope of coverage makes clear that it applies only to '... (b) investments of investors of another Party in the territory of the Party', thus leading the tribunal in *Methanex v United States* to state that Article 1101 is 'the gateway leading to the dispute resolution provisions of Chapter 11';[78] a gateway that limits the powers of Chapter Eleven tribunals. Accordingly, NAFTA tribunals have consistently held that 'in order to be an "investor" under Article 1139 one must make an investment in the territory of another NAFTA State, not in one's own'.[79] Thus, for example

---

[74] ibid ¶¶ 101–102.   [75] *SGS v Paraguay* (n 68 above) ¶ 111.   [76] ibid ¶ 113.
[77] ibid ¶ 115.
[78] *Methanex Corp v United States*, NAFTA/UNCITRAL (First Partial Award) (7 August 2002) ¶ 106.
[79] *Bayview Irrigation District et al v United Mexican States*, ICSID Case No ARB(AF)/05/1 (Award on Jurisdiction) (19 June 2007) ¶ 105. See also *Canadian Cattlemen for Fair Trade v United States*, NAFTA/UNCITRAL (Award on Jurisdiction) (28 January 2008) ¶ 126; *Grand River Enterprises Six Nations Ltd v United States*, NAFTA/UNCITRAL (Award) (12 January 2011) ¶ 87, stating that NAFTA Chapter Eleven is applicable 'only to investors of one NAFTA Party who seek to make, are making, or have made an investment in another NAFTA Party: absent those conditions, both the substantive protection of Section A and the remedies provided in Section B of Chapter Eleven are unavailable to an investor'.

in *Apotex Inc v United States*,[80] a Canadian pharmaceutical company instituted an arbitration against the United States under Chapter Eleven of NAFTA on the grounds that US regulatory agencies and federal courts violated their obligations under the treaty because of the measures they had taken against Apotex's efforts to obtain approval to bring certain new generic drugs to market in the United States. The tribunal dismissed the complaint for lack of jurisdiction because all of Apotex's activities occurred in Canada, not the United States, and because the claimant neither resided nor had a place of business in the United States, had no equity or debt interest in any US company, had not claimed to have purchased property, built facilities, or hired a workforce in the United States, and did not claim to have developed, tested, or manufactured its drugs in the United States. Furthermore, the claimant developed pharmaceutical products in Canada for the domestic market and for export to many other countries. The products at issue in the case were formulated, developed, manufactured, tested, and labelled outside the United States and then exported thereto. The tribunal held that activity by an exporter in its own country did not constitute an investment under Article 1139 of NAFTA.[81]

(c) Temporal requirements

Most treaties extend the definition of 'investment' to cover all investments existing at the date of the treaty's signature or entry into force, whether such investments were made before or after that date. For example, Article 1 of the Canada–Peru BIT provides that 'covered investment' means 'an investment of an investor of the other Party existing on the date of entry into force of this Agreement, as well as investments made or acquired thereafter'.[82] Article 1 of the Ghana–Guinea BIT provides that the term 'investment' includes 'all investments, whether made before or after the date of entry into force of this Agreement'.[83] Under these provisions all investments existing at the treaty's effective date enjoy the benefit of its protection. The inclusion of all existing investments within an investment treaty's scope of application may also signal the seriousness of the host state's commitment to ensuring a favourable investment climate.

This issue of whether investments made prior to the entry into force of a treaty should nonetheless benefit from its provisions has not been without contention in some treaty negotiations. Developing countries have sometimes sought to limit

---

[80] *Apotex Inc v United States*, UNCITRAL (Award on Jurisdiction and Admissibility) (14 June 2013).

[81] Ibid. ¶¶ 160–176.

[82] Agreement between Canada and the Republic of Peru for the Promotion and Protection of Investments (14 November 2006).

[83] Agreement between the Government of the Republic of Ghana and the Government of the Republic of Guinea for the Promotion and Protection of Investments (18 May 2001).

a treaty's application only to future investment or at least to investments made in the relatively recent past.[84] Viewing treaties primarily as investment promotion mechanisms, they have claimed to see little purpose in granting additional protection to investments already made in the host country. Moreover, they argue that their governments might not have approved previous investments if they had realized that an investment treaty could later expand the investor's rights and privileges.[85] Capital-exporting states, on the other hand, have generally sought to protect all their nationals' investments and companies, regardless of when they were made. For example, the US Model BIT defines 'covered investment' as 'an investment in its territory of an investor of the other Party in existence as of the date of entry into force of this Treaty or established, acquired, or expanded thereafter'.[86]

Investment treaties, including the ECT and most BITs, also seek continued treaty protection for investors after the treaty has terminated or the host country has withdrawn. For example, the ECT states that it will continue to apply to investments for a period of twenty years from the effective date of withdrawal.[87] This continuing effects provision is designed to protect investors who have made investments in reliance on the expectation of treaty protection. In many BITs, the period of continued protection is between fifteen and twenty years.[88]

However, where a new treaty supersedes obligations under an earlier treaty, the definition of 'investment', while continuing to cover existing investments, may exclude investment disputes arising before the new treaty's entry into force from arbitration. For example, Article 1 of the UK–Croatia BIT provides that 'the term investment includes all investments whether made before or after the date of entry into force of this Agreement, but the provisions of this Agreement shall not apply to a dispute concerning an investment which arose before its entry into force'.[89] One reason behind this clause may be a desire by the contracting states to preclude investors from shopping among different international legal regimes and to ensure that investment disputes arising prior to a new treaty's conclusion are decided in accordance with the provisions of the treaty under which the investment was originally made.

---

[84] See eg Agreement between the Government of the United Kingdom of Great Britain and Northern Ireland and the Government of the Republic of Indonesia for the Promotion and Protection of Investments (27 April 1976), Art 2(3) ('The rights and obligations of both Contracting Parties with respect to investments made before 10 January 1967 shall be in no way affected by the provisions of this Agreement').

[85] UNCTAD, *Bilateral Investment Treaties in the Mid-1990s* (1998) 42.

[86] 2012 US Model BIT, Art 1; see also Malaysia–Australia Free Trade Agreement (22 May 2012), Art 12.2(a).

[87] ECT, Art 47(3).   [88] UNCTC, *Bilateral Investment Treaties* (1988) 36–40.

[89] Agreement between the Government of the United Kingdom and Northern Ireland and the Government of the Republic of Croatia for the Promotion and Protection of Investments (11 March 1997).

(d) Sector requirements

Some treaties provide that for an asset to qualify as an investment that asset must be made in a specified sector of the economy. For example, Article III(1) of the Egypt–Belgo-Luxemburg Economic Union BIT contains the following general definition of investment: 'The term "investments" shall comprise every direct or indirect contribution of capital and any other kind of assets, invested or reinvested in enterprises in the field of agriculture, industry, mining, forestry, communications, and tourism'.[90] Thus, under this definition, for a contribution of capital to constitute an investment it must be made in one of the specified economic sectors.

The challenges that may arise in interpreting provisions of this kind are illustrated in *Jan de Nul NV and Dredging International NV v Arab Republic of Egypt*.[91] In that dispute, the tribunal was faced with the question of whether a contribution of capital was invested in one of the fields specified in Article III(1), as just quoted. More specifically, the issue was whether the dredging of the Suez Canal was related to 'communications' within the meaning of that Article. Egypt argued that the dredging of the Canal did not relate to communications, since the ordinary meaning of 'communications' in English is limited to the exchange of information. In response, the claimants relied on authoritative English language dictionaries to support the argument that the word 'communications' is not limited to the transmission of information but includes a geographical dimension. For example, it may include: 'any connective passage or channel', 'a system of routes for moving troops, supplies, and vehicles', or 'passage or an opportunity or means of passage between places'. The tribunal ultimately decided the issue in favour of the claimants, stating that it failed 'to see how the Respondent can argue that including "road of communication" or "transport of persons and goods" in the meaning of "communications" under Article III(1) can be "at odds with the common and ordinary meaning of the term communications"'. The tribunal also found that just because the claimants' activities related to dredging the canal, and not communicating through the canal, did not mean that the claimants had not invested in an enterprise in the field of communications within the meaning of the BIT.[92]

Although limiting an investment to certain economic sectors may be justified by economic development or the protection of a national economy, most modern BITs have not followed this practice.[93] While the definition of investment is broad in virtually all BITs, the area of economic activity defined as an investment in the ECT is subject to limitations because it is only intended to

---

[90] Agreement between the Arab Republic of Egypt on the One Hand, and the Belgo-Luxemburg Economic Union on the Other Hand, on the Encouragement and Reciprocal Protection of Investments (28 February 1977), Art III.

[91] *Jan de Nul NV and Dredging International NV v Arab Republic of Egypt*, ICSID Case No ARB/04/13 (Decision on Jurisdiction) (16 June 2006).

[92] ibid ¶¶ 101–102, 104.

[93] See generally UNCTAD, *Bilateral Investment Treaties in the Mid-1990s* (1998) 7–12.

cover the energy sector. Therefore, its drafters had to define that sector with some precision. Article 1(6) of the ECT states: '"Investment" refers to any investment Associated with an Economic Activity in the Energy Sector and to investments or classes of investments designated by a Contracting Party as "Charter efficiency projects" and so notified to the [Energy Charter] Secretariat'. Under Article 1(4), '"Economic Activity in the Energy Sector" is defined broadly as "an economic activity concerning the exploration, extraction, refining, production, storage, land transportation, transmission, distribution, trade, marketing or Sale of Energy Materials and Products"' with certain specified exceptions. The Understandings in the Final Act of the European Energy Charter Conference give examples of permitted 'Economic Activity in the Energy Sector' and further underscore the sectoral character of the Treaty by stating that it confers no right to engage in economic activities other than in the Energy Sector.

Because most other investment treaties are general rather than sectoral in scope, they have usually not employed such elaborate provisions to define the sectors in which investments are permitted. On the other hand, investment treaties rarely allow investments in all economic sectors. Most BITs either specifically identify sectors in which nationals from the other country may not invest, for example banking or maritime shipping, or they state that investments are allowed only in those sectors permitted by domestic law, a provision that incorporates legislation prohibiting foreign investment in defined economic areas into the treaty by reference.[94]

(e) Approved project requirements

Some treaties may also limit their scope to investments in projects classified by appropriate governmental authorities as 'approved projects'. The aim of this provision is to confine a treaty's encouragement and protection only to investment in projects perceived by a host country's governing authorities to be contributing to the state's economic development or national interest. For example, Article 1 of the Sweden–Malaysia BIT, like many treaties, defines 'investment' as 'any kind of asset'; however, the definition also contains an important proviso:

provided that such asset when invested:
(i) in Malaysia, *is invested in a project classified by the appropriate Ministry in Malaysia in accordance with its legislation and administrative practice as an 'approved project.'* The classification as an 'approved project' may, on application, be accorded to investments made prior to the date of the entry into force of this Agreement on conditions to be stipulated for each individual case (emphasis added).[95]

Although this provision contains a broad asset-based definition of 'investment', it attaches a condition limiting the BIT's application to assets classified as 'approved

[94] UNCTC, *Bilateral Investment Treaties* (1988) 27.
[95] Agreement between the Government of Sweden and the Government of Malaysia concerning the Mutual Protection of Investments of 1979, Art 1.

projects'. A failure to satisfy this condition would deprive an asset of the BIT's protection because it would not constitute a covered investment within the meaning of the treaty.

The ICSID case of *Gruslin v Malaysia*,[96] which involved an alleged investment made in securities listed on the Malaysian Stock Exchange (KLSE), required the tribunal to interpret a provision similar to that quoted earlier. Relying on that provision, Malaysia argued that the assets in question did not constitute an investment within the meaning of the treaty because they were not made in an approved project and because 'mere investment in shares in the stock market, which can be traded by anyone and are not connected to the development of an approved project, are not protected'. The sole arbitrator upheld Malaysia's position and rejected the claimant's contention that the approval given to participate in the KLSE listing processes was sufficient to satisfy the 'approved project' requirement. The arbitrator noted: 'What is required is something constituting regulatory approval of a "project", as such, and not merely the approval at some time of the general business activities of a corporation.'[97] He therefore concluded that the shares in question did not satisfy the treaty's definition of 'investment' and consequently were not protected by the BIT. Thus, it would seem that clauses similar to the proviso found in the Sweden–Malaysia BIT require specific governmental authorization for the investment. The fact that an investment was made in accordance with the host country's laws and regulations, as was discussed earlier in section 7.6(a), is not sufficient to meet this requirement.

7.7 Arbitral Applications of Investment Definitions in Special Situations

Arbitral tribunals have increasingly been called upon to interpret treaty definitions of 'investment' and apply them to a variety of assets and transactions. As noted earlier in this chapter, tribunals have found construction contracts,[98] loan agreements,[99] shares,[100] locally incorporated corporations,[101] promissory notes,[102] and public concession agreements,[103] among others, to come within the meaning of 'investment' in different investment treaties. Still, categories of assets exist

---

[96] *Gruslin v Malaysia*, ICSID Case No ARB/99/3 (Final Award) (27 November 2000).

[97] ibid ¶ 25.5.

[98] *Salini Construtorri SpA and Italstrade SpA v Morocco*, ICSID Case No ARB/00/4 (Decision on Jurisdiction) (23 July 2001).

[99] *Ceskoslovenska Obchodni Banka, AS v The Slovak Republic*, ICSID Case No ARB/97/4 (Award on Jurisdiction) (24 May 1999).

[100] *Asian Agricultural Products Ltd v Sri Lanka*, ICSID Case No ARB/87/3 (Final Award) (27 June 1990) (UK–Sri Lanka BIT); *American Manufacturing and Trading, Inc v Zaire*, ICSID Case No ARB/93/1 (Award) (21 February 1997); *CMS Gas Transmission Co v The Argentine Republic*, ICSID Case No ARB/01/8 (Decision on Jurisdiction) (17 July 2003).

[101] *Tokios Tokelés v Ukraine*, ICSID Case No ARB/02/18 (Decision on Jurisdiction) (29 April 2004).

[102] *Fedax NV v Venezuela*, ICSID Case No ARB/96/3 (Award on Jurisdiction) (11 July 1997).

[103] *Lanco International Inc v Argentina*, ICSID Case No ARB/97/6 (Decision on Jurisdiction) (8 December 1998).

where there is controversy as to whether they constitute protected investments. Among such complex situations are (a) pre-investment expenditures; (b) shareholdings; and (c) indirect holdings. This section examines each of these situations.

(a) Pre-investment expenditures

One interesting question is whether expenses incurred by an investor in developing a project that does not ultimately come to fruition can be considered an 'investment' for the purposes of an investment treaty. A financial expert would probably consider such expenses to be investments, since they are a commitment of funds for a business purpose in the expectation of a return. However, that determination is not necessarily conclusive under investment treaties.

One of the first reported cases dealing with this issue is *Mihaly International Corporation v Sri Lanka*.[104] In 1993, Mihaly entered into a series of arrangements with the Sri Lankan government in the hope of concluding a contract for constructing a 300 megawatt power plant in Sri Lanka on a build-own-transfer basis. This arrangement included a letter of intent, a letter of agreement, and a letter of intention. The letter of intent, however, specified that it 'constitutes a Statement of Intention and does not constitute an obligation binding on any party' and that 'the project and contract details are subject to Cabinet approval'. The other two documents also clearly specified that they did not create binding obligations on either party. After the execution of those arrangements, and after Mihaly incurred significant expense, the government decided not to sign a project agreement. Seeking reimbursement of its expenses and compensation for lost profits, Mihaly filed a request for ICSID arbitration based on the US–Sri Lanka BIT, claiming that it had not received fair and equitable treatment at the hands of the Sri Lankan government. Sri Lanka defended itself by claiming that such pre-contractual expenses did not constitute an investment and were therefore not subject to international legal protection; consequently, ICSID and the tribunal did not have jurisdiction over Mihaly's claim.

The tribunal found that the pre-contract expenditures did not constitute an investment within the meaning of Article 25 of the ICSID Convention and did not fall under the protection of the US–Sri Lanka BIT. It based its decision on two grounds. First, Sri Lanka had taken great care to state that none of the documents created a contractual obligation for building the power plant. Second, the negotiations between the parties never evolved into a contract.[105] The tribunal also observed that 'it is always a matter for the parties to determine at what point in their negotiations they wish to engage the provisions of the Convention by entering into an investment'.[106]

---

[104] *Mihaly International Corp v Sri Lanka*, ICSID Case No ARB/00/2. For further comments, see R Hornick, 'The *Mihaly* Arbitration Pre-Investment Expenditure as a Basis for ICSID Jurisdiction' (2003) 20(2) J Int'l Arb 189; Yala (n 2 above) 105–26.
[105] *Mihaly International* (n 104 above) ¶ 48.
[106] ibid ¶ 51. It further observed:

If the negotiations during the period of exclusivity, or for that matter, without exclusivity, *had come to fruition, it may well have been the case that the moneys expended during the*

At the same time, the tribunal was careful to confine its holding to the facts of the case before it. It said that it 'is not unmindful of the need to adapt the Convention to changes in the form of cooperation between investors and host States. However, these changes have to be considered in the context of the specific obligations which the parties respectively assume in the particular case'. The tribunal repeated that, in other circumstances, similar expenditure might be found to be an investment.[107]

It is interesting to note that the claimant did not present any arguments on whether its expenditures were investments within the meaning of the US–Sri Lanka BIT. Its only BIT-based arguments were based on Article II, which dealt with the standards of treatment for investments, and Article VI, which specified what investment disputes were subject to ICSID arbitration. The BIT, however, contained a very broad asset-based definition of the term 'investment' with no requirement that the asset arise out of a contract or that it be admitted, approved, or registered by the host state. This factor prompted one commentator to suggest that it would have been possible for Mihaly to argue that its rights fell within the BIT's concept of investments and that therefore under the BIT pre-investment expenditures could be considered as a protected investment.[108]

A second case involving pre-investment expenses, *PSEG v Turkey*,[109] dealt with claims under the US–Turkey BIT that arose from the cancellation of a concession contract by the Turkish government before any works commenced. Turkey argued that, while the parties signed and approved the concession contract, the contract did not constitute an investment because it did not contain essential agreed commercial terms and, at best, constituted a framework for further negotiation. Therefore, analogizing to *Mihaly*, Turkey argued that the claimants had incurred expenditures on a project that never materialized, but had not made an investment under the BIT.

The tribunal approached the question in two steps: first it had to determine whether a contract existed and then decide whether it was valid. On this issue, the tribunal found that the concession contract existed because it was couched in proper legal language, duly signed, approved, and later executed with all the necessary legal formalities and requirements. According to the tribunal, the existence of that contract was a substantive difference from the facts in *Mihaly*, where the

---

period of negotiations might have been capitalised as part of the cost of the project and thereby become part of the investment. By capitalising expenses incurred during the negotiation phase, the parties in a sense may retrospectively sweep those costs within the umbrella of an investment. (emphasis added)

[107] ibid ¶ 49.

[108] WB Hamida, 'The *Mihaly v. Sri Lanka* Case: Some Thoughts Relating to the Status of Pre-investment Expenditures' in T Weiler (ed), *International Investment Law and Arbitration: Leading Cases from the ICSID, NAFTA, Bilateral Treaties and Customary International Law* (Cameron May, 2005) 53, 64–6.

[109] *PSEG Global, Inc, The North American Coal Corp, and Konya Ingin Electrik Uretim ve Ticaret Ltd Sirketi v Turkey*, ICSID Case No ARB/02/5 (Decision on Jurisdiction) (4 June 2004).

parties never signed a concession contract and Sri Lanka had expressly disclaimed any legal obligations arising from the preparatory work undertaken.[110]

On the second issue, the tribunal also determined that the contract was valid. It looked to both the language of the contract as well as the circumstances of the case, which demonstrated an intent by the parties to be bound despite the fact that certain terms needed to be agreed upon at a later date.[111] Moreover, it added:

Theoretically, on the basis of the Contract as signed and executed, the Claimants could still undertake the project on the commercial terms therein specified, which the Respondent has admitted was a possibility... [and the] fact that economically the project might be difficult to execute or even become unfeasible does not render the Contract invalid... [n]either does the fact that the project could become impossible to perform.[112]

Having thus established the existence and the validity of the contract, the tribunal determined that the contract was a protected investment within the meaning of the applicable treaties.

These two BIT cases demonstrate that a distinction can be drawn between disputes where expenses have been incurred before a contract or governmental approval has become effective and those arising after the government has approved a contract. This distinction may have serious implications for investors and host states alike. As one commentator observed, expenditures incurred in preparatory work for the making of an investment certainly represent a 'pre-investment and development' activity, which is a common feature of modern-day commercial activity. Investors may spend large amounts of money to prepare the resources necessary to fulfil the final stage of a contract for a major investment project. Thus, they may commit several million dollars on financing, negotiating, and engineering, as well as on legal work, environmental studies, and financial advice.[113] In this connection, the concurring opinion in *Mihaly* by arbitrator D Suratgar underscored an important consideration:

if private foreign investors are to be encouraged to pursue transparency in seeking such... opportunities the international community must address the lessons of this case. Expenditure incurred by successful bidders do [sic] indeed produce 'economic value' as specified by Article 1 of the US–Sri Lanka BIT and the protection mechanism developed under the aegis of the World Bank in the form of the ICSID Convention should be available to those who are encouraged to embark on such expensive exercises.[114]

On the other hand, one can argue that expanding treaty protection to pre-investment expenses would create too heavy a burden for host states and arbitral institutions such as ICSID.[115] The pre-investment bidding process typically

---

[110] ibid ¶ 81.   [111] ibid ¶ 88.   [112] ibid ¶¶ 83, 85.

[113] Hamida (n 108 above) 60–1.

[114] Individual Concurring Opinion by Mr David Suratgar of 15 March 2000 in *Mihaly International Corp v Sri Lanka* (n 104 above) ¶ 10.

[115] The tribunal in *Nordzucker v Poland* stated:

It is not surprising that the host States that waive a part of their sovereign rights by their agreement to arbitrate the disputes concerning the investments made and admitted in accordance with their legislation do not agree to arbitration of disputes related to

involves a large number of potential investors, only one of which, ultimately, can be successful. Consequently, every project has many losers, some of whom may be motivated to file frivolous claims in the hope that the costs of defending the claim or the potential embarrassment and deterrent effect on future investment of an investor–state arbitration will induce the host state to settle rather than fight. The ICSID mechanism should not be extended to a new category of disputes unless the benefits to foreign investment clearly outweigh the costs—a result that is not at all clear in the case of pre-investment expenses. Moreover, further expanding access to ICSID and other arbitral institutions to encompass pre-investment expenditure disputes risks alienating developing countries, slowing down the BIT-making process, overburdening arbitral institutions, and perhaps even compromising the legitimacy of investor–state arbitration. Of course, potential investors and host states are always free to enter into binding, pre-investment agreements on a case-by-case basis and to provide for arbitration of pre-investment disputes in a non-ICSID forum.[116]

(b) Minority shareholdings

For reasons of economic convenience or host government requirements, investors frequently carry out investments through companies incorporated in host states. To achieve this end, a foreign investor may establish a new local company or acquire shares in a pre-existing one. However, if a host state commits a wrongful act against the locally incorporated company, that company, in the absence of a specific provision to the contrary,[117] may not have legal standing to bring a

> pre-investment relations with persons merely intending to invest. Taking into account the fact that tenders...attract usually a large number of foreign bidders only one of whom can be successful, the State would be exposed to many international arbitration proceedings commenced by unsuccessful bidders. For this reason the States in principle...agree to grant the full Treaty protection only with regard to investments actually made and admitted in accordance with the law of the host State and not to intended investments.

Nordzucker AG v Republic of Poland, UNCITRAL (Partial Award Jurisdiction) (10 December 2008) ¶ 189. The case was brought under the Germany–Poland BIT, which stated in Art 2(1):

> Each Contracting Party shall in its territory promote as far as possible investments by investors of the other Contracting Party and admit such investments in accordance with its respective laws. Investments that have been admitted in accordance with the respect law of one Contracting Party shall enjoy the protection of this Treaty. Each Contracting Party shall in any case accord investments fair and equitable treatment.

The tribunal interpreted this language to require that the contracting states accord fair and equitable treatment to potential as well as admitted investments. For the treaty to cover such intended investments, however, the investment must be in the making or about to be made, there must be more than a mere intention in the mind of the investor, and the host state must be aware of the investment and be ready to admit it. ibid ¶ 185. The tribunal found that two of the claimant's projects had reached a sufficient stage to qualify for FET protection: Poland knew of the claimant's intention to invest, the claimant was the winning bidder and had deposited a bid bond, and only the final step of formal approval remained. ibid ¶¶ 202–208.

[116] Hornick (n 104 above) 192–3.
[117] NAFTA provides that an investor who owns or controls a company directly or indirectly that is registered in the state of another party may submit a claim to arbitration on behalf of that

treaty claim for damages if that treaty does not consider the company to be an investor or investment of the other contracting party. In such cases, the applicable treaty may give the shareholder-investor the ability to bring claims for damages done to the corporate entity. As discussed earlier, many treaties define the term 'investment' to include *'assets'* that an investor *'owns or controls, directly or indirectly'* and specify that *'shares in stock or other interests in a company or interests in the assets thereof'* may constitute one of the forms of a foreign investment. The plain meaning of such language does not require that the investor's participation in a company be a controlling or direct one, and so covers portfolio investments (less than 10% of shares) and investments made indirectly through intermediaries. Accordingly, participation in a locally incorporated company qualifies as a foreign investment under applicable treaties. Thus, the owner of that investment may bring claims under the treaty against a host state for wrongful conduct that damages a locally incorporated company.

The prevailing treaty approach to this question stands as a repudiation of any suggestion that customary international law does not protect portfolio investments.[118] As discussed in Chapter 3, a decision of the International Court of Justice (ICJ), *Barcelona Traction Power and Light Co, Ltd,*[119] has been cited to support the opposing view. In that case, a Canadian corporation, Barcelona Traction, Light and Power Co, Ltd, supplying electricity to the city of Barcelona, Spain, allegedly went bankrupt as a result of certain actions taken by Spain. Many of the shareholders in the company were Belgian nationals, whose investments were lost as a result of the bankruptcy. Belgium brought an action against Spain in the ICJ for the alleged injury to the Belgian shareholders, claiming that Spain had breached its obligations to the shareholders under international law. The ICJ rejected the Belgian claim because the injury was done to a Canadian entity, Barcelona Traction Power and Light Co, Ltd and only incidentally to the shareholders. The Court held that Belgium lacked *jus standi* to exercise diplomatic protection of shareholders in a Canadian company with respect to measures taken against that company in Spain. Scholars have criticized the decision over the years as ignoring the realities of international business and denying fair treatment to investors.[120]

---

company. The NAFTA Agreement, Art 1117 states: 'An investor of a Party, on behalf of an enterprise of another Party that is a juridical person that the investor owns or controls directly or indirectly, may submit to arbitration under this Section a claim that the other Party has breached an obligation under...Section A [protection of investments]'.

The ICSID Convention provides that a host state and a foreign investor may agree that a locally incorporated company should be treated as a foreign company because it operates under foreign control. ICSID Convention, Art 25(2)(b) reads, in relevant parts: '"National of another Contracting State" means:...any juridical person which had the nationality of the Contracting State party to the dispute on that date and which, because of the foreign control, the parties have agreed should be treated as a national of another Contracting State for the purposes of this Convention'. Convention on the Settlement of Investment Disputes between States and Nationals of Other States (18 March 1965).

[118] Sornarajah (n 11 above) 8, 12 (without citing supporting authority for the statement).
[119] *Barcelona Traction, Light and Power Co, Ltd (Belgium v Spain)* [1970] ICJ Rep 3.
[120] eg RB Lillich 'Two Perspectives on the Barcelona Traction Case' (1971) 65 AJIL 522–32.

It seems clear that one of the purposes of employing a broad definition of the term 'investment' in treaties is to avoid any suggestion that the *Barcelona Traction* approach should be used in defining the scope of treaty protection. Indeed, it can be argued that most investment treaties seek to avoid the *Barcelona Traction* holding by making clear that shares, as well as companies, are meant to receive international law protection under relevant investment treaties. As a result, virtually all modern investment treaties reject the approach of *Barcelona Traction* with respect to the protection of corporate shares as a form of investment.

Nonetheless, in various investor–state arbitrations under investment treaties respondent states have sought to rely on *Barcelona Traction* to defend against actions brought by shareholders.[121] Indeed, despite the usual breadth of treaty language in defining investment, the matter has been the subject of controversy and litigation on several occasions. These disputes usually arise in cases in which foreign investors have invested in a company organized in the host country in which they hold shares. Where governmental action has injured the company, those investors have brought actions based on the shares they hold and asserted that their shares constitute 'investments' under the treaty in question. Host countries have defended themselves by relying on *Barcelona Traction*; however, arbitration tribunals have unanimously rejected the argument where the investment treaty in question makes clear that 'investment' includes shares in companies.[122]

Respondent states have also repeatedly argued that foreign investors do not have standing to bring BIT claims because the foreign investors are either minority or indirect shareholders. As illustrated in the following decisions, arbitral tribunals have rejected this argument.

In *AAPL v Sri Lanka*,[123] a dispute arose between AAPL, a minority shareholder in a locally incorporated company named Serendib, and Sri Lanka, when government security forces destroyed Serendib's property during a military operation. As a direct consequence, AAPL allegedly suffered a total loss of its investment and made a claim for compensation from the Sri Lankan government. The arbitration tribunal noted that the UK–Sri Lanka BIT defined 'investments' to include 'shares, stock and debentures of companies or interests in the property of such companies'. It concluded that the claimant's shareholdings fell within that

---

[121] See eg *Suez, Sociedad General de Aguas de Barcelona SA and Vivendi Universal v Argentine Republic*, ICSID Case No ARB/03/19 (Decision on Jurisdiction) (3 August 2006).

[122] See ibid. The tribunal stated, referring to *Barcelona Traction*:

> That decision, which has been criticized by scholars over the years, concerned diplomatic protection of its nationals by a State, an issue that is in no way relevant to the current case. Unlike the present case, *Barcelona Traction* did not involve a bilateral treaty which specifically provides that shareholders are investors and as such are entitled to have recourse to international arbitration to protect their shares from host country actions that violate the treaty.

ibid ¶ 50.

[123] *Asian Agricultural Products Ltd v Sri Lanka*, ICSID Case No ARB/87/3 (Final Award) (27 June 1990).

definition. Consequently, it upheld the investor's right to bring a damage claim under the BIT, stating:

The undisputed 'investments' effected since 1985 by AAPL in Sri Lanka are in the form of acquiring shares in Serendib Company, which has been incorporated in Sri Lanka under the domestic Companies Law. Accordingly... [t]he scope of international law protection granted to the foreign investor in the present case is limited to a single item: the value of his share-holding in the joint-venture entity.[124]

In *CMS v Argentina*,[125] the claimant alleged that Argentina breached the US–Argentina BIT by modifying the legal and regulatory framework that had initially induced CMS, a US incorporated company, to acquire a 29.42 per cent share in TGN, a gas transportation company incorporated in Argentina. Argentina's subsequent forced change from a dollar tariff regime to one based on the Argentine peso at a one-to-one exchange rate (when the real exchange rate dropped to one to three) and the subsequent freeze of those tariffs were alleged to be a breach of Argentina's obligation to treat CMS's investment fairly and equitably and to observe certain obligations Argentina had entered into with regard to the investment. Argentina advanced two principal arguments against the admissibility of CMS's claims. First, as TGN was the licensee and CMS was only a minority shareholder, Argentina argued that the claimant did not hold the rights upon which it based its claim. According to this reasoning, only TGN as a corporation could make a claim for damages. However, since TGN was an Argentine company, it did not qualify as a foreign investor under the BIT. Second, Argentina asserted that CMS's claim was not for *direct damages* arising from measures affecting the shares, such as expropriation of shares or interference with the property rights tied to those shares, but rather was for *indirect damages*, that is, claims connected to damage suffered by TGN as a separate corporate entity. While admitting that claims for direct damages are allowed by international law, Argentina asserted that the right to claim for indirect damages had to be explicitly provided in the BIT.

The tribunal rejected Argentina's objections on several grounds. First, it found no bar in current international law to allowing claims by shareholders independently from those of the corporation concerned, even if those shareholders were minority or non-controlling shareholders.[126] It based this finding on two important conclusions. First, although *Barcelona Traction* ruled out the protection of investors by the state of their nationality when that state was different from the state of incorporation of the corporate entity concerned in a case dealing with damages suffered in a third state, *Barcelona Traction* only concerned the exercise of diplomatic protection in that particular setting and did not deal with the possibility of extending protection to shareholders in different contexts. Second, the

[124] ibid ¶ 95.
[125] *CMS Gas Transmission Co v The Argentine Republic*, ICSID Case No ARB/01/8 (Decision on Jurisdiction) (17 July 2003).
[126] ibid ¶ 48.

tribunal pointed to the fact that the very concept of diplomatic protection had been dwindling in international law in recent years and now constituted a residual mechanism only resorted to in the absence of other specific arrangements recognizing a direct right of action by individuals. Because of the rapid proliferation of international investment agreements, which do provide an arrangement for individuals to bring a direct action, such arrangements, previously considered as *lex specialis*, have become prevalent enough to now be considered the *general rule*.

Second, the tribunal held that in the light of the ICSID convention there was no bar to the exercise of jurisdiction over the claims brought by a minority shareholder investor.[127] It noted that because the ICSID Convention does not define 'investment', it does not purport to define the requirements that an investment must meet to qualify for ICSID jurisdiction. Therefore, 'there is indeed no requirement that an investment in order to qualify, must necessarily be made by shareholders controlling a company or owning the majority of its shares'.[128]

Third, the tribunal concluded that since the US–Argentina BIT defines 'investments' as including 'shares of stock or other interests in a company or other assets thereof' without providing any qualifications concerning the measure of control by a shareholder, the latter enjoys an independent right of action for direct and indirect damages and that right is not tied to the legal and economic performance of its investment.[129]

(c) Indirect shareholdings

For a variety of financial and economic reasons, investors often make their investments in host countries *indirectly* through one or more subsidiaries or other intermediaries. This practice has raised the question of whether the holders of such indirect investments may seek treaty protection for injurious actions done directly to the underlying enterprise but which, as a result, also diminish the value of the claimants' indirect investments. Various cases have dealt with this issue.

In *Siemens v Argentina*,[130] the dispute concerned the indirect shareholding through the investor's home state intermediary. It arose out of the termination of an investment contract that Argentina concluded with Siemens IT Services SA (SITS), a company incorporated in Argentina by the German-based company Siemens through its wholly-owned affiliate Siemens Nixdorf Informationssysteme AG (SNI). Argentina argued that since the shares in SITS were held through SNI, and not by Siemens directly, Siemens had no right to claim damages. The tribunal rejected Argentina's submission on the following grounds.

Having conducted a detailed analysis of the definition of 'investment' and 'investor' in the Germany–Argentina BIT, the tribunal observed that the treaty contained no explicit distinction between direct and indirect investments and that, in fact, the broad definition of 'investment' seemed to cover any kind of

---

[127] ibid ¶ 56.   [128] ibid ¶ 51.   [129] ibid ¶¶ 57–65.
[130] *Siemens v Argentina*, ICSID Case No ARB/02/8 (Decision on Jurisdiction) (3 August 2004).

asset, including 'shares, rights of participation in companies and other types of participation in companies'. The tribunal thus concluded:

a plain meaning of [such a] provision is that shares held by a German shareholder are protected under the Treaty. The Treaty does not require that there be no interposed companies between the investment and the ultimate owner of the company. Therefore, a literal reading of the Treaty does not support the allegation that the definition of investment excludes indirect investments.[131]

In *Enron v Argentina*,[132] the dispute arose out of allegedly excessive taxes imposed by Argentina on the gas distribution company Transportadora de Gas del Sur (TGS). TGS was incorporated in Argentina but the US company Enron indirectly held shares in it through locally registered companies and several layers of ownership. That complex structure can be summarized as follows. Enron owned 50 per cent of the shares of CIESA, an Argentine-incorporated company that controlled TGS by owning 55.30 per cent of its shares. Enron's participation in CIESA was held by two wholly-owned companies, EPCA and EACH. Through EPCA, EACH, and ECIL, another corporation controlled by Enron, Enron also owned 75.93 per cent of EDIDESCA, another Argentine corporation that owned 10 per cent of the shares of TGS. Enron also acquired an additional 0.02 per cent of TGS through EPCA. The investment, as a whole, amounted to 35.263 per cent of TGS.

Argentina asserted that Enron's complex shareholding in TGS could not qualify as an investment and consequently was not protected by the US–Argentina BIT. The tribunal, relying on the broad definition of 'investment' in the BIT, found that that treaty did not exclude the independent claims of shareholders, even if they were not in the majority or did not control the corporation concerned.[133] At the same time, the tribunal was sympathetic to Argentina's concerns that the ability of minority shareholders to pursue arbitration claims independently of an affected corporation could trigger a potentially endless chain of claims, since any shareholder in a company that had made an investment in another company could potentially invoke a right of action for measures affecting the corporation at the end of the chain. The tribunal noted that while minority shareholders can claim their own rights under the provisions of the treaty, 'there is indeed a need to establish a *cut-off* point beyond which claims would not be permissible as they would have only a remote connection to the affected company'.[134] According to the tribunal, the cut-off point should be determined by the extent of the consent to arbitration of the host state:

if consent has been given in respect of an investor and an investment, it can be reasonably concluded that the claims brought by such investors are admissible under the treaty; but if the consent cannot be considered as extending to another investor or investment, these

---

[131] ibid ¶ 136.
[132] *Enron Corp and Ponderosa Assets, LP v Argentine Republic*, ICSID Case No ARB/01/3 (Decision on Jurisdiction) (14 January 2004).
[133] ibid ¶¶ 39, 44.   [134] ibid ¶ 52.

other claims should then be considered inadmissible as being only remotely connected with the affected company and the scope of the legal system protecting that investment.[135]

The tribunal cited the following factors as among those to be considered in evaluating the extent of Argentina's consent to arbitration: that Argentina gave a specific invitation to Enron to undertake the investment, that the investment was made in an approved project, that the investors had decision-making power in the management of TGS, and that the pertinent officials of the Argentine government were kept informed of the corporate structures related to the investment.[136]

In *Standard Chartered Bank v Tanzania*,[137] the tribunal had to interpret language in the UK–Tanzania BIT that granted jurisdiction to ICSID over disputes arising between a contracting party and a national or company of the other contracting party 'concerning an investment *of* the latter in the territory of the former' (emphasis added).[138] The claimant was Standard Chartered Bank, a UK company whose subsidiary, Standard Chartered Bank (Hong Kong), acquired a loan to finance a power plant in Tanzania.[139] The dispute over the jurisdictional clause of the treaty concerned the meaning of the word 'of'. The claimant contended that an investment may be 'of' an entity by virtue of an ownership interest, while the respondent argued that 'of' required an association between the investor and investment beyond indirect ownership, such as a contribution or flow of funds.[140] After interpreting the text and object and purpose of the treaty, the tribunal concluded that to benefit from the treaty a claimant must demonstrate 'that the investment was made at the claimant's direction, that the claimant funded the investment or that the claimant controlled the investment in an active and direct manner. Passive ownership of shares in a company not controlled by the claimant where that company in turn owns the investment is not sufficient'.[141] A transfer of something of value, such as money, know-how, contacts, or expertise would suffice.[142] Because the claimant did not show such contribution or control over the loans, the tribunal found that the claimant was not an investor under the treaty and declined jurisdiction.[143]

7.8 'Investors' Covered by Investment Treaties

Even though an asset qualifies as an 'investment' under an investment treaty, a person or entity will not be able to claim treaty protection for that asset unless that person or entity is deemed to be an 'investor' as that term is defined in the applicable treaty. Defining which investors can benefit from the treaty is important, as

---

[135] ibid ¶ 52.   [136] ibid ¶¶ 53–56.

[137] *Standard Chartered Bank v United Republic of Tanzania*, ICSID Case No ARB/10/12 (Award) (2 November 2012).

[138] Agreement between the Government of the United Kingdom of Great Britain and Northern Ireland and the Government of the United Republic of Tanzania (7 January 1994), Art 8(1).

[139] *Standard Chartered Bank* (n 137 above) ¶¶ 2–3.   [140] ibid ¶¶ 209–211.

[141] ibid ¶ 230.   [142] ibid ¶ 232.   [143] ibid ¶ 271.

the goal of the contracting state is to secure benefits for its own nationals, companies, and investors, and not those of other countries. The problem is essentially one of determining what *link* needs to exist between an investor and a party to a treaty for the investor to benefit from the treaty's provisions. In examining this problem, one must distinguish between two types of investors: (a) natural persons and (b) legal entities. Virtually all treaties make this distinction in setting out their definitions of 'investor'. Most treaties provide a definition of investor that applies equally to natural and legal persons of both Contracting parties; however, some treaties may apply different definitions to legal investors of each of the two contracting states in order to take account of special needs or conditions within one of such states. Thus, for example, Saudi Arabia's BITs normally adopt this approach by specifying that with respect to Saudi Arabia the term 'investor' means *inter alia* 'the Kingdom of Saudi Arabia and its financial institutions and authorities such as the Saudi Arabian Monetary Agency, public funds, and other similar governmental institutions existing in Saudi Arabia'.[144]

(a) Natural persons as 'investors'

In the case of physical persons or individuals, investment treaties specify the necessary link between the individual and a contracting state primarily on the basis of nationality or citizenship and to a lesser extent by domicile, permanent residence, or some combination thereof. Thus, for example, Article 1(7)(a)(i) of the ECT defines 'investor' as including a 'natural person having the citizenship or nationality of or who is permanently residing in that Contracting Party in accordance with its applicable law'.[145] Whether a person has the necessary link is determined by the domestic law of the country with which the link is claimed.

Persons having more than one nationality pose a special problem under investment treaties. Unless the treaty specifically treats this question, a variety of possible solutions present themselves. One possibility is to follow the principle of international law that a person with more than one nationality is a national of the state of that person's dominant and effective nationality.[146] Another approach is to hold that if a person is a national of both contracting states that fact automatically denies that person protection, since the treaty is not meant to provide protection to nationals who invest in their own state. Such individuals receive protection from the legal system of the state of which they are nationals.

---

[144] eg Agreement Between the Kingdom of Saudi Arabia and the Government of Malaysia Concerning the Promotion and Reciprocal Protection of Investment (25 October 2000), Art 1.3(b)(iii).

[145] ECT, Art 1(7)(a)(i).

[146] UNCTAD, *Bilateral Investment Treaties 1995–2006: Trends in Investment Rulemaking* (2007) 14. It is to be noted that the Uruguay–US BIT, Art 1 specifically adopts this position in its definition of 'investor', which states 'provided however, that a natural person who is a dual citizen shall be deemed to be exclusively a citizen of the State of his or her dominant and effective citizenship'. Treaty between the United States of America and the Oriental Republic of Uruguay concerning the Encouragement and Reciprocal Protection of Investment (4 November 2005).

(b) Companies and other legal entities as 'investors'

For investors that are companies or other legal entities, the problem of determining an appropriate link with a contracting state is more complex. Such legal entities may be created and owned by persons who have no real connection with the countries that are a party to the treaty. In particular, three types of cases raise problems: (1) companies organized in a treaty country by nationals of a non-treaty country; (2) companies organized in a non-treaty country by nationals of a treaty country; and (3) companies in which nationals of a non-treaty country hold a substantial interest. For a company to be covered by the treaty, most treaties require that a treaty partner at least be one of the following: (1) the country of the company's incorporation;[147] (2) the country of the company's seat, registered office, or principal place of business;[148] or (3) the country whose nationals have control over, or a substantial interest in, the company making the investment.[149] Sometimes these requirements are combined so that an investing company must satisfy two or more conditions to qualify for coverage under a particular investment treaty. For example, the Switzerland–Slovakia BIT provides that the term 'investor' refers to 'legal entities, including companies, corporations, business associations and other organizations, which are constituted or otherwise duly organized under the law of that Contracting party and have their seat, together with real economic activities, in the territory of that same Contracting Party'.[150] In *Alps Finance and Trade AG v Slovak Republic*,[151] the tribunal, in order to establish jurisdiction, had to determine whether the claimant, a Swiss corporation, had

---

[147] See eg Treaty between the United States of America and the Democratic Socialist Republic of Sri Lanka Concerning the Encouragement and Reciprocal Protection of Investment (20 September 1991), Art 1(b) ('"company" of a Party means any kind of corporation, company, association, partnership or other organization, legally constituted under the laws and regulations of a Party or a political subdivision thereof...'). BITs concluded by Denmark, the Netherlands, the UK, and the US are frequently of this type. UNCTAD, *Bilateral Investment Treaties in the Mid-1990s* (1998) 39.

[148] See eg Treaty between the Federal Republic of Germany and the Kingdom of Swaziland Concerning the Encouragement and Reciprocal Protection of Investments (5 April 1990), Art 1(4)(a) ('The term "companies" means...in respect of the Federal Republic of Germany: any juridical person as well as any commercial or other company or association with or without legal personality having its seat in the German area of application of this Treaty, irrespective of whether or not its activities are directed at profit'). BITs concluded by Belgium, Germany, and Sweden are frequently of this type. UNCTAD, *Bilateral Investment Treaties in the Mid-1990s* (1998) 40.

[149] See eg Agreement on Encouragement and Reciprocal Protection of Investments between the Government of the Kingdom of the Netherlands and the Government of the Republic of Lithuania (26 January 1994), Art 1(b)(iii):

> The term 'investor' shall comprise with regard to either contracting party:...(iii) legal persons not constituted under the law of that Contracting Party but controlled, directly or indirectly, by natural persons as defined in (i) [of the Contracting Party's nationality] or by legal persons as defined in (ii) [legal persons constituted under the law of the Contracting Party] above, who invest in the territory of either Contracting Party.

'Ownership or control', as these provisions are called, are used in BITs concluded by the Netherlands, Sweden, and Switzerland. UNCTAD, *Bilateral Investment Treaties in the Mid-1990s* (1998) 39.

[150] Agreement between the Czech and Slovak Federal Republic and the Swiss Confederation on the Promotion and Reciprocal Protection of Investments (5 October 1990), Art 1(1)(b).

[151] *Alps Finance and Trade AG v Slovak Republic*, UNCITRAL (Award) (5 March 2011).

a 'seat' in Switzerland as required by the BIT. To support its claim to a seat in Switzerland, the claimant argued that it was registered in the commercial registry of the Swiss locality where it had its headquarters, that the company books were held in Switzerland, that it had a bank price list for the costs of its bank account in Switzerland, and that it had a tax receipt showing the company's revenues, profits, and losses for the year 2007. Defining the term 'business seat' as meaning 'an effective center of administration of business operations', the tribunal stated that proof of a seat requires regular board or shareholder meetings, top management, a certain number of employees, an address with phone and fax numbers, and expenses and overhead costs in the location of the seat. Since the claimant had proved none of these elements, the tribunal concluded that the claimant corporation did not have a seat in Switzerland and was therefore not an investor under the BIT.[152]

Another example of an approach taken with respect to corporate investors in a treaty regime is the ECT, which adopts the relatively simple rule that a company is an investor of a contracting party if it has been organized in accordance with the law applicable in the contracting state. Thus, even if nationals of a non-ECT state organize a company in an ECT state, such a company would qualify as an investor of a contracting party under the treaty. Moreover, unlike most BITs, the ECT explicitly recognizes the possibility that a natural or legal person from a 'third state' (ie a non-ECT state) can be considered an investor if it fulfils the treaty conditions, *mutatis mutandis*, specified for contracting states.[153] So, if under the laws of an ECT state a company organized in another state was considered to be organized under the laws of the ECT state, that company would still qualify as an investor under the treaty. In order to prevent these provisions from being abused by nationals and companies of non-ECT states, Article 17 of the ECT, in terms almost identical to those of the United States Model BIT,[154] gives each contracting party the right to deny the advantages of the treaty to a legal entity if it is owned or controlled by third country nationals and has no substantial business activities in the state of the contracting party. A contracting party may also deny the advantages of the treaty to the investments of third country investors with which the host country does not maintain diplomatic relations or prohibits transactions.

To be protected under many investment treaties, an investor must 'own' or 'control' the investment. While determining ownership is usually easy, control is a more vague and ambiguous concept. In order to give some specificity to the term, some treaties contain an annexed or supplementary agreement defining the term 'control' in the treaty. For example, the Understandings of the Final Act, IV 3, of the European Energy Charter Conference that adopted the ECT provides as follows:

control of an Investment means control in fact, determined after examining the actual circumstances in each situation. In any such examination, all relevant factors should be considered, including the Investor's

---

[152] ibid ¶¶ 215–218.   [153] ECT, Art 1(7)(b).   [154] 2012 US Model BIT, Art 17.

(a) financial interest, including equity interest in the Investment;
(b) ability to exercise substantial influence over the management and operation of the Investment; and
(c) ability to exercise substantial influence over a selection of members of the board of directors or other managing body.

States have sometimes dealt with the issue of control in the text of the BIT itself or in separate protocols or an exchange of letters.[155] The concern in most investment treaties has been the same: to prevent persons and companies having no genuine link with treaty partners from obtaining benefits under the treaty.

Two arbitration decisions are of interest with respect to the interpretation and application of treaty provisions concerning the ability of corporations to qualify as 'investors'. In *Tokios Tokelés v Ukraine*,[156] a Lithuanian corporation brought an arbitration proceeding against the government of Ukraine under the Ukraine–Lithuania BIT for Ukraine's alleged violation of the BIT's guarantees of investor treatment. Ukraine argued that Tokios Tokelés was not an 'investor' under the treaty, since 99 per cent of its shares were owned by Ukrainian nationals, who also constituted two-thirds of its management. Ukraine argued that, therefore, while Tokios Tokelés was technically a Lithuanian corporation it was effectively owned and operated by Ukrainian nationals. Relying on the BIT's definition of investor, which included 'any entity established in the territory of the Republic of Lithuania in conformity with its laws and regulations', the tribunal, with strong dissent by its president, found that Tokios Tokelés satisfied the requirements of the treaty. The majority acknowledged that many investment treaties expressly provide that an entity controlled by nationals of the host country shall not be considered an investor of the other contracting party. Regardless, it found no such limitation in the Ukraine–Lithuania BIT. In a statement that negotiators and drafters of investment treaties should bear in mind, the majority observed: 'We regard the absence of such a provision as a deliberate choice of the Contracting Parties. In our view, it is not for tribunals to impose limits on the scope of BITs not found in the text, much less limits nowhere evident from the negotiating history.'[157]

In a second ICSID case, *Rompetrol Group NV v Romania*,[158] the claimant, a Dutch corporation whose principal shareholder was a Romanian national, commenced arbitration against Romania under the Netherlands–Romania BIT, which defined 'investors' of a contracting party as 'legal persons constituted under

---

[155] See *Mobil Corp Venezuela Holdings, BV, Mobil Cerro Negro Holding Ltd, Mobil Venezolana de Petróleos Holdings, Inc, Mobil Cerro Negro Ltd, and Mobil Venezolana de Petróleos, Inc v Bolivarian Republic of Venezuela*, ICSID Case No ARB/07/27 (Decision on Jurisdiction) (10 June 2010) ¶¶ 150–160 for a discussion of the control requirement in the Netherlands–Venezuela BIT and Protocol and its application to wholly-owned subsidiaries incorporated in third party states.

[156] *Tokios Tokelés v Ukraine*, ICSID Case No ARB/02/18 (Decision on Jurisdiction) (29 April 2004).

[157] ibid ¶ 36.

[158] *Rompetrol Group NV v Romania*, ICSID Case No ARB/06/3 (Decision on Respondent's Preliminary Objections on Jurisdiction and Admissibility) (18 April 2008).

the law of that Contracting Party'. Romania sought dismissal of the case on the grounds that Rompetrol was merely a shell company controlled by Romanian nationals and that it therefore did not qualify as an 'investor' under the BIT. The tribunal rejected this argument and found that the treaty very clearly stated that an entity merely had to be constituted under the law of a contracting party to establish a legal link with that state and qualify it as an investor. On the basis of these two cases, it would seem that tribunals are reluctant to impose on corporate investors substantive conditions that the applicable investment treaty does not specifically require.

(c) States and state-owned entities as 'investors'

The growing role of states and state-owned entities, such as government corporations and sovereign wealth funds, in international investment raises a question as to whether they are to be considered 'investors' under international investment treaties and whether their investments therefore are subject to treaty protections, including investor–state dispute settlement.[159] Some treaties provide a clear answer to this question by expressly including such state-entities within their definitions of 'investor'. Indeed, this seems to be the growing trend. Thus, for example, Article 4(d) of the 2009 ASEAN Comprehensive Investment Agreement defines investor as 'any juridical person of a member state' and then Article 4(e) clarifies that '"juridical person" means any legal person duly constituted or otherwise organized under the law of a Member State, whether for profit or otherwise, and whether privately-owned or governmentally-owned'. Similarly, Article 1 of the 2012 Model US BIT states that '"investor of a Party" means a Party or state enterprise thereof, or a national or an enterprise of a Party, that attempts to make, is making, or has made an investment in the territory of the other Party; provided, however, that a natural person who is a dual national shall be deemed to be exclusively a national of the State of his or her dominant and effective nationality'. Examples of other treaties that expressly include state-owned entities with their definition of 'investor' include the US BITs with Azerbaijan,[160] Argentina,[161] Armenia,[162] and Bahrain;[163] Canada's

---

[159] On the role of states and state-owned entities in international investment, see Ch 2, section 2.4(b).

[160] Treaty Between the Government of the United States of America and the Government of the Republic of Azerbaijan Concerning the Encouragement and Reciprocal Protection of Investment (1 August 1997).

[161] Treaty Between the United States of America and the Argentine Republic Concerning the Reciprocal Encouragement and Protection of Investment (14 November 1991).

[162] Treaty Between the United States of America and the Republic of Armenia Concerning the Encouragement and Reciprocal Protection of Investment (23 September 1992).

[163] Treaty Between the Government of the United States of America and the Government of the State of Bahrain Concerning the Encouragement and Reciprocal Protection of Investment (29 September 1999).

BITs with Armenia,[164] Costa Rica,[165] and Panama;[166] and Saudi Arabia's BITs with Italy,[167] Belgium-Luxembourg,[168] and Korea.[169]

Most investment treaties, however, do not expressly provide that state entities fall within the definition of investor.[170] In defining investors who are physical persons such treaties simply refer to 'legal persons', 'juridical persons', or 'companies' under the laws of a contracting party.[171] For example, Article 1 (1)(7) (a) (ii) of the ECT merely states that an '"investor"...means a company or other organization organized in accordance with the law applicable in that Contracting Party' and the France–Argentina BIT defines an investor ('*investisseur*') as 'legal persons organized on the territory of one of the Contracting Parties and having its administrative headquarters (*siège sociale*) there'.[172] If one were to give such terms as 'company or other organization in accordance with...law' and 'legal person' their ordinary meaning as required by Article 31(1) of the Vienna Convention on the Law of Treaties, one would have to conclude that such entities as state corporations, sovereign wealth funds, and government-owned corporations are indeed investors under these treaties since they ordinarily have separate legal personality, headquarters in a contracting party, and are organized according to that party's law. And in fact it appears that no tribunal has refused jurisdiction in an investor–state dispute because a claimant is owned or controlled by a government. And although questions have also been raised about whether the ICSID Convention should properly apply to a case in which a state-entity is a complaining party, tribunals that have dealt with the question have always found that such entities are within the tribunal's jurisdiction.[173]

---

[164] Agreement between the Government of Canada and the Government of the Republic of Armenia for the Promotion and Protection of Investments (8 May 1997).

[165] Agreement between the Government of Canada and the Government of the Republic of Costa Rica for the Promotion and Protection of Investments (18 March 1998).

[166] Treaty between the Government of Canada and the Government of the Republic of Panama for the Protection and Promotion of Investments (12 September 1996).

[167] Tra Il Governo Della Repubblica Italiana Ed Il Regno Dell'arabia Saudita Sulla Reciproca Promozione E Protezione Degli Investimenti (10 September 1996).

[168] Agreement between the Kingdom of Saudi Arabia and the Belgo-Luxembourg Economic Union (b.l.e.u.) concerning the Reciprocal Promotion and Protection of Investments (22 April 2001).

[169] For a detailed listing of investment treaties that specifically define the term 'investor' as including state entities, see C Annacker, 'Protection and Admission of Sovereign Investment Under Investment Treaties,' (2011) 10 Chinese J Int'l L 531.

[170] ibid 542.   [171] ibid 539.

[172] Accord entre La République Francaise and La République Argentine sur l'encouragement and la protection réciproques des investissements (3 July 1991), Art.1.2(b) ('personnes morales constituées sur le territoire de l'une des Parties contractantes, conformément a la législation de celle-ci et y possédant leur siége sociale').

[173] See generally, M Feldman, 'The Standing of State-owned Entities Under Investment Treaties' in K Sauvant (ed) *Yearbook on International Investment Law and Policy 2010–2011* (OUP, 2012) 615–37.

8

Investment Promotion, Admission, and Establishment

8.1 State Sovereignty and Foreign Investment

International law recognizes that by virtue of its sovereignty a state has the right to control the entry and exit of persons and things from its territory and also to regulate the activities of nationals or foreign persons and companies within that territory. A corollary of that principle is that a state is not required to allow foreign nationals or companies to establish or acquire an enterprise or investment within its territory.[1] With respect to foreign investment, states have complete legislative jurisdiction to determine to what extent foreign nationals and companies may undertake investments, which sectors and industries they may or may not enter, and whether or not they must fulfil additional conditions in order to undertake and operate an investment within state territory.[2]

Recognizing the importance of investment, and particularly foreign investment, to the economic prosperity and well-being of their populations while also being conscious of the potential costs that certain types of investment may entail, all states have exercised their sovereign authority to develop policies and laws to govern the admission and operation of foreign investment. For example, many if not most developing countries have enacted 'foreign investment laws', 'foreign investment codes', or 'joint venture laws', which in effect create a special legal regime for foreign investment. This legal regime defines the types of investments that foreigners are permitted to make, the incentives they may receive, the controls to which they are subject, and the governmental agencies that have special responsibility for promoting and regulating foreign investment.[3] While developed countries may not have similar foreign investment laws or codes, a close analysis of their legislation invariably reveals special legal provisions relating to foreign investment and investors.[4]

---

[1] I Brownlie, *Principles of Public International Law* (7th edn, OUP, 2008) 520; D Carreau and P Juillard, *Droit international economique* (Librairie générale de droit et de jurisprudence, 2003) 361.

[2] R Dolzer and C Schreuer, *Principles of International Investment Law* (OUP, 2008) 80.

[3] J Salacuse, *Three Laws of International Investment: National, Contractual, and International Frameworks for Foreign Capital* (OUP, 2013) 89–136.

[4] Even the US, which strongly supports the liberal economic model, restricts or limits the ability of foreigners to invest in certain sectors, including commercial aviation, telecommunications, and maritime industries. Moreover, several states restrict the ability of foreigners to own real estate. RH

Policies and laws on foreign investment differ greatly from country to country. Some are more restrictive than others with respect to the entry and operation of foreign investment. Countries also exhibit significant differences in their treatment of foreign investment over time. For example, the end of the twentieth century witnessed openness and liberalization in many countries that had previously been highly restrictive and closed to foreign investment. A study by the United Nations Conference on Trade and Development (UNCTAD) found that between 1991 and 2002, '1551 (95%) out of 1641 changes introduced by 165 countries in their FDI laws were in the direction of greater liberalization'.[5] While the trend towards liberalization had slowed in certain countries by the beginning of the twenty-first century, it was still strong on a global scale in 2014.[6] Despite this worldwide trend towards investment liberalization, and despite declarations of various national governments regarding their 'openness' to foreign capital and foreign enterprises, no country appears to have enacted national legislation granting foreign investors total freedom to enter the country, undertake investments, establish enterprises, and otherwise conduct economic activities. Numerous factors have shaped individual countries' attitudes towards foreign investment and have militated against a policy of complete liberalization. These factors include perceived national security concerns, the desire to protect national enterprises from potentially damaging competition from better financed and more technologically advanced foreign enterprises, and the need to safeguard public order, morals, health, safety, and the environment. These concerns have not only shaped national laws and policies on foreign investment, but they have also influenced countries' positions in investment treaty negotiations. One of the aims of the investment treaty movement has been to reduce these internal barriers to foreign investment, particularly through treaty provisions on investment promotion, admission, and establishment.

8.2 Foreign Investment Promotion

Believing that increased foreign investment will foster economic prosperity and global well-being, numerous countries have undertaken to negotiate investment treaties as a means to facilitate the entry of capital, technology, and people from their territories into the territories of their treaty partners. In doing so, these states hoped that such treaty commitments would lead potential host countries to reduce or lower their own barriers to foreign investment. This goal has been apparent

---

Cummings, 'United States Regulation of Foreign Joint Ventures and Investment' in DN Goldsweig and RH Cummings (eds), *International Joint Ventures: A Practical Approach to Working with Foreign Investors in the U.S. and Abroad* (American Bar Association, 1990) 137, 139.

[5] UNCTAD, *World Investment Report 2003: FDI Policies for Development: National and International Perspectives* (2003) 20; see also World Bank, *World Development Report 2005: A Better Investment Climate for Everyone* (2004) 111–12.

[6] UNCTAD, *World Investment Report 2014* (2014) 18, stating that in 2014 '[n]ational investment policymaking remained geared towards investment promotion and liberalization'.

from the titles given to most investment treaties—'A Treaty for the *Promotion and Protection of Investment*'[7] or 'A Treaty for the Reciprocal *Encouragement and Protection of Investment*'.[8] This goal is also clear from the objectives given in treaty preambles, stating that the contracting parties desire to 'create favourable conditions for greater investment by nationals of one state in the territory of the other state',[9] wish 'to develop economic cooperation between the two states and to create favourable conditions for investments',[10] or seek 'to intensify economic cooperation for the economic benefit of both countries'.[11] Thus, it would seem that many investment treaties seek more than a lack of resistance or even passivity towards investment by the contracting parties; rather, they contemplate that treaty partners will somehow actively promote and encourage the entry of investment into their territories.

In pursuit of this goal, all treaties impose an obligation on each contracting party 'to promote' or 'encourage' investments by nationals and companies of other contracting parties; however, the nature of that obligation is usually very general and vague. For example, the BIT between Egypt and France simply states that '[e]ach of the contracting parties shall encourage investment made in its territory by nationals and companies of the other contracting party'.[12] Notably, it does not specifically state what each country must do to encourage investment from the other. Even in the absence of treaties, as a matter of national policy many countries promote specific kinds of foreign investment to secure needed capital and technology. These countries undertake promotional activities such as placing advertisements in international publications, holding investment conferences in their countries to which potential investors are invited, and sending missions abroad to conduct 'road shows' that give presentations about investment opportunities in their countries. No investment treaty, however, obliges a contracting state to undertake such specific promotional activities.

---

[7] eg Agreement between the Government of the United Kingdom of Great Britain and Northern Ireland and the Government of the Republic of Albania for the Promotion and Protection of Investments (30 March 1994); Treaty Concerning the Promotion and Reciprocal Protection of Investments (Germany–Poland) (10 November 1989); Agreement between the Government of the United Kingdom of Great Britain and Northern Ireland and the Government of the Republic of Indonesia for the Promotion and Protection of Investments (27 April 1976).

[8] Treaty between the United States of America and the Republic of Armenia Concerning the Encouragement and Reciprocal Protection of Investment (23 September 1992).

[9] 'Draft Agreement between the Government of the United Kingdom of Great Britain and Northern Ireland and the Government of Albania for the Promotion and Protection of Investments' in Dolzer and Schreuer (n 2 above) 376.

[10] Convention entre le Gouvernement de la République Française et le Gouvernement de la République Arabe d'Egypte sur l'Encouragement et la Protection Réciproques des Investissements (22 December 1974).

[11] Acuerdo para la Promoción y la Protección Reciproca de Inversiones entre el Reino de España y la Republica Argentina (3 October 1991) ('Deseando intensificar la cooperación económica en beneficío económico de ambos países').

[12] Convention entre le Gouvernement de la République Française et le Gouvernement de la République Arabe d'Egypte sur l'Encouragement et la Protection Réciproques des Investissements (22 December 1974).

Investment treaties generally impose an obligation to promote or encourage investments in the following terms: 'Each contracting state shall encourage and create favourable conditions for investors of the other Contracting party to make investments in its territory.'[13] A variation of this obligation is found in Article 10 of the Energy Charter Treaty (ECT), entitled 'Promotion, Protection, and Treatment of Investment', which states: 'Each Contracting Party shall, in accordance with the provisions of this Treaty, encourage and create stable, equitable, favourable and transparent conditions for Investors of other Contracting Parties to make Investments in its Area.'

Thus, investment treaties place an obligation upon host countries to promote investment from treaty partners by creating 'favourable conditions' within their territories for making and operating such investments. The notion of 'favourable conditions' can conceivably cover a wide range of political, economic, and social situations in areas from exchange rates to security in rural areas: however, investment treaties do not normally specify the precise kinds of conditions that a contracting state must create. Presumably, a country is to create favourable conditions through its laws, policies, and administrative actions; however, investment treaties are rarely that specific. Often they do not even indicate the kind of laws and administrative actions that must be enacted to meet their investment promotion obligations.

In view of its generality and vagueness, it is difficult to determine whether the obligation to promote investment has been effective in influencing the behaviour of host country governments. Only one arbitration case appears to have considered a claim by an investor that a host government had failed to meet its treaty obligation to encourage and create favourable conditions for investments from a treaty partner. In *White Industries Australia Limited v The Republic of India*, an Australian company that had invested in a failed coal venture with an Indian public enterprise in India sought compensation from the Indian government on various treaty grounds, including its failure to 'encourage and promote favourable conditions for investors of the other Contracting Party' under Article 3(1) of the Australia–India BIT. The specific alleged violations included India's failure to create (1) a suitable governance framework for supervising the action of state-owned enterprises in their dealings with foreign investors; (2) to ensure that its arbitration laws are administered in accordance with India's obligations under the New York Convention; and (3) to take steps to reduce the backlog of cases in its courts. Finding that a consensus exists among commentators that provisions requiring states to encourage and promote favourable conditions do not give rise to substantive rights, the tribunal concluded that in the case at hand the language used in Article 3(1) was far too general to support the three specific obligations the investors sought to impose on India.[14] While the promotion clause may not

---

[13] eg Agreement between the Government of the United Kingdom of Great Britain and Northern Ireland and the Government of the Republic of India for the Promotion and Protection of Investments (14 March 1994), Art 3(1).

[14] *White Industries Australia Ltd v The Republic of India*, UNCITRAL (Final Award) (30 November 2011) ¶¶ 9.2.7–9.2.10.

grant an investor an actionable right against a state, in diplomatic negotiations between states on the reception granted to foreign investors, that treaty provision could be useful in efforts to persuade a treaty partner to improve its investment climate.

The generality and vagueness of the language in which treaties express the obligation to promote investments give contracting states great latitude to argue that the nature of such conditions makes their application a matter fully within a host country's legislative and administrative discretion. On the other hand, it is clear from the language of most treaties that a contracting party has no obligation to encourage and promote investors from *its own* country to make investments in the territory of a treaty partner, a goal sometimes sought by developing countries when negotiating bilateral investment treaties with wealthy industrialized states. Investment treaties impose the duty to promote investment on the potential host country, not the prospective investor's home country.[15] Moreover, whatever the scope and nature of the obligation to promote, such obligations do not include a duty to admit investments from other contracting states to their territories. Investment treaties usually view investment promotion and investment admission as two separate and distinct functions governed by different treaty provisions.

8.3 Admission of Investments

Although the investment treaty movement has caused more than 3,300 agreements to be concluded in the last half-century, that movement has not created a truly open door to the flow of capital among treaty partners nor led to the total dismantling of all the pre-existing laws and policies restricting the entry of foreign investors and investment. While countries have participated in the investment treaty movement in the hope of obtaining increased foreign capital and technology vital for their economic development and prosperity, they have also perceived a need to protect important national interests that might be threatened by the uncontrolled entry of foreign investment. Consequently, no country has been willing to sacrifice those interests by creating an unrestricted 'open door' to investors from treaty partners. In their treaty negotiations and the agreements that have ultimately been concluded by them, countries have had to balance two imperatives: their need for foreign investment and their need to protect certain

---

[15] See, however, the Convention between the Belgo-Luxembourg Economic Union and the United Republic of Cameroon Concerning the Reciprocal Promotion and Protection of Investments (27 March 1980), Art 2(3) which states: 'Aware of the importance of investments for the promotion of its development and cooperation, the Belgo-Luxembourg Economic Union shall adopt measures to encourage its economic agents to participate in the development of the United Republic of Cameroon, in accordance with its priority objectives.' While one interpretation of this provision might lead to the conclusion that the Belgo-Luxembourg Economic Union encourages its own companies and nationals to invest in Cameroon, an equally plausible interpretation is that the Union is only obliged to encourage governmental agencies to participate in Cameroon's development.

domestic interests. In effect, this means that no state has been willing to make an unconditional treaty commitment to admit all investments from a treaty partner.

That fact does not mean, however, that treaties have no effect on the admission and establishment of investment. Investment treaties refer to the totality of treaty obligations that a host country owes to foreign investors as the 'treatment' to be accorded to the investor or the investment. Most treaties make a distinction between the treatment to be accorded in making an investment and the treatment to be given after that investment is made. The former is referred to as 'pre-entry' or 'pre-establishment' treatment, while the latter is referred to as 'post-entry' or 'post-establishment' treatment. While most investment treaties establish firm obligations with respect to the latter, they express much more tentative and general commitments with respect to the former.

Despite a contracting state's obligation to promote investment and create favourable conditions for investment, no treaty requires a host country to admit any or all investments proposed by investors from another treaty country. On the other hand, all investment treaties endeavour to restrain host countries' discretion regarding the admission of investment to a greater or lesser extent. A review of investment treaties to this point reveals three approaches: (1) the admission of investment according to host country law, which one might call the 'controlled entry model';[16] (2) the grant of a relative right of admission or establishment, which can be described as the 'liberalized entry model'; and, in rare cases, (3) the grant of an absolute right of admission or establishment (the 'establishment model'). The remaining sections of this chapter will examine each of these approaches.

8.4 Admission According to Host Country Law

Most investment treaties admit investments of other contracting parties only if they comply with the host country's legislation.[17] This type of provision is normally referred to as an 'admission clause'.[18] An example of such a clause is Article 2(1) of the Germany–Antigua and Barbuda BIT of 1998, which provides: 'Each Contracting State shall in its territory promote as far as possible investments by investors of the other Contracting State and *admit such investments*

---

[16] I Gomez-Palacio and P Muchlinski, 'Admission and Establishment' in P Muchlinski et al (eds), *The Oxford Handbook of International Investment Law* (OUP, 2008) 240.

[17] UNCTAD, *Bilateral Investment Treaties 1995–2006: Trends in Investment Rulemaking* (2007) 21.

[18] ibid. See also *Aguas del Tunari SA v Republic of Bolivia*, ICSID Case No ARB/02/3 (Decision on Respondent's Objections to Jurisdiction) (21 October 2005), in which the tribunal interpreted the 1992 Bolivia–Netherlands BIT, Art 2 which provided: 'Each Contracting Party shall, within the framework of its laws and regulations, promote economic cooperation through the protection in its territory of investments of nationals of other Contracting Parties. Subject to its right to exercise powers conferred by its laws or regulations, each Contracting Party shall admit such investments.' The tribunal stated: 'This obligation to allow the entry of foreign investment is a common provision in bilateral investment treaties, and is often termed an "admission clause".' (ibid ¶ 147).

in accordance with its legislation' (emphasis added).[19] Similarly, Article 2(1) of the China–Bosnia-Herzegovina BIT of 2002 represents a variation on this approach: 'Either Contracting Party shall encourage and create favourable, stable and transparent conditions for investors of the other Contracting Party to make investment in its territory and *shall admit such investments, within the framework of its laws and regulations*' (emphasis added).[20]

These admission clauses have two important implications. The first and most obvious is that under a treaty containing an admission clause a host country agrees to allow investments from a treaty partner only to the extent that it decides they meet the requirements of its national laws and regulations. Consequently, the admission clause allows the host state to retain control over the entry of foreign capital; to screen investments to ensure their compatibility with the state's national security, economic development, and public policy goals; and to determine the conditions under which foreign investments will be permitted, if at all. For example, in *Aguas del Tunari SA v Republic of Bolivia*, a tribunal interpreted a Bolivia–Netherlands BIT in which the contracting parties agreed to admit investments of the other contracting party '[s]ubject to its right to exercise powers conferred by its laws or regulations'. Based on this language, the tribunal found in the case of Bolivia that 'the obligation to admit investments was subject to the decision of Bolivia to exercise powers conferred by its laws or regulations'.[21]

Furthermore, unless the treaty provides otherwise, when considering the admission of investments from a treaty partner the host state is under no obligation to grant investors from treaty partners the same treatment that it grants to its own nationals or to investors of third parties. Similarly, it is not required to amend its laws and regulations subsequent to a treaty's ratification to facilitate their entry. Indeed, each contracting party is free to change its legislation after the treaty has entered into effect in ways that create new barriers to investments. Thus, a host government may subject the admission of investments from a treaty partner to less favourable treatment than is enjoyed by host country nationals or investors from third countries.

Similarly to the definition of 'investment' discussed in Chapter 7, a treaty's reference in an admission clause to the phrase 'in accordance with laws and regulations' may serve as a limitation on a treaty's scope of protection and the host state's consent to arbitral jurisdiction over related investment disputes. Thus, if a treaty protects only investments made in accordance with host country law and an investment in an arbitration case is shown not to have been made in accordance with such law, a tribunal may conclude that it has no jurisdiction to hear the dispute. For example, in *Inceysa Vallisoletana SL v Republic of El Salvador*,[22] a

---

[19] Treaty between the Federal Republic of Germany and Antigua and Barbuda concerning the Encouragement and Reciprocal Protection of Investments (5 November 1998).

[20] Agreement between the People's Republic of China and the Republic of Bosnia-Herzegovina on the Promotion and Protection of Investments (26 June 2002).

[21] *Aguas del Tunari SA v Republic of Bolivia*, ICSID Case No ARB/02/3 (Decision on Respondent's Objections to Jurisdiction) (21 October 2005) ¶ 147.

[22] *Inceysa Vallisoletana SL v Republic of El Salvador*, ICSID Case No ARB/03/26 (Award) (2 August 2006).

Spanish company brought a claim against El Salvador based on a concession that had been granted to the company. The tribunal found that in the bidding process for the concession the claimant provided false information on important matters relating to its financial condition and experience. As a result, the tribunal concluded that the claimant had not made an investment according to El Salvador law. It therefore dismissed the claim for lack of jurisdiction because El Salvador had consented to arbitrate only claims arising out of lawful investments. On this point, the tribunal stated:

the clause 'in accordance with law' appears both in the article on 'Protection,' and in the article that regulates 'Promotion and Admission,' indicating that investments that do not comply with the requisite of having been made 'in accordance with the laws' of the signatory State will not be Admitted (Article II(1)). This clearly indicates that the BIT leaves investments made illegally outside of its scope and benefits.... [b]ecause Inceysa's investment was made in a manner that was clearly illegal, it is not included within the scope of consent expressed by Spain and El Salvador in the BIT and, consequently, the disputes arising from it are not subject to the jurisdiction of [ICSID]. Therefore, this Arbitral Tribunal declares itself incompetent to hear the dispute brought before it.[23]

A similar result occurred in *Fraport AG Frankfurt Airport Services Worldwide v Philippines*,[24] in which the tribunal, in order to determine whether it had subject-matter jurisdiction, had to analyse the BIT's definition of 'investment' and its clause on 'admission and promotion of investments' in the light of violations of the host state's laws by the investor. The Germany–Philippines BIT defined 'investment' as 'any kind of asset accepted in accordance with the respective laws and regulations of either Contracting State'.[25] Article 2(1) of the treaty provided that each contracting state 'shall admit such investments in accordance with its Constitution, laws and regulations'.[26] The tribunal found that since Fraport had knowingly and intentionally circumvented Philippine law restricting foreign ownership and management of public utilities, it could not claim to have made an investment 'in accordance with law'. Neither could it defend itself by asserting that high Philippine government officials had subsequently waived the legal requirements and validated Fraport's investment because those officials could not have been aware of the violation. Stating that compliance with the host state's laws is an explicit and reasonable treaty requirement and that Fraport's ostensible purchase of shares concealed an unlawful investment, the tribunal concluded that the

---

[23] ibid ¶¶ 206, 257.
[24] *Fraport AG Frankfurt Airport Services Worldwide v Philippines*, ICSID Case No ARB/03/25 (Award) (16 August 2007) (Germany–Philippines BIT). See also *Alasdair Ross Anderson and Ors v Republic of Costa Rica*, ICSID Case No ARB(AF)/07/3 (Award) (19 May 2010) (Canada–Costa Rica BIT) in which the tribunal held that it had no jurisdiction to hear a case brought by a group of Canadian nationals who lost funds in a Ponzi scheme operated in violation of the Costa Rican Central Bank Law since their investments in the scheme was not according to Costa Rican law.
[25] Agreement between the Federal Republic of Germany and the Republic of the Philippines for the Promotion and Reciprocal Protection of Investments (18 April 1997), Art 1(1).
[26] ibid Art 2(1).

claimant's alleged asset was not an 'investment' covered by the BIT. It therefore rejected Fraport's claim for lack of subject-matter jurisdiction.[27]

With respect to the effect of admission clauses, the tribunal also stated that principles of fairness require a tribunal to hold a government estopped from raising violations of its own law as a jurisdictional defence when it knowingly overlooked them and chose to endorse an investment that did not comply with its law. However, a covert arrangement unknown to the government officials who may have approved a project would not be a basis for estoppel.[28] The tribunal made the following additional observation with respect to the effect of treaty admission clauses:

As for policy, BITs oblige governments to conduct their relations with foreign investors in a transparent fashion. Some reciprocal if not identical obligations lie on the foreign investor. One of those is the obligation to make the investment in accordance with the host state's law. It is arguable that even an investment which is not made in accordance with host state law may import economic value to the host state. But that is not the only goal of this sector of international law. Respect for the integrity of the law of the host state is also a critical part of development and a concern of international investment law.[29]

These two cases[30] contain an important lesson for persons and companies seeking investment treaty protection for their investment: scrupulously respect host country law in all matters concerning the investment or risk the loss of treaty protection should a tribunal find that the investment was made in violation of that law.

8.5 Grants of a Relative Right of Establishment

In negotiating investment treaties, some capital-exporting states have sought to protect their nationals and companies from unfavourable discrimination by securing admission treatment no less favourable than that given to investments made by the nationals of the host country, nationals of a third country, or both, whichever is the more favourable. This approach has been labelled a 'right of establishment';[31] however, it is only a conditional and relative right in that it exists only if other parties have been treated in a more favourable way.

The United States has traditionally sought this type of relative right of establishment in its BIT negotiations. Canada and Japan have subsequently adopted a similar approach. As a result, with respect to the admission of investment, investment treaties increasingly reflect two models: a 'controlled entry model' (found mostly in BITs with European countries), in which investment admission is subject to the application of local law, and a 'liberalized entry model' (mainly found

---

[27] *Fraport* (n 24 above) ¶¶ 401, 404.   [28] ibid ¶¶ 346–347.   [29] ibid ¶ 402.
[30] See also *Aguas del Tunari SA v Republic of Bolivia*, ICSID Case No ARB/02/3 (Decision on Respondent's Objections to Jurisdiction) (21 October 2005) ¶ 141.
[31] UNCTAD, *Bilateral Investment Treaties 1995–2006: Trends in Investment Rulemaking* (2007) 22.

in treaties concluded by the United States, Japan, Turkey, and Canada), in which contracting parties are to treat the admission of investments from other contracting parties no less favourably than investors and investments from nationals or third countries.[32] The purpose of these provisions is to equalize competitive conditions for market entry among potential investors.

With respect to the latter model, the Kuwait–Japan BIT provides an example of a provision granting a relative right of establishment.[33] Article 2(1) provides, 'Each Contracting Party shall in its Area accord to investors of the other Contracting Party and to their investments treatment no less favourable than the treatment it accords in like circumstances to its own investors and to their investments with respect to investment activities.'[34] Article 3(1) provides, 'Each Contracting Party shall in its Area accord to investors of the other Contracting Party and to their investments treatment no less favourable than the treatment it accords in like circumstances to investors of a third party and to their investments with respect to investment activities.'[35] The treaty defines 'investment activities' as 'establishment, acquisition, expansion, operation, management, maintenance, use, enjoyment and sale or other disposal of investments'.[36]

A similar approach is found in the 2012 US Model BIT,[37] the US–Uruguay BIT of 2005,[38] and free trade agreements (FTAs) between the United States and several other countries. For example, the US–Chile FTA grants national treatment and most-favoured-nation treatment for the 'establishment, acquisition, expansion, management, conduct, operation, and sale or other disposition of investments in its territory'.[39] In addition, among multilateral treaties, both the North American Free Trade Agreement[40] and the ASEAN Comprehensive Investment Agreement[41] also grant investments from contracting states a relative right of establishment in similar terms.

---

[32] ibid 23.
[33] Agreement Between Japan and the State of Kuwait for the Promotion and Protection of Investment (22 March 2012).
[34] ibid Art 2(1).   [35] ibid Art 3(1).   [36] ibid Art 1(d).
[37] The 2012 US Model BIT, Art 3(1) states: 'Each Party shall accord to investors of the other Party treatment no less favorable than that it accords, in like circumstances, to its own investors with respect to the establishment, acquisition, expansion, management, conduct, operation, and sale or other disposition of investments in its territory.'
[38] Treaty Between the United States of America and the Oriental Republic of Uruguay Concerning the Encouragement and Reciprocal Protection of Investment (4 November 2005), Art 3(1).
[39] The Free Trade Agreement between the Government of the United States of America and the Government of the Republic of Chile (6 June 2003) provides in Art 10.2:

1. Each Party shall accord to investors of the other Party treatment no less favorable than that it accords, in like circumstances, to its own investors with respect to the establishment, acquisition, expansion, management, conduct, operation, and sale or other disposition of investments in its territory.
2. Each Party shall accord to covered investments treatment no less favorable than that it accords, in like circumstances, to investments in its territory of its own investors with respect to the establishment, acquisition, expansion, management, conduct, operation, and sale or other disposition of investments.

[40] NAFTA, Arts 1102 and 1103.
[41] ASEAN Comprehensive Investment Agreement, Arts 5 and 6.

With respect to the entry of foreign investment, it should be noted that while treaty provisions establishing the controlled entry model usually refer to 'the admission' of investments, clauses on a relative right of establishment refer to the 'establishment, admission, acquisition, [and] expansion' of investments. No treaty specifically defines these terms or seeks to explain the difference between admission and establishment. One suggested explanation is that while 'admission' and 'establishment' both imply the entry of foreign capital into a host state, the notion of 'establishment' carries with it an investor's implicit right to create a permanent enterprise and establish a long-term business presence in the host country.[42]

The implication of provisions granting a relative right of establishment is clear: in deciding on the admission of foreign investment projects, the host country authorities must treat applications by investors of its treaty partners in the same way as it treats applications by its own national investors and those from other countries. For host countries seeking to encourage investments by their own nationals, such provisions may be problematic. For one thing, the host country may have closed certain sectors to foreign investment for strategic or political reasons. For another, many countries give special preference to national investors in order to strengthen national enterprises in particular sectors or because they believe that national investors cannot compete on an equal footing with foreign firms. Such countries would be likely to find it easier to grant most-favoured-nation treatment on the entry of foreign investment than national treatment. Thus, one finds two subcategories of treaties using the relative right of establishment approach: (1) treaties granting both most-favoured-nation treatment and national treatment upon admission; and (2) treaties granting most-favoured-nation treatment only.[43]

The concepts of national treatment and most-favoured-nation treatment arose out of the field of international trade.[44] It should be noted, however, that applying them to foreign investment projects, no two of which are exactly alike, is a far more difficult task than is the case with the international trade in fungible goods. The qualifying words 'in like situations', quoted previously, and the standard limitations found in virtually all treaty grants of relative rights of admission, might allow differing treatment to the entry of investments if the nature of projects or the circumstances surrounding them are sufficiently dissimilar. Moreover, treaties with this type of entry provision also often contain a specific list of economic areas and sectors in which foreign investment may be prohibited or partially restricted. For example, the United States–Grenada Treaty grants most-favoured-nation and national treatment to the entry of investment from each country but also stipulates that such treatment is 'subject to the right of each Party to make or maintain exceptions falling within one of the sectors to which the respective host countries may restrict investment by

---

[42] Gomez-Palacio and Muchlinski (n 16 above) 230.

[43] UNCTAD, *Bilateral Investment Treaties 1995–2006: Trends in Investment Rulemaking* (2007) 22–6.

[44] For a discussion of national and most-favoured-nation treatment within the context of admitted investments, see Ch 9, sections 9.6 and 9.7.

the other country'.[45] The list of exceptions with respect to Grenada consists of the following areas: air transportation, government grants, government insurance and loan programs, ownership of real estate, use of land, and natural resources.

The ECT adopts a unique approach to the admission of investments from treaty partners. It recognizes the possibility of non-discriminatory treatment on entry but does not oblige contracting parties to grant this treatment to potential investors. Under Article 10(2) and (3) of the ECT, '[e]ach Contracting Party shall *endeavour* to accord Investors of other Contracting Parties, as regards the making of investments, treatment...which is no less favourable than that which it accords to its own investors or to investors of any Contracting party or of any third state, whichever is the most favourable' (emphasis added). The use of the term 'endeavour' only obliges ECT countries to use their best efforts to grant non-discriminatory treatment to investors making investments.[46] One may view this provision as falling between a firm obligation desired by many capital-exporting states in their BIT negotiations and the complete freedom desired by many countries to approve or disapprove proposed foreign investment.

The ECT contemplates going beyond this 'soft' commitment on non-discrimination to a 'hard' one. Article 10(4) of the Treaty contemplates a supplementary treaty embodying a firm obligation to accord national and most-favoured-nation treatment to investors from ECT countries when making investments. To provide momentum towards the creation of a non-discrimination obligation for the admission of foreign investment, the ECT contains two additional provisions not ordinarily found in BITs. First, under Article 10(5) each contracting party makes a commitment to attempt to limit exceptions to the non-discriminatory treatment of the entry of foreign investment. Each country also pledges to progressively remove existing restrictions affecting investors from other ECT countries. This provision does not prevent a country from introducing new restrictions; however, Article 10(6)(a) allows a contracting party to declare to the Energy Charter Conference that it will not introduce new restrictions. Moreover, an ECT country may also make a voluntary commitment to grant non-discriminatory treatment to investments in some or all economic activities in the energy sector. Thus, a country could voluntarily make a commitment to grant national or most-favoured-nation treatment, whichever is more favourable, to the making of an investment in the hydropower generation area without being obliged to grant similar treatment to investments in petroleum exploration or other energy sector activities. These kinds of provisions, which envisage progressive development of a host country's obligations towards the making of foreign investments, are not ordinarily found in BITs. If this approach is successful within the context of the ECT, it may one day be included in BIT negotiations as well.

One specific type of discriminatory treatment that host countries often impose when approving foreign investments is a 'performance requirement' or

[45] Treaty between the United States of America and Grenada Concerning the Reciprocal Encouragement and Protection of Investment (2 May 1986).

[46] Legal Counsel of the IEA, *The Energy Charter Treaty: A Description of its Provisions* (1994) 17.

'trade-related investment measure' (TRIM).[47] TRIMs might require an investment project—as a condition for entry—to export a certain proportion of its production, restrict its imports to a certain level, or purchase a minimum quantity of local goods and services. Although most BITs have not dealt with performance requirements, the United States, with only limited success, has sought to protect its investors from them through BIT negotiations. The US Model BIT provides: 'Neither Party may, in connection with the establishment, acquisition, expansion, management, conduct, operation, or sale or other disposition of an investment of an investor of a Party or of a non-Party in its territory, impose or enforce any requirement or enforce any commitment or undertaking' related to certain performance requirements.[48] The ASEAN Comprehensive Agreement also endeavours to limit the ability of contracting states to impose performance requirements on ASEAN members.[49]

Viewed as measures that unjustifiably burden trade and investment, concerns by governments about performance requirements prompted the Uruguay Round of the GATT to conclude an Agreement on Trade-Related Investment Measures forbidding the imposition of measures that are inconsistent with Article II of GATT, on national treatment, and Article XI, on the elimination of quantitative restrictions. GATT members are thereby prevented from making local content and trade balancing requirements conditions for making or operating foreign investment projects. In similar fashion, Article 5 of the ECT, deals with this problem by incorporating GATT obligations into the treaty by reference. The Charter provides that a contracting party shall not apply any TRIM that is inconsistent with Article III and Article XI of GATT. It does not specifically refer to the new GATT agreement on TRIMs. On the other hand, the ECT does provide for certain exceptions that allow TRIMs as a condition of eligibility for a host country's export programmes, foreign aid, government procurement, or preferential tariff programmes. It also permits contracting parties to phase out existing performance requirements gradually.

8.6 Grants of an Absolute Right of Establishment

A true right of establishment would allow investors from other treaty partners to invest freely and unconditionally in a host state. The only significant international treaty that grants such an absolute right is the Treaty on the Functioning of the European Union (TFEU).[50] The TFEU is constitutional in nature, but it is also partly an investment treaty designed to promote and protect the flow of capital among EU members. One of the basic purposes of the European Union is to create

---

[47] See the discussion in Ch 13, section 13.2.   [48] 2012 US Model BIT.

[49] ASEAN Comprehensive Investment Agreement, Art 7 ('Prohibition of Performance Requirements').

[50] Consolidated Versions of the Treaty on European Union and the Treaty on the Functioning of the European Union [2010] OJ C83/1.

an internal market among its member states, an internal market which, according to the TFEU, 'shall comprise an area without internal frontiers in which the free movement of goods, persons, services and capital is ensured in accordance with the provisions of the Treaties'.[51] Various specific treaty provisions seek to achieve this result with respect to the movement of capital. Thus, Articles 49 to 55 of the TFEU grant all member state firms and nationals the right of establishment in all EU member countries and guarantee that such firms will receive national treatment. Article 49 provides that 'restrictions on the freedom of establishment of nationals of a Member State in the territory of another Member State shall be prohibited' and that '[s]uch prohibition shall also apply to restrictions on the setting-up of agencies, branches or subsidiaries by nationals of any Member State established in the territory of any Member State'. Freedom of establishment is defined to include 'the right to take up and pursue activities as self-employed persons and to set up and manage undertakings in particular companies or firms...., under the conditions laid down for its own nationals by the law of the country where such establishment is effected'.

Article 54 states that '[c]ompanies or firms formed in accordance with the law of a Member State and having their registered office, central administration or principal place of business within the Community shall, for the purposes of this Chapter, be treated in the same way as natural persons who are nationals of Member States', thereby guaranteeing such firms national treatment. Furthermore, under Articles 63 to 66 of the TFEU, investors from other EU member states have the right to transfer capital and earnings freely and are guaranteed national treatment on expropriation. Indeed, Article 63 of the EU Treaty specifically prohibits restrictions on the movement of capital and payments between member states and between member states and third countries.

Finally, the European Court of Justice (ECJ) may adjudicate any violation of these rights. The ECJ may hear cases related to the violation of treaty rights directly or overturn national court decisions found inconsistent with the Treaty. The TFEU authorizes the European Commission to reduce barriers to investment among EU members and from third countries, a task that the Commission has pursued quite energetically.[52] For example, in 2008 Greece had passed a law stating that any investor seeking to acquire more than 20 per cent of the total equity with 20 per cent voting rights in any privatized enterprise must first receive

---

[51] TFEU, Art 26(2).

[52] eg in June 1997, the European Commission issued an interpretative Communication clarifying the scope of EU Treaty provisions on capital movements and the right of establishment. It took this initiative because certain member states had imposed limits on the number of voting shares that investors from other member states could acquire in privatization operations. The Communication stresses that free movement of capital and freedom of establishment constitute fundamental and directly applicable freedoms established by the EU Treaty. Nationals of other member states should, therefore, be free to acquire controlling stakes, exercise the voting rights attached to these stakes, and manage domestic companies under the same conditions that a member state has prescribed for its own nationals. Communication of the European Commission on Certain Legal Aspects Concerning Intra-EU Investment [1997] OJ C220/15–18. In April 2001, the Commission reaffirmed the validity of its interpretative Communication on investment.

prior authorization from the Interministerial Privatization Committee. In addition, decisions of these privatized entities were subject to the authorization of the Minister of Finance. The Commission brought an action before the ECJ, claiming, among other things, that the Greek law violated TFEU provisions on the right of establishment. The ECJ held that in laying down the requirements with respect to *ex ante* and *ex post* investment controls, Greece had not fulfilled its obligations under Article 43 on freedom of establishment.[53]

Although no other investment treaty has gone so far as that of the European Union to create an 'open door' for investments from treaty partners, the TFEU may stand as a model for countries that desire increased economic integration through the treaty-making process.

---

[53] Case C-244/11, *European Commission v Hellenic Republic*, European Court of Justice (Judgment of 8 November 2012).

9

General Treatment Standards

9.1 The Nature of Investment and Investor Treatment

In order to protect foreign investors against the political risk resulting from placing their assets under a host country's jurisdiction, investment treaties stipulate obligations regarding the 'treatment' that host countries must give to investors and their investments. Although the treaties do not usually define the meaning of 'treatment', that term in its ordinary dictionary sense includes the 'actions and behaviour that one person takes towards another person'. In other words, by entering into an investment treaty, a state makes promises about the actions and behaviours it will take towards investments and investors of treaty partners.[1] The treaty provisions on investor and investment treatment are intended to restrain host country government behaviour and impose a discipline on governmental actions. To achieve this goal, treaties define a standard to which host countries must conform in their treatment of investors and investments. State actions that fail to meet the defined standard constitute treaty violations that engage the offending state's international responsibility and render it potentially liable to pay compensation for the injury it has caused.

Investment treaties normally contain treatment provisions with respect to numerous matters that investors consider important. One may categorize the various treatment standards included in treaties as 'general' or 'specific'. General standards of treatment apply to all facets of an investment's activities in the host country. These include host government commitments to grant investors and investments 'fair and equitable treatment', 'full protection and security', and 'treatment in accordance with international law'. Specific treatment standards concern particular matters relating to an investment, such as monetary transfers, expropriation, and investor rights in times of war, revolution, or civil disturbance.[2] This

---

[1] In the ICSID case of *Suez, Sociedad General de Aguas de Barcelona SA, and Vivendi Universal SA v The Argentine Republic*, the tribunal defined 'treatment' as follows: 'The word "treatment" is not defined in the treaty text. However, the ordinary meaning of that term within the context of investment includes the rights and privileges granted and the obligations and burdens imposed by a Contracting State on investments made by investors covered by the treaty.' *Suez, Sociedad General de Aguas de Barcelona SA, and Vivendi Universal SA v The Argentine Republic*, ICSID Case No ARB/03/19 (Decision on Jurisdiction) (3 August 2006) ¶ 55.

[2] UNCTAD, *Bilateral Investment Treaties 1995–2006: Trends in Investment Rulemaking* (2007) 28.

chapter is concerned with general treatment standards, while succeeding chapters will discuss individual, specific treatment standards.

It should be noted that while investment treaties specify standards for state behaviour towards investors, they generally do not impose standards for the behaviour of investors towards the host country or its government. Presumably, the reason for this is the assumption by treaty negotiators that host country laws and legal institutions are sufficient to ensure proper investor behaviour.

9.2 Overview of General Treatment Standards

General treatment standards consist of two types: (a) *absolute standards*, which are not contingent upon specified factors, happenings, or government behaviour towards other investors or persons; and (b) *relative standards*, which are dependent upon the host government's treatment of other investments or investors. Examples of absolute standards include guarantees of full protection and security, fair and equitable treatment, or treatment in accordance with the minimum standard of international law. Examples of relative standards are most-favoured-nation treatment and national treatment. Whereas the latter type of standard requires a comparator for its application,[3] the former does not.

The present chapter discusses the absolute and relative general treatment standards used most frequently in international investment treaties. These include full protection and security, fair and equitable treatment, minimum treatment according to international law, most-favoured-nation treatment, and national treatment. That these standards exist in one form or another in most investment treaties gives the treaties a strong similarity—indeed, some would say a significant commonality. It must also be acknowledged, however, that not all treaties include all of these general standards and that significant differences exist in the way individual treaties articulate them. For example, particular treaties may grant investments 'complete protection and security', 'full protection and security', 'full legal protection and security', or simply 'protection and security'. Moreover, some treaties may articulate specific treatment standards as independent commitments, while others may link them to or condition them on another standard. For example, while many early US bilateral investment treaties (BITs) simply required host countries to grant investors 'full protection and security', the 2005 US–Uruguay BIT specifies that 'full protection and security' requires each party to provide 'the level of police protection required under customary international law'.[4] As a result of these differences, the degree of protection afforded individual investments may vary significantly among treaties. Consequently, persons interpreting investment

---

[3] TJ Grierson-Weiller and IA Laird, 'Standards of Treatment' in P Muchlinski et al, *The Oxford Handbook of International Investment Law* (OUP, 2008) 262.

[4] Treaty between the United States of America and the Oriental Republic of Uruguay Concerning the Encouragement and Reciprocal Protection of Investment (4 November 2005), Art 5(2)(b). See also 2012 US Model BIT, Art 5.2(b).

treaty provisions should give careful attention to the differing ways individual treaty texts articulate their protections. At the same time, it should be emphasized that treatment standards are almost always expressed in general and even vague terms and thus render the task of applying them to concrete, complex fact situations, like those that usually arise in investment disputes, even more difficult.

9.3 Protection and Security

(a) In general

In virtually all investment treaties, contracting parties promise to give some degree of 'protection' and 'security' to the investors and investments of other contracting parties. The precise formulation of that promise varies among treaties. For example, the first BIT ever concluded, the agreement between Germany and Pakistan in 1959, provided that investments by nationals or companies of either party are to 'enjoy *protection and security* in the territory of the other party'.[5] On the other hand, Article 4(1) of the Germany–Argentina BIT of 1991 states that investments should enjoy 'full legal protection and full legal security',[6] and Article IV(2) of the Ecuador–El Salvador BIT of 1994 provides for 'full legal protection' for the investments of either party's nationals.[7] Article 3 of the China–Qatar BIT of 1999 merely states that the contracting party investments and the activities associated with those investments 'shall be accorded fair and equitable treatment and shall *enjoy protection* in the territory of the other Contracting Party'.[8] Despite the generality and vagueness of these provisions, they do seem to imply that the host state has an obligation to take measures to protect covered investors and investments from certain negative actions that may affect them.[9] Beyond this

---

[5] Treaty between the Federal Republic of Germany and Pakistan for the Promotion and Protection of Investments (25 November 1959).

[6] Artikel 4:

　(1) Kapitalanlagen von Staatsangehoerigen oder Gesellschaften einer Vertragspartei geniessen im Hohheitsgebiet der abderen Vertragspartei vollen rechtlichen Schutz und volle rechtliche Sicherheit. Vertrag zwischen der Bundesrepublik Deutschland und der Argentinischen Republik über die Förderung und den gegenseitigen Schutz von Kapitalanlagen (9 April 1991).

[7] ARTICULO IV 'Protección de inversiones':

　(2) Cada Parte Contratante, una vez que haya admitido en su territorio inversiones de inver-sionistas de la otra Parte Contratante, concederá plena protección legal a tales inversiones y les acordará un tratamiento no menos favorable que el otorgado a las inversiones de sus propios inversionistas nacionales o de inversionistas de terceros Estados. Convenio entre el Gobierno de la Republica del Ecuador y el Gobierno de la Republic de El Salvador para la Promoción y Protección Reciprocas de Inversiones (16 May 1994).

[8] Agreement between the Government of the People's Republic of China and the Government of the State of Qatar Concerning the Encouragement and Reciprocal Protection of Investments (9 April 1999), Art 3.1.

[9] R Dolzer and C Schreuer, *Principles of International Investment Law* (OUP, 2008) 149.

basic observation, treaty provisions on full protection and security do little to answer three difficult but essential questions:

1. Against whom is the host state to protect covered investors and investments?
2. Against what actions is the host state to protect investors and their investments?
3. Precisely what measures must a host state take in order to meet its treaty obligations?

To answer these questions, one must consider the historical origins of this standard that has now become a common feature of investment treaties.

(b) Historical origins of the standard

The origin of the terms 'full protection and security', 'constant protection and security', or simply 'protection and security' appears to lie in the bilateral commercial treaties that many countries concluded in the nineteenth and early twentieth centuries. One example is the friendship, commerce, and navigation (FCN) treaties made by the United States during that period.[10] Of the twenty-two commercial treaties concluded by the United States before 1920, fourteen contained reference to 'special protection' and the remaining eight required 'full and perfect protection' of persons' private property.[11] As an illustration, Article 3 of the 1850 FCN treaty between the United States and Brunei provided that His Highness the Sultan 'engages that such Citizens of the United States of America shall as far as lies within his power, within his dominions enjoy *full and complete protection and security* for themselves and for any property which they may acquire' (emphasis added).[12] The bilateral treaties of other countries also employed this term.[13]

Arbitral decisions, judicial decisions, and other forms of international practice have given meaning to the term 'protection and security' over the years. Indeed, it is only through jurisprudence that one can fully understand the content of this standard. Most cases involved actions by third persons, such as mobs, revolutionaries, or insurgents, who had physically damaged investments covered under the treaty. Injured investors sought compensation from the host government on the grounds that the government had not taken sufficient measures to protect the investment or the investor. For example, in the *Sambiaggio* case,[14] the

---

[10] K Vandevelde, 'The Bilateral Investment Treaty Program of the United States' (1988) 21 Corn Int'l LJ 203, 204.

[11] R Wilson, 'Property-protection Provisions in United States Commercial Treaties' (1951) 45 AJIL 84, 92–6.

[12] Treaty of Friendship, Commerce and Navigation with Brunei (entered into force 11 July 1853) 10 Stat 909; Treaty Series 331.

[13] See eg the bilateral treaty between Italy and Venezuela, stating that 'citizens of each state should enjoy in the territory of the other "the fullest measure of protection and security of person and property, and should have in this respect the same rights and privileges accorded to nationals"'. Quoted in the *Sambiaggio* case, Italy–Venezuela Mixed Claims Commission, UN Reports of International Arbitral Awards, vol 10, p 512.

[14] ibid.

Italy–Venezuela Mixed Claims Commission in 1903 had to adjudicate whether Venezuela was monetarily liable to Italian nationals for damage resulting from the acts of revolutionaries operating in Venezuelan territory. Article 4 of the Italy–Venezuela Treaty of 1861 stated that each state's citizens should enjoy 'the fullest measure of protection and security of person and property, and should have in this respect the same rights and privileges accorded to nationals' of the territory. The umpire in the case declared that he 'accepts the rule that if in any case of reclamation submitted to him it is alleged and proved that Venezuelan authorities failed to exercise due diligence to prevent damages from being inflicted by revolutionists, that country should be held responsible'.[15] He ultimately denied Italy's claims that the treaty imposed strict liability.

Probably the most authoritative case interpreting the FCN treaty provisions on protection and security was a 1989 decision of a chamber of the International Court of Justice (ICJ) in the *ELSI* case.[16] In that case, the United States brought a claim against Italy under the US–Italy FCN treaty for injuries incurred by Raytheon, a US company, with respect to its subsidiary in Sicily. A factory of Raytheon's subsidiary in Palermo was taken over by workers and then requisitioned by the mayor in order to forestall its closure by the investor for economic reasons. The United States alleged that such actions violated Italy's obligation to give US investors 'the most constant protection and security', as required by Article V(1) of the FCN treaty. The United States did not contend, however, that the obligation constituted a guarantee resulting in strict liability. Instead, it pointed to the 'well-established aspect of the international standard of treatment…that States must use "due diligence" to prevent wrongful injuries to the person or property of aliens within their territory'. The ICJ Chamber found that the Italian government had taken adequate measures to protect the investor and its property, stating that '[t]he reference in Article V to the provision of "constant protection and security" cannot be construed as the giving of a warranty that property shall never in any circumstances be occupied or disturbed'.[17]

In general, jurisprudence relating to the FCN provisions on protection and security recognizes that this standard requires host countries to take steps to protect investors against physical injury to their persons or properties, whether by government agents or third persons. However, the FCN provision does not make the host state a guarantor of the safety of the investor or its property. It requires only that the host state exercise due diligence in carrying out its obligations under the treaty. As one commentator has observed, the decisions of tribunals and the other sources offer no definition of 'due diligence', noting: 'No doubt the application of this standard will vary according to the circumstances, yet, if "due diligence" be taken to denote a fairly high standard of conduct the exception will overwhelm the rule.'[18] A host state satisfies its due diligence obligation when it

---

[15] ibid 534.
[16] *Elettronica Sicula SpA (ELSI) (United States v Italy)* (Judgment) (20 July 1989) [1989] ICJ Rep 15.
[17] ibid ¶108, p 65.
[18] J Crawford, *Brownlie's Principles of Public International Law* (8th edn, OUP, 2012) 552.

takes all the reasonable measures of protection that a well-administered government would take in a similar situation.[19]

(c) Full protection and security in the modern era

With the development of bilateral and other investment treaties since 1960, the inclusion of provisions granting investors some form of protection and security has become standard. It can thus be found in countless BITs, NAFTA,[20] the Energy Charter Treaty (ECT),[21] and the 2009 ASEAN Comprehensive Investment Agreement,[22] among others. These provisions have also been the basis of several investor–state arbitrations, and so arbitral tribunals have had to interpret and apply them in a new era. In doing so, contemporary tribunals have relied on the jurisprudence interpreting FCNs to a significant extent but have also extended the scope of protection in certain instances.

The first such BIT case was *Asian Agricultural Products Limited v Sri Lanka (AAPL)*.[23] In *AAPL*, an ICSID tribunal considered the claims of a UK investor in shrimp farming in Sri Lanka which had suffered injuries as a result of the destruction of its facilities by Sri Lankan security forces during an alleged operation against rebels. The claimant maintained that the UK–Sri Lanka BIT's provision guaranteeing 'full protection and security' went beyond the minimum standard of customary international law and imposed an unconditional obligation of protection on the host country. Therefore, failure to comply with the obligation entailed 'strict or absolute liability' for the host state once damage to the investor's property was established. In response, Sri Lanka contended that the 'full protection and security' standard incorporates, rather than supplants, the customary international legal standard of responsibility requiring due diligence on the part of states and reasonable justification for the destruction of property, but not

---

[19] On the meaning of due diligence, tribunals and scholars have often referred to the statement of Professor AV Freeman in his lectures at the Hague Academy of International Law: 'The "due diligence" is nothing more nor less than the reasonable measures of prevention which a well-administered government could be expected to exercise under similar circumstances.' AV Freeman, 'Responsibility of States for the Unlawful Acts of Their Armed Forces' (1956) 88 *Receuil des Cours* 261. See also *Asian Agricultural Products Ltd v Sri Lanka*, ICSID Case No ARB/87/3 (Final Award) (27 June 1990) ¶ 170.

[20] NAFTA, Art 1105, entitled 'Minimum Standard of Treatment', provides: '1. Each Party shall accord to investments of investors of another Party treatment in accordance with international law, including fair and equitable treatment and full protection and security.'

[21] ECT, Art 10, entitled 'Promotion, Protection, and Treatment of Investments', provides in part in para 1: '[s]uch investments shall enjoy the most constant protection and security'.

[22] Art 11(1), on the Treatment of Investments states: 'Each member state shall accord to covered investments of investors of any other member state fair and equitable treatment and full protection and security.' Art 11 (2) further provides: 'For greater certainty... (b) full protection and security requires each Member State to take such measures as may be reasonably necessary to ensure the protection and security of covered investments.'

[23] *Asian Agricultural Products Ltd v Sri Lanka*, ICSID Case No ARB/87/3 (Final Award) (27 June 1990). The Sri Lanka–United Kingdom Agreement on the Promotion and Protection of Investments (entered into force 18 December 1980) (1980) 19 ILM 886.

imposing strict liability. A central issue throughout the case was the standard of liability to be applied to the Sri Lankan security forces.

The tribunal unanimously rejected the UK investor's contentions that the 'full protection and security' standard imposed 'strict liability' on the host state; however, a majority of the arbitrators did find the Sri Lankan government responsible for the property destruction under the customary international law standard requiring 'due diligence' protection from the host state. The tribunal acknowledged that customary international law contemplated a 'sliding scale of liability related to the standard of due diligence'. This scale would range from the older 'subjective' criteria that take into account the relatively limited existing possibilities of local authorities in a given context to an 'objective' standard of vigilance in assessing the required degree of protection and security with regard to what one should legitimately expect from a reasonably well-organized modern state with respect to the level of security afforded to foreign investors.[24] Applying this reasoning to the facts of the case, the tribunal concluded that the Sri Lankan government could reasonably have used other means than those employed by its troops to exclude suspected rebel elements from the shrimp farm staff. Further, those other actions would have minimized the risk of death and destruction in the counter-insurgency operation. The tribunal also found that the failure to take such precautionary measures was especially significant because such measures fall within the normal exercise of governmental inherent powers. The tribunal concluded that Sri Lanka, both through inaction and omission, 'violated its due diligence obligation which requires undertaking all possible measures that could be reasonably expected to prevent the eventual occurrence of killings and property destructions'.[25]

Subsequent cases have found host governments liable for not taking steps to protect an investor's factory from looting by government troops in Zaire, and for not employing measures to prevent the seizure of a hotel by disgruntled employees in Egypt. In the case of *American Manufacturing and Trading, Inc v Zaire* (*AMT*),[26] the tribunal rejected Zaire's defence that it should not be liable for the acts of marauding soldiers who looted the investor's factory on at least two consecutive occasions without any intervention by government authorities. The tribunal stated that the protection and security treatment standard constituted an objective obligation 'which must not be inferior to the minimum standard of vigilance and of care required by international law'.[27] It therefore found it unnecessary to discuss whether Zaire was bound by an obligation of result or simply an obligation of conduct, but found it sufficient that Zaire took no measures whatsoever to ensure the protection and security of the investment in question. Consequently, Zaire's failure to take any protective measures to ensure the security of AMT's investment engaged its international responsibility. The tribunal stated:

---

[24] ibid ¶ 170.   [25] ibid ¶ 85(B).

[26] *American Manufacturing and Trading, Inc v Zaire*, ICSID Case No ARB/93/1 (Award) (21 February 1997).

[27] ibid ¶ 6.06.

the obligation incumbent upon Zaire is *an obligation of vigilance*, in the sense that Zaire as the receiving State of investments made by AMT, an American company, shall take all measures necessary to ensure the full enjoyment of protection and security of its investment and should not be permitted to invoke its own legislation to detract from any such obligation. Zaire must show that it has taken all measure of precaution to protect the investments of AMT on its territory. It has not done so... (emphasis added).[28]

A similar result can be found in *Wena Hotels Ltd v Arab Republic of Egypt*,[29] in which an ICSID tribunal considered a UK investor's claim under the UK–Egypt BIT. The case concerned the seizure of a hotel by its employees. Relying solely on the standards developed in the *AAPL* and *AMT* cases, the tribunal found Egypt responsible for the failure to accord the investment 'fair and equitable treatment' and 'full protection and security' because it did not take any action to prevent the seizures or to immediately restore control over the hotel to Wena.

A finding of liability for failure to provide promised protection and security is necessarily fact driven. It must be based on the details of the threat as well as the government's response to that threat. The burden of proving the facts that constitute the threat, the nature and inadequacy of the government's response, and the connection of these factors to the injury suffered by the investor all rest on the claimants. Failure to carry that burden will result in a denial of government liability. For example, in the case of *Técnicas Medioambientales Tecmed SA v United Mexican States*,[30] a Spanish company that had invested in a Mexican waste disposal facility brought a claim under the Spain–Mexico BIT. It alleged that Mexico had breached its obligation to provide 'full protection and security' from various social movements, disturbances, and demonstrations against the investor's activities. The investor claimed that Mexican authorities had encouraged the community to react adversely to the landfill and its operation. The investors also asserted that the authorities did not act as quickly, efficiently, and thoroughly as they should have to prevent or terminate the adverse actions of the local population. The tribunal found that the claimant failed to provide sufficient evidence to establish a causal link between the public protests and Mexico's inaction or to show that Mexico acted unreasonably under the circumstances.[31] Like many previous tribunals, the tribunal concluded that 'the guarantee of full protection and security is not absolute and does not impose strict liability upon the State that grants it'.[32]

A lack of evidence led to similar results in *Eureko v Poland*,[33] which involved the alleged harassment and intimidation of the investor's local representatives, as well as in *Noble Ventures v Romania*,[34] which concerned protests and demonstrations by employees.

---

[28] ibid ¶ 6.05.
[29] *Wena Hotels Ltd v Arab Republic of Egypt*, ICSID Case No ARB/98/4 (Award on Merits) (8 December 2000).
[30] *Técnicas Medioambientales Tecmed SA v United Mexican States*, ICSID Case No ARB(AF)/00/2 (Award) (29 May 2003).
[31] ibid ¶¶ 176, 177.   [32] ibid ¶ 177.
[33] *Eureko BV v Republic of Poland*, UNCITRAL (Partial Award) (19 August 2005).
[34] *Noble Ventures Inc v Romania*, ICSID Case No ARB/01/11 (Award) (12 October 2005).

Traditionally, tribunals have interpreted provisions guaranteeing protection and security as protecting investors and their investments from *physical* injury caused by the actions of host governments, their agents, or third parties. The US–Uruguay BIT quoted earlier appears to adopt this position by making explicit that '"full protection and security" requires each Party to provide the level of police protection required under customary international law'.[35] At the beginning of the twenty-first century, a few cases have sought to expand the term's scope to include protection against allegedly unjustified governmental actions that injure an investor's legal rights but cause no physical injury. The first such case to take this position was *CME Czech Republic v Czech Republic*,[36] a dispute brought under the Netherlands–Czech Republic BIT in which the investor claimed that certain acts and omissions of the Czech Media Council (a quasi-governmental media regulatory body) amounted to a violation of the obligation to provide full protection and security. The tribunal found that the Media Council's conduct was aimed at removing the security and legal protection from the investor's investment and so violated the standard of full protection and security. The tribunal stated: 'The host State is obligated to ensure that neither by amendment of its laws nor by actions of its administrative bodies is the agreed and approved security and protection of the foreign investor's investment withdrawn or devalued.'[37]

The decision in *CME* could be seen as a strong precedent for the expansion of the full protection and security clause to cover non-physical injuries sustained by investors. However, its precedential force would seem to be weakened by two factors. First, in the related case of *Lauder v Czech Republic*,[38] which involved the same parties and the same set of facts as in *CME*, the tribunal found no violation of the full protection and security clause. Second, the *CME* tribunal did not provide a historical analysis of the concept of full protection and security, failed to give any clear reason as to why it departed from the historical interpretation traditionally employed by courts and tribunals, and instead chose to expand the concept to cover non-physical actions and injuries.[39]

Other cases have nonetheless followed the approach of *CME*. In *Azurix v Argentina*,[40] a US investor argued that the limits of 'full protection and security' were not confined to physical protection but also included the kind of protection described in *CME*. The investor alleged that Argentina breached the standard in question by failing to apply the relevant regulatory framework and the concession

[35] Treaty between the United States of America and the Oriental Republic of Uruguay Concerning the Encouragement and Reciprocal Protection of Investment (4 November 2005), Art 5(2)(b).

[36] *CME Czech Republic BV v Czech Republic*, UNCITRAL (Partial Award) (13 September 2001).

[37] ibid ¶ 613.

[38] *Lauder v Czech Republic*, UNCITRAL (Award) (3 September 2001).

[39] On this point, see *Suez, Sociedad General de Aguas de Barcelona SA, and Vivendi Universal SA v The Argentine Republic*, ICSID Case No ARB/03/19 and *AWG Group Ltd v The Argentine Republic*, UNCITRAL (Decision on Liability) (30 July 2010) ¶ 177.

[40] *Azurix v Argentine Republic*, ICSID Case No ARB/01/12 (Award) (14 July 2006).

agreement applicable to the claimant's investment. Argentina thereby destroyed the security provided to those investments. In response, Argentina contested the relevance of the *AAPL* and *AMT* cases on the grounds that they involved physical destruction of the investor's facilities by the armed forces. As for the relevance of *CME*, it pointed out that relying on *CME* was questionable without referring to *Lauder*, where, on the same facts, the tribunal reached the opposite conclusion. As a final argument, Argentina requested that the tribunal consider that during the period under review the country was undergoing the worst economic, social, and institutional crisis in its history.

Relying on *AAPL*, *AMT*, *Wena Hotels*, and *Occidental*,[41] the tribunal concluded that the interrelation between the 'fair and equitable treatment' and 'full protection and security' 'indicates that full protection and security may be breached even if no physical violence or damage occurs'.[42] Focusing on the specific language of the clause in which full protection and security is granted, the tribunal stated:

The cases referred to above show that full protection and security was understood to go beyond protection and security ensured by the police. It is not only a matter of physical security; the stability afforded by a secure investment environment is as important from an investor's point of view. The Tribunal is aware that in recent free trade agreements signed by the United States, for instance, with Uruguay, full protection and security is understood to be limited to the level of police protection required under customary international law. However, when the terms "protection and security" are qualified by "full" and no other adjective or explanation, they extend, in their ordinary meaning, the content of this standard beyond physical security.[43]

Thus, *Azurix* seems to suggest that the omission of the words 'full' or 'fully', which are included in some investment treaties, restricts the scope of protection to physical security and protection but that the inclusion of those words expands the scope of protection to cover non-physical injuries. On the other hand, in the later case of *Parkerings-Compangiet AS v The Republic of Lithuania*,[44] the tribunal took a different view, stating: 'It is generally accepted that the variation of language

---

[41] *Occidental Exploration and Production Co v The Republic of Ecuador*, LCIA Case No UN3467 (Final Award) (1 July 2004). The tribunal pointed out the fact that in some BITs fair and equitable treatment and full protection and security appear as a single standard, in others as separate protections. Under the BIT in question, the tribunal observed that, since 'fair and equitable treatment' and 'full protection and security' appeared sequentially, they constituted different obligations. The tribunal subsequently held:

> the Respondent has breached its obligations to accord fair and equitable treatment under Article II(3)(a) of the Treaty. In the context of this finding the question of whether in addition there has been a breach of full protection and security under this Article becomes moot as a treatment that is not fair and equitable automatically entails an absence of full protection and security of the investment.

ibid ¶ 187.

[42] *Azurix v Argentine Republic*, ICSID Case No ARB/01/12 (Award) (14 July 2006) ¶ 406.
[43] ibid ¶ 408.
[44] *Parkerings-Compangiet AS v The Republic of Lithuania*, ICSID Case No ARB/05/08 (Award) (11 September 2007).

between the formulation *"protection"* and *"full protection and security"* does not make a difference in the level of protection a host State is to provide.'[45]

Another later case, also involving Argentina, justified the expansion of full protection and security to non-physical injuries in a different way. In *Siemens v Argentina*,[46] the investor initiated arbitration under the German–Argentina BIT and alleged, *inter alia*, that Argentina breached its obligation to accord full protection and security by engaging in conduct that frustrated the contract. According to Argentina, 'security' implied only physical security. The investor, however, gave the term a wider meaning, particularly because of the treaty's reference to 'legal security'. Having noted that the definition of investment included tangible and intangible assets, the tribunal found that 'the obligation to provide full protection and security is wider than "physical" protection and security'. It offered the following reasoning:

It is difficult to understand how the physical security of an intangible asset would be achieved. In the instant case, 'security' is qualified by 'legal'. In its ordinary meaning 'legal security' has been defined as 'the quality of the legal system which implies certainty in its norms and, consequently, their foreseeable application.' It is clear that in the context of this meaning the Treaty refers to security that is not physical. In fact, one may question given the qualification of the term 'security', whether the Treaty covers physical security at all. Arguably it could be considered to be included under 'full protection', but that is not an issue in these proceedings.[47]

Based on this textual interpretation of the standard, the tribunal concluded that Argentina's initiation of the renegotiation of the contract constituted a violation of its obligations under the BIT because it was done for the sole purpose of reducing its costs, was unsupported by any declaration of public interest, and affected the legal security of Siemens' investment. Moreover, the qualifying adjective 'legal' was meant to extend the scope of the full protection and security clause. One may question the tribunal's reasoning regarding the emphasis it placed on the fact that intangible assets are not subject to physical injury. Merely because some assets are subject to physical injury and others are not does not necessarily mean that a treaty's contracting parties intended to depart from the traditional definition and scope of full protection and security. One could equally well conclude from reading the treaty's provisions that the contracting parties only intended to protect assets from physical injury that are capable of physical injury.

Some awards since the *CME* decision have maintained the more traditional approach to interpreting full protection and security. In *Saluka Investments BV*

---

[45] ibid ¶ 354, citing N Rubins and S Kinsella, *International Investment, Political Risk and Dispute Resolution* (Oceana Publications, 2005) to justify this proposition.
[46] *Siemens v Argentina*, ICSID Case No ARB/02/8 (Award) (6 February 2007).
[47] ibid ¶ 303.

(The Netherlands) v The Czech Republic, the tribunal determined that the Czech Republic did not violate the Netherlands–Czech Republic BIT when it took measures to stop trading in the claimant's securities. Under the BIT, investors were promised 'full security and protection'. In reaching its decision, the tribunal stated: 'The practice of arbitral tribunals seems to indicate however that the "full protection and security clause" is not meant to cover just any kind of impairment of an investor's investment but to protect more specifically the physical integrity of an investment against interference by the use of force.'[48] The tribunals in *BG v Argentina*,[49] *PSEG v Turkey*,[50] *Rumeli v Kazakhstan*,[51] and *Suez, Sociedad General de Aguas de Barcelona SA, and Vivendi Universal SA v The Argentine Republic*[52] reached a similar conclusion. Many cases since, however, have found that full protection and security does extend beyond physical protection.[53]

In addition to the apparent divergence of views on the scope of the full protection and security clause, it would seem that the treaty provisions and cases represent two different views of the nature of full protection security. On the one hand, some, such as the tribunal in *Saluka*, view it as part of a minimum standard of international law elaborated in customary international law. On the other hand, some, such as the tribunal in *CME*, view it as an independent, self-contained treaty standard to be interpreted without reference to the limitations of customary international law. The NAFTA Free Trade Commission, which is empowered under the NAFTA treaty to make authoritative interpretations of the treaty, has sought to clarify the issue by opting for the traditional approach. In 2001, it issued such an interpretation for the term 'full protection and security' as found in Article 1105(1) of NAFTA: 'The concepts of "fair and equitable treatment" and "full protection and security" do not require treatment in addition to or beyond that which is required by the customary international law minimum standard of treatment of aliens'.[54]

---

[48] *Saluka Investments BV (The Netherlands) v The Czech Republic*, UNCITRAL (17 March 2006) ¶ 484.

[49] *BG Group plc v Republic of Argentina*, UNCITRAL (Award) (24 December 2007) ¶ 326.

[50] *PSEG Global, Inc, The North American Coal Corp, and Konya Ingin Electrik Üretim ve Ticaret Ltd Sirketi v Republic of Turkey*, ICSID Case No ARB/02/5 (Award) (19 January 2007) ¶¶ 258–259.

[51] *Rumeli Telekom AS and Telsim Mobil Telekomunikasyon Hizmetleri AS v Republic of Kazakhstan*, ICSID Case No ARB/05/16 (Award) (29 July 2008) ¶ 668.

[52] *Suez, Sociedad General de Aguas de Barcelona SA, and Vivendi Universal SA v The Argentine Republic*, ICSID Case No ARB/03/19 and *AWG Group Ltd v The Argentine Republic*, UNCITRAL (Decision on Liability) (30 July 2010) ¶ 179.

[53] See eg *Unglaube v Republic of Costa Rica*, ICSID Case No ARB/08/1 and ARB/09/20 (Award) (16 May 2012) ¶ 281 (rejecting the standard expressed by the tribunal in *Saluka*); *Total SA v Argentine Republic*, ICSID Case No ARB/04/01 (Decision on Liability) (27 December 2010) ¶ 343; *Frontier Petroleum Services Ltd v Czech Republic*, UNCITRAL (Final Award) (12 November 2010) ¶ 263; *Mohammad Ammar Al-Bahloul v Republic of Tajikistan*, SCC Case No V064/2008 (Partial Award on Jurisdiction and Liability) (2 September 2009) ¶ 246.

[54] NAFTA Free Trade Commission, *Notes of Interpretation of Certain Chapter 11 Provisions* (31 July 2001) B(2).

(d) Conclusion

In reviewing the jurisprudence related to the meaning of the term 'full protection and security' and the variations of the term found in investment treaties, one may conclude the following:

1. The core element under this standard is an obligation on the part of a contracting state to exercise due diligence in providing physical protection and security from injurious acts by government agents or third parties to the investor and its investment. The standard imposes an objective obligation that must not be less than the minimum standard of vigilance and care required by international law. Qualifying words such as 'constant' or 'full' that are found in many treaties might strengthen the required standard of 'protection and security' by requiring a standard of 'due diligence' higher than the 'minimum standard' of general international law.

2. The due diligence obligation requires a host state to undertake all measures that could be reasonably expected to prevent damage to foreign investments. Since due diligence means, according to the cases and commentators, 'nothing more nor less than the reasonable measures of prevention which a well-administered government could be expected to exercise under similar circumstances',[55] it would seem that a state's lack of resources or the existence of crisis conditions are not defences to a state's obligation to meet this objective standard. A state may breach its obligation by action, failure to act, omission to act, or by instigation or connivance. Moreover, a state may not absolve itself of international responsibility arising out of a treaty violation by invoking its legislation as a defence.

3. The nature and scope of the protection and security standard under a given treaty depends on its precise wording and its place in the treaty relative to other standards of investment treatment.

4. Certain arbitral cases indicate that protection may be expanded to cover non-physical injuries caused by host states or their instrumentalities. Thus, the host state may be held responsible for the failure to provide 'legal security', which is defined by tribunals as the quality of the legal system and particularly the certainty of its norms and their foreseeable application. Additionally, the interrelationship of 'fair and equitable treatment' and 'full protection and security' might allow for full protection and security to be breached without physical violence or damage; however, the force and durability of this trend is not yet clear or certain.

---

[55] Freeman (n 19 above).

9.4 Fair and Equitable Treatment

(a) Background

Virtually all investment treaties contain promises by the contracting parties to give 'fair and equitable treatment' to investors and the investments of other contracting parties. Although the precise formulation of these promises of fair and equitable treatment and the conditions attached thereto vary considerably among treaties, fair and equitable treatment is a core concept embedded in nearly all international investment agreements. Indeed, one might say that it represents the 'golden rule' of investment treaties.

While the term 'fair and equitable' is vague and ambiguous on its face and is never defined within the treaties themselves, it is invoked so often in contemporary investor–state arbitrations that one scholar has labelled it 'an almost ubiquitous presence' in investment litigation.[56] Its undefined and potentially elastic nature has made it a favourite of aggrieved investors and their lawyers when seeking compensation for the allegedly injurious acts of host country governments. Indeed, some have claimed that a majority of successful claims in investor–state arbitrations have been based on the fair and equitable clause.[57] As a result of its wide use, tribunals have interpreted and applied the fair and equitable standard in a large number of arbitral cases, and scholars have analysed and commented upon it extensively.

Unlike the full protection and security clause, which dates from the development of friendship, commerce, and navigation treaties in the nineteenth century, the concept of fair and equitable treatment in investment treaties has its origins in the post-World War II era. Whereas the concept of full protection and security was developed within treaties whose fundamental purpose was to facilitate trade, the fair and equitable treatment standard arose within international efforts to foster international investment specifically. These early developments took place at both the multilateral and bilateral levels.

Commentators[58] seem to agree that the fair and equitable treatment standard became part of the international legal landscape with the attempts to establish an International Trade Organization (ITO) through the Havana Charter of 1948 after World War II. In Article 11(2), the Havana Charter provided that the ITO had authority to make recommendations for and promote bilateral or multilateral agreements on measures designed: '(i) to assure *just and equitable treatment* for the enterprise, skills, capital, arts and technology brought from one Member country to another' (emphasis added).[59] The ITO would never become a reality due to

---

[56] R Dolzer, 'Fair and Equitable Treatment: A Key Standard in Investment Treaties' (2005) 39 Int'l Lawyer 87.
[57] Dolzer and Schreuer (n 9 above) 119.
[58] UNCTAD, *Fair and Equitable Treatment*, UNCTAD/ITE/IIT/11 (1999) vol 3, p 26.
[59] UNCTAD, *International Investment Instruments: A Compendium* (1996) vol 1, p 4.

the failure of certain countries to ratify it,[60] but the concept of just and equitable treatment and fair and equitable treatment persisted in subsequent efforts to shape multilateral frameworks for investment. Such efforts can be seen in the failed 1948 Economic Agreement of Bogota among Latin American States,[61] the private initiative in 1959 known as the Abs-Shawcross Draft Convention on Investment Abroad,[62] and the 1963 OECD Draft Convention on the International Protection of Foreign Property, subsequently revised in 1967.[63]

Although none of these multilateral efforts resulted in an enforceable treaty, their discussion and elaboration of the fair and equitable concept seem to have implanted the idea into the minds of the epistemic community of international lawyers and negotiators, who would become a principal channel for its diffusion and development among countries. Eventually, these ideas found their way into national programmes to negotiate BITs, and through this process the fair and equitable treatment standard has become a principle of international law and a fundamental norm of the emerging global regime for international investment. Indeed, one would say that fair and equitable treatment is, to employ Hans Kelsen's concept from his *Pure Theory of Law* (1934), the *grundnorm* or basic norm of the investment treaty system.

The first country to adopt the fair and equitable concept in treaty practice was the United States. With the expansion of American investment abroad after World War II, the United States negotiated a series of modern friendship, commerce, and navigation (FCN) treaties whose primary goal was to protect US foreign investments by obtaining treaty commitments from other countries on new absolute standards of investment treatment, one of which was 'equitable treatment'. For example, US FCN treaties with Uruguay and Ireland contained the obligation to accord 'equitable' treatment to the capital of nationals and companies of the other party.[64] Subsequent FCN treaties routinely employed the term 'fair and equitable treatment' in their texts.[65]

European countries launched their programmes to negotiate BITs around 1960 and the fair and equitable treatment standard would eventually also become a

---

[60] ibid vol 1, p 3.

[61] The Bogota Agreement, Art 22 included the following provision:

Foreign capital shall receive equitable treatment. The States therefore agree not to take unjustified, unreasonable or discriminatory measures that would impair the legally acquired rights or interests of nationals of other countries in the enterprises, capital, skills, arts or technology they have supplied.

[62] This draft, prepared under the leadership of Herman Abs (Director-General of the Deutsche Bank) and Lord Shawcross (the UK Attorney-General), stipulated in Art 1 that 'each party shall at all times ensure fair and equitable treatment to the property of the nationals of the other Parties'. H Abs and L Shawcross, 'The Proposed Convention to Protect Foreign Investment: A Round Table: Comment on the Draft by the Authors' (1960) 9 J Pub L 119, 119–24.

[63] Draft Convention, Art 1 stated: 'Each Party shall at all times ensure fair and equitable treatment to the property of the nationals of the other Parties.'

[64] Wilson (n 11 above) 101, 104.

[65] R Wilson, *United States Commercial Treaties and International Law* (Hauser Press, 1960) 120. The US FCN treaties with Belgium and Luxembourg, France, Greece, Ireland, Israel, Nicaragua,

basic feature of those agreements. For example, in the period from the early 1960s to the early 1990s, the fair and equitable treatment standard was incorporated into over 300 BITs. One study of 335 of these treaties found that only twenty-eight did not expressly include the standard and 196 combined the fair and equitable standard with the national treatment and most-favoured-nation treatment standards.[66]

In recent years, the number of capital-exporting countries that have proposed draft BITs for negotiations with their capital-importing counterparts has broadened, so that countries such as Chile and China, not traditionally regarded as capital-exporting states, now have model BITs that incorporate norms of fair and equitable treatment. BITs between developing countries, such as Peru and Thailand, the United Arab Emirates and Malaysia, and Argentina and Chile, as well as those between states in transition and developing countries, such as Bulgaria and Ghana and Russia and the Republic of Korea, are additional evidence of the concept's broad acceptance. There are still deviations in practice, but the inclusion of the fair and equitable standard is clearly a dominant trend in investment treaty-making.[67]

(b) Formulation of the standard

The precise formulation of the fair and equitable standard varies among investment treaties. In some treaties, the standard is given a prominent and independent position at the beginning of the general treatment clauses. A number of French treaties, as well as Belgium–Luxembourg and Swedish agreements, adopt this approach. German BITs, on the other hand, tend to refer to the standard in the admission clause.[68] In still other treaties, the fair and equitable treatment standard is combined with provisions on the protection and security of the investment, as is the case in UK and US treaties. Yet other treaties have combined the clause with provisions prohibiting discriminatory measures, or with national and most-favoured-nation standards.[69] NAFTA includes it as part of the section discussing the protection to be accorded under international law. Thus, Article 1105(1) of NAFTA provides: 'Each Party shall accord to investments of investors of another Party treatment in accordance with international law, including fair and equitable treatment and full protection and security.'

A treaty that offers fair and equitable treatment and combined national and most-favoured-nation treatment provides foreign investors with both

---

and Pakistan contained the express assurance that foreign persons, properties, enterprises, and other interests would receive 'equitable' treatment, while other US FCN treaties—including those with Ethiopia, the Federal Republic of Germany, Oman, and the Netherlands—contemplated 'fair and equitable' treatment for a similar set of items in the foreign investment process.

[66] M Khalil, 'Treatment of Foreign Investment in Bilateral Investment Treaties' (1992) 8 ICSID Rev—FILJ 339, 351–5.

[67] S Vasciannie, 'The Fair and Equitable Treatment Standard in International Investment Law and Practice' (1999) 70 BYIL 100, 105, 130.

[68] R Dolzer and M Stevens, *Bilateral Investment Treaties* (Kluwer Law International, 1995) 58.

[69] ibid 59.

non-contingent and contingent forms of protection. From the perspective of the investor, the fair and equitable component establishes an important fixed reference point because it provides an apparently definite standard that will not vary according to external considerations—its content turns solely on what is fair and reasonable in the circumstances. The fair and equitable standard also prevents discrimination against the beneficiary when discrimination would amount to unfairness or inequity under the circumstances. Simultaneously, national and most-favoured-nation treatment, as contingent standards, protect investments by ensuring equality or non-discrimination in relation to investments by other persons. A foreign investor might believe that even if a state promises protection under national and most-favoured-nation treatment standards that level of protection is insufficient because nationals and investors from the most favoured nation are themselves receiving inadequate protection. In such cases, the fair and equitable treatment standard helps to ensure that the investor will receive a minimum level of protection based on notions of fairness and equity.[70]

(c) The complexities of interpreting and applying the standard

Interpreting the fair and equitable standard and applying it to the kind of complicated fact situations that usually present themselves in investor–state disputes are not easy tasks. Indeed these tasks are complicated by at least three factors. First the term 'fair and equitable' is, one may say without exaggeration, maddeningly vague, frustratingly general, and treacherously elastic. Second, the treaty provisions and the agreements in which the terms are embedded offer no definition for them, nor any real guidance on how to apply them. Third, despite the abundant scholarly commentary on the subject and a growing volume of arbitral decisions, application of the fair and equitable standard is so tied to the facts of the specific cases as to limit the utility of the arbitral decisions and doctrinal analysis.

For persons attempting to apply the treaty standard, one initial question is whether the term 'fair and equitable' embodies a single standard or two distinct standards, one concerning fairness and the other equity. As a matter of practice, the two words are employed as a single standard of treatment. For one thing, most treaty texts and other instruments providing for fair and equitable treatment for investments combine the two words to refer to a single treatment standard—'fair and equitable treatment'. For example, the model BITs prepared by Chile, China, France, Germany, the United States, and the United Kingdom, as well as regional instruments such as NAFTA, the 1993 Treaty Establishing the Common Market for Eastern and Southern Africa (COMESA), the 1994 ECT, and the 2009 ASEAN Comprehensive Investment Treaty all use the phrase 'fair and equitable treatment' as part of a single concept. An UNCTAD study concluded that this fact points to 'fair and equitable treatment' being a single standard and not two separate standards. Two considerations support this view. First, the consistency

---

[70] UNCTAD, *Fair and Equitable Treatment* (1999) 16.

with which states have linked the two terms in the verbal formula of 'fair and equitable' treatment supports the view that states believe there is a single standard. The history of the term's use in various efforts to draft a multilateral treaty in the post-World War II era further supports this view. Second, if states intended 'fair and equitable' to refer to two separate standards, they would have made that meaning explicit in the treaty texts. No state has chosen to do so. They could, for example, set out the fairness standard in one treaty provision, and the equity standard in another. The fact that they have not done so indicates that the contracting states intended the phrase 'fair and equitable treatment' to connote a single standard.[71]

One may speculate as to whether a promise in an investment treaty of 'equitable' treatment or 'just and equitable' treatment grants weaker legal protection to investors than a commitment to 'fair and equitable' treatment. However, up to this point there seems to be little basis for making such a distinction. For one thing, a reference to fairness and equity together would seem to afford investors at least as much protection as 'equitable' treatment. Moreover, in view of the similarity in meaning between fairness, on the one hand, and equity, on the other, in the context of investment relations it is difficult to identify ways in which the combination of the two provides greater protection in practice than the equitable standard alone. Similarly, while the term 'just and equitable' treatment occurs in some treaties, it is difficult to determine how this formulation differs in substance from the fair and equitable standard.[72]

(d) Differing concepts of the fair and equitable standard

An examination of treaty practice, jurisprudence, and scholarly commentary reveals two different conceptions of the nature of the fair and equitable standard: (1) that fair and equitable treatment merely reflects the *international minimum standard* required by customary international law; or, (2) that the standard is *autonomous and additional* to general international law. Let us examine each of these views briefly.

(i) Fair and equitable treatment as the international minimum standard

As was discussed in Chapter 3, the traditional position of western governments and commentators has been that states owe aliens and their property a certain minimum level of treatment regardless of the treatment each state gives to its own nationals. Treatment short of this required minimum creates state responsibility for any resulting injuries. One view of the fair and equitable treatment standard is that it merely refers to that minimum international standard and does not give investors any additional rights. This position has

---

[71] ibid 14.   [72] ibid 19.

often been advanced by developing countries, which have sought to limit the scope of the fair and equitable treatment standard. For example, during the negotiations for the Draft United Nations Code of Conduct on Transnational Corporations, it has been claimed that the Group of 77, which is constituted exclusively of developing countries, collectively took the position that the fair and equitable treatment language was equivalent to the international minimum standard.[73]

The treaty practice of certain countries also seems to support this view of fair and equitable treatment. Article 5 of the 2012 US Model BIT, entitled 'Minimum Standard of Treatment', as well as the investment chapters of the recently concluded US Free Trade Agreements go even further and attempt to define a minimum standard of treatment. They provide as follows: '1. Each Party shall accord to covered investments treatment in accordance with customary international law, including fair and equitable treatment and full protection and security.' Paragraph 2 of Article 5 makes clear that the fair and equitable treatment standard does not go beyond the minimum standard:

2. For greater certainty, paragraph 1 prescribes the customary international law minimum standard of treatment of aliens as the minimum standard of treatment to be afforded to covered investments. The concepts of 'fair and equitable treatment' and 'full protection and security' do not require treatment in addition to or beyond that which is required by that standard, and do not create additional substantive rights.[74]

Canada has taken a similar approach in its model Foreign Investment Protection and Promotion Agreement and recent treaty practice.[75]

Certain arbitral decisions have also adopted this concept of fair and equitable treatment. In *Genin v Estonia*,[76] the tribunal considered whether certain actions by Estonia amounted to a violation of its obligation to accord 'fair and equitable treatment' and 'non-discriminatory and non-arbitrary treatment' under the 1994 US–Estonia BIT. The tribunal ultimately dismissed the claim, viewing the fair and equitable treatment standard as incorporating the minimum standard under international law:

Article II(3)(a) of the [US–Estonia] BIT requires the signatory governments to treat foreign investment in a 'fair and equitable' way. Under international law, this requirement is generally understood to 'provide a basic and general standard which is detached from the host State's domestic law.' While the exact content of this standard is not clear [citing

[73] P Robinson, 'The June 1985 Reconvened Special Session on the Code' (1985) 20 C TC Reporter 15 (published by the Commission on Transnational Corporations).

[74] 2012 US Model BIT, Art 5.

[75] C Yannaca-Small, *Fair and Equitable Treatment Standard in International Investment Law* (OECD, 2005) 87. See eg Agreement Between the Government of Canada and the Government of the People's Republic of China for the Promotion and Reciprocal Protection of Investments (9 September 2012), Art 4.2; Agreement between the Government of Canada and the Government of Romania for the Promotion and Reciprocal Protection of Investments (8 May 2009), Art II.2(b).

[76] *Alex Genin, Eastern Credit Ltd, Inc and AS Baltoil (US) v Republic of Estonia*, ICSID Case No ARB/99/2 (Award) (25 June 2001).

Brownlie], the Tribunal understands it to require an 'international minimum standard' that is separate from domestic law, but that is, indeed, a *minimum* standard.[77]

In *Occidental v Ecuador*,[78] the tribunal asked 'whether the fair and equitable treatment mandated by the Treaty is a more demanding standard than that prescribed by customary international law' and concluded that 'the BIT standard was not different from the minimum standard required under customary international law concerning both the stability and predictability of the legal and business framework of the investment'.[79]

The most significant and explicit adoption of the concept of fair and equitable treatment as a minimum international standard is found in the text of NAFTA and related practice. Article 1105(1) of NAFTA, entitled 'Minimum Standard of Treatment' states: 'Each Party shall accord to investments of investors of another Party treatment in accordance with international law, including fair and equitable treatment and full protection and security.'

Two elements of this text reveal its conceptual basis. The first is its heading, the 'Minimum Standard of Treatment', which is a clear reference to customary international law. The second is the inclusion of the fair and equitable treatment standard in referring to international law ('international law, including fair and equitable treatment'). Both these elements indicate that the NAFTA considers the fair and equitable treatment as part of the minimum standard of treatment under international law, not autonomous from it.[80]

In spite of these indications, some early NAFTA tribunals did not regard the fair and equitable treatment standard in Article 1105(1) as being restricted to customary international law. Instead, the tribunals viewed it as having an additive character. For example, the Partial Award in *SD Myers*[81] stated that the breach of a rule of international law might not be decisive in determining whether fair and equitable treatment had been denied. The tribunal said:

In some cases, the breach of a rule of international law by a host Party may not be decisive in determining that a foreign investor has been denied 'fair and equitable treatment', but the fact that a host Party has breached a rule of international law that is specifically designed to protect investors will tend to weigh heavily in favor of finding a breach of Article 1105.[82]

The tribunal in *Pope & Talbot*[83] was even more explicit. The tribunal discussed the issue of the relationship between Article 1105 of NAFTA and customary international law at some length, and found that the fairness elements in Article 1105

---

[77] ibid ¶ 367.
[78] *Occidental Exploration and Production Co v Ecuador*, LCIA Case No UN3467 (Award) (1 July 2004).
[79] ibid ¶¶ 188, 190.
[80] C Schreuer, 'Fair and Equitable Treatment in Arbitral Practice' (2005) 6 JWIT 357, 362.
[81] *SD Myers v Government of Canada*, UNCITRAL (Partial Award) (12 November 2000).
[82] ibid ¶ 64.
[83] *Pope & Talbot Inc v The Government of Canada*, UNCITRAL (Award) (10 April 2001).

were additional to the requirements imposed by international law. It based this conclusion on the view that the language of Article 1105 grew out of bilateral treaties that had conceived of the fair and equitable standard as extending beyond the minimum international law standard. According to the tribunal, 'the language and evident intention of the BITs makes the discrete (i.e. additive) standards of interpretation the proper one. A contrary reading would do violence to the BIT language'.[84] It followed that 'compliance with the fairness elements must be ascertained free of any threshold that might be applicable to the evaluation of measures under the minimum standard of international law'.[85]

In reaction to these arbitral determinations, the NAFTA Free Trade Commission (FTC), a body composed of representatives of the three states, which has the power to adopt binding interpretations under Article 1131(2) of the treaty, issued the following Note of Interpretation on 31 July 2001:

Minimum Standard of Treatment in Accordance with International Law
1. Article 1105(1) prescribes the customary international law minimum standard of treatment of aliens as the minimum standard of treatment to be afforded to investments of investors of another Party.
2. The concepts of 'fair and equitable treatment' and 'full protection and security' do not require treatment in addition to or beyond that which is required by the customary international law minimum standard of treatment of aliens.
3. A determination that there has been a breach of another provision of the NAFTA, or of a separate international agreement, does not establish that there has been a breach of Article 1105(1).[86]

In a subsequent decision on damages,[87] the tribunal in *Pope & Talbot* criticized the FTC's power to issue the Interpretation[88] as well as its correctness,[89] but reluctantly accepted the FTC's Interpretation.[90] Later NAFTA tribunals in the *Mondev*,[91] *UPS*,[92] *ADF*,[93] and *Loewen*[94] cases relied on the FTC's Notes of Interpretation in applying the fair and equitable standard. Nonetheless, some scholars have argued that the concept of fair and equitable treatment in NAFTA has little application to the interpretation of other investment treaties. The reason is that the NAFTA standard is expressed in a provision entitled 'Minimum

---

[84] ibid ¶ 13.   [85] ibid ¶ 111.

[86] NAFTA Free Trade Commission, *Notes of Interpretation of Certain Chapter 11 Provisions* (31 July 2001).

[87] *Pope & Talbot Inc v The Government of Canada*, UNCITRAL (Award in Respect of Damages) (31 May 2002).

[88] ibid ¶¶ 17–24.   [89] ibid ¶¶ 25–47.

[90] ibid ¶¶ 48–69. See also P Dumberry, 'The Quest to Define "Fair and Equitable Treatment" for Investors under International Law—the Case of the NAFTA Chapter 11 Pope & Talbot Awards' (2004) 3 JWIT 4658.

[91] *Mondev International Ltd v United States of America*, ICSID Case No ARB(AF)/99/2 (Award) (11 October 2002).

[92] *United Parcel Service v Canada*, UNCITRAL (Award on the Merits) (24 May 2007).

[93] *ADF Group, Inc v United States of America*, ICSID Case No ARB(AF)/00/1 (Award) (9 January 2003).

[94] *Loewen Group, Inc and Raymond L Loewen v United States of America*, ICSID Case No ARB(AF)/98/3 (Award) (26 June 2003).

Standard of Treatment', which is not widely used in other treaties, and because NAFTA, unlike other treaties, specifically states that the fair and equitable standard falls within the international law minimum treatment standard. Moreover, other treaties have not been subject to an authoritative interpretation like that issued by the FTC.[95]

(ii) Fair and equitable treatment standard as an autonomous standard additional to international law

Many scholars and non-NAFTA tribunals have concluded that the fair and equitable standard, when expressed without qualification or condition, is an autonomous, additional standard whose scope is not limited by the minimum standards required by international law. According to this view, the fair and equitable clause imposes a higher standard of treatment on host states than customary international law does. For example, FA Mann states:

The terms 'fair and equitable treatment' envisage conduct which goes far beyond the minimum standard and afford protection to a greater extent and according to a much more objective standard than any previously employed form of words. A tribunal would not be concerned with a minimum, maximum or average standard. It will have to decide whether in all circumstances the conduct in issue is fair and equitable or unfair and inequitable. No standard defined by other words is likely to be material. The terms are to be understood and applied independently and autonomously.[96]

Various arguments support this view. First, if states and investors believed that the fair and equitable standard was entirely interchangeable with the international minimum standard, they could have stated so clearly in their investment treaty texts; instead, most investment instruments do not make an explicit link between the two in the way that NAFTA has done. Therefore, one may reasonably infer that most contracting states do not believe that fair and equitable treatment is implicitly the same as the international minimum standard. Second, attempts to equate the two standards fail to take into account the significant historical debate between developed, capital-exporting countries and developing capital-importing countries concerning the very existence of the international minimum standard. While developed countries have strongly supported the existence of a minimum international standard, many developing countries have denied its very existence in customary international law. Against this uncertain background, it is difficult to assume that countries participating in investment treaties intended to incorporate the international minimum standard into their treaties without expressly stating so.[97] One may therefore conclude that the fair and equitable standard

---

[95] Dolzer and Schreuer (n 9 above) 126. See also Schreuer (n 80 above) 360.
[96] FA Mann, 'British Treaties for the Promotion and Protection of Investments' (1981) 52 BYIL 241, 244.
[97] UNCTAD, *Fair and Equitable Treatment* (1999) 13.

is autonomous and is not necessarily equivalent to the international minimum standard. Indeed, in view of the various historical challenges to the international minimum standard (as discussed in Chapter 3), and the fact that capital-exporting countries have been the driving force behind the investment treaty movement, it is likely that the fair and equitable treatment provision is intended to be a higher standard of protection than that provided under the disputed international minimum standard. The inclusion of the fair and equitable standard, unknown to customary international law prior to the advent of investment treaties, seems to be intended to provide investors with a basic level of protection in situations where the other substantive provisions of international and national law are inapplicable.[98] Its function in the treaty can thus be seen as filling gaps not covered by other treaty provisions.[99] It also serves to guide the interpretation of other treaty provisions and assure that the general standard of fair and equitable treatment of foreign investment, a fundamental treaty goal, is attained.

These arguments are weakened, however, by the fact that neither the texts of individual BITs nor the available negotiating history demonstrates a clear, mutual intent by the contracting parties to adopt a standard that is higher than that required by customary international law in specific treaties.

Regardless of the different arguments on this issue, it must be admitted that the minimum international standard and the fair and equitable treatment standard overlap significantly with respect to issues like arbitrary treatment, discrimination, and unreasonableness. Moreover, the presence of a provision assuring fair and equitable treatment in an investment instrument does not automatically incorporate the international minimum standard for foreign investors. On the other hand, as at least one tribunal has suggested, the difference between the two standards may for all practical purposes be more apparent than real.[100] Indeed, one might say that for the purpose of applying and interpreting a fair and equitable clause in an investment treaty that makes no reference to the minimum international standard, the debate is largely irrelevant. When a claimant invokes the fair and equitable provision of a treaty, the central issue for arbitral tribunals is whether the alleged government conduct was unfair and inequitable, not whether it violated some minimum international standard to which the treaty does not

---

[98] K Vandevelde, *United States Investment Treaties: Policy and Practice* (Kluwer Law and Taxation, 1992) 76.

[99] Dolzer and Schreuer (n 9 above) 123.

[100] *Azurix v Argentine Republic*, ICSID Case No ARB/01/12 (Award) (14 July 2006) ¶ 361. In interpreting the Argentina–US BIT, Art II.2(a) which states: '[i]nvestment shall at all times be accorded fair and equitable treatment, shall enjoy full protection and security and shall in no case be accorded treatment less than required by international law', the tribunal stated:

> The purpose of the third sentence is to set a floor, not a ceiling, in order to avoid a possible interpretation of these standards below what is required by international law. While this conclusion results from the textual analysis of this provision, the Tribunal does not consider that it is of material significance for its application of the standard of fair and equitable treatment to the facts of the case. As it will be explained below, the minimum requirement to satisfy this standard has evolved and the Tribunal considers that its content is substantially similar whether the terms are interpreted in their

refer. The challenge is one of interpreting and applying this vague and general term to a usually highly complex fact situation.

(e) The content of the standard

The application of the fair and equitable standard in most cases is difficult for a variety of reasons. First, investment treaties do not define the term. Thus, arbitrators, government officials, investors' legal counsel, and others who would apply the term must begin interpretation by confronting two words, 'fair' and 'equitable', that because of their vagueness and generality allow for great subjectivity. Second, as a result, the standard created will be highly flexible and may result in a subjective decision-making process that disappointed litigants may consider unprincipled. Third, the fact situations to which the term must be applied are highly complex and in many cases involve troubled relationships between investors and host governments stretching over significant periods of time and involving multiple interactions. Thus, determining whether a particular governmental action violates the fair and equitable standards depends greatly on the facts of the individual case.[101]

In actual practice, it is impossible to anticipate the entire range of state actions that may injure an investor.[102] Some might consider this lack of precision a virtue rather than a shortcoming because it promotes flexibility in the investment process. Like other broad legal principles (such as 'due process of law', a term found in many domestic legal systems), the fair and equitable standard has been and will continue to be elaborated and given specific content through judicial and arbitral practice.[103] Thus, its very vagueness and generality endow it with a flexibility that will permit it to evolve in the light of experience by investors, host countries, and international arbitration tribunals. At the same time, interpreters of the standard must guard against the danger of subjectivity, bias, and lack of discipline in the interpretation process.

Usually, the process of interpreting the fair and equitable clause in most arbitral proceedings begins with a reference to the Vienna Convention on the Law of Treaties (VCLT), particularly Article 31(1), which provides: '(1) A treaty shall be interpreted in good faith in accordance with the *ordinary meaning* to be given the terms of the treaty *in their context and in light of its object and purpose*' (emphasis added). Thus, three elements are of particular importance in interpreting the fair and equitable standard: (1) the ordinary meaning of the term 'fair and equitable'; (2) the context in which the term 'fair and equitable' is used; and (3) the object

ordinary meaning, as required by the Vienna Convention, or in accordance with customary international law.
ibid ¶ 361.

[101] *Noble Ventures, Inc v Romania*, ICSID Case No ARB/01/11 (Award) (12 October 2005) ¶ 181.
[102] Vasciannie (n 67 above) 100, 104, 145.
[103] P Weil, 'The State, the Foreign Investor, and International Law: The no Longer Stormy Relationship of Ménage À Trois' (2000) 15 ICSID Rev—FILJ 401, 415.

and purpose of the investment treaty in question.[104] An inquiry into the ordinary meaning of the words 'fair' and 'equitable' usually yields very little. As the tribunal in Saluka stated after making its own strenuous efforts in this regard:

The 'ordinary meaning' of the 'fair and equitable treatment' standard can only be defined by terms of almost equal vagueness. In *MTD*, the tribunal stated that: 'In their ordinary meaning, the terms "fair" and "equitable"...mean "just", "even handed", "unbiased" "legitimate."' On the basis of such and similar definitions, one cannot say more than the tribunal did in *S.D. Meyers* by stating that an infringement of the standard requires 'treatment in such an unjust or arbitrary manner that the treatment rises to a level that is unacceptable from an international perspective'.[105]

The context of the term 'fair and equitable' is the whole treaty in which it is employed. Thus, the term must be interpreted not just as three words plucked from the text but instead must be construed from within the context of the various rights and responsibilities and conditions and limitations to which the contracting parties agreed.

And finally, following the directives of Article 31(1) of the VCLT, the tribunal must take into account the objects and purposes of the treaty. Here, most tribunals turn to the treaty's preamble to understand those objects and purposes. Individual treaties differ in their stated objectives, but while the treaty's title states that its immediate goal is the protection and promotion of investments, treaties' preambles often express far broader goals, such as economic cooperation between the treaty partners, economic development of the contracting parties, or mutual prosperity. As the Saluka tribunal noted, these broad goals lead to the conclusion that the promotion and protection of investment is not the only goal of the treaties and a balanced approach that takes into account these diverse goals must be used in interpreting fair and equitable treatment:

That in turn calls for a balanced approach to the interpretation of the Treaty's substantive provisions for the protection of investments, since an interpretation which exaggerates the protection to be accorded to foreign investments may serve to dissuade host States from admitting foreign investments and so undermine the overall aim of extending and intensifying the parties' mutual economic relations.[106]

Thus, it would appear that tribunals should take these broader goals into consideration when interpreting and applying the term 'fair and equitable treatment' and other treaty provisions.

In the end, an analysis of the treaty's text is necessary, but not sufficient, for the interpretation and application of the fair and equitable standard to an investment dispute. Normally, one must also consider decisions of tribunals in other cases to gain a better understanding of a term now found in virtually all investment treaties. Within a relatively short time, numerous arbitral tribunals have applied the

---

[104] See eg *Saluka Investment BV (Netherlands) v The Czech Republic*, UNCITRAL (Partial Award) (May 17, 2006) ¶ 297, which adopted a similar tripartite approach.
[105] ibid.   [106] ibid ¶ 300.

fair and equitable standard in numerous investment treaties in diverse situations and in many countries and industries. While these decisions only bind the parties in those specific cases, they also elaborate and give content to what is, by its terms, an imprecise standard. Arbitrators, legal counsel, and government officials all refer to this accumulated jurisprudence when seeking to apply the standard to new situations. Moreover, such cases have been the subject of much doctrinal commentary by scholars, yet another source of information for those seeking to apply the fair and equitable standard to specific situations.

An examination of the cases applying the fair and equitable standard reveals that arbitral tribunals have developed specific criteria, norms, and principles to determine whether host states have given fair and equitable treatment to investors. In general, tribunals have been called upon to determine whether specific governmental actions, such as amending legislation, revising administrative regulations, and modifying contracts in ways that adversely affect an investor's interests, have denied investors fair and equitable treatment. Not all such actions are a violation of the fair and equitable standard. States have a right to regulate persons and activities on their territories and do not cede that right when they sign an investment treaty. Therefore, in interpreting the meaning of fair and equitable treatment with respect to investors, tribunals must balance the legitimate and reasonable expectations of investors with the host country's legitimate regulatory interests.[107]

Among the principles most often relied upon by tribunals when applying the fair and equitable standard is whether the host state has: (1) failed to protect the investor's legitimate expectations; (2) failed to act transparently; (3) acted arbitrarily or subjected the investor to discriminatory treatment; (4) denied the investor access to justice or procedural due process; or (5) acted in bad faith. Let us examine each of these arbitration-based interpretations of the fair and equitable standard in turn. It must also be recognized, however, that these five general principles are not separate and distinct, but often overlap and blend into one another. It should also be noted that some of these principles, such as the prohibition on arbitrary or discriminatory actions or on measures that are denials of access to justice, are stated in particular treaties as explicit, independent standards in addition to being subsumed within the meaning of fair and equitable treatment.

(i) Failure to protect the investor's legitimate expectations

Investor expectations are fundamental to the investment process. It is the investor's expectations with respect to the risks and rewards of the contemplated investment that have a crucial influence on the investor's decision to invest. States seek to influence these investment decisions through their actions, laws, regulations, and policies. Indeed, the very idea of investment promotion, which is a fundamental

---

[107] ibid ¶ 306.

goal of virtually all investment treaties, is to create an expectation of profit in the minds of potential investors that will lead them to commit their capital and technology to the country in question. Thus, when a state has created certain expectations through its laws and acts that have led the investor to invest, it is generally considered unfair for the state to take subsequent actions that fundamentally deny or frustrate those expectations.

Respecting legitimate expectations is not only important to be fair to the individual but also important to the effectiveness of a country's economic system. The renowned German sociologist Max Weber emphasized the role of 'calculability' in the development of modern capitalism. He saw the main contribution of the legal system in modern capitalism as making economic life more calculable or predictable.[108] In the economic context, calculability refers to the likelihood that an economic actor will achieve its legitimate economic expectations. Economic activity is negatively affected if calculability is reduced by governmental or other action.

Various bodies of municipal law support the idea that governing authorities must respect the legitimate expectations they create. For example, the concept of 'legitimate expectations' is central to EU law and, in fact, forms a 'general principle of law' that can justify the European Court of Justice overturning offensive national measures.[109] It is also a basic principle of English public law that government entities honour statements of policy or intention, particularly those directed at particular individuals or groups, as part of a general duty of fairness. Such statements may create 'legitimate expectations', either procedural or substantive in nature, the disappointment of which can create a cause of action against the government entities concerned.[110] And in US law, courts have identified claimants' 'investment-backed expectations' as being a 'relevant consideration' in determining whether or not public entities have 'taken' property in violation of the Fifth Amendment.[111]

Numerous decisions of arbitral tribunals seeking to interpret and apply the fair and equitable standard have adopted a similar approach. Underlying these cases is the fundamental notion that it is unfair for a state to create certain expectations in the minds of investors through its laws, regulations, and actions; and then, once the investment is made, to change those laws and regulations in ways that significantly frustrate or cancel the expectations that the state itself has been instrumental in creating. Over thirty years ago, Professor Raymond Vernon characterized foreign investments as 'obsolescing bargains'.[112] By this he meant that

---

[108] R Swedberg, 'Max Weber's Contribution to the Economic Sociology of Law' (2006) 2 Ann Rev L Soc Sci 61.

[109] De Smith, Woolf, and Jowell, *Judicial Review of Administrative Action* (Sweet & Maxwell, 1995) 867. See eg Cases C-104/89 and 307/90, *Mulder v Council and Commission* [1992] ECR 1–3061; Case C-152/88, *Sofrimport Sour v Commission* [1990] ECR 1–2477; and Case 74/74, *CNTA SA v Commission* [1975] ECR 533.

[110] H Wade and C Forsyth, *Administrative Law* (OUP, 2000) 498.

[111] See eg *Penn Central Transportation Co and Ors v New York City and Ors*, 438 US 104; 98 S Ct 2646.

[112] R Vernon, *Sovereignty at Bay: The Multinational Spread of U.S. Enterprises* (Basic Books, 1971) 46.

once an investment was made, the host country had the power to change the terms of the investment agreement between the host government and the investor through the use of the former's sovereign authority. In many cases, arbitral tribunals have found such unilateral action not to be fair and equitable and have therefore held host states liable for rendering their bargains with investors obsolete. Governments may change policies in their continuing search for the best options available to discharge their functions. However, to the extent that earlier policies might have created legitimate procedural and substantive expectations for investors, they may not be abandoned without compensating the investor if the result would be so unfair as to amount to an abuse of power.[113]

The state is certainly not responsible for all the imaginable factors that could frustrate an investor's expectations. Thus, changes in a country's natural conditions, such as its weather, political stability, and markets, among a host of other factors that may have induced certain expectations in the investor, are not what the fair and equitable treatment standard is aimed to guard against. Rather, it is directed at actions of the state through its legal and policy framework. An initial step in most investor–state arbitral cases focuses on the nature of the host country legal order at the time the investment was made. In the case of an allegation that the host country violated the fair and equitable standard, the legal order must be evaluated to determine the reasonable, legitimate expectations that it created in the mind of the investor. The legal order must also be evaluated to determine the extent to which the host government had a legitimate and reasonable right to substantively and procedurally change that legal order. The application of the fair and equitable treatment standard therefore requires an inquiry into the investor's reasonable expectations and the host country's reasonable right to regulate.

The principle of respecting investors' legitimate expectations is not absolute and does not require the host state to freeze its legal system for the investors' benefit. Such a general stabilization requirement goes beyond what an investor can legitimately expect. It is clear that reasonable evolutions in host state law are part of the environment that investors must contend with. For instance, the adjustment of environmental regulations to internationally accepted standards or the improvement of labour laws to benefit the host state's workforce would not lead to violations of the fair and equitable treatment standard if applied in good faith and without discrimination.

While the concept of legitimate expectations has helped to refine the even vaguer concept of fair and equitable treatment, its application in particular cases is by no means automatic. That application requires tribunals to carefully evaluate numerous factors in individual fact situations. Although previous arbitral decisions are helpful in understanding how to apply the fair and equitable standard in cases involving alleged disappointed legitimate expectations, such decisions are highly fact specific and that specificity complicates the application of the principles

[113] F Vicuna, 'Regulatory Authority and Legitimate Expectations: Balancing the Rights of the State and the Individual under International Law in a Global Society' (2003) 5 *International Law Forum Du Droit International* 188, 194.

to conflicts in other arbitrations. Nonetheless, a few such cases are now reviewed for illustrative purposes. Many of these cases involve licences, permissions, and regulatory frameworks that were changed after an investment had been made.

In the NAFTA case of *International Thunderbird Gaming Corporation v United Mexican States*,[114] the claimant company, which was engaged in operating gaming facilities, requested an official opinion from Mexican authorities concerning the legality under Mexican law of a planned investment. Its written request (or *solicitud*), which was submitted to the *Secretaria de Gobernacion* (SEGOB), described Thunderbird's planned investment as concerning 'the commercial exploitation of video game machines for games of skills and ability' and explained that '[i]n these games, chance and wagering or betting is not involved'. In its formal response (or *oficio*), SEGOB referred to the Federal Law of Games and Sweepstakes, which prohibited 'gambling and luck related games' on Mexican territory and also laid out Mexican law regarding the regulation and authorization of gambling establishments. The *oficio* stated that, if the machines used by Thunderbird operated in the form and on the conditions stated in the *solicitud*, SEGOB would be unable to prohibit their use pursuant to Mexican law. Thunderbird subsequently opened a number of gaming facilities in Mexico. However, following a change of government, SEGOB began closing down those facilities and issued a resolution declaring Thunderbird's machines to be prohibited, causing Thunderbird to bring a Chapter Eleven NAFTA claim against Mexico.

Thunderbird based a significant part of its complaint on an argument that the *oficio* had created a 'legitimate expectation' that it would be able to operate its machines without regulation by SEGOB. The tribunal addressed the 'legitimate expectation' issue in general terms in its award. It stated:

the concept of 'legitimate expectations' relates, within the context of the NAFTA framework, to a situation where a Contracting Party's conduct creates reasonable and justifiable expectations on the part of an investor (or investment) to act in reliance on said conduct, such that a failure by the NAFTA Party to honour those expectations could cause the investor (or investment) to suffer damages.[115]

The tribunal concluded that for the purposes of this test the *oficio* had not generated a legitimate expectation upon which Thunderbird could reasonably rely. In doing so, it pointed out that the information presented in the *solicitud* had been incomplete and inaccurate. Furthermore, it found that the *oficio* had done no more than convey a message to the effect that, if the machines operated in accordance with the representations made in the *solicitud*, SEGOB would not have jurisdiction over them. The tribunal was therefore of the view that Thunderbird could not have reasonably relied to its detriment on the *oficio*. Indeed, Thunderbird had known when it chose to invest in Mexico that gambling was illegal under

---

[114] *International Thunderbird Gaming Corp v United Mexican States*, UNCITRAL (Award) (26 January 2006).
[115] ibid ¶ 147.1x(12).

Mexican law. As a result, it was incumbent on Thunderbird to exercise 'particular caution' in pursuing its business venture.

In *CME v The Czech Republic*,[116] the investor complained that interference with its contractual rights by the Czech Media Council, a quasi-governmental media regulatory body, created a violation of the fair and equitable standard promised under the Netherlands–Czech Republic BIT. In an important change, the Council reversed its previous position on the legal situation of the investor as a licence holder, a move that had allowed the investor's local partner to terminate the contract the investment depended upon. The tribunal found that '[t]he Media Council breached its obligation of fair and equitable treatment by evisceration of the arrangements in reliance upon which the foreign investor was induced to invest'.[117] In finding a breach of the obligation of fair and equitable treatment, the tribunal determined that the Media Council intentionally undermined CME's investments because it had both the power and the obligation under Czech law to remedy the partner's unlawful actions in severing the service agreement with CME.[118] It also found that CME had a legitimate expectation of reliance on the investment structure that had been arranged by the Media Council and that the Media Council should not have acted, without a bona fide purpose, to undermine the investor's business.[119]

Although the facts in *Ronald Lauder v The Czech Republic*[120] were the same as in *CME*, the *Lauder* tribunal rejected the investor's claims. In its discussions of the obligations owed under the fair and equitable treatment standard, the tribunal noted that the investor's claim could not be sustained because the Media Council had not reversed any prior express permissions.[121] The implication of this statement is that a reversal of a prior express permission by a state agency could constitute a breach of fair and equitable treatment in that such an express permission would have created a legitimate expectation on the part of the investor.

In *Tecmed v Mexico*,[122] the dispute concerned the Mexican government's replacement of an unlimited licence with a licence of limited duration for the operation of a landfill in which the claimant had invested. Applying the provision in the Spain–Mexico BIT guaranteeing fair and equitable treatment, the tribunal concluded that the provision required transparency and protection of the investor's basic expectations. It noted in particular that '[t]he foreign investor also expects the host State to act consistently, ie without arbitrarily revoking any preexisting decisions or permits issued by the State that were relied upon by the investor to assume its commitments as well as to plan and launch its commercial and business activities'.[123] The tribunal concluded that Mexico's behaviour

---

[116] *CME v The Czech Republic*, UNCITRAL (Partial Award) (13 September 2001).
[117] ibid ¶ 611.   [118] ibid ¶¶ 133, 611.   [119] ibid ¶ 611.
[120] *Ronald Lauder v The Czech Republic*, UNCITRAL (Final Award) (3 September 2001).
[121] ibid ¶ 291.
[122] *Tecnicas Medioambientales Teemed SA v The United Mexican States*, ICSID Case No ARB (AF)/00/2 (Award) (29 May 2003).
[123] ibid ¶ 154.

frustrated the investor's fair expectations. That behaviour was 'characterized by its ambiguity and uncertainty which are prejudicial to the investor in terms of its advance assessment of the legal situation surrounding its investment and the planning of its business activity and its adjustment to preserve its rights'.[124]

The case of *MTD v Republic of Chile*,[125] which involved a BIT between the developing countries of Chile and Malaysia, also raised an issue of fair and equitable treatment. The Malaysian investor had signed an investment contract with Chile's Foreign Investment Commission (FIC) to construct a large planned community. The project was halted after it was discovered that it was not consistent with existing zoning regulations. The tribunal found that Chile had violated the BIT's fair and equitable treatment standard by 'the inconsistency of action between two arms of the same Government vis-à-vis the same investor'.[126] While it was the investor's duty to inform itself of the country's law and policy, 'Chile also has an obligation to act coherently and apply its policies consistently, independently of how diligent an investor is'.[127] The fact that one arm of the Chilean government had approved a project that was against the country's urban zoning policy was a breach of the government's obligation to treat the investor fairly and equitably.

Other cases have held that to establish that government action failed to protect legitimate expectations the investor needs to prove an outright and unjustified repudiation of government regulations.[128] Fundamental changes in policy that negatively affect existing contracts are not necessarily violations of fair and equitable treatment.[129]

When an investor makes a contract with a host government, it expects that the government will respect that contract. However, in the realm of investment treaties and investor–state arbitration, whether the fair and equitable treatment clause protects investors against failures to respect those contracts is an extremely difficult issue. The question is equally difficult if the non-performance of a contract between the investor and the host state, or one of its territorial subdivisions or entities, is contrary to the investor's legitimate expectations and so a violation of the fair and equitable treatment standard.[130] The essential question is whether reliance on contractual undertakings is protected by the obligation to provide fair and equitable treatment. If the answer is affirmative, then investors could use the fair and equitable treatment standard as an 'umbrella clause',[131] which would effectively elevate contractual breaches to treaty breaches.[132]

---

[124] ibid ¶ 172.
[125] *MTD Equity Sdn Bhd & MTD Chile SA v Chile*, ICSID Case No ARB/01/7 (Award) (25 May 2004).
[126] ibid ¶ 163.   [127] ibid ¶ 165.
[128] *GAMI Investments, Inc v United Mexican States*, UNCITRAL (Award) (15 November 2004).
[129] *Eureko BV v Republic of Poland*, UNCITRAL (Partial Award) (19 August 2005).
[130] Dolzer (n 56 above) 104.   [131] Ch 11 discusses the umbrella clause.
[132] Schreuer (n 80 above) 360, 379.

Answering this question is not easy. On the one hand, an investor's contract with the government may be viewed as part of the legal framework of the investor's project and so a failure to respect it would result in a failure to protect the investor's legitimate expectations. On the other hand, the breach of a contract can also be viewed as one of the ordinary business risks of an investment, which would make such risks objectively in the contemplation of the investor when it enters into the agreement. In an effort to balance these two views, one might draw a line between two situations: (1) simple breaches of contract arising out of a host state's financial difficulties or legitimate differences between the parties about contractual terms; and (2) wilful refusals by a government authority to abide by its contractual obligations, abuse of government authority to evade agreements with foreign investors, or actions in bad faith in the course of contractual performance.[133] Only the latter situation would justify a finding of a violation of fair and equitable treatment on the ground that the host government had failed to respect the investor's legitimate expectations.

The tribunal in *Waste Management* seemed to recognize this distinction. One of the investor's claims, based on Article 1105(1) of NAFTA, involved the failure of the City of Acapulco to make payments under a concession agreement. The tribunal found that the evidence did not support the conclusion that the city had acted arbitrarily or in a grossly unfair way, since it was in a genuinely difficult financial situation. The tribunal said: 'even the persistent non-payment of debts by a municipality is not to be equated with a violation of Article 1105, provided that it does not amount to an outright and unjustified repudiation of the transaction and provided that some remedy is open to the creditor to address the problem'.[134]

Other tribunals have indicated that a failure to perform a contract may, under certain circumstances, amount to a violation of the fair and equitable treatment standard. For example, the tribunal in the NAFTA case of *Mondev* stated that 'a governmental prerogative to violate investment contracts would appear to be inconsistent with the principles embodied in Article 1105 and with contemporary standards of national and international law concerning governmental liability for contractual performance'.[135]

Eureko BV v Republic of Poland[136] similarly found that the Polish government's wilful refusal to sell shares to an investor as it had previously agreed 'consciously and overtly, breached the basic expectations of Eureko that are at the basis of its investments' and so treated the investor unfairly and inequitably. It will remain for future tribunals to develop criteria for determining which breaches of contract qualify as ordinary risks because a host government is 'in difficulty' and which breaches are wilful and abusive.

---

[133] ibid.

[134] *Waste Management Inc v United Mexican States (II)*, ICSID Case No ARB(AF)/00/3 (Award) (30 April 2004) ¶ 115.

[135] *Mondev International Ltd v United States of America*, ICSID Case No ARB(AF)/99/2 (Award) (11 October 2002) ¶ 134. See also *SGS Société Générale de Surveillance SA v Republic of the Philippines*, ICSID Case No ARB/02/6 (Decision on Jurisdiction) (29 January 2004).

[136] *Eureko BV v Republic of Poland*, UNCITRAL (Partial Award) (19 August 2005).

(ii) Failure to act transparently

The failure of a host state to act 'transparently' towards an investor may also constitute a violation of the fair and equitable standard. Transparency is considered an important element of good governance generally, and it is especially important to investors. To make effective investment decisions, investors need to know the applicable legal rules. It is these rules that create an investor's legitimate expectations and facilitate the Weberian concept of calculability. Thus, governments need to be transparent about what rules are in force. Once the investor makes an investment, fairness requires that the government inform the investor of changes in the applicable rules so that the investor may plan and manage operations accordingly. The foregoing suggests that even where an investment treaty does not specifically provide for transparency, a fair and equitable treatment clause implicitly requires transparency by the host government.

Governmental transparency clearly affects an investor's legitimate expectations. An investor's legitimate expectations will be based on the host state's legal framework and on any undertakings or representations made by it explicitly or implicitly. As the late Thomas Wälde has pointed out, the principle of protecting legitimate, investment-backed expectations 'is often combined with the principle of transparency: that government administration has to make clear what it wants from the investor and cannot hide behind ambiguity and contradiction itself'.[137] Thus, in many investor–state disputes, one finds that arbitral tribunals have ruled that a violation of fair and equitable treatment has occurred where a host government has both failed to act transparently and to protect the investor's legitimate expectations. For example, in the NAFTA case of *Metalclad Corporation v United Mexican States*,[138] the federal government of Mexico and the state government of San Luis Potosi issued construction and operating permits for the investor's landfill project and also assured the investor that it had all the permits it needed. However, the municipality of Guadalcazar refused to grant a construction permit, effectively blocking the project. The tribunal held that the investor was entitled to rely on the representations of the federal officials and therefore Mexico had violated the fair and equitable standard under Article 1105(1) of NAFTA. It stated:

Mexico failed to ensure a transparent and predictable framework for Metalclad's business planning and investment. The totality of these circumstances demonstrates a lack of orderly process and timely disposition in relation to an investor of a Party acting in the expectation that it would be treated fairly and justly in accordance with the NAFTA.[139]

Similarly, many of the arbitral cases discussed earlier in this chapter with respect to the requirement of respecting legitimate investor expectations also made reference to transparency in analysing whether a state had acted fairly and

---

[137] T Wälde, 'Energy Charter Treaty-based Investment Arbitration' (2004) 5 JWIT 3 387.
[138] *Metalclad Corp v United Mexican States*, ICSID Case No ARB(AF)/97/1 (Award) (30 August 2000).
[139] ibid ¶ 99. The Award was set aside in part by the Supreme Court of British Columbia.

equitably. As will be seen in Chapter 13, at section 13.5, some recent investment treaties contain a specific provision, separate from the fair and equitable treatment clause, that requires host states to act transparently. As of 2014, no investor–state case appears to have alleged a violation of this new treaty standard of treatment.

(iii) Arbitrary and discriminatory actions

Host government actions that are arbitrary and/or discriminatory towards an investor or an investment covered by an investment treaty also violate the fair and equitable treatment standard. The plain meaning of 'fair and equitable treatment' indicates that if there is discrimination on arbitrary grounds or the investment is subject to arbitrary or capricious treatment by the host state, then the fair and equitable standard has been violated. This conclusion flows from the idea that fair and equitable treatment inherently precludes arbitrary actions against investors.[140] Thus, governmental conduct categorized as arbitrary or discriminatory will generally breach the fair and equitable treatment standard. The problem is to determine whether in a specific situation the particular action of a government towards an individual investor within the framework of a relationship that is complex and long-standing is actually discriminatory or arbitrary. Inevitably, states that take questionable actions justify them as rational and necessary to protect the public interest, while the investors whose interests have been injured claim them to be arbitrary and discriminatory.

In the *ELSI* case,[141] the ICJ, while not specifically interpreting a fair and equitable treatment clause, did seek to determine what would constitute an 'arbitrary' measure. Its approach may offer some guidance in deciding what government actions are arbitrary under an investment treaty. The Court stated that an act that is illegal under domestic law is not necessarily arbitrary. Indeed, it suggested that even if a domestic court concluded that an act was arbitrary or unreasonable, that finding would not necessarily make the act arbitrary under international law. Arbitrariness, it stated, 'is not so much something opposed to a rule of law, as something opposed to the rule of law.... It is a willful disregard of due process of law, an act which shocks, or at least surprises, a sense of juridical propriety'.[142]

When determining whether an investor had received fair and equitable treatment, arbitration tribunals have focused on what they characterized as arbitrary governmental actions. In some cases, they did so in order to interpret the term 'fair and equitable treatment'; in others, they did so to apply treaty

---

[140] Vasciannie (n 67 above) 100, 133.

[141] *Elettronica Sicula SpA (ELSI) (United States v Italy)* (Judgment) (20 July 1989), [1989] ICJ Rep 15.

[142] ibid 73–7. In his dissent, Judge Schwebel concurred in the Chamber's concept of what constitutes an arbitrary act in international law but interpreted Article I of the Supplementary Agreement of 1951 as creating an obligation of result (as opposed to an obligation of conduct). He stated that 'failure to correct an arbitrary measure constitutes a violation of the FCN treaty regardless of the existence of local remedies'.

provisions that specifically prohibit arbitrary or discriminatory treatment. In applying NAFTA's fair and equitable treatment standard in *Pope & Talbot*, the tribunal did not emphasize the legitimate expectations of the investor but focused instead on the aggressive and hostile actions of Canada's Softwood Lumber Division (SLD), a government agency, towards the investor. In particular, it found that SLD's denials of reasonable requests by the investor for pertinent information, its threats to the investor's business, and its misleading statements regarding the investor's actions to the Minister, all contributed to a breach of the fair and equitable treatment standard contained in Article 1105(1) of NAFTA.[143]

On the other hand, in *Genin*[144] the tribunal considered whether a decision by the Bank of Estonia to withdraw Genin's banking licence amounted to 'arbitrariness' under Article II(3)(b) of the US–Estonia BIT. After examining the totality of the evidence, the tribunal concluded that for Estonia's action to violate the BIT, 'any procedural irregularity that may have been present would have to amount to bad faith, a willful disregard of due process of law or an extreme insufficiency of action'.[145] It found none of these factors present in the case, stating that the withdrawal of the licence was not 'an arbitrary act that violates the tribunal's "sense of juridical propriety"'. The tribunal also attached importance to the fact that the political and economic transition occurring in Estonia at the time justified heightened scrutiny of the banking sector and that the state's action reflected 'a clear and legitimate public purpose'.[146] Thus, it would seem that to find a government measure arbitrary, that country's special circumstances and the reasonableness of the government goals in taking that action must be taken into account.

The importance of the context for judging the arbitrariness of a governmental action is also illustrated in *LG&E Energy*.[147] In *LG&E Energy*, an ICSID tribunal considered whether the measures taken by Argentina during a severe economic and financial crisis and which adversely affected the investors' gas-distribution licences were arbitrary and therefore in violation of Article II(2)(b) of the US–Argentine BIT,[148] which prohibits the host state from taking arbitrary or discriminatory measures against an investor. The investor claimed that the standard for an arbitrary act is 'disregard for the rule of law' and that by wilfully repudiating its legal obligations Argentina had followed 'the rule of power, not

---

[143] *Pope & Talbot Inc v The Government of Canada*, UNCITRAL (Award on the Merits Phase II) (10 April 2001) ¶¶ 177–179.

[144] *Alex Genin, Eastern Credit Ltd, Inc and AS Baltoil (US) v Republic of Estonia*, ICSID Case No ARB/99/2 (Award) (25 June 2001).

[145] ibid ¶ 371.   [146] ibid.

[147] *LG&E Energy Corp v Argentine Republic*, ICSID Case No ARB/02/1 (Decision on Liability) (3 October 2006).

[148] The 1994 BIT, Art II(2)(b) provides: 'Neither Party shall in any way impair by arbitrary or discriminatory measures the management, operation, maintenance, use, enjoyment, acquisition, expansion, or disposal of investments.'

the rule of law'. Because the BIT did not define the term 'arbitrary', the tribunal looked to international law to define the term and so considered the *ELSI* case, described earlier. It then examined the BIT text and interpreted the intent of the contracting parties 'prohibiting themselves from implementing measures that affect the investments of nationals of the other Party without engaging in a rational decision-making process'.[149] A 'rational decision-making process', according to the tribunal, would include a consideration by Argentina of the effect of a proposed measure on foreign investments and a balancing of state interests against the burden placed on the investor. After reviewing the process by which Argentina arrived at the measures taken, the tribunal—emphasizing that Argentina was seeking to avert a complete economic collapse—concluded that the measures were not arbitrary because they resulted from reasoned judgment rather than a disregard for the rule of law.

Arbitrary conduct is also often discriminatory against the investor; consequently, the two words 'arbitrary and discriminatory' are often part of a single treaty standard or are considered inherent in the concept of unfair and inequitable treatment. The question of whether a measure is discriminatory also arises in the application of the required standards in treaties of national and most-favoured-nation treatment, both of which are discussed later in this chapter. When investment treaties are meant to prohibit discrimination against foreign investors, a measure is considered discriminatory if its intent is to discriminate or if it has a discriminatory *effect*.[150] In determining whether specific actions are discriminatory, and so violate the fair and equitable treatment standard or other specific provisions against discrimination, tribunals often refer to the *ELSI* case. In *ELSI*, the ICJ determined that the elements of a discriminatory measure include: (i) an intentional treatment, (ii) in favour of a national, (iii) against a foreign investor, and (iv) that is not taken under similar circumstances against another national.[151] However, proving these elements to the satisfaction of a tribunal can be difficult. For example, in the *ADF* case,[152] which concerned the US domestic-contents requirements for the government procurement of a construction project, alleged by the claimant to be discriminatory, the tribunal refused to find a violation of fair and equitable treatment. The tribunal noted that the investor had not claimed that other companies in like circumstances had been granted requirements waivers while the investor was denied, that the investor did not allege that the requirements under the project contract had been 'tailored' so that only a particular US company could comply with its specifications, or that the US measures had imposed 'extraordinary costs or other burdens' on the investor that were not imposed on the successful project bidders.[153]

---

[149] ibid ¶ 158.   [150] Vandevelde (n 98 above) 77.   [151] ibid 61–2.
[152] *ADF Group, Inc v United States of America*, ICSID Case No ARB (AF)/00/1 (Award) (9 January 2003).
[153] ibid ¶ 191.

(iv) Denial of justice or due process

Procedural fairness by governmental and judicial authorities when dealing with nationals or foreigners is a basic requirement of the rule of law and a vital element of fair and equitable treatment. The failure to respect procedural fairness is therefore considered a 'denial of justice'. According to Brownlie, the term 'denial of justice' has been employed by claims tribunals in a way that is coextensive with the general notion of state responsibility for harm to aliens. Regardless, it is widely seen as a particular category of deficiencies in host state governmental organs, particularly those involved in the administration of justice.[154] Other commentators have identified at least three different meanings—broad, narrow, and intermediate—of the term 'denial of justice'. In its broadest sense, 'denial of justice' covers all of state responsibility and applies to all kinds of wrongful acts by the state towards an alien. In its narrowest sense, it refers to direct intervention by government authorities in the workings of the judicial system, for example by taking affirmative action to deny an alien access to the courts or to prevent a court from pronouncing its judgment. The intermediate meaning of the term 'denial of justice' is related to the improper administration of civil and criminal justice with respect to a foreigner, including a denial of access to courts, inadequate procedures, and unjust decisions.[155] It has been observed by three leading scholars of international law that 'the term may thus be usefully employed to describe a particular type of international wrong for which no other adequate phrase exists in the language of the law' and that '[t]he tendency of the jurisprudence of international tribunals and of previous codifications of the law of responsibility of States has been to give only a generalized meaning to "denial of justice" and to refrain from establishing a list of those wrongful acts and omissions which would constitute a "denial of justice"'.[156]

The *Third Restatement of the Foreign Relations Law of the United States* takes the position that although the term 'denial of justice' has sometimes been used to refer to any injury done to an alien, it is used more commonly in a narrow sense 'to refer only to injury consisting of, or resulting from, denial of access to courts, or denial of procedural fairness and due process in relation to judicial proceedings, whether criminal or civil'.[157] From the foregoing, it is clear that an actionable failure of justice must be manifest and must constitute a gross deficiency in the administration of justice in the individual case. An error of law by a national court or an incorrect finding of fact by an administrative authority would not constitute such a denial of justice.

A denial of justice may arise out of either procedural or substantive deficiencies. As Freeman has noted, 'steady international practice as well as the overwhelming

---

[154] Crawford (n 18 above) 619.

[155] FV Garcia-Amador, L Sohn, and R Baxter, *Recent Codification of the Law of State Responsibility for Injuries to Aliens* (Oceana Publications, 1974) 180.

[156] ibid.

[157] *Restatement (Third) of the Foreign Relations Law of the United States*, § 711, comm a.

preponderance of legal authority, recognizes that not only flagrant procedural irregularities and deficiencies may justify diplomatic complaint, but also gross defects in the substance of the judgment itself'.[158]

The US Model BIT of 2012 specifically clarifies that the fair and equitable treatment standard protects against a denial of justice and also guarantees due process. Article 5(2)(a) provides that 'fair and equitable treatment' includes an obligation not to deny justice in any criminal, civil, or administrative adjudicatory proceedings in accordance with the principle of due process 'embodied in the principal legal systems of the world'.[159] Free trade agreements signed by the United States specifically prescribe the inclusion of due process rights as a part of the fair and equitable standard. Recent bilateral treaties signed by other states also include similar protections.[160] In addition, the 2009 ASEAN Comprehensive Investment Agreement specifies that for purposes of 'greater certainty', 'fair and equitable treatment requires each Member State not to deny justice in any legal or administrative proceedings in accordance with the principles of due process'.[161]

The jurisprudence of international tribunals indicates that a state's failure to comply with its duty to grant due process to aliens constitutes a violation of fair and equitable treatment. Both courts and other state agencies may violate this duty. In the field of investor–state arbitration, tribunals have found a denial of justice and a breach of the fair and equitable treatment standard when government or judicial processes affecting investors' interests failed to give the investor proper notification of the hearing or processes, did not invite or allow the investor to participate or appear, or were influenced by bias or prejudice. For example, in *Metalclad*[162] the tribunal found a violation of the fair and equitable treatment under Article 1105(1) of NAFTA because the construction permit requested by the investor 'was denied at a meeting of the Municipal Town Council of which Metalclad received no notice, to which it received no invitation, and at which it was given no opportunity to appear'.[163] Similarly, in *Middle East Cement*,[164] an investor complained that the Egyptian government had seized and auctioned its ship without proper notice. The tribunal determined that the auction procedure applied to the claimant was not 'under due process of law' as required by Article 4

---

[158] A Freeman, *The International Responsibility of States for Denial of Justice* (Longmans, Green & Co, 1938) 309.

[159] 2012 US Model BIT.

[160] See eg Malaysia–Australia Free Trade Agreement (22 May 2012), Art 12.7(2); Agreement for the Promotion and Protection of Investments between the Republic of Colombia and the Republic of India (10 November 2009), Art 3.4(a); Bilateral Agreement for the Promotion and Protection of Investments between the Government of the United Kingdom of Great Britain and Northern Ireland and the Republic of Colombia (17 March 2010), Art II.4(b); Agreement between the Government of Canada and the Government of Romania for the Promotion and Reciprocal Protection of Investments (8 May 2009), Annex D.

[161] 2009 ASEAN Comprehensive Investment Agreement, Art 11(2)(b).

[162] *Metalclad Corp v United Mexican States*, ICSID Case No ARB(AF)/97/1 (Award) (30 August 2000).

[163] ibid ¶ 91.

[164] *Middle East Cement Shipping and Handling Co SA v Arab Republic of Egypt*, ICSID Case No ARB/99/6 (Award) (12 April 2002).

of the Greece–Egypt BIT and specifically found that the notification procedure had been insufficient.[165]

(v) Good faith

If their actions are taken in bad faith, states will fail to meet the minimum international standard and the fair and equitable treatment standard. On the one hand, there is considerable authority indicating that bad faith is *not* an essential element of a violation of the fair and equitable treatment standard. For example, the *Mondev* tribunal stated, 'what is unfair or inequitable need not equate with the outrageous or the egregious. In particular, a State may treat foreign investment unfairly and inequitably without necessarily acting in bad faith'.[166]

The notion of bad faith is particularly concerned with the motivations of a government or public authority when interacting with an investor. While conceptually it would seem that bad faith actions by a government would violate the fair and equitable treatment standard owed an investor, no modern arbitral decision has actually found a state to have acted in bad faith towards an investor under an applicable investment treaty. Three reasons would seem to explain this result. First, it is not necessary to find governmental bad faith in order to establish a breach of the fair and equitable treatment standard. Second, proving a state's bad faith can be an extremely difficult task, since a government can usually offer some public policy justification for its actions. And third, most arbitral tribunals would be loath to make such a finding against a sovereign state, particularly if they could give redress to an injured investor without taking such action.

(f) Conclusion

Based on the existing jurisprudence of investor–state arbitral tribunals, one may conclude that the core of the fair and equitable treatment standard includes the previously discussed elements. Thus, a state treats an investor fairly and equitably when its actions respect the investor's legitimate expectations, are transparent, are not arbitrary or discriminatory, respect due process and access to justice, and are done in good faith. The foregoing, however, do not constitute an exhaustive list. Claims based on the denial of fair and equitable treatment will continue to be a constant feature of investor–state arbitration, and so the standard will continue to be subject to interpretation and refinement in the years ahead.[167]

---

[165] ibid ¶ 147.

[166] *Mondev International Ltd v United States of America*, ICSID Case No ARB(AF)/99/2 (Award) (11 October 2002) ¶ 116.

[167] Investors and their lawyers should also be aware of the potential for a 'creeping' violation of the fair and equitable standard. The tribunal in *El Paso v Argentina* found such a violation, noting:

> in the same way as one can speak of *creeping expropriation*, there can also be creeping violations of the FET standard...*A creeping violation of the FET standard* could thus be described as a process extending over time and comprising a succession or an

Moreover, some states have taken to defining the scope of the fair and equitable treatment standard more precisely, and in some cases limiting it by using more precise definitions in the treaty itself. An example of this approach is the 2005 treaty between the United States and Uruguay. Article 5 of that BIT, entitled 'Minimum Standard of Treatment', stipulates that '[e]ach Party shall accord to covered investments treatment in accordance with customary international law, including fair and equitable treatment and full protection and security'. A footnote to the Article requires that it be interpreted in accordance with Annex A to the treaty, which states a shared understanding of the parties that 'customary international law...result[s] from a general and consistent practice of States that they follow from a sense of legal obligation'.[168]

Some recent treaties have included separate provisions on administrative procedures and transparency that may affect the scope of the fair and equitable standard.[169] Article 10 of the China–Japan–Korea Trilateral Investment Agreement, for instance, provides:

1. Each Contracting Party shall promptly publish, or otherwise make publicly available, its laws, regulations, administrative procedures and administrative rulings and judicial decisions of general application as well as international agreements to which the Contracting Party is a party and which pertain to or affect investment activities. The Government of each Contracting Party shall make easily available to the public, the names and addresses of the competent authorities responsible for such laws, regulations, administrative procedures and administrative rulings.
2. When a Contracting Party introduces or changes its laws or regulations that significantly affect the implementation and operation of this Agreement, the Contracting Party shall endeavor to provide a reasonable interval between the time when such laws or regulations are published or made publicly available and the time when they enter into force...
4. Each Contracting Party shall, in accordance with its laws and regulations:
   (a) make public in advance regulations of general application that affect any matter covered by this Agreement; and
   (b) provide a reasonable opportunity for comments by the public for those regulations related to investment and give consideration to those comments before adoption of such regulations.[170]

---

accumulation of measures which, taken separately, would not breach that standard but, when taken together, do lead to such a result.

El Paso Energy International Co v Argentine Republic, ICSID Case No ARB/03/15 (Award) (31 October 2011) ¶¶ 518–519.a.

[168] Treaty between the United States of America and the Oriental Republic of Uruguay Concerning the Encouragement and Reciprocal Protection of Investment (4 November 2005), Annex A. See also 2012 US Model BIT, Annex A.

[169] For a discussion on transparency provisions see Ch 13, section 13.5.

[170] Agreement among the Government of Japan, the Government of the Republic of Korea and the Government of the People's Republic of China for the Promotion, Facilitation and Protection of Investment (13 May 2012), Art 10.

This provision would seem to require that states provide investors with access to laws and administrative proceedings that affect their interests, notice of new laws and regulatory changes, and the opportunity to comment on regulations. The US–Rwanda BIT extends these protections to include a right of review, stating that '[e]ach Party shall establish or maintain judicial, quasi-judicial, or administrative tribunals or procedures for the purpose of the prompt review and, where warranted, correction of final administrative actions regarding matters covered by this Treaty'.[171] The treaty requires that parties in a review proceeding receive an opportunity to present their case and that any resulting decision be based on the record.[172]

These new provisions that specifically outline states' administrative obligations and explain how a state must act transparently and in accordance with due process encroach on territory that the fair and equitable standard has traditionally covered. These provisions will therefore affect the fair and equitable standard. When confronted with a treaty that includes a separate transparency provision in addition to the vague fair and equitable standard, it would be difficult for a tribunal to incorporate transparency into the fair and equitable standard, as the parties have expressly and specifically addressed it elsewhere. In this sense, the transparency and administrative due process provisions could be interpreted in one of three ways depending on the specific language employed: (a) as limiting certain aspects of the fair and equitable standard; (b) as giving content to the transparency and due process aspects of the fair and equitable standard; or (c) as creating a separate treatment standard, apart from the fair and equitable standard, that requires states to act transparently towards investors and that grants protected investors a cause of action in cases where states fail to meet the transparency standard. Under these interpretations, such separate provisions would limit the scope of those aspects of the fair and equitable standard that are separately addressed. As seen in the previous examples, the new treaties that incorporate separate provisions on transparency and administrative procedures can use different language. Those tasked with interpreting these provisions must therefore carefully evaluate the extent of a state's obligations and an investor's rights and how they relate to the fair and equitable standard. Those tasked with drafting these provisions might in the first instance consider clearly stating their relationship to the fair and equitable standard. Chapter 13, section 13.5 will consider in more detail the third of the previously-mentioned possibilities—the creation of a separate treatment standard requiring host states to act transparently towards protected investors.

In interpreting and applying the fair and equitable treatment clause, tribunals have focused primarily on the behaviour of the respondent state. The reason is that most investment treaties set down standards of behaviour for states, not

---

[171] Treaty between the United States of America and the Government of the Republic of Rwanda Concerning the Encouragement and Reciprocal Protection of Investment (19 February 2008), Art 11.5(a).
[172] ibid Art 11.5(b).

investors. It is important to recognize, however, that the investor's behaviour may influence a tribunal in applying the fair and equitable standard. For one thing, whether a state has acted fairly and equitably is not an abstract question but one that requires an examination of the way a state behaved in a particular situation. Investor behaviour is very much a part of that situation, and it is therefore a legitimate area of inquiry by a tribunal. Determining whether a state has acted fairly and equitably towards an investor depends to a significant extent on the acts of the investor as well as the state. An investor that has engaged in corrupt business practices, has conducted its operations recklessly or in an unreasonable manner, or has not appropriately evaluated and protected itself against the risks posed by an investment may well have less standing to claim that a state measure was unfair or inequitable than an investor whose operations have been scrupulously honest, well managed, and attentive to risks. As one scholar has written, 'if equity means anything it suggests a balancing process and weighing what is right in all the circumstances'.[173]

9.5 Other General Standards of Treatment

(a) In general

Individual investment treaties often stipulate other general treatment standards, most of which could be subsumed within the meanings of either fair and equitable treatment or full protection and security. Thus, alone or in conjunction with such basic general standards of treatment, treaties may require treatment that accords with international law, complies with an international minimum standard, is not arbitrary or discriminatory, or allows access to justice or due process. One might refer to these as 'limited general treatment standards' in that their scope is more restricted than that of the sweeping language of fair and equitable treatment or full protection. All of these limited general treatment standards have been discussed earlier in connection with the fair and equitable treatment standard and that discussion should be born in mind in seeking to understand and interpret them when they are stated individually in investment treaties. They become particularly important in two situations: (1) when the applicable treaty does not contain a provision on fair and equitable treatment or full protection and security; and (2) when the treaty concerned does include such provisions but the challenged governmental actions do not constitute a violation of those two basic general standards. In both of these situations, investors may be able to establish that a government has not complied with such other limited general standards of treatment and has therefore committed a

---

[173] P Muchlinski, '"Caveat Investor?": The Relevance of the Conduct of the Investor under the Fair and Equitable Treatment Standard' in F Ortino et al (eds), *Investment Treaty Law, Current Issues II* (British Institute of International and Comparative Law, 2007) 209–10.

treaty violation requiring the payment of compensation for any resulting injury to a protected investment. Two of such limited general standards particularly have potential importance: (1) treatment in accordance with international law; and (2) avoidance of arbitrary, discriminatory, or unreasonable measures. They are each considered briefly.

(b) Treatment in accordance with international law

Many investment treaties specifically provide that protected investments are to be given treatment in accordance with international law. For example, the Benin–Belgium BIT,[174] after promising covered investments fair and equitable treatment and protection and security, further provides: 'The treatment and protection defined in paragraph 1 and 2 will be at least equal to that enjoyed by investors from third states and will not, in any case, be less favorable than that recognized by international law.'[175] The implication of this and similar treaty provisions is that it is possible for states to take measures that do not violate fair and equitable treatment and full protection and security but may nonetheless violate international law, and that the intent of such provisions is to protect investments against that eventuality.

Similar provisions are to be found in some of the BITS negotiated by the United States before the beginning of the twenty-first century. Thus, the 1986 US BIT with Egypt stipulates: 'The treatment, protection and security of investments shall never be less than that required by international law and national legislation.'[176] The application of such treaty provisions raises an important question of interpretation: What is the scope of the term 'international law'? As was discussed in Chapter 3, at section 3.3, international law is derived from three sources: treaties and conventions, custom, and general principles of law. Does the term 'international law' as used in such treaty provisions include the whole of international law as derived from all its sources or is it limited to customary international law? If the term international includes a host state's treaty obligations, the effect could be far reaching. For example suppose an investor covered by a BIT established a factory in a host country in reliance on its ability to import certain raw materials allowed by a bilateral trade treaty or a treaty of the World Trade Organization by which the host state was bound, but that thereafter the host government adopted measures to prevent such imports in violation of its obligations under those treaties, thereby causing a financial injury to the investment in the factory. Even though the government's failure

---

[174] Accord entre la République de Benin, d'une part, et l'Union Belgo-Luxembourgeoise, d'autre part, Concernant l'Encouragement et la Protection Réciproques des Investissments (18 May 2001).

[175] ibid Art 3(3). ('Le traitement et la protection definis aux paragraphes 1 et 2 seront au moins egaux a ceux dont jouissent les investisseurs d'un Etat tiers et ne seront, en aucun cas, moins favorables que ceux reconnus par le droit international.')

[176] Treaty between the United States of America and the Arab Republic of Egypt Concerning the Reciprocal Encouragement and Protection of Investments (13 March 1986), Art 2(4).

to comply with its trade treaty obligations might not constitute a violation of the fair and equitable treatment standard, it might nevertheless violate the host state's obligation not to afford such investments a treatment less than that required by international law.

In support of that conclusion, one might argue that the plain meaning of the term 'international law' is that it includes international law from all sources including treaties. On the other hand, some scholars have argued that this interpretation would create an extremely broad right and that if states intended such a result they would have made that intent clear in the text of the treaty.[177] For example, Article 10(1) of the ECT clearly states: 'In no case shall such Investments be accorded treatment less favorable than that required by international law, *including treaty obligations*' (emphasis added). One may contrast that formulation with that of Article 1105 of NAFTA which stipulates: 'Each Party shall accord to investments of investors of another Party treatment in accordance with international law, including fair and equitable treatment and full protection and security.'

More recent treaties seemed to have become more specific in delineating the scope of the term international law. Thus, in contrast to the provision from the Egypt–US BIT cited earlier, Article 5(1) of the 2012 US Model BIT, following the pattern established by the 2004 US Model BIT, provides: 'Each Party shall accord to covered investments treatment in accordance with *customary international law*, including fair and equitable treatment and full protection and security' (emphasis added).

Since the adoption of the 2004 Model, US treaty practice has employed the term 'customary international law' rather than simply 'international law' in defining this international law standard of treatment, and has also made clear that 'a determination that there has been a breach of this Treaty, or *of a separate international agreement*, does not establish that there as been a breach of this article' (emphasis added).[178] The intent of such provision is that the determination of whether a host government's actions have denied an investment treatment in accordance with international law is to be made only by reference to international custom and not to treaty law. On the other hand, an argument could be made that since the obligation of a state to respect its international agreements is based on international customary law, any failure of a state to respect its treaty commitments is a violation of customary law (ie *pacta sunt servanda*) and therefore a denial of treatment according to international customary law. Recent Canadian BITs avoid this interpretational problem by limiting the scope of protection under

---

[177] A Newcombe and L Paradell, *Law and Practice of Investment Treaties* (Kluwer Law International, 2009) 254.

[178] See eg Treaty between the United States of America and Oriental Republic of Uruguay Concerning the Encouragement and Reciprocal Protection of Investment (11 April 2005), Art 5(1) and (3); Treaty Between the Government of the United States of America and the Government of the Republic of Rwanda (19 February 2008), Art 5(1) and (3).

international law to that accorded by 'the customary international law minimum standard of treatment of aliens'.[179]

(c) Avoidance of arbitrary, discriminatory, or unreasonable measures

A common provision found in many international investment treaties is a commitment by the contracting states not to impair protected investments by unreasonable, discriminatory, or arbitrary measures. For example, the 2003 BIT between Germany and China provides:

Neither Contracting Party shall take any arbitrary or discriminatory measures against the management, maintenance, use, enjoyment and disposal of the investments by the investors of the other Contracting Party.[180]

Sometimes such a treatment standard is stated in a separate treaty provision, but it may also be combined with the fair and equitable treatment standard, as in the Netherlands–Argentina BIT:

Each Contracting Party shall ensure fair and equitable treatment to investments of investors of the other Contracting Party and shall not impair, by *unreasonable or discriminatory measures*, the operation, management, maintenance, use, enjoyment or disposal thereof by those investors. (emphasis added)[181]

Although included within a single treaty provision, the two treatment standards are separate and distinct. It is possible that a governmental action against a protected investment may violate the fair and equitable treatment standard without contravening the provision against unreasonable or discriminatory measures, and the opposite situation may also come to pass.

The precise phraseology employed in a treaty to express this standard may vary. Thus, the Germany–China BIT quoted previously referred to 'arbitrary or discriminatory measures', while the Netherlands–Argentina BIT required 'unreasonable or discriminatory measures'. The Jordan–Italy BIT adopts yet another variation:

Both Contracting Parties shall ensure that the management, maintenance, use, transformation, enjoyment or assignment of the investments effected in their territory by investors of the other Contracting Party, as well as companies and enterprises in which these

---

[179] eg Agreement between Canada and the Slovak Republic for the Promotion and Protection of Investments (20 July 2010, terminating and replacing the 1997 BIT), Art III 1(a); Agreement Between the Government of Canada and the Government of the Republic of Latvia for the Promotion and Protection of Investments (5 May 2009, terminating and replacing the 1995 BIT), Art II 2(a); Agreement Between Canada and the Czech Republic for the Promotion and Protection of Investments (6 May 2009, terminating and replacing the 1990 BIT) Art III(1)(a).

[180] Agreement between the People's Republic of China and the Federal Republic of Germany on the Encouragement and Reciprocal Protection of Investments (1 December 2003), Art 2(3).

[181] Agreement on Reciprocal Protection and Encouragement of Investments between the Kingdom of the Netherlands and the Argentine Republic (20 October 1992), Art 3(1).

investments have been effected, *shall in no way be subject to unjustified or discriminatory measures* (emphasis added)[182]

In analysing and applying treaty provisions governing this standard, three elements must be found: (1) there must be a 'measure'; (2) such measure must impair or negatively affect a protected investment; and (3) the measure must possess the specified negative quality required by the treaty, that is, it must be arbitrary, discriminatory, or unreasonable. It is important at the outset of that analysis to recognize that the focus of the standard is 'measures', not 'treatment'. Thus the objective of an aggrieved investor's complaint is a 'measure' taken by an organ of a host state. Like the term 'treatment' discussed at the beginning of this chapter, investment treaties do not define the meaning of 'measure'.[183] The ICJ in the *Fisheries Jurisdiction Case* adopted a broad definition of the term, stating that 'in its ordinary sense the word is wide enough to cover any act, step or proceeding, and imposes no particular limit on their material content or on the aim pursued thereby'.[184] As a result, an action by a governmental organ, as well as any decision not to act, would be considered a measure for purposes of an investment treaty. Actions taken by third parties, for example business competitors, labour unions, or brigands, would not be considered 'measures'; however, a decision by a governmental organ not to protect an investment against the actions of such persons would constitute a measure. The measure must affect the investment in a negative way, which in most instances would mean that it diminishes to some extent the financial value of the investment. And finally, the measure must be shown to be arbitrary, discriminatory or unreasonable, as required by the treaty text. This third part of the analysis is usually the most difficult because it requires the application of imprecise, vague, and general concepts to complex fact situations and demands a careful evaluation of a host of competing factors. In that respect, it is similar to the analysis that must be undertaken in judging whether a violation of the fair and equitable treatment standard, and particularly that standard's application to arbitrary and discriminatory actions, has taken place, as discussed earlier in section 9.4(e)(iii). That discussion should also be consulted when considering the application of treaty provisions on arbitrary, discriminatory, and unreasonable measures.

---

[182] Agreement between the Hashemite Kingdom of Jordan and the Government of the Italian Republic on the Promotion and Protection of Investments (30 September 2001) Art 2(3).

[183] It is interesting to note that the 2012 United States Model BIT, which unlike its predecessors omits a general prohibition of arbitrary or discriminatory measures while prohibiting specific types of measures, states that '"measure" includes any law, regulation, procedure, requirement, or practice' (Art 1).

[184] *Fisheries Jurisdiction Case (Spain v Canada)* [1998] ICJ Rep 432, ¶ 66.

9.6 National Treatment

(a) Competition and discrimination

Economic and business activity is a competitive process. Economic actors constantly seek to gain advantage over their competitors and to remove advantages that their competitors may have over them. In response to their perceived national interests, governments often seek through their laws, regulations, and administrative actions to: (1) assist their nationals and companies in the competitive process by taking measures that favour their interests and disfavour the interests of others; or (2) favour certain foreign nationals and companies over other foreign nationals and companies. Government measures may thus have a discriminatory effect on economic activity.

Such discriminatory measures can impede international investment. In encouraging increased foreign investment, investment treaties often seek to remove the competitive disadvantages that may be placed on foreigners by eliminating such discriminatory treatment. Treaties do this by making non-discrimination a standard that host countries must grant to investors and investment from other contracting states.

Non-discriminatory treatment has two dimensions. The first, known as national treatment, requires host states to treat foreign investors and foreign investments no less favourably than they treat their own national investors and investments. The second, known as most-favoured-nation treatment, demands that host countries treat investments and investors covered by the treaty no less favourably than they treat other foreign investors and investments. The purpose of these treatment standards is to place all economic actors in an equal position on the assumption that such equality of treatment will foster competition and economic growth. Most treaties include, in some form, both of these relative treatment standards. This section will discuss national treatment and section 9.7 will consider most-favoured-nation treatment.

(b) National treatment in investment treaties

For many countries, agreeing to grant national treatment to foreign investment is often more difficult politically than granting most-favoured-nation treatment. The reason is that national treatment may require difficult changes in existing laws and policies favouring national companies, while most-favoured-nation treatment usually does not. For example, many countries encourage national industries by granting subsidies or other benefits that the country would be unwilling to provide equally to foreigners and thereby undermine the competitive position of those industries. For that reason, the negotiation and drafting of national treatment provisions in investment treaties has often been fraught with difficulty. It is also for this reason that treaties demonstrate a wide variety of formulations in expressing national treatment standards.

Resistance to the national treatment standard was stronger in the early days of the investment treaty movement, when many countries had large state-owned industries to protect. Today, as a result of large-scale privatizations and the resulting shrinkage of the public sector, countries more readily accept national treatment clauses in treaties of one type or another, and a large majority of treaties now include them.[185] On the other hand, as was discussed in Chapter 8, many treaties distinguish between requiring this treatment standard for the admission of an investment and imposing it once an investment has been made. Thus, the ECT avoids a firm commitment to grant investors national or most-favoured-nation treatment with respect to the making of an investment, but it does commit the contracting parties to granting national treatment or most-favoured-nation treatment, whichever is the more favourable, to investments, once made, and to their associated activities. These 'associated activities' would include the investments' management, maintenance, use, enjoyment, and disposal.[186] On the other hand, the Treaty on the Functioning of the European Union (TFEU),[187] which seeks to create a single market for the movement of persons, goods, and capital among the twenty-eight EU states, gives persons and companies of one member state broad rights of national treatment in all other member states. Thus, Article 49 of the TFEU prohibits member states from enacting measures that restrict the freedom of establishment of nationals of other member states and defines the freedom of establishment as including 'the right to take up and pursue activities as self-employed persons and to set up and manage undertakings, in particular companies or firms...under the conditions laid down for its own nationals by the law of the country where such establishment is effected'. Article 54 provides that companies formed under the laws of an EU state and having their registered office or principal place of business within the Union shall be treated in the same way as natural persons who are nationals of member states. Furthermore, Article 55 states that 'Member States shall accord nationals of the other Member States the same treatment as their own nationals as regards participation in the capital of companies or firms within the meaning of Article 54'. As discussed in Chapter 8, at section 8.6, the European Court of Justice has the power to judge and strike down member state measures that offend these principles of national treatment. Its jurisprudence may therefore be a source of assistance for scholars, lawyers, and arbitrators interpreting the provisions on national treatment found in other investment treaties.

For investment treaties granting national treatment, one must thus make a fundamental distinction between treaties that promise non-discriminatory treatment during the entire investment process and those that limit national treatment

---

[185] UNCTAD, *Bilateral Investment Treaties 1995–2006: Trends in Investment Rulemaking* (2007) 33.

[186] ECT, Art 10(7).

[187] Consolidated Versions of the Treaty on European Union and the Treaty on the Functioning of the European Union [2010] OJ C83/1.

to investments after they have been established in the host country. These latter treaties usually provide that each contracting party shall accord protection to 'investment in its territory'[188] or 'investments made in accordance with its laws'.[189] This type of provision allows the host country to deal with competitively threatening foreign investments by simply refusing them the right of establishment while granting that right to those it has admitted into the country. Even after establishment, some treaties make national treatment tentative by making it contingent upon national legislation. Thus, an investment treaty may provide that '[e]ach Contracting Party shall, subject to its laws and regulations, accord to investments of investors of the other Contracting party treatment no less favorable than that which is accorded to investments of its investors'.[190] This provision gives host countries the power to enact laws favouring national investments when their governments judge it important to advance certain national interests. A variation of this approach is to define the aspects of investment activity that will receive national treatment while stating or implying that other aspects will not receive the same treatment. Many treaties, particularly those negotiated by the United States, make clear that national treatment will be granted to investors or investments of parties that are in 'like circumstances' to those of national investors.

On the other hand, many treaties grant full national treatment in the pre- and post-establishment phase. In addition, some treaties grant national treatment to 'investments of the other Party', to 'investors of the other Party', and still others to both. Thus, NAFTA has separate Articles for investors and investments. It provides:

Article 1102: National Treatment
1. Each Party shall accord to investors of another Party treatment no less favorable than that it accords, in like circumstances, to its own investors with respect to the establishment, acquisition, expansion, management, conduct, operation and sale or other disposition of investments.
2. Each Party shall accord to investments of investors of another Party treatment no less favorable than that it accords, in like circumstances, to investments of its own investors with respect to the establishment, acquisition, expansion, management, conduct, operation and sale or other disposition of investments.

While discussions of 'national treatment' often seem to imply that its meaning is constant and uniform across treaties, that is not the case. Because of the many variations that it takes in particular treaty texts, it is essential for those interpreting

---

[188] Agreement between the Government of the Republic of Mauritius and the Government of the Republic of Zimbabwe for the Promotion and Protection of Investments (17 May 2000), Art 4.

[189] Agreement between the Government of the Kingdom of Thailand and the Government of the Russian Federation on the Promotion and Reciprocal Protection of Investments (17 October 2002), Art 3.

[190] Agreement between the Government of the Republic of Indonesia and the Government of the Republic of India for the Promotion and Protection of Investments (8 February 1999), Art 4(3).

and applying the national treatment commitments contained in particular treaties to examine carefully the specific language of the text in question.

(c) The application of the national treatment standard

The application of the national treatment standard depends not only on how the standard is articulated in a particular treaty but also on the specific facts of the case in question. Applying national treatment standards in investor–state disputes, like cases involving the fair and equitable standard, is highly fact-specific and not easily amenable to a mechanistic application of treaty provisions.[191] But, unlike the fair and equitable treatment standard, tribunals in national treatment standard cases appear to have developed a more or less common, three-step analytical approach. This is particularly the case within the context of NAFTA. The first step involves identifying a group of national investors to be compared with the claimant foreign investor. The second step is to compare the relative treatment the two groups have received and evaluate whether the treatment of the claimant is less favourable than that given to the compared group of national investors. The final step is to determine whether the two are, in the words of NAFTA and similar treaties, in 'like circumstances' or whether factors justifying differential treatment exist.[192] The completion of each step requires the answer to a particular question. Let us examine each step in greater detail.

(i) With whom should the claimant be compared?

The application of the national treatment standard is inherently a comparative process. The foreign investor is complaining because it has compared the treatment it has received from the host government with that received by someone else and found its treatment wanting. In order to determine the validity of such a claim, a tribunal first has to determine whether the investor has compared itself with an appropriate comparator. For example, suppose that a host country provides subsidized electricity to small farmers but not to a foreign investor operating an aluminium smelter. Would such differential treatment constitute a breach of the national treatment standard? Has the foreign investor selected an appropriate basis of comparison? For one thing, the subsidized small farmer and the aluminium producer are operating in two very different economic sectors: agriculture and heavy industry. For another, the size of the the two economic actors and the scale of their respective operations are vastly different. Moreover, the relative costs and benefits of the electricity subsidy are disproportionate because in the production of aluminium electricity is a much higher percentage of total

---

[191] Dolzer and Schreuer (n 9 above) 179.
[192] UNCTAD, *Investor–State Dispute Settlement and Impact on Investment Rulemaking* (2007) 48.

production costs that in a small farm. An arbitral tribunal analysing all of these factors would conclude that it would be inappropriate, for purposes of determining a breach of national treatment, to compare a small farmer with an aluminium smelter.

Several NAFTA cases provide guidance in the determination of an appropriate comparator. In the NAFTA case of *Pope & Talbot*, the tribunal declared that 'as a first step, the treatment accorded a foreign owned investment protected by Article 1102(2) should be compared with that accorded domestic investments in the same business or economic sector'.[193] Applying this principle to specific cases can prove difficult. An individual tribunal may opt for either a broad or narrow approach in delineating the comparator group. For example, in *Feldman v Mexico*, the claimant was a trading company that was engaged, among other things, in purchasing Mexican cigarettes from local retailers and then selling those cigarettes abroad. The company alleged that the Mexican government had granted tax rebates to competing exporters of Mexican cigarettes but had denied the same rebates to the claimant. In determining the basis of comparison, the tribunal stated that the 'universe of firms' to which the claimant was to be compared were those in the business of 'reselling/exporting cigarettes'. Other firms that might also export cigarettes, such as cigarette manufacturers, were not in that group.[194]

In *Occidental v Ecuador*,[195] the host government had originally granted the claimants and other oil producers a rebate on the value-added tax (VAT) they paid on goods purchased for their exploration activities. In 2001, however, Ecuador's tax authorities stopped granting those rebates to the claimant and other oil exploration companies on the grounds that the participation formulas in their government contract already accounted for such rebates. Although all the companies in the oil sector were treated equally with respect to these value-added tax rebates, the tribunal determined that the relevant comparison group for national treatment purposes was not the oil sector but 'local producers in general... since the purpose of national treatment is to protect foreign investors as compared to local producers and this cannot be done by addressing exclusively the sector in which that particular activity is undertaken'.[196]

This conclusion could be criticized as being an overly broad interpretation of the national treatment standard in the US–Ecuador BIT, which requires that national investors in the comparison group be 'in like situations'. In interpreting this provision, the tribunal would have done well to ask a fundamental question: What does the national treatment clause seek to protect US investors from? One answer is that the purpose of the clause is to protect the investor from unfair

---

[193] *Pope & Talbot Inc v The Government of Canada*, UNCITRAL (Award) (10 April 2001) 7 ICSID Reports 102, ¶ 78.
[194] *Marvin Feldman v Mexico*, ICSID Case No ARB(AF)/99/1 (Award) (16 December 2002) ¶ 171.
[195] *Occidental Exploration and Petroleum Co v The Republic of Ecuador*, London Court of Arbitration Case No UN 3467 (Final Award) (1 July 2004).
[196] ibid ¶ 173.

competitive disadvantages and that the claimant in the *Occidental* case was not in competition with all other 'local producers'. The claimant competed only against other oil companies, all of which had been treated similarly, since the VAT rebates had been denied to all. Applying the *Occidental* tribunal's reasoning to the example given earlier in this section, one would conclude that, because the small farmer and the foreign-owned aluminium smelter are both 'local producers', the host government breached the national treatment standard by denying the smelter subsidized electricity.

(ii) What is the nature of the difference in treatment?

The second step in the analysis is to determine whether the treatment of the aggrieved foreign investor differs from that accorded to local investors, and if so, in what way it differs. Most tribunals have concluded that discrimination may be either *de jure* or *de facto*. Thus, one needs to look not only at discrimination in the text and application of legal provisions but also treatment that, while not being discriminatory in law, nonetheless has a discriminatory impact. In *SD Meyers v Canada*,[197] a NAFTA case, the tribunal pointed to two factors in particular that need to be evaluated in determining differential treatment: (1) whether the practical effect is to create a disproportionate benefit for nationals over non-nationals; and (2) whether on its face the contested measure appears to favour the host country's nationals over non-nationals protected by the treaty.[198] Arbitral tribunals have also generally held that in order to demonstrate discriminatory treatment an aggrieved investor need not show discriminatory intent on the part of the host country,[199] nor that the host country's discriminatory action was specifically due to the foreign investor's nationality.[200] On the other hand, the existence of a discriminatory intent without some differential impact is insufficient. As the tribunal stated in *SD Meyers*, '[t]he word "treatment" suggests that practical impact is required to produce a breach of Article 1101, not merely a motive or intent that is in violation of Chapter 11'.[201]

(iii) Is the difference in treatment justified?

Tribunals will often not find a breach of the national treatment standard if the foreign investor and the compared national investors are not in 'like circumstance', 'similar situations', or if there is a justified policy reason for the differential

---

[197] *SD Meyers Inc v Canada*, UNCITRAL (First Partial Award) (13 November 2000).

[198] ibid ¶ 252.

[199] ibid ¶ 254, stating: 'Intent is important, but protectionist intent is not necessarily decisive on its own. The existence of an intent to favour nationals over non-nationals would not give rise to a breach of Chapter 1102 of the NAFTA if the measure in question were to produce no adverse effect on the non-national complainant.'

[200] *International Thunderbird Gaming Corp v United Mexican States*, UNCITRAL (Award) (26 January 2006) ¶ 177.

[201] ibid ¶ 254.

treatment. This requirement gives host country governments room to make regulations in the public interest. The tribunal in *Pope & Talbot* suggested the importance of considering the policy justifications in measures that have a discriminatory effect when it stated that '[d]ifferences in treatment will presumptively violate Article 1102(2) unless they have a reasonable nexus to national policies that (1) do not distinguish, on their face or de facto, between foreign-owned and domestic companies, and (2) do not otherwise unduly undermine the investment liberalizing objectives of NAFTA'.[202] Thus, in the example given earlier in the section, even if a tribunal found that both the foreign-owned aluminium smelter and local small farmers were local producers, it might nevertheless hold that no breach of national treatment occurred. The reason is that the process of providing subsidized electricity to small farmers does not distinguish on its face between foreigners and nationals, is done for the justified purpose of supporting small-scale agriculture and raising the standard of living of farming families, and does not affect the basic goal of the treaty, which is to promote and protect investment.

The precise boundaries of justified public policy and 'like circumstances' are by no means clear and will no doubt be the subject of continuing litigation and debate in the years ahead.

9.7 Most-Favoured-Nation Treatment

Virtually all investment treaties contain a most-favoured-nation (MFN) provision whose purpose is to prevent host states from treating investors and investments of its treaty partners less favourably than investors from third countries. The provision's aim is to assure non-discrimination among foreign investors. Countries that have been unwilling to grant national treatment in investment treaties out of a concern to protect domestic industries have been more willing to grant MFN treatment, which they view as less threatening to national enterprises and interests.

In some treaties, the MFN treatment commitment is limited to post-establishment investments and does not apply to the process of making investments. Thus, for example, the ECT avoids a firm commitment to investors regarding MFN treatment when making investments, but grants national treatment or MFN treatment, whichever is the more favourable, to contracting parties once their investments have been made. MFN treatment under the ECT covers the investments' associated activities, including their management, maintenance, use, enjoyment, and disposal.[203]

As has been the case for centuries in international economic treaties, the purpose of the MFN clause in investment treaties is to assure equal treatment at the international level so that covered investors and investments receive treatment

---

[202] *Pope & Talbot Inc v The Government of Canada*, UNCITRAL (Award) (10 April 2001) ¶ 78.
[203] ECT, Art 10(7).

no less favourable than that which the host country grants investors from any third country. Like provisions on national treatment, MFN clauses are formulated in different ways in different treaties. As a result, the scope of protection that the clause provides and the stipulated exceptions to it vary from treaty to treaty. For example, some treaties grant MFN treatment only to *investments* of a treaty partner, while others grant it to *investors*. Some may specify the particular matters to which MFN treatment applies, for example 'to the establishment, acquisition, expansion, management, conduct and sale or other disposition of an investment',[204] while others may state generally that '[i]nvestments by nationals and companies of either Contracting State...shall not be subjected to treatment less favorable than that accorded to investments by nationals and companies of third states'.[205] As a result of the wide variety of MFN treatment formulations found in investment treaties, persons interpreting them need to focus carefully on the particular language of the treaty in question and should not assume that the nature and scope of protection is uniform among treaties.

A host country may favour an investment or an investor from another country in one of two general ways: (1) by using its legislation, regulations, or administrative acts to grant those investments and/or investors a special benefit not generally granted to foreign investors or investments; and (2) by entering into treaties with third countries assuring their investors and/or investments special benefits or treatment. An example of the first way might be a national law that grants investors from a neighbouring country tax exemptions that are denied to investors from all other countries. An example of the latter way might be a country that makes a bilateral investment agreement promising national treatment to investors and investments from a treaty partner when all other treaties with third countries omit the promised treatment. To set limits on the effects of MFN clauses, most investment treaties contain stated exceptions as to matters, such as customs unions and free trade zones, to which the clause does not apply.

Most of the litigation surrounding MFN treatment clauses in investment treaties involves a situation in which an investor that is covered under a treaty from one country is seeking to take advantage of benefits that the host country has granted by treaty to an investor or investment from a third country. MFN provisions allow a country that was not able to negotiate a desired standard with a treaty partner to nonetheless attain that standard if the treaty partner has granted it to a third country in another treaty. Accordingly, one of the effects of the MFN clause is to increase a country's bargaining power.[206] It achieves this result by allowing the investor to import the standards of protection from other treaties

---

[204] Agreement between the Government of the Republic of Korea and the Government of His Majesty the Sultan and Yang Di-Pertuan of Brunei Darussalam Concerning the Encouragement and Reciprocal Protection of Investments (14 November 2000), Art 3.2.

[205] Treaty between the Government of Malaysia and the Government of the Republic of Chile on the Promotion and Protection of Investments (11 November 1992), Art 3(1).

[206] UNCTAD, *Bilateral Investment Treaties 1995–2006: Trends in Investment Rulemaking* (2007) 38.

into the treaty applicable to its investment. For example, in the case of *Bayindir v Pakistan*,[207] the claimant, a Turkish construction company, brought an ICSID case against Pakistan under the 1995 bilateral investment treaty between Turkey and Pakistan. That BIT provided that '[e]ach Party shall accord to these investments, once established, treatment no less favourable than that accorded in similar situations to investments of its investors or to investments of investors of any third country, whichever is the most favourable'.[208] The Turkey–Pakistan BIT contained no provision specifically guaranteeing Turkish investors fair and equitable treatment; however, Pakistan had made investment treaties with various European countries explicitly promising such treatment. The Turkish claimant argued, and the tribunal eventually agreed, that by virtue of the MFN clause in the Turkey–Pakistan BIT Pakistan was obliged to treat the claimant in a fair and equitable manner.[209]

Similarly, in *MTD Equity v Chile*,[210] Malaysian investors, who had been denied the zoning changes necessary to undertake a land development project, successfully argued that the MFN clause in the Malaysia–Chile BIT made the provisions in the Croatia–Chile BIT and the Denmark–Chile BIT applicable. Both of those BITs provided that '[w]hen a Contracting Party has admitted an investment in its territory, it shall grant the necessary permits in accordance with its laws and regulations'.[211] The tribunal in *MTD* considered the incorporation of the protections of the Denmark and Croatia BITs into the Malaysia–Chile BIT as consistent with the treaty's purpose, which is to protect investment and create conditions favourable to investments. Moreover, the fact that the Malaysia–Chile BIT specifically excluded certain matters from MFN protection, and that the protections provided in the Denmark and Croatia BITs were not among those excluded matters, also supported the applicability of the Malaysia–Chile MFN clause.[212]

While it is generally agreed that an appropriately drafted MFN clause will import into an investment treaty substantive protective standards, controversy exists as to whether the clause also extends to procedural rights, particularly those relating to dispute settlement in other treaties. The case of *Maffezini v Spain*[213] first provoked this controversial issue. The claimant, an Argentine national who invested in an enterprise in Spain for the production and distribution of chemicals, initiated an ICSID arbitration against Spain under the Spain–Argentina BIT. That BIT required resort to local courts for a period of eighteen months before an investor could invoke international arbitration. Although Maffezini did

---

[207] *Bayindir Insaat Turizm Ticaret VeSanayi AS v Islamic Republic of Pakistan*, ICSID Case No ARB/03/29 (Decision on Jurisdiction) (14 November 2005).
[208] Agreement between the Republic of Turkey and the Islamic Republic of Pakistan Concerning the Reciprocal Promotion and Protection of Investments (16 March 1995), Art II(2).
[209] *Bayindir Insaat Turizm Ticaret VeSanayi* (n 207 above) ¶ 231.
[210] *MTD Equity Sdn Bhd and MTD Chile SA v Republic of Chile*, ICSID Case No ARB/01/7 (Award) (25 May 2004).
[211] ibid ¶ 197.   [212] ibid ¶ 104.
[213] *Emilio Agustín Maffezini v The Kingdom of Spain*, ICSID Case No ARB/97/7 (Award on Jurisdiction) (25 January 2000).

not have recourse to the Spanish courts as required by the treaty, he argued that he was not required to do so because the Spain–Chile BIT did not contain a similar eighteen-month requirement and, by virtue of the MFN clause in the Spain–Argentina BIT, he was entitled to avail himself of the lesser requirements in the Spain–Chile BIT.

Interpreting the broad MFN clause, which provided that 'in all matters subject to this agreement treatment shall be no less favourable than that extended...to investors of a third country', the ICSID tribunal concluded that Maffezini was entitled to avail himself of the lighter procedural burden included in the Spain–Chile BIT. Therefore, Maffezini did not have to pursue his claim for eighteen months in Spanish courts before requesting ICSID arbitration. Some subsequent cases followed this approach.[214] On the other hand, some tribunals have refused to allow the claimants to import dispute resolution provisions from other treaties.[215] The difference in the result in these cases can be explained largely by the fact that the MFN clauses in the latter cases were much narrower in scope than the MFN clause in the former cases.

[214] eg *Siemens v Argentina*, ICSID Case No ARB/02/8 (Decision on Jurisdiction) (3 August 2004); *Suez, Sociedad General de Aguas de Barcelona SA, and InterAguas ServiciosIntegrales del Agua SA v The Argentine Republic*, ICSID Case No ARB/03/17 (Decision on Jurisdiction) (16 May 2006); *Suez, Sociedad General de Aguas de Barcelona SA and Vivendi Universal SA v Argentine Republic*, ICSID Case No ARB/03/19 (Decision on Jurisdiction) (3 August 2006); *RosInvestCo UK Ltd v Russian Federation*, SCC Case No Abr. V 079/2005 (Award on Jurisdiction) (5 October 2007) ¶¶ 132–133; *HOCHTIEF Aktiengesellschaft v Argentine Republic*, ICSID Case No ARB/07/31 (Decision on Jurisdiction) (24 October 2011) ¶ 75; *Teinver SA, Transportes de Cercanías SA and Autobuses Urbanos del Sur SA v Argentine Republic*, ICSID Case No ARB/09/1 (Decision on Jurisdiction) (21 December 2012) ¶ 186; *Garanti Koza LLP v Turkmenistan*, ICSID Case No ARB/11/20 (Decision on the Objection to Jurisdiction for Lack of Consent) (3 July 2013) ¶ 96.

[215] eg *Salini Costruttori SpA and Italstrade SpA v Jordan*, ICSID Case No ARB/02/13 (Decision on Jurisdiction) (9 November 2004) ¶¶ 118–119; *Plama Consortium Ltd v Bulgaria*, ICSID Case No ARB/03/24 (Decision on Jurisdiction) (8 February 2005) ¶ 184; *Telenor Mobile Communications AS v Republic of Hungary*, ICSID Case No ARB/04/15 (Award) (13 September 2006) ¶¶ 91–95; *Wintershall Aktiengesellschaft v Argentine Republic*, ICSID Case No ARB/04/14 (Award) (8 December 2008) ¶ 167; *ICS Inspection and Control Services Ltd (United Kingdom) v Argentine Republic*, PCA Case No 2010-9 (Award on Jurisdiction) (10 February 2012) ¶ 318; *Kilic Insaat Ithalat Ihracat Sanayi ve Ticaret Anonim Sirketi v Turkmenistan*, ICSID Case No ARB/10/1 (Award) (2 July 2013) ¶ 7.9.1.

10

Monetary Transfers and Treatment

10.1 The Significance of Monetary Transfers

The ability of a foreign investor to make international monetary payments freely both into and out of a host country is crucial to the success of any foreign investment. Investors need to transfer funds into the host country in order to establish an investment, operate it, expand it, and support it during economic hard times. They need to transfer funds out of the country in order to purchase raw materials and spare parts, make royalty and technology payments, service debts, distribute profits made by the enterprise, and repatriate capital when the investment is sold. The aim of all foreign investors is not just to make a profit, but to make a profit that can be freely transferred to its home country or elsewhere. Investors want the freedom to engage in these monetary transactions whenever they see fit in response to market conditions and without the need to secure government approvals for them. They thus consider the rights granted to them by the host country with respect to international monetary transactions as important matters affecting their treatment.

States, on the other hand, have the right under international law to control the transfer of all funds into and out of their territory. While host country governments understand that giving foreign investors the right to make international payments freely is important for the promotion of investment, they also know that granting them total freedom to transfer funds poses certain risks. Sudden large infusions of foreign capital can lead to inflation and appreciation of a country's currency, which in turn may have negative effects on the export of its goods and the country's overall macroeconomic situation. Large outflows of funds can dangerously reduce monetary reserves, create undesirable volatility in exchange rates, inhibit a country's ability to secure goods and services needed for the public welfare, and negatively affect the host government's ability to meet its international financial obligations. Moreover, governments also perceive that supervision and control over international payments are necessary to prevent crime and security threats, to facilitate the collection of taxes, and to protect creditors. As a result of these considerations, host governments, while seeking to promote foreign investment through treaties, are also concerned with maintaining their ability to regulate monetary transactions so as to protect these important interests. Accordingly, states may enact legislation and regulations, known generally as 'exchange controls' or 'capital controls', to regulate such monetary transactions.[1] Investment treaties do not prevent states from adopting such controls, but they may forbid governments from applying them to investments and investors protected by such treaties.

Nearly all investment treaties grant covered investors or investments the freedom to make monetary transfers; however, the precise nature of such provisions in particular treaties depends upon the differing interests of host country governments. While investors want broad and unrestricted guarantees on monetary transfers, host states seek, in varying degrees, to limit their commitments with respect to monetary transfers and to subject them to qualifications and exceptions. The tension between these two competing sets of interests has affected the language of many treaty provisions on monetary transfers and payments. Unlike general standards of treatment such as full protection and security, fair and equitable treatment, and national treatment, which consist of statements of general norms, provisions on monetary treatment and transfers are fairly specific and detailed. As a result, they have rarely been the subject of investor–state arbitration.[2]

Although the provisions on monetary transfers vary from treaty to treaty, they all tend to address six basic issues: (1) the general scope of the investor's rights to make monetary transfers; (2) the types of payments that are covered by such rights; (3) the nature of the currency in which payments may be made; (4) the applicable exchange rate; (5) the time within which the host state must allow the investor to make transfers; and (6) exceptions to the right to make monetary transfers. Let us examine each of these issues.

10.2 The General Scope of the Right to Make Transfers

Virtually all investment treaties refer to the various international payments made by investors and investments as 'transfers'.[3] Indeed, the term 'transfer' in this very special sense has become an established term of art in investment treaty practice. Because of the importance of this issue to investors, and therefore to the promotion of investment, investment treaties include provisions on transfers as part of

---

[1] For a discussion of the nature of such controls, see JW Salacuse, *The Three Laws of International Investment: National, Contractual, and International Frameworks for Foreign Capital* (OUP, 2013) 75–88. Although the International Monetary Fund (IMF) has traditionally taken a position against such controls, in 2012 it endorsed a new 'institutional view' on capital controls, meaning that states should open capital accounts in an orderly manner based on the strength of their institutions, rather than requiring full liberalization of capital accounts without considering institutional development. IMF, *The Liberalization and Management of Capital Flows: An Institutional View* (14 November 2012). The IMF's new position does not alter the specific obligations that states have undertaken in treaties, though it may suggest a change in the general view on capital flows and shape future investment agreements.

[2] R Dolzer and C Scheurer, *Principles of International Investment Law* (OUP, 2008) 192.

[3] MI Khalil, 'Treatment of Foreign Investment in Bilateral Investment Treaties' (1999) 7 ICSID Rev—FILJ 339, 360.

the treatment that host states grant to covered investors and investments. Unlike 'repatriation', a term found in some treaties[4] that refers only to payments from the host country to the investor's home country, transfers include payments both to the host state and from the host state to any other state.

Most investment treaties recognize the investor's right to make monetary transfers to and from the host country; however, they express that right in different ways. Some explicitly require that each contracting party guarantee to the investors of the other contracting party that the free transfer of payments operates in both directions.[5] For example, Article 13 of the China–Japan–Korea Trilateral Investment Agreement states: '1. Each Contracting Party shall ensure that all transfers relating to investments in its territory of an investor of another Contracting Party may be made *freely into and out of its territory* without delay'[6] (emphasis added). Others employ less specific language that obliges contracting states to allow investors of other contracting states to make transfers that are 'in connection with an investment'[7] freely. Despite this more general language, the ordinary meaning of 'in connection with an investment' would seem to cover transfers in both directions; however, such an interpretation is not beyond plausible challenge.

Still another approach in defining monetary transfer rights is to grant investors a general freedom to make transfers but then to include a non-exclusive list of transactions that investors may undertake. For example, Article 14 of the Energy Charter Treaty (ECT), entitled 'Transfers Related to Investments', obliges contracting parties to 'guarantee the freedom of transfer' with respect to investments and it then provides, in terms nearly identical to those employed in the 2012 US Model BIT, a non-exclusive list of what may be transferred freely. The list includes initial capital, returns, payments under contracts, proceeds from the sale or liquidation of any part of an investment, and payments arising out of the settlement of any dispute. In its declaration of a general 'freedom of transfer', the ECT appears to have been influenced by the Netherlands Model BIT, which also specifically recognizes a freedom of transfer.[8] In similar terms, Article 1109 of

---

[4] Some UK BITs refer to 'repatriation of investments and returns'; eg Agreement between the Government of the United Kingdom of Great Britain and Northern Ireland and the Government of the Republic of Albania (30 March 1994), Art 6.

[5] eg Agreement between the People's Republic of China and Bosnia and Herzegovina on the Promotion and Protection of Investments (26 June 2002), Art 6; Treaty between the United States of America and the Oriental Republic of Uruguay Concerning the Encouragement and Reciprocal Protection of Investment (4 November 2005), Art 7; Agreement between Canada and the Republic of Peru for the Promotion and Protection of Investments (14 November 2006), Art 14.

[6] Agreement among the Government of Japan, the Government of the Republic of Korea and the Government of the People's Republic of China for the Promotion, Facilitation and Protection of Investment (13 May 2012).

[7] eg Treaty between the Federal Republic of Germany and Bosnia and Herzegovina concerning the Encouragement and Reciprocal Protection of Investments (18 October 2001), Art 5; Agreement between the Government of the Kingdom of Saudi Arabia and the Government of Malaysia Concerning the Promotion and Reciprocal Protection of Investments (25 October 2000), Art 6.

[8] The Netherlands Model Agreement on Encouragement and Reciprocal Protection of Investments (1979 version), Art IV, reprinted in UNCTC, *Bilateral Investment Treaties* (1988) 167, 168.

NAFTA states: 'Each Party shall permit all transfers and international payments ("transfers") relating to an investment of an investor of another Party in the territory of the Party to be made freely and without delay.' It then proceeds to provide a non-exclusive list of permitted transfers, including, among others, 'profits, dividends, interest, capital gains, royalty payments, management fees, technical assistance and other fees, returns in kind, and other amounts derived from the investment'.[9]

In considering the scope of the right to make transfers under an investment treaty, one interesting question is whether foreign employees and contractors of a covered investment can benefit from transfer provisions with respect to compensation or other funds they have earned from a covered investment project. The issue may well be important to investors, since their ability to recruit foreign managers and specialists as well as the determination of how much they must pay them will depend on whether such foreign employees can repatriate their compensation freely. Some international investment treaties specifically discuss the transfer rights of employees. The ECT, for example, lists among permitted transfers 'unspent earnings and other remuneration of personnel engaged from abroad in connection with that investment'.[10] US BITs also often provide that permitted transfers should include 'earnings and other remuneration of personnel engaged from abroad in connection with an investment',[11] although this language is not in the 2004 and 2012 Model BIT.

Even if a treaty does not specifically grant employees and contractors the right to transfer their earnings, a treaty's general grant of transfer rights may cover such transactions. For example, a provision that allows transfers of 'payments in connection with an investment' could arguably be interpreted to cover compensation and other payments earned by employees and contractors from the investment. Whether the scope of the transfer rights extends to such persons may depend, among other things, on whether the subject of the right in the treaty is 'the investment' or the 'investor'. If the right belongs to the investment, one could interpret transfers by employees and contractors as 'made in connection with an investment'. If, on the other hand, the right is the investor's, then it may be more difficult to bring payments received by employees and contractors within its scope.

Because of their vulnerability to international monetary volatility and their concern about preserving foreign exchange reserves, some developing countries have sought to place limitations or conditions on investors' ability to transfer funds. They have therefore avoided an obligation to grant investors complete freedom to make transfers. For example, some contracting parties have made their obligation to guarantee the right of transfer subject to domestic laws. Thus, Article 3 of the China–Djibouti BIT provides: 'Each Contracting party shall, *subject to its*

---

[9] NAFTA, Art 1109(1).   [10] ECT, Art 14(1)(d).
[11] eg Treaty between the United States of America and the Republic of Armenia Concerning the Encouragement and Reciprocal Protection of Investment (23 September 1992), Art 7(1)(g).

laws and regulations, guarantee to the investors of the other Contracting Party the transfer of their investments and returns held in its territory' (emphasis added).[12]

Similarly to the 'controlled entry' approach employed in many treaties with respect to the admission of investment and discussed in Chapter 7, this provision would appear to grant investors a 'controlled transfer right' subject to the host government authorities' discretion, since national laws usually give governments significant discretionary authority over international monetary transfers. Therefore, foreign investors might well be concerned about the strength and reliability of such treaty commitments, particularly in difficult economic times when a state may decide that its desire to protect certain domestic interests is greater than its need to protect foreign investor interests. Such a decision would cause host governments to exercise their discretion in ways that would inhibit the making of transfers by investors. Aware of investor concerns on this issue, in some cases treaty negotiators have sought to include both an explicit right to make unrestricted transfers and a requirement to respect local law in the text. For example, the Denmark–Hong Kong BIT states:

Each Contracting Party shall, *in accordance with its laws and regulations in respect of investments*, allow to investors of the other Contracting Party the *unrestricted transfer* of their investments and returns abroad, including funds in repayment of loans related to an investment, the proceeds of the total or partial liquidation of an investment, and the earnings of individuals allowed to work in an investment made in its area (emphasis added).[13]

Nearly all countries, developed and developing, have laws that regulate international monetary payments in one respect or another. For example, some states grant the government authority to control or oversee the transfer of payments to assure that they do not finance crime or terrorism, defraud an investor's creditors, or evade legitimate taxes owed by the investor or the investment. Thus, under treaty provisions similar to the Denmark–Hong Kong BIT just quoted, investors of a contracting party have the right to make unrestricted transfers provided they respect applicable laws and regulations. The provision thus seeks to strike a reasonable balance between the investor's interest in the free transfer of money and the host government's interest in assuring that important public interests are protected. For foreign investors, the problem posed by such provisions is how they will be applied in times of economic difficulties, for example when governments enact measures that severely restrict the ability of persons in their territories to make monetary transfers abroad. Will such measures apply to investors covered by the treaty, severely restricting their transfer rights? Or will the government (and

---

[12] Agreement between the Government of the People's Republic of China and the Government of the Republic of Djibouti on the Promotion and Protection of Investments (18 August 2003). See also the Czechoslovakia–Denmark BIT, Art 7(1)(d) which guarantees the transfer of 'an approved portion of the earnings of the non-nationals who are allowed to work on an investment'. Agreement between the Czech and Slovak Federal Republic and the Kingdom of Denmark for the Promotion and Reciprocal Protection of Investments (6 March 1991).

[13] Agreement between the Government of Hong Kong and the Government of the Kingdom of Denmark for the Promotion and Protection of Investments (2 February 1994), Art 6.

potentially an investor–state tribunal) interpret the provision to allow regulation, but only to the point that it does not limit the right to make legitimate unrestricted transfers under the treaty? No investor–state case has arisen to resolve this question.

The scope of an individual investor's transfer rights would also ordinarily be influenced by a most-favoured-nation (MFN) clause in the investment treaty. Thus, if the host country gave more expansive transfer rights to a third country's investors than those accorded to investors under a particular treaty, by virtue of the treaty's MFN clause the treaty investors would be entitled to equivalent treatment. As was discussed in Chapter 9, the ability of an investor to use an MFN clause to expand its rights under a treaty depends on the precise wording of the clause and, in particular, on whether the investment or investor under the treaty and the third country investors that are allegedly receiving better treatment are 'in like circumstance'. Some treaties make that principle explicitly applicable to monetary transfers by providing that the contracting parties will accord to transfers by investors of their treaty partners a treatment no less favourable than that accorded to transfers originating from investors of third states.[14]

Through investment treaties, host states generally grant treatment rights to investors and investments of *other* contracting parties, not to their own investors. One notable exception to this principle is the provision in some treaties, including NAFTA[15] and the Canadian Model BIT, which states that no contracting party may require *its* investors to transfer, or penalize *its* investors for failing to transfer, income, earnings, profits or other amounts derived from investments in another party's territory.[16] As a result of this provision, home countries make an unusual international commitment regarding the treatment they accord domestic investors. While the stated beneficiary of the provision is the home country investor, the provision's actual intent is to benefit the host country by preventing treaty partners from using their sovereign powers to influence the transfer decisions of investors in the other treaty partner's territory. All things being equal, most host countries would prefer that foreign investments in their territories retain and reinvest their profits rather than transfer them abroad.

10.3 Types of Payments Covered by Transfer Provisions

As the introduction to this chapter indicated, investors often need to transfer a wide diversity of payments in order to operate their investments effectively. Investment treaties employ different approaches to specifying the kinds of

---

[14] Agreement on Facilitating and Protecting Investment between the People's Republic of China and the Republic of Bosnia-Herzegovina (26 June 2002), Art 6.4.

[15] NAFTA, Art 1109(3) states: 'No Party shall require its investors to transfer, or penalize its investors who fail to transfer, the income, earnings, profits or other amounts derived from, or attributable to, an investment in the territory of another Party.'

[16] 2004 Canada Model BIT, Art 14(4).

payments they cover. Whereas some treaties simply grant a general right to transfer 'capital and returns',[17] others go into significant detail as to what kinds of payments are covered. Those that adopt the latter approach employ either a closed list or an open list.

A treaty using a closed list will state the specific transactions permitted. The implication is that any transfer not specified does not benefit from the treaty's protection. For example, Article 7 of the 1980 Unified Agreement for the Investment of Arab Capital in the Arab States[18] provides:

1. The Arab investor shall have the freedom to make periodic transfers, both of Arab capital for investment in the territory of any State Party and of the revenues therefrom, and subsequently to make retransfers to any State Party following settlement of his outstanding obligations without this being subject to any discriminatory banking, administrative or legal restrictions and without the transfer process incurring any taxes or duties. This shall not apply in respect of banking services.

This provision would seem to limit the transfer guarantee to payments of capital and earnings while excluding loans, technology transfers, royalty payments, and numerous other international monetary transfers necessary for the operation of an investment.

Most treaties that adopt a closed-list approach are more detailed with respect to the types of payments that are covered than the Unified Arab Agreement. Thus, many treaties grant a general right to make transfers and then provide a lengthy, detailed list of permitted transactions. These may include contributions to capital, profits, dividends, capital gains, proceeds from the sale of the covered investment or from liquidation of the covered investment, interest, royalty payments, management fees, technical assistance, payments made under a contract, payments received as a result of expropriation or losses owing to armed conflict, civil strife, and payments arising out of disputes. Some Danish BITs follow this model by providing:

(1) Each Contracting Party shall with respect to investments in its territory by investors of the other Contracting Party allow the *free transfer in and out* of its territory of:
   (a) the initial capital and any additional capital for the maintenance and development of the investment;
   (b) the investment capital or the proceeds from the sale or liquidation of all or any part of an investment;
   (c) interests, dividends, profits and other returns realized;

---

[17] Similar to many UK BITs, the UK–Bangladesh BIT, Art 6 states: 'Each Contracting Party shall in respect of investments guarantee to nationals or companies of the other Contracting Party the free transfer of their capital and their returns from it.' Agreement between the Government of the United Kingdom and Northern Ireland and the Government of the People's Republic of Bangladesh for the Promotion and Protection of Investments (19 June 1980).

[18] League of Arab States (1982). 'Unified Agreement for the Investment of Arab Capital in the Arab States', *Economic Documents*, No 3 (Tunis: League of Arab States).

(d) payments made for the reimbursement of the credits for Investments, and interests due;

(e) payments derived from rights enumerated in Article 1, section 1, iv of this Agreement;

(f) unspent earnings and other remunerations of personnel engaged in connection with an investment;

(g) compensation, restitution, indemnification or other settlement pursuant to articles [relating to compensation for losses and expropriation] (emphasis added).[19]

Even if drafted in broad terms, a treaty that employs a closed-list approach may not be satisfactory to an investor because it may not take account of newly emerging forms of investment. For that reason, many treaties employ open lists by permitting all transfers 'related to an investment' or 'payments resulting from investment activities'. These descriptions are then combined with an illustrative, non-exclusive list of transfers. Thus, Article 1106 of NAFTA states that '[e]ach Party shall permit all transfers and international payments ("transfers") relating to an investment of an investor of another Party in the territory of the Party to be made freely and without delay'. Article 1106 then proceeds to stipulate that such transfers 'include' a long list of items including profits, dividends, interest, capital gains, royalty payments, management fees, technical assistance, proceeds from the sale of all or any part thereof, loan payments, and other payments under contract. Another specific example of the open-list approach is the Austria–Philippines BIT, which provides:

(1) Each Contracting Party shall guarantee *without undue* delay to investors of the other Contracting Party free transfer in freely convertible currency of *payments in connection with an investment, in particular but not exclusively*, of the
   (a) capital and additional amounts for the maintenance or extension of the investment;
   (b) amounts assigned to cover expenses relating to the management of the investment;
   (c) returns;
   (d) repayment of loans;
   (e) proceeds from total or partial liquidation or sale of the investment;
   (f) compensation payment for expropriation, damage or loss; or
   (g) payments arising out of a settlement of a dispute (emphasis added).[20]

Among more modern investment treaties, the dominant approach is to state a general obligation to allow transfers and then to combine it with a non-exclusive list of permitted transactions.

[19] Agreement between the Government of the Kingdom of Denmark and the Government of the Lao People's Democratic Republic Concerning the Promotion and Reciprocal Protection of Investments (28 September 1998), Art 7; Agreement between the Government of the Kingdom of Denmark and the Government of the Republic of Cuba Concerning the Promotion and Reciprocal Protection of Investments (19 February 2001), Art 8.

[20] Agreement between the Republic of Austria and the Republic of the Philippines for the Promotion and Reciprocal Protection of Investments (11 April 2002), Art 6.

10.4 The Currency of Transfer

The specific currency in which the transfer will be made is also a matter of concern to investors. Normally, investors want to be able to make transfers in their home currency or another currency that is readily convertible. Most investment treaties therefore permit a covered investment's transfers to be made in a 'freely *usable* currency' or 'freely *convertible* currency'. The ECT, for example, provides that transfers are to be made without delay and in a 'freely convertible currency', which Article 1(14) defines as 'currency which is widely traded in international foreign exchange markets and widely used in international transactions'.

Other treaties employ more restrictive language. For example, the Canada–Peru BIT provides: 'Each Party shall permit transfers relating to a covered investment to be made in the *convertible currency* in *which the capital was originally invested*, or in *any other convertible currency agreed by the investor and the Party concerned*' (emphasis added).[21] Such a provision gives a host state flexibility with respect to the currency of payment by providing for the possibility of negotiating an agreement with an investor as to the specific convertible currency for making transfers. However, in the absence of such an agreement, the host state's only obligation is to allow transfers in the convertible currency in which the capital was originally invested, a common provision in some older treaties. Thus, if a Swiss investor makes an investment in Swiss francs, the host state is only required to permit transfers in Swiss francs.

As a result of production-sharing agreements with host countries some investors, such as oil and mineral companies, gain returns from their investment in the form of the minerals or petroleum they produce. A few treaties have expanded the concept of 'transfers' to cover such payments in kind and provided that, subject to a written agreement with the host government, an investor may be permitted to transfer out of the country returns in kind relating to a covered investment.[22] Both NAFTA and the ECT[23] also make clear that returns in kind are, with certain limitations, to be treated as monetary returns under the treaty.[24]

---

[21] Agreement between Canada and the Republic of Peru for the Promotion and Protection of Investments (14 November 2006), Art 14.

[22] eg Treaty between the United States of America and the Oriental Republic of Uruguay Concerning the Encouragement and Reciprocal Protection of Investment (4 November 2005), Art 7: '3. Each Party shall permit returns in kind relating to a covered investment to be made as authorized or specified in a written agreement between the Party and a covered investment or an investor of the other Party'.

[23] ECT, Art 14(1) and (6).

[24] NAFTA, Art 1109(6): 'A Party may restrict transfers of returns in kind only in circumstances in which it could otherwise restrict such transfers under this Agreement'.

10.5 The Applicable Exchange Rate

Investment treaties do not protect investors against exchange rate risk. Normally, investors expect to convert inward transfers at the prevailing currency exchange rate and then to convert subsequent outward transfers at the exchange rate prevailing at that time, which, of course, may be much higher or lower than at the time of the original investment. The exchange rate for the conversion of host country currency is a key element in a covered investment's monetary transfer. For that reason, investment treaties normally provide that covered transfers have to be effected at the rate of exchange prevailing on the day of the transfer. However, since exchange rates may be either officially set or determined by the market, some treaties specify that transfers are to be made on the basis of the *market rate of exchange*. This approach is illustrated by Article 6 in the Austria–Philippines BIT:

(2) The payments referred to in this Article shall be effected at the *market rate of exchange prevailing on the day of the transfer*.
(3) The rates of exchange shall be determined according to the quotations on the stock exchanges or in the absence of such quotations according to the spot transactions conducted through the respective banking system in the territory of the respective Contracting Party (emphasis added).[25]

In cases where a market rate of exchange does not exist, the contracting parties may agree upon a specific framework for its determination, as reflected in the China–Brunei BIT:

Transfers shall be made at the market rate of exchange of the Contracting Party accepting the investment on the day of transfer. In the event that the market rate of exchange does not exist, the rate of exchange shall correspond to the cross rate obtained from those rates which would be applied by the International Monetary Fund on the date of the payment for conversions of the currencies concerned into Special Drawing Rights.[26]

With respect to currency rates of exchange, the ECT, which includes countries of vastly different monetary strengths, follows US BIT practice fairly closely. It states that 'transfers shall be made at the market rate of exchange existing on the date of the transfer with respect to spot transactions in the currency to be transferred'.[27] In the absence of a market for a foreign currency, the Treaty provides two alternative reference rates: (1) the most recent rate applied to inward investments; or, (2) the most recent rate for the conversion of currency into Special Drawing Rights, whichever is the more favourable to the investor.

---

[25] Agreement between the Republic of Austria and the Republic of the Philippines for the Promotion and Reciprocal Protection of Investments (11 April 2002), Art 6.
[26] Agreement between the Government of the People's Republic of China and the Government of His Majesty the Sultan and Yang Di-Pertuan of Brunei Darussalam Concerning the Encouragement and Reciprocal Protection of Investment (11 November 2000), Art 6.
[27] ECT, Art 14(3).

10.6 The Time for Effecting Transfers

The time within which a host state permits an investor to make transfers is another crucial element in the efficient and profitable operation of an investment project. For this reason, treaties usually provide a guarantee that transfers shall be effected 'without delay' or 'without undue delay'.[28] Since the term 'without undue delay' may invite several interpretations due to its vagueness, some contracting parties have chosen to clarify the term to remove any uncertainty. The Austria–Philippines BIT, for example, provides: 'The term "without undue delay" means such period as is normally required for the completion of necessary formalities for the transfer of payments. The said period shall commence on the day on which the request for transfer has been submitted and may on no account exceed two months.'[29]

10.7 Exceptions

As indicated earlier in this chapter, in negotiating investment treaties states are motivated both by a desire to promote investment and by a concern to maintain control over international monetary payments in order to assure proper governance of their territories and protect important national financial and monetary interests. Examples of such interests include the preservation of foreign currency reserves, currency stability, and the avoidance of monetary crises. In order to accommodate these two potentially competing interests, countries have negotiated exceptions to their general treaty commitments with respect to the monetary treatment of protected investors and investment. The resulting provisions thus represent an attempt to balance the interests of the host country with those of the foreign investor.[30] However, treaties that include such exceptions also stipulate that contracting parties must respect the requirements of good faith and non-discrimination and follow certain specified procedures. Friendship, commerce and navigation (FCN) treaties, the predecessors to BITs, included provisions with exceptions to enable transfers by protected nationals. For example, Article VII(1) of the 1955 Treaty of Amity, Economic and Consular Rights between the United States of America and Iran provided:

---

[28] eg Agreement on Facilitating and Protecting Investment between the People's Republic of China and the Republic of Bosnia-Herzegovina (26 June 2002), Art 6: '[t]ransfers shall be effected without delay in a convertible currency at the market rate of exchange applicable on the date of transfer'; Agreement among the Government of Japan, the Government of the Republic of Korea and the Government of the People's Republic of China for the Promotion, Facilitation and Protection of Investment (13 May 2012), Art 13.

[29] Agreement between the Republic of Austria and the Republic of the Philippines for the Promotion and Reciprocal Protection of Investments (11 April 2002), Art 6(4).

[30] UNCTAD, *Bilateral Investment Treaties 1995–2006: Trends in Investment Rulemaking* (2007) 63.

Neither High Contracting Party shall apply restrictions on the making of payments, remittances, and other transfers of funds to or from the territories of the other High Contracting Party, except (a) to the extent necessary to assure the availability of foreign exchange for payments of goods and services essential to the health and welfare of its people, or (b) in the case of a member of the International Monetary Fund, restrictions specifically approved by the Fund.

Article VII (2) of the Treaty established procedures for applying the exceptions: 'If either High Contracting Party applies exchange restrictions, it shall promptly make reasonable provision for the withdrawal, in foreign exchange in the currency of the other High Contracting Party, of... (b) earnings'. In *Hood Corporation v the Islamic Republic of Iran*,[31] the Iranian government, following the revolution of 1979, instituted exchange controls and refused to allow an Iranian bank to transfer funds of a US corporation in Deutschmarks to its bank account in Munich, Germany. The Iran–US Claims Tribunal denied recovery to the US corporation on the grounds that its claim for the unpaid funds was not protected by the Treaty since it made no request for transfer of the funds to the United States or into US dollars as the Treaty required.

The nature of monetary transfer exceptions varies among treaties. For example, the BITs concluded by Sweden and Austria with many developing countries contain no exceptions at all.[32] Others provide a general exception in times of emergency economic situations. Thus, for example, the 1980 UK–Bangladesh BIT obliges the contracting parties to guarantee the free transfer of capital and returns to investors of either party 'subject to the right of each Contracting Party in exceptional financial or economic circumstances to exercise equitably and in good faith powers conferred by its laws'.[33] Most, particularly the more recent treaties, have detailed and lengthy exceptions. The reason for the development of these more elaborate provisions no doubt has to do with countries' experiences with various economic and political emergencies in recent years, such as developing country debt defaults, the Asian financial crisis, and the Argentine economic emergency, as well as governments' growing need, in a time of increasing globalization, to control international payments to protect vital security and fiscal interests.

In general, the monetary exceptions in treaties fall into two categories: those aimed at helping countries to confront economic emergencies and those designed to facilitate good governance in the host country. An example of the former is the detailed Article 17 of the 2002 Korea–Japan BIT, which was probably influenced by Korea's difficult experience during the Asian financial crisis of the late 1990s. It states:

---

[31] *Hood Corp v The Islamic Republic of Iran*, 7 Iran-USCTR 36 (1984).

[32] eg Agreement between the Government of Sweden and the Government of the Arab Republic of Egypt on the Mutual Protection of Investments (15 July 1978); Agreement between the Government of Hong Kong and the Government of the Republic of Austria for the Promotion and Protection of Investments (11 October 1996).

[33] Agreement between the Government of the United Kingdom and Northern Ireland and the Government of the People's Republic of Bangladesh for the Promotion and Protection of Investments (19 June 1980), Art 6.

1. A Contracting Party may adopt or maintain measures not conforming with its obligations under paragraph 1 of Article 2 relating to cross-border capital transactions and Article 12 of this Agreement:
    (a) in the event of serious balance-of-payments and external financial difficulties or threat thereof; or
    (b) in cases where, in exceptional circumstances, movements of capital cause or threaten to cause serious difficulties for macroeconomic management, in particular, monetary and exchange rate policies.
2. Measures referred to in paragraph 1 of this Article:
    (a) shall be consistent with the Articles of Agreement of the International Monetary Fund so long as the Contracting Party taking the measures is a party to the said Articles of Agreement;
    (b) shall not exceed those necessary to deal with the circumstances set out in paragraph 1 of this Article;
    (c) shall be temporary and shall be eliminated as soon as conditions permit; and
    (d) shall be promptly notified to the other Contracting Party.
3. Nothing in this Agreement shall be regarded as altering the rights enjoyed and obligations undertaken by a Contracting Party as a party to the Articles of Agreement of the International Monetary Fund.[34]

Good governance requires that governments have the legal authority to oversee and regulate transfers in order to protect creditors, fight crime and terrorism, and prevent tax evasion. Exceptions designed to deal with these issues are found in Article 7 of the US–Uruguay BIT, which provides:

4. Notwithstanding paragraphs 1 through 3, a Party may prevent a transfer through the equitable, non-discriminatory, and good faith application of its laws relating to:
    (a) bankruptcy, insolvency, or the protection of the rights of creditors;
    (b) issuing, trading, or dealing in securities, futures, options, or derivatives;
    (c) criminal or penal offenses;
    (d) financial reporting or record keeping of transfers when necessary to assist law enforcement or financial regulatory authorities; or
    (e) ensuring compliance with orders or judgments in judicial or administrative proceedings.[35]

The Canada–Peru BIT illustrates yet another type of exception that relates to transfers by financial institutions:

Notwithstanding the provisions of paragraphs 1, 2 and 4, and without limiting the applicability of paragraph 5, a Party may prevent or limit transfers by a financial institution to, or for the benefit of, an affiliate of or person related to such institution, through the equitable, non-discriminatory and good faith application of measures relating to maintenance of the safety, soundness, integrity or financial responsibility of financial institutions.[36]

---

[34] Agreement between the Government of Japan and the Government of the Republic of Korea for the Liberalization, Promotion and Protection of Investment (22 March 2002), Art 17.
[35] Treaty between the United States of America and the Oriental Republic of Uruguay concerning the Encouragement and Reciprocal Protection of Investment (4 November 2005).
[36] Agreement between Canada and the Republic of Peru for the Promotion and Protection of Investment (14 November 2006), Art 14(6).

Another approach is illustrated by the ECT, which provides for three exceptions to the freedom of transfer:

1. A host country may limit monetary transfers in order to protect the rights of creditors or ensure compliance with securities laws or with laws on the satisfaction of judgments, provided such measures are 'equitable, non-discriminatory, and a good faith application of its laws and regulations'. For example, this provision might allow a central bank, before authorizing a transfer, to require a showing by the investor that it is not subject to an unsatisfied judgment or attachment in connection with a debt it owes. Such a requirement, of course, could serve to delay the transfer and thus avoid one of the essential elements of the freedom of transfer—that it be made without delay.

2. The Contacting Parties of the former Soviet Union may provide among themselves by agreement that their own investors may be paid in their own currencies, provided that the investors of other contracting parties are not treated less favourably than those investors or the investors of any third party in respect of monetary transfers.

3. Returns in kind, for example payments in crude oil pursuant to production sharing agreements, may be restricted by the host country in circumstances where they are permitted by the GATT, except that such returns must be permitted if authorized in a written agreement between the host country and either an investor of another Contracting Party or its investment.[37]

While in the early years of the BIT movement, capital-exporting countries tended to oppose all exceptions to transfer rights, recently they seem to have become more appreciative of their utility, particularly with respect to those related to good governance.

In this regard, three rulings[38] by the European Court of Justice in 2009 are important. In the three cases, the Court held that the monetary clauses in Sweden, Austria, and Finland's BITs with several developing countries were incompatible with their obligations as EU members under the EU Treaty. While Article 56 of the EU Treaty prohibited restrictions on the movement of capital and on payments between member states, as well as between member states and third countries, Articles 57, 59, and 60 authorized the EU Council to introduce exceptions to these principles of free movement of capital and payments in order to protect general EU interests in exceptional situations. The Court found that the BITs concluded by Sweden, Austria, and Finland, which guaranteed investors the right to make transfers without delay and without exceptions, were incompatible with their obligations under the EU Treaty. Further, the Court held that by not taking

---

[37] Legal Counsel of the IEA, *The Energy Charter Treaty* (1994) 19.
[38] Case C-249/06 *Commission of the European Communities v Kingdom of Sweden* (ECJ 3 March 2009); Case C-205/06 *Commission of the European Communities v Republic of Austria* (ECJ 3 March 2009); Case C-118/07 *Commission of the European Communities v Republic of Finland* (ECJ 19 November 2008).

appropriate steps to eliminate the incompatibilities, Sweden, Austria, and Finland failed to fulfil their obligations under the Treaty. As was discussed in Chapter 4, at section 4.2(l), foreign investment as a result of the Treaty of Lisbon is now constitutionally a Union, rather than a member state function. Consequently, one can expect that future investment treaties affecting European countries will take account of the EU treaty requirements on monetary payments and transfers and that the EU institutions will actively seek to renegotiate existing European BITs to introduce appropriate exceptions to accord with the decisions of the European Court of Justice. More generally, in recent years it seems that capital-exporting countries have developed a heightened appreciation of the importance of exceptions to monetary transfer clauses when compared to the position that they took on the question during the early years of the investment treaty movement, and that such sensitivity will be reflected in their future investment treaties.

11

Treatment of State Obligations
(the 'Umbrella Clause')

11.1 The Problem of the Obsolescing Bargain

In order to attract foreign investment, host states make various commitments and representations to foreign investors. Some of these undertakings are embodied in formal bilateral agreements such as investment accords, development contracts, public service concessions, and tax stabilization agreements, to mention only a few. Others are found in unilateral acts like foreign investment legislation, licences, and regulatory permissions. Still others are less formal governmental actions, such as the oral statements by government officials and promises about investments published by a government in the press or promotional literature.

In varying degrees, investors rely on such obligations and undertakings in making decisions about investing their capital in a host country. They usually consider the continued willingness of the host state to respect its commitments to be crucial to the profitability of an investment, and sometimes to its very survival. Since these arrangements are governed by the law of the host country and are subject to the actions of its institutions, their continued viability is premised on the assumption that the host government will not unilaterally modify or terminate them at some later time—a phenomenon that has in fact taken place on numerous occasions. Thus, a mineral development agreement made with a foreign investor by one government may be cancelled by a subsequent government as a result of a change in policy or economic conditions. A government may grant a foreign investor the right to operate a landfill one year and cancel it the next as a result of changes in environmental legislation. A host government's obligations to foreign investors are therefore, in the oft-quoted words of Raymond Vernon, 'obsolescing bargains' between the investor and the host country.[1]

The cause of their obsolescence has much to do with two important factors: (1) changing circumstances; and (2) the decline in the investor's bargaining power after making the investment. With regard to the first factor, states, like rational private parties, will generally continue to respect their obligations to the extent that the perceived net benefits of performance exceed those of

---

[1] R Vernon, *Sovereignty at Bay: The Multinational Spread of U.S. Enterprises* (Basic Books, 1971) 46.

non-performance. But when, for whatever reason, a state judges the net costs of continuing performance to exceed the perceived net benefits, the result will usually be rejection of the obligation or, at the very least, a demand to renegotiate the original undertaking.[2] For example, a developing country that is attracted to a mining project proposed by a French mining company because of the prospect of high revenues may eagerly enter into a mineral development contract with that company. But, if after a few years revenues do not meet governmental expectations, or if another mining company promises higher income, the government will cancel the contract if it concludes that the cost of doing so will not exceed the benefits to be derived from a new arrangement. In making this calculation, the host government weighs the expected benefits from a new arrangement against such political and economic costs as defending against a lawsuit or arbitration claim brought by the French company as well as any sanctions that the French government might impose, such as a reduction in foreign aid.

The concept of costs and benefits is not limited to purely economic factors. When states are involved, the costs and benefits of both political and social effects will weigh heavily in any decision to continue or end an undertaking. For example, in one case involving a foreign investment project designed to build a luxury resort near the Giza pyramids in Egypt, the Egyptian government originally signed the agreement believing the economic benefits of the project would exceed its costs. But, when public and international opposition became strong and persistent, the government cancelled the project. The government judged that the project's political costs would outweigh the economic benefits to be derived from its construction.[3]

A second factor that contributes to the obsolescence of state undertakings is the decline in the investor's bargaining power after making an investment. When proposing an investment, the investor has a certain amount of bargaining power to secure favourable treatment and conditions for its investment because of the government's desire to acquire the investment. However, once the investor has invested and so placed its capital under the sovereignty of the host state, its bargaining power with the host state diminishes and the commitment runs the risk of becoming obsolete in the eyes of the host government.

All foreign investors therefore face a fundamental problem: How can they be certain that host states will continue to respect the commitments made at the time the investment was made? One approach is to increase the perceived costs to the host state for failing to fulfil its undertakings by making such a failure a violation of the treaty subject to investor–state arbitration and whatever other enforcement mechanisms are available under the treaty. As a consequence, a state deciding whether or not to continue to respect its obligations towards a particular investment would at least in theory have to include in its calculations the significant costs of defending and losing an

---

[2] J Salacuse, *The Global Negotiator* (Palgrave Macmillan, 2003) 223–7.
[3] *SPP (Middle East) Ltd, and Southern Pacific Properties Ltd v The Arab Republic of Egypt*, ICC Case No 3493 (Award) (11 March 1983) (1983) 22 ILM 752.

investor–state arbitration. The state would also have to consider the resulting negative impact on its investment climate. From a foreign investor's point of view, elevating such costs through treaty provisions constitutes an inducement to host countries to fulfil their obligations in the face of opposing pressures. Moreover, by giving an individual investor the right to bring an investor–state arbitration and obtain compensation for the non-performance of state obligations, such a treaty provision increases the bargaining power of investors in their dealings with the host government and works to ensure continued state compliance. It is for these reasons that a large number of investment treaties contain provisions, often referred to as 'umbrella clauses', to achieve just these results by making performance of state undertakings a part of the treatment owed to investors.

This chapter will examine the general nature of umbrella clauses, their historical background, the various formulations that they take, and their application by arbitral tribunals. It will conclude with a suggested framework of analysis for applying umbrella clauses to specific investments.

11.2 Umbrella Clauses in General

The breach of state contracts and other obligations to investors is not ordinarily considered a breach of international law. The Permanent Court of International Justice in the *Serbian Loans* case[4] stated that 'any contract which is not a contract between States in their capacity as subjects of international law is based on the domestic law of some country'. More recently, in *Noble Ventures v Romania*,[5] a case involving alleged breaches of an agreement to privatize a Romanian steel enterprise made by Romanian authorities, an ICSID tribunal stated:

the well established rule of general international law that in normal circumstances *per se* a breach of a contract by the State does not give rise to direct international responsibility on the part of the State. This derives from the clear distinction between municipal law on the one hand and international law on the other, two separate legal systems (or orders) the second of which treats the rules contained in the first as facts, as is reflected in *inter alia* Article Three of the International Law Commission's Articles on State Responsibility adopted in 2001.[6]

Even if an investor is protected by an investment treaty, usually the treatment provisions contained therein do not make breaches of state obligations to investors violations of the treaty, unless the state has acted so flagrantly towards its obligation that its actions constitute a denial of fair and equitable treatment, full

---

[4] *Case Concerning the Payment of Various Serbian Loans Issued in France (France v Kingdom of Serbs, Croats and Slovenes)* (1929) PCIJ Rep Series A, No 20, at 41.
[5] *Noble Ventures, Inc v Romania*, ICSID Case No ARB/01/11 (Award) (12 October 2005).
[6] ibid ¶ 53.

protection and security, or another treatment standard specified in the treaty. Thus, for example, many tribunals have pointed out that contractual breaches are not necessarily violations of an investment treaty. As the ICSID Annulment Committee stated in *Vivendi*: 'A state may breach a treaty without breaching a contract and vice versa.' And further:

whether there has been a breach of the BIT and whether there has been a breach of contract are different questions. Each of these claims will be determined by reference to its own proper or applicable law—in the case of the BIT, by international law; in the case of the Concession Contract by the proper law of the contract.[7]

The rules regarding the legal status of state contracts and breaches thereof do not mean that states cannot agree by treaty that state contracts and other obligations will be governed by international law and that breaches of those obligations will make states responsible under international law.[8] Such a provision would increase the costs to host states for violating their obligations to investors and thus encourage states to continue fulfilling those obligations. Accordingly, in order to protect investor–state commitments and obligations from obsolescence, many investment treaties—approximately 1,000 by some estimates[9]—contain a clause defining the treatment that the host state will give to obligations it has made to investors or investments covered by the treaty. Known commonly as 'umbrella clauses', such provisions generally stipulate that '[e]ach Contracting Party shall observe any obligation it may have entered into with regard to the investments of investors of the other Contracting Party'.[10] Similar clauses can

[7] *Compañía de Aguas del Aconquija SA and Vivendi Universal (formerly Compagnie Générale des Eaux) v Argentine Republic*, ICSID Case No ARB/97/3 (Decision on Annulment) (3 July 2002) ¶¶ 95, 96.

[8] In *Noble Ventures, Inc v Romania*, ICSID Case No ARB/01/11 (Award) (12 October 2005), the tribunal stated:

That being said, none of the above mentioned general rules is peremptory in nature. This means that, when negotiating a bilateral investment treaty, two States may create within the scope of their mutual agreement an exception to the rules deriving from the autonomy of municipal law, on the one hand and public international law, on the other hand. In other words, two States may include in a bilateral investment treaty a provision to the effect that, in the interest of achieving the objects and goals of the treaty, the host State may incur international responsibility by reason of a breach of its contractual obligations towards the private investor of the other Party, the breach of contract being thus 'internationalized', i.e. assimilated to a breach of the treaty. In such a case, an international tribunal will be bound to seek to give useful effect to the provision that the parties have adopted.

ibid ¶ 54.

[9] R Dolzer and C Schreuer, *Principles of International Investment Law* (OUP, 2008) 153. See also J Gill et al, 'Umbrella Clauses and Bilateral Investment Treaties: A Comparative Study of the SGS Cases' (2004) 21 J Int'l Arb 397, 403, n 43 (reporting that approximately 40% of a sample drawn from *Investment Treaties* (2003) contained umbrella clauses), and UNCTAD, *Bilateral Investment Treaties 1995–2006: Trends in Investment Rulemaking* (2007) 73, stating that 40% of all BITs contain umbrella clauses.

[10] Agreement between the Government of the United Kingdom of Great Britain and Northern Ireland and the Government of the Republic of Argentina for the Promotion and Protection of Investments (11 March 1990).

also be found in multilateral arrangements such as the Energy Charter Treaty (ECT)[11] and the 1987 ASEAN Investment Agreement.[12] The NAFTA chapter on investments, however, contains no umbrella clause. Thus, the umbrella clause creates an exception to a well-established principle of international law concerning state contracts with, and obligations to, foreign investors.

The intention of an umbrella provision is to impose an international treaty obligation on host countries that requires them to respect obligations they have entered into with respect to investments protected by the treaty. This places such obligations under the protective umbrella of international law, not just the domestic law that would otherwise normally apply exclusively. The effect of the umbrella clause is not to transform a contractual or other obligation governed by domestic law into an international obligation governed by international law. The source of the obligation, as well as its nature and scope, are delineated by the law under which it was originally made—in most cases, the law of the host country. As the Annulment Committee stated in the *CMS* case, which involved alleged breaches by the Argentine government of obligations under Argentine law with respect to investments in natural gas transmissions: 'The effect of the umbrella clause is not to transform the obligation which is relied upon into something else; the content of the obligation is unaffected, as is its proper law.'[13] By virtue of the umbrella clause, a host state has an international duty to respect its obligations concerning foreign investments despite the fact that those obligations remain subject to the law under which they were originally made. The failure to respect such obligations, while remaining subject to local courts or the contractually specified dispute settlement procedures, also renders an offending state subject to the jurisdiction of investor–state arbitration or whatever other dispute settlement mechanisms are provided for by treaty. Thus, by imposing a treaty-based international duty on host states to fulfil their obligations towards foreign investments, the umbrella clause seeks to slow or stop entirely the obsolescence of state bargains that Professor Vernon described.

---

[11] ECT, Art 10(1) in articulating the protection to be afforded to investments, states: 'Each Contracting Party shall observe any obligations it has entered into with an Investor or an Investment of an Investor of a Contracting Party.'

[12] III(3), which is entitled 'General Obligations', states: 'Each Contracting Party shall observe any obligation arising from a particular commitment it may have entered into with regard to a specific investment of nationals or companies of the other Contracting Parties.' Agreement among the Government of Brunei Darussalam, the Republic of Indonesia, Malaysia, the Republic of the Philippines, the Republic of Singapore and the Kingdom of Thailand for the Promotion and Protection of Investments (15 December 1987). The 2009 ASEAN Comprehensive Investment Agreement does not appear to contain a similar provision.

[13] *CMS Gas Transmission Co v Argentine Republic*, ICSID Case No ARB/01/8 (Annulment Proceeding) (25 September 2007) ¶ 95(c).

11.3 Historical Background of the Umbrella Clause

Scholars trace the idea of an umbrella clause, sometimes also called a 'mirror', 'parallel effect', or *pacta sunt servanda* clause',[14] to a recommendation by the eminent international law scholar Elihu Lauterpacht. The recommendation was made in connection with a proposed settlement of the Anglo-Iranian Oil Company's claim against Iran in 1954, which followed the nationalization of its interests in that country. The company, along with others affected by the nationalization, entered into a tentative 'Consortium Agreement' with the Iranian government under which it would continue to operate certain oil facilities in Iran. In order to stabilize the agreement and protect it from subsequent unilateral changes by the Iranian government, Lauterpacht proposed the conclusion of an 'umbrella treaty' between the United Kingdom and Iran that would incorporate the consortium agreement in a way that would make any breach of the consortium a breach of the treaty itself.[15] By this method, Lauterpacht sought to give the consortium agreement the protection of international law and make any breaches subject to the enforcement mechanisms of the umbrella treaty.

Although the umbrella treaty never became a reality because the Anglo-Iranian Oil Company settled its claims against Iran by other means, the idea of seeking to protect investor–state obligations through an international treaty did not die. As Chapter 9 noted, a private initiative by leading European lawyers called the Abs-Shawcross Draft Convention on Investments Abroad sought to develop a set of provisions that would protect foreign investment. Just as the Draft Convention would become one of the foundations for the fair and equitable treatment standard that is now a basic principle in virtually all investment treaties, so it would also lay the basis for the umbrella clause. The Draft's Article II provided: 'Each party shall at all times ensure the observance of any undertakings which it may have given in relation to investment made by nationals of any other Party.'[16] Unlike the 'umbrella treaty' suggested by Lauterpacht in the Anglo-Iranian Oil case, the provision in the Abs-Shawcross Draft applied to all 'undertakings' of the host state towards covered investors and not to a particular, named agreement. The scope of the Draft Convention's language made clear that it covered undertakings made directly to investors as well as those made to the investor's home state. Moreover, the word 'undertaking' is broad enough to cover not only written contracts but all commitments a state makes to an investor, in whatever form.

The umbrella clause in Article II of the Abs-Shawcross Draft influenced subsequent efforts to develop investment treaty provisions, including the 1967 OECD

---

[14] J Wong, 'Umbrella Clauses in Bilateral Investment Treaties: Of Breaches of Contract, Treaty Violations, and the Divide between Developing and Developed Countries in Foreign Investment Disputes' (2006) 14 George Mason L Rev 135, 142.

[15] AC Sinclair, 'The Origins of the Umbrella Clause in the International Law of Investment Protection' (2004) 20 Arb Int'l 411, 415.

[16] 'Proposed Convention to Protect Private Foreign Investment: A Roundtable' (1960) 9 J Pub L 115, 116.

Draft Convention on the Protection of Foreign Property. Article 2 of the OECD Draft Convention stated: 'Each Party shall at all times ensure the observance of undertakings given by it in relation to property of nationals of any other party.'[17] Although the OECD Draft Convention was never adopted by its members, it and the Abs-Shawcross initiative had a strong influence on the bilateral treaty movement because many states incorporated an umbrella clause into the model treaties that they used in conducting BIT negotiations.[18] The very first BIT ever negotiated, the 1959 Germany–Pakistan BIT, included an umbrella clause, stating: 'Each Party shall observe any other obligations it may have entered into with regard to investments by nationals or companies of the other Party.'[19] It is to be noted that this BIT employed the word 'obligation' rather than 'undertaking', which was used in the Abs-Shawcross Draft and some BITs;[20] however, the two words would seem to be synonymous within the context of umbrella clauses.[21] As subsequent BITs were concluded in the following years, more and more included umbrella clauses, but they employed a variety of formulations. Moreover, the fact that some capital-exporting countries included them in their model treaties and others did not, significantly influenced the degree to which they would become part of binding international investment agreements among particular countries.

11.4 Formulations of the Umbrella Clause

One of the most common formulations of the umbrella clause in investment treaties is the following: 'Each party shall observe any obligation it may have entered into with regard to investments in its territory by investors of the other contracting Party.'[22] As an UNCTAD study has pointed out, such language is clearly intended to cover not only investment agreements between investors and host states but also is broad enough to apply to 'all kinds of obligations, explicit or

---

[17] OECD, Draft Convention on the Protection of Foreign Property and Resolution of the Council of the OECD on the Draft Convention (12 October 1967) OECD Publication No 23081 (1968) 7 ILM 117.

[18] Whereas the US Model BITs of 1983, 1984, and 1987 contained umbrella clauses, the 2004 and 2012 US Model BITs, like NAFTA, do not. One may infer from this omission that the US government does not want to restrict its range of action when dealing with foreign investors in the US by making its obligations towards them matters of international, rather than US, law.

[19] Pakistan and the Federal Republic of Germany Treaty for the Promotion and Protection of Investments (with Protocol and exchange of notes) (25 November 1959), Art 7.

[20] eg the 1988 Australia–China BIT, Art XI, entitled 'Undertakings given to investors', states: 'A Contracting Party shall, subject to its law, adhere to any written undertakings given by a competent authority to a national of the other Contracting Party with regard to an investment in accordance with its law and the provisions of this Agreement.' Agreement between the Government of Australia and the Government of the People's Republic of China on the Reciprocal Encouragement and Protection of Investments (11 July 1988).

[21] eg Webster's Third International Dictionary defines 'undertaking' as 'to put oneself under an obligation to accept a charge'. *Webster's Third New International Dictionary of the English Language* (3rd edn, Merriam-Webster, 2002).

[22] eg Agreement between the Government of the United Kingdom of Great Britain and Northern Ireland and the Government of the Republic of Argentina for the Promotion and Protection of

implied, contractual or non-contractual, undertaken with respect to investment generally'.[23] Such breadth of scope would in effect make the respect by host governments of all their commitments to investors a treaty obligation governed by international law and all disputes related to their failure to fulfil those commitments potentially subject to international arbitration. Thus, depending on the precise terms of an umbrella clause, states become obliged under international law to respect state concession contracts to operate public services, government permits to operate landfills, tax exemptions promised in foreign investment codes, and even representations made by ministers to investors during investment promotion 'road shows'.

Many countries have viewed the consequences of such a treatment standard as undesirably broad and an unjustified intrusion into what they consider their natural right to regulate persons and activities within their territories. As a result, certain treaties have sought to reduce the scope of the umbrella clause by introducing qualifications into the language of the provision. For example, some treaties may require that the obligation covered by the umbrella clause be in writing and be made with respect to a specific investment.[24] Such a qualification would exclude from umbrella clause protection, for example, a government minister's oral statements about his department's intentions towards an investor, as well as provisions in a host country's foreign investment code. Other treaty provisions specify that a contracting state is to respect obligations 'subject to its law',[25] a provision that makes clear that the state's obligations under the umbrella clause are dependent on host country law.

Another approach to limiting the impact of the umbrella clause is to require that the host state observe all obligations made with respect to covered investments while simultaneously specifying 'any disputes arising from such obligations being only redressed under the terms of the contract underlying the obligations'.[26] Thus, although the treaty creates an international obligation to observe the treaty's contractual provisions, aggrieved investors must resort to the dispute settlement mechanism put in place by the contract rather than investor–state arbitration.

The prevalence of a variety of formulations of umbrella clauses has led investors to allege their existence in treaties where it is not clear that they exist at all. For example, the BIT between Jordan and Italy provides in Article 2(4) that: 'Each

---

Investments (11 March 1990), Art 2(2); Agreement between the Kingdom of Denmark and the Republic of Lithuania for the Promotion and Protection of Investment (30 March 1992), Art 3(1).

[23] UNCTAD, *Bilateral Investment Treaties in the Mid-1990s* (1998) 56.

[24] eg the Greece–Mexico BIT, Art 19 states: 'Each contracting party shall observe any other obligation it may have entered into in writing with regard to a specific investment of an investor of the other Contracting Party.' Agreement between the Government of the United Mexican States and the Government of the Hellenic Republic on the Promotion and Reciprocal Protection of Investments (30 November 2000).

[25] eg Agreement between the Government of Australia and the Government of the People's Republic of China on the Reciprocal Encouragement and Protection of Investments (11 July 1988), Art XI.

[26] UNCTAD, *Bilateral Investment Treaties 1995–2006: Trends in Investment Rulemaking* (2007) 74.

Contracting Party shall create and maintain in its territory a legal framework apt to guarantee to investors the continuity of legal treatment, including the compliance, in good faith, of all undertakings assumed with regard to each specific investor.'[27] In *Salini v Jordan*,[28] which dealt with a dispute arising out of a construction contract between Jordanian and Italian contractors, the Italian claimants argued that the provision just quoted was an umbrella clause that had the effect of internationalizing all of Jordan's obligations towards investors. The tribunal rejected this argument, stating that a treaty provision concerning the creation and maintenance of a 'legal framework' favourable to investment was only intended to set norms and establish institutions to facilitate the investment by investors of the other party. The provision did not make each contracting state responsible under international law for the breach of any of its contractual obligations vis-à-vis the private investors of the other party. Ultimately, the tribunal in *Salini* concluded that the provision was not an umbrella clause as that term is normally understood and that Jordan had not violated the provision with respect to the construction contract.

11.5 Application of the Umbrella Clause

At first glance, the usual formulations of the umbrella clause would not seem to require a complicated exercise in interpretation. The meaning of the language seems clear and forthright: a state must respect any obligations that it has made to an investment covered by the treaty. If it does not respect such obligations, it violates its treaty commitments and is consequently liable to compensate the investor for any resulting loss. If it does not make compensation, it is subject to investor–state arbitration. For example, in the UNCITRAL case of *Eureko BV v Republic of Poland*, which arose out of an alleged breach of an agreement between foreign investors and the Polish government in connection with the privatization of a major Polish state-owned insurance company, the tribunal was required to interpret Article 3(5) of the 1992 Netherlands–Poland BIT. That Article provides: 'Each Contracting Party shall observe any obligations it may have entered into with regard to investment of investors of the other Contracting Party.' In finding that Poland had violated its obligations to the claimants under the umbrella clause, the majority of the tribunal stated:

The plain meaning—the 'ordinary meaning'—of a provision that a state 'shall observe any obligations it may have entered into' with regard to certain foreign investments is not obscure. The phrase 'shall observe' is imperative and categorical. 'Any' obligations is capacious; it means not only obligations of a certain type, but 'any'—that is to say,

---

[27] Agreement between the Hashemite Kingdom of Jordan and the Government of the Italian Republic on the Promotion and Protection of Investments (21 July 1996).
[28] *Salini Costruttori SpA and Italstrade SpA v Jordan*, ICSID Case No ARB/02/13 (Decision on Jurisdiction) (9 November 2004).

'all'—obligations entered into with regard to investments of investors of the other Contracting Party.[29]

The majority also pointed out that the umbrella clause in the Netherlands–Poland BIT could not be overlooked, equated with, or subsumed within other treatment standards in the treaty, like fair and equitable treatment or full protection and security. The umbrella clause had to be interpreted to mean something in and of itself.

Despite their apparent clarity and brevity, umbrella clauses have been the subject of interpretations in at least twenty-three investor–state arbitrations between 2003 and 2013. The resulting arbitral jurisprudence has by no means been uniform. The differing interpretations of apparently similar umbrella clauses by different tribunals raise concerns with respect to the consistency and development of the law of investment treaties. Part of the reason for the divergence in arbitral decisions is certainly due, to some extent, to the differing formulations of the clause that have confronted tribunals in individual cases. Equally significant is that different tribunals have had differing conceptions of the nature of a clause and, in particular, the intended scope of application that contracting states were seeking when they agreed to it.

In order to understand the divergent jurisprudence on umbrella clauses, one may divide arbitral decisions into those which focus primarily on the specific language of the provision in question and those that seem to be influenced by the consequences to states and to the arbitral system of giving too broad an interpretation to the clause. Thus, some tribunals have claimed that the 'ordinary meaning' of the clause, an analysis required by Article 31 of the Vienna Convention on the Law of Treaties (VCLT), leads to a broad interpretation and that arbitrators should interpret the clear meaning of the terms without regard to possible policy consequences. Others argue that ordinary meaning is not enough—that the VCLT obliges tribunals to interpret treaties by giving their words their ordinary meaning in context and in the light of a treaty's objects and purposes. A consideration of a treaty's context, object, and purpose has led some tribunals to adopt a more nuanced and narrower interpretation of the umbrella clause.[30] This view is often reflected in the tribunal's stated concern that too broad an interpretation will lead to a flood of all sorts of claims that are better settled under domestic law and by domestic institutions.

The first reported case to consider an umbrella clause was *Fedax v Venezuela*,[31] which dealt with a claim by investors that Venezuela had failed to honour promissory notes it made and, as a result, breached the umbrella clause in the Netherlands–Venezuela BIT. Article 3 of that BIT provides: 'Each Contracting Party shall observe any obligation it may have entered into with regard to the

---

[29] *Eureko BV v Republic of Poland* (Partial Award) (19 August 2005) ¶ 246.
[30] L Halonen, 'Containing the Scope of the Umbrella Clause' in TJG Weiler (ed), *Investment Treaty Arbitration and International Law* (JurisNet, 2008) 27.
[31] *Fedax NV v The Republic of Venezuela*, ICSID Case No ARB/96/3 (Award) (9 March 1998) (1998) 37 ILM 1391.

treatment of investments of nationals of the other Contracting Party.' Although the merits of the case were partially settled by agreement of the parties, the tribunal did state in its award that 'the Republic of Venezuela is under the obligation to honor precisely the terms and conditions governing such investment, laid down mainly in Article 3 of the Agreement [ie the BIT], as well as to honor the specific payments established in the promissory notes issued'.[32]

A few years later, a divergence would begin to develop in two cases that involved the same claimants and similar transactions but were against two different countries subject to two different BITs. In *SGS Société Générale de Surveillance SA v Islamic Republic of Pakistan*,[33] Pakistan entered into a five-year agreement with SGS, a Swiss corporation, under which SGS would perform pre-shipment inspection services of goods to be exported from certain countries to Pakistan. Subsequently, SGS claimed that Pakistan wrongfully terminated the agreement, and it therefore brought an ICSID arbitration proceeding for damages. Among its claims, SGS asserted that the umbrella clause in the Pakistan–Switzerland BIT makes all violations of the pre-inspection services agreement in effect violations of the BIT. The umbrella clause in Article 11 of the BIT had a somewhat different formulation from similar clauses in other BITs. It provided: 'Either Contracting Party shall constantly guarantee the observance of the commitments it has entered into with respect to the investments of the investors of the other Contracting Party.'

The tribunal rejected SGS's argument that Article 11 had the effect of elevating breaches of the contract into breaches of the treaty. It advanced several grounds to support this conclusion. First, it stated that the obligations referred to in Article 11 were not limited to contractual obligations and that, therefore, Article 11 appeared to be capable of 'infinite expansion'. According to the tribunal, the legal consequences of the claimants' interpretation of the treaty were 'so far-reaching in scope, and so automatic and unqualified and sweeping in their operation, so burdensome in their potential impact upon a Contracting Party, that clear and convincing evidence had to be adduced by the Claimant' that the two contracting states in fact had such an intention.[34] The tribunal found no evidence in the treaty of such intent and no other supporting evidence was presented to it. Moreover, accepting the investor's interpretation would amount to incorporating an unlimited number of state contracts, as well as an unlimited number of municipal law obligations, into the treaty. This would mean that the other treatment standards in the treaty were 'substantially superfluous', since virtually any injurious action by a contracting party against an investor would constitute a violation of Article 11. That, in turn, would allow an investor to nullify a state contract's freely

---

[32] ibid ¶ 29.
[33] *SGS Société Générale de Surveillance SA v Islamic Republic of Pakistan*, ICSID Case No ARB/01/13 (Decision on Objections to Jurisdiction) (6 August 2003) (2003) 42 ILM 1290.
[34] ibid ¶ 167.

negotiated dispute resolution clause by claiming a treaty breach and invoking investor–state arbitration.

SGS Société Générale de Surveillance SA v Republic of the Philippines,[35] decided just a few months later by a different tribunal, involved the same claimant and a similar transaction for pre-shipment services as was at issue in *SGS v Pakistan*. SGS claimed that the Philippines breached the pre-shipment services contract and that, by virtue of the umbrella clause in the Philippines–Switzerland BIT, the breach was a violation of the treaty itself. Relying on the decision in *SGS v Pakistan*, the Philippines argued that contractual breaches were not treaty breaches and so the tribunal had no jurisdiction over the contractual claims.

The applicable umbrella clause differed from the one in *SGS v Pakistan* in that, in Article X(2), it provided: 'Each Contracting Party shall observe any obligation it has assumed with regard to specific investments in its territory by investors of the other Contracting Party.'

The tribunal in *SGS v Philippines* found that the umbrella clause 'means what it says'[36] and that it obliged contracting states to respect all the obligations they make, whether by contract or otherwise. It specifically rejected the Philippines' argument that the clause only applied to obligations found in international instruments, stating that if the parties had so intended they would have said so specifically. It also reasoned that the object and purpose of the treaty—to promote investment—was consistent with the view that a state must observe all obligations, contractual and otherwise, which a state assumes with regard to investments in its territory. It then rigorously criticized the *SGS v Pakistan* case, analysing and disputing each of the reasons on which the decision was based.

First, it pointed out that the umbrella clause in the Switzerland–Philippines BIT, unlike the Pakistan–Switzerland BIT, was limited to 'obligations assumed with regard to specific investments'. This provision would not have the effect of elevating all municipal obligations to the level of international obligations, a concern of the tribunal in *SGS v Pakistan*. Second, it challenged the notion that international law maintained a presumption against a broad interpretation of the umbrella clause. The tribunal argued that the issue was one of treaty interpretation, not presumption. In summary, it found the reasons advanced in *SGS v Pakistan* to be unconvincing and, moreover, concluded that the tribunal in that case failed to provide a clear interpretation of the clause.

Subsequent cases have rejected a restrictive approach to interpreting umbrella clauses and so have followed *SGS v Philippines*, rather than *SGS v Pakistan*. It would appear that the majority view in current arbitral jurisprudence is that umbrella clauses mean what they say, and that tribunals should give them a literal interpretation when applying them in individual cases. Cases following this

---

[35] *SGS Société Générale de Surveillance SA v Republic of the Philippines*, ICSID Case No ARB/02/6 (Decision on Jurisdiction) (29 January 2004).
[36] ibid ¶119.

approach include *Noble Ventures v Romania*,[37] *Eureko BV v Republic of Poland*,[38] *BIVAC BV v The Republic of Paraguay*,[39] and *SGS v Paraguay*,[40] which interpreted language identical to that at issue in *SGS v Pakistan*.

On the other hand, while *SGS v Pakistan* now seems to be an isolated decision that has not strongly influenced subsequent tribunals, some tribunals, perhaps influenced by the same concerns that motivated the *SGS v Pakistan* tribunal, have found certain limitations to exist explicitly or implicitly in the treaty language. Accordingly, these tribunals have been unwilling to give a broad interpretation to the umbrella clauses that they have been called upon to interpret. For example, some tribunals have indicated that only sovereign obligations, as opposed to commercial obligations, are covered, and so states entering into such obligations must be acting as sovereigns and not as merchants.[41] This approach, however, seems problematic. For one thing, the precise distinction between the two types of obligations is not clear. For another, umbrella clauses generally refer only to 'obligations' and do not make a distinction between those that are commercial and those that are sovereign in nature. Neither do they distinguish between treaties entered into by the state as a merchant and as a sovereign. It should also be pointed out that where states have wanted to limit the scope of umbrella clauses, tribunals have found that they have the power to do so and, in fact, in many treaties have imposed such limitations. Where states have chosen not to impose such limitations, one may question the soundness of arbitral decisions that assume to impose them or assume that states intended to so impose them even though they did not explicitly state that intent. Nonetheless, the current state of the jurisprudence on this question is not uniform, and more divergence and more litigation can be expected in the years ahead.

11.6 A Framework for Applying Umbrella Clauses

In view of the unsettled state of the jurisprudence on umbrella clauses, the following framework of analysis is offered for applying umbrella clauses to specific

---

[37] The tribunal stated: 'Art. II(2)(c) of the BIT perfectly assimilates to breach of the BIT *any* breach by the host State of *any* contractual obligation as determined by its municipal law *or* whether the expression "any obligation", despite its apparent breadth, must be understood to be subject to some limitation in the light of the nature and objects of the BIT', ibid ¶ 61.

[38] In which the tribunal stated that it found the analysis of the umbrella clause in *SGS v Pakistan* 'less convincing', ibid ¶ 257.

[39] The tribunal stated: 'The words "any obligation" are all encompassing. They are not limited to international obligations, or non-contractual obligations, so that they appear without apparent limitation with respect to commitments that impose legal obligations. On a plain meaning they are undoubtedly capable of being read to include a contractual arrangement.' *BIVAC BV v The Republic of Paraguay*, ICSID Case No ARB/07/09 (Decision of the Tribunal on Objections to Jurisdiction) (29 May 2009) ¶ 141.

[40] *SGS Société Générale de Surveillance SA v The Republic of Paraguay*, ICSID Case No ARB/07/29 (Decision on Jurisdiction) (12 February 2010) ¶ 167.

[41] eg *Joy Mining Machinery Ltd v The Arab Republic of Egypt*, ICSID Case No ARB/03/11 (Award on Jurisdiction) (6 August 2004) ¶ 72; *CMS Gas Transmission Co v The Argentine Republic*,

investments. In particular, persons applying umbrella clauses should seek to address the following questions:

1. *The Nature and Source of the Obligation.* What is the specific nature and source of the obligation or obligations that the investor claims the host state has violated? First, it is important to determine the specific content of the obligation and the source from which it is derived. States make commitments, obligations, or undertakings to investors in a variety of ways. These include but are not limited to specific contracts signed by the investors, legislation applicable to investments generally, administrative orders applicable to a specific investment or investments generally, and oral and written statements made by state authorities at various levels.

2. *State Attribution.* Is the obligation in question attributable to the host state? If the obligation is not a state obligation, then the umbrella clause is not applicable. Undertakings made by certain quasi-governmental agencies and enterprises may not be considered state obligations under the investment treaty.

3. *Sovereign and Non-Sovereign Obligations.* Does the umbrella clause govern all obligations or only sovereign obligations? What are the distinguishing criteria between the two?

4. *Consensual and Non-Consensual Obligations.* Does the umbrella clause cover both contractual and non-contractual obligations, such as those that may have been created through legislation, regulations, or even governmental statements on which the investor has relied?

5. *Nature and Source of Non-Consensual Obligations.* If the umbrella clause does cover non-contractual obligations, which non-contractual obligations are covered and how must they have been created to be covered by the clause in question?

6. *The Obligee.* To whom must the state owe the obligation to be covered by the umbrella clause? Must the obligation be specifically to the aggrieved investor or injured investment to justify a claim under the treaty in question? Or may it be directed to investments in general covered by the treaty? In cases in which an obligation is made in respect of an investment, rather than to an investor, may investors, such as shareholders or creditors, in that investment and therefore not a direct party to the obligation or contract covered by the umbrella clause nonetheless be protected by the umbrella clause?[42]

ICSID Case No ARB/01/08 (Award) (12 May 2005) ¶ 299; *El Paso Energy International Co v The Argentine Republic*, ICSID Case No ARB/03/15 (Decision on Jurisdiction) (27 April 2006) ¶¶ 79–81; *Pan American and BP v The Argentine Republic*, ICSID Case No ARB/03/13, ICSID Case No ARB/04/08 (Decision on Preliminary Objections) (27 July 2006) ¶¶108–109.

[42] CS Miles, 'Where's My Umbrella? An "Ordinary Meaning" Approach to Answering Three Key Questions that have Emerged from the "Umbrella Clause" Debate' in TJG Weiler (n 30 above) 3.

12

Protection Against Expropriation, Nationalization, and Dispossession

12.1 The Risk of Expropriation, Nationalization, and Dispossession

An age-old, overriding concern of all foreign investors is that host country governments will seize their assets. Such uncertainty over the security of property rights is the essence of political risk.[1] Whenever a foreign investor places its assets in a foreign territory, it thereby subjects them to the jurisdiction of the host country government. Those assets then become susceptible to host country legislative and administrative acts, including expropriation, nationalization, dispossession, and alteration of property rights.

In contemplating an investment in a foreign country, investors always calculate the risk of expropriation and dispossession. That calculation is invariably rendered difficult by the fact that investments are long-term transactions, often projected to extend over many years and even decades into an always uncertain future. While conditions may appear safe for investment property at the time the investment is made, those conditions can change rapidly and dramatically as a result of shifting political and economic dynamics in host countries, the regions in which they are located, and indeed the world itself. Popular uprisings, wars, regime changes, coups, economic crises, and insurrections are just a few of the events that can place investor property rights in jeopardy. In response to such events, governments may use their legislative and administrative powers to revise investors' legal rights in ways they consider to be in the public interest.

One may view an investment at the time it is made as a bargain between the investor and the host country government as to their respective rights to benefit from that investment. In response to subsequent political and economic realities, governments often seek to change the terms of that bargain unilaterally by altering investors' legal rights in ways that increase the government's benefits from the investment and decrease the investor's.

The most dramatic way in which governments can change this bargain is by seizing an investment and thereby cancelling the investor's property rights. Thus, for

[1] N Rubins and NS Kinsella, *International Investment, Political Risk and Dispute Resolution: A Practitioner's Guide* (Oceana Publications, 2005) 1–29.

example, governments can simply seize factories, mines, plantations, and other physical assets owned and controlled by foreign investors. Such direct expropriations were a constant concern throughout the nineteenth and twentieth centuries. As was discussed in Chapter 3, the twentieth century witnessed significant expropriations of foreign investment in Latin America, the Soviet Union, the Middle East, and Eastern Europe. In those cases, the governments asserted their legal rights to take the property and denied any obligation to compensate investors for what they had taken. As will be recalled, such actions raised a fundamental question as to the standard of treatment that host countries legally owed to foreign investors. Host governments asserted that they owed no more than 'national treatment', that is, treatment no better than they gave their own nationals, while capital-exporting states claimed that host countries had an obligation to accord foreign investors an international minimum standard of treatment. With specific reference to expropriation, the United States and western European governments claimed that the international standard allowed host governments to expropriate foreign investments only for a public purpose, in a non-discriminatory manner, in accordance with due process of law, and upon payment, in the words of the Hull formula, of 'prompt, adequate, and effective compensation'. The dispute over the conditions under which a host state could expropriate continued into the post-World War II era when newly decolonized countries in the 1960s and 1970s called for a New International Economic Order. The investment treaty movement was an effort to resolve that debate by securing agreement on international rules to protect the property rights of foreign investors. Thus, the modern international regime for the protection of investor property evolved through a treaty-making process that, among other things, sought to establish clear and enforceable international legal rules to protect investor property rights. This chapter examines the nature and effect of those treaty provisions.

Just as international investment law has evolved over time so, too, have the methods by which governments seek to modify or interfere with investor property rights. Whereas outright expropriation through government seizure was common until the 1980s, it has become an increasingly less common phenomenon thereafter. In the twenty-first century, governments dissatisfied with the original bargains made with foreign investors rarely send their troops to seize a factory or occupy a mine; instead, they use their legislative and regulatory power in more subtle ways to alter the benefits flowing to the investor from the investment. Thus, a government may impose new regulations on the way the investment is operated, raise taxes on the investment substantially, or unilaterally change a contract to reduce the revenues flowing to a concessionaire. The investor remains in possession of the investment, but the amount and nature of the benefits originally contemplated are significantly reduced. In legal terms, these regulatory actions diminish the nature of the investor's property rights over the investment and, if sufficiently extreme, may constitute a form of expropriation or dispossession. Such actions may rise to the level of an 'indirect' expropriation, sometimes referred to as 'regulatory taking'.[2] They have become the most common type of intervention with foreign

---

[2] SR Ratner, 'Regulatory Takings in the Institutional Context: Beyond the Fear of Fragmented International Law' (2008) 102 AJIL 475.

investments by host governments in the twenty-first century. As will be seen, one challenge in interpreting treaty provisions on expropriation is determining whether and to what extent such provisions protect covered assets against various forms of administrative and regulatory actions that negatively affect but nonetheless leave the investor in possession of the investment. This shift in governmental tactics has led to a change in the legal debate about the definition of expropriation and nationalization and also whether traditional principles of international law apply to legislative and regulatory actions that leave investors in possession of investment assets but diminish their freedom to control, manage, and derive benefits from them. In short, the challenge for scholars, arbitrators, and lawyers, is to determine the dividing line between investors' property rights and the host governments' reasonable right to regulate investments.

One should not assume, however, that old fashioned techniques of expropriation are things of the past. Two highly publicized direct expropriations that did take place in the early twenty-first century were the seizure in 2004 by the Russian government of the assets of Yukos, at the time a leading privately owned Russian oil company, and the nationalization in 2012 by the Argentine government of a 51 per cent interest in YPF, an Argentine oil company, whose majority shareholder was Repsol, a Spanish energy corporation. In both cases, title to the investor's assets was transferred to the state or state-owned enterprises through a variety of legal means undertaken by the governments concerned. Both cases would result in arbitration under investment treaties in which the investors challenged such actions as illegal under international law. In 2005, shareholders in Yukos would bring three separate UNCITRAL arbitrations employing the institutional auspices of the Permanent Court of Arbitration under the Energy Charter Treaty (ECT),[3] claiming a total of US$114 billion. In 2012, Repsol would commence an ICSID arbitration[4] against Argentina under the Argentina–Spain bilateral investment treaty (BIT) for US$10.5 billion. Both arbitrations would conclude in 2014. In March 2014, Repsol and Argentina agreed to settle their dispute with the payment of US$5billion in bonds issued by Argentina, and in July of the same year, the tribunal in the Yukos cases issued awards[5] totalling more than US$50 billion, the largest amount of damages ever awarded in the history of international arbitration.

---

[3] *Hulley Enterprises Ltd (Cyprus) v The Russian Federation*, PCA AA 226 (Final Award) (18 July 2014); *Yukos Universal Ltd (Isle of Man) v the Russian Federation*, PCA AA 227 (Final Award) (18 July 2014); and *Veteran Petroleum Ltd (Cyprus) v the Russian Federation*, PCA AA 228 (Final Award) (18 July 2014).

[4] *Repsol SA and Repsol Butano SA v Argentine Republic*, ICSID Case No ARB/12/28 (Discontinued) (19 May 2014).

[5] *Hulley Enterprises Ltd (Cyprus) v The Russian Federation*, PCA AA 226 (Final Award) (18 July 2014) ¶ 339; *Yukos Universal Ltd (Isle of Man) v the Russian Federation*, PCA AA 227 (Final Award) (18 July 2014); *Veteran Petroleum Ltd (Cyprus) v the Russian Federation*, PCA AA 228 (Final Award) (18 July 2014). The three awards probably also set a historic record for length, since each was nearly 600 pages long.

12.2 Investment Treaty Provisions
on Expropriation, Nationalization, and Dispossession

Because the investment treaty movement arose during a period when many expropriations and nationalizations had taken place and states exhibited significant disagreement about the applicable international law, one of the primary goals of capital-exporting countries in promoting investment treaties was to protect their investors and investments from acts of expropriation, nationalization, and dispossession by host governments.[6] In other words, their goal was to preserve the original bargain that the investor had made with the host government when it entered the country. As a result, virtually all investment treaties contain a provision concerning the expropriation or nationalization of covered investments; however, the nature of those provisions, their scope, and the limitations they place on governmental action, vary among treaties.

All treaties use similar words to refer to the phenomenon of governmental interference with the property rights of investors: expropriation, nationalization, dispossession, or some combination thereof. Most treaties refer to both expropriation and nationalization. Thus, Article 1110 of the North American Free Trade Agreement (NAFTA) provides that '[n]o Party may directly or indirectly nationalize or expropriate an investment of an investor of another Party in its territory'; however, NAFTA does not define expropriation or nationalization or explain how or whether the two terms differ.[7] Some scholars have argued that the term 'nationalization' applies only to state seizure of an entire industry while implementing a new economic policy, whereas 'expropriation' refers to the seizure of a particular asset or investment.[8] Although investment treaties do not specifically recognize this distinction, their use of both words arguably indicates an intention to cover both situations and to avoid any suggestion that a governmental taking labelled as a 'nationalization' is somehow exempt from treaty coverage. This chapter will use the term 'expropriate' or 'expropriation' to apply to the various forms of state takings, however they may be denominated.

All treaty provisions on expropriation are alike in two fundamental respects. First, they all recognize the right of host countries to nationalize, expropriate, or dispossess an investor's investment. Such treaty provisions thus acknowledge an important incident of a state's territorial sovereignty and embody the classical principle of international law that a state has the right to expropriate an alien's

---

[6] UNCTAD, *Bilateral Investment Treaties in the Mid-1990s* (1998) 65.

[7] See also Agreement among the Government of Japan, the Government of the Republic of Korea and the Government of the People's Republic of China for the Promotion, Facilitation and Protection of Investment (13 May 2012), Art 11.1: 'No Contracting Party shall expropriate or nationalize investments in its territory of investors of another Contracting Party or take any measure equivalent to expropriation or nationalization (hereinafter referred to in this Agreement as "expropriation")...'.

[8] M Sornarajah, *The International Law on Foreign Investment* (2nd edn, Cambridge University Press, 2004) 347–48; UNCTAD, *Bilateral Investment Treaties in the Mid-1990s* (1998) 65.

property.[9] The justification for this principle is that the fundamental purpose of the state is to protect and preserve the public interest of its citizens and that if such interest will be properly safeguarded by expropriation, then the state must be free to pursue that course of action.[10] Second, all treaties purport to place limitations or conditions on a state's exercise of its right to expropriate, nationalize, or dispossess a covered investment. Thus, while a state has a right to expropriate, the exercise of that right, to be legal under the applicable treaty, must be done according to specified conditions. Accordingly, nearly all treaties adopt a specific linguistic formula that first states that no contracting party shall nationalize or expropriate investments of the other contracting party, but then proceeds to specify the exceptions to the purported ban. Article 1110 of NAFTA is one example:

1. No Party may directly or indirectly nationalize or expropriate an investment of an investor of another Party in its territory or take a measure tantamount to nationalization or expropriation of such an investment ('expropriation'), except:
   (a) for a public purpose;
   (b) on a non-discriminatory basis;
   (c) in accordance with due process of law and Article 1105(1); and
   (d) on payment of compensation in accordance with paragraphs 2 through 6.[11]

Article 13(1) of the ECT adopts a similar approach:

(1) Investments of Investors of a Contracting Party in the Area of any other Contracting Party shall not be nationalized, expropriated or subjected to a measure or measures having effect equivalent to nationalization or expropriation (hereinafter referred to as 'Expropriation') except where such Expropriation is:
   (a) for a purpose which is in the public interest;
   (b) not discriminatory;
   (c) carried out under due process of law; and
   (d) accompanied by the payment of prompt, adequate and effective compensation.[12]

As will be seen later in this chapter, it is in the nature of the conditions and limitations placed on expropriation that one finds significant variation among treaties. Before considering such conditions, it is important to determine the scope and meaning of the expropriatory acts that are covered by the expropriation treaty clauses. An act that falls outside that scope is not an expropriation or nationalization and so is not subject to the limitations and conditions of the investment treaty—including the obligation of the host state to pay compensation. This chapter will first examine the scope of coverage of expropriation provisions as they apply to direct and indirect takings of investor property by a state. It will then consider the various conditions and limitations that treaties place upon such state actions, including the obligation to pay compensation.

---

[9] R Dolzer and C Schreuer, *Principles of International Investment Law* (OUP, 2007) 89.
[10] I Delupis, *Finance and Protection of Investments in Developing Countries* (Gower Technical Press, 1975) 31.
[11] North American Free Trade Agreement (17 December 1992), (1994) 32 ILM 612.
[12] The Energy Charter Treaty (17 December 1994), 2080 UNTS 100 (ECT).

12.3 The Scope of Expropriation, Nationalization, and Dispossession Clauses

In interpreting expropriation clauses, three elements are of fundamental concern: (1) the nature of the expropriating actor; (2) the nature of the property expropriated; and (3) the nature of the expropriatory act.

(a) The nature of the expropriating actor

Treaty provisions on expropriation are aimed at actions by the contracting states, not by private persons, organizations, or non-contracting states. The act complained of as expropriatory must be attributable to a contracting state. For example, the seizure of an investor's factory by workers without government authority or connivance would not ordinarily constitute an expropriation; however, the host government's failure to restore the property to the investor might be a denial of full protection and security required by the applicable treaty. In all investment treaties, an expropriation is a governmental action that is forbidden by the treaty except upon specified conditions. Governments take all kinds of actions constantly. The challenge in applying an investment treaty is to determine *which* governmental actions fall within the category of expropriation under the applicable treaty.

(b) The nature of the property expropriated

Investment treaties protect 'investments' from expropriation. As Chapter 7 indicated, treaties define the term 'investments' broadly to include both tangible and intangible assets. Thus, depending on the breadth of that definition, expropriation clauses may not only protect physical property, such as land and buildings, but also intangible forms of property, such as contractual rights, intellectual property rights, and government business concessions.

Even before the advent of investment treaties, courts and tribunals recognized that contractual rights could also be subject to expropriation. In *Norwegian Shipowners' Claims*, one of the very first cases to decide the question, the US government seized ships built for Norwegian nationals in US shipyards during World War I and cancelled ship construction contracts with Norwegian nationals. A government entity, 'the Fleet Corporation', took over the ships and the contracts. In response to Norwegian claims of expropriation, the United States argued that contractual rights could not be considered property for purposes of international law. The arbitral tribunal rejected this broad assertion, referring to both US and Norwegian domestic law. It held that 'the Fleet Corporation took over the legal rights and duties of the ship owners toward the shipbuilders'[13]

---

[13] *Norwegian Shipowners' Claims (Norway v United States)* (Perm Ct Arb 1922) 1 RIAA 307, 332, 233. See also A Reinisch, 'Expropriation' in P Muchlinski et al (eds), *The Oxford Handbook of International Investment Law* (OUP, 2008) 407, 411–12.

and that the cancellation of existing ship-building contracts amounted to *de facto* expropriation.[14] Consequently, it ordered the payment of appropriate compensation.

The *Chorzów Factory* case concerned the effect of Polish measures directed against Bayerische, a German company that had the contractual right to manage and operate a nitrate plant, the Chorzów Factory, owned by another German company. The Permanent Court of International Justice held that the Polish measures expropriated both the factory owner and the company holding contractual rights to the factory: 'it is clear that the rights of the Bayerische to the exploitation of the factory and to the remuneration fixed by the contract for the management of the exploitation and for the use *of its patents, licenses, experiments, etc.,* have been directly prejudiced by the taking over of the factory by Poland'.[15] The Iran-US claims tribunal[16] and other international tribunals have relied on and reaffirmed the *Chorzów Factory* holding when deciding claims of interference with rights arising under a contract and other forms of intangible property.

Following the development of investment treaties, arbitration tribunals have consistently recognized that intangible as well as tangible property may be the subject of expropriation.[17] As was stated very clearly in the *Methanex* case: 'Certainly, the restrictive notion of property as a material "thing" is obsolete and has ceded its place to a contemporary conception which includes managerial control over components of a process that is wealth producing.'[18] Indeed, in contemporary practice the most prevalent types of alleged expropriations under treaties, and usually the most difficult legal questions, involve governmental measures affecting intangible rights.

[14] '[W]hatever the intentions may have been, the United States took, both in fact and in law, the contracts under which the ships in question were being or were to be constructed'. *Norwegian Shipowners' Claims* (n 13 above) 325.

[15] *Case Concerning Certain German Interests in Polish Upper Silesia (FRG v Poland)* (1926) PCIJ Series A, No 7, at 44.

[16] In the *Amoco* case, the tribunal determined that '[i]n spite of the fact that it is nearly sixty years old, this judgment is widely regarded as the most authoritative exposition of the principles applicable in this field, and is still valid today'. *Amoco International Finance Corp v Iran* (1987) 15 Iran-USCTR 189, ¶ 191.

[17] *Fireman's Fund Insurance Co v United Mexican States*, ICSID Case No ARB(AF)/02/1 (Award) (17 July 2006) ¶ 176. See also *Biloune and Marine Drive Complex Ltd v Ghana Investments Centre and the Government of Ghana*, UNCITRAL (Award on Jurisdiction and Liability) (27 October 1989), a non-treaty case in which the investor concluded a ten-year lease contract to renovate and manage a restaurant with an agency of the Ghana government. The Accra City Council subsequently ordered work to stop on the project and demolished the facility. In its award in favour of the claimant, the ad hoc tribunal stated: 'such prevention of [an investor] from pursuing its approved project would constitute constructive expropriation of [the investor]'s contractual rights in the project... unless the Respondents can establish by persuasive evidence sufficient justification for these events'.

[18] *Methanex v United States*, UNCITRAL (Final Award) (3 August 2005), Part IV, Ch D, p 7.

(c) The nature of the expropriating act

Most expropriation provisions refer to governmental actions as 'measures'. For example, the BIT between Peru and Paraguay provides: 'Neither of the Contracting Parties shall adopt, directly or indirectly, measures of expropriation, nationalization or any other measure of the same nature or effect against the investments of the other Contracting Party.'[19] Investment treaties do not usually define 'measure', but one accepted dictionary definition is 'a course of action intended to obtain some object'.[20] It is unclear whether a government's failure or refusal to act can constitute a 'measure' under an expropriation clause. For example, suppose a government has induced a foreign investor to buy land and build a factory, but once the factory is built, fails to grant the necessary operating permit because of conflict within the government bureaucracy. Would the failure to deliver the permit constitute a 'measure of expropriation'? In one of the few arbitral decisions to consider the meaning of 'measure' in an expropriation clause, the tribunal in *Mr Euduro Armando Olguín v Republic of Paraguay*, applying the Peru–Paraguay BIT just quoted, stated:

For an expropriation to occur, there must be actions that can be considered reasonably appropriate for producing the effect of depriving the affected party of the property it owns, in such a way that whoever performs those actions will acquire, directly or indirectly, control, or at least the fruits of the expropriated property. Expropriation therefore requires a teleologically driven action for it to occur; omissions, however egregious they may be, are not sufficient for it to take place.[21]

On the other hand, a formal decision by a government not to grant a requested licence probably would fit the definition of a 'measure', since it could be viewed as an act done to achieve a desired end. What is less clear is whether a government's inaction or mere failure to decide, in response to a licence request by an investor, constitutes a 'measure' under the applicable treaty.

As can be seen from the expropriation provisions in NAFTA and the ECT set out earlier, treaty provisions on expropriation do not generally define 'expropriation' or 'nationalization' or specify the elements that must be present to constitute an expropriatory governmental action. Nor do they specify the difference between direct and indirect expropriation or provide guidance in determining whether a governmental act is 'tantamount to' or has the 'equivalent effect' of expropriation. The brevity and conciseness of such formulations do not make their application

---

[19] Convenio Entre La República del Perú y La República del Paraguay Sobre Promoción y Protección Reciproca de Inversiones (31 January 1994), Art 6.1. The original Spanish version of this provision (the only official language of the treaty) states: 'Ninguna de las Partes Contratantes adoptará, directa o indirectamente, medidas de expropiación, nacionalización o cualquier otra medida de la misma naturaleza o efecto, contra inversiones de nacionales de la otra Parte Contratante.'

[20] *Oxford English Dictionary* (2nd edn, OUP, 1989).

[21] *Mr Euduro Armando Olguín v Republic of Paraguay*, ICSID Case No ARB 96/5 (Award) (26 January 2001) ¶ 84. For a contrary view, see A Newcombe and L Paradell, *Law and Practice of Investment Treaties: Standards of Treatment* (Kluwer Law International, 2009) 337.

to the inevitably complex fact situations presented in expropriation cases easy. Their failure to define or establish any criteria to identify 'indirect expropriations' or 'measures having an effect equivalent to expropriation or nationalization' further exacerbates the problem.[22] The apparent reluctance by contracting states to define these concepts in their treaties may be explained both by the difficulty treaty negotiators face in predicting the infinite variety of state measures that may be taken as well as the equally infinite variety of potential investment arrangements.[23] The adoption of these open-ended formulations allows expropriation treaty provisions to capture the multiplicity of host state acts that might have an expropriatory effect on foreign investment. Such an approach assumes that principles of general international law will work to clarify and guide the application of treaty provisions to specific situations.

A reasonable reading of treaty expropriation provisions, such as those quoted earlier, indicates that they prohibit three kinds of expropriation: (1) direct expropriations or nationalizations; (2) indirect expropriations or nationalizations; and (3) governmental actions that are tantamount or equivalent to expropriation or nationalization.

Treaties differ in the way they deal with these three possible types of expropriation. Not all of them follow the comprehensive approach employed by NAFTA and the ECT. BITs, for example, display a variety of approaches in protecting against expropriation: (a) some contain provisions that refer only to 'expropriation' and 'nationalization'; (b) others combine the reference to 'expropriation' and 'nationalization' with 'measures tantamount to' or 'measures having effect of' expropriation and nationalization; and (c) yet others provide protection against direct and indirect expropriation.

Treaties in the first category contain only a general clause providing that the contracting parties 'shall abstain from taking any measures of expropriation'[24] and then specify the conditions under which an expropriation will be considered lawful. Questions may arise as to whether an investor may invoke such a provision with respect to an indirect expropriation or regulatory taking. One interpretation of such provisions is that because they use the plural form *'any measures* of expropriation' such provisions are intended to cover various types of expropriatory

---

[22] The tribunal in *LG&E Energy Corp* stated: 'Generally, bilateral treaties do not define what constitutes an expropriation—they just make an express reference to "expropriation" and add the language "any other action that has equivalent effects".' *LG&E Energy Corp et al v The Argentine Republic*, ICSID Case No ARB/02/1 (Decision on Liability) (26 September 2006) ¶ 185.

[23] R Dolzer and M Stevens, *Bilateral Investment Treaties* (Kluwer Law International, 1995) 99.

[24] eg Agreement between the Government of the Lebanese Republic and the Government of Malaysia for the Promotion and Protection of Investments (26 February 1998), Art 5:

Neither Contracting Party shall take any measures of expropriation or nationalization against the investments of an investor of the other Contracting Party except under the following conditions:

(a) the measures are taken for a lawful or public purpose and under due process of law;
(b) the measures are non-discriminatory;
(c) the measures are accompanied by provisions for the payment of prompt, adequate and effective compensation.

actions, including those having an effect equivalent to that of a direct expropriation. On the other hand, it could also be argued, relying on the interpretation principle of *expressio unius est exclusio alterius* (the expression of one thing is the exclusion of another), that one could interpret the provision as referring to measures of a direct expropriation only, and not to other kinds of measures, regardless of whether the latter have an effect equivalent to that of the former. To avoid possible ambiguities and ensure better investment protection from expropriatory measures, many international investment agreements provide for more comprehensive and specific expropriation clauses.

In addition to referring to 'expropriation' and 'nationalization', some treaties extend the concept of expropriation to measures whose effect on investors' property rights and investments is equivalent to what results from direct expropriation. The expressions most utilized by such investment treaties are 'measures having similar effects', 'any measures having effect equivalent to nationalization or expropriation', or 'any other measure the effects of which would be tantamount to expropriation or nationalization'. For example, Article 6 of the 1998 Chile–Tunisia BIT provides: 'Neither Contracting Party shall nationalize, expropriate or *subject the investments* of an investor of the other Contracting Party *to any measures having an equivalent effect*'[25] (emphasis added).

In another variation, Article 5 of the UK–Sierra Leone BIT of 2000 contains the following provision:

(1) Investments of nationals or companies of either Contracting Party *shall not be nationalised, expropriated* or subjected to *measures having effect equivalent to nationalisation or expropriation* (hereinafter referred to as 'expropriation') in the territory of the other Contracting Party except for a public purpose related to the internal needs of that Party on a non-discriminatory basis and against prompt, adequate and effective compensation[26] (emphasis added).

The following sections of this chapter examine the three types of expropriatory actions covered in most investment treaties: (1) direct expropriations; (2) indirect expropriations; and (3) actions tantamount or equivalent to an expropriation.

12.4 Direct Expropriations, Nationalizations, and Dispossessions

The essential element of an expropriation is a 'taking' by the state of property that belongs to the investor. In a direct expropriation, that taking comes through state action that deprives the investor of legal title or control of its investments. As

---

[25] Agreement between the Republic of Chile and the Republic of Tunisia on the Reciprocal Promotion and Protection of Investments (23 October 1998).

[26] Agreement between the Government of the United Kingdom of Great Britain and Northern Ireland and the Government of the Republic of Sierra Leone for the Promotion and Protection of Investments (13 January 2000).

the tribunal in *Feldman v Mexico* observed: 'Recognizing direct expropriation is relatively easy: governmental authorities take over a mine or factory, depriving the investor of all meaningful benefits of ownership and control.'[27] In the NAFTA case of *Fireman's Fund Insurance Company v United Mexican States*, the tribunal, summarizing the jurisprudence of ten previous decisions on expropriation under Article 1110, identified the key elements necessary to sustain an investor's claim of expropriation and the requirements of a 'taking':[28]

a. Expropriation requires a taking (which may include destruction) by a government-type authority of an investment by an investor covered by the NAFTA.
b. The covered investment may include intangible as well as tangible property.[29]
c. The taking must be a substantially complete deprivation of the economic use and enjoyment of the rights to the property, or of identifiable distinct parts thereof (ie it approaches total impairment).
d. The taking must be permanent, and not ephemeral or temporary.
e. The taking usually involves a transfer of ownership to another person (frequently the government authority concerned), but that need not necessarily be so in certain cases (eg total destruction of an investment due to measures by a government authority without transfer of rights).
f. The effects of the host state's measures are dispositive, not the underlying intent, for determining whether there is expropriation.
g. The taking may be *de jure* or *de facto*.
h. The taking may be 'direct' or 'indirect'.[30]
i. The taking may have the form of a single measure or a series of related or unrelated measures over a period of time (the so-called 'creeping' expropriation).[31]

Although this summary of the elements necessary for expropriatory taking was made with specific reference to NAFTA, it is applicable to the expropriation provisions of most investment treaties, which, like NAFTA, do not define expropriation or specify its essential elements.

---

[27] *Feldman v Mexico*, ICSID Case No ARB(AF)/99/1 (Award on Merits) (16 December 2002) ¶ 100.
[28] *Fireman's Fund Insurance Co v United Mexican States*, ICSID Case No ARB(AF)/02/1 (Award) (17 July 2006) ¶ 176.
[29] Citing *Mondev International Ltd v United States*, ICSID Case No ARB(AF)/99/2 (Award) (11 October 2002) ¶ 98.
[30] On this point, the *Fireman's Fund* tribunal stated: '"Indirect" expropriation is contemplated by Article 1110(1) of the NAFTA: "No Party may directly or *indirectly* nationalize or expropriate . . . or take a *measure tantamount to* nationalization or expropriation"' (emphasis added). According to certain case law, the expression 'a measure tantamount to nationalization or expropriation' in NAFTA, Art 1110 means nothing more than 'a measure equivalent to nationalization or expropriation'. *Pope & Talbot Inc v The Government of Canada*, UNCITRAL (Interim Award) (26 June 2000) ¶¶ 96, 104; *SD Myers, Inc v The Government of Canada*, UNCITRAL (Partial Award) (13 November 2000) ¶¶ 285–286; *Feldman Kappa v Mexico*, ICSID Case No ARB(AF)/99/1 (Award) (16 December 2002) ¶ 100.
[31] 'Creeping expropriation is a form of indirect expropriation with a distinctive temporal quality in the sense that it encapsulates the situation whereby a series of acts attributable to the State *over a period of time* culminate in the expropriatory taking of such property.' *Generation Ukraine Inc v Ukraine*, ICSID Case No ARB/00/9 (Final Award) (16 September 2003) ¶ 20.22. Creeping expropriation applies when no single measure alone is expropriatory. *Burlington Resources Inc v Republic of Ecuador*, ICSID Case No ARB/08/5 (Decision on Liability) (14 December 2012) ¶¶ 345–346.

Although cases of direct expropriation have been rare in recent years, they do sometimes occur. In addition to the Yukos and Repsol cases discussed at the beginning of this chapter, the 2000 arbitration case of *Swembalt v Latvia*[32] is of interest. Swedish investors, believing they had an agreement with appropriate Latvian authorities, purchased and renovated a ship to be used as a floating trade centre, which they towed to and docked in the port of Riga, Latvia. Without notice to the investors, the port authorities subsequently moved the ship and, ultimately, sold it at auction. The Swedish investors brought a claim against Latvia under the 1992 Agreement between the Government of the Kingdom of Sweden and the Government of the Republic of Latvia on the Promotion and Reciprocal Protection of Investments, alleging that Latvia had deprived them of their investment. The tribunal found Latvia's conduct to be a direct expropriation: 'The Republic of Latvia, by taking the ship away, preventing SwemBalt from using it and, finally, by auctioning it and permitting that it be scrapped without any compensation to SwemBalt, has breached its obligations under the Investment Agreement and general international law.'[33]

The tribunal, which awarded the investors over US$2.5 million in compensation, relied upon Article 4(1) of the Sweden–Latvia BIT,[34] which prohibits expropriation except upon the conditions stated earlier. The facts of the case presented a clear instance of direct expropriation because the Latvian authorities took actions that deprived the investors of control of the ship and ultimately its legal title.

In the Yukos cases, the Russian government, apparently for political motives due to the fact that Yukos' principal shareholder Mikhail Khordokovsky was a political opponent of Russian President Vladimir Putin, caused its taxation authorities to launch a number of tax cases against Yukos, leading to the freezing of Yukos assets, the rendering of tax claims amounting to billions of dollars against the company, and ultimately the holding of auctions of Yukos assets to secure payment of those claims but which allowed state enterprises to obtain Yukos assets at bargain prices. Reviewing the complex facts of the cases, the arbitration tribunal concluded: 'the auction of YNG [Yukos' main oil production subsidiary] was not driven by motives of tax collection but by the desire of the State to acquire Yukos' most valuable asset and bankrupt Yukos. In short, it was in effect a devious and calculated expropriation by Respondent of YNG'.[35] It acknowledged,

---

[32] *Swembalt AB, Sweden v Latvia*, UNCITRAL (Award) (23 October 2000).

[33] ibid ¶ 38.

[34] Agreement between the Government of the Kingdom of Sweden and the Government of the Republic of Latvia on the Promotion and Reciprocal Protection of Investments (10 March 1992), Art 4(1), provides:

(1) Neither Contracting Party shall take any measures depriving, directly or indirectly, an investor of the other Contracting Party of an investment unless the following conditions are complied with:
(a) the measures are taken in the public interest and under due process of law;
(b) the measures are distinct and not discriminatory; and
(c) the measures are accompanied by provisions for the payment of prompt, adequate and effective compensation, which shall be transferable without delay in a freely convertible currency.

[35] *Hulley Enterprises Ltd (Cyprus) v The Russian Federation*, PCA AA 226 (Final Award) (18 July 2014) ¶ 1037; *Yukos Universal Ltd (Isle of Man) v the Russian Federation*, PCA AA 227, (Final Award)

however, that 'Respondent has not explicitly expropriated Yukos or the holdings of its shareholders, but the measures that Respondent has taken in respect of Yukos...have had an effect "equivalent to nationalization or expropriation"',[36] an implicit reference to the language of Article 13 of the ECT which states that 'investment...shall not be nationalized, expropriated or subjected to measures having effect equivalent to nationalization or expropriation...'.

Where a situation presents a clear case of a taking or seizing control of an investor's assets, determining that an expropriation or nationalization has taken place is usually not difficult. However, a difficulty may arise in determining whether the asset expropriated is a protected 'investment' under the treaty. It should be noted that treaties do not protect all investor assets from expropriation—only those that are considered 'investments' under the relevant treaty. Chapter 7 discusses the meaning of 'investment' as it is used in investment treaties. Thus, in the *Swembalt* case, Latvia argued that the ship and the lease of the area where it was to be docked did not constitute an investment 'made in accordance with the laws and regulations' of Latvia, as required by the treaty, and therefore it was not protected against expropriation. The tribunal concluded otherwise in deciding in favour of the investors.

12.5 Indirect Expropriations, Nationalizations, and Dispossessions

In the investment climate of the early twenty-first century, direct expropriations happen infrequently. Far more frequent are *indirect* expropriations, situations in which host states invoke their legislative and regulatory powers to enact measures that reduce the benefits investors derive from their investments but without actually changing or cancelling investors' legal title to their assets or diminishing their control over them. There are various possible explanations for the shift by host governments from direct expropriations to regulatory actions that may constitute indirect expropriations. First, host states that need foreign capital may be reluctant to harm their countries' investment climate by taking the drastic and conspicuous step of openly seizing foreign property. Official acts that seize title or control of a foreign investor's property will attract negative publicity and are likely to do serious damage to the state's reputation as a site for foreign investments. Second, complex contemporary investment transactions, such as concessions, mineral development agreements, and long-term economic development contracts, which are based on shared benefits and risks between the host country and the investor are susceptible to being altered to the benefit of the host country through its regulatory power. In short, effective use of regulatory powers allows the host country

(18 July 2014) ¶1037; *Veteran Petroleum Ltd (Cyprus) v the Russian Federation*, PCA AA 228 (Final Award) (18 July 2014) ¶ 1037 .

[36] ibid ¶ 1580.

to have many of the benefits of an expropriation without actually taking title or seizing control. And third, all host countries have a legitimate right to regulate investors and investments in their territory, but the precise boundary between legitimate regulation and acts that violate a Treaty's expropriation provisions is often difficult to determine. Thus, while the *Feldman* tribunal, quoted earlier, stated that recognizing a direct expropriation was relatively easy, it also said, 'it is much less clear when governmental action that interferes with broadly-defined property rights... crosses the line from valid regulation to a compensable taking, and it is fair to say that no one has come up with a fully satisfactory means of drawing this line'.[37] This lack of a clear line between valid regulation and illegal indirect expropriation may lead governments to use their regulatory power more aggressively against foreign investments than they would otherwise, when they deem it in the public interest.

Because of these factors, cases alleging indirect expropriations have become increasingly important in recent years and instances of direct expropriations have become less frequent. An indirect expropriation leaves the investor's title untouched but significantly reduces an investor's ability to utilize or benefit from the investment. A typical feature of indirect expropriation is that the state denies the very existence of an expropriation and justifies its actions as a legitimate exercise of its regulatory or 'police powers', thereby rejecting the investor's claim of compensation.[38] In many cases, aggrieved investors will allege that a governmental action negatively affecting their investment is both an indirect expropriation and a violation of the fair and equitable treatment standard discussed in Chapter 10. For example, in arbitral decisions arising from the Argentine economic crisis at the beginning of the twenty-first century, tribunals found that governmental actions did not constitute an expropriation but did deny the investor fair and equitable treatment.[39]

In determining whether a regulatory action by a host state constitutes an indirect expropriation, tribunals look primarily to its effect on the investment rather than to the form of the state action or the intent of the government in making it. Thus, in the Energy Charter case of *Nykomb Synergetics Technology Holding AB v Latvia*, the claimant argued that the Latvian government's refusal to pay a double tariff, as was allegedly promised, constituted an 'indirect' or 'creeping' expropriation under Article 13(1), asserting that the denial of such a substantial part of the project's expected income made the enterprise economically unviable and the investment worthless. In that case, the tribunal said:

[37] *Feldman v Mexico*, ICSID Case No ARB(AF)/99/1 (Award on Merits) (16 December 2002) ¶ 100.

[38] Dolzer and Schreuer (n 9 above) 92.

[39] eg *LG&E v Argentine Republic*, ICSID Case No ARB/02/1 (Decision on Liability) (3 October 2006); *CMS Gas Transmission Co v The Argentine Republic*, ICSID Case No ARB/01/8 (Award) (12 May 2005); *Sempra Energy International v The Argentine Republic*, ICSID Case No ARB/02/16 (Award) (28 September 2007).

regulatory takings may under the circumstances amount to expropriation or the equivalent of an expropriation. The decisive factor for drawing the border line towards expropriation must primarily be the degree of possession taking or control over the enterprise the disputed measures entail. In the present case, there is no possession taking of Windau or its assets, no interference with the shareholder's rights or with the management's control over and running of the enterprise—apart from ordinary regulatory provisions laid down in the production license, the off-take agreement, etc.[40]

Thus, despite the fact that a regulatory act may have a negative effect on an investment, expropriation will not be found if the investor retains control of the investment.

As numerous cases have indicated, in evaluating a claim of expropriation it is important to recognize a state's legitimate right to regulate and exercise its police power in the interests of public welfare. Such actions should not be confused with acts of expropriation. The *American Law Institute's Restatement (Third) of the Foreign Relations Law of the United States* underscores this point when it states that 'a state is not responsible for loss of property or for other economic disadvantage resulting from *bone fide* general taxation, regulation, forfeiture for crime, or other action that is commonly accepted as within the police power of states, if it is not discriminatory'.[41]

12.6 Governmental Actions Equivalent or Tantamount to Expropriation

Some investment treaties appear to recognize a third category of expropriatory acts: acts that are tantamount to or equivalent in effect to an expropriation or nationalization. The precise differentiation between this category and the category of indirect expropriations is ephemeral at best, and tribunals have struggled to articulate a meaningful distinction.

Two views towards this category seem to have emerged. One is that the category is somehow broader and more expansive than simple 'indirect expropriations'. Thus, the tribunal in the *Waste Management* case pointed out that Article 1110(1) of NAFTA distinguished between direct or indirect expropriation, on the one hand, and measures tantamount to an expropriation, on the other. It stated that an indirect expropriation was still a taking of property, but a measure tantamount to an expropriation might involve no actual transfer, taking, or loss of property by any person or entity. It might only require 'an effect on property which makes formal distinctions of ownership irrelevant'. It argued that the phrase 'take a measure tantamount to nationalization or expropriation of such an investment' in Article

---

[40] *Nykomb Synergetics Technology Holding AB v Latvia*, SCC 118/2001 (Award) (16 December 2003) ¶ 4.3.1.
[41] American Law Institute, *Restatement of the Law (Third), The Foreign Relations Law of the United States* (3rd edn, 1987) vol 1, § 712, Committee g.

1110(1) was intended to add to the meaning of the prohibition, over and above the reference to indirect expropriation and so to broaden it.[42]

On the other hand, one may also view the concept of 'measures equivalent to expropriation' as simply stating that the concept is co-extensive with that of expropriation or indirect expropriation. Thus, the tribunal in *Pope & Talbot* interpreted 'a measure tantamount to nationalization or expropriation' as referring simply to indirect expropriation. In the tribunal's opinion, the expression 'a measure tantamount to nationalization or expropriation' means nothing more than 'a measure equivalent to nationalization or expropriation'. It therefore rejected the argument that measures tantamount to expropriation can encompass less severe government acts than expropriation itself because 'something that is equivalent to something else cannot logically encompass more.... Thus, measures are covered only if they achieve the same result as expropriation'.[43] In the NAFTA *Metalclad* case, the tribunal stated that expropriation under Article 1110:

includes not only open, deliberate and acknowledged takings of property, such as outright seizure or formal or obligatory transfer of title in favour of the host State, but also covert or incidental interference with the use of property which has the effect of depriving the owner, in whole or in significant part, of the use or reasonably-to-be-expected economic benefit of property even if not necessarily to the obvious benefit of the host State.[44]

In practice, the distinction between indirect expropriations and measures equivalent to expropriations does not appear to be a meaningful one. No case has yet identified a measure that was tantamount to an indirect expropriation but not itself an indirect expropriation. The more important and more challenging distinction for arbitral tribunals is the distinction between legitimate regulatory acts and regulatory actions that amount to an indirect expropriation or that have effects equal or tantamount to an expropriation.

12.7 Types of Government Measures that May Constitute Indirect Expropriation

As illustrated by the decisions of arbitral tribunals, investors have sought with mixed success to challenge the following types of host government measures as expropriation: (1) disproportionate tax increases; (2) interference with contract rights; (3) interference with the management of an investment; and (4) revocation or denial of government permits or licences. Each of these types of measures is now examined briefly.

---

[42] *Waste Management, Inc v United Mexican States (No 2)*, ICSID Case No ARB(AF)/00/3 (Final Award) (30 April 2004) ¶¶ 143–144.
[43] *Pope & Talbot Inc v The Government of Canada*, UNCITRAL (Interim Award) (26 June 2000) ¶¶ 96, 104.
[44] *Metalclad Corp v Mexico*, ICSID Case No ARB(AF)/97/1 (Award) (30 August 2000) ¶ 103.

(a) Disproportionate tax increases

Host countries may use their power to levy taxes as a means to limit and even curtail the activities of foreign investors and investments. While taxation, even if onerous, may be a legitimate means of raising public revenue, it is possible for taxes to be so high that they are confiscatory and constitute expropriation. *Revere Copper v OPIC*[45] arose out of a concession contract with the Jamaican government that contained a stabilization clause concerning taxes and other financial burdens. Subsequently, in violation of contractual obligations, the government drastically increased the taxes and royalties on Revere Copper to the point that its investments became economically unviable. Revere thereafter sought to recover compensation from the US Overseas Private Investment Corporation (OPIC) because OPIC's political risk insurance policy provided coverage against 'expropriatory action'. OPIC refused the request on the grounds that Revere Copper continued to have all the property rights it had had before the tax increase. Revere then instituted arbitral proceedings, as was permitted by its insurance policy. The tribunal, by a vote of 2 to 1, rejected OPIC's argument, but with a lengthy and vigorous dissenting opinion. The majority based its decision on the grounds that the Jamaican government's repudiation of its commitments had rendered the investor's control, use, and operation of its properties no longer effective.[46]

The *Revere Copper* case did not arise under an investment treaty and was not an example of investor–state arbitration. Nonetheless, its conclusion does support the proposition that a drastic tax increase, particularly when it violates a pre-existing government agreement, can amount to expropriation. This understanding accords with the approach taken by the tribunal in *Link-Trading Joint Stock Co v Moldova*,[47] a case that arose out of the US–Moldova BIT. The tribunal there stated:

As a general matter, fiscal measures only become expropriatory when they are found to be an abusive taking. Abuse arises where it is demonstrated that the State has acted unfairly or inequitably towards the investment, where it has adopted measures that are arbitrary or discriminatory in character or in their manner of implementation, or where the measures taken violate an obligation undertaken by the State in regard to the investment.[48]

Two other investor–state cases based on treaty provisions also raised the issue of whether an increase in taxes can constitute an expropriation. Both cases were brought against Ecuador. *EnCana Corporation v Republic of Ecuador*[49] and

---

[45] *Re Revere Copper and Brass Inc v Overseas Private Investment Corp* (Award) (24 August 1978) (1978) 17 ILM 1321.

[46] ibid 1348–53.

[47] *Link-Trading Joint Stock Co v Department for Customs Control of the Republic of Moldova*, UNCITRAL (Final Award) (18 April 2002). See also *Burlington Resources, Inc v Republic of Ecuador*, ICSID Case No ARB/08/5 (Decision on Liability) (14 December 2012) ¶ 393, which found that customary international law limits the power to tax in two ways: taxes may not be discriminatory and they may not be confiscatory.

[48] ibid ¶ 64.

[49] *EnCana Corp v Republic of Ecuador*, LCIA Case No UN3481 (Award) (3 February 2006).

Occidental Exploration and Production Company v The Republic of Ecuador[50] each alleged indirect expropriation through taxation. At issue were the claimants' right to value-added tax (VAT) refunds to which they believed themselves entitled under the law at the time of investment and Ecuador's right to issue interpretative rulings retroactively excluding petroleum companies from such refunds. In *EnCana*, the tribunal rejected the indirect expropriation claim on the ground that, despite the denial of VAT refunds, the companies continued to operate profitably. It stated that 'in the absence of a specific commitment from the host state, the foreign investor has neither the rights nor any legitimate expectations that the tax regime will not change, perhaps to its disadvantage, during the period of investment'. It added that 'only if a tax is extraordinary, punitive in amount or arbitrary in its incidence would issues of indirect expropriation be raised'.[51] The tribunal recognized that a law cancelling a state's accrued liability to an investor might amount to direct expropriation, but it rejected the investors' direct expropriation claim on the grounds that Ecuador's refusal to refund VAT payments was not 'merely willful' and that independent national courts were available to the investors.[52] In *Occidental*, the tribunal dismissed the expropriation claims on the ground that the measure did not affect a substantial portion of the investment.[53]

Based on the foregoing, one must conclude that since taxation falls within a state's normal police power, for a tax measure to constitute indirect expropriation it would need to be extraordinarily excessive and arbitrary and to violate an existing agreement with the investor.

(b) Interference with contractual rights

Many governmental actions taken for public policy reasons can negatively affect an investor's contractual rights. As indicated earlier in the chapter, international law protects contract rights from expropriation, and investment treaties have sought to broaden and deepen that protection significantly. On the basis of such treaty provisions, investors have brought arbitral claims against host countries with varying degrees of success by claiming that government measures affected their contractual rights to the point that they constituted expropriation.

In *CME v Czech Republic*, an investor–state dispute based on the Netherlands–Czech Republic BIT, the investor complained about interference with its contractual rights by a government-established regulatory authority, the Media Council. It argued that such interference undermined the contractually guaranteed licence of the local partner of the investor, which was crucial for the investment project because of its exclusivity. The tribunal found that the

---

[50] *Occidental Exploration and Production Co v The Republic of Ecuador*, LCIA Case No UN3467 (Award) (1 July 2004).

[51] *EnCana Corp v Republic of Ecuador*, LCIA Case No UN3481 (Award) (3 February 2006) ¶¶ 173, 177.

[52] ibid ¶ 194.

[53] *Occidental Exploration and Production Co v The Republic of Ecuador*, LCIA Case No UN3467 (Award) (1 July 2004) ¶ 89.

regulatory authority had breached the treaty's provision against indirect expropriation by reversing its earlier position and forcing the investor to accept the amendments to the contract. This act resulted in a loss of legal security.[54] The tribunal found irrelevant the respondent's view that the Media Council's actions did not deprive the investor of value because there had been no physical taking of property by the state and because the original licence always had been held by the original licensee and kept untouched. It found that 'what was touched and indeed destroyed was the investor's investment and the commercial value of the investment by reason of coercion exerted by the Media Council'.[55] It should be noted, however, that in *Lauder v Czech Republic*, a different tribunal deciding the same set of facts under a different BIT, came to the opposite conclusion. It found that the respondent state 'did not take any measure of, or tantamount to, expropriation of the Claimant's property rights within any of the time periods, since there was no direct or indirect interference by the Czech Republic in the use of Mr. Lauder's property or with the enjoyment of its benefits'.[56] Moreover, it pointed to the fact that there was no evidence that any measure of the Czech government transferred, deprived, or interfered with the claimant's property rights.[57]

Not every failure by a government to perform a contract amounts to an expropriation, even if the violation leads to a loss of contractual rights. A simple contractual breach by a state is not an expropriation.[58] Tribunals have found that a determining factor is whether the state acted in an official, governmental capacity.[59] In *Siemens v Argentina*, the tribunal observed that a host state party breaching a contract only breaches the applicable treaty if the behaviour goes beyond what an ordinary contracting party could adopt.[60] It stated:

for the State to incur international responsibility it must act as such, it must use its public authority. The actions of the State have to be based on its superior governmental power. It is not a matter of disappointment in the performance of the State in the execution of a contract but rather of interference in the contract execution through governmental actions.[61]

---

[54] *CME Czech Republic BV v Czech Republic*, UNCITRAL (Partial Award) (13 September 2001) ¶¶ 591–609.

[55] ibid ¶ 591.

[56] *Ronald S Lauder v Czech Republic*, UNCITRAL (Final Award) (3 September 2001), ¶ 201.

[57] ibid ¶ 202.

[58] SM Schwebel, 'On Whether a Breach by a State of a Contract with an Alien is a Breach of International Law' in *International Law at the Time of its Codification, Essays in Honor of Roberto Ago, III* (Giuffrè, 1987) 401.

[59] *Impregilo SpA v Islamic Republic of Pakistan*, ICSID Case No ARB/03/3 (Decision on Jurisdiction) (22 April 2005) ¶ 281; *Bayindir Insaat Turizm Ticaret Ve Sanayi AS v Islamic Republic of Pakistan*, ICSID Case No ARB/03/29 (Decision on Jurisdiction) (14 November 2005) ¶ 257; *Azurix v Argentine Republic*, ICSID Case No ARB/01/12 (Award) (14 July 2006) ¶ 315; *Parkerings-Compagniet AS v Republic of Lithuania*, ICSID Case No ARB/05/8 (Award) (11 September 2007) ¶ 443; *Biwater Gauff (Tanzania) Ltd v United Republic of Tanzania*, ICSID Case No ARB/05/22 (Award) (24 July 2008) ¶ 458.

[60] *Siemens v Argentina*, ICSID Case No ARB/02/8 (Award) (6 February 2007) ¶ 248.

[61] ibid ¶ 253.

In the NAFTA case of *Waste Management*, the tribunal adopted a similar position:

The mere non-performance of contractual obligations is not to be equated with a taking of property, nor (unless accompanied by other elements) is it tantamount to expropriation. Any private party can fail to perform its contracts, whereas nationalization and expropriation are inherently governmental acts.... The tribunal concludes that it is one thing to expropriate a right under a contract and another to fail to comply with the contract. Non-compliance by the government with contractual obligations is not the same thing as, or equivalent or tantamount to, an expropriation.[62]

Despite the guidance offered by this jurisprudence, determining when a state is invoking its governmental powers with respect to a contract and when it is engaged in simple non-performance is not always easy, clear, or self-evident.

(c) Unjustified interference with the management of the investment

An indirect expropriation may also take place as a result of governmental measures that significantly interfere with or entirely remove an investor's actual management control over an investment. This can occur when an investor is physically or legally impeded from its management tasks or when investor-controlled management is replaced with government-appointed management. Such interference may constitute an indirect expropriation alone or in conjunction with other acts or omissions that effectively deprive an investor of its property rights. The crucial element in such a determination is the degree or magnitude of the interference resulting from such conduct.

An example of such interference occurred in *Biloune v Ghana*, which concerned an investment project to build a restaurant complex through the investor's local subsidiary, MDCL. The project was substantially under way when local governmental authorities issued a stop work order and arrested and expelled the investor. The tribunal noted that given the central role of Mr Biloune in promoting, financing, and managing MDCL, his expulsion from the country effectively prevented MDCL from pursuing its project and, therefore, constituted an indirect expropriation of MDCL's contractual rights in the project and consequently an indirect expropriation of the value of Mr Biloune's interest in MDCL.[63]

In *Benvenuti & Bonfant*, the tribunal concluded that the cumulative effect of a series of governmental acts and omissions amounted to a *de facto* expropriation. These acts and omissions included interference with the marketing of the investors' products by fixing sales prices, dissolving a marketing company, instituting criminal proceedings against the investor who then left the country, and finally

---

[62] *Waste Management, Inc v United Mexican States (II)*, ICSID Case No ARB(AF)/00/3 (Final Award) (30 April 2004) ¶¶ 184–185.

[63] *Biloune and Marine Drive Complex Ltd v Ghana Investments Centre and the Government of Ghana*, UNCITRAL (Award on Jurisdiction and Liability) (27 October 1989).

the physical takeover of the investors' premises.[64] Thus, the host state's measures may amount to an expropriation when they are directed against an investor who is crucial for the profitable management and operation of the investment.

Although they did not involve investment treaties, two Iran–US claims tribunal cases, *Starrett Housing Corporation v Government of the Islamic Republic of Iran*[65] and *Tippetts, Abbett, McCarthy, Stratton v TAMS-AFFA Consulting Engineers of Iran*,[66] also found expropriations as a result of the Iranian Revolutionary government's appointment of new managers of investments owned by US nationals.

(d) Revocation or denial of government permits or licences

Several cases have found that a government's revocation of approved licences or permits constitutes an expropriation. The cases of *Goetz* and *Middle East Cement* involved investment disputes in which a government's revocation of an investor's free zone benefits was determined to have an effect similar to expropriation. In *Goetz*, Burundi revoked the investor's free zone status without any formal taking of property. Applying the Belgium-Luxembourg Economic Union–Burundi BIT, the tribunal held that 'the government's actions fell within the concept of measures having the effect similar to expropriation, ie they constituted indirect expropriation'. It also stated:

Since...the revocation by the Minister for Industry and Commerce of the free zone certificate forced [the investors] to halt all activities...which deprived their investments of all utility and deprived the claimant investors of the benefit which they could have expected from their investments, the disputed decision can be regarded as a 'measure having similar effect' to a measure depriving of or restricting property within the meaning of Article 4 of the Investment Treaty.[67]

Middle East Cement concerned the revocation of a free zone licence by the Egyptian government when it prohibited importation of cement. The tribunal found that the investor had been deprived of the use and benefit of its investment even though it retained the nominal ownership of its rights. It therefore concluded that Egypt had breached the Egypt–Greece BIT's clause prohibiting measures whose effects are tantamount to expropriation.[68]

Governmental permits are essential for businesses to operate in many economic areas. The revocation or non-renewal of permits by the government can in some circumstances amount to an indirect expropriation even though the

---

[64] *Benvenuti & Bonfant v Congo*, ICSID Case No ARB/77/2 (Award) (8 August 1980).

[65] *Starrett Housing Corp v Government of the Islamic Republic of Iran* (19 December 1983) 4 Iran-USCTR 122, 154.

[66] *Tippetts, Abbett, McCarthy, Stratton v TAMS-AFFA Consulting Engineers of Iran* (29 June 1984) 6 Iran-USCTR 219, 225.

[67] *Goetz and Ors v Republic of Burundi*, ICSID Case No ARB/95/3 (Award) (2 September 1998) ¶ 124.

[68] *Middle East Cement Shipping and Handling Co SA v Arab Republic of Egypt*, ICSID Case No ARB/99/6 (Award) (12 April 2002) ¶ 107.

investor retains full ownership and control of business assets. For example, in *Técnicas Medioambientales Tecmed SA v The United Mexican States*,[69] the claimant, a Spanish company, purchased a hazardous waste landfill from a Mexican government agency in 1995 and operated it under an annually renewable authorization. When the agency of the Mexican government charged with enforcing environmental policy adopted a resolution refusing to renew the authorization and ordering the landfill to be closed, the claimant instituted arbitration against Mexico on grounds that the agency's actions amounted to indirect expropriation under the Mexico–Spain BIT. The tribunal, focusing on the effects of such action, concluded that the agency's action was equivalent to an expropriation.[70]

The NAFTA case of *Metalclad Corporation v The United Mexican States*[71] also dealt with the refusal to issue a permit for a landfill in Mexico. In that case, the Mexican federal government specifically assured the investor that its landfill project complied with all the relevant environmental and planning regulations; however, in response to local opposition and without legal authority, the municipality of Guadalcazar denied the project a construction permit. The arbitral tribunal determined that the denial, as well as a subsequent action by the governor declaring the land in question a protected area because it was the site of a rare cactus, constituted indirect expropriation of the investor's investment. The tribunal stated:

by permitting or tolerating the conduct of Guadalcazar in relation to Metalclad which has already been found to amount to unfair and inequitable treatment breaching Article 1105 and by thus participating or acquiescing in the denial to *Metalclad* of the right to operate the landfill, notwithstanding the fact that the project was fully approved and endorsed by the federal government, Mexico must be held to have taken a measure tantamount to expropriation in violation of NAFTA Article 1110(1).[72]

The cited cases illustrate some of the circumstances that give rise to indirect expropriations by host state regulatory measures. In each case, the respondents stated in defence that their action was an exercise of their police powers and necessary to protect the public welfare. The question, as many arbitral tribunals have stated, is: Where should the line be drawn between an indirect expropriation that entails the international responsibility to compensate for the inflicted damages and a non-compensable regulatory measure? No definitive answer exists. However, arbitrators and scholars have pointed to certain criteria that may be useful in determining that elusive dividing line.

---

[69] *Técnicas Medioambientales Tecmed SA v The United Mexican States*, ICSID Case No ARB(AF) 00/2 (Award) (29 May 2003).

[70] ibid ¶ 151.

[71] *Metalclad Corp v The United Mexican States*, ICSID Case No ARB(AF)/97/1 (Award) (3 August 2000).

[72] ibid ¶ 128.

12.8 Criteria for Distinguishing Indirect Expropriation from Legitimate Regulation

In applying the expropriation clauses to modern concrete situations, most contemporary arbitral tribunals have struggled to define the precise boundary between legitimate host country regulation and illegitimate regulatory takings. In its summary of expropriation jurisprudence under NAFTA, the tribunal in *Fireman's Fund Insurance Company v United Mexican States*[73] listed the following factors as relevant: (1) whether the measure is within the recognized police powers of the host state; (2) the public purpose and effect of the measure; (3) whether the measure is discriminatory; (4) the proportionality between the means employed and the aim sought to be realized; and (5) the bona fide nature of the measure. It also stated that the investor's reasonable 'investment-backed expectations' may be a relevant factor in determining whether an indirect expropriation occurred. While these elements constitute a useful framework for evaluating whether a specific governmental measure constitutes a regulatory taking or an indirect expropriation, their application to specific cases is by no means easy or automatic.

Although the texts of investment treaties do not ordinarily provide guidance on how to distinguish between indirect expropriation and legitimate regulation, an examination of arbitral jurisprudence on this question does provide some illumination. As a group, relevant arbitral decisions point to a number of criteria that may be helpful in drawing a line between a compensable indirect expropriation and non-compensable regulatory measures. These include: (1) the degree of intensity of interference with investor property rights; (2) the frustration of investors' legitimate expectations; (3) lack of proportionality; (4) non-transparency, arbitrariness, and discrimination; and (5) the effects and purpose of the measure.

(a) Degree of interference with investor property rights

The purpose of expropriation provisions in treaties is to protect investors' property rights. Therefore, the greater the interference with those rights by governmental regulatory measures, the more likely it is that a tribunal will find an indirect expropriation. Two factors in particular are relevant in evaluating the magnitude of a host government's interference through a regulatory measure with an investor's property rights: (1) the severity of its economic impact and effect on the investor's control over the investments; and (2) the duration of the regulatory measure.

---

[73] *Fireman's Fund Insurance Co v United Mexican States*, ICSID Case No ARB(AF)/02/1 (Award) (17 July 2006) ¶ 176.

(i) Severity of economic impact and loss of effective control

International tribunals treat the severity of the economic impact caused by a regulatory measure as an important element in determining whether the measure constitutes an expropriation requiring compensation. One question often asked is whether the measure in question resulted in 'substantial deprivation' of the investment or its economic benefits. Thus, the tribunal in *Occidental v Ecuador*,[74] discussed earlier in this chapter, had to consider whether Ecuador's refusal to refund to Occidental VAT to which the state was entitled to under Ecuadorian law constituted a measure tantamount to an expropriation. It concluded that the measure in question did not constitute indirect expropriation because 'the criterion of "substantial deprivation" was not present in that case, since in fact, there has been no deprivation of the use of the investment, let alone measures affecting a significant part of the investment'.[75]

Tribunals have also applied the test of substantial deprivation in cases challenging measures taken by Argentina to deal with the severe financial and economic crisis it experienced in 2001–02.[76] For example, in *CMS v Argentina*, the claimant, an investor in a gas transportation company, alleged that Argentina's decision to suspend a tariff adjustment formula for gas transportation during the crisis constituted an indirect expropriation. In evaluating this claim, the tribunal, after reviewing the relevant arbitral jurisprudence, stated that 'the essential question is to establish whether the enjoyment of the property has been effectively neutralized' because 'the standard...where indirect expropriation is contended is that of substantial deprivation'.[77] Although the tribunal recognized that the measures under dispute had an important effect on the investor's business, it found no substantial deprivation and thus no breach of the expropriation provision of the Argentina–US BIT. It also noted that 'the investor is in control of the investment; the government does not manage the day-to-day operations of the company; and the investor has full ownership and control of the investment'.[78]

Similarly, in *LG&E v Argentina*,[79] which also arose out of the Argentine crisis, the investors brought indirect expropriation claims when the value of their licences was reduced by more than 90 per cent as a result of Argentina's abrogation of the principal guarantees of the tariff system. The tribunal observed that in order to establish whether state measures constitute expropriation under the relevant BIT expropriation clause, one 'must balance two competing interests: the degree of the

---

[74] *Occidental Exploration and Production Co v The Republic of Ecuador*, LCIA Case No UN3467 (Final Award) (1 July 2004).

[75] ibid ¶ 89.

[76] See *BG Group plc v The Republic of Argentina*, UNCITRAL (Final Award) (24 December 2007) ¶ 271; *El Paso Energy International Co v The Argentine Republic*, ICSID Case No ARB/03/15 (Award) (31 October 2011) ¶ 256.

[77] *CMS Gas Transmission Co v The Argentine Republic*, ICSID Case No ARB/01/8 (Award) (12 May 2005) ¶ 262.

[78] ibid ¶ 263.

[79] *LG&E Energy Corp, LG&E Capital Corp, LG&E International INC v Argentine Republic*, ICSID Case No ARB/02/1 (Decision on Liability) (3 October 2006).

measure's interference with the right of ownership and the power of the State to adopt its policies'.[80] According to the tribunal, an evaluation of the measure's interference with the investor's right of ownership must take into account the measure's economic impact—its interference with the investor's reasonable expectations—and the measure's duration.[81] In considering the severity of the economic impact, 'the analysis must focus on whether the economic impact unleashed by the measure adopted by the host State was sufficiently severe as to generate the need for compensation due to expropriation'.[82] The tribunal noted that sufficient interference with the investment's ability to carry on its business does not meet this standard when the investment continues to operate, even if profits are diminished. It held that 'the impact must be substantial in order that compensation may be claimed for the expropriation'.[83] In the circumstances of that case, the tribunal found that, although Argentina adopted severe measures that undoubtedly had an impact on the investment's expected earnings, the measures did not deprive the investors of the right to enjoy their investment, nor did they lose control of their shares in its licensees, even though the value of the shares may have fluctuated during the economic crisis. The tribunal also found relevant that the investor was able to direct the day-to-day operations of the licensees in a manner similar to what had been possible before the measures were implemented; consequently, it rejected the claims of indirect expropriation.

Several NAFTA cases have also considered the severity of the economic impact of a challenged state measure to determine whether an indirect expropriation occurred.[84] In addition, the first case to be decided under the ECT also dealt with the issue. In *Nykomb Synergetics Technology Holding AB v Latvia*[85] the investor contended that the non-payment of an allegedly promised double tariff by Latvia constituted an indirect expropriation, since the non-payment resulted in a substantial loss of sales income and made the enterprise economically unviable. The tribunal, like others concerned with drawing the line between legitimate regulation and illegal indirect expropriation, acknowledged that under certain circumstances regulatory measures may be equivalent to expropriation. '[T]he decisive factor for drawing the borderline towards expropriation must primarily be the degree of possession taking or control over the enterprise the disputed measures entail.'[86] Since Latvia did not take possession of the investor or its assets and did not interfere with shareholders' rights or with management's control of the enterprise—apart from ordinary regulatory provisions—the tribunal concluded that the challenged governmental measures were not equivalent to expropriation.[87]

---

[80] ibid ¶ 189.　　[81] ibid ¶ 190.　　[82] ibid ¶ 191.　　[83] ibid ¶ 194.

[84] eg *SD Myers, Inc v Canada*, UNCITRAL (First Partial Award) (13 November 2000); *Pope & Talbot Inc v The Government of Canada*, UNCITRAL (Interim Award) (26 June 2000); *GAMI Investments, Inc v Mexico*, UNCITRAL (Final Award) (15 November 2004).

[85] *Nykomb Synergetics Technology Holding AB v Latvia*, SCC 118/2001 (Award) (16 December 2003).

[86] ibid ¶ 4.3.1.

[87] See also *Generation Ukraine, Inc v Ukraine*, ICSID Case No ARB/00/9 (Award) (16 September 2003), in which the tribunal, applying the US–Ukraine BIT, concluded that the failure of the Kyiv City State Administration to provide lease agreements for a construction project of an office building did not amount to an expropriation because the respondent's conduct 'did not come close to

However, the arbitral tribunal in *Revere Copper*, discussed previously, found an expropriation by looking at the impact of the regulation on effective control over the use and operation of the investor's property.[88] Although formal ownership was not affected by the governmental measures, the tribunal found that the investor's control, use, and operation of its investments were no longer 'effective'.

(ii) Duration of the governmental measure

The duration of the challenged measure is another element considered in deciding whether it is tantamount to an expropriation. In *SD Myers*, the NAFTA tribunal reinforced the distinction between indirect expropriation and regulation by observing that 'an expropriation usually amounts to a lasting removal of the ability of an owner to make use of its economic rights', although it did acknowledge that in some contexts even a partial or temporary deprivation could amount to expropriation.[89] In that case, the tribunal did not find the temporary export ban on certain hazardous waste to amount to expropriation because it lasted only a short time.

Similarly, the tribunal in *LG&E* held that in evaluating the degree of the interference with the investor's right of ownership one should analyse not only the measure's economic impact but also 'the duration of the measure as it relates to the degree of interference with the investor's ownership rights'.[90] The tribunal observed that 'generally, the expropriation must be permanent, that is to say, it cannot have a temporary nature unless the investment's successful development depends on the realization of certain activities at specific moments that may not endure variations'.[91] In that case, the effect of Argentina's regulatory measures on the value of the investments in question was not found to be permanent. Therefore, the tribunal concluded that 'without a permanent, severe deprivation of LG&E's rights with regard to its investment, or almost complete deprivation of the value of LG&E's investment'[92] Argentina's challenged measure could not be held as equivalent to expropriation.

The tribunals in the *Tecmed* and *Generation Ukraine* cases also considered the temporal quality of the challenged regulatory measure to be important in assessing the degree of its interference with the investor's property rights. The former held that measures adopted by a state constitute an indirect expropriation if they are, among other things, irreversible and permanent.[93] The latter found that the

---

creating a persistent or irreparable obstacle to the investor's use, enjoyment, or disposal of its investments'. ibid ¶ 20.32.

[88] *Re Revere Copper and Brass, Inc v Overseas Private Investment Corp* (Award) (24 August 1978) (1978) 17 ILM 1321.

[89] *SD Myers, Inc v Canada*, UNCITRAL (First Partial Award) (13 November 2000) ¶ 283.

[90] *LG&E Energy Corp, LG&E Capital Corp, LG&E International INC v Argentine Republic*, ICSID Case No ARB/02/1 (Decision on Liability) (3 October 2006) ¶ 190.

[91] ibid ¶ 194.   [92] ibid ¶ 200.

[93] *Técnicas Medioambientales Tecmed SA v The United Mexican States*, ICSID Case No ARB(AF) 00/2 (Award) (29 May 2003) ¶ 116.

challenged regulatory measure 'did not come close to creating a persistent or irreparable obstacle to the Claimant's use, enjoyment or disposal of its investment'.[94]

Thus, the severity of the economic impact is a crucial test in determining whether a regulatory measure gives rise to indirect expropriation. Arbitral jurisprudence provides broad support for the proposition that to constitute an expropriation, a challenged measure has to interfere with an investment to the point that it deprives the investor of his or her fundamental rights of ownership, use, enjoyment, or management in a permanent or persistent way.

(b) Frustration of the investor's legitimate expectations

The concept of the investor's legitimate expectations, discussed in Chapter 9 with respect to fair and equitable treatment, has been acknowledged in international jurisprudence[95] as important in protecting investors' property rights. A host state's frustration of such expectations may play a crucial role in finding a breach of the fair and equitable treatment standard and also in a determination of indirect expropriation.[96]

Foreign investors invest not only to acquire assets but also to achieve particular economic benefits that they reasonably expect to derive from such assets. Most governments, through their laws and representations to the investors, often encourage and sometimes create these expectations. Government statements, whether expressed in advertisements, during promotional 'road shows', or during direct negotiations with specific foreign investors, may also create expectations upon which investors rely in making investment decisions. Consequently, a host country's failure to honour its assurances may adversely affect investors' reasonably expected economic benefits and so is a factor in judging whether a measure constitutes indirect expropriation. Thus, in *Metalclad v Mexico*, the tribunal found that 'Metalclad was led to believe, and did in fact believe, that federal and state permits allowed for the construction and operation of the landfill',[97] and as a result it was

---

[94] *Generation Ukraine, Inc v Ukraine*, ICSID Case No ARB/00/9 (Award) (16 September 2003) ¶ 20.32.

[95] *Kuwait v American Independent Oil Co* (Final Award) (24 March 1982) (1982) 21 ILM 976, 1034; *Metalclad Corp v The United Mexican States*, ICSID Case No ARB(AF)/97/1 (Award) (3 August 2000) ¶ 99; *International Thunderbird Gaming Corp v United Mexican States*, UNCITRAL (Award) (26 January 2006) ¶ 147; *INA Corp v Iran* (1985) 8 Iran-USCTR 373, 385 (Lagergren, J, separate opinion); *National & Provincial Building Society v United Kingdom*, ECHR App Nos 21319/93, 21449/93, 21675/93 (Judgment) (23 October 1997) Reports 1997-VII, 2325, 2347–50; *Prince Hans-Adam II of Liechtenstein v Germany*, ECHR App No 42527/98 (Judgment) (12 July 2001) 83.

[96] See, however, the tribunal in *El Paso v Argentina*, which determined that because '[t]here is not always a clear distinction between *indirect expropriation* and *violation of legitimate expectations*...the violation of a legitimate expectation should rather be protected by the fair and equitable treatment standard'. *El Paso Energy International Co v The Argentine Republic*, ICSID Case No ARB/03/15 (Award) (31 October 2011) ¶ 227. This approach could not apply if the treaty expressly included investor expectations within the indirect expropriation standard.

[97] *Metalclad Corp v The United Mexican States*, ICSID Case No ARB(AF)/97/1 (Award) (3 August 2000) ¶ 100.

led to rely on 'the reasonably-to-be-expected economic benefit'.[98] Consequently, its inability to carry out the investment project frustrated those expectations and so constituted an additional factor in finding that the governmental measures were tantamount to expropriation. Similarly, when asking whether the revocation of a permit amounted to an expropriation, the tribunal in *Tecmed* also referred to the legitimate expectations of the investor. It stated that 'even before the investor made its investment, it was widely known that it expected its investments in the project to last for a long term and that it took this into account to estimate the time and business required to recover such investment and obtain the expected return upon making its tender offer for the acquisition of the assets related to that investment project'.[99] Therefore, as the tribunal stressed, 'the Mexican governmental authorities could not be unaware of that and of the need to act in line with such legitimate expectations to avoid rendering unfeasible any private investment of the scale required to confine hazardous waste in the United Mexican States under acceptable technical operating conditions'. Investor expectations, according to the tribunal, 'should be considered legitimate and should be evaluated in light of the Agreement and of international law when ascertaining whether the host state's actions violate the investment treaty that accords protection against measures equivalent to an expropriation'.[100]

In response to the growing number of arbitral claims challenging regulatory measures as indirect expropriations, and the difficulty in judging them against traditional treaty provisions, some recent treaties have sought to provide more detailed guidance regarding the factors to be considered in determining whether a measure violates expropriation clauses. Examples of such treaties include various US free trade agreements (FTAs),[101] the Malaysia-Australia FTA,[102] recent Canadian BITs,[103]

---

[98] ibid ¶ 103.

[99] *Tecnicas Medioambientales Tecmed SA v The United Mexican States*, ICSID Case No ARB(AF) 00/2 (Award) (29 May 2003) ¶ 149.

[100] ibid ¶ 150.

[101] US–Singapore Free Trade Agreement (6 May 2003); US–Chile Free Trade Agreement (6 June 2003).US–Australia Free Trade Agreement (18 May 2004); US–Morocco Free Trade Agreement (15 June 2004).

[102] Malaysia–Australia Free Trade Agreement (22 May 2012).

[103] Agreement between Canada and the Republic of Peru for the Promotion and Protection of Investments (14 November 2006); Agreement between the Government of Canada and the Government of the Republic of Latvia for the Promotion and Protection of Investments (5 May 2009); Agreement between Canada and the Czech Republic for the Promotion and Protection of Investments (6 May 2009); Agreement between the Government of Canada and the Government of Romania for the Promotion and Reciprocal Protection of Investments (8 May 2009); Agreement between Canada and the Hashemite Kingdom of Jordan for the Promotion and Protection of Investments (28 June 2009); Agreement between Canada and the Slovak Republic for the Promotion and Protection of Investments (20 July 2010); Agreement between the Government of Canada and the Government of the People's Republic of China for the Promotion and Reciprocal Protection of Investments (8 September 2012); Agreement Between the Government of Canada and the Government of the Republic of Benin for the Promotion and Reciprocal Protection of Investments (9 January 2013).

recent Indian BITs,[104] the US–Uruguay BIT,[105] the 2012 US Model BIT, and the Japan–Korea–China Trilateral Investment Agreement.[106] Thus, the US–Uruguay BIT states that its expropriation provisions are to be interpreted in accordance with Annex B of the treaty. Annex B provides that in determining whether an action constitutes indirect expropriation one of the factors to be considered is 'the extent to which the government action interferes with distinct, reasonable investment-backed expectations'.[107] In general, treaties adopting this approach have been fairly specific in defining the nature of such investment-backed expectations. In particular, they must be 'distinct' and 'reasonable' to be weighed by a tribunal in determining whether a government measure constitutes indirect expropriation. The Malaysia–Australia FTA is even more specific, providing for consideration of 'whether the government action breaches the government's prior binding written commitment, where applicable, to the investor whether by contract, licence or other legal document'.[108] Thus, these treaties generally appear to adopt the approach of traditional international law jurisprudence and state practice that requires a regulatory measure be held equivalent to expropriation only if it interferes with clearly ascertainable and reasonable investment-backed expectations, not just the investor's subjective hopes.[109]

(c) Lack of proportionality

In judging whether a government's measure constitutes indirect expropriation, tribunals have also examined whether the challenged measure is reasonably proportional to the purpose the government seeks to achieve. One important factor of this analysis is the impact of the measure on a foreign investor versus the impact on host country nationals. A lack of proportionality may be found if foreign investors bear an excessive amount of the burden imposed by the measure.

[104] Agreement for the Promotion and Protection of Investments between the Republic of Colombia and the Republic of India (10 November 2009); Agreement between the Government of the Republic of India and the Government of Latvia for the Promotion and Protection of Investments (18 February 2010); Agreement between the Government of the Republic of India and the Government of the Republic of Lithuania for the Promotion and Protection of Investments (31 March 2011); Agreement between the Government of the Republic of India and the Government of the Republic of Slovenia on the Mutual Promotion and Protection of Investments (14 June 2011); Agreement between the Government of India and the Government of Nepal for the Promotion and Protection of Investments (21 October 2011).

[105] Treaty between the United States of America and the Oriental Republic of Uruguay Concerning the Encouragement and Reciprocal Protection of Investment (4 November 2005).

[106] Agreement among the Government of Japan, the Government of the Republic of Korea and the Government of the People's Republic of China for the Promotion, Facilitation and Protection of Investment (13 May 2012).

[107] Treaty between the United States of America and the Oriental Republic of Uruguay Concerning the Encouragement and Reciprocal Protection of Investment (4 November 2005) Annex B, at 4(a)(ii).

[108] Malaysia–Australia Free Trade Agreement (22 May 2012), Annex on Expropriation, at 3(b).

[109] eg *Oscar Chinn* Case (*UK v Belgium*) (Judgment) (12 December 1934) (1934) PCIJ Series A/B, No 63, at 88; *Starrett Housing Corp v The Government of the Islamic Republic of Iran* (19 December 1983) 4 Iran-USCTR 122, 256.

One important source of the proportionality test is found in the jurisprudence of the European Court of Human Rights. That Court has held:

Not only must a measure depriving a person of his property pursue, on the facts as well as in principle, a legitimate aim 'in the public interest,' but there must also be a reasonable relationship of proportionality between the means employed and the aim sought to be realised... [t]he requisite balance will not be found if the person concerned has had to bear an individual and excessive burden... [therefore,] the Court considers that a measure must be both appropriate for achieving its aim and not disproportionate thereto.[110]

In reaching this conclusion, the Court took into account the fact that 'non-nationals are more vulnerable to domestic legislation: unlike nationals, they will generally have played no part in the election or designation of its authors nor have been consulted on its adoption'. Additionally, it noted that 'although a taking of property must always be effected in the public interest, different considerations may apply to nationals and non-nationals and there may well be legitimate reason for requiring nationals to bear a greater burden in the public interest than non-nationals'.[111]

The test for proportionality, as developed by the European Court of Human Rights, has influenced the approach of investor–state arbitration tribunals when applying treaty provisions to governmental measures that allegedly amount to indirect expropriation. In *Tecmed v Mexico*, the tribunal stated that in addition to the negative financial impact of regulatory measures on foreign investments, the question of whether such measures were proportional to the public interest protected and to the protection legally granted to the investments should also be considered. While acknowledging that the starting point for such an analysis should be due deference to the state's determination of issues affecting public policy and society as a whole, as well as what actions are necessary to protect those interests, the tribunal found that that deference would not prevent it from examining the actions of Mexico in the light of the Spain–Mexico BIT's expropriation clause.[112] The tribunal determined that the expropriation clause asked whether such measures 'are reasonable with respect to their goals, the deprivation of economic rights and the legitimate expectations of who suffered such deprivation'.[113] Affirming that 'there must be a reasonable relationship of proportionality between the charge or weight imposed to the foreign investor and the aim sought to be realized by any expropriatory measure', the *Tecmed* tribunal explained that 'to value such charge or weight, it is very important to measure the size of the ownership deprivation caused by the actions of the state and whether such deprivation was compensated or not'.[114] Additionally, drawing on the jurisprudence of

---

[110] *James and Ors v the United Kingdom*, ECHR App No 8793/79 (Judgment) (21 February 1986) Series A, No 98, at 19–20.

[111] ibid 24.

[112] Acuerdo para la Promoción y Protección Recíproca de Inversiones entre el Reino de España y los Estados Unidos Mexicanos (10 October 2006), Art V.

[113] *Técnicas Medioambientales Tecmed SA v The United Mexican States*, ICSID Case No ARB(AF) 00/2 (Award) (29 May 2003) ¶ 122.

[114] ibid.

the European Court of Human Rights, the tribunal found it necessary to consider the fact that foreign investors have little or no impact on the decision-making that affects them, since they are not entitled to exercise domestic political rights, such as voting.[115] Having analysed the circumstances surrounding the revocation of the landfill permit, the tribunal found that the situation contained no emergency circumstances, serious social situation, or even any urgency. Therefore, it determined that the measures undertaken by the Mexican authorities were not proportional to the aim sought and so were equivalent to an expropriation.

In *LG&E v Argentina*, the tribunal cited the *Tecmed* decision and applied the proportionality test. It stated:

with respect to the power of the State to adopt its policies, it can generally be said that the State has the right to adopt measures having a social or general welfare purpose, and in such a case, the measure must be accepted without any imposition of liability, except in cases where the State's action is obviously disproportionate to the need being addressed.[116]

According to the tribunal, the relevant proportionality test for questions regarding the right to regulate is whether the measures are proportional to the public interest protected and to the legal protection accorded to investments. The tribunal also found that the significance of a regulatory measure's impact on foreign investments should be taken into account as well.[117] Although *LG&E* thus reaffirmed *Tecmed's* proportionality test,[118] it concluded that the measures taken by Argentina to deal with its crisis did not deprive the claimants of the economic value of their investment and therefore did not constitute an indirect expropriation; however, it did not specifically state whether the measures challenged were proportional to the aims they sought to achieve.

(d) Non-transparency, arbitrariness, and discrimination

Another factor that may contribute to a finding of indirect expropriation is that the challenged measure or the process by which it was enacted is non-transparent, arbitrary, or discriminatory. The degree to which this factor will affect an ultimate judgment on the legality under an expropriation clause of such measure will usually depend on the facts of the individual case. For example, in *Feldman v Mexico*, a case that concerned the Mexican tax authorities' allegedly non-transparent and arbitrary treatment of a US investor, a tribunal rejected claims of indirect expropriation because it considered it 'doubtful that lack of transparency alone rises to the level of violation of NAFTA and international law, particularly given

---

[115] ibid.

[116] *LG&E Energy Corp, LG&E Capital Corp, LG&E International INC v Argentine Republic*, ICSID Case No ARB/02/1 (Decision on Liability) (3 October 2006) ¶ 195.

[117] ibid.

[118] The proportionality requirement was more recently confirmed by the tribunal in *Deutsche Bank AG v Democratic Socialist Republic of Sri Lanka*, ICSID Case No ARB/09/2 (Award) (31 October 2012) ¶ 522.

the complexities not only of Mexican but most other tax laws'.[119] The tribunal thought it was undeniable that the investor had experienced great difficulty in dealing with tax officials and in some respects was treated in a less than reasonable manner. Nevertheless, it found that such treatment did not rise to the level of a violation of Article 1110 of NAFTA, adding with evident sympathy that 'unfortunately, tax authorities in most countries do not always act in a consistent and predictable way'.[120]

On the other hand, in *Metalclad v Mexico* the tribunal found that the challenged measures, taken together with the representations of the Mexican federal government, on which Metalclad relied, and the *absence of a timely, orderly, or substantive basis for the denial* by the municipality of the local construction permit, amounted to an indirect expropriation.[121] And in *SD Myers*, a NAFTA tribunal also had to examine whether the practical effect of the Canadian regulatory measures aimed at protecting the environment actually created a disproportionate benefit for Canadian nationals versus foreign investors and whether those measures prima facie favoured the nationals over non-nationals. Based on an extensive review of the facts, the tribunal concluded that the measures in question were designed for protectionist purposes and so were discriminatory against the claimants.[122] This finding of discrimination lent additional support to the tribunal's determination that the challenged Canadian regulatory measures were tantamount to expropriation. Thus, in certain cases, instances of non-transparent, arbitrary, and discriminatory conduct by a host state may aid in establishing that a regulatory measure ostensibly enacted for public policy purposes actually concealed *de facto* expropriatory conduct.

Recent treaties, such as the investment chapters of US FTAs, the investment chapter of the Malaysia–Australia FTA, the US–Uruguay BIT, Turkish BITs,[123] Canadian BITs, Indian BITs, and the Japan–Korea–China Trilateral Investment Agreement, have made non-discrimination an explicit criterion for judging the legality of governmental measures. The Canada–China BIT, for example, states:

Except in rare circumstances, such as if a measure or series of measures is so severe in light of its purpose that it cannot be reasonably viewed as having been adopted and applied in *good faith*, a *non-discriminatory measure* or series of measures of a Contracting Party that is designed and applied to protect the legitimate public objectives for the well-being of

---

[119] *Feldman v Mexico*, ICSID Case No ARB(AF)/99/1 (Award on Merits) (16 December 2002) ¶ 133.

[120] ibid ¶ 113.

[121] The tribunal stated: 'These measures, taken together with the representations of the Mexican federal government, on which Metalclad relied, and the absence of a timely, orderly or substantive basis for the denial by the Municipality of the local construction permit, amount to an indirect expropriation.' *Metalclad Corp v Mexico*, ICSID Case No ARB(AF)/97/1 (Award) (30 August 2000) ¶ 107.

[122] *SD Myers, Inc v Canada*, UNCITRAL (First Partial Award) (13 November 2000) ¶¶ 221–255.

[123] See eg Agreement between the Government of the Republic of Turkey and the Government of the People's Republic of Bangladesh Concerning the Reciprocal Promotion and Protection of Investments (12 April 2012), Art 6(2).

citizens, such as health, safety and the environment, *does not constitute indirect expropriation*.[124] (emphasis added)

(e) Sole effects versus purpose and context of the measure

As indicated previously, one of the crucial factors in determining whether a host state measure is equivalent to expropriation is the severity of its effects on the investment. At the same time, a controversial question still remains unresolved: whether tribunals should focus solely on the effects of the challenged measure or whether they should consider the purpose and context of the measure. The dominant view is that the measure's effects should be the sole criterion[125] and that the state's intentions in making the measure should be given little weight.[126] Early support for this view is found in the *Norwegian Shipowners' Claims*[127] and *Chorzów Factory*[128] cases. The jurisprudence of the Iran–US claims tribunal,[129] non-treaty expropriation cases,[130] and NAFTA cases[131] have all served to emphasize the importance of effects over intentions[132] in evaluating the expropriatory character of governmental measures.

Some cases have given weight to the intention of the state and the context of the measures adopted when evaluating whether they constituted indirect expropriation. In *LG&E v Argentina*, which arose out of the measures taken by Argentina to confront its economic crises, the tribunal acknowledged that 'there is no doubt that the facts relating to the severity of the changes on the legal status and the practical impact endured by the investors in this case, as well as the possibility of enjoying the right of ownership and use of the investment are decisive in establishing whether an indirect expropriation is said to have occurred'. However, an important question for the tribunal was 'whether one should only take into

---

[124] Agreement between the Government of Canada and the Government of the People's Republic of China for the Promotion and Reciprocal Protection of Investments (8 September 2012), Annex B.10, at 3.

[125] R Dolzer, 'Indirect Expropriations: New Developments?' (2002) 14 NYU Envir LJ 64, 64; Reinisch (n 13 above) 405.

[126] See *Compañía de Aguas del Aconquija SA and Vivendi Universal SA v Argentine Republic*, ICSID Case No ARB/97/3 (Award) (20 August 2007) ¶ 7.5.20 ('There is extensive authority for the proposition that the state's intent, or its subjective motives are at most a secondary consideration'); *Spyridon Roussalis v Romania*, ICSID Case No ARB/06/1 (Award) (1 December 2011) ¶ 330 ('The intention or purpose of the State is relevant but is not decisive of the question whether there has been an expropriation').

[127] *Norwegian Shipowners' Claims (Norway v United States)* (Perm Ct Arb 1922) 1 RIAA 307.

[128] *Case Concerning Certain German Interests in Polish Upper Silesia (FRG v Poland)* (1926) PCIJ Series A, No 7.

[129] See eg *Tippets et al v TAMSEFTA* (1984) 6 Iran-USCTR 219.

[130] See eg *Biloune and Marine Drive Complex Ltd v Ghana Investments Centre and the Government of Ghana*, UNCITRAL (Award on Jurisdiction and Liability) (27 October 1989).

[131] See eg *Metalclad Corp v Mexico*, ICSID Case No ARB(AF)/97/1 (Award) (30 August 2000) in which the tribunal stated that it 'need not decide or consider the motivation or intent of the adoption of the Ecological Decree . . . [h]owever, [it] considers that the implementation of the Ecological Decree would, in and of itself, constitute an act tantamount to expropriation' ibid ¶ 111.

[132] Reinisch (n 13 above) 405, 446.

account the effects produced by the measure or if one should consider also the context within which a measure was adopted and the host state's purpose'. The tribunal answered in the following way: 'It is this tribunal's opinion that there must be a balance in the analysis both of the causes and the effects of a measure in order that one may qualify a measure as being of an expropriatory nature.'[133] Relying on a balancing approach, the tribunal concluded that Argentina's gas tariff measures were not the equivalent of an expropriation.

Despite the overwhelming importance attached to analysing the effects of a measure by arbitral jurisprudence and scholarly doctrine, it is suggested that the *LG&E* decision offers a useful reminder of the importance of also considering intention and context when judging whether a measure is expropriatory. *LG&E's* approach of balancing effects with context and purposes seems a prudent way to give due deference to a state's legitimate right to regulate. Moreover, giving an exclusive role only to the 'effects' of the challenged measure without placing those effects in a broader context may lead to an incomplete analysis that is unintentionally biased in favour of a foreign investor. It is not solely the 'effects' of a regulatory measure that should matter but also what purpose the regulation serves, how that regulation is implemented (transparently, non-arbitrarily, without discrimination), whether the means employed are proportionate to the ends pursued, and whether there are less restrictive alternatives available. Only through a contextual analysis that allows for the weighing of many relevant factors will it be possible to achieve a balanced approach when considering indirect expropriation claims. Such an approach would lead to more objective awards and contribute to the perception of legitimacy and justice in the international investment legal regime.

The prudence of this approach can also be seen in recent state practice. For example, some international investment treaties[134] now explicitly provide that determining whether an action or series of actions constitutes an indirect expropriation requires a case-by-case, fact-based inquiry that considers: (1) the economic impact of the government action; (2) the extent to which the government action interferes with distinct, reasonable, investment-backed expectations; and (3) the character of the government action, among other factors. More importantly, such provisions stipulate that although the fact that an action or series of actions has an adverse effect on the economic value of an investment may be relevant, economic impact *standing alone* does not establish that an indirect expropriation has occurred.[135]

---

[133] *LG&E Energy Corp, LG&E Capital Corp, LG&E International INC v Argentine Republic,* ICSID Case No ARB/02/1 (Decision on Liability) (3 October 2006) ¶ 194.

[134] US–Australia Free Trade Agreement (18 May 2004); US–Chile Free Trade Agreement (6 June 2003); US–Morocco Free Trade Agreement (15 June 2004); US–Singapore Free Trade Agreement (6 May 2003); Treaty between the United States of America and the Oriental Republic of Uruguay Concerning the Encouragement and Reciprocal Protection of Investment (4 November 2005); Agreement between Canada and the Republic of Peru for the Promotion and Protection of Investments (14 November 2006).

[135] See Agreement between the Government of the Republic of India and the Government of Latvia for the Promotion and Protection of Investments (18 February 2010), Ad Art 5(4)(b): 'Actions by a Government or Government controlled bodies, taken as a part of normal business activities, will not constitute indirect expropriation unless it is prima facie apparent that it was taken with an intent to create an adverse impact on the economic value of an investment.'

Faced with applying such a provision, an international tribunal will be bound to recognize the dispositive character of that language and extend its indirect expropriation analysis to include factors outside economic impact. Moreover, that such treaties do not set down an exhaustive list of factors allows tribunals to refer to other relevant facts and sources of international law for guidance.

12.9 Newer Treaties' Approach to Distinguishing Legitimate Regulation from Indirect Expropriation

Although investment treaties have not traditionally provided specific guidance on how to distinguish indirect expropriations from legitimate regulatory measures, a few more recent treaties appear to have moved in this direction by giving explicit criteria on how to determine whether a particular regulatory measure amounts to an indirect expropriation. In particular, the 2004 and 2012 US Model BITs[136] and the 2004 Canadian Model Foreign Investment Protection Agreement (FIPA) have adopted this approach, presumably in response to the two countries' experience in investment arbitrations under NAFTA's Chapter 11. The basic approach taken is to state the provision on expropriation in the traditional manner but then indicate that those provisions are to be interpreted in accordance with attached treaty annexes that set down criteria to be used when determining whether a governmental measure constitutes an indirect expropriation. These new models became the basis for multiple BITs and the investment chapters in various US FTAs.

Article 6 of the US–Uruguay BIT states the traditional rule against expropriation,[137] but also requires that it be interpreted in accordance with Annexes A and B of the treaty. Among other things, the Annexes make clear that (1) Article 6(1) is intended to reflect customary international law concerning the obligation of

---

[136] For a discussion of innovations in US investment treaty practice, see D Gantz, 'The Evolution of FTA Investment Provisions: From NAFTA to the United States–Chile Free Trade Agreement' (2004) 194 Amer U Intl L Rev 679; N Rubins, 'The Arbitral Innovations of Recent U.S. Free Trade Agreements: Two Steps Forward, One Step Back' (2003) 8 Int'l Bus LJ 865; M Kantor, 'Investor–State Arbitration over Investments in Financial Services: Disputes under New U.S. Investments Treaties' (2004) 121 Banking LJ 579.

[137] US–Uruguay BIT, Art 6(1) states:

> Neither Party may expropriate or nationalize a covered investment either directly or indirectly through measures equivalent to expropriation or nationalization ('expropriation'), except:
> (a) for a public purpose;
> (b) in a non-discriminatory manner;
> (c) on payment of prompt, adequate, and effective compensation; and
> (d) in accordance with due process of law and Article 5(1) through (3).

Treaty between the United States of America and the Oriental Republic of Uruguay Concerning the Encouragement and Reciprocal Protection of Investment (4 November 2005).

states with respect to expropriation; (2) an action or a series of actions by a party cannot constitute an expropriation unless it interferes with a tangible or intangible property right or interest in an investment; (3) an indirect expropriation occurs 'where an action or series of actions by a Party has an effect equivalent to direct expropriation without formal transfer of title or outright seizure'; and (4) 'the determination of whether an action or series of actions by a Party, in a specific fact situation, constitutes an indirect expropriation, requires a case-by-case, fact-based inquiry'. This inquiry itself requires a consideration of various factors, including:

(i) the economic impact of the government action, although the fact that an action or series of actions by a Party has an adverse effect on the economic value of an investment, standing alone, does not establish that an indirect expropriation has occurred;

(ii) the extent to which the government action interferes with distinct, reasonable investment-backed expectations; and

(iii) the character of the government action.

Article 13 of the Canada–Peru 2006 BIT parallels the language of Article 6 of the US–Uruguay 2005 BIT and requires it be interpreted in the light of Annex B.13(1), which states the criteria for distinguishing indirect expropriations from legitimate regulation in terms almost identical to those of the US model. One of the purposes of the US and Canadian annexes is to limit and provide guidance to investor–state arbitral tribunals that interpret expropriation clauses in disputes over the nature of governmental measures

One finds a similar approach in the 2009 ASEAN Comprehensive Investment Agreement in which Article 14 obliges the contracting states not to nationalize or expropriate covered investments except for a public purpose, in a non-discriminatory way, on payment of prompt adequate and effective compensation, and in accordance with due process of law. A footnote note to Article 14 stipulates that the article is to be read with Annex 2 of the treaty, which states that the determination of whether a particular action or series of actions by a member state constitutes an expropriation 'requires a case-by-case fact-based inquiry' that considers the following three factors, among others: (1) the economic impact of the action, although the existence of an adverse economic effect on the value of an investment does not establish the existence of an expropriation; (2) whether the government's action breaches the government's prior written commitments to the investor; and (3) the character of the government action and whether it is disproportionate to the public purpose for which the action was taken.[138]

---

[138] ASEAN Comprehensive Investment Agreement, available at <http://www.asean.org/images/2012/Economic/AIA/Agreement/ASEAN%20Comprehensive%20Investment%20Agreement%20(ACIA)%202012.pdf> Art 14 and Annex 2, accessed 15 September 2014.

12.10 Conditions for the Legality
of Expropriations, Nationalizations, and Dispossessions

Even if an act of a government is found to expropriate an investment, it may still be legal if it meets certain specified conditions. Traditionally, customary law considers an expropriation to be legal if the expropriatory measure is: (1) for a public purpose; (2) not arbitrary or discriminatory; (3) done in accordance with due process of law; and (4) accompanied by compensation. To a significant degree, modern investment treaties have incorporated these conditions for determining an expropriation's legality.[139] Indeed, they have become so common in investment treaties that one can argue with justification that they constitute customary international law on expropriation of property held by foreign nationals. The following sections consider each condition briefly.

(a) Expropriation measure must be for a public purpose

Virtually all investment treaties adopt the traditional customary international law position that an expropriation must be for a 'public purpose'. Since virtually any taking by a government can ostensibly be justified on these grounds, investors are rarely successful in challenging the legality of government taking because it is not for a public purpose. One exception was *ADC Affiliate Ltd and ADC & ADMC Management Ltd v Republic of Hungary*, an ICSID case that arose when the Hungarian government expropriated the claimants' interest in the operation of a terminal at Budapest airport. The claimants alleged that in expropriating its interest the Hungarian government did not meet any of the four conditions required by the applicable Cyprus–Hungary BIT, including the requirement that '[t]he measures are taken in the public interest'. The tribunal found that although the concept of 'public interest' is inherently broad, the requirement of 'public interest' in the treaty nonetheless necessitated some genuine interest of the public: 'If mere reference to "public interest" can magically put such interest into existence and therefore satisfy this requirement, then this requirement would be rendered meaningless since the Tribunal can imagine no situation where this requirement would not have been met.'[140] Ultimately, the tribunal found that no public interest was served by depriving the claimants of their investment.[141] That finding contributed to the tribunal's decision that the Hungarian government had illegally expropriated the claimants' investment and that Hungary was therefore liable to pay compensation.[142]

---

[139] UNCTAD, *Bilateral Investment Treaties in 1995–2006: Trends in Investment Rulemaking* (2007) 47.

[140] *ADC Affiliate Ltd and ADC & ADMC Management Ltd v Republic of Hungary*, ICSID Case No ARB/03/16 (Award) (2 October 2006) ¶ 432.

[141] ibid ¶ 476.

[142] Other arbitral cases treating this issue but which did not involve the application of investment treaties were *British Petroleum v Libya* (Award) (10 October 1973) (1 August 1974) (1974) 53 ILR 297, 329, in which ad hoc arbitrator explicitly assessed the public purpose requirement and

In the Yukos cases, Russia had argued that it had acted for a public purpose in seizing Yukos assets; however the tribunal rejected this argument, stating:

whether the destruction of Russia's leading oil company and largest taxpayer was in the public interest is profoundly questionable. It was in the interest of the largest State-owned oil company, Rosneft, which took over the principal assets of Yukos virtually cost-free, but that is not the same as saying that it was in the public interest of the economy, polity and population of the Russian Federation.[143]

(b) Expropriation must not be discriminatory

As has been shown, international investment agreements consistently provide that nationalization and expropriation must be 'not discriminatory', taken 'on a non-discriminatory basis', and done 'in a non-discriminatory manner'. In *ADC v Hungary*, in which the claimants alleged discriminatory expropriation of their investment in the operation of a terminal at Budapest airport, Hungary argued that the claimants were unable to raise that argument, since the claimants were the only foreign parties involved in the airport's operation. The tribunal responded that while it was true that 'for discrimination to exist there must be different treatments to different parties',[144] the relevant comparison was between the treatment granted to the replacement operator appointed by Hungary and the treatment given to foreign investors as a whole. By this standard, the tribunal found that Hungary's actions against the claimants had indeed been discriminatory.

International jurisprudence in non-treaty cases also affirms non-discrimination as a basic element of the international law governing expropriation. In *LIAMCO*, the arbitrator held: '[It is] clear and undisputed that nondiscrimination is a requisite for the validity of a lawful nationalization. This is a rule well-established in international legal theory and practice... Therefore, a purely discriminatory nationalization is illegal and wrongful.'[145] In *LETCO* the tribunal stressed that even if the Liberian government sought to justify its action as one of nationalization, it would still have to prove that the action was non-discriminatory. Since

---

found that the expropriation was unlawful because it was adopted 'for purely extraneous political reasons as an act of retaliation for a British foreign policy decision'; and *LETCO v Liberia* (Award) (31 March 1986) (1986) 26 ILM 647, 665, in which the tribunal found that the revocation of a concession was not for a bona fide public purpose, stating:

There was no legislative enactment by the Government of Liberia. There was no evidence of any stated policy on the part of the Liberian Government to take concessions of this kind into public ownership for the public good. On the contrary, evidence was given to the tribunal that areas of the concession taken away from LETCO were granted to other foreign-owned companies.

[143] *Hulley Enterprises Ltd (Cyprus) v The Russian Federation*, PCA AA 226 (Final Award) (18 July 2014) ¶ 1581; *Yukos Universal Ltd (Isle of Man) v the Russian Federation*, PCA AA 227 (Final Award) (18 July 2014) ¶ 1581; *Veteran Petroleum Ltd (Cyprus) v the Russian Federation*, PCA AA 228, (Final Award) (18 July 2014).

[144] *ADC Affiliate Ltd and ADC & ADMC Management Ltd v Republic of Hungary*, ICSID Case No ARB/03/16 (Award) (2 October 2006) ¶ 442.

[145] *Libyan American Oil Co (LIAMCO) v Libya* (1977) 62 ILR 140, 194.

the tribunal found that areas of concession taken from LETCO were granted to other foreign-owned companies run by people who were 'good friends of Liberian authorities', it concluded that the taking was discriminatory.[146]

(c) Expropriation must take place in accordance with due process of law

Many investment treaties, like NAFTA, the ECT, and the ASEAN Comprehensive Investment Agreement provide that expropriation, nationalizations, or dispossessions of protected investment must take place according to 'due process of law'. The treaties themselves usually do not define this term, which, of course, has deep roots in many legal systems. In *ADC v Hungary*, in which the claimants argued that Hungary had not respected due process of law when it expropriated their investment, the tribunal sought to define the term. It stated:

due process of law demands an actual and substantive legal procedure for a foreign investor to raise its claims against the depriving actions already taken or about to be taken against it. Some basic legal mechanisms, such as reasonable advance notice, a fair hearing and an unbiased and impartial adjudicator to assess the actions in dispute, are expected to be readily available and accessible to the investor to make such legal procedure meaningful. In general, the legal procedure must be of a nature to grant an affected investor a reasonable chance within a reasonable time to claim its legitimate rights and have its claims heard. If no legal procedure of such nature exists at all, the argument that '*the actions are taken under due process of law*' rings hollow.[147]

The tribunal found that Hungary had not made any of these procedures and mechanisms available to the claimants and that expropriation in violation of the due process requirement of the treaty had indeed taken place. Similarly in the Yukos cases, although Russia claimed that the seizure of the assets and treatment of the investors had been done according to law, the tribunal concluded that it had not been 'carried out under due process of law', as required by Article 13(1) (c) of the ECT. In particular it found that 'Russian courts bent to the will of Russian executive authorities to bankrupt Yukos, assign its assets to a State controlled company, and incarcerate a man who gave signs of becoming a political competitor'.[148]

Some investment treaties contain language explaining the due process requirements necessary for expropriation and compensation. For example, Article 5(3) of the 2000 Austria–Bosnia-Herzegovina BIT provides:

Due process of law includes the right of an investor of a Contracting Party which claims to be affected by expropriation by the other Contracting Party to prompt review of its case, including the valuation of its investment and the payment of compensation in accordance

---

[146] *LETCO v Liberia* (Award) (31 March 1986) (1986) 26 ILM 647, 665.
[147] *ADC Affiliate Ltd and ADC & ADMC Management Ltd v Republic of Hungary*, ICSID Case No ARB/03/16 (Award) (2 October 2006) ¶ 435.
[148] *Yukos* (n 143 above) ¶ 1583.

with the provisions of this Article, by a judicial authority or another competent and independent authority of the latter Contracting Party.[149]

(d) Expropriation must be accompanied by compensation

A simple determination by a tribunal or other body that a host state has expropriated assets in violation of treaty provisions is, by itself, of little comfort to the loser of those assets. What is important to that investor is that the offending state fully compensates it for the lost investment. However, the importance of securing compensation for treaty violations serves a greater purpose than achieving justice in an individual case. It also serves the important goal of assuring respect for investment treaty rules and fostering investment regime effectiveness, ultimately preserving the regime itself. From the point of view of regime maintenance, being able to obtain compensation effectively from treaty violators raises the costs of treaty violations and will therefore induce other potential violators to respect their bargains with foreign investors protected by investment treaties.

As Chapter 3 indicated, one of the most debated issues among negotiators and scholars has been the extent to which customary international law requires states to pay compensation to foreigners for expropriated assets. Investment treaties have sought to settle that debate by affirming that the payment of compensation for expropriation is an international obligation and by articulating the principles that should be applied in determining the amount of compensation required.

Unlike violations of other treatment standards, virtually all investment treaties make the payment of compensation a specific condition for expropriation. However, it is one thing for a treaty to enunciate a general principle requiring compensation, it is quite another for a tribunal to determine precisely the amount of compensation that an offending state must pay to an investor for the expropriation of particular assets at a particular time. To accomplish that task, one must value the loss resulting from expropriation and that requires at least three elements: (1) a standard of compensation; (2) a method for applying that standard; and (3) the actual application of the chosen valuation method to the specific assets that have been expropriated. Each of these three elements is examined briefly.

(i) *The standard of compensation*

Compensation for injury requires a standard for determining precisely what an injured party should receive as a result of a state's wrongful conduct. As noted in Chapter 3, before the development of investment treaties, considerable disagreement existed within the international community regarding what standard should be applied in cases of expropriation. One of the purposes of the investment treaty movement was to end that debate by agreeing to an international standard. In a

---

[149] Agreement between the Republic of Austria and Bosnia and Herzegovina for the Promotion and Protection of Investments (2 October 2000).

reflection of the increasing convergence on the issue, many treaties have adopted some version of the 'Hull formula', which requires that compensation should be 'prompt, adequate and effective'.[150] The term 'prompt' generally means that payment should be made without undue delay. 'Effective' means that the payment should be made in realizable and readily transferable currency; accordingly, payment in forty-year bonds denominated in local currency, for example, would not be considered effective. 'Adequate' compensation has been much more difficult to define. In a real sense, in the contentious relationships between offending states and aggrieved investors, adequacy exists in the eye of the beholder. Treaties have therefore sought to give greater precision to the standard.

Rather than leave the interpretation of the standard of prompt, adequate, and effective compensation solely to the discretion of arbitrators, many investment treaties define the terms in detail and provide instruction for their application. For instance, it is common for investment treaties to specify that the investor shall be owed the 'market value' of the investment before the expropriatory act was taken or became known to the public. Moreover, treaties also authorize tribunals to award interest on the amount owing from the date of expropriation until the respondent state pays the injured investor. For example, Article 5 of the Korea–Congo BIT, while requiring compensation for expropriation to be 'prompt, adequate and effective' also provides that such compensation shall amount to:

the fair market value of the expropriated investments immediately before the expropriation took place or before the impending expropriation became public knowledge, whichever is the earlier, shall include interest at the applicable commercial rate from the date of expropriation until the date of payment, and shall be made without undue delay, be effectively realizable, and be freely transferable.[151]

Similarly, the second paragraph of Article 1110 of NAFTA seeks to set down a standard for compensation with some degree of specificity:

2. Compensation shall be equivalent to the fair market value of the expropriated investment immediately before the expropriation took place ('date of expropriation'), and shall not reflect any change in value occurring because the intended expropriation had become known earlier. Valuation criteria shall include going concern value, asset value (including declared tax value of tangible property) and other criteria, as appropriate to determine fair market value.

Subsequent paragraphs of Article 1110 specify that compensation is to be paid without delay, that it shall include interest at commercial rates from the date of expropriation to the date of payment, and that upon payment the compensation will be freely transferable.

---

[150] UNCTAD, *Bilateral Investment Treaties in 1995–2006: Trends in Investment Rulemaking* (2007) 48; Dolzer and Schreuer (n 9 above) 91.

[151] Agreement between the Government of the Republic of Korea and the Government of the Democratic Republic of Congo for the Promotion and Protection of Investments (17 March 2005).

A few treaties are less specific in establishing standards of compensation. Instead of market value, they may require 'real value',[152] 'reasonable compensation',[153] or simply 'compensation'.[154] These formulations of a treaty's standard for compensation provide ample room for controversy as to their meaning and application in specific expropriation cases. Therefore, they may have the net effect of increasing investors' insecurity about their rights in cases of expropriation. For example, a standard of 'just compensation' would allow a state to offset environmental or other damage, while the 'market value' is less amenable to such an interpretation. Indeed, the concept of market value seems to be more concrete and so may be more easily applied than other options employed in international treaties.

Even a treaty's specific promise to pay market value for expropriated investments may be problematic in specific cases. For one thing, investment treaties rarely define in detail the specific meaning of 'market value' or 'effective compensation'. Consequently, the very content of the standard may become a subject of controversy between aggrieved investors and offending host states. Arbitral tribunals have defined the term by drawing on the notion of a market transaction between willing buyers and sellers. Thus, one useful definition of market value, elaborated by the Iran–US claims tribunal in *Starrett Housing Corporation v Iran* is 'the price that a willing buyer would pay to a willing seller in circumstances in which each had good information, each desired to maximize his financial gain, and neither was under duress or threat, the willing buyer being a reasonable person'.[155]

(ii) *The question of compensation for legal and illegal expropriations*

One common reading of treaty provisions on compensation for expropriation would lead to the conclusion that tribunals are to apply the stipulated standard of compensation not only to determine whether a state has *lawfully* expropriated an investment but also to determine the amount to be awarded to the investor in the event that the tribunal decides that the state has *unlawfully* expropriated that same investment. In short, the treaty standard of compensation is not only a *condition* for a lawful expropriation but it also states the *consequence* of an unlawful one. A different interpretation would suggest that the valuation principles stipulated in investment treaties apply only to 'legal expropriations', that is, expropriations that meet the treaty's required conditions. Compensation for illegal expropriation, on the other hand, is governed not by the treaty provisions

---

[152] Agreement between the Government of the Kingdom of Thailand and the Government of the Hong Kong Special Administrative Region of the People's Republic of China for the Promotion and Protection of Investments (19 November 2005), Art 5(1).

[153] Agreement between the Government of Australia and the Government of the People's Republic of China on the Reciprocal Encouragement and Protection of Investments (11 July 1988), Art 8.1.

[154] Agreement on the Encouragement and Protection of Investments between the Government of Hong Kong and the Government of the Kingdom of the Netherlands (19 November 1992), Art 5(1).

[155] *Starrett Housing Corp v The Government of the Islamic Republic of Iran* (19 December 1983) 4 Iran-USCTR 122, 201.

on expropriation compensation but on the principles of customary international law, as illustrated by the *Chorzów Factory* case, which requires that to the extent possible the offending state restore the investor to the situation that would have existed before illegal expropriation took place.[156] Under this view, while market value immediately prior to expropriation might be the applicable standard in cases of legal expropriation, in cases of illegal expropriation the appropriate standard is the amount necessary to restore the investor to the situation it would have been in had the illegal act never taken place. The application of these two standards to the same set of facts can lead to very different results. For example, the latter might well take into account lost profits and any increase in enterprise value following the expropriation, while the former might not. The tribunal in *ADC v Hungary* was faced with this precise issue in determining the appropriate standard of compensation to apply to Hungary's expropriation of the claimants' investments in a Budapest airport terminal. Hungary argued that the appropriate standard was 'market value', since the applicable BIT provided that the 'amount of compensation must correspond to the market value of the expropriated investments at the moment of the expropriation'.[157] The tribunal concluded, however, that this standard applied only to cases of legal expropriation and not to illegal expropriations.[158] The treaty made no reference to the standard to be applied to illegal expropriations, which included Hungary's expropriation of the claimants' investment. Consequently, the tribunal turned to customary international law to find a standard. The tribunal concluded that the appropriate standard was found in the *Chorzów Factory* case judgment: 'reparation must, as far as possible, wipe out all the consequences of the illegal act and re-establish the situation which would, in all probability, have existed if that act had not been committed'.[159]

One may question whether the tribunal's interpretation of the applicable BIT was correct. The treaty provision in question provided that '[n]either Contracting Party shall take any measures depriving, directly or indirectly, investors of the other Contracting Party of their investments unless... the measures are accompanied by provision for the payment of just compensation'.[160] As indicated earlier, just compensation was to be market value and the treaty makes no distinction between legal and illegal deprivation measures. The treaty refers only to measures depriving investors of their property. By not making provision for the payment of market value Hungary undoubtedly violated its treaty obligation, but according to the treaty the proper remedy is the payment of compensation equal to the market value of the investment. Moreover, a strict application of the tribunal's reasoning

---

[156] Dolzer and Schreuer (n 9 above) 92, who state that the latter position is 'the better view'.

[157] Agreement between the Government of the Republic of Cyprus and the Government of the Hungarian People's Republic on Mutual Promotion and Protection of Investments (24 May 1989), Art 4(2).

[158] *ADC Affiliate Ltd and ADC & ADMC Management Ltd v Republic of Hungary*, ICSID Case No ARB/03/16 (Award) (2 October 2006) ¶ 481.

[159] ibid ¶ 484.

[160] Agreement between the Government of the Republic of Cyprus and the Government of the Hungarian People's Republic on Mutual Promotion and Protection of Investments (24 May 1989), Art 4(1).

would lead to the curious result that in cases in which an expropriation meets all the conditions for a legal expropriation except for a determination by the tribunal that the host state had not paid market value for the property expropriated, such an expropriation would have to be considered 'illegal' and compensation would therefore be awarded not on the basis of the valuation standard in the treaty but on the basis of the *Chorzów Factory* principle and customary international law. It is suggested that such a result may not accord with the intention of the contracting states as evidenced by the treaty text.

(iii) Valuation methods

Once a tribunal or other body has determined an appropriate standard of compensation, it must apply that standard to a specific set of circumstances to arrive at the appropriate amount of compensation to award to the injured investor. In order to accomplish that task, an appropriate valuation methodology must be employed.

It is often said that 'valuation is more art than science'. One of the reasons for this sentiment is that many diverse, seemingly scientific valuation methods can be applied in different ways to arrive at different results. This diversity of valuation methods is apparent in the calculation of investor compensation in cases of expropriation.[161] One of the reasons for this diversity of methods is that investment treaties do not provide guidance on the methodology to be applied in deciding on 'fair market value', 'real value', 'adequate compensation', or whatever compensation standard is specified in the treaty. So, while the definitions of market value quoted earlier in this chapter are helpful, neither they nor investment treaties employing them explain precisely how to apply the concept to expropriated assets in particular cases. Indeed, often the determination of what a willing buyer would pay a willing seller for an expropriated asset prior to the expropriation is a highly speculative exercise. In fact, in many cases no willing buyer or willing seller for such an asset exists to provide concrete data for such a determination.

In the absence of such treaty-based guidance, parties and their experts have employed a variety of valuation techniques from the fields of finance and economics, none of which are specifically authorized by investment treaty provisions. Among the principle valuation methods employed are the following:

1. book value, which is based on the actual costs incurred to establish the investment as those costs are reflected on the books (ie the balance sheet) of the affected enterprise;

2. replacement value, which is the amount needed to acquire an asset of the same type as that which was expropriated;

---

[161] TW Wälde and B Sabhi, 'Compensation, Damages, and Valuation' in P Muchlinski (n 13 above) 1049, 1070–82; M Ball, 'Assessing Damages in Claims by Investors Against States' 16 ICSID Rev—FILJ (2001) 408; A Newcombe and L Paradell (n 21 above) 385–93.

3. liquidation value, which is what a willing buyer would pay for the assets of the expropriated enterprise in liquidation; and

4. going-concern value or discounted cash flow (DCF), which is a forward-looking method that values the enterprise on the basis of its future expected cash and then, using a discount rate that takes account of the cost of capital and risk, discounts that estimated cash flow to arrive at a present value.

When applied to the same set of facts, each of these methods may result in a considerable variation in values. The choice of the appropriate method and how it should be applied is always the subject of significant dispute among the parties. While individual tribunals and negotiators usually arrive at a pragmatic answer, the law of investment treaties gives little guidance to them in choosing and using valuation methods. Chapter 16, which considers the consequences of treaty violations, will examine these issues at greater length.

13

Other Treatment Standards

13.1 Introduction to Other Treaty Standards

In addition to the usual treaty standards of treatment discussed in previous chapters, individual investment treaties, depending on the policies of the countries concerned and the negotiation dynamics between contracting states, may impose other obligations on host states with respect to their treatment of investments and investors. Such treatment provisions do not appear in all treaties and are subject to a variety of linguistic formulations. Moreover, although they were rarely the subject of arbitration or litigation in the early years of the bilateral investment treaty (BIT) movement, investors have increasingly alleged their violation in investor–state arbitral proceedings, beginning with the second decade of the twenty-first century. This chapter will briefly survey these treatment standards.

13.2 Treatment with Respect to Performance Requirements

Performance requirements are conditions imposed by a host country government on the establishment and operation of a foreign investment in connection with the admission of the investment or in exchange for a special benefit granted to it.[1] Examples of performance requirements include the requirement that an approved investment project export a minimum percentage of its production, that it use a minimum amount of local content in the goods it manufactures, or that it hire a minimum number of local workers. Rather than leave important decisions on matters like exports, inputs, and employment to investment managers to be made solely on the basis of market factors, performance requirements seek to influence the manner in which an investment is operated. The purpose of performance requirements is to increase the amount of benefits flowing from the investment to the host government and its citizens. Host countries often view performance requirements as important policy tools in fostering economic development.

Opponents of performance requirements have argued that when they are imposed as a condition of investment they actually deter, rather than promote,

---

[1] UNCTAD, *Bilateral Investment Treaties 1995–2006: Trends in Investment Rulemaking* (2007) 64. See also JW Salacuse, *The Three Laws for International Investment: National, Contractual, and International Frameworks for Foreign Capital* (OUP, 2013) 98, 251, 382–3.

foreign investment. Opponents also claim that such requirements distort economic decisions that should be based on market conditions and not on governmental decrees. Economic efficiency is best served, it is argued, when enterprises make decisions about exporting or not exporting their goods on the basis of economic costs and benefits.

The concern that performance requirements, some of which are known as 'trade-related investment measures' (TRIMs), are unjustifiable burdens on trade and investment was formally addressed in the General Agreement on Tariffs and Trade (GATT) Uruguay Round of multilateral trade negotiations that would lay the foundation for the World Trade Organization (WTO).[2] Among many other multilateral trade agreements, that round of negotiations produced an Agreement on TRIMs that forbade the imposition of measures that are inconsistent with Article III of GATT on national treatment,[3] and Article XI on the elimination of quantitative restrictions.[4] The Agreement's purpose is to prevent WTO members from imposing local content and trade balancing requirements as conditions for the creation or operation of foreign investment projects. The treaty applies only to trade in goods. In an early case applying the TRIMs agreement in 1998, a WTO dispute settlement panel determined that certain import duty exemptions granted to components for the production of Indonesia's 'national car' violated the TRIMs Agreement.[5] Thus, even without BIT provisions on performance requirements, the WTO's over 150 members are subject to the treatment standards set out in the TRIMs Agreement. Some investment treaties make this obligation explicit either by requiring the contracting parties to follow other rules governing the treatment of investors or by directing them to respect any obligations that they have assumed with regard to investments in their territories. In effect, such provisions incorporate the TRIMs Agreement into investment treaties. Thus, barring specified performance requirements, even if a BIT makes no reference to performance requirements the presence of such language may make it become an additional means of enforcing TRIMs provisions.[6]

Even before the adoption of the TRIMs Agreement, some capital-exporting countries sought to limit or curtail performance requirements through the BITs they negotiated with other countries. The United States was a leader in this regard. Its first model BIT, which dates from 1984, contained the following provision: 'Neither Party shall impose performance requirements as a condition of establishment, expansion or maintenance of investments, which require or enforce

---

[2] Final Act Embodying the Results of the Uruguay Round of Multilateral Trade Negotiations (15 April 1994), 'Legal Instruments—Results of the Uruguay Round' (1994) 33 ILM 1125.
[3] General Agreement on Tariffs and Trade III (30 October 1947), 55 UNTS 194; 61 Stat A-11; TIAS 1700.
[4] ibid Art XI.
[5] WTO Dispute Settlement, DS 54, *Indonesia—Certain Measures Affecting the Automobile Industry*, 'Panel Report' (2 July 1998).
[6] UNCTAD, *Bilateral Investment Treaties 1995–2006: Trends in Investment Rulemaking* (2007) 65.

commitments to export goods produced, or which specify that goods or services must be purchased locally, or which impose any other similar requirements.'[7]

Subsequent US model BITs have continued this trend through the development of detailed, lengthy provisions intended to curtail the imposition of performance requirements on US investors.[8] Indeed, the United States has succeeded in incorporating provisions on performance requirements into the BITs it has concluded.[9] Although the initial approach of the United States was to seek a broad ban on all performance requirements, as indicated by the 1984 Model BIT quoted earlier, more recent model BITs have taken a more nuanced approach. The 2012 US Model BIT makes clear that a host state's conditioning an advantage granted to an investor on certain requirements, such as the location of an investment in a particular area, the training of workers, or the undertaking of research and development, is not a prohibited performance requirement.[10]

The actual treaty practice of the United States has reflected the evolution of its model BITs on the subject of performance requirements. Thus, while during the 1980s its BITs contained a single clause in the article on treatment of investments, sometimes expressed in precatory rather than mandatory language,[11] its more recent BITs contain more fully elaborated, mandatory provisions which not only prohibit the imposition of performance requirement on US investments but on the investments of other countries ('investments of an investor of a non-Party') as well.[12]

---

[7] 'Model Bilateral Investment Treaty (BIT) and Sample Provisions from Negotiated BITs' Art II(5) in S Zamora and R Brand (eds), 1 *Basic Documents in International Economic Law* (CCH International, 1990) 655, 657.

[8] 2012 US Model BIT, Art 8 is a lengthy provision that curtails or limits specific performance requirements. These include obligations:

    (a) to export a given level or percentage of goods or services;

    (b) to achieve a given level or percentage of domestic content;

    (c) to purchase, use, or accord a preference to goods produced in its territory, or to purchase goods from persons in its territory;

    (d) to relate in any way the volume or value of imports to the volume or value of exports or to the amount of foreign exchange inflows associated with such investment;

    (e) to restrict sales of goods or services in its territory that such investment produces or supplies by relating such sales in any way to the volume or value of its exports or foreign exchange earnings…

[9] eg Treaty between the Government of the United States of America and the Government of the Republic of Albania Concerning the Encouragement and Reciprocal Protection of Investments (11 January 1995), Art VI (prohibiting four specified types of performance requirements).

[10] 2012 US Model BIT, Art 8(3)(a).

[11] eg Treaty Between the United States of America and the Kingdom of Morocco Concerning the Encouragement and Reciprocal Protection of Investments (22 July 1985), Art II(6) ('Each Party shall seek to avoid performance requirements as condition of establishment, expansion or maintenance of investments, which require or enforce commitments to export goods produced, or which specify that goods or services must be purchased locally, or which impose any other similar requirements.'); Treaty Between the United States of America and the Arab Republic of Egypt Concerning the Reciprocal Encouragement of Protection of Investments (11 March 1986), Art II(6) ('In the context of its national economic policies and objectives, each Party shall seek to avoid the imposition of performance requirements of the investment of nationals and companies of the other Party.').

[12] eg Treaty Between the Government of the United States of America and of the Republic of Rwanda Concerning the Encouragement and Reciprocal Protection of Investment (19 February

At first, relatively few other capital-exporting countries followed the US lead by incorporating limitations on performance requirements into their BITs. Although most BITs do not have performance requirement provisions, the number that does has been increasing since 1995, which was the year the TRIMs Agreement came into effect. Basically, these BITs reflect three approaches to the problem of regulating performance requirements. One approach is to limit the use of performance requirements in general terms but to make clear that the obligations assumed by the contracting parties do not go beyond the restrictions of the TRIMs Agreement.[13] The 2009 ASEAN Comprehensive Investment Agreement takes a similar approach[14] but also commits the ASEAN member states to undertake a joint assessment of their performance requirements to determine what additional treaty commitments need to be made. A second approach is to limit the imposition of performance requirements after an investment has been established. Thus, a host country may impose performance requirements as conditions for permitting the investments, or for the grant of a special benefit or incentive to that investment, but it cannot impose them thereafter. A third approach used since the beginning of the twenty-first century by the United States, Canada, and Japan is to include in the treaty a list of specific performance requirements that are prohibited at both the pre-investment and post-investment phases. The implication of such a provision, of course, is that all other types of performance requirements do not violate the treaty. Canada, Mexico, and the United States employed this approach in the investment chapter of NAFTA, which is in effect an investment treaty among the countries. Chapter 11 of NAFTA lists a total of seven specific performance requirements that the contracting states may not impose on investments with their treaty partners:

2008), Art 8 (stating that '[n]either Party may, in connection with the establishment, acquisition, expansion, management, conduct, operation, or sale or other disposition of an investment of an investor of a Party or of a non-Party in its territory, impose or enforce any requirement or enforce any commitment or undertaking' with respect to seven defined performance requirements); Treaty Between the Government of the United States of America and the Oriental Republic of Uruguay Concerning the Encouragement and Reciprocal Protection of Investment (11 April 2005), Art 8.

[13] eg Agreement between the Government of Canada and the Government of the Republic of Costa Rica for the Promotion and Protection of Investments (1998), Art VI:

> Neither Contracting Party may impose, in connection with permitting the establishment or acquisition of an investment, or enforce in connection with the subsequent regulation of that investment, any of the requirements set forth in the World Trade Organization Agreement on Trade Related Investment Measures contained in the Final Act Embodying the Results of the Uruguay Round of Multilateral Trade Negotiations, done at Marrakech on April 15, 1994.

[14] 2009 ASEAN Comprehensive Investment Agreement, Art 7(1) ('The provisions of the Agreement on Trade-Related Investment Measures in Annex 1A to the WTO Agreement (TRIMS), which are not specifically mentioned in or modified in this Agreement, shall apply, *mutatis mutandis*, to this Agreement.').

Article 1106: Performance Requirements[15]

1. No Party may impose or enforce any of the following requirements, or enforce any commitment or undertaking, in connection with the establishment, acquisition, expansion, management, conduct or operation of an investment of an investor of a Party or of a non-Party in its territory:
   (a) to export a given level or percentage of goods or services;
   (b) to achieve a given level or percentage of domestic content;
   (c) to purchase, use or accord a preference to goods produced or services provided in its territory, or to purchase goods or services from persons in its territory;
   (d) to relate in any way the volume or value of imports to the volume or value of exports or to the amount of foreign exchange inflows associated with such investment;
   (e) to restrict sales of goods or services in its territory that such investment produces or provides by relating such sales in any way to the volume or value of its exports or foreign exchange earnings;
   (f) to transfer technology, a production process or other proprietary knowledge to a person in its territory, except when the requirement is imposed or the commitment or undertaking is enforced by a court, administrative tribunal or competition authority to remedy an alleged violation of competition laws or to act in a manner not inconsistent with other provisions of this Agreement; or
   (g) to act as the exclusive supplier of the goods it produces or services it provides to a specific region or world market.

Some treaties that take this approach provide for exceptions under specified circumstances. These seven specified performance requirements now also appear in the US 2012 Model BIT, the Canada Model BIT, and various treaties that have been negotiated on the basis of these these models. Despite their length and specificity, the application of performance requirement treaty provisions like those found in NAFTA can raise difficult questions of interpretation. Three investor–state arbitrations involving the interpretation and application of Article 1106 of NAFTA are of interest in this regard. In *Cargill, Inc v United Mexican States*,[16] the claimant, a US food company, had established an investment in Mexico in order to sell high fructose corn syrup to the Mexican market. The claimant argued that a tax advantage given to soft drink bottlers that used domestically produced cane sugar violated Article 1106(3)(b) of NAFTA which prohibits a state from conditioning an advantage, in connection with an investment, on the purchase of goods produced in the territory or from producers in the territory. The tribunal had to decide whether a reduced tax on soft drinks not containing high fructose corn syrup was an advantage 'in connection with' the claimant's investment. It therefore had to determine the nature of the necessary relationship between the legal advantage and investment under Article 1106 (3)(b). The purpose of the tax,

---

[15] Cases addressing NAFTA, Art 1106 include *Merrill & Ring Forestry L P v Government of Canada*, UNCITRAL, ICSID Administrated (Award) (31 March 2010); and *Mobil Investments Canada Inc and Murphy Oil Corp v Government of Canada*, ICSID Case No ARB(AF)/07/4 (Decision on Liability and on Principles of Quantum) (22 May 2012).
[16] ICSID Case No ARB(AF)/05/2 (Award) (18 September 2009).

which was imposed on bottlers, not on the claimant, was to restrict opportunities for the sale of high fructose corn syrup in Mexico by conditioning the receipt of a tax advantage on the use of domestic cane sugar. The tribunal concluded that even though the tax was imposed on bottlers, not on the claimant, the tax involved a performance requirement on the claimant's investment.[17]

In *Mobil Investments Canada Inc and Murphy Oil Corporation v Government of Canada*[18] the claimants had invested in two petroleum development projects off the coast of Newfoundland and Labrador, which under guidelines issued by Canadian provincial authorities were required to make certain minimum expenditures on research and development and education and training. The claimants alleged that such required fixed expenditures violated the prohibitions of Article 1106 of NAFTA on performance requirements, specifically Article 1106(1)(c) which prohibits requirements to purchase goods or services in the territory or from persons in the territory.[19] The tribunal had to determine whether the term 'services' in Article 1106(1)(c) encompassed research and training. Drawing on the NAFTA provisions relating to trade in services and procurement, the tribunal concluded that research and development and education and training are recognized as categories of services for those purposes and that they should also be recognized as such for purposes of Article 1106(1)(c). It therefore concluded that the expenditures required of the claimants' investments violated NAFTA's prohibition against performance requirements.[20] On the other hand, in *Merrill & Ring Forestry L P v Government of Canada*,[21] a case in which the claimant challenged certain Canadian regulations governing the export of logs as constituting impermissible performance requirements, the tribunal concluded that while these regulations may have had some effect on exports, 'these effects are incidental and not prohibited by the terms of Article 1106(1)'.[22]

In one of the few investor–state cases interpreting a US BIT's provisions on performance requirements, the tribunal in *Joseph C Lemire v Ukraine*[23] had to determine whether a Ukrainian law requiring that either the author, the composer, and/or the performer of 50 per cent of the music broadcast by a radio organization in Ukraine be Ukrainian violated Article II.6 of the Ukraine–US BIT, which provides: 'Neither party shall impose performance requirements as a condition of establishment, expansion or maintenance of investments, which require or enforce commitments to export goods produced, or which specify that goods and services must be purchased locally, or which impose any other similar requirement.' The tribunal acknowledged that the plain meaning of the law on

---

[17] ibid ¶¶ 306–319.

[18] *Mobil Investments Canada Inc and Murphy Oil Corp v Government of Canada*, ICSID Case No ARB(AF)/07/4 (Decision on Liability and on Principles of Quantum) (22 May 2012).

[19] ibid ¶ 172.   [20] ibid ¶ 246.

[21] *Merrill & Ring Forestry L P v Government of Canada*, UNCITRAL, ICSID Administrated (Award) (31 March 2010).

[22] ibid ¶ 120.

[23] *Joseph C Lemire v Ukraine*, ICSID Case No ARB/06/18 (Decision on Jurisdiction and Liability) (21 January 2010).

its face did not require radio stations to purchase any goods or services locally; however, it recognized that an argument could be made that although the law did not prohibit radio stations from obtaining Ukrainian music from non-Ukrainian sources, *de facto* the market for Ukrainian-authored, -composed or -produced music is located in Ukraine.[24] It therefore undertook to interpret the BIT article by reference to the object and purpose of the treaty. It found that the purpose of Article II.6 is 'to avoid that States impose local content requirements as a protection of local industries against competing imports',[25] and that the purpose of the Ukrainian broadcasting law was not to protect local industries but rather to promote Ukrainian culture. It therefore concluded that the law did not violate the BIT's provisions on performance requirements.[26]

In general, treaty provisions on performance requirements are not uniform. Instead, they adopt a variety of formulations that have evolved in response to the contracting states' national interests. To interpret and apply individual provisions, one needs to ask the following questions: (1) What is the specific nature and scope of the performance requirements that are prohibited? (2) To what extent do they go beyond those performance requirements outlawed by the TRIMs Agreement? (3) May a host state impose performance requirements on investments as a condition for investment establishment? Or is the ban limited to the post-investment phase? (4) May a host state impose performance requirements in exchange for granting an investment an incentive or benefit? (5) What kinds of actions by the investor or investment may the host government demand in exchange for granting a benefit or incentive? (6) Does the treaty exempt certain performance requirements from the general prohibition?

13.3 Entry and Residence of Foreign Nationals and Managerial Personnel

A direct foreign investment not only involves the transfer of capital from one country to another but also entails the transfer of skills, technology, know-how, and managerial ability. The effective transfer of these intangible factors usually requires the movement of the people who possess them from their home countries to the site of the investment. A basic concern of any foreign investor is whether those managers, technicians, and experts will be able to enter and stay in the host country for enough time to carry out managerial and technical functions that are vital to the success of the investment. A second, related question is the extent to which an investor will be able to hire sufficient numbers of the personnel of its choice—regardless of their nationality—to carry out those same functions. Moreover, if an investor is to effectively manage and control a branch or a subsidiary in another country, its managerial personnel must be able to enter and reside

---

[24] ibid ¶ 509.   [25] ibid ¶ 510.   [26] ibid ¶ 511.

within the host country. Thus, the effectiveness of an investment often depends on the free movement of persons across a host country's borders.

On the other hand, free movement and free employment of aliens raises serious issues with respect to a country's national security and employment policies, which all governments consider important to regulate. As a result, in the domain of foreign investment, one often detects strong tensions between two imperatives: (1) free movement of persons to advance investment; and (2) controlled movement of persons to protect national security and the jobs of host country citizens. Thus, two questions are fundamental. First, to what extent may personnel associated with the investment enter and reside in the country? Second, to what extent may the investor employ persons of its own choosing to work on the investment project?

Many, perhaps most, investment treaties do not contain provisions dealing with the entry and sojourn of foreign nationals associated with an investment. Thus, the issue remains subject to host country legislation. Some treaties, however, have sought to deal with this obvious investor concern. While very few treaties impose an obligation on the contracting parties to allow the entry and sojourn of all persons associated with a covered investment, some have included language that is non-obligatory in nature but requires the host country to give favourable consideration to requests for entry by persons associated with an investment. Some treaties, while affirming that the entry and sojourn of foreign nationals remains subject to host country law, simultaneously provide that each contracting party shall give 'sympathetic consideration'[27] to applications for entry and work permits or that the contracting party 'shall provide assistance' in securing applications for investment personnel.[28] Thus, German BITs provide that each contracting party will give 'sympathetic consideration' to applications for entry[29] and US BITs give 'nationals' of contracting parties the right to enter other contracting states for the purpose of establishing or operating investments.[30]

The Energy Charter Treaty (ECT) offers another example of treatment granted to foreign managers and employees associated with investments by contracting parties. Article 11 of the ECT, entitled 'Key Personnel', deals with the two related questions in this area: the right of an investor or its employees to enter the host country and the right of an investor to employ persons in connection with its investments. With respect to the former issue, Article 11(1) of the ECT requires a contracting party to 'examine in good faith' requests both by investors of another contracting party and by 'key personnel' employed by them to enter and remain

[27] Treaty between the Federal Republic of Germany and Bosnia and Herzegovina concerning the Encouragement and Reciprocal Protection of Investments (18 October 2004), Art 3(c).

[28] Agreement between the Government of the Republic of Botswana and the Government of the People's Republic of China (12 June 2000), Art 2.4.

[29] eg Protocol to the Treaty between the Federal Republic of Germany and the Islamic Republic of Afghanistan concerning the Encouragement and Reciprocal Protection of Investments (20 April 2005), Art 3(c).

[30] eg Agreement between the Government of the Republic of Botswana and the Government of the People's Republic of China (12 June 2000), Art 2.4.

in the host country in connection with the making, development, management, maintenance, use, enjoyment, or disposal of an investment. Thus, the ECT does not grant a right of entry to investors or their employees. Nor does the ECT define 'key employee', which is a term not found in any BIT. Obviously, differences may arise between an investor and a host country government as to whether a particular employee is 'key'. For example, to be 'key', must a person be indispensable to an investment project? Or must he or she be simply one who has an important role to play? It should also be noted that the ECT makes no reference to such a key employee's nationality; consequently, the term could cover persons who are not nationals of any ECT country.

The second paragraph of Article 11 of the ECT gives investors or their investments the right to employ key persons, regardless of nationality and citizenship, provided that they have been given permission by the host government to enter, stay, and work in the country. This provision would appear to override local legislation that limits the ability of foreign nationals to work in certain jobs or gives nationals of the host country employment priority.

Article 1107(2) of NAFTA also provides that no contracting state may require the appointment of individuals of any particular nationality to 'senior management positions'; however, the second paragraph of that article does give contracting parties the right to use nationality as a factor in appointments to governing boards. It states:

A Party may require that a majority of the board of directors, or any committee thereof, of an enterprise of that Party that is an investment of an investor of another Party, be of a particular nationality, or resident in the territory of the Party, provided that the requirement does not materially impair the ability of the investor to exercise control over its investment.

Similar provisions can be found in some recent US BITs,[31] US Free Trade Agreements (FTAs),[32] Canadian BITs,[33] and the ASEAN Comprehensive Investment Agreement.[34]

With respect to the interplay of local legislation and treaty rights concerning a covered investment's foreign employees, one might refer to the US Supreme Court decision in *Sumitomo Shoji America, Inc v Avagliano*.[35] In that case, the Court had to interpret whether the provisions of the US–Japan Treaty of Friendship, Commerce, and Navigation gave companies operating in the territory of the other party the right to engage executive personnel and technical experts 'of their choice'. The facts were that a wholly-owned US subsidiary of a Japanese company

---

[31] eg Treaty between the United States of America and the Oriental Republic of Uruguay Concerning the Encouragement and Reciprocal Protection of Investment (4 November 2005), Art 9.

[32] eg US–Australia Free Trade Agreement (18 May 2005) Implementation Act, Pub L No 108–286, § 102(1)(1) 118 Stat 919, 921 (2004); codified at 19 USC § 3805 note (2006), Art 11.10.

[33] eg Agreement Between the Government of Canada and the Government of the People's Republic of China for the Promotion and Reciprocal Protection of Investments (9 September 2012), Art 7.

[34] ASEAN Comprehensive Investment Agreement, Art 8.   [35] 457 US 176 (1982).

was sued by a group of female employees under US civil rights legislation for hiring only Japanese males in executive positions. In defence, the Japanese subsidiary argued that the treaty in question granted it the right to hire managers and technical experts of its choice, and this exempted it from US laws banning discrimination in employment and promotion. The Court held against the Japanese subsidiary on the grounds that since it had been incorporated in the United States it was an American company, not a company of 'the other Party' (ie Japan), as required by the treaty.

In the case of the ECT, it should be noted that the right to hire 'key personnel' is given to both the investor and the investment. The ECT's specific reference to the investment would presumably avoid the result in the *Sumitomo* case and protect an investment from local employment legislation purporting to deny its right to hire key personnel without regard to nationality and citizenship.

While no investment treaty overrides a contracting party's immigration laws, some treaties seek to grant investments the right to hire managers, technicians, and professionals of their choice or to exempt them from numerical immigration quotas. Thus, for example, the BIT between Japan and Kuwait provides that '[n]either Contracting Party shall impose or enforce, as a condition for investment activities' the requirement that an investor of the other contracting party 'appoint, as executives, managers or members of boards of directors, individuals of any particular nationality'.[36]

Even if a treaty contains no provisions on the ability of the investor to enter and reside in the host country, it is worth remembering that a host country's unjustified expulsion of an investor who is crucial to the functioning of the investment may constitute an expropriation under the investment treaty, a conclusion justified by the decision in *Biloune*,[37] discussed in Chapter 12.[38]

13.4 Compensation for Losses Due to War, Revolution, and Civil Disturbance

As was noted in the discussion of full protection and security in Chapter 9,[39] customary international law does not make host states guarantors of all injuries that might befall a foreign investor or investment. The duty owed by host states to foreign investors is to exercise due diligence. Thus, if an investor sustains a loss due to war, civil disturbance, revolution, or natural calamities, the host state will not be liable for compensation unless it failed to exercise due diligence to protect the investor. A state acts with due diligence when it makes reasonable efforts and

[36] Agreement between Japan and the State of Kuwait for the Promotion and Protection of Investment (22 March 2012), Art 6.
[37] eg *Biloune and Marine Drive Complex Ltd v Ghana Investments Centre and the Government of Ghana*, UNCITRAL (Award on Jurisdiction and Liability) (27 October 1989).
[38] See the discussion in Ch 12, section 12.7(c).
[39] See the discussion in Ch 9, section 9.3.

uses the forces at its command, such as the army and the police, to protect the investor's interests to the extent practicable and feasible.[40]

Investment treaties have not really changed international law in this respect. No treaty makes the host state an insurer against all injuries that might befall foreign investors. On the other hand, capital-exporting states have been concerned that their nationals and companies not be adversely discriminated against with respect to whatever protection a host state affords to its own investors in times of emergency.[41] As a result, capital-exporting states have incorporated provisions ensuring non-discriminatory treatment of investors in the event of injury arising from war, civil strife, and in some cases natural disasters into their negotiating models and, eventually, into their BIT provisions. Thus, for example, Article 5(3) of the BIT between Argentina and France provides:

Investors of either Contracting Party whose investments have suffered losses as a result of war or any other armed conflict, revolution, state of national emergency or uprising in the territory or maritime zone of the other Contracting Party shall be accorded by the latter Party treatment which is no less favourable than that accorded to its own investors or to investors of the most-favoured nation.[42]

Most investment treaties also deal with the treatment to be accorded investors for investment losses due to armed conflict or internal disorder; however, they do not normally establish an absolute right to compensation. Instead, many promise that foreign investors will be treated in the same way as nationals of the host country. Thus, if a host country compensates or assists its nationals with regard to damaged property, it would be required to give similar assistance to covered foreign investors. Many treaties also provide for most-favoured-nation treatment in this situation. The ICSID case of *Asian Agricultural Products Ltd v The Republic of Sri Lanka*[43] was the first to consider this type of treatment provision in connection with a dispute between an injured investor and a host country. Among other things, the tribunal concluded that in addition to any specific compensatory actions taken for the benefit of other investors, this provision would also grant injured investors any *promised* higher standard, for example in another BIT, that had been granted to other countries' investors.

Article 12 of the ECT adopts a position on losses similar to that found in many BITs. It provides that with regard to an investor suffering a loss with respect to an investment due to 'war or other armed conflict, state of national emergency, civil disturbance or other similar event' an ECT host country shall, except in cases where Article 13 on expropriation applies, accord that investor treatment with respect to restitution, indemnification, compensation, or settlement, which

---

[40] R Dolzer and C Schreuer, *Principles of International Investment Law* (OUP, 2007) 166.

[41] UNCTAD, *Bilateral Investment Treaties 1995–2006: Trends in Investment Rulemaking* (2007) 52.

[42] Accord Entre le Gouvernement de la République Française et le Gouvernement de la République Argentine sur l'Encouragement et la Protection Réciproques des Investissements (3 July 1992), Art 5(3).

[43] (Award) (27 June 1990) ¶¶ 57–68, (1991) 30 ILM 580.

the contracting party accords to its own investors, investors of other contracting parties, or investors of any third country, whichever treatment is most favourable.

The ECT, like many BITs, also provides protection in cases where property is requisitioned or damaged by the host country's forces or government authorities. In the case of requisition, ECT countries are to provide injured investors with compensation or restitution that is prompt, adequate, and effective.[44] In the case of losses caused by the host country's forces or authorities, the ECT, like many BITs, requires compensation or restitution only if the destruction was not wholly 'required by the necessity of the situation'. A key question, which may lead to disputes between an injured investor and the host government, is whether particular damage was required by the situation.

NAFTA, along with most US BITs, also seeks to secure non-discriminatory treatment for its investors in emergency situations. Article 1105(2) of NAFTA, in defining the minimum level of protection to be granted to investors of the three contracting parties, states: 'Each Party shall accord to investors of another Party, and to investments of investors of another Party, non-discriminatory treatment with respect to measures it adopts or maintains relating to losses suffered by investments in its territory owing to armed conflict or civil strife.'

It would seem that treaties that do not make special provisions for emergency situations but do contain national treatment and most-favoured-nation treatment provisions also oblige contracting states to abstain from discriminatory treatment of covered investments in times of war, revolution, and civil disturbance by virtue of these later provisions. Thus, if in times of war, a host state that granted special protection or compensation to its own injured nationals denied that treatment to foreigners covered by a BIT with a national treatment clause, it would seem to be in violation of its treaty obligations.

In view of that conclusion, one might well ask what the purpose of such special provisions is in times of emergency. Argentina has argued in a number of cases arising out of the severe Argentine economic and political crisis of 2001–02 that compensation for loss provisions constitute a special regime applicable to investors.[45] Under this reasoning, in the emergencies specified the only treatment that a host state owes to foreign investors is to treat them no less favourably than

---

[44] In the *Elsi* case, the ICJ, dealing with an instance of alleged requisition, noted that there must be a causal link between the injury complained of and the requisition. *Elettronica Sicula Spa (Elsi) (United States v Italy)* [1989] ICJ 15 (July 20).

[45] *Enron Corp and Ponderosa Assets LP v Argentine Republic*, ICSID Case No ARB/01/3 (Award) (22 May 2007) ¶¶ 314–321; *Sempra Energy International v Argentine Republic*, ICSID Case No ARB/02/16 (Award) (28 September 2007) ¶¶ 356–363; *BG Group plc v Republic of Argentina*, UNCITRAL (Award) (24 December 2007) ¶¶ 369–387; *Suez, Sociedad General de Aguas de Barcelona SA and Vivendi Universal SA v Argentine Republic*, ICSID Case No ARB/03/19, *AWG Group Ltd v Argentine Republic*, UNCITRAL (Decision on Liability) (30 July 2010) ¶¶ 266–270; *Total SA v Argentine Republic*, ICSID Case No ARB/04/01 (Decision on Liability) (27 December 2010) ¶¶ 225–230; *Impregilo SpA v Argentine Republic*, ICSID Case No ARB/07/17 (Award) (21 June 2011) ¶¶ 339–341; *El Paso Energy International Company v Argentine Republic*, ICSID Case No ARB/03/15 (Award) (31 October 2011) ¶¶ 558–560; *EDF International SA, SAUR International SA and León Participaciones Argentinas SA v Argentine Republic*, ICSID Case No ARB/03/23 (Award) (11 June 2012) ¶¶ 1153–1162.

national or third country investors and no other treatment obligations are applicable. In support of this position, one could argue that if such an interpretation is not given to the provision, it would be meaningless, since the national treatment and most-favoured-nation treaty provision would serve to protect investors to the same extent as the special provisions on treatment in emergency situations. Yet all of the tribunals that considered this issue rejected Argentina's position. The *CMS* tribunal stated:

The plain meaning of the Article [Article IV(3)] is to provide a floor treatment for the investor in the context of the measures adopted in respect of the losses suffered in the emergency, not different from that applied to nationals or other foreign investors. The Article does not derogate from the Treaty rights but rather ensures that any measures directed at offsetting or minimizing losses will be applied in a non-discriminatory manner.[46]

Additional arguments supporting this conclusion are that such treatment provisions only apply in situations where: (a) an investor has suffered damage as a result of armed conflict or similar circumstances; but (b) such investor does not have a specific entitlement to reparation under another provision of the treaty or customary international law; and (c) another investor, whether domestic or foreign, has been granted reparation, whether by operation of another treaty, domestic law, or simply on a discretionary basis. In short, by their terms and structure these treaty provisions do not establish an excuse for measures that otherwise breach the treaty—they create an additional legal cause for compensation. Moreover, as a matter of treaty interpretation, the intent of these provisions is to compensate for physical damage caused by war, revolution, or civil disturbance, not injuries resulting from a state's regulatory measures.

13.5 Transparency and Regulatory Due Process

The beginning of the twenty-first century witnessed the introduction of a new investment treaty standard—the obligation of contracting states to maintain some degree of governmental transparency. Although it is generally agreed that transparency of governmental operations is a key element of good governance, no definitive, accepted definition of 'transparency' has emerged.[47] One scholar has defined transparency as 'the broadest doctrine of openness', 'the doctrine that the general conduct of executive government should be predictable and operate according to published (and as far as possible non-discretionary) rules rather than arbitrarily'.[48]

---

[46] *CMS Gas Transmission Co v The Argentine Republic*, ICSID Case No ARB/01/8 (Award) (12 May 2005) ¶ 375.

[47] M Bauhr and M Grimes, 'What is Transparency? New Measures and Relevance for Quality of Government', Working Paper Series 2012:16, University of Gothenburg (December 2012), 4, available at <http://www.qog.pol.gu.se/digitalAssets/1418/1418047_2012_16_bauhr_grimes.pdf> accessed 15 January 2015; see also C Hood and D Heald, (eds), *Transparency in Government: The Key to Better Governance?* (OUP, 2006).

[48] Hood and Heald (n 47 aove) 14.

A Committee of Experts on Public Administration functioning under the auspices of the UN Economic and Social Council has stated:

Transparency and accountability are interrelated and mutually reinforcing concepts. Without *transparency*, that is, unfettered access to timely and reliable information on decisions and performance, it would be difficult to call public sector entities to account. Unless there is *accountability*, that is, mechanisms to report on the usage of public resources and consequences for failing to meet stated performance objectives, transparency would be of little value. The existence of both conditions is a prerequisite to effective, efficient and equitable management in public institutions.[49]

The concept of transparency can therefore be narrowly defined as simply the release of relevant information, for example the publication of laws, or much more broadly to include elements of the rule of law, particularly with respect to the functioning of the executive institutions of government, and indeed may be conflated with what one might call 'regulatory due process'.

Transparency of laws and other governmental measures is critical for investors desiring a stable and predictable investment environment. Such information helps investors decide whether to invest and assists them to evaluate the conditions and rules governing their investments.[50] In varying degrees, it may also place a check on arbitrary governmental action. The fair and equitable treatment standard has traditionally included the principle of transparency and many tribunals have addressed transparency within the context of fair and equitable treatment.[51] Most BITs have lacked a specific provision on transparency and those that included such clauses focused on relations between the contracting states.[52] Some of the earlier treaties contained a paragraph committing the contracting parties to publish their laws (certainly an important element of transparency), often as part of treaty articles on investment promotion or investment treatment,[53] but they did not employ the term 'transparency' and did not include a separate article on transparency that elaborated in any detail on this obligation. A number of recent treaties, however, include separate provisions on transparency that enumerate specific obligations involving 'interested persons' or the 'public'. These clauses could be

---

[49] United Nations Economic and Social Council, 'Definition of basic concepts and terminologies in governance and public administration', E/C.16/2006/4, 5 January 2006, available at <http://unpan1.un.org/intradoc/groups/public/documents/un/unpan022332.pdf>accessed 19 January 2015.

[50] UNCTAD, *Bilateral Investment Treaties 1995–2006: Trends in Investment Rulemaking* (2007) 77.

[51] See the discussion in Ch 9, section 9.4.

[52] UNCTAD, *Bilateral Investment Treaties 1995–2006: Trends in Investment Rulemaking* (2007) 76.

[53] eg Treaty Between the United States of America and the Arab Republic of Egypt Concerning the Reciprocal Encouragement and Protection of Investments (1986), Art II ('Encouragement and Protection of Investments'), ¶ 8 provides: 'Each Party and its subdivisions shall make public all laws, regulations, administrative practices and procedures, and adjudicatory decisions that pertain to [or] affect investments in its territory of nationals or companies of the other Party.'

interpreted to provide a cause of action to wronged investors. For example, Article 19 of the Canada–Jordan BIT[54] states:

1. Each Party shall ensure its laws, regulations, procedures, and administrative rulings of general application respecting any matter covered by this Agreement are promptly published or otherwise made available in such a manner as to enable interested persons and the other Party to become acquainted with them.
2. To the extent possible, each Party shall:
   (a) publish in advance any such measure that it proposes to adopt; and
   (b) provide interested persons and the other Party a reasonable opportunity to comment on such proposed measures.
3. Upon request by a Party, the other Party shall provide information on the measures that may have an impact on covered investments.

This right to information, however, is qualified. The Canada–Jordan BIT includes a separate provision that lists exceptions to the treaty, one of which states: '[n]othing in this Agreement shall be construed: to require any Party to furnish or allow access to any information the disclosure of which it determines to be contrary to its essential security interests'.[55]

Other treaties include more elaborate requirements and limitations within the transparency provisions. Article 10 of the China–Japan–Korea Trilateral Investment Agreement[56] is a particularly complex and thorough transparency clause:

1. Each Contracting Party shall promptly publish, or otherwise make publicly available, its laws, regulations, administrative procedures and administrative rulings and judicial decisions of general application as well as international agreements to which the Contracting Party is a party and which pertain to or affect investment activities. The Government of each Contracting Party shall make easily available to the public, the names and addresses of the competent authorities responsible for such laws, regulations, administrative procedures and administrative rulings.
2. When a Contracting Party introduces or changes its laws or regulations that significantly affect the implementation and operation of this Agreement, the Contracting Party shall endeavor to provide a reasonable interval between the time when such laws or regulations are published or made publicly available and the time when they enter into force, except for those laws or regulations involving national security, foreign exchange rates or monetary policies and other laws or regulations the publication of which would impede law enforcement.
3. Each Contracting Party shall, upon the request by another Contracting Party, within a reasonable period of time and through existing bilateral channels, respond to specific questions from, and provide information to, the latter Contracting Party with respect to any actual or proposed measure of the former Contracting Party, which

---

[54] Agreement between Canada and the Hashemite Kingdom of Jordan for the Promotion and Protection of Investments (28 June 2009).

[55] ibid Art 10(4)(a).

[56] Agreement among the Government of Japan, the Government of the Republic of Korea and the Government of the People's Republic of China for the Promotion, Facilitation and Protection of Investment (13 May 2012).

might materially affect the interests of the latter Contracting Party and its investors under this Agreement.

4. Each Contracting Party shall, in accordance with its laws and regulations:
   (a) make public in advance regulations of general application that affect any matter covered by this Agreement; and
   (b) provide a reasonable opportunity for comments by the public for those regulations related to investment and give consideration to those comments before adoption of such regulations.

5. The provisions of this Article shall not be construed so as to oblige any Contracting Party to disclose confidential information, the disclosure of which:
   (a) would impede law enforcement;
   (b) would be contrary to the public interest; or
   (c) could prejudice privacy or legitimate commercial interests.

In addition, the first two US BITs concluded in the twenty-first century, one with Rwanda and one with Uruguay, each contain two articles that directly affect governmental transparency; the first is entitled 'Publication of Law and Decisions Respecting Investment' and the second 'Transparency', both of which enumerate the obligations of contracting states in considerable detail.[57] With respect to multilateral treaties, Article 20 of the ECT and Article 21 of the ASEAN Comprehensive Investment Treaty both address transparency, specifying various requirements and exceptions. The investment chapter of NAFTA, however, does not include a provision on transparency.

The inclusion of transparency provisions in investment treaties should also be considered in relation to another recent trend, which will be discussed in Chapter 14: the introduction of treaty provisions that give host countries greater scope, sometimes referred to as 'increased policy space', to exercise their regulatory powers without violating basic treaty standards such as fair and equitable treatment or full protection and security. Together these two trends may be viewed as a new dimension of the basic bargain between host states and some countries: the grant of increased regulatory authority, provided such authority is exercised in conformity with basic notions of transparency and regulatory due process.

The growth of investment treaty transparency provisions both in number and scope also raises an important question: Do these clauses actually create obligations for states on which investors may sue if states fail to meet them? Or do they simply set a goal for states to achieve? An investor arguing a claim under the China–Japan–Korea Agreement could compare the language of the transparency provision, Article 10, with the entry of personnel provision,[58] Article 8, which states: 'Each Contracting Party shall *endeavor*, to the extent possible ...' (emphasis added). The language in the former provision seems to require the state to act in a

---

[57] Treaty Between the Government of the United States of America and of the Republic of Rwanda Concerning the Encouragement and Reciprocal Protection of Investment (19 February 2008), Arts 10 and 11; Treaty Between the Government of the United States of America and the Oriental Republic of Uruguay Concerning the Encouragement and Reciprocal Protection of Investment (11 April 2005), Arts 10 and 11.

[58] See the discussion in section 13.3 above.

specific manner, rather than encourage the state to make a reasonable effort. The former seems to create an obligation, while the latter provides a goal. By this logic, the second paragraph of Article 10 of the China–Japan–Korea Agreement would not bind the parties.

If transparency clauses can in theory be breached, what facts and circumstances would allow investors to bring transparency claims? Tribunals would have to interpret the language of specific treaties to determine whether the government acted efficiently and transparently enough. Clear cases may arise where states withhold critical information for an extended period of time or completely fail to provide information to an investor. It would be particularly obvious if a state failed to abide by its own internal procedures for publishing information. More difficult cases could result from situations where an investor claims that a state's procedures are inadequate. Not only would a tribunal struggle to define the meaning of promptness, easy availability, and reasonableness in this context, it could also be politically challenging and controversial for a tribunal to hold that a government does not function properly according to an abstract international standard.

13.6 The Subrogation Obligation

Nearly all major capital-exporting countries have established or supported programmes and entities to provide political risk insurance to their nationals and companies investing abroad. In addition, certain large developing countries, such as China, India, and South Africa, whose nationals undertake significant foreign investments, have established similar programmes.[59] Some offer only political risk insurance on investment while others combine this service with credit insurance on exports.

Most such programmes will not insure investments in countries whose governments have not entered into an agreement permitting such programmes to operate in that country and agreeing to abide by certain principles, including the right of the insurer, if it has paid compensation to an insured investor under an insurance contract, to seek reimbursement from the host government. That right under general principles of insurance law is known as subrogation. Certain insuring countries also require that the host country has concluded a BIT with them before they will provide political risk insurance to investments in those countries. Moreover, many investment agreements specifically recognize the right of the insurer country to be subrogated to the rights of the insured and

---

[59] For a list of political risk insurance providers, both public and private, see the website of the Multilateral Investment Guarantee Agency at <http://www.miga.org/documents/flagship09e-book_chap3.pdf> accessed 17 January 2015. Only three OECD governments, Ireland, Mexico, and New Zealand, do not provide some form of political risk insurance. K Gordon, *Investment Guarantees and Political Risk Insurance: Institutions, Incentives and Development* (OECD, 2009) 6. See generally Salacuse (n 1 above) 243–73.

to seek reimbursement from the offending host country. For example, Article 8 ('Subrogation') of the India–China BIT provides:

Where one Contracting Party or its designated agency has guaranteed any indemnity against non-commercial risks in respect of an investment, covered under this agreement, by any of its investors in the territory of the other Contracting Party and has made payment to such investors in respect of their claims, the other Contracting Party shall recognise that the first Contracting Party or its designated agency is entitled by virtue of subrogation to exercise the rights and assert the claims of those investors. The subrogated rights or claims shall not exceed the original rights or claims of such investors.[60]

In addition, similar provisions may also be found in the ECT[61] and the ASEAN Comprehensive Investment Agreement.[62] On the other hand, United States BITs do not include a similar clause since the United States requires that countries benefiting from its political risk insurance program under the Overseas Private Investment Corporation (OPIC) enter into a separate agreement governing OPIC operations in that country and granting OPIC the right of subrogation to the rights of insured investors.

Technically, BIT provisions on subrogation do not constitute a standard of treatment that a contracting state owes to an investor but rather an obligation that contracting states have towards one another. The failure of a contracting state to respect that obligation would not be adjudicated in investor–state arbitration but instead in inter-state arbitration, which is provided by all investment treaties for the resolution of disputes between contracting states.

---

[60] Agreement between the Republic of India and the People's Republic of China for the Protection and Promotion of Investments (21 November 2006).
[61] ECT, Art 15.   [62] ASEAN Comprehensive Investment Agreement, Art 15.

14

Investment Treaty Exceptions, Modifications, and Terminations

14.1 The Tensions of Investment Treaties

The negotiation and implementation of any treaty has the potential to confront a state with the tension between its perceived national interests and its requested or ratified treaty obligations. Such tensions seem to be a permanent feature of investment treaty practice. On the one hand, a state seeking the benefits of foreign investment contemplates or agrees to international obligations regarding the treatment it will accord to such investors and investments during the long years of their existence in its territory; on the other, those same states wish to retain the maximum amount of freedom possible to enact legislation and regulations during the same period in order to pursue their perceived national interests in an uncertain future. The tension between these two imperatives is present at the bargaining table when representatives of concerned states negotiate investment treaties, in government offices when officials consider how existing or proposed laws or regulations may affect their treaty obligations, and in arbitration hearings when tribunals deciding an investor–state dispute must determine whether a government measure, ostensibly taken for the public welfare, conflicts with a respondent state's investment treaty commitments.

A state has three basic devices to mediate the tensions created by investment treaty practice. The first, which is employed as part of the negotiating process, is to create specific exceptions in the treaty to assure a host state sufficient latitude of action for the future. The other two, which are invoked after the investment treaty enters into effect, are for a state to modify the treaty provisions by agreement with other contracting parties or terminate participation in the treaty and thus end its international investment obligations. This chapter considers the investment treaty devices of exceptions, modifications, and terminations.

14.2 Treaty Exceptions

(a) In general

Nearly all investment treaties include one or more exceptions in order to protect certain important interests from the treaty's coverage and allow the contracting states to maintain their ability to exercise legislative and regulatory authority in that area. Some of these exceptions (many of which have been discussed earlier in this book) are narrowly drafted and only restrict the application of a specific treaty provision to a particular circumstance or transaction. For example, treaty provisions that grant investors the freedom to make monetary transfers often contain provisions clarifying that such commitments do not prohibit a contracting state from preventing a transfer through a good faith and non-discriminatory application of its laws relating to bankruptcy, insolvency, and the protection of creditors' rights.[1]

Other exceptions are broader in scope and exempt a specified class of persons, transactions, or situations from the application of all investment treaty provisions. For example, many treaties contain what might be called a 'denial of benefits' clause. This exception allows the contracting states to deny the benefits of a treaty to investments of companies controlled by third country nationals if the companies lack 'substantial business activities' in the home country or if the controlling persons are nationals of a country with which the denying party does not maintain 'normal economic relations'.[2] Accordingly, US BITs usually include the following provision:

Each Party reserves the right to deny to any company the advantages of this Treaty if nationals of any third country control such company and, in the case of a company of the other Party, that company has no substantial business activities in the territory of the other Party or is controlled by nationals of a third country with which the denying Party does not maintain normal economic relations.[3]

This exception explicitly carves out a class of 'investors' that would otherwise be entitled to protections under the treaty. For many years the United States has maintained economic sanctions against Libya and Cuba, and these two countries have been cited by the US State Department as examples of countries that the United States does not maintain normal economic relations with and whose nationals and companies would therefore not benefit from US BITs with third countries. In 2004, the United States lifted economic sanctions against Libya and thereby recognized Libyan-controlled entities with substantial business activities

---

[1] eg Agreement between the Government of the United Mexican States and the Government of the Republic of Korea for the Promotion and Reciprocal Protection of Investments (14 November 2000), Art 6(3). See the discussion in Ch 10, section 10.7.

[2] eg Treaty between the United States of America and the Republic of Kazakhstan Concerning the Encouragement and Reciprocal Protection of Investment (19 May 1992), Art I(2).

[3] ibid. See also the ASEAN Comprehensive Investment Agreement, Art 19 ('Denial of Benefits').

in treaty partners as being able to benefit from investment treaties with those countries.[4]

A searching examination of the body of investment treaties reveals a wide diversity of exceptions, which includes differences in their nature, breadth, and conditions for application. A 2007 study by UNCTAD found that the number of exceptions finding their way into newly negotiated treaties was increasing.[5] An examination of treaties signed since that time confirms this trend. One reason for the increase is that the experience of host countries with investor–state arbitration has revealed various situations in which investment treaty provisions can intrude into and inhibit domestic law-making and regulation, sometimes in unexpected and undesired ways. As a result, states negotiating investment treaties have perceived a need to demarcate clearly the latitude that host countries reserve to themselves in order to protect their vital national interests. The following are some of the principal types of exceptions found in investment treaties.

(b) Exceptions to protect essential security interests and the maintenance of public order

Many investment treaties contain provisions that except contracting parties from core treaty obligations under exceptional circumstances in which a country's important national interests are at stake. Such important interests include national security, the maintenance of public order, and the restoration of peace and security. For example, Article XI of the bilateral investment treaty (BIT) between the United States and Argentina states: 'This Treaty shall not preclude the application by either Party of measures necessary for the maintenance of public order, the fulfillment of its obligations with respect to the maintenance or restoration of international peace or security, or the Protection of its own essential security interests.'[6]

Because of the use of the term 'preclude' in some treaty texts, exception clauses are sometimes referred to as 'non-precluded measures provisions'.[7] Many treaties, however, seek to arrive at the same result without using the term 'preclude'. Thus, Article 24 of the Energy Charter Treaty (ECT), on exceptions, states that the

---

[4] CNN, 'Bush signs order lifting sanctions on Libya' (21 September 2004), at <http://www.cnn.com/2004/WORLD/africa/09/20/libya.sanctions/> accessed 18 December 2013.

[5] UNCTAD, *Bilateral Investment Treaties 1995–2006: Trends in Investment Rulemaking* (2007) 81.

[6] Treaty between the United States of America and the Argentine Republic Concerning the Reciprocal Encouragement and Protection of Investment (14 November 1991). cf the UK–Argentina BIT, which does not have such a broad exceptions clause. Art 7, entitled 'Exceptions', applies only to exclude the BIT's national treatment provisions to three specified situations. Agreement between the Government of the United Kingdom and Northern Ireland and the Government of the Republic of Argentina for the Promotion and Protection of Investments (11 December 1990). See also ASEAN Comprehensive Investment Agreement, Art 18 ('Security Exception').

[7] WW Burke-White and A von Staden, 'Investment Protection in Extra-Ordinary Times: The Interpretation and Application of Non-Precluded Measures Provisions in Bilateral Investment Treaties' (2008) 48 Va J Int'l L 307.

treaty's provisions are not to be construed 'to prevent any Contracting Party from taking any measure which it considers necessary', 'for the protection of essential security interests', and 'the maintenance of public order', among others. Many other treaties also follow this linguistic pattern.[8] Some treaties also provide exceptions to allow states to pursue other objectives, including public health, public morality, and emergency situations.[9] It should be noted, however, that such exception clauses rarely refer specifically to *economic* crisis or *economic* interests as creating a basis for justifying an exception to treaty obligations.

These general exception clauses or non-precluded measures provisions have the justifiable goal of giving host countries the legislative and regulatory latitude to deal with threats to important national interests. On the other hand, their existence in treaties raises the risk that host countries will invoke them in unjustified circumstances in order to avoid their legal obligations and thwart the justified expectations of investors. This risk is particularly severe because of the vagueness and generality of key terms such as 'protection of essential security interests'. For example, can a state facing difficult economic challenges justify the expropriation of foreign investments on the grounds that such action was necessary to protect its essential security interests?

In order to provide some safeguards against the abusive invocation of exception clauses, many investment treaties establish conditions that must be met for

---

[8] eg the Colombia–India BIT, Art 13 which states:

    4. Nothing in this Agreement precludes either Contracting Party from taking action, which it considers necessary for the protection of its essential security interests or in circumstances of extreme emergency in accordance with its laws normally, and reasonably applied on a non-discriminatory basis.

    5. Subject to the requirement that such measures are not applied in a manner which would constitute a means of arbitrary or unjustifiable discrimination against the investors of the other Contracting Party or a disguised restriction on investment of investors of a Contracting Party in the territory of the other Contracting Party, nothing in this Agreement shall be construed to prevent the adoption or enforcement by a Contracting Party of measures:

    a. necessary to maintain public order;
    b. necessary to protect human, animal, plant life or health;
    c. relating to the protection of the environment or the conservation of exhaustible natural resources, if such measures are made effective in conjunction with restrictions on domestic production or consumption;
    d. in pursuance of its obligation under the United Nations Charter for the maintenance of international peace and security.

Agreement for the Promotion and Protection of Investments between the Republic of Colombia and the Republic of India (10 November 2009).

[9] eg the Malaysia–Australia FTA, Art 12.18 which states:

    1. Subject to the requirement that such measures are not applied in a manner which would constitute a means of arbitrary or unjustifiable discrimination between Parties where like conditions prevail, or a disguised restriction on investment flows, nothing in this Chapter shall be construed to prevent the adoption or enforcement by any Party of measures:

    (a) necessary to protect national security and public morals;
    (b) necessary to protect human, animal or plant life or health....

Malaysia–Australia Free Trade Agreement (22 May 2012).

a host country legitimately to invoke the clauses and avoid treaty obligations. One example is a requirement that the invoking party notify the other party of its intention to invoke the exception clause and provide pertinent information regarding the proposed measure. The treaty may also attempt to specify the conditions that must be legitimately met to allow for the exception. For example, the Kuwait–Japan BIT states: 'the public order exception may only be invoked where a genuine and sufficiently serious threat is posed to one of the fundamental interests of society'.[10] More generally, it would seem that the treaty provisions, discussed in Chapter 13, at section 13.5, requiring contracting states to act with transparency and to respect various principles of regulatory due process in their treatment of investors, would also apply to many situations in which a host state invokes and applies treaty exceptions.

Despite the existence of such restrictions, the interpretation and application of exceptions clauses can generate controversy because of their breadth, ambiguity, and potential for abuse. They raise at least three basic questions: (1) To what extent are such clauses self-judging so that the legality of invoking them is solely within the judgment of the host country and not effectively reviewable by an arbitral tribunal? (2) May a host government invoke the exception clause in cases of economic and financial crisis on the grounds that such crises threaten 'essential security interests'? (3) What specifically are the elements of the threat that justify invoking the exception?

The Argentina financial and economic crisis at the beginning of the twenty-first century gave rise to claims by aggrieved investors that led arbitral tribunals to consider these questions. In order to cope with the crisis, which caused significant political turmoil in the country, Argentina took measures that included a significant devaluation and a refusal to meet certain contractual commitments to investors. American investors alleged that these actions violated the US–Argentina BIT. One of the grounds on which Argentina defended its actions was that the treaty did not preclude it from taking the steps necessary to deal with its essential security interests and to preserve public order because of the exception clause, Article XI, quoted earlier. It further argued that the exception clause was self-judging and that Argentina's decision to invoke it was not reviewable by an arbitral tribunal. An examination of relevant Argentine cases provides some guidance in answering the questions; however, as will be seen, tribunals have not given uniform answers on all three questions.

(i) The self-judging nature of the exception clause

As with any treaty clause, one must focus on the specific language of the exception provision being applied, since there is a wide variation among treaties. For one thing, some clauses appear to be self-judging while others do not. For example,

---

[10] Agreement Between Japan and the State of Kuwait for the Promotion and Protection of Investment (22 March 2012), Art 17.

the exception clause in the US–Bahrain BIT states: 'This Treaty shall not preclude a party from applying measures *which it considers* necessary for the fulfillment of its obligations with respect to international peace and security, or the protection of its own essential security interests' (emphasis added).[11] The exception clause of the ECT contains similar language.[12] The use of the phrase 'which it considers' gives rise to the inference that the exception clause is self-judging. On the other hand, the US–Argentina BIT quoted earlier does not include that phrase and therefore might be interpreted as non-self-judging.

Thus, in approaching an exception clause it is important to determine whether there is some specific language as to its self-judging character. Even if the exception contains self-judging language, however, that fact does not mean that a host state may invoke it at its unfettered discretion. By virtue of Article 23 of the Vienna Convention on the Law of Treaties (VCLT), states have a duty to carry out their treaty obligations 'in good faith'; consequently, a tribunal or court applying an investment treaty is required to determine whether a contracting state has invoked an exception clause in good faith. As a result, even an explicitly self-judging clause is not completely beyond the jurisdiction of an investor–state tribunal.[13]

Tribunals in four cases involving Argentina concluded that the exception clauses invoked by Argentina (including the US–Argentina BIT quoted earlier) were not self-judging. They appear to have been motivated by different factors. In *CMS v Argentina*,[14] the tribunal compared the language of the US BIT with treaties, such as the General Agreement on Tariffs and Trade (GATT), which were explicitly self-judging. It then found that the language in the US BIT did not contain sufficiently similar indications of a self-judging nature. In *LG&E v Argentina*,[15] the tribunal also held the provision to be non-self-judging because it found no evidence that the contracting parties had a contrary intent.[16]

(ii) Application of exception clauses to economic crises

Some general exception clauses expressly include economic crises. The Kenya–Slovakia BIT states: 'Nothing in this Agreement shall be construed as preventing a Contracting Party from taking any action that it considers necessary for the protection of its essential security interests in time of war or armed conflict,

---

[11] Treaty between the Government of the United States of America and the Government of the State of Bahrain Concerning the Encouragement and Reciprocal Protection of Investment (29 September 1999), Art 14.

[12] ECT, Art 24(5).   [13] Burke-White and von Staden (n 7 above).

[14] *CMS Gas Transmission Co v The Argentine Republic*, ICSID Case No ARB/01/8 (Award) (12 May 2005).

[15] *LG&E Energy Corp v Argentine Republic*, ICSID Case No ARB/02/1 (Decision on Liability) (3 October 2006).

[16] Other cases that also found that Article XI of the Argentina–US BIT was not self-judging include *Continental Casualty Co v The Argentine Republic*, ICSID Case No ARB/03/9 (Award) (5 September 2008) and *El Paso Energy International Co v The Argentine Republic*, ICSID Case No ARB/03/15 (Award) (31 October 2011).

financial, economic, social crisis or other emergency in international relations'.[17] Japan has included in its recent agreements a 'prudential measures' provision, which states:

1. Notwithstanding any other provisions of this Agreement, a Contracting Party shall not be prevented from taking measures relating to financial services for prudential reasons, including measures for the protection of investors, depositors, policy holders or persons to whom a fiduciary duty is owed by an enterprise supplying financial services, or to ensure the integrity and stability of the financial system.
2. Where the measures referred to in paragraph 1 do not conform with the provisions of this Agreement, they shall not be used as a means of avoiding the Contracting Party's obligations under this agreement.[18]

This language is very similar to that in the General Agreement on Trade in Services (GATS) Annex on Financial Services and the 2012 US Model BIT includes a similar provision.[19]

Although most exception clauses do not specifically refer to economic crises or economic emergencies as reasons justifying their application, all tribunals that have considered the matter thus far have interpreted the clauses broadly enough to include such crises and emergencies within the scope of essential security and public order provisions. Tribunals have not limited the exceptions to extreme physical threats such as war and revolution. On this point the tribunal in *LG&E v Argentina*, interpreting the exception clause in the US–Argentina BIT, stated:

The Tribunal rejects the notion that Article XI is only applicable in circumstances amounting to military action and war. Certainly, the conditions in Argentina in December 2001 called for immediate, decisive action to restore civil order and stop the economic decline. To conclude that such a severe economic crisis could not constitute an essential security interest is to diminish the havoc that the economy can wreak on the lives of an entire population and the ability of the Government to lead. When a State's economic foundation is under siege, the severity of the problem can equal that of any military invasion.[20]

(iii) Elements justifying the exception

A basic problem in interpreting and applying an exception clause is determining what must be established and what degree of severity is necessary in order to release a host country from its obligations under an investment treaty. Thus, the *CMS* tribunal, while affirming that 'economic difficulties' were within the scope

---

[17] Agreement between the Government of the Slovak Republic and the Government of the Republic of Kenya for the Promotion and Reciprocal Protection of Investments (14 December 2011), Art 14.

[18] eg Agreement among the Government of Japan, the Government of the Republic of Korea and the Government of the People's Republic of China for the Promotion, Facilitation and Protection of Investment (13 May 2012), Art 20.

[19] 2012 US Model BIT, Art 20.

[20] *LG&E Energy Corp v Argentine Republic*, ICSID Case No ARB/02/1 (Decision on Liability) (3 October 2006) ¶ 238.

of the exception clause, went on to say: 'The question is, however, how grave these economic difficulties might be.'[21]

The tribunals deciding the cases arising out of the Argentine crisis have not given a uniform answer to this question. Three of the tribunal decisions[22] took a strict approach to interpreting exception clauses and essentially viewed them as incorporating the very limited customary international law defence of state of necessity. Thus, the tribunal in *Enron v Argentina*, believing that a restrictive interpretation of any 'escape route' from treaty obligations was required, decided that as the treaty itself provided no guidance as to the meaning of essential security interests it was 'necessary to rely on the requirements of the state of necessity under customary law'.[23]

One of the most authoritative statements of the state of necessity defence is found in Article 25 of the Draft Articles on the Responsibility of States for Internationally Wrongful Acts (2001), a document that tribunals have relied upon in interpreting the exception clauses in investment treaties.[24] It states:

necessity may not be invoked by a State as a ground for precluding the wrongfulness of an act not in conformity with an international obligation of that State unless the act (a) is the only way for the State to safeguard an essential interest against a grave and imminent peril; and (b) does not seriously impair an essential interest of the State or States towards which the obligation exists, or of the international community as a whole.

It further provides that 'necessity may not be invoked by a State as a ground for precluding wrongfulness if: (a) the international obligation in question excludes the possibility of invoking necessity; or (b) the State has contributed to the situation of necessity'. All three tribunals that equated the exception provision in the US–Argentina BIT with the state of necessity defence found that the required elements for the necessity defence did not exist. As the tribunal stated in *Enron*:

As the Tribunal has found above that the crisis invoked does not meet the customary law requirements of Article 25 of the Articles on State Responsibility, thus concluding that necessity or emergency are not conducive to the preclusion of wrongfulness, there is no need to undertake a further judicial review under Article XI as this Article does not set out conditions different from customary law in this respect.[25]

---

[21] ibid ¶ 354.
[22] *CMS Gas Transmission Co v Argentine Republic*, ICSID Case No ARB/01/8 (Award) (12 May 2005); *Enron Corp and Ponderosa Assets LP v Argentine Republic*, ICSID Case No ARB/01/3 (Award) (22 May 2007); *Sempra Energy International v Argentine Republic*, ICSID Case No Arb/02/16 (Award) (28 September 2007). The annulment committee in *CMS* heavily criticized the tribunal's approach to Art XI as an error of law but did not annul the award, while the decisions in *Enron* and *Sempra* were both annulled. *CMS* (see earlier in this note) (Annulment Proceeding) (25 September 2007) ¶¶ 130–136. The *Sempra* decision was annulled for failing to apply Article XI of the treaty. *Sempra* (see earlier in this note) (Annulment Proceeding) (29 June 2010) ¶¶ 159–207.
[23] *Enron Corp and Ponderosa Assets LP v Argentine Republic*, ICSID Case No ARB/01/3 (Award) (22 May 2007) ¶¶ 6, 333.
[24] Draft Articles on the Responsibility of States for Internationally Wrongful Acts (2001), Art 25.
[25] *Enron Corp and Ponderosa Assets LP v Argentine Republic*, ICSID Case No ARB/01/3 (Award) (22 May 2007).

The tribunal's decision, however, has been annulled for failing to interpret fully the language of Article 25. Specifically, the annulment committee found that the tribunal failed to consider whether the 'only way' language in Article 25 could be interpreted to mean there must be no alternative measures that the state could have taken that did not involve a similar or graver breach of international law. The committee also criticized the tribunal for failing to consider the questions of who decides whether there is a relevant alternative available and whether the state should receive some margin of appreciation.[26]

The tribunal in *LG&E v Argentina*[27] arrived at a different result after interpreting the exception clause in the US–Argentina BIT. It found that a state of necessity existed in Argentina between 1 December 2001 and 26 April 2003 because conditions in the country had deteriorated to the point that 'the essential interests of the Argentine state were threatened'.[28] In reaching this conclusion, it applied the elements of the state of necessity defence as presented in Article 25 of the Draft Articles on State Responsibility and found that they were satisfied by the situation in Argentina during the crisis. The tribunal stated that Article XI of the US–Argentina BIT establishes the state of necessity as a ground for exempting Argentina from liability from what would otherwise be a wrongful act under the treaty. However, it concluded that the exemption would only be justified in emergency situations and that, once the emergency had ended, the state would no longer be exempted from liability. Thus, in the case of the Argentine crisis, Argentina would be liable for its actions after 26 April 2003, which was the date when the tribunal determined the crisis to have ended. The tribunal also determined that although Article XI of the BIT and the Draft Article on State Responsibility make no mention of whether a state has an obligation to compensate investors during a state of necessity or emergency, damages suffered during such period should be borne by the investor and not by the host country.[29]

Tribunals have properly recognized that a defence under Article XI is distinct from the state of necessity as determined under customary international law.[30] Since it is based in customary international law, the state of necessity defence is theoretically always available to a respondent state whether or not a specific exception clause exists in the applicable treaty. To some extent, conflating the two defences negates the intention of the contracting states that specifically negotiated

[26] *Enron Corp and Ponderosa Assets LP v Argentine Republic*, ICSID Case No ARB/01/3 (Annulment Proceeding) (30 July 2010) ¶¶ 368–406.
[27] *LG&E Energy Corp v Argentine Republic*, ICSID Case No Arb/02/1 (Decision on Liability) (3 October 2006).
[28] ibid ¶ 257.   [29] ibid ¶ 264.
[30] *El Paso Energy International Co v The Argentine Republic*, ICSID Case No ARB/03/15 (Award) (31 October 2011) ¶ 553; *Continental Casualty Co v The Argentine Republic*, ICSID Case No ARB/03/9 (Award) (5 September 2008) ¶ 167; *LG&E Energy Corp v Argentine Republic*, ICSID Case No ARB/02/1 (Decision on Liability) (3 October 2006) ¶ 245. In *CMS Gas Transmission Co v The Argentine Republic*, ICSID Case No ARB/01/8, the Decision of the ad hoc Committee on the Application for Annulment of 25 September 2007, the Committee stated: 'Article XI is a threshold requirement: if it applies, the substantive obligations under the Treaty do not apply. By contrast, Article 25 is an excuse which is only relevant once it has been decided that there has otherwise been a breach of those substantive obligations.' ibid ¶ 129.

and included an exception clause in the treaty. By including such a treaty provision while making no reference to the state of necessity defence, one would normally assume that the contracting states intended their exception clause to mean something different from the state of necessity as expressed in Article 25 of the Draft Articles on State Responsibility. Moreover, normal principles of treaty interpretation require that the exception clause be read on its own terms and that the state of necessity defence not be unjustifiably incorporated into the treaty.

It should be pointed out that the difference between the two defences may be significant. Thus, the customary international law defence of state of necessity requires that a state raising such defence meet certain strict requirements. For example, the state may not have contributed to the state of emergency and the measures taken must be the only way available for the state to protect essential interests. Article XI of the US–Argentina BIT and indeed most investment treaty exception clauses do not contain such strict limitations, nor do they imply such a result. The possibility exists, therefore, that a state could meet the requirements of a treaty exception clause and therefore be exempt from liability under an investment treaty without satisfying the state of emergency requirements envisioned by Article 25.[31]

(c) Exceptions for specified national legislation

Investment treaties may also contain specified exceptions that permit host country legislation in areas deemed by contracting parties to be of great national importance. Two are particularly worthy of note: environmental and tax laws.

With the rise in environmental concern throughout the globe, investment treaties have increasingly sought to give host countries wide latitude to legislate on matters relating to the natural environment. For instance, the US–Uruguay BIT provides: 'Nothing in this Treaty shall be construed to prevent a party from adopting, maintaining, or enforcing any measure otherwise consistent with the Treaty that it considers appropriate to ensure that investment activity in its territory is conducted in a manner sensitive to environmental concerns.'[32] This particular provision would appear to be self-judging, since it refers to measures that the host states 'consider' appropriate. The phrase 'otherwise consistent with the Treaty' would seem to mean that the measures in question would be consistent but for the fact that they were taken to assure that investments will be conducted in an environmentally sensitive manner.

Generally, tax matters fall outside the scope of investment treaties and instead are treated in separate bilateral tax treaties. However, in recognition of the potential overlap between tax matters and investment rights, many investment treaties allow the application of their dispute settlement procedures to specified tax-related

---

[31] Burke-White and von Staden (n 7 above).

[32] Treaty between the United States of America and the Oriental Republic of Uruguay Concerning the Encouragement and Reciprocal Protection of Investment (November 2005), Art XII.

disputes.[33] For example, many US BITs apply their dispute settlement procedures to tax matters relating to expropriation, monetary transfers, and the observance and enforcement of the terms of investment agreements or authorizations.[34] In *El Paso v Argentina*,[35] the claimants alleged that various measures taken by Argentina during its financial crisis violated provisions of the US–Argentina BIT and specifically that the imposition of a high export duty on hydrocarbons rendered the claimant's business unprofitable. Although Argentina argued that the part of the claim based on the export duty related to tax matters and, therefore, was exempt from dispute resolution under the BIT, the tribunal took a different view. It found that the tax aspect of the issue was 'part and parcel' of the expropriation dispute and concluded that it had jurisdiction over the entire matter.[36] In *Burlington v Ecuador*,[37] Ecuador objected to jurisdiction based on Article X of the US–Ecuador BIT, which excludes matters of taxation, except those relating to expropriation, transfers, or the observance and enforcement of terms of an investment agreement. The claimant challenged a law that granted the Ecuador government 50 per cent of unforeseen surpluses from oil contracts. The tribunal first found that the law was a tax because '(i) there is a law (ii) that imposes a liability on classes of persons (iii) to pay money to the State (iv) for public purposes'.[38] The tribunal then found that some of the claimant's claims raised matters of taxation, specifically those based on fair and equitable treatment, arbitrary impairment, and full protection and security, while others, such as the umbrella clause claims, did not.[39] After determining that the parties had not entered into an investment agreement, the tribunal found that it did not have jurisdiction over the non-expropriation claims.[40]

The exception to the general rule that tax matters belong to tax treaties also contains an exception: BITs' dispute settlement procedures apply to specified tax disputes 'to the extent they are not subject to the dispute settlement provisions of a Convention for the avoidance of double taxation between the two Parties', or if so subject, are not resolved in a reasonable period of time.[41] This clause resolves the potential conflict regarding the choice of forums in favour of the tax treaty. However, bilateral tax treaties do not generally cover expropriatory taxation or tax terms included in investment agreements. Thus, although BITs claim to except these matters to the extent they are covered by the tax treaty, in practice few are actually covered.

---

[33] Treaty between the United States of America and the Republic of Kazakhstan Concerning the Encouragement and Reciprocal Protection of Investment (19 May 1992), Art XI.

[34] ibid.

[35] *El Paso Energy International Co v Argentina*, ICSID Case No ARB/03/15 (Decision on Jurisdiction) (27 April 2006).

[36] ibid ¶ 115.

[37] *Burlington Resources Inc v Republic of Ecuador*, ICSID Case No ARB/08/5 (Decision on Jurisdiction) (2 June 2010).

[38] ibid ¶ 165.   [39] ibid ¶¶ 181, 205–215.   [40] ibid ¶¶ 248–249.

[41] Treaty between the United States of America and the Republic of Kazakhstan Concerning the Encouragement and Reciprocal Protection of Investment (19 May 1992), Art XI.

A small number of US BITs also except the application of minimum standards of treatment to tax matters. For instance, both the US–Turkey and US–Morocco BITs except all tax matters from the obligations of national, MFN, non-discriminatory, and fair and equitable treatment under the BIT.[42]

14.3 Treaty Modifications

The experience of arbitral tribunals or other bodies applying a particular investment treaty, often in ways and in circumstances not contemplated at the time of negotiation, may cause one or more of the contracting states to view the international obligations they have assumed with dissatisfaction and as being in conflict with their national interests. One way in which parties may resolve tensions that arise after the conclusion of a treaty is by conducting negotiations to modify it. Most BITs do not make reference to amending or modifying their texts, although they do provide for consultations between the contracting states. Moreover, Article 39 of the VCLT states what is accepted as the general rule with regard to treaty modifications: 'A treaty may be amended by agreement between the parties.' That rule, of course, is equally applicable to modifying investment treaties.

Treaty modifications can take place through explicit renegotiations or through less formal processes. In 2006, for example, Bolivia announced that it was dissatisfied with the constraints of its investment treaties and that it planned to renegotiate all of its BITs,[43] a process that clearly contemplated a formal effort to modify the treaty texts. Another approach to modification, without using that label, was taken by the Czech and Netherlands governments after a partial award was made in the case of *CME v Czech Republic*.[44] Dissatisfied with the way the tribunal in that case had interpreted the Czech–Netherlands BIT, the Czech government, as provided for in the text of the treaty, called for consultations with the Netherlands. Delegations from the two countries met at The Hague in April 2002 to arrive at a common understanding of the three issues of treaty interpretation that arose out of the partial award. The two sides agreed on a 'common position' and incorporated it into Agreed Minutes that were signed on 1 July 2002. The Czech Republic then submitted the Agreed Minutes to the tribunal as a binding statement of the meaning and application of the treaty.[45] The tribunal considered itself to be bound by the common position of the two contracting parties. Although the procedure engaged by the two governments did not result in a formal modification of the text of the BIT, this subsequent agreement, embodied in

[42] Treaty between the United States of America and the Republic of Turkey Concerning the Reciprocal Encouragement and Protection of Investments (3 December 1985), Art XI.

[43] US Department of State, '2009 Investment Climate Statement—Bolivia', available at <http://www.state.gov/e/eb/rls/othr/ics/2009/117852.htm> accessed 17 December 2013.

[44] *CME Czech Republic BV v Czech Republic* (Partial Award) (13 September 2001).

[45] *CME Czech Republic BV v Czech Republic* (Final Award) (14 March 2003) ¶¶ 87–93.

the Agreed Minutes, had the effect of modifying the treaty in that the BIT before and the agreement after The Hague meeting are not the same.

Multilateral treaties often contain express provisions on modification because the number of members involved necessitates an explicit and formal process. For example, NAFTA states that the parties may agree on any modification of, or addition to, that agreement. When so agreed and approved in accordance with the applicable legal procedures, a modification or addition constitutes an integral part of the Agreement.[46] The ECT, which is a multilateral convention with over fifty members, contains elaborate provisions on treaty modification. Article 42 provides that any contracting party may propose amendments to that treaty. The text of any proposed amendment must be communicated by the Secretariat to the contracting parties at least three months before it is proposed for adoption in a Charter Conference. Amendments to the ECT must be communicated by the Secretariat to the Depository, which then submits them to the contracting parties for ratification, acceptance, or approval. If accepted by at least three-quarters of the contracting parties, the Amendments enter into force for the parties that have ratified, accepted, or approved them ninety days after the deposit of the instruments with the Depository. Thereafter, the amendments will enter into force for any other contracting party that deposits its instrument of ratification, acceptance, or approval of the amendments ninety days after their deposit occurs.[47]

14.4 Treaty Terminations

The termination of treaties is governed by the VCLT and customary international law. The VCLT permits the termination of a treaty or the withdrawal of a party only in conformity with the provisions of the treaty or 'at any time by consent of all the parties after consulting with the other contracting States'.[48] It further provides that if a treaty contains no provision for denunciation or withdrawal it is not subject to such denunciation or withdrawal unless: (1) it is established that the parties intended to admit the possibility of denunciation or withdrawal; or (2) such right may be implied by the treaty's nature.[49] These principles of course apply to the interpretation and application of investment treaties.

Most investment treaties contain specific provisions on treaty termination and party withdrawal. Foreign investments are often long-term transactions. To give foreign investors assurance of a predictable and stable legal framework, investment treaties: (1) establish an initial period for which the treaty will be in force without providing for a right to terminate the treaty during that period; and (2) specify

---

[46] North American Free Trade Agreement (17 December 1992) (1992) 32 ILM 612, Art 2202.

[47] The Energy Charter Treaty (17 December 1994) 2080 UNTS 100. See also ASEAN Comprehensive Investment Agreement, Art 46 ('Amendments') which simply provides: 'The provisions of this Agreement may be modified through amendments mutually agreed upon in writing by the Member States.'

[48] VCLT, Art 54.   [49] VCLT, Art 56.

how long and under what circumstances the treaty will continue following the expiration of its initial period or its termination.

Investment treaties generally provide that they shall be in force for ten[50] or fifteen[51] years. Upon the expiry of this initial period, the treaty may continue either for a fixed additional period or until it is terminated by one of the parties. For example, the Indonesia–Algeria BIT provides: 'The present Agreement...shall remain in force for a period of *ten years* and shall continue in force thereafter for *another period of ten years* and *so forth* unless denounced in writing by either Contracting Party one year before its expiration' (emphasis added).[52]

A party may terminate a treaty only after the end of the initial period and after submitting advance written notice.[53] Investment treaties make no provision for termination or withdrawal before that time nor does the VCLT. Once a treaty is lawfully terminated, that fact does not result in the immediate denial of treaty protection for investments made while the treaty was in effect. Most treaty termination provisions contain a 'continuing effects' or 'survival' clause, which provides that for investments made, acquired, or approved prior to the date of termination the treaty will remain in force for a further period of ten, fifteen, or twenty years.[54] In view of the time and expense necessary to prepare investments, the Canada–Peru BIT continuing effects clause stipulated in Article 52.3 covers not only investments but 'commitments to invest made prior to the effective date of termination'.[55] An interpretative footnote to this provision explains that for the purposes of that Article 'commitments to invest' means concrete steps taken by an investor to make an investment. For example, a commitment to invest would occur when an investor has applied for a permit or licence authorizing the establishment of an investment.

The termination provisions of the ECT generally follow the pattern found in BITs, although the initial period of effectiveness is much shorter. Its termination provision provides that a contracting party may give written notification to the

[50] eg Agreement between the Government of the Republic of Botswana and the Government of the People's Republic of China on Promotion and Protection of Investments (12 June 2000), Art 14.

[51] eg Agreement on Encouragement and Reciprocal Protection of Investments between the State of Eritrea and the Kingdom of the Netherlands (14 April 2004), Art 13.

[52] Agreement between the Government of the Republic of Indonesia and the Government of the People's Democratic Republic of Algeria Concerning the Promotion and Protection of Investments (21 March 2000), Art XIII.

[53] eg the Jordan–Yemen BIT, Art 10 provides: 'Each Contracting Party has the right to terminate this agreement at the end of its duration or at any time after the expiry of the initial ten years period by a written notice served to the other Contracting party one year prior to the intended termination date.' Agreement between the Government of the Hashemite Kingdom of Jordan and the Government of the Republic of Yemen on the Mutual Promotion and Protection of Investments (8 May 1999).

[54] eg the Japan–Bangladesh BIT, Art 14.3 provides: 'In respect of investments and returns acquired prior to the date of termination of the present Agreement, the provisions of Articles 1 to 13 shall continue to be effective for a further period of fifteen years from the date of termination of the present Agreement.' Agreement between Japan and the People's Republic of Bangladesh Concerning the Promotion and Protection of Investment (10 November 1998).

[55] Agreement between Canada and the Republic of Peru for the Promotion and Protection of Investments (14 November 2006), Art 52.3.

depository of its withdrawal from the treaty five years after the ECT has entered into force for a contracting party. Such a withdrawal takes effect one year after the notification is received by the Depository, or as specified in the notification of withdrawal. The provisions of the ECT continue to apply to investments made in the territory of a contracting party by investors of other contracting parties or in the area of other contracting parties by investors of that contracting party for a period of twenty years after the withdrawal takes effect.[56] Article 45 of the ECT provides for its provisional application to each signatory state 'to the extent that such provisional application is not inconsistent with its constitution, laws or regulations'. That article also has a continuing effects clause which stipulates that if a member state withdraws from provisional application of the ECT, investments made during provisional application will continue to benefit from its provisions for twenty years following termination.[57] In 2009, a tribunal hearing claims against Russia under the ECT in the much publicized Yukos expropriation cases held that Russia's termination of the Treaty's provisional application did not affect the continuing protection of investment under its provisions, including dispute settlement, of investments made before the withdrawal of provisional application for another twenty years.[58] The tribunal would ultimately award the claimants over US$50 billion in damages, the highest arbitral award in history.

A number of states have recently begun to terminate treaties in accordance with treaty provisions.[59] Venezuela terminated its BIT with the Netherlands in 2008.[60] Ecuador terminated nine of its BITs in 2008 (with Cuba, the Dominican Republic, El Salvador, Guatemala, Honduras, Nicaragua, Paraguay, Romania, and Uruguay) for not bringing enough investment.[61] Ecuador has since terminated BITs with

---

[56] The Energy Charter Treaty (17 December 1994) 2080 UNTS 100, Art 47.

[57] ECT, Art 45(3)(2).

[58] *Hulley Enterprises Ltd (Cyprus) v The Russian Federation*, PCA AA 226 (Interim Award on Jurisdiction and Admissibility) (30 November 2009) ¶ 339; *Yukos Universal Ltd (Isle of Man) v the Russian Federation*, PCA AA 227, (Interim Award on Jurisdiction and Admissibility) (30 November 2009) ¶ 339; *Veteran Petroleum Ltd (Cyprus) v the Russian Federation*, PCA AA 228 (Interim Award on Jurisdiction and Admissibility) (30 November 2009) ¶ 339, stating:

> Furthermore, pursuant to Article 45(3)(b) of the Treaty, investment-related obligations, including the obligation to arbitrate investment-related disputes under Part V of the Treaty, remain in force for a period of 20 years following the effective date of termination of provisional application. In the case of the Russian Federation, this means that any investments made in Russia prior to 19 October 2009 will continue to benefit from the Treaty's protections for a period of 20 years—*i.e.*, until 19 October 2029. As a result, the Tribunal finds that the provisional application of the ECT, including the continuing provisional application of Article 26 in this case, does provide a basis for the Tribunal's jurisdiction over the merits of this claim.

[59] In addition, Bolivia, Ecuador, and Venezuela have denounced the ICSID Convention. See footnotes to ICSID, List of Contracting States and Other Signatories of the Convention (1 November 2013), available at <http://www.academia.edu/5423492/ICSID_3_LIST_OF_CONTRACTING_STATES_AND_OTHER_SIGNATORIES_OF_THE_CONVENTION> accessed 17 January 2015.

[60] UNCTAD, Issues Note, *International Investment Policymaking in Transition: Challenges and Opportunities of Treaty Renewal* (June 2013) 3.

[61] ibid.

France, Sweden, Germany, and the United Kingdom and Northern Ireland and professed its intent to end all remaining treaties.[62] Bolivia terminated its BIT with the United States with effect from June 2012.[63] Since 2012, South Africa has given notice of termination of BITs with the Belgo-Luxembourg Economic Union, Spain, the Netherlands, Italy, Greece, the United Kingdom, France, Germany, Denmark, Switzerland, and Austria.[64] According to UNCTAD, more than 1,300 treaties will have reached the stage where they may be renegotiated or terminated by the end of 2013, and an additional 103 treaties was to have reached that stage in 2014.[65] As more treaties approach the end of their initial fixed period, the world may witness additional investment treaty terminations and renegotiation.

[62] M Alvaro, 'China Worried About Ecuador Move to End Bilateral Investment Treaties', *Wall Street Journal* (16 October 2013), available at <http://adrresources.com/doc/headlines/20131016_China_Worried_About_Ecuador_Move_to_End_Bilateral_Investment_Treaties.PDF> accessed 17 December 2013.

[63] United States Federal Register, Notice of Termination of United States–Bolivia Bilateral Investment Treaty (23 May 2012), available at <https://www.federalregister.gov/articles/2012/05/23/2012-12494/notice-of-termination-of-united-states-bolivia-bilateral-investment-treaty> accessed 17 December 2013.

[64] Discussions by the Department of International Relations and Cooperation with European and non-European countries to terminate bilateral investment treaties without automatic renewal clauses and their terminal dates, Republic of South Africa Department of International Relations and Cooperation (25 October 2013), available at <http://www.dfa.gov.za/docs/2013pq/pq2958.html> accessed 17 December 2013.

[65] UNCTAD, Issues Note, *International Investment Policymaking in Transition: Challenges and Opportunities of Treaty Renewal* (June 2013) 3.

15

Investment Treaty Dispute Settlement

15.1 The Significance of Investment Treaty Dispute Settlement

The potential for conflict over a treaty's interpretation or application always exists in international relations, no matter how well drafted the treaty or how detailed its provisions. Although the causes of conflict vary in individual cases, they may generally be attributed either to an imperfect agreement over the subject of the treaty or to changes in circumstance after the agreement has been concluded. The goal of all treaty negotiations is to express in writing the full meaning of the parties' agreement; however, the parties' ability do so is limited by two factors: (1) the fact that treaty negotiators from different countries have been shaped by differing national cultures, ideologies, legal traditions, and interests (factors that profoundly influence and complicate communications at the bargaining table); and (2) the inherent inability of treaty negotiators to foresee all of the circumstances to which the treaty may be applied in the coming years. Moreover, even if negotiators had perfect foresight, there is no assurance that persons applying the treaty in the future would interpret treaty provisions exactly as the negotiators had intended. As a result, it can fairly be said that all treaties are imperfect agreements. Moreover, changes in circumstances that are beyond the control or expectation of either party may make fulfilling treaty commitments extremely costly or impossible for one of the parties. That party will, in turn, then seek to avoid or reinterpret its commitments in a way that will lighten its burden, an action that will naturally be resisted by the other contracting party.

In view of these considerations, it is important for a treaty to have mechanisms for the resolution of conflict through the effective and objective application and enforcement of treaty provisions. This element is particularly important in the case of investment treaties because their purpose is to encourage investors to make long-term, substantial financial commitments on the basis of the treatment that host states promise in the treaty. Indeed, although investment treaties are made only between states, their principal purpose is to benefit the nationals and companies of the contracting states by granting them specified treatment and protection under international law. Virtually all disputes that arise under investment treaties do so because an investor believes the host state did not provide the level of protection and treatment promised. Unlike the customary international law on foreign investment, which lacks an obligatory mechanism for resolving disputes, all investment treaties provide such mechanisms. The importance of these mechanisms is twofold. First, they are a means for resolving disputes and securing the payment of compensation to injured investors. Second, such enforcement mechanisms deter states from disregarding their treaty commitments to other investors. The existence of effective and efficient methods for resolving investment disputes is, as an UNCTAD study has stated, 'the ultimate guarantee of protection for foreign investors'.[1] This chapter will examine the nature of conflicts between investors and states and the various means provided by treaties to resolve them.

15.2 The Nature of Disputes between States and Investors

Disputes between states and investors can arise in many different contexts, take various forms, and have differing degrees of importance. These disputes may arise from the contested seizure of a foreign investor's factory, the promulgation of new environmental regulations increasing costs to an investor's enterprise, or the simple refusal of host state authorities to grant a visa to a foreign technician needed by an investment project. More generally, investor–state disputes governed by treaties occur because a host state has taken a 'measure' that allegedly violates that state's treaty commitments on the treatment it has promised to accord to investments protected by that treaty. Three of the most common measures that may lead to an investor–state dispute are governmental actions that (1) cancel or change contractual or licence rights enjoyed by an investment; (2) seize or cancel property rights owned by an investor; or (3) change legislation or regulations, causing economic detriment of the investment protected by a treaty.

Because of the broad treatment standards articulated in investment treaties, such as 'full protection and security' and 'fair and equitable treatment', virtually all disputes between investors and host governments are potentially subject to the applicable investment treaty. Nonetheless, it is important to understand at the outset that disputes arising under international investment treaties are not ordinary commercial disputes. Treaty-based investor–state disputes are unique and that uniqueness needs to be understood because it affects the ways that disputants approach their conflicts and the utility and effectiveness of dispute resolution techniques used to resolve them.

First, such disputes are not just a matter of simple contract claims governed by contract law. While they are certainly subject to the domestic law of the host country, they are also governed by public international law in the form of treaties—instruments of international law—entered into by two or more states.[2]

---

[1] UNCTAD, *Bilateral Investment Treaties in the Mid-1990s* (1998) 87.

[2] As the ICSID Annulment Committee stated in the *Vivendi* case, which involved a dispute under the Argentina–France BIT: '[a] state may breach a treaty without breaching a contract, and vice versa'; 'whether there has been a breach of the BIT and whether there has been a breach of contract are different questions. Each of these claims will be determined by reference to its own proper or applicable law—in the case of the BIT, by international law; in the case of the Concession Contract by the proper law of the contract'. *Compañía de Aguas del Aconquija SA and Vivendi*

Given the international legal nature of these disputes, unilateral attempts by a host state to deal with them through domestic laws and regulations may well be unsuccessful.

Second, public policy questions are often at the heart of investor–state conflicts. The host government has taken certain public policy measures—for example legislative or administrative acts meant to preserve the environment, regulate business, or impose a tax—which it considers important for the public welfare but which an investor believes violate its rights under a treaty. The resolution of such disputes has significant implications for the ability of sovereign governments to regulate enterprises within their territories.[3] If an arbitral tribunal ultimately judges contested measures to be illegal under the applicable treaty, the resulting award may not only require the offending government to pay the investor damages and to incur heavy arbitration costs but also to repeal or modify such measures in order to avoid similar arbitration claims from other foreign investors.

Third, because they involve public policy issues, investor–state disputes are political in nature. Moreover as political groups, non-governmental organizations, the media, and ultimately the general public come to have definite views on the dispute and how it should be settled, the controversy may become highly politicized. The political nature of these disputes influences the strategies of both the governments and investors involved in seeking to resolve them.

Fourth, underlying the dispute is an intended long-term investment relationship—a complex connection, often amounting to a state of interdependence, between the investor and the host country. In the case of privatization of public services, such as water, gas, or telecommunications, the investor and the host country are linked in a more or less permanent relationship. Such relationships are far more difficult to unravel, for example, than undoing a simple contract for the sale of a commodity in international commerce. In these more complicated relationships, the host country is dependent on the continued supply by the investor of a needed public service and, at least in the short run, has no option but to continue to deal with the investor. Similarly, the investor, having committed substantial capital to the privatized enterprise, is dependent on the host country for continued revenues. For this reason, at least in the short run, the investor also has few opportunities to disengage from the investment.

Fifth, the amounts of money at stake in investor–state disputes are large, sometimes staggeringly so, amounting in some cases to hundreds of millions, even billions of US dollars. As a result, in most investor–state, treaty-based disputes, host countries face the risk of having to pay substantial negotiated settlements or arbitration awards that might prove burdensome in relation to the country's budget and financial resources. Whereas the average award in ordinary international commercial arbitration is less than a million dollars, an award in an investor–state

---

Universal (formerly Compagnie Générale des Eaux) v Argentine Republic, ICSID Case No ARB/97/3 (Decision on Annulment) (3 July 2002) ¶¶ 95 and 96.

[3] G Van Harten, 'Private Authority and Transnational Governance: The Contours of the International System of Investor Protection' (2005) 12 Rev Int'l Political Economics 600, 610–11.

arbitration may well be many times that amount.[4] For example, arbitral tribunals have rendered awards of US$353 million (against the Czech Republic),[5] US$71 million (against Ecuador),[6] US$824 million (against Slovakia),[7] US$133.2 million (against Argentina),[8] and in the much publicized Yukos case in 2014 more than US$50 billion (against Russia).[9]

Moreover, aside from settlements or awards, the costs of investor–state arbitration are usually substantially greater than those incurred in an ordinary commercial dispute and may prove a significant burden for developing countries. In addition to indirect costs, such as the time of government officials and corporate executives devoted to preparing and participating in the matter, there are substantial direct costs. Direct costs usually consist of two elements: (1) the expenses of the party's legal representation; and (2) its share of the costs of administering the arbitration. The precise amount of such costs varies depending on the case's complexity, the amount in dispute, and the extent of time needed to reach a resolution. In a highly complicated and lengthy case, the costs of legal representation can be extremely heavy. For example, in *CME v Czech Republic*, the Czech Republic reportedly spent US$10 million on its legal defence.[10] A more typical investor–state case may be *International Thunderbird Gaming Corporation v United Mexican States*, a NAFTA case under UNCITRAL rules that was decided in January 2006. There, the total cost was US$3,170,692, which included US$405,620 in arbitrators' fees, US$99,632 in administrative expenses, US$1,502,065 in costs for Mexico's legal representation, and US$1,163,375 in costs for Thunderbird's representation.[11]

It is possible for a successful host country to recoup some of these costs from an investor who brought the case; however, the rules on apportionment of costs vary and in any case are subject to the tribunal's discretion. On the other hand, a host

---

[4] N Rubins, 'The Allocation of Costs and Attorney's Fees in Investor–State Arbitration' (2003) 18 ICSID Rev—FILJ 109, 125 (observing that whereas 58 per cent of commercial arbitration claims brought to the ICC in 1999 were for less than US$1 million, the average claim for ICSID cases in 1997 was US$10 million).

[5] *CME Czech Republic BV v Czech Republic* (Final Award) (14 March 2003), UNCITRAL (The Netherlands–Czech Republic BIT) ¶ 161. See also PS Green, 'Czech Republic Pays $355 Million to Media Concern', *New York Times*, 16 May 2003, W1.

[6] *Occidental Exploration & Production Co v Republic of Ecuador*, London Ct Intl Arb Case No UN3467 (Final Award) (1 July 2004) (US–Ecuador BIT) ¶ 73.

[7] *Československá Obchodní Banka AS v Slovak Republic*, ICSID Case No ARB/97/4 (Final Award) (29 December 2004) (Czech Republic–Slovak Republic BIT) ¶ 126.

[8] *CMS Gas Transmission Co v Argentine Republic*, ICSID Case No ARB/01/8 (Final Award) (12 May 2005) (US–Argentina BIT) ¶ 139.

[9] *Hulley Enterprises Ltd (Cyprus) v The Russian Federation*, PCA AA 226, (Final Award) (18 July 2014) ¶ 339; *Yukos Universal Ltd (Isle of Man) v the Russian Federation*, PCA AA 227, (Final Award) (18 July 2014); *Veteran Petroleum Ltd (Cyprus) v the Russian Federation*, PCA AA 228 (Final Award) (18 July 2014).

[10] International Institute for Sustainable Development, 'Czech Republic Hit with Massive Compensation Bill in Investment Treaty Dispute', *Investment Law and Policy Weekly News Bulletin*, 21 March 2003. See also *CME Czech Republic* (n 5 above).

[11] See <http://naftaclaims.com/disputes/mexico/Thunderbird/award.pdf> accessed 24 March 2015.

state that loses a case may, in certain circumstances, be required to pay a portion of the investor's costs.

15.3 Traditional, Non-Treaty Methods of Resolving Investor–State Disputes

Before the advent of investment treaties, investors basically had three methods to seek resolution of their disputes with host states: (a) direct negotiation with host state governments; (b) domestic courts in the host country; and (c) diplomatic protection by their home states.

(a) Direct negotiations with host governments

Many disputes between foreign investors and host countries have been resolved by direct negotiations between the disputants. Indeed, nearly all investment treaties provide that in the event of a dispute between an investor and the host country the two parties are required to engage in consultations and negotiations,[12] often for a specified period of time (for example six months),[13] before the investor may pursue other remedies. As a result, virtually all disputes go through a period of negotiation before either reaching settlement or advancing to formal investor–state arbitration. Because of the confidentiality that usually surrounds such settlements, accurate, comprehensive statistics on negotiated settlements of investor–state conflicts are not available. One example of a successful investor–state negotiation that did not involve an investment treaty took place between India and Enron, a large US energy company. In 1993, Enron, a US corporation, and the Maharashtra State Electricity Board (MSEB) in India signed a contract whereby a consortium led by Enron would build the Dabhol Power Project. The total investment was US$2 billion. MSEB signed an agreement to buy all the electricity produced by the project for twenty years. When a newly elected government came to power

---

[12] eg Agreement Between the Czech Republic and Malaysia for the Promotion and Protection of Investments (9 September 1998), Art 7(1): 'Any dispute which may arise between an investor of one Contracting Party and the other Contracting Party in connection with an investment on the territory of that other Contracting Party shall be subject to negotiations between the parties in dispute.'

[13] eg Agreement between the Czech Republic and Canada for the Promotion and Protection of Investments (6 May 2009), Art X:

1. Any dispute between one Contracting Party and an investor of the other Contracting Party relating to the effects of a measure or series of measures taken by the former Contracting Party on the management, use, enjoyment or disposal of an investment made by the investor, and in particular, but not exclusively, relating to expropriation referred to in Article VI (Expropriation) of this Agreement or to the transfer of funds referred to in Article VII (Transfer of Funds) of this Agreement, shall, to the extent possible, be settled amicably between them.
2. If the dispute has not been settled amicably within a period of six months from the date on which the dispute was initiated, it may be submitted by the investor to arbitration.

in Maharashtra state, it cancelled the contract, alleging that the power tariff was too high and that the contract was not in the state of Maharashtra's best interests. Later negotiations between the state and Enron were successful and resulted in a modification of the contract, a reduction in power tariffs, and the continuation of the project.[14]

(b) Local courts

A second option for resolving investor–state disputes is for aggrieved investors to have recourse to the courts of the host country. Depending on the country involved, this option, which is required by some investment treaties prior to arbitration,[15] may pose a variety of problems for foreign investors. First, depending on the country concerned, local courts may lack judicial independence and might be subject to the control of the host government, depriving the investor of an impartial forum. Second, even if the judiciary is independent, it may nonetheless harbour prejudice towards foreign investors, as the courts of the state of Mississippi demonstrated in the NAFTA case of *Loewen Group, Inc v United States*.[16] Third, local courts may not have the expertise to apply complex principles of international law to complicated foreign investment transactions. Fourth, even if courts have such expertise, domestic law may limit or prohibit them from adjudicating their state's international commitments. And finally, local courts often have a heavy backlog of cases and inefficient procedures that deny expeditious justice and make obtaining a final judicial determination difficult. For these reasons, in many countries foreign investors do not consider local courts an effective and reliable means for resolving disputes with host governments, and they therefore often

---

[14] J Salacuse, *The Global Negotiator: Making, Managing, and Mending Deals Around the World in the Twenty-first Century* (Palgrave Macmillan, 2003) 236–55.

[15] eg Agreement between the Government of the United Kingdom and Northern Ireland and the Government of the Republic of Argentina for the Promotion and Protection of Investments (11 December 1990), Art 8:

(1) Disputes with regard to an investment which arise within the terms of this Agreement between an investor of one Contracting Party and the other Contracting Party, which have not been amicably settled shall be submitted, at the request of one of the Parties to the dispute, to the decision of the competent tribunal of the Contracting Party in whose territory the investment was made.

(2) The aforementioned disputes shall be submitted to international arbitration in the following cases:

(a) if one of the Parties so requests, in any of the following circumstances:

(i) where, after a period of eighteen months has elapsed from the moment when the dispute was submitted to the competent tribunal of the Contracting Party in whose territory the investment was made, the said tribunal has not given its final decision;

(ii) where the final decision of the aforementioned tribunal has been made but the Parties are still in dispute;

(b) where the Contracting Party and the investor of the other Contracting Party have so agreed.

[16] ICSID Case No ARB (AF)/98/3 (19 July 2002), available at <http://worldbank.org/icsid> accessed 8 June 2009.

try to avoid them. Indeed, one of the principal reasons for creating treaty-based, investor–state arbitration was to enable investors to avoid the courts of the countries in which they invest.

(c) Diplomatic protection

A third method available to aggrieved investors is to enlist the aid of their home countries to assist them in obtaining a satisfactory settlement from the host government. This method is known as diplomatic protection. As was discussed in Chapter 3, foreign investors consider it a far from perfect means of resolving their disputes for several reasons. First, under international law, before a state can make formal claim against another state on behalf of one of its nationals, that national must first ordinarily exhaust local remedies available in the host state. The International Court of Justice (ICJ) has stated that the principle of exhaustion of local remedies is 'a well-established rule of customary international law'[17] whose purpose is to ensure that 'the State where the violation occurred should have an opportunity to redress it by its own means within the framework of its own domestic legal system'.[18] Nonetheless, from the point of view of the investor, exhausting local remedies can be a long, slow, complicated process that merely serves to delay reparation of the injury sustained.

Second, the availability of diplomatic protection for investors depends entirely on their home country's willingness to extend assistance in a given situation. Home country governments were not then, and are not now, required to espouse claims against offending states, no matter how egregious their conduct has been. The decision to espouse a claim or not, and to pursue it vigorously or not, is completely within the discretion of the home government.

Third, once the home country government has espoused the claim, it effectively 'owns' it. This means that it controls how the claim will be made, what settlement it will accept, and whether any portion of the settlement will be paid to the aggrieved national. Thus, for example, a home country might abandon an injured national's claim if it judges that other factors in its relations with the host country, such as security or trade, require it. In such a situation, the injured investor is left without redress against the offending host country and its unsympathetic home government.

A further complication involves a home country's ability to extend diplomatic protection to nationals who are shareholders in foreign corporations. In the famous *Barcelona Traction* case,[19] Belgium sued Spain in the ICJ on behalf of injured Belgian shareholders of Barcelona Traction, which was a Canadian

---

[17] *Interhandel (Switzerland v United States)* (Judgment) (21 March 1959) [1959] ICJ Rep 25. See also *Elettronica Sicula SpA (ELSI) (United States v Italy)* (Judgment) (20 July 1989) [1989] ICJ Rep 15, ¶ 50, referring to the obligation of exhaustion of local remedies as 'an important principle of customary international law'.

[18] *Interhandel* (n 17 above).

[19] *Barcelona Traction, Light and Power Co, Ltd (Belgium v Spain)* [1970] ICJ Rep 3; (1970) 64 AJIL 653.

corporation. Barcelona Traction was supplying electricity to the city of Barcelona when the Spanish government expropriated it. The Court ruled that Belgium had no right to make a claim on behalf of the Belgian shareholders, since the primary party injured by the expropriation was the Canadian corporation, and not the Belgian shareholders. Although this decision has been strongly criticized over the years,[20] it remains difficult for shareholders of one nationality to press claims for injuries to a corporation that was incorporated in another country. This is particularly vexing, since purchasing shares in companies and corporations organized in other countries is a common investor practice.

And finally, once the era of gunboat diplomacy ended, diplomatic protection of aliens and foreign investors did not necessarily result in meaningful redress in many cases. Often, it yielded little by way of concrete results except the exchange of oral or written statements, and the injured investor received no material compensation. And, of course, the matter could only be brought to an international tribunal if the offending state agreed, which rarely occurred. Thus, diplomatic protection was and is an uncertain remedy for injured international investors. Investment treaties have sought to establish a dispute settlement process that does not suffer from these defects.

15.4 Treaty Methods for Resolving Investment Disputes

In order to establish a stable, rule-based system for international investment, treaties provide means to resolve disputes about the interpretation and application of treaty provisions. Whereas treaties traditionally only recognized states as participants in the dispute settlement process, many now also grant investors a distinct role and specific rights as disputants. Most investment treaties provide four separate dispute settlement methods: (1) consultations and negotiations between contracting states; (2) arbitration between contracting states; (3) consultations and negotiations between covered investors and host governments; and (4) investor–state arbitration. The following sections of this chapter will examine each of these methods.

15.5 Interstate Consultations and Negotiations

Most investment treaties contain a separate article on dispute settlement between contracting states. That article usually provides that attempts to resolve disputes concerning the interpretation and application of a treaty should first proceed by 'negotiation', 'consultations', or 'diplomatic means'.[21] A common formulation of

---

[20] eg RB Lillich 'Two Perspectives on the Barcelona Traction Case' (1971) 65 AJIL 522–32.
[21] eg the 1987 Switzerland–Bolivia BIT (Accord entre la Confédération suisse et la République de Bolivie concernant la promotion et la protection réciproques des investissements), Art 10(1), entitled 'Les différends entre Parties Contractantes' (Disputes between the Contracting Parties)

this requirement is found in Article 11 of the 1989 bilateral investment treaty (BIT) between the United Kingdom and Ghana. It states: 'Disputes between the Contracting Parties concerning the interpretation and application of this Agreement shall be settled through the diplomatic channel.'[22]

Even if an investment treaty does not have a similarly specific provision on dispute settlement, by virtue of customary international law and Article 33 of the United Nations Charter, the contracting parties have a duty to seek peaceful solutions to their disputes and engage in good faith negotiations to that end.[23]

Such treaty provisions clearly indicate that conflicts over the interpretation and application of treaty provisions, which will often involve the contested application of the treaty to one or more investors of the contracting states, are to be settled by discussions and negotiations between diplomatic representatives of the two states at whatever level the two states choose. For example, these discussions could take the form of a telephone call from the vice consul of the investor's home country to officials in the local ministry of finance, reminding them of their BIT commitments on monetary transfers, or of formal discussions by the foreign ministers of the two countries concerning the alleged nationalizations of investment properties.

Often an appropriate intervention by representatives of the investor's home country can help to settle an investor–state dispute. On the other hand, it must also be recognized that the nature and vigour of that intervention will depend not only on the nature of the investment dispute but also on the overall political and economic relationship between the two countries. For example, if an investor's home country has an important military base located in the host country or if the two share a valuable trade relationship, the investor's home country may be unwilling to jeopardize the status quo by advocating too vigorously for an investor.

The consultations and negotiation provisions serve a useful function in preserving investment relationships under the treaty. They facilitate conflict settlement that might otherwise evolve into costly arbitrated disputes that could endanger the contracting parties' relationship. Second, the provisions may provide the host state with useful information and insights about developing investment policies that will advance its national interests while respecting investment treaty commitments. In many situations, the consultation process may be structured to guide the overall application of the treaty. Thus, for example, the Denmark–Poland BIT, in addition to providing for dispute settlement between the contracting

---

states: 'Les différends entre Parties Contractantes au sujet de l'interprétation ou de l'application des dispositions du présent Accord seront réglés par la voie diplomatique.'

[22] Agreement between the Government of the United Kingdom of Great Britain and Northern Ireland and the Government of the Republic of Ghana for the Promotion and Protection of Investment (22 March 1989).

[23] UN Charter, Art 33(1) provides: 'The parties to any dispute, the continuance of which is likely to endanger the maintenance of international peace and security, shall, first of all, seek a solution by negotiation, enquiry, mediation, conciliation, arbitration, judicial settlement, resort to regional agencies or arrangements, or other peaceful means of their own choice.'

states, contains a provision authorizing consultation to 'review the implementa-tion of this Agreement' and requires the first consultation to take place within five years of the treaty entering into force.[24]

One of the most elaborate consultation mechanisms for contracting par-ties is the Free Trade Commission created by the North American Free Trade Agreement (NAFTA).[25] The NAFTA Free Trade Commission, endowed with its own secretariat, is composed of cabinet-level representatives of the three contract-ing states. It is authorized, among other things, to supervise the implementa-tion of the NAFTA treaty, oversee its further elaboration, and resolve disputes regarding its interpretation or application. Moreover, under Article 1132(2) of the treaty, the Commission can issue 'interpretations' of NAFTA provisions that are binding on arbitral tribunals deciding investor–state disputes. In exercising this power the Commission has issued interpretations concerning access to documents in Chapter 11 investor–state cases, the meaning of Article 1105, which requires a minimum standard of treatment in accordance with international law,[26] and the transparency and efficiency of Chapter 11 arbitrations.[27] The ASEAN Comprehensive Investment Agreement adopts still another approach. Rather than specify procedures for consultations in the event of disputes, the Agreement incor-porates by reference the 2004 ASEAN Protocol on Enhanced Dispute Settlement Mechanism,[28] an elaborate set of dispute settlement procedures that the ASEAN states have adopted to handle all of their interstate disputes.[29]

15.6 Interstate Arbitration

In the event that states are unable to settle a dispute through negotiations and diplomacy, nearly all investment treaties give disputing states the right to invoke arbitration to settle their conflict. Interstate arbitration is an old and traditional method for the peaceful resolution of state disputes. Basically, arbitration is a dis-pute resolution method by which the disputants agree to submit their dispute to a third party (the arbitrator or arbitrators) for a decision according to agreed-upon

[24] Agreement between the Government of the Kingdom of Denmark and the Government of the Republic of Poland for the Promotion and the Reciprocal Protection of Investments (1 May 1990), Art 13(1) states: '(1) The representatives of the Contracting Parties shall, whenever needed, hold meetings in order to review the implementation of this Agreement. These meetings shall be held on the proposal of one of the Contracting Parties at a place and at a time agreed upon through diplomatic channels.'

[25] North American Free Trade Agreement United States–Canada–Mexico (1 January 1994) (1993) 32 ILM 289, Arts 2001–2002.

[26] NAFTA Free Trade Commission, *Notes of Interpretation of Certain Chapter 11 Provisions* (31 July 2001).

[27] NAFTA Free Trade Commission, *Statement of the Free Trade Commission on Non-Disputing Party Participation* (7 October 2003).

[28] Available at <http://www.asean.org/news/item/asean-protocol-on-enhanced-dispute-settlement-mechanism> acccessed 17 January 2015.

[29] ASEAN Comprehensive Investment Agreement, Art 27.

norms and procedures and to carry out that third party's decision. Arbitration is thus a means for converting a diplomatic dispute into a legal or judicial dispute.

The modern history of interstate arbitration dates from the 1794 Jay Treaty between the United States and Great Britain.[30] The Jay Treaty sought to resolve contentious issues resulting from the American Revolutionary War. It influenced the development of interstate arbitration in that it provided for the final settlement of disputes between two states by an arbitral tribunal and also indicated the standards that should apply in arriving at a decision. Moreover, it set down some of the principles that have come to characterize modern international arbitration in the resolution of disputes between both states and private parties. For example, the Treaty and the awards made by the treaty-constituted tribunals established the important rule that arbitration tribunals are competent to decide their own jurisdiction. The practice of including arbitration clauses in commercial and other treaties became widespread following Italy's repeated use of such clauses in its treaty practice.[31] By the end of the nineteenth century, over a hundred treaties referred to interstate dispute settlement by arbitration.[32]

While some of the US friendship, commerce, and navigation (FCN) treaties provided for the settlement of interstate disputes by the ICJ,[33] nearly all investment treaties today provide for interstate arbitration as a means to resolve disputes between the contracting states. Moreover, nearly all follow the same interstate arbitration model. First, the stated purpose of interstate arbitration in investment treaties is to settle disputes between contracting states concerning 'the interpretation or application' of the treaty. Thus, for example, Article 8 of the Chile–United Kingdom BIT provides, in part:

(1) Disputes between the Contracting Parties concerning the interpretation or application of this Agreement should, if possible, be settled through the diplomatic channel.
(2) If a Dispute between the Contracting Parties cannot thus be settled, it shall upon the request of either Contracting Party be submitted to an arbitral tribunal.[34]

---

[30] H Neufeld, *The International Protection of Private Creditors from the Treaties of Westphalia to the Congress of Vienna* (Sijthof, 1971) 69–78.

[31] LB Sohn, 'International Arbitration in Historical Perspective: Past and Present' in AHA Soons (ed), *International Arbitration: Past and Prospects* (Carnegie Endowment for International Peace, 1990) 12.

[32] B Descamp, 'General Survey of the Clauses of Mediation and Arbitration Affecting the Powers Represented at the Conference' in JB Scott (ed), *The Proceedings of the Hague Peace Conferences* (OUP, 1920) 191.

[33] eg the Treaty of Friendship, Commerce and Navigation between the United States of America and the Italian Republic (26 July 1949), Art XXVI provides:

Any dispute between the High Contracting Parties as to the interpretation or the application of this Treaty, which the High Contracting Parties shall not satisfactorily adjust by diplomacy, shall be submitted to the International Court of Justice, unless the High Contracting Parties shall agree to settlement by some other pacific means.

Under this treaty, a dispute between the US and Italy concerning an alleged expropriation gave rise to the ICJ *Case Concerning Elettronica Sicula SPA (ELSI) (United States v Italy)* (Judgment) (20 July 1989) [1989] ICJ Rep 15.

[34] Agreement between the Government of the United Kingdom of Great Britain and Northern Ireland and the Government of the Republic of Chile for the Promotion and Protection of Investments (8 January 1996).

While similar language may also be found in certain multilateral investment agreements such as the Energy Charter Treaty (ECT),[35] it is worth noting that the ASEAN Comprehensive Investment Agreement takes a different approach by incorporating by reference the ASEAN Protocol on Enhanced Dispute Settlement Mechanism signed in Vientiane, Lao PDR, on 29 November 2004, which applies to all disputes between ASEAN member states.[36]

As will be seen in section 15.8, this language on the settlement of interstate disputes contrasts with that employed by the same treaties in stating the purpose of investor–state arbitration, which is to settle 'investment disputes'. Thus, it has been argued that the two dispute settlement systems created by most investment treaties not only have different disputing parties—that is, investors and states in one, and contracting states in the other—but also have two different mandates—that is, adjudication of investment disputes in one, and interpretation or application of the treaty in the other.[37]

Interstate, investment treaty arbitration is ad hoc, rather than institutional, and tribunals consist of three arbitrators: one appointed by each contracting party and a third, a national of a third country, who is agreed upon by the other two arbitrators. If the arbitrators cannot agree on a third member, or if one of the parties refuses to appoint an arbitrator, the treaty provides for an 'appointing authority', such as the President of the International Court of Justice, the Secretary-General of the United Nations, or some other distinguished international figure, to make the appointment. Many treaties require a minimum period of negotiation between the contracting parties before one of them may resort to arbitration. As a general rule, the tribunal is free to determine its own rules of procedure, but nearly all treaties provide that decisions must be made by a majority in order to avoid the paralysis that a rule requiring unanimity might create. The decision of the arbitrators is final and binding on the contracting parties to the treaty.

The coexistence of the two forms of dispute settlement—interstate and investor–state—raises important questions about the relationship between the two and how and under what conditions states may invoke interstate arbitration in practice. Virtually all investment treaties are silent on these questions. A few of China's BITs, in setting the rules for investor–state arbitration, specifically provide that 'the provisions of this Article shall not prejudice the Contracting Parties from using the procedures specified in Article 14 [on interstate arbitration] where a dispute concerns the interpretation or application of this Agreement'.[38] Similar language is not to be found in other investment treaties.

---

[35] ECT, Art 27.

[36] ASEAN Comprehensive Investment Agreement, Art 27. ('The ASEAN Protocol on Enhanced Dispute Settlement Mechanism signed in Vientiane, Lao PDR on 29 November 2004, as amended, shall apply to the settlement of disputes concerning the interpretation or application of this Agreement.')

[37] A Roberts, 'State-to-State Investment Treaty Arbitration: A Hybrid Theory of Interdependent Rights and Shared Interpretative Authority' (2014) 55 Harv Int'l LJ 1, 7.

[38] Agreement between the Government of the People's Republic of China and the Government of the Republic of Singapore on the Promotion and Protection of Investments (1985), Art 13.12. See also Agreement between the Government of the Democratic Socialist Republic of Sri Lanka

In theory, there would seem to be three basic situations in which states might invoke interstate arbitration. The first would include a difference of opinion between contracting states concerning the interpretation of treaty language unconnected to an actual conflict between a national of one state and the government of another. For example, one state might believe that the other state is not actively promoting and facilitating investment to the extent promised in the treaty. The second situation might arise where one state believes that the other state has violated the treaty in its treatment of specific investors from the first state. Invoking interstate arbitration would in effect constitute a form of diplomatic protection. The third situation would occur where a state that is an actual or potential respondent in an investor–state arbitration over an alleged treaty violation invokes interstate arbitration in order to secure an interpretation of the treaty that will favour its position in its investor–state dispute.

Each of these situations raises a variety of important legal issues; however, answers to them remain in the realm of speculation since contracting states to investment treaties seem to have invoked interstate arbitration on only three occasions. The first case occurred in 2003, when Peru, in response to an International Centre for Settlement of Investment Disputes (ICSID) claim against it by Chilean investors, instituted an interstate arbitration against Chile and requested the ICSID tribunal to suspend its proceedings until the interstate arbitration was resolved. The tribunal declined the request, and Peru ceased to press its case against Chile.[39]

The second known interstate case also took place in 2003, when Italy invoked interstate arbitration against Cuba under their 1993 BIT[40] because of alleged injuries to some sixteen Italian companies in various industries caused by Cuban government measures taken in violation of the treaty. Unlike the Peru–Chile case, the *Republic of Italy v Republic of Cuba* case would result in both an interim award[41] in 2005 and a final award[42] in 2008, both of which dealt at length with important legal issues.

The interim award dealt with three important objections raised by Cuba. First, Cuba objected to Italy's invocation of interstate arbitration as vehicle for diplomatic protection of its nationals' interests when the treaty granted Italian investors the right to initiate investor–state arbitration on their own initiative. On this point, the tribunal concluded that the mere existence in the treaty of a provision

---

and the Government of the People's Republic of China on the Reciprocal Promotion and Protection of Investments (1986), Art 13.11; and New Zealand and China: Agreement on the Promotion and Protection of Investments (1988), Art 13.12.

[39] *Empresas Lucchetti SA and Lucchetti Peru SA v Peru*, ICSID Case No ARB/03/4 (Award) (7 February 2005) (Peru–Chile BIT) ¶¶ 7 and 9 (also known as *Industria Nacional de Alimentos SA and Indalsa Perú SA v Peru*).

[40] Tra Il Governo della Repubblica Italiana e Il Governo della Repubblica di Cuba sulla Promozione e Protezione degli Investimenti (1993).

[41] *Republic of Italy v Republic of Cuba*, Interim Award (Sentence préliminaire) (Ad Hoc Tribunal, 15 March 2005). See M Podesta, 'Note: Republic of Italy v. Republic of Cuba,' (2012) 106 AJIL 341.

[42] *Republic of Italy v Republic of Cuba*, Final Award (Sentence Finale) (Ad Hoc Tribunal, 15 January 2008).

for investor–state arbitration did not bar a state from pursuing interstate arbitration as a means of affording diplomatic protection to its nationals; however, once an investor had brought an investor–state claim against the host government or given its advance consent to such a process, its home state would be barred from invoking interstate arbitration as a means of diplomatic protection. Cuba also raised a jurisdictional objection to the effect that the transactions that Italy was seeking to protect were not 'investments' under the Cuba–Italy BIT. Although the treaty defined investment in the usual broad fashion as 'any kind of asset' and among its enumerated examples included 'claims to money or to any performance having an economic value' and 'any economic right accruing by law or contract', the tribunal took the view that three elements, not specifically stipulated in the treaty, were nonetheless required for an investment: a contribution of capital, a sufficiently long duration, and risk assumed by the investor. Such requirements, according to the tribunal would exclude ordinary sales transactions from the definition of investment. Finally, with respect to Cuba's objection that the investors had not exhausted their local remedies as required by customary international law, the tribunal held that the requirement of exhaustion of local remedies did not apply to those claims that Italy was bringing in its own right but that it did apply to the diplomatic protection claims that Italy was bringing on behalf of Italian investors. It also found that the contracting parties did not waive the requirement of exhausting local remedies merely because the treaty also provided for investor–state arbitration.

Taking account of the principles set forth in the Interim Award, Italy pursued only six of the original sixteen investor claims in the second phase of the proceeding; however, the tribunal would dismiss all of them in its final award on various jurisdictional and substantive grounds.

The third interstate arbitration occurred in 2011, when Ecuador, disagreeing with the interpretation by the tribunal in the investor–state case of *Chevron v Ecuador*[43] of a clause in the US–Ecuador BIT requiring each host country to provide foreign investors with 'effective means' for asserting claims and enforcing rights, invoked interstate arbitration against the United States, seeking a correct interpretation of the clause.[44] The tribunal in the *Chevron* case had held that Article II(7) of the treaty protected foreign investors against 'undue' delay in local court systems, and this obligation might require a higher standard of governmental behaviour than that demanded for 'denial of justice' under international law. Here then was an instance when a state, disappointed by its fate in investor–state arbitration, sought to use interstate arbitration to thwart or mitigate that result. The interstate tribunal rendered a decision in 2012 but as of 2015 it had not been publicly released. It seems that the tribunal dismissed Ecuador's claims. Nonetheless, in future, respondent host states disappointed by rulings in

---

[43] *Chevron Corp (US) v Ecuador*, PCA Case No 34877 (Partial Award on the Merits) (Perm Ct Arb, 2010).

[44] *Ecuador v United States*, PCA Case No 2012-5 (Request for Arbitration) (Pt Ct Arb, 2011).

investor–state cases may turn to interstate arbitration increasingly as a means to correct what they consider a miscarriage of justice.

15.7 Investor–State Consultations and Negotiations

Many disputes between foreign investors and host countries are resolved through negotiation. Indeed, nearly all investment treaties provide that in the event of a dispute the parties are to engage in consultations and negotiations, often for a specified period of time (six months in many cases), before another remedy is sought.[45] As a result, it is safe to say that almost all such disputes go through a period of negotiation before reaching settlement or advancing to formal investor–state arbitration. Because of the confidentiality that often surrounds such settlements, accurate and comprehensive statistics on these negotiated settlements are not available.

Negotiations may be conducted before or after arbitration has begun. For example, a 2006 ICSID case by the Western NIS Enterprise Fund against Ukraine[46] was terminated when the disputants agreed to a settlement in which Ukraine reimbursed the Fund for certain loans it had made.[47] As of the beginning of 2014, UNCTAD estimated that of the 274 known concluded investor–state arbitrations, approximately 26 per cent had been settled.[48] On the other hand, ICSID determined that in 2014, 35 per cent of its concluded cases were 'settled or otherwise discontinued'.[49]

A variety of factors can prevent successful negotiated settlements. These might include, for example, the host government's belief that vital national interests are at stake, the investor's perception that crucial economic interests are in play, the political dynamics of the host country, the inability of the investor to mitigate its loss, and the appointment by the parties of incompetent or dysfunctional

---

[45] eg the Agreement between the Government of the Republic of Chile and the Government of the Republic of Finland on the Promotion and Reciprocal Protection of Investments (1 May 1996), Art 8 provides:

    (1) With a view to an amicable solution of disputes between a Contracting Party and an investor of the other Contracting Party consultations will take place between the parties concerned.

    (2) If these consultations do not result in a solution within six months from the date of request for settlement, the investor may submit the disputes:

        either to the competent tribunal of the Contracting Party in whose territory the investment was made; or

        to international arbitration of the International Centre for the Settlement of Investment Disputes (ICSID).

[46] *Western NIS Enterprise Fund v Ukraine*, ICSID Case No ARB/04/2 (US–Ukraine BIT).

[47] 'Ukraine Reaches Settlement in BIT claim by US-govt Venture Capital Fund', *Investment Treaty News*, 4 July 2006, available at <http://www.iisd.org/pdf/2006/itn_july4_2006.pdf.> accessed 17 January 1915.

[48] UNCTAD, *World Investment Report 2014* (2014) 126.

[49] ICSID, *The ICSID Caseload—Statistics* (Issue 2014–2) 13.

negotiators to represent them. Any of these factors can inhibit or halt the negotiation process.

Depending on the circumstances, the threat of initiating arbitration can either favour or discourage negotiated settlements of investor–state disputes. On the one hand, faced with the hard realities of the costs, slow pace, and unpredictability of arbitration, some parties might negotiate a settlement rather than incur additional expenses and delay. On the other hand, initiating arbitration may create a psychological barrier to settlement by causing the parties to harden their positions and become less flexible in dealing with one another.

Unrealistic expectations by the parties can create a further obstacle to successful negotiations. In most cases, the alternative to successful negotiation is arbitration in which the investor will be the claimant and the state refusing that claim the respondent. Investor–state arbitration has risks and costs for both sides, and it is important that both sides understand those costs and benefits thoroughly so that they can accurately evaluate settlement proposals advanced by the other side. Not surprisingly, parties to a dispute, influenced by psychological and political factors, tend to view their conflict from their own points of view. This factor often leads them to overestimate their chances of success in later litigation. When the investor overestimates the strength of its claims and the host state undervalues the worth of the claimant's case, the opportunities for a successful negotiated settlement decline. Various factors may contribute to such a miscalculation, including the failure of lawyers to give their clients a frank assessment of the strength of their case and their likelihood of prevailing in arbitration. One possible means of overcoming these barriers is through the intervention of a skilful, well-intentioned third party who can provide the disputants with a neutral, disinterested evaluation of their respective cases and can advise them on ways to reach a negotiated settlement.

Although mediation, conciliation, and other forms of alternative dispute resolution (ADR) are becoming increasingly popular in settling domestic disputes, their use in investor–state disputes seems relatively rare. Nonetheless, persons involved in disputes with host governments should consider them as a potential option.[50]

In theory and in law, there is no reason why mediation and other forms of ADR could not be applied to investor–state disputes just as successfully as they are applied elsewhere. Certainly, nothing in international investment treaties prohibits the parties from engaging in mediation or other ADR processes to settle treaty disputes. On the other hand, until recently relatively few investment treaties specifically authorized or recognized the applicability of ADR procedures to investor–state disputes. Those that do, generally only make reference to conciliation, which is a form of ADR but does not necessarily encompass the range of techniques and approaches usually associated with ADR.

---

[50] JW Salacuse, 'Is There a Better Way? Alternative Methods of Treaty-Based, Investor–State Dispute Resolution' (2007) 31 Ford Int'l LJ 138.

With respect to non-adjudicative methods for the resolution of investor–state disputes, the traditional formulation found in investment treaties is that in the event of a dispute 'the parties shall initially seek to resolve the dispute by consultations and negotiations',[51] 'the dispute shall as far as possible be settled amicably through negotiations between the parties',[52] or 'the dispute shall as much as possible be settled amicably between the parties'.[53]

Although these treaty provisions, which require the parties to negotiate and consult prior to arbitration, do not specify how those negotiations and consultations are to be conducted, they also do not prevent the parties from seeking assistance from mediators, conciliators, or facilitators to help them to conduct their negotiations and consultations. On the other hand, specific language authorizing the use of ADR might serve as a signal to governments and investors that the contracting parties intended to encourage disputants to use ADR and that they should seek to resolve their dispute accordingly. Although no corroborative evidence exists, it is possible that a treaty's failure to authorize ADR up to this point has inhibited disputants' willingness to use it.

Some treaties specifically authorize the use of conciliation; in fact, it is the only form of non-binding third party procedure that most treaties recognize. For example, the 1988 Japan–China BIT gives investors the option to engage in either conciliation or arbitration.[54] However, no treaty requires its use.

Other treaties contain language specifically authorizing the use of alternative resolution techniques as part of the negotiation and consultation process. For instance, the 1990 US–Poland BIT states: 'In the event of an investment dispute...the parties shall initially seek to resolve the dispute by consultation and negotiation, which may include the use of non-binding, third-party procedures.'[55] Article 6(2) of the 1985 US–Turkey BIT provides that if negotiations are unsuccessful, 'the dispute may be settled through the use of non-binding, third party procedures mutually agreed upon'.[56] And Article 23 of the 2012 US Model BIT provides: 'In the event of an investment dispute, the claimant and the respondent should initially seek to resolve the dispute through consultation and negotiation,

---

[51] Agreement between Australia and the Socialist Republic of Vietnam on the Reciprocal Promotion and Protection of Investments (signed 5 March 1991, entered into force 11 September 1991) 1991 Austl TS No 36, Art 129(1), available at <http://www.unctad.org/sections/dite/iia/docs/bits/ australia_vietnam.pdf> accessed 25 August 2009.

[52] Agreement between the Government of the People's Republic of China and the Government of the Republic of Singapore on the Promotion and Protection of Investments (21 November 1985), Art 13(1).

[53] 'Tout différend relatif aux investissements entre l'une des Parties contractantes et un national ou une société de l'autre Partie contractante est autant que possible réglé a l'amiable entre les deux Parties concernées.' L'accord sur le traitement et la protection des investissements, Fr-Pan (5 November 1982) 1985 J officiel 12067, Art 8(1).

[54] Agreement between Japan and the People's Republic of China Concerning the Encouragement and Reciprocal Protection of Investment (1 August 1988) (1990) 1555 UNTS 238, Art 11(2).

[55] Treaty between the United States of America and the Republic of Poland Concerning Business and Economic Relations (21 March 1990), Art 9(2).

[56] Treaty between the United States of America and the Republic of Turkey Concerning the Reciprocal Encouragement and Protection of Investments (signed 3 December 1985, entered into force 18 May 1990), Art 6(2).

which may include the use of non-binding, third party procedures.'[57] This language appears to be an attempt to underscore the importance of alternative dispute resolution techniques and to introduce them into the investor–state dispute resolution process.

It is difficult to determine the extent to which third party intervention actually takes place in investor–state disputes. It may well be that third parties, such as local business leaders, diplomats, politicians, and others, play an important role in facilitating the negotiations that successfully settle investor–state disputes. While these third parties may not be formally designated as mediators, they nevertheless exercise mediation functions.

The willingness of disputants to resort to mediation or another ADR technique depends, among other factors, on their knowledge of and experience with these processes. In general, companies engaged in international business disputes have not sought the help of mediators to the degree that they have in the domestic context. Generally, they first try to resolve the matter themselves through negotiation, but when that fails, they immediately proceed to arbitration or litigation. Various factors explain this failure to attempt mediation or another form of voluntary third party intervention. These factors include a lack of knowledge about the processes, persons, and institutions that provide the services in question, the fact that companies tend to give control of their disputes to lawyers whose professional inclination is to litigate, and the belief that mediation is merely a stalling tactic that only serves to delay an inevitable arbitration proceeding.[58]

With parties increasingly recognizing the disadvantages of arbitration, some companies are turning to more explicit forms of mediation to resolve business disputes.[59] Increasingly, when a dispute can be quantified (for example calculating the extent of damage done to an asset by a partner or the amount of a licensor's royalty fee), the parties will engage an independent third party, possibly an international accounting or consulting firm, to examine the matter and give an opinion. The opinion is not binding on the parties, but it allows them to make a more realistic prediction of what may happen in an arbitration proceeding.

Host countries' lack of experience with and knowledge of ADR as it applies to investor–state disputes may also explain why they have not resorted to it more often. The politics of investor–state disputes may also be a complicating factor. Once an investor has initiated arbitration against a host state, the host government may fear that its willingness to resort to ADR will be perceived by the investor or the public as weakness or as compromising national interests. A treaty

---

[57] Treaty Concerning the Encouragement and Reciprocal Protection of Investment, US–[Country] (2004), Art 23 ('Model US BIT').

[58] JW Salacuse, 'Mediation in International Business' in J Bercovitch (ed), *Studies in International Mediation* (Palgrave Macmillan, 2002) 213–28.

[59] eg General Electric Corporation has developed a programme known as the Early Dispute Resolution Initiative, which seeks to save money and time through the effective use of dispute resolution techniques outside formal litigation and arbitration, often with external mediators. See Harvard Business School, GE's *Early Dispute Resolution Initiative*, HBS Case N9-801-395 (2001).

provision specifically authorizing the use ADR techniques might help to counter this reaction.

One type of voluntary third party intervention that has particular relevance for investor–state conflicts is *conciliation*. ICSID, the International Chamber of Commerce, and other arbitration institutions offer this service, which is normally governed by a set of rules.[60] Indeed, certain investment treaties specifically provide for conciliation as an option during investor–state disputes. Generally, a party to a dispute seeking institutional conciliation addresses a request for conciliation to the institution offering conciliation services. If the institution secures the agreement of the other disputant, it will appoint a conciliator. While the conciliator has broad discretion to conduct the process, in practice he or she will often invite both sides to state their views of the dispute. He or she will then make a report proposing an appropriate settlement. The parties may accept the report or reject it and proceed to arbitration. In many cases, the report will be used as the basis for a negotiated settlement.

Conciliation, therefore, is a kind of non-binding arbitration.[61] Its function is predictive. It tends to take a rights-based approach and gives the parties a third person's evaluation of their respective rights and obligations. If, as indicated earlier, mediators work on the process, communication, and substance of disputes, conciliators usually focus almost exclusively on the substance of the dispute. They do not normally adopt a problem-solving or relationship-building approach to resolving the dispute, nor do they seek to eliminate the various psychological, strategic, and structural barriers that might obstruct negotiations. The conciliation process is confidential and completely voluntary. Either party may withdraw from conciliation at any time.

One theoretical question is how to categorize conciliation. It has been argued that it is a process separate and distinct from mediation;[62] however, if one defines mediation as a voluntary process by which a third person assists the disputants in negotiating a settlement to their dispute, conciliation clearly falls within the definition of mediation. As it is currently practised, conciliation would appear to be a form of mediation, albeit narrower in scope; its primary focus is to propose a solution that may be used as the basis of a negotiated settlement and not to work on process and communications or seek to eliminate other barriers to agreement. The conciliator has no power to impose a decision. The primary function of the conciliator's report is to help the parties to negotiate a settlement.

Since conciliation is confidential, public information on the process itself is scant. One of the few published accounts concerning the practice discusses the first conciliation conducted under ICSID auspices. In that case, a retired English

[60] See eg ICSID, 'Rules of Procedure for Conciliation Proceedings' in ICSID Convention, Regulations and Rules, available at <https://icsid.worldbank.org/ICSID/StaticFiles/basicdoc/CRR_English-final.pdf> accessed 3 November 2014.

[61] U Onwuamaegbu, 'The Role of ADR in Investor-State Dispute Settlement: The ICSID Experience' (2005) 22 News from ICSID 12, 14.

[62] JJ Coe, Jr, 'Toward a Complementary Use of Conciliation in Investor–State Disputes—A Preliminary Sketch' (2005) 12 U California Davis J Int'l L & Policy 7, 14.

judge, Lord Wilberforce, successfully acted as a conciliator to assist in resolving a dispute involving the distribution of the US$143 million accumulated profits of a joint venture between Tesoro Petroleum Corporation and the state of Trinidad and Tobago. The conciliation, which started in 1984, took less than two years and cost only US$11,000.[63] Despite the success of ICSID's first conciliation and the reference to conciliation in some investment treaties, conciliation has not become widely used to resolve investor–state disputes. By 30 June 2014, ICSID since its creation in 1966 had received only nine requests for conciliation, while receiving 464 requests for arbitration during that same period.[64] The success rate for ICSID conciliation does not appear to be high. In only 20 per cent of concluded conciliation proceedings did the parties report reaching agreement.[65] These figures do not necessarily indicate that mediation is infrequently used to settle international business and investment disputes. It is possible that third parties other than formally designated 'mediators', 'conciliators', or 'facilitators' have played an important role in helping parties involved in investment disputes to negotiate a settlement. Nonetheless, many countries, concerned by the costs of investor–state arbitration, have sought to give great prominence to conciliation and ADR in the treaties they have negotiated in the twenty-first century.[66]

In considering the applicability of ADR to investor–state disputes, it must be stressed that many attorneys only view conciliation as a rather limited form of mediation. In contrast to the passive and restricted role Lord Wilberforce played in ICSID's first conciliation case, other third parties may actively intervene in disputes to help the parties to negotiate a settlement of their investor–state conflict.[67]

15.8 Investor–State Arbitration

(a) The nature and evolution of international arbitration

Arbitration is an ancient dispute settlement method whereby the disputants agree to submit their dispute to a third party (the arbitrator or arbitrators) for a decision according to agreed norms and procedures and to carry out the decision of that third party. The arbitration process is based on agreement by the parties and the authority of the arbitrator is founded on that agreement. In addition to its traditional role as a means to resolve interstate conflicts, arbitration has also become an

---

[63] L Nurick and SJ Schnably, 'The First ICSID Conciliation: Tesoro Petroleum Corporation v. Trinidad and Tobago' (1986) 1 ICSID Rev—FILJ 340.

[64] ICSID, *The ICSID Caseload—Statistics* (Issue 2014–2) 8.   [65] ibid 16.

[66] See eg Comprehensive Economic Partnership Agreement Between Japan and the Republic of India (16 February 2011), Art 96(4).

[67] See eg the very different, proactive approach taken by a multidisciplinary team of mediators in successfully mediating an investment dispute between Vattenfall, a Swedish state-owned electricity company, and Polskie Sieci Elektroenergetyczne (PSE), a Polish integrated electricity company, as reported by the team's chief mediator. TW Wälde, 'Efficient Management of Transnational Disputes: Mutual Gain by Mediation or Joint Loss in Litigation' (2006) 22 Arb Int'l 205, 206.

important means for resolving international commercial disputes between private parties and for the settlement of investor–state conflicts.

After World War II, with the growth in international business activity, arbitration became an increasingly common method to resolve international commercial disputes. Thus, arbitration agreements and clauses found their way with increasing frequency into international contracts for the sale of goods, the transfer of technology, and the undertaking of foreign investments. In certain particularly significant contracts with foreign companies, such as those involving mineral development, states might also agree to submit future disputes to international arbitration as well. As a result, a discrete system of international commercial arbitration developed to deal with disputes involving private parties engaged in trans-border commerce. Institutional centres of international commercial arbitration, such as the London Court of Arbitration and the International Chamber of Commerce, emerged and grew into important structures to support this process. These institutions developed rules to govern the arbitral process, and parties in their contracts would specifically opt for a particular centre and its rules in the event of a contract dispute. In addition, further support for the international arbitral system came with the 1958 conclusion of the Convention on the Recognition and Enforcement of Foreign Arbitral Awards[68] and the adoption in 1966 of the UNCITRAL Arbitration Rules.[69] Often referred to as the New York Convention, the former has been ratified by 152 countries as of 2014.[70] Under the treaty, member states commit their courts to enforcing international arbitration agreements and awards in accordance with specific rules and conditions. The UNCITRAL Arbitration Rules, prepared after several years of work by a group of international jurists operating under the authority of the United Nations Commission on International Trade Law (UNCITRAL), are designed to provide a set of accepted arbitration rules not tied to any particular arbitral institution. They may be used either in ad hoc arbitrations or arbitral proceedings administered by arbitration institutions. Although both sets of international legal rules were designed primarily to support international commercial arbitration, they would also become relevant for investment treaties and investor–state arbitration.

The jurisdictional basis of any arbitration resides in the agreement by the parties to submit their dispute to the arbitral process. Without such an agreement, the parties cannot be compelled to submit to arbitration and any arbitral award can be successfully attacked by demonstrating that the agreement to arbitrate was absent or defective. In international business, agreements to arbitrate take one of two forms: (1) a

---

[68] Convention on the Recognition and Enforcement of Foreign Arbitral Awards (10 June 1958) 330 UNTS 3; 21 UST 2517; TIAS No 6997.

[69] United Nations Commission on International Trade Law Arbitration, 31 UN GAOR Supp (No 17), 35-50 UN Doc A/31/17 (1976) (hereinafter 'UNCITRAL Arbitration Rules'). The text of the UNCITRAL Arbitration Rules is reprinted in (1972) 2 YB Comm Arb 161, 161–71; (1979) 27 Amer J Comp L 489, 489–503.

[70] UNCITRAL, Status: Convention on the Recognition and Enforcement of Foreign Arbitral Awards (New York, 1958), available at <http://www.uncitral.org/uncitral/en/uncitral_texts/arbitration/NYConvention_status.html> accessed 17 January 2015.

provision—usually referred to as an 'arbitration clause'—in a contract, stipulating that future disputes arising under or in connection with the contract are to be submitted to arbitration; and (2) an agreement—usually called a 'submission agreement'—by which the parties to a specific, existing dispute agree to submit that dispute to arbitration.

It must be stressed that as applied in the international business setting, arbitration is a principled and rational method of dispute resolution that seeks a result based on the evidence, the applicable law, and the arguments presented to the arbitral panel. It is by no means a form of conciliation, mediation, or 'palm tree justice'. On the contrary, it is a highly structured and formal process that operates through a set of specific rules and procedures. Although an arbitral proceeding may not exhibit all of the hallowed ritual and procedural technicalities common to judicial hearings, it must nevertheless conform to the minimal standards of justice common to the world's legal systems. Indeed, a tribunal's failure to respect minimal requirements of justice may mean that a court of law will refuse to enforce the resulting arbitral award. Thus, the parties must be given an opportunity to be heard, the arbitrator must be impartial, and the decision-making process must be fair.

The arbitral process, like a court case, goes through a series of procedural stages. Thus, the aggrieved party must initiate the process by filing a demand for arbitration, which the respondent must answer. The arbitrator or arbitrators must then be selected and their powers defined. The time and place of the arbitration hearing must be determined, along with the appropriate procedures. Once these preliminary matters are determined and any challenges to the jurisdiction of the arbitrators are resolved, each side submits its evidence and presents its case. Based on the evidence, the arguments of the parties, and the applicable rules and principles of law, the arbitrators decide the dispute and prepare an award embodying their decision. An arbitral award, however, is not self-enforcing. If the losing party refuses to respect the award, the winning party will need to rely on state power and particularly on state courts to enforce it.

Although the stages of arbitration are fairly uniform, the requirements and rules applicable to each stage may differ significantly among various arbitration systems. The procedural rules applicable to an arbitration depend on the consent of the parties. Most commonly, an arbitration agreement will contain a provision adopting the entire body of rules promulgated by an institution such as the International Chamber of Commerce, the American Arbitration Association, or UNCITRAL. To supplement or replace these rules, the parties may agree on special rules for their particular arbitration. Most legal systems will respect the procedures selected unless they are fundamentally unfair or are the product of fraud or overreaching. Indeed, the failure of the arbitral tribunal to follow the agreed-upon procedures may be grounds for invalidating any eventual award. If the parties have not specified a particular rule or if the adopted set of rules is silent on a particular matter, the arbitral tribunal is normally competent to select the necessary procedures.[71] Generally speaking, arbitration rules are not as well

---

[71] eg UNCITRAL Arbitration Rules, Art 15(1) provide: 'Subject to these Rules, the arbitral tribunal may conduct the arbitration in such manner as it considers appropriate, provided that the

defined and detailed as judicial procedural rules. Failing agreement by the parties or if a lacuna exists in the applicable rules, arbitrators have significant discretion in shaping the applicable arbitration procedures.

Tribunals' decisions and jurisprudence over time have also shaped the international arbitral system. Tribunals have articulated the notion of 'party autonomy' and fashioned a body of law, *lex mercatoria*, gleaned from existing arbitral awards, the writings of commentators, and general principles of law, and applied it to commercial agreements often independently of municipal laws. However, no matter how effective this mechanism was for settling private party disputes, the involvement of a foreign sovereign in an arbitration inevitably makes the procedures of international commercial arbitration insufficient for the settlement of investor–state disputes. This is so because of sovereign nations' state immunity, especially with regard to absolute foreign sovereign immunity, and also the difficulty in enforcing awards against the sovereign, an issue not settled until the adoption of the 1958 New York Convention and the 1965 ICSID Convention.

In contrast to these developments, the possibility of dispute settlement between an alien and a state through international arbitration, despite an increased need due to the rise in foreign investment activity, was precluded by positivist views of international law and state practice. The adoption of the ICSID Convention was necessary to achieve a major breakthrough in this area.

An initial theoretical problem for applying arbitration to investor–state disputes came from the positivist school of legal thought, which regarded international law as governing relations between sovereign states alone. Thus, individual or corporate persons, lacking legal personality under international law, could not obtain an international remedy through an international arbitral tribunal. Consequently, disputes arising out of contracts between sovereign states and private foreign individuals were considered to be subject only to the host state's municipal law. The Permanent Court of International Justice affirmed that view in the *Serbian Loans* case when it held that the dispute was exclusively the relationship between the borrowing state and private person, 'that is to say, relations which are in themselves, within the domain of the municipal law'.[72] *Lena Goldfield Limited v USSR*

---

parties are treated with equality and that at any stage of the proceedings each party is given a full opportunity of presenting his case.' ICSID Convention, s 44 states:

> Any arbitration proceeding shall be conducted in accordance with the provisions of this Section and, except as the parties otherwise agree, in accordance with the Arbitration Rules in effect on the date on which the parties consented to arbitration. *If any question of procedure arises which is not covered by this Section or the Arbitration Rules or any rules agreed by the parties, the Tribunal shall decide the question.* (emphasis supplied).

See Order in Response to a Petition by Five Non-Governmental Organizations for Permission to make an Amicus Curiae Submission (12 February 2007) in the ICSID case of *Suez, Sociedad General de Aguas de Barcelona SA and Vivendi Universal SA v Argentine Republic*, ICSID Case No ARB/03/19, in which the tribunal relied on Art 44 to allow non-parties to make *amicus curiae* submissions on the merits of the case, available at <https://icsid.worldbank.org/ICSID/FrontSer vlet?requestType=CasesRH&actionVal=showDoc&docId=DC519_En&caseId=C19> accessed 17 January 2015.

[72] *Serbian Loans* (1926) PCIJ Series A, No 20, at 17.

was one of the very first arbitrations involving a foreign investor and a state, and at the time it was considered a curious exception to the dominant view.[73] In 1935, Sir Hersch Lauterpacht reluctantly noted the *Lena* award in his *Annual Digest*, stating with regard to the exact nature of the *Lena* decision: '[I]n a sense [it] stand[s] half-way between international and municipal arbitrations.'[74] The Soviet Union, Latin American countries influenced by the Calvo Doctrine, and the newly decolonized countries seeking a New International Economic Order, also tended to support the view that international law dealt exclusively with the regulation of relations between states, and therefore did not apply to relations and transactions between states and private foreign investors.[75]

In situations where a large number of disputes involving nationals of a particular country had to be settled, states have agreed to the establishment of claims commissions. Such procedures did not upset the positivist theory that states needed to be the only parties involved, since the basis of such commissions' power and jurisdiction was agreement between the two states involved in the dispute.[76] To resolve investment disputes between investors and capital-importing countries, capital-exporting countries relied upon the interstate arbitration mechanism in various bilateral commercial agreements, such as FCN treaties. Early BITs would also adopt this approach. Thus, the very first BIT, an agreement between Germany and Pakistan signed in 1959, provided for interstate arbitration as a mechanism for investment dispute settlement.[77] Under Article 11 of that BIT, which followed the pattern of earlier FCN treaties, the contracting parties undertook to resolve disputes regarding treaty interpretation and application through consultations in a spirit of friendship. Failing that, they agreed to submit the dispute to the ICJ by mutual agreement or, if the two states could not so agree, to an arbitration tribunal.

---

[73] According to V Veeder:

Historically, the Lena case remains a baleful monument to the absolute power of a State able by force alone to thwart the consensual process of international arbitration, a threat to transnational trade still present in many parts of the world. Juridically, over the last years, its direct beneficiary has been the modern system of international commercial arbitration to which the *Lena* tribunal applied several innovative and hugely important ideas: (1) the application of a non-national system of law to the merits of the private law dispute, namely 'general principles of law'; (2) the power of the majority of an arbitration tribunal to continue the proceedings in the absence of the minority (notion of 'truncated tribunal'); (3) the related jurisdictional concepts of '*Kompetenz-Kompetenz*', the legal autonomy or 'separability' of an arbitration clause and the scope of the reference of a specific dispute to a particular arbitration tribunal. In the broadest sense, the *Lena* case represents the development of modern commercial arbitration.

VV Veeder, 'The *Lena Goldfields* Arbitration: The Historical Roots of Three Ideas' (1998) 47 ICLQ 747–8

[74] H Lauterpacht, *Annual Digest* (Cambridge University Press, 1935) 428.
[75] See generally GI Tunkin, *Theory of International Law* (Wildy, Simmonds & Hill, 1974).
[76] AH Feller, *The Mexican Claims Commissions: 1923–1934* (Macmillan, 1935) cited in M Sornarajah, *The International Law on Foreign Investment* (2nd edn, Cambridge University Press, 2005) 38.
[77] Treaty for the Promotion and Protection of Investments (with Protocol and exchange of notes) Germany–Pakistan (signed 25 November 1959, entered into force 26 March 1963), Art 11.

With the growth of international investment, resolving investor–state disputes through interstate arbitration proved deficient in several ways, at least from the perspective of foreign investors. First, the remedy was highly politicized because it necessitated involvement by the investor's home government. The initiation and pursuit of a claim against a host state in interstate arbitration or before another body required energetic and prolonged action by the home country government. Moreover, an investor might be prevented from even seeking intervention if a host country required foreign investors to waive diplomatic protection by their home government as a condition of entry. Moreover, no home government would take action solely on the basis of the investor's claim. Rather, its decision on whether or not to pursue interstate arbitration would be based on a comprehensive evaluation of the home country's diplomatic, political, and economic relations with the offending country. Moreover, regardless of the merits of the investor's claim, a home state would be likely to refuse to take any formal action on behalf of an investor if it determined that such an action would damage valuable relations with the host country. Thus, an investor could well find that its national government refused to espouse a meritorious case simply because it feared doing so would be received badly by the host government and would thus harm important national interests. A government would be even more reluctant to invoke interstate arbitration if the merits of the investor's case were unclear. Second, if the home government did decide to initiate an interstate arbitration, the claim would then belong to the home country government, not the investor. This meant that the investor would have no control over the case, no formal role in the interstate proceedings, and no voice in decisions with respect to litigation strategy, settlement, or abandonment of the claim. Third, losing states faced with awards against them often sought to avoid payment by invoking the doctrines of foreign sovereign immunity and the act of state, both of which deny an aggrieved investor a remedy. Fourth, if an offending host state did not comply with an ICJ decision, the only enforcement mechanism available under Article 94(2) of the United Nations Charter is a UN Security Council resolution, a practical impossibility in virtually any investor–state dispute.

In an attempt to overcome these difficulties, some investors, mostly large corporations in the mineral and extractive industries, negotiated arbitration clauses in concession contracts. These clauses provided for disputes arising under their contracts with a host country to be decided by an independent international tribunal located in a third country, rather than in local courts. Such arbitration clauses also provided that any arbitral award would be accepted by and enforceable against the host government, and they set down detailed rules regarding the selection of arbitrators, the arbitral procedure, and, in many cases, the law to be applied by the arbitral tribunal. However, only a few investors had the negotiating power to make such agreements with host governments. Moreover, the validity of such agreements was sometimes questioned. If the government refused to proceed with the arbitration, the investor's only remedies would again be to make a request to its national state either for diplomatic intervention or to espouse the investor's claim before an international tribunal. Moreover, attempts to agree on an appropriate mode of dispute settlement were frustrated by an absence of adequate arbitration mechanisms. For example, arbitration processes organized by private entities such as the International Chamber of Commerce were frequently unacceptable to governments, particularly in the non-western world, and the only public international arbitral tribunal, the Permanent Court of Arbitration, was not yet open to private claimants.

(b) The development of investor–state arbitration

As a result of the lack of any established arbitration mechanism recognized by both investors and governments as adequate, individual disputants and other parties approached the World Bank, as an institution, and the President of the Bank, in his personal capacity, to assist in the settlement of financial disputes involving private parties and states on several occasions.[78] The World Bank's involvement in investment dispute settlement fell into three categories. The first category included two cases involving conciliation in the Suez Canal Compensation and City of Tokyo Bond cases. Disputants in other cases made similar requests for help, but the President declined to accept. The second category included a large number of cases in which the President designated impartial arbitrators, umpires, or experts to assist in resolving existing or future disputes. The third category consisted of cases in which the World Bank attempted to help the parties to agree on a method for solving their disputes outside the World Bank's framework, for instance, by recourse to commercial arbitration, as was the case in the dispute between Columbia and Parsons & Whittemore.[79] Although the World Bank succeeded in facilitating settlements of some of these investment disputes, it was not really equipped to handle that task in addition to its regular activities. At the same time, the World Bank's staff were acutely aware that one of the bank's fundamental purposes was, as stated in Article I of its Articles, 'to assist in the reconstruction and development of territories of members by facilitating the investment of capital for productive purposes'.[80] This laudable goal might well be furthered by a fair and efficient means of dispute resolution that had the confidence of both investors and host states.

In the early 1960s, the staff of the World Bank concluded that an institution specifically designed to deal with the special problems of settling investment disputes between foreign private investors and host country governments would facilitate the international flow of capital. In 1962, the World Bank's Board of Governors requested the Executive Directors to study the matter. After a series of discussions within the World Bank and meetings with legal experts in various

---

[78] Address by World Bank President Eugene Black to the Annual Meeting of the Board of Governors (19 September 1961) ICSID History, vol 2, part 1, p 3.

[79] Note by the General Counsel transmitted to the Executive Directors (19 January 1962) SecM 62–17, 2.

[80] Articles of Agreement of the International Bank for Reconstruction and Development (Washington, DC) 2 UNTS 134, Art I.

parts of the world, the staff recommended an international convention to establish an institution to provide arbitration and conciliation facilities to settle such investment disputes.

The approach suggested by the World Bank included the following principles:

1. a recognition by states of the possibility of direct access by private individuals and corporations to an international tribunal in the field of financial and economic disputes with governments;

2. a recognition by states that agreements made by them with private individuals and corporations to submit such disputes to arbitration are binding international undertakings;

3. the provision of international machinery for the conduct of arbitration, including the availability of arbitrators, methods for their selection, and rules for the conduct of arbitral proceedings;

4. the provision for conciliation as an alternative to arbitration.

The World Bank's approach was motivated by a strong commitment to promote the flow of private investment to areas in need of capital, an objective of special concern to the World Bank.[81] The staff decided that improving the investment climate in developing countries could be done best from a procedural angle, by creating international machinery that would be freely available for the conciliation and arbitration of investment disputes.[82] In other words, the establishment of adequate methods for settling investment disputes was considered vital in improving the investment climate and, thus, the promotion of foreign private investments for development.

Accordingly, in 1964 the World Bank's Board of Governors directed the Executive Directors to 'formulate a convention establishing facilities and procedures which would be available on a voluntary basis for the settlement of investment disputes between contracting States and Nationals of other contracting States through conciliation and arbitration'.[83] The World Bank chose a multilateral convention, whose members would include both capital-exporting and capital-importing states, as the international legal instrument to foster a climate of confidence by providing basic rules that dealt with the protection of both governments' and foreign investors' legitimate interests.[84] In order to allay the concerns of foreign investors that host states might repudiate agreements with investors providing for the conciliation or arbitration of investment disputes, one purpose of the proposed convention was to establish that such agreements were valid

---

[81] Paper prepared by the General Counsel and transmitted to the members of the Committee of the Whole, SID/63-2 (18 February 1963) 3, ICSID, History, vol 2, part 1, p 73.

[82] Note by the President of the Executive Directors, R 61-128 (28 December 1961) ICSID, History, vol 2, part 1, pp 4–6.

[83] IBRD, Report of the Executive Directors on the Convention on the Settlement of Investment Disputes between States and the Nationals of Other States (1965).

[84] Report of the World Bank Executive Directors on the ICSID Convention, Doc ICSID/2, ICSID, History, vol 2, part 2, pp 1072–4.

international obligations. Governments that were asked to enter into arbitration agreements and that were willing to agree to international, rather than national, procedures for dispute resolution feared that notwithstanding that acceptance they might remain subject to diplomatic or other governmental representations or claims by the national government of the foreign investor. The convention would remove this fear by excluding such representation or claims when an arbitration agreement was in effect and respected by the host government. After entering into an agreement for conciliation or arbitration, both parties wished to be sure that the agreement could not be frustrated by a unilateral act and that, in the case of arbitration, any award would be complied with.[85] To give these assurances, the convention would embody the following principles:

1. It provided that a non-state party, an investor, could have direct access to an international forum against a state party without the need for espousal of its cause by its national government. In signing the convention, states accepted that principle, but no signatory state would be compelled to submit to the facilities provided by the convention and no foreign investor could initiate proceedings against a signatory state unless that state and the investor had specifically so agreed. However, once they did agree, their agreement was irrevocable and the parties were bound to carry out their agreement in accordance with the dispute settlement rules established by the convention.

2. While the Convention implied that local courts were not the final forum for the settlement of disputes between states and a foreign investor, it did not suggest that local remedies could not play a major role. In consenting to arbitration, the parties were free to agree either that local remedies might be pursued in lieu of arbitration or that local remedies needed to be exhausted before a dispute could be submitted for arbitration under the Convention. If the parties did not make either stipulation, the Convention provided that arbitration would take the place of local remedies.

3. As a corollary to the principle that an investor could bring a claim in arbitration directly against a foreign state without its home government's intervention, the proposed convention provided that an investor's national state would no longer be able to espouse a claim on the investor's behalf. The Convention, therefore, was designed to offer a means of settling investment disputes between states and foreign investors directly, on a legal basis, and to insulate those disputes from politics and diplomacy.

4. Arbitral tribunals' awards rendered under the Convention would be recognized and enforceable in all contracting states as if they were final judgments of their national courts, even if the state in which enforcement is sought was not a party to the dispute in question. The proposal made clear, however, that if the law of the state where enforcement was being sought

---

[85] Paper prepared by the General Counsel and transmitted to the members of the Committee of the Whole, SID/63-2 (18 February 1963) 11, ICSID, History, vol 2, part 1, p 81.

prevented enforcement against a state as opposed to execution against a private party, the convention would not change that law. The proposal only sought to place arbitral awards on the same footing as final judgments of national courts. If the judgments could be enforced under the domestic laws in question, so could the award; if that judgment could not be so enforced, neither could the award.

5. The proposed convention would not establish standards for the treatment of aliens' property and did not prescribe standards for foreign investors' conduct in their relations with the host state. Accordingly, the Convention would not contain provisions concerning the substantive law or the merits of investment disputes—it would focus instead solely on the procedure for their settlement.[86]

By 1965, the Executive Directors and the World Bank staff had completed their work, which resulted in the Convention on the Settlement of Investment Disputes between States and Nationals of other States.[87] This Convention was then submitted for approval to the member states of the World Bank and entered into force on 14 October 1966. The Convention has steadily gained state acceptance since that time. As of 30 June 2013, 158 countries had signed the Convention and 149 deposited their instruments of ratification.[88]

The Convention on the Settlement of Investment Disputes between States and Nationals of other States (sometimes referred to as the 'Washington Convention') created an international institution named the International Centre for Settlement of Investment Disputes (ICSID) to provide facilities for the conciliation and arbitration of investment disputes. Located in Washington, DC at the headquarters of the World Bank, the Centre itself does not engage in conciliation or arbitration; instead, it facilitates the establishment of arbitral tribunals and conciliation commissions in accordance with the provisions of the Convention. The Centre's governing body, known as the Administrative Council, is composed of one representative from each contracting state. The ex-officio chairman of the Administrative Council is the President of the World Bank.

The Convention establishes a system of arbitration that is distinct from interstate and international commercial arbitration. In a sense, it stands between those two forms of arbitration, while sharing features of both systems. It creates a complete, self-contained jurisdictional system for the settlement of investor–state disputes. Thus, the Convention laid the foundation for future investment treaties

---

[86] See eg Paper prepared by the General Counsel and transmitted to the members of the Committee of the Whole SID/63-2 (18 February 1963); Summary Record of Proceedings, Adis Ababa Consultative Meetings of Legal Experts (16–20 December 1963) Z7 (30 April 1964).

[87] (18 March 1965) 575 UNTS 159; 17 UST 1270; TIAS No 6090. For a history of the Convention, see ICSID, Convention on the Settlement of Investment Disputes between States and Nationals of Other States: Analysis of Documents Concerning the Origin and Formation of the Convention (Washington, DC, 1970). See also C Schreuer, *The ICSID Convention: A Commentary* (Cambridge University Press, 2001), which is the most comprehensive and authoritative scholarly analysis of the text of the Convention.

[88] ICSID, *ICSID 2013 Annual Report* (2008) 7.

to incorporate this mechanism into their texts. Therefore, an investor can bring suit without the aid or intervention of its national state and litigate on a procedurally equal footing with a host state.[89] The establishment of the ICSID institutional investor–state arbitration became a catalyst for offering other institutional, as well as ad hoc, forms of arbitration.

The Convention created ICSID as an institution distinct from the World Bank but at the same time linked to it. This linkage allows the Centre to take advantage of the World Bank's administrative resources and perceived prestige and reputation for impartiality. On the other hand, the Convention sought to design dispute resolution processes that are not influenced by the World Bank or its staff. At the same time, the fact that the Centre was created under the sponsorship of the World Bank from which it continues to receive support has tended to assure investors and governments that it is an acceptable forum for investor–state dispute resolution.

It should be emphasized that by becoming a member of the ICSID Convention a state does not automatically become subject to ICSID jurisdiction for all disputes arising out of foreign investment in its territory. The state must have specifically consented in writing to be subject to arbitration of such a dispute. Thus, Article 25(1) of the Convention establishes the basis of ICSID jurisdiction over investment disputes:

(1) The jurisdiction of the Centre shall extend to any legal dispute arising directly out of an investment, between a Contracting State (or any constituent subdivision or agency of a Contracting State designated to the Centre by that State) and a national of another Contracting State, which the parties to the dispute consent in writing to submit to the Centre. When the parties have given their consent, no party may withdraw its consent unilaterally.

Although ICSID would not hear its first case until 1972, it has become an important institution for international investment dispute resolution and handles the majority of known investor–state disputes. In 1978, ICSID's Administrative Council authorized its Secretariat to administer certain proceedings that were not covered by the Washington Convention. There were three types of such proceedings: (a) conciliation or arbitration of legal disputes arising out of an investment that is not within the jurisdiction of ICSID because either the state party or the state whose national is a party is not a contracting state of the Convention; (b) conciliation or arbitration proceedings between parties where at least one is a contracting state or a national of a contracting state and where the settlement of the legal dispute may not directly arise out of an investment; and (c) fact-finding proceedings. The procedures governing each of these proceedings are set out in ICSID Additional Facility Rules.[90] These procedures enable states that are not

---

[89] A Broches, 'Bilateral Investment Protection Treaties and Arbitration of Investment Disputes' in J Schultz and J van den Berg (eds), *The Art of Arbitration, Essays on International Arbitration, Liber Amicorum Pieter Sanders* (Kluwer Law International, 1982) 64.

[90] Known formally as the Rules Governing the Additional Facility for the Administration of Proceedings by the Secretariat of the International Centre for Settlement of Investment Disputes (Additional Facility Rules). In addition to a brief set of rules prescribing the basic conditions

ICSID members to commit to investor–state arbitration in investment treaties through the Additional Facility Rules. Many have done so, and several additional facility cases have been registered. It should be noted, however, that the ICSID Convention and its enforcement provisions do not apply to these three types of proceedings. The enforcement of awards under the Additional Facility Rules would ordinarily be governed by the UN Convention on the Recognition and Enforcement of Foreign Arbitral Awards. For this reason the Rules provide that Additional Facility Arbitration may only be held in a state that is a party to the Convention.

In addition to these investor–state dispute settlement mechanisms, investment treaties often offer investors ad hoc investor–state arbitration under UNCITRAL rules or at other arbitral institutions such as the Stockholm Chamber of Commerce.

Between 1987 and the beginning of 2014, the total number of investor–state disputes submitted to arbitration was estimated at 568, with a total of ninety-eight countries involved as a respondent in at least one case.[91] The majority of these arbitration cases have taken place under ICSID's auspices. The reason for this growth is the rapid increase in investment treaties and their imposition of ICSID and other forms of investor–state arbitration for resolving disputes.

(c) The incorporation of investor–state arbitration into treaties

Shortly after the adoption of the ICSID Convention, investment treaties began to provide for settling investor–state disputes through arbitration. The first BIT to include an ICSID clause was the Netherlands–Indonesia treaty,[92] signed in 1968, just two years after the ICSID Convention went into effect. That treaty, which set the pattern for subsequent investment agreements, provided that if the investor–state dispute could not be settled amicably, 'the dispute shall, at the request of the national concerned, be submitted either to the judicial procedures provided by the Contracting Party concerned or to international arbitration or conciliation'. It further provided that each contracting party to the treaty 'hereby consents to submit any legal dispute arising between that Contracting Party and a national of the other Contracting Party concerning an investment of that national in the territory of the former Contracting Party to' ICSID. Through the treaty, each contracting state provided the essential jurisdictional element of consent to arbitration but left the decision as to whether or not to arbitrate to the investor.

Unlike the arbitration clauses used in contracts, these treaty provisions could not be considered an arbitration agreement with the investor because the investor, while a national of a contracting state, was not a party to the treaty. Conceptually,

---

necessary for access to the facility, the Additional Facility Rules contained detailed schedules setting out Additional Facility Administrative and Financial Rules, Additional Facility Conciliation Rules, Additional Arbitration Rules, and Additional Facility Fact-Finding Rules.

[91] UNCTAD, *World Investment Report 2014* (2014) 125.

[92] Agreement between the Government of the Kingdom of the Netherlands and the Government of the Republic of Indonesia on Promotion and Protection of Investment (7 July 1968), Art 9(4).

such a provision constitutes an irrevocable offer to arbitrate disputes concerning the interpretation and application of the treaty. An investor may accept that offer in different ways, including the submission of a request for arbitration or some other mechanism offered in the treaty. The offer includes the various terms and conditions contained in the applicable investment treaty.[93]

Treaties negotiated in the following years provided for investor–state arbitration, and today such provisions have become standard in investment treaty practice. Moreover, multilateral treaties such as NAFTA and the ECT have also adopted investor–state arbitration as their fall-back dispute resolution mechanism. However, the specific nature of those provisions, their scope, and their conditions and legal consequences are not uniform among investment treaties. For example, whereas most BITs and NAFTA grant investors the right to invoke arbitration against a host state, the ECT gives a more nuanced approach that is worth considering in some depth.

The dispute settlement provisions of the ECT, found in Articles 26 to 28 (Part V), are like most BITs in that they create separate mechanisms for state-to-state disputes and disputes between aggrieved investors and host countries. With regard to the former, the ECT follows BITs in providing for ad hoc arbitration if diplomatic negotiations fail. In this respect, one should note Article 15 of the ECT on subrogation, which specifically recognizes the ability of a national or company to assign its rights and claims to a contracting party and the right to pursue those rights and claims against another contracting party.

In its provisions on the settlement of investment disputes between investors and host countries, the ECT departs from the approach of more recent BITs and does not allow for automatic recourse to international arbitration by the investor. Under Article 26, disputes between a contracting party and an investor of another party over an alleged breach of the ECT may be submitted by the investor only after an attempt at amicable settlement for a period of at least three months. Following that period, an investor may choose one of the following dispute settlement procedures: (1) the courts or administrative tribunals of the host country; (2) any previously agreed dispute settlement procedure; and (3) binding international arbitration under the auspices of the International Centre for Settlement of Investment Disputes, the Arbitration Institute of the Stockholm Chamber of Commerce, or ad hoc arbitration under the UNCITRAL Arbitration Rules. However, an investor's right to invoke international arbitration can be limited at the option of a host country. Article 26(3) provides that ECT contracting parties may choose to be listed in Annex ID, which identifies them as denying investor access to international arbitration when an investor has previously submitted an investment to local courts or to other dispute settlement procedures. The effect of this provision is that if local law requires disputes to be heard first by local courts, by opting to be listed in Annex ID an ECT country can prevent an aggrieved investor from initiating international arbitration. This resistance to granting

[93] Schreuer (n 87 above) 210–22.

aggrieved investors automatic access to international arbitration in disputes with the host country is in distinct contrast to the prevailing BIT trend to provide for such a right.

The first investor–state arbitration to establish jurisdiction on the basis of an investment treaty was the 1990 case of *AAPL v Sri Lanka*.[94] The tribunal in *AAPL* relied on Article 8 of the 1980 UK–Sri Lanka BIT, which provided that '[e]ach Contracting Party hereby consents to submit to' ICSID 'for settlement by concili-ation or arbitration...any legal disputes arising between that Contracting Party and a national or company of the other Contracting Party concerning an invest-ment of the latter in the territory of the former'.[95] Without a specific arbitration clause in a contract between the investor and the Sri Lankan government and with little discussion, the tribunal decided the treaty provision was sufficient to establish Sri Lanka's consent to arbitrate and that the filing of a request for arbitra-tion was adequate evidence of the UK investor's consent. Many subsequent cases would proceed in a similar manner.[96] It is established investment treaty practice, therefore, that an investor may accept a host country's offer to arbitrate in an investment treaty simply by instituting arbitral proceedings.[97] On the other hand, most treaties do not specifically state how an investor must manifest its consent or even if consent must be manifested at all. In most instances, the nature and form of investor consent will be determined by the rules of the arbitral process under the treaty. Thus, in the case of an ICSID arbitration, one would look to the ICSID Convention and Rules to determine whether the consent manifested meets ICSID requirements.

(d) Governing law

Investor–state arbitration, it must be emphasized, is a rule-driven process. Arbitrators have the duty to decide investor–state disputes according to law. In the domain of international commercial arbitration, the principle of 'party auton-omy' is generally accepted, which means that arbitrators will apply the law that the parties have agreed will govern their transaction. Similarly, most investment treaties state what laws arbitral tribunals are to apply in deciding investor–state disputes. Thus, for example, Article 26(6) of the ECT directs tribunals to 'decide the issues in dispute in accordance with this treaty and the applicable rules and principles of international law'. Some treaties will also include the legislation of

---

[94] *AAPL v Sri Lanka*, 4 ICSID Reports 246, 250/1 (Award) (27 June 1990). See also CF Amerasinghe, 'The Prawn Farm (AAPL) Arbitration' (1992) 4 Sri Lanka J Int'l L 155.

[95] Agreement between the Government of the United Kingdom of Great Britain and Northern Ireland and the Government of the Democratic Socialist Republic of Sri Lanka for the Promotion and Protection of Investments (13 February 1980), Art 8(1).

[96] eg *AMT v Zaire* (Award) (21 February 1997) (1997) 36 ILM 1531, 1545; *Fedax v Venezuela* (Decision on Jurisdiction) (11 June 1997) (1998) 37 ILM 1378, 1384.

[97] R Dolzer and C Schreuer, *Principles of International Investment Law* (OUP, 2008) 243. See also the award in *Generation Ukraine v Ukraine* (16 September 2003), in which the tribunal stated at ¶ 12.2, 'it is firmly established that an investor can accept a State's offer of ICSID jurisdiction contained in a bilateral investment treaty by instituting ICSID proceedings'.

the host country among the bodies of law that may be applied. Thus, the BIT between Bulgaria and Belgium provides that investor–state arbitration tribunals shall decide cases on the basis of:

- the national law of the Contracting Party on whose territory the investment is situated, including the rules relating to conflict of laws;
- the provisions of the present agreement;
- the terms of the particular obligation which involves the investment;
- the generally accepted rules and principles of international law.[98]

This provision, and other similar provisions that refer to national legislation, cannot be read as creating a prioritized list of sources indicating that national law is to be applied even when it conflicts with treaty provisions. It is an established principle of international law, as reaffirmed by the Vienna Convention on the Law of Treaties (VCLT), that a state party to a treaty 'may not invoke the provisions of its internal law as justification for its failure to perform a treaty'.[99] Indeed, to arrive at a decision, tribunals in many investor–state disputes must evaluate whether a particular item of internal legislation and its application to a covered investment violates a treaty provision. To hold that a provision gives preference to national legislation over a treaty provision would nullify the treaty's goal of restraining state action by requiring that it conform to international standards in its treatment of covered investments and investors.

Not all treaties contain a specific governing law clause.[100] In such situations, if the treaty provides for dispute resolution according to the ICSID Convention, a tribunal would be guided on governing law by Article 42(1) of the Convention. That article provides that in the absence of an agreement with respect to choice of law, the tribunal will apply the law of the host country and such rules of international law as may be applicable. If a treaty contains no provision on governing law and no reference to choice of law rules, the tribunal would first apply the investment treaty provisions itself, since it is directed by the treaty to decide disputes arising under the treaty, and then to other rules of international law such as the VCLT.

(e) The differing natures of investor–state arbitration provisions

While the majority of investment treaties now contain provisions on investor–state arbitration, those provisions are by no means uniform. Although a survey of the individual differences among the vast array of existing treaties is beyond the scope

---

[98] Accord entre la République Populaire de Bulgarie et L'Union Belgo-Luxembourgeoise concernant l'Encouragement et la Protection Réciproques des Investissements (25 October 1988), Art 8(5).

[99] VCLT, Art 27.

[100] eg Agreement between the Government of the United Kingdom of Great Britain and Northern Ireland and the Government of the Republic of Albania for the Promotion and Protection of Investments (30 March 1994).

of this book,[101] there are certain important issues on which persons interpreting such treaty provisions should focus, including the following: (1) the unequivocal nature of the state's consent to arbitrate; (2) the scope of the consent to arbitrate; (3) the conditions precedent to arbitration; and (4) available dispute forums. Each of these issues is examined briefly.

(i) The unequivocal nature of the state's consent to arbitrate

Although the majority of contracting states make unequivocal commitments in their treaties to arbitrate disputes with covered investors, in some treaties the state's commitment is less firm and unequivocal. Some clauses, found principally in older BITs, simply state that investor–state arbitration will be resorted to if the parties agree to it. This requires the creation of a subsequent, specific agreement to arbitrate between the investor and the host state. In other treaties, contracting states promise 'sympathetic consideration' of requests to arbitrate disputes by investors of another contracting party.[102] Such a provision is much less than a firm, unequivocal consent to arbitration; however, it can be interpreted as an implied obligation not to withhold consent unreasonably.[103]

In several treaties, contracting states, while refraining from giving their unequivocal consent to arbitrate, have nonetheless promised to give their consent to any investor who requests it. For example, Article 10 of the Netherlands–Pakistan BIT of 1988 provides: 'The Contracting Party in the territory of which a national of the other Contracting Party makes or intends to make an investment, shall assent to any demand on the part of such national to submit, for arbitration or conciliation, to the Centre…any dispute that may arise in connection with the investment.'

If the host state refuses to give its consent after receiving a request from a covered investor, the other contracting party could demand that the refusing party carry out its obligation under the treaty. If the state persists in its refusal, the insisting party would have recourse to the remedies available under the treaty or other applicable rules of international law.[104] Alone such a clause would not allow an investor to begin arbitration because ICSID and other forums require both parties' consent to establish arbitral jurisdiction.

---

[101] For a survey of the issues posed by investor–state arbitration and the current challenges it faces, see generally UNCTAD, *Investor–State Dispute Settlement* (2014).

[102] eg the Netherlands–Yugoslavia BIT of 1976, Art VI which provides:

> The competent authority of the Contracting Party in the territory of which a national of the other Contracting Party makes or intends to make an investment, shall give *sympathetic consideration* to any request of such national to assume the obligation to submit, for arbitration or conciliation, to the Centre…any dispute that may arise in connection with that investment, and shall inform that national in writing of its decision. (emphasis added)

[103] Schreuer (n 87 above) 217.　　　　[104] ibid 216.

(ii) The scope of consent

Arbitral jurisdiction requires on the consent of the parties. Normally, the extent of arbitrators' jurisdiction depends the scope of the authority that parties give them. For anyone interpreting and applying investor–state treaty provisions, therefore, it is essential to determine whether the specific dispute at issue falls within the scope of the provision on investor–state arbitration.

In general, most treaty provisions have a wide scope and stipulate that consent to arbitration covers 'any dispute' or 'all disputes...concerning an investment'. For example, Article X of the Spain–Argentina BIT covers '[d]isputes arising between a Party and an investor of the other Party in connection with investments within the meaning of this Agreement'.[105] US BITs, on the other hand, contain an elaborate and broad definition of investment disputes, which specifically defines the disputes covered as including: (a) disputes concerning the interpretation or application of an investment contract; (b) disputes concerning the interpretation or application of an investment authorization; and (c) disputes concerning breaches of rights created under the terms of the BIT.[106]

Some treaties seek to limit, rather than broaden, the scope of disputes that are subject to investor–state arbitration. For example, Romanian BITs from the 1970s restricted international arbitration to disputes about the amount of compensation due to an investor after expropriation and even then only after the dispute had been decided by the host country's courts. Thus, an investor dissatisfied with the amount of compensation granted after exhausting local remedies is entitled to ICSID arbitration, but in the case of any other dispute, including disputes about the legality of the expropriation, the local court's decision is final. China takes this approach in its BITs. Article 8 of its 1994 investment treaty with Jamaica only allows arbitration for disputes relating to the amount of compensation owed as a result of an expropriation.[107] In the ICSID case of *Plama Consortium Limited v Republic of Bulgaria*,[108] the tribunal would not allow claimants to avoid a similarly limited consent clause in the Bulgaria–Cyprus BIT by using the MFN clause in that BIT to take advantage of a broader consent clause in the Bulgaria–Finland BIT.

(iii) Conditions precedent to invoking investor–state arbitration

Even if the contracting parties to an investment treaty give an unequivocal consent to the arbitration of investment disputes with other contracting parties' investors,

---

[105] Agreement between the Government of Spain and the Government of the Argentine Republic on the Reciprocal Promotion and Protection of Investments (3 October 1991), Art X(1).

[106] eg Treaty between the United States of America and the Republic of Armenia Concerning the Promotion and Reciprocal Protection of Investment (signed 23 March 1992), Art VI(1).

[107] Agreement between the People's Republic of China and the Government of Jamaica Concerning the Encouragement and Reciprocal Protection of Investment (signed 26 October 1994).

[108] *Plama Consortium Ltd v Republic of Bulgaria*, ICSID Case No Arb/03/24 (Decision on Jurisdiction) (8 February 2005).

all treaties set down certain conditions, sometimes procedural, that an investor must fulfil before commencing arbitration proceedings. One common condition discussed earlier in this chapter is a requirement that an investor first try to resolve the dispute amicably, through direct negotiations and consultations with host country government authorities. In order to forestall delaying tactics and make clear when a party has satisfied this condition, treaties often specify time limits for such negotiations. If the parties are unable to settle the dispute within the designated time period, which may range from three to twelve months, the investor is free to commence arbitration. Arbitral jurisprudence on whether the passage of the specified time is a required element to establish jurisdiction appears to be divided. One the one hand, in *SGS v Pakistan*,[109] the tribunal, applying a Pakistan–Switzerland BIT requiring a twelve-month period of consultation, held that the completion of the period was not a condition precedent to jurisdiction.[110] On the other hand, the tribunal in *Enron v Argentina*, applying an Argentina–US BIT calling for six months of consultation, specifically stated that it was a jurisdictional requirement and that failure to fulfil it would result in a lack of jurisdiction.[111] While the specific language of the treaty in question will influence this issue, from a policy perspective it would seem that the better view is that periods of consultation and negotiation are jurisdictional in nature and a condition precedent to arbitration. All treaties evince a preference by the contracting parties to settle investor–state disputes through negotiations and other amicable means rather than by arbitration and litigation. The stipulated consultation period is one means of achieving this desirable public policy goal. Arbitral tribunals should not diminish the condition's importance by asserting jurisdiction before it is fulfilled.[112] On the other hand, in order to foster an expeditious settlement process of investor claims, NAFTA, unlike most other investment treaties, provides what is effectively a three-year statute of limitations after which an investor is barred from seeking arbitration.[113]

Beyond mere negotiations and consultations, some treaties require that parties to an investor–state dispute seek a resolution through local judicial and

---

[109] *SGS v Pakistan* (Decision on Jurisdiction) (6 August 2003) 184.

[110] Other cases taking a similar view that specified amicable settlement procedures that were not jurisdictional in nature were *Ethyl Corp v Canada*, UNCITRAL (Decision on Jurisdiction) (24 June 1998) ¶ 85; *Biwater Gauff v Tanzania* (Award) (24 July 2008) ¶¶ 343–344; and *Occidental v Ecuador*, ICSID Case No ARB/06/11 (Decision on Jurisdiction) (9 September 2008) ¶ 94.

[111] *Enron Corp and Ponderosa Assets LP v Argentina* (Decision on Jurisdiction) (14 January 2004) 88. Other cases that adopted a similar view that such procedures are jurisdictional in nature were *Burlington v Ecuador*, ICSID Case No ARB/08/5 (Decision on Jurisdiction) (2 June 2010) ¶¶ 312, 315; *Murphy Exploration and Production Co International v Ecuador*, ICSID Case No ARB/08/04 (Award on Jurisdiction) (15 December 2010) ¶ 149; *Wintershall v Argentina*, ICSID Case No ARB/04/14 (Award) (8 December 2008) ¶¶ 114–156.

[112] For an opposing view, see Dolzer and Schreuer (n 97 above) 248–9.

[113] The North American Free Trade Agreement, Art 1116(2) provides:

An investor may not make a claim if more than three years have elapsed from the date on which the investor first acquired, or should have first acquired, knowledge of the alleged breach and knowledge that the investor has incurred loss or damage.

administrative means. Normally, these efforts are limited to specific periods of time and are not a requirement for the exhaustion of local remedies in the traditional meaning of that term.

(iv) Available dispute resolution forums

A wide variety of arbitral and judicial forums exist in the world. Investment treaties normally indicate to which particular forums an investor may have recourse in order to settle a dispute with a host country. Many treaties specify only one such forum, which is often ICSID. Others give investors a choice of various arbitral options. For example, unless a contracting state has specifically limited dispute resolution, the ECT offers investors the following options: (1) the courts or administrative tribunals of the host country; (2) any previously agreed dispute settlement procedure; or (3) binding international arbitration under the auspices of ICSID, the Arbitration Institute of the Stockholm Chamber of Commerce, or ad hoc arbitration under the UNCITRAL Arbitration Rules.[114] Other treaties refer to other arbitral institutions, including the International Chamber of Commerce and certain regional centres.

(f) The growth and significance of investor–state arbitration

In a significant departure from customary international law and earlier bilateral commercial treaties, contemporary international investment treaties commonly grant investors the right to bring claims in arbitration against host states for violations of treaty provisions with respect to investor treatment. The novelty and power of this remedy cannot be overstated. There are few other instances where international law gives private persons and companies the right to force a sovereign to appear before an international tribunal, compel that state to defend its actions ostensibly taken to protect the public interest, and, if those actions are judged to violate international law, to pay the injured investor compensation. Unlike the situation prevailing before the advent of the investment treaty movement, investors have the right to bring claims autonomously and without reference to or the permission of their home governments, to control and direct their case against a host state as they see fit, and to have full entitlement to any monetary award that an arbitral tribunal may grant them. Indeed, it should also be emphasized that investment treaties usually grant aggrieved investors the right to prosecute their claims autonomously, with complete disregard for the concerns and interests of their home countries. For capital-exporting states and foreign investors, it is this mechanism that gives important, practical significance to international investment agreements and enables the treaties to afford true protection to foreign investment.

---

[114] ECT, Art 26.

Particularly in recent years, investors have taken advantage of that remedy. At the end of the twentieth and the beginning of the twenty-first centuries, one of the most significant developments in international investment law has been the growth of investor–state arbitration to settle investment disputes. From 1987 to the beginning of 2014, at least 568 investor–state treaty arbitrations had been brought,[115] virtually all of which involved private investors as claimants and states as respondents. The precise number cannot be ascertained because some investor–state arbitrations are not made public by the involved parties. As of 2014, known cases involved ninety-eight different governments. The three investment treaties most frequently invoked as a basis for investor–state arbitration were NAFTA (fifty-one cases), the ECT (fifty-one cases), and the Argentina–United States BIT (seventeen cases).[116] Of the total number of arbitral cases brought, UNCTAD estimates that 43 per cent were decided in favour of states, 31 per cent were decided in favour of investors, and 26 per cent were settled.[117] The frequency of investor–state litigation has also grown substantially from only two cases begun in 1994 to record levels of fifty-eight and fifty-six registered in 2012 and 2013, respectively

In the realm of international investment, investor–state, treaty-based arbitration has become increasingly common. Similarly, arbitral awards interpreting and applying investment treaty provisions have become increasingly numerous. For international law firms, investor–state arbitration—once an arcane field only of interest to a few scholars and specialists—has become an important and lucrative area of practice.

In almost all investor–state arbitrations, the investor is the claimant and the host state is the respondent. Three reasons explain why states rarely initiate international arbitration cases against investors. First, host states generally consider their internal legal processes—for example their regulatory powers and judicial systems—sufficient to handle their claims against investors during disputes. Second, BITs grant investors rights but rarely impose obligations on them that host states can enforce through arbitration. Third, ICSID and other forms of arbitration require the consent of *both* parties to establish jurisdiction. Under nearly all investment treaties, the state alone, not the investor, consents to arbitration; consequently, unless the investor has specifically consented to arbitration in some other way, it is not subject to arbitral jurisdiction. Thus, among all the arbitration cases registered at ICSID as of 2007, only two were initiated by states, and jurisdiction in both cases was based on contracts with the investor and not on investment treaties.[118]

One may argue that the recent growth in treaty-based investor–state disputes is purely a function of the vast increase in international investment generally

---

[115] UNCTAD, *World Investment Report 2014* (2014) 125.   [116] ibid.
[117] ibid 126.
[118] *Tanzania Electric Supply Co Ltd v Independent Power Tanzania Ltd*, ICSID Case No ARB/98/8 and *Gabon v Société Serte*, ICSID Case No ARB/79/1. See the listing of registered cases on the ICSID website, at <https://icsid.worldbank.org/apps/ICSIDWEB/cases/Pages/AdvancedSearch.aspx> accessed 17 January 2015.

and the inevitability of conflict in investment relationships and that, therefore, investor–state disputes are a natural and inevitable fact of international economic life. On the other hand, one must also acknowledge that investor–state disputes have certain potential negative consequences for both the states and the investors involved.

The costs of investor–state disputes are imposing growing financial hardships on individual states, particularly on poor, developing countries. The OECD estimates that the average cost to the parties of an investor–state arbitration is US$8 million, with costs exceeding US$30 million in some cases.[119] In addition to the costs of actually conducting the arbitration, there are two other costs. First, a host country risks having to pay awards that, in relation to its budget and financial resources, may be extremely burdensome. Second, the 'policy cost' of an investor–state arbitration is that a substantial award to the investor may require the host government to repeal or modify other similar but unrelated measures.

The growing number of investor–state disputes may impose other, indirect burdens on governments, as well. Investment policy, like any other government policy, needs to be sustained by popular support. Public realization of the costs incurred by host countries during investor–state, treaty-based disputes, which are often accompanied by significant publicity and media comment, might lead to declining support for foreign investment or for the economic liberalization policies many countries have adopted over the last two decades.[120] In other words, continued public support for policies favouring foreign investment is not a foregone conclusion, and increases in investor–state arbitration may contribute to additional restrictions if popular support leans the other way. Moreover, a high-profile investor–state arbitration may be seen by other foreign investors as a negative reflection on the investment climate in the host country, and as an indication that the country concerned is not as receptive to foreign investors as its government contends. After all, the basis of any claim in a treaty-based, investor–state arbitration is that the host country violated its international treaty commitments.

In addition to the cost incurred by host countries and investors, investor–state arbitrations may also have negative consequences for international relationships between host countries and investor home countries. A highly publicised, hotly litigated arbitration between a foreign investor and a host country can negatively affect governmental and public opinion in the investor's home country towards the host country and vice versa.

Despite a few investors who have won large awards as a result of treaty-based, investor–state arbitration, the idea that it is the road to vast riches for investors

---

[119] D Gaukrodger and K Gordon, 'Investor–State Dispute Settlement: A Scoping Paper for the Investement Policy Community', OECD Working Papers on International Investment, 2012/03, 19, available at <http://www.oecd.org/daf/inv/investment-policy/WP-2012_3.pdf> accessed 17 January 2015.

[120] eg an UNCTAD study found that from 1991 to 2002, '1551 (95%) out of 1641 changes introduced by 165 countries in their FDI laws were in the direction of greater liberalization'. UNCTAD, *World Investment Report 2003: FDI Policies for Development: National and International Perspectives*, UN Doc UNCTAD/WIR/2003 (4 September 2003) 20.

is a gross exaggeration. Investor–state arbitration also entails significant costs for the investor—costs that may not be recouped from any eventual arbitral award. The costs to the investor have several dimensions. First, there are the financial costs incurred by the investor by hiring legal representation and paying its portion of the arbitration's administrative costs. Second, there are the costs incurred by having to devote significant executive time, effort, and concentration to arbitration rather than the investor's core business. Third, there are relationship costs. A transnational corporation requires productive relationships with host governments, business communities, and the publics where it operates. Initiating arbitration against a host government might serve to rupture those relationships and put into question its relationships with countries that are sympathetic to the host country respondent. Other host countries may ask themselves: If this investor was willing to sue country X, may it not also be willing to sue us? It was perhaps an evaluation of these costs that led the former CEO of Metalclad, which won an award of US$17 million against Mexico in a much noted case,[121] to state publicly that he found the whole arbitration process a burden and he wished he had settled his company's claim through informal mechanisms, or what he called Metalclad's 'political options'.[122] Presumably, he was indicating that, in hindsight, informal processes of dispute resolution might have been less costly than the formal processes involved in investor–state arbitration.

(g) Waiver of investor rights to investor–state arbitration

Over the past six decades, the nations of the world have engaged in the process of constructing a treaty regime that grants specific rights under international law to private investors who undertake investments in foreign countries. A potentially important question is whether those private investors may waive any or all of the rights granted to them by individual treaties, particularly the right to bring a claim in arbitration directly against a host state. No investment treaty specifically deals with this issue, and no arbitral award appears to have decided it.

The question is not purely theoretical. It is possible that host countries, having entered into numerous investment treaties in an earlier era, might later seek to extricate themselves from treaty commitments towards particular investors by asking them to waive certain rights, for example recourse to compulsory international arbitration, as a condition for the host government's permission to make an investment or its grant of a particularly desirable benefit. For example, if a country has discovered vast mineral or petroleum resources, could it require investors seeking to invest in the development of those resources to waive some or all of their rights under an otherwise applicable BIT? If subsequent to such an investment, the host state takes actions that injure the investment and the investor then seeks to assert its rights under the applicable treaty, could the host state raise the

---

[121] *Metalclad Corp v United Mexican States (United States v Mexico)*, ICSID Case No ARB(AF)/97/1 P 31 (30 August 2000) (2001) 40 ILM 36 (NAFTA).
[122] J Coe (n 62 above) 7, 8, n 2.

investor's earlier waiver as a defence to a claim in an investor–state arbitration proceeding? While it is generally agreed that an injured alien may waive an existing claim against a state,[123] it does not follow from that principle that a prospective waiver of rights will be binding and irrevocable.

One approach to resolving this question is to inquire whether the investment treaty in question confers rights directly on investors as subjects of international law or whether investors derive those rights from the treaty state to which they belong.[124] If the former situation prevails and investors, by virtue of the investment treaty, are endowed directly with a right to make a claim in arbitration in their own capacity, neither acting on behalf of their home state nor deriving their capacity from it to make such a claim, then, according to some scholars, an investor should be able to waive that right to the same extent that an individual is able to waive any other right.[125] On the other hand, if the right to bring an action under the treaty is derived from its home state, which is a party to the treaty, then a waiver of the right to make a claim in investor–state arbitration under the treaty should be ineffective because the right is not the investor's to give away.

Another approach to the problem is to inquire into the intent of the contracting states that concluded the treaty granting an aggrieved investor the right to institute arbitration against a host state for treaty violations. As revealed by treaty preambles, the purpose of investment treaties is not merely to give rights to individual investors, but to achieve the larger aims of strengthened economic relations between the two countries concerned, the promotion of capital flows between them, and their economic development and increased prosperity. To achieve these goals, states, through the treaty-making process, have constructed an elaborate regime of international rights and duties binding the contracting parties, of which the right of investors to bring claims is an important part. Investor–state arbitration plays an important role in sustaining that regime. Investor–state arbitration is not only a means to protect individual investor rights but also to assure respect of the reciprocal treaty obligations and rights by the states concerned. Thus, investor–state arbitration, like other private rights of action granted under domestic law to individuals, serves as a mechanism created by the contracting states to assure respect for treaty obligations and therefore the preservation of the treaty structure. Investors should not be allowed to permanently waive those

---

[123] *Eureko BV v Republic of Poland* (Partial Award) (19 August 2005), in which the tribunal stated:

> International law thus recognizes that an investor may, after a claim against a state has arisen, enter into a settlement agreement with that State and commit to a final waiver of those claims. The State can subsequently rely on that waiver and assert it as a defense against the investor, should such investor attempt to raise those claims again.

ibid ¶ 175.

[124] JJ Van Haersolte-Van Hof and AK Hoffmann, 'The Relationship between International Tribunals and Domestic Courts' in P Muchlinski et al (eds) *The Oxford Handbook of International Investment Law* (OUP, 2008) 962, 984.

[125] ibid 1002–3.

rights and thus risk undermining the international legal structure between the contracting states.

The only arbitral case to consider the question of waiver of the right to investor–state arbitration was *Aquas del Tunari v Bolivia* in which Bolivia argued that a provision in a concession contract by which the parties agreed to the exclusive jurisdiction of Bolivian courts to settle concession disputes constituted a waiver of ICSID jurisdiction. The tribunal concluded that the dispute resolution clause in the concession did not constitute such a waiver; however, it did state in passing that 'it would appear that an investor could also waive its right to invoke the jurisdiction of ICSID'.[126] The strength of that statement is undermined by the fact that it was irrelevant to the holding in the case but more important because the tribunal did not fully analyse the role of investor–state arbitration in the preservation of the investment regime created by investment treaties.

(h) The impetus for reform of investor–state dispute settlement

The element of the international investment regime that has drawn the most concern and criticism has been investor–state arbitration. The concerns and criticisms have several dimensions. First, the very legitimacy of a system that entrusts to private persons the power to judge the legality of regulations and measures ostensibly taken in the public interest by lawful governments, often democratically elected, has been challenged. Partisans of this view argue that it is wrong to allow arbitrators to thwart regulations and laws enacted to protect and advance vital public interests such as health, safety, security, and environmental protection. Second, the costs of the system and damage awards against state parties place a great burden on public finances and are not worth the questionable benefits to be derived from this form of dispute settlement. Third, the system is not transparent since it is possible for the parties to invoke confidentiality to prevent the public from fully understanding the workings of a process that can affect the public interest. Fourth, in individual cases, investor–state tribunals have rendered erroneous and inconsistent decisions but the investment regime affords no mechanism, such an appellate institution, by which such decisions may be corrected and a consistent jurisprudence developed. Fifth, serious questions have been raised about the impartiality and independence of arbitrators. It is often claimed that some arbitrators assume their arbitral responsibilities with preconceived notions of the facts and the applicable law and are also influenced by their other activities and interests.[127]

These concerns have provoked significant comment and thought among scholars, arbitrators, and practitioners and within government departments, NGOs,

---

[126] *Aguas El Tunari SA v Republic of Bolivia*, ICSID Case No ARB/02/3 (Decision on Respondent's Objection to Jurisdiction) (21 October 2005) 118.

[127] See generally, M Waibel et al (eds), *The Backlash Against Investment Arbitration: Perceptions and Reality* (Kluwer Law International, 2010); Gaukrodger and Gordon (n 119 above) 19; UNCTAD, *World Investment Report 2013* (2013) 111–12.

and international institutions. They have also led individual governments to take certain actions. Thus dissatisfaction with investor—state arbitration was the primary cause for countries such as South Africa, Bolivia, and Venezuela to decide not to renew BITs that have reached their termination dates, and for Venezuela, Bolivia, and Ecuador to withdraw from ICSID by denouncing its Convention.

Other countries, while leaving in place their existing investment treaties, have sought to limit or control investor—state arbitration more tightly in the new treaties they have made. Indeed, one may say that the development of a new generation of investment treaties has been prompted by the results observed over several years in investor state—arbitrations interpreting and applying the earlier generation of international investment agreements. The new generation of treaties contains more detailed definitions and other provisions, for example with regard to particularly problematic concepts such as 'fair and equitable treatment', in order to limit the discretion of arbitrators in applying them in the future. They may also provide more detailed provisions on treatment exceptions, arbitral procedure, transparency of proceedings, and submissions by non-disputing parties.[128]

Yet others have sought to narrow the scope of investor—state arbitration in their new agreements and a few countries have determined to reject any type of investor—state arbitration in their investment treaties on the grounds that it imposes unacceptable constraints on national policy-making,[129] thereby leaving their investors to local and intergovernmental remedies to resolve investor—state disputes. As of the middle of the second decade of the twenty-first century, the investment regimes dispute settlement process seemed in a state of flux and open to various possible options for reform.[130]

---

[128] eg Agreement Between the Government of Canada and the Government of the People's Republic of China for the Promotion and Reciprocal Protection of Investments (9 September 2012).
[129] eg Australia–US Free Trade Agreement (2004); Australia–Malaysia Free Trade Agreement (2011); Japan–Philippines Economic Partnership Agreement (2006).
[130] UNCTAD, *World Investment Report 2014* (2014) 125–32.

16

The Consequences of Treaty Violations

16.1 The Question of Consequences

This book began by defining international investment treaties as 'instruments of international law by which states make commitments to other states with respect to the treatment that they will accord to investors and investments from those states'. The individual chapters of this book have sought to explain the nature and content of the various treatment commitments embodied in the texts of those treaties, treaty texts that on the whole are strikingly similar in content. A final question, however, must be addressed: what are the consequences both for the state concerned and the affected foreign investment when a state acts towards an investment protected by a treaty so as to violate that state's treaty commitments? More particularly, what remedies are available to an investment when a host state fails to provide the treatment it has promised? This chapter explores that question.

16.2 The Silence of the Treaty Texts

As a general rule, investment treaties do not specifically state the consequences of a state's breach of treaty provisions. In fact, many, if not most investment treaties make no reference at all to the obligation of an offending state to pay compensation or make reparation to investors injured by a breach. In view of the fact that capital-exporting states have by and large driven the movement to negotiate and conclude investment treaties for the specific purpose of protecting investments made by their nationals in other countries, it is indeed curious that such capital-exporting states did not include a specific treaty article requiring the contracting states to abide by their provisions and pay compensation to protected investments for any injuries caused by a state's failure to do so. One can only speculate on the reason for the absence of such a clause; however, two possible explanations are worth considering. The first is that an explicit provision on damages might complicate and even frustrate entirely treaty negotiations with developing countries, which would be especially sensitive to this issue. The second is that such a clause in a negotiated treaty might prevent ratification by the legislatures of both capital-exporting and capital-importing states when confronted with the task of approving a treaty that would render their state treasuries potentially liable to pay substantial damages to a foreign government.

One cannot say that the drafters of investment treaties had no useful examples and precedents in this regard. The Abs-Shawcross Draft Convention on Investments Abroad,[1] a private initiative begun in 1957 and issued in 1959 under the leadership of Hermann Abs, then Chairman of Deutsche Bank in Germany, and Lord Shawcross, former Attorney-General of the United Kingdom, which greatly influenced the development of later investment treaty texts,[2] contained a specific provision with respect to the consequences of a treaty breach. Article IV of the Draft Convention states:

Any breach of this Convention shall entail the obligation to make full reparation. The Parties shall not recognise or enforce within their territories any measures conflicting with the principles of this Convention and affecting the property of nationals of any of the Parties until reparation is made or secured.

Although this provision does not specify the nature of the reparation to be made by the offending state, it is broad in scope in that it covers 'any' violation and obliges the offending state to make 'full' reparation. The authors' commentaries to the Draft Convention confirm that the first sentence deliberately incorporates the *Chorzów Factory restitutio in integrum* standard.[3]

One will search in vain among investment treaty texts to find a provision of equal clarity and precision with respect to the consequences of a treaty breach. For some reason, states have chosen not to follow the example set down in the Abs-Shawcross Draft Convention on treaty breaches. Indeed, most investment treaties do not specifically oblige an offending to state to make reparation for failure to fulfil its treaty commitments, grant no specific authorization to investor–state arbitral tribunals to award damages, and do not stipulate the standard of compensation that is to be applied in determining the appropriate amount of compensation to which an injured investment is entitled. Thus the France–Argentina BIT,[4] the Spain–Argentina BIT,[5] the UK–Argentina BIT,[6] and the US–Morocco BIT,[7] to mention just a few, are equally silent on these matters.

---

[1] 'Proposed Convention to Protect Private Foreign Investment: A Roundtable' (1960) 9 J Pub L 115, 116. See also UNCTAD, 'Draft Convention on Investments Abroad', International Investment Instruments: A Compendium (2005) 395, available at <http://unctad.org/en/docs/dite4volxiv_en.pdf> accessed 17 January 2015.

[2] See eg the discussion in Ch 11, section 11.3, which considers the impact of the Abs-Shawcross Draft Convention on the development of the umbrella clause.

[3] Comment on the Draft Convention by Its Authors, April 1959, (1960) 9 J Pub L 119, 122 (1960) (now Emory LJ).

[4] Accord entre le Gouvernement de la République française et le Gouvernement de la République Argentine sur l'encouragement et la protection réciproques des investissements (3 July 1991).

[5] Acuerdo para la promoción y protección recíprocas de inversiones entre el Reino de España y la República Argentina (3 October 1991).

[6] Agreement between the Government of the United Kingdom of Great Britain and Northern Ireland and the Government of the Republic of Argentina for the Promotion and Protection of Investments (11 December 1990).

[7] Treaty between the United States of America and the Kingdom of Morocco Concerning the Encouragement and Reciprocal Protection of Investments (22 July 1985).

It is true, however, that these treaties and virtually all others do have more or less detailed provisions on compensation with respect to the expropriation of protected investments. Thus, as was discussed in Chapter 12, investment treaties normally provide that a state may legally take an investment only if certain conditions are met, one of the most important of which is that the expropriating state pay compensation to the investor for the expropriated investment. The treaty will normally also stipulate in varying degrees of detail and specificity the standard of acceptable compensation and the method to be used in applying that standard in specific cases. For example, Article 5 of the France–Argentina BIT states: 'Any such dispossession measures shall give rise to the payment of prompt and adequate compensation the amount of which, calculated in accordance with the real value of the investments in question, shall be assessed of a normal economic situation prior to any threat of dispossession.'

Many scholars have noted that it is only in the context of expropriation that treaties provide guidance on compensation but that texts are generally silent about the consequences of breaches of other treaty provisions.[8] One may indeed interpret these treaty provisions on compensation for expropriation as stipulating a state's obligation to pay compensation in the event of an expropriation treaty breach and also providing for the amount of compensation that the state must pay in such circumstances. In short, according to this view, the compensation provisions on expropriation stipulate the *consequence* to an offending state of its failure to respect the treaty's provisions on dispossession of a protected investment. One may, however, also interpret such provisions in another vein: the provisions on compensation state the *conditions* for a *legal* expropriation, that is, an expropriation that does not violate the treaty. According to this interpretation, one would need to look elsewhere to find the appropriate standard to apply to an *illegal* expropriation, that is, an expropriation that did not meet the specified treaty conditions for a legal taking by a host state of an investment. The fact that no other treaty provision stipulates the consequences of its violation strengthens the view that the provisions on expropriation are intended to specify the conditions for a legal expropriation only, not the consequences of one that is illegal. At least one arbitration award, *ADC v Hungary*,[9] has adopted this interpretation. In that case, the tribunal stated:

---

[8] See eg M Kinnear, 'Damages in Investment Treaty Arbitration' in K Yannaca-Small (ed), *Arbitration Under International Investment Agreements: A Guide to the Key Issues* (OUP, 2010) 551: 'The quantum of damages to be awarded in investment treaty arbitration is often the main pre-occupation of the investor and of officials in the respondent State. As a result, it is ironic that investment treaties and investment awards give comparatively little guidance concerning the basis upon which damages ought to be awarded.' See also C Söderlund, 'Compensation under International Law in Cases of Treaty Breach Resulting in Impairment of Business Performance' (2012) 13 JWIT 279, 280; S Jagusch and N Duclos, 'Compensation for the Breach of Relative Standards of Treaty Protection' (2009) 10 JWIT 515, 522.

[9] *ADC Affiliate Ltd and ADC & ADMC Management Ltd v Republic of Hungary*, ICSID Case No ARB/03/16 (Award) (2 October 2006).

But in the present case the BIT does not stipulate any rules relating to damages payable in the case of an unlawful expropriation. The BIT only stipulates the standard of compensation that is payable in the case of a lawful expropriation, and these cannot be used to determine the issue of damages payable in the case of an unlawful expropriation since this would be to conflate compensation for a lawful expropriation with damages for an unlawful expropriation. This would have been possible if the BIT expressly provided for such a position, but this does not exist in the present case.[10]

A similar interpretational issue arises in connection with common treaty provisions, discussed in Chapter 13, concerning losses sustained by protected foreign investments due to war, armed conflict, insurrections and other similar events. Many of these provisions also mention damages, compensation, or remuneration for losses sustained in such situations. However, normally they do not grant investors an absolute right to compensation. Instead, they merely promise that protected foreign investors are to be treated in the same way as are nationals of the host country with respect to injuries suffered as a result of war, revolution, insurrections, and similar events. Thus, the Czech Republic–Ireland BIT provides:

Compensation for Losses
1. Where investments of investors of either Contracting Party suffer losses owing to war, armed conflict, a state of national emergency, revolt, insurrection, riot or other similar events in the territory of the other Contracting Party, such investors shall be accorded by the latter Contracting Party, treatment, as regards restitution, indemnification, compensation or other settlement, not less favorable than that which the latter Contracting Party accords to its own investors or to investors of any third State.
2. Without prejudice to paragraph 1 of this Article, investors of one Contracting Party who in any of the events referred to in that paragraph suffer losses in the territory of the other Contracting Party resulting from:
   a) requisitioning of their property by the forces or authorities of the latter Contracting Party; or
   b) destruction of their property by the forces or authorities of the latter Contracting Party which was not caused in combat action or was not required by the necessity of the situation,
shall be accorded restitution or prompt, adequate and effective compensation for the losses sustained during the period of the requisitioning or as a result of the destruction of the property. Resulting payments shall be freely transferable in freely convertible currency without delay.[11]

Here, too, the treaty does not specify the consequences for the host country if it fails to grant such national treatment to protected foreign investments. One may read texts of such provisions as stating the *consequences* of such failure as obliging the state to pay the investor compensation comparable to what it has paid its national investors. On the other hand, the provision may also be interpreted as

---

[10] ibid ¶ 481.
[11] Agreement between the Czech Republic and Ireland for the Promotion and Reciprocal Protection of Investments (28 June 1996), Art 4.

stipulating the conditions necessary for the host state to comply with the treaty, but not the consequences if it fails to do so.

While no treaty is as explicit and as far-reaching as Article IV of the Abs-Shawcross Draft Convention, quoted earlier, some international investment agreements have specifically authorized and recognized the power of arbitral tribunals to award compensation in investor–state arbitrations. For example, Article 1135 of the North American Free Trade Agreement (NAFTA), which governs final awards in investor–state disputes, provides:

Article 1135: Final Award
1. Where a Tribunal makes a final award against a Party, the Tribunal may award, separately or in combination, only:
   (a) monetary damages and any applicable interest;
   (b) restitution of property, in which case the award shall provide that the disputing Party may pay monetary damages and any applicable interest in lieu of restitution.
   A tribunal may also award costs in accordance with the applicable arbitration rules.
2. Subject to paragraph 1, where a claim is made under Article 1117(1):
   (a) an award of restitution of property shall provide that restitution be made to the enterprise;
   (b) an award of monetary damages and any applicable interest shall provide that the sum be paid to the enterprise; and
   (c) the award shall provide that it is made without prejudice to any right that any person may have in the relief under applicable domestic law.
3. A Tribunal may not order a Party to pay punitive damages.

The 2012 United States Model BIT,[12] the ASEAN Comprehensive Investment Agreement of 2012,[13] and other more recent treaties contain similar language.[14] While the Energy Charter Treaty (ECT) contains no specific authorization for tribunals to award damages in case of breaches of the treaty, there appears to be an implicit authorization in Article 26(8), which states that 'arbitration awards may include an award of interest', a provision which would only be feasible if the award contained monetary damages, and also that '[a]n award of arbitration concerning a measure of a sub-national government or authority of the disputing Contracting Party shall provide that the Contracting Party may pay monetary damages in lieu of any other remedy granted'.[15]

---

[12] 2012 US Model BIT, Art 34.
[13] ASEAN Comprehensive Investment Agreement, Art 41.
[14] See eg Agreement Between the Government of Canada and the Government of the Republic of Latvia for the Promotion and Protection of Investments (5 May 2009), Art XIII(9), which provides:

A tribunal may award, separately or in combination, only:

a. monetary damages and any applicable interest;
b. restitution of property, in which case the award shall provide that the disputing Contracting Party may pay monetary damages and any applicable interest in lieu of restitution.

A tribunal may also award costs in accordance with the applicable arbitration rules.

[15] ECT, Art 26(8).

On the other hand, Article 48(3) of the ICSID Convention states that 'The award shall deal with every question submitted to the Tribunal'. Furthermore, Article 54 of the ICSID Convention imposes on member states the obligation 'to recognize an award rendered pursuant to this Convention as binding and enforce the *pecuniary obligations* imposed by that award' (emphasis added), thus recognizing implicitly the power of an ICSID tribunal to award compensation in appropriate cases. However, the Arbitration Rules of the United Nations Commission on International Trade Law (UNCITRAL), commonly applicable in cases not covered by the ICSID Convention, contains no similar specific reference to the award of damages or the imposition of pecuniary obligations on a respondent.

16.3 Application of Customary International Law on State Responsibility

The foregoing discussion raises a fundamental question of investment treaty interpretation: what inference is one to draw from the fact that most investment treaties do not specifically state the consequences to a contracting state for a failure to meet its treaty obligations to foreign investments ostensibly protected by such treaties? How is one to interpret the failure of most treaty texts to specifically authorize arbitration tribunals to award monetary damages and the absence in virtually all treaties of any guidance on how tribunals should determine the amount of damages to award in the event of a treaty breach? The silence of treaty texts on these matters might lead one to conclude that the contracting states did not intend to authorize the payment of monetary damages for breaches of investment treaties and that therefore arbitral tribunals have no such power. The purpose of investor–state arbitration, according to this view, would merely be to render a determination of the respective legal rights and obligations of the parties, not to determine the consequences of a violation of those rights and obligations, including the amount of damages to be paid. In such instance, investor–state arbitration would seem to have little effect, except perhaps to afford the parties an authoritative statement of their respective rights and obligations that might serve as a basis for negotiating a settlement of an investor's claims against a host state. In view of the traditional role accorded arbitration in the international domain in determining damages for international wrongs, it would not seem reasonable for a treaty to establish an investor–state arbitral mechanism without such power, unless the treaty text explicitly so provided. Moreover, no arbitration tribunal appears to have taken the position that it has no power to award damages, and it appears that no state, facing a claim of damages for a treaty breach, has seriously pressed this argument. Indeed, arbitral tribunals have consistently held implicitly or explicitly that if a tribunal has jurisdiction to decide a dispute it also has jurisdiction to decide on reparation and damages.[16]

While investment treaties generally do not specify rules on damages for failure to respect their provisions, they nearly always provide that tribunals are to decide disputes not only in accordance with the applicable treaty provisions but also in accordance with 'the relevant principles of international law',[17] 'the general principles of international law',[18] or 'the applicable principles of international law'.[19] Thus, all investment treaties stipulate that international law, customary international law, or some variation of that formulation is the source of law that tribunals are to apply in deciding the issues that they confront, which of course includes compensation for investments that have been injured by a contracting state's failure to respect treaty provisions. As a result, arbitral tribunals in treaty-based, investor–state disputes look to customary international law for the applicable principles to follow in determining and quantifying compensation that states must make to investments injured by failures to respect investment treaty commitments on investment treatment.[20]

Pursuant to Article 26 (*Pacta Sunt Servanda*) of the Vienna Convention of the Law of Treaties (VCLT), a provision that also embodies a fundamental principle of customary international law: 'Every treaty in force is binding upon the parties to it and must be performed by them in good faith.'[21] The treatment promised by a state to investments from a treaty partner therefore constitutes an obligation under international law. Article 2 of the Draft Articles on Responsibility of States for Internationally Wrongful Acts,[22] which is generally considered as an

---

[16] *AIG Capital Partners, Inc and CJSC Tema Real Estate Co v Republic of Kazakhstan*, ICSID Case No ARB/01/6 (Award) (7 October 2003). ¶ 12.1: 'It is settled law that where a Court or a Tribunal has jurisdiction to determine a dispute, it also has jurisdiction to determine reparation or compensation.'; *SwemBalt AB, Sweden v Republic of Latvia*, UNCITRAL (Decision by the Court of Arbitration) (23 October 2000) ¶ 38: 'It seems clear that when Article 7 of the Investment Agreement refers disputes concerning the interpretation or application of the Agreement to arbitration, the intention has been to permit the arbitral tribunal to decide not only the existence or not of a breach of the Agreement, but also any consequences of such breach.'

[17] Accord entre le Gouvernement de la République française et le Gouvernement de la République Argentine sur l'encouragement et la protection réciproques des investissements (3 July 1991), Art 8.

[18] Acuerdo para la promoción y protección recíprocas de inversiones entre el Reino de España y la República Argentina (3 October 1991), Art X(5).

[19] Agreement between the Government of the United Kingdom of Great Britain and Northern Ireland and the Government of the Republic of Argentina for the Promotion and Protection of Investments (11 December 1990), Art 8(4).

[20] See eg *National Grid plc v The Argentine Republic*, UNCITRAL (Award) (3 November 2008) ¶ 269; *LG&E v The Argentine Republic*, ICSID Case No ARB/02/1 (Award) (25 July 2008) ¶¶ 29–32; *SD Meyers, Inc v Government of Canada*, UNCITRAL (Partial Award) (13 November 2000) ¶¶ 310, 315; *BG Group plc v Republic of Argentina*, UNCITRAL (Final Award) (24 December 2007) ¶ 422.

[21] Vienna Convention on the Law of Treaties (23 May 1969) 1155 UNTS 331 (VCLT).

[22] United Nations, *Draft Articles on Responsibility of States for Internationally Wrongful Acts, with commentaries*, 2001 (2008), adopted by the International Law Commission at its fifty-third session, in 2001, and submitted to the General Assembly as part of the Commission's Report covering that session, available at <http://legal.un.org/ilc/texts/instruments/english/commentaries/9_6_2001.pdf> accessed 17 January 2015.

authoritative restatement of international law, and one on which many tribunals have relied,[23] states:

There is an international wrongful act of a State when conduct consisting of an act or omission:
(a) is attributable to the State under international law; and
(b) constitutes a breach of an international obligation of the State.

The acts and omissions of a state in denying an investment the treatment promised under an applicable treaty are therefore internationally wrongful acts. An act or omission is attributable to a contracting state if such act or omission is done by a state organ.[24] Article 1 of the Draft Articles provides: '[e]very wrongful act of a State entails the international responsibility of that state'. The comment to Article 1 makes clear that the term 'international responsibility' 'covers the new legal relations which arise under international law by reason of the internationally wrongful act of a State'.[25] A state, by reason of not respecting its obligations under a treaty, is therefore subject to a new relationship towards the injured investment. Inherent in that relationship is the obligation to compensate the parties injured as a result of the state's failure to fulfil its international obligations.

16.4 Investment Treaty Remedies in General

A state responsible for an internationally wrongful act is, according to Article 31(1) of the Draft Articles, 'under an obligation to make full reparation for the injury caused by [its] internationally wrongful act'. 'Injury', in this sense, 'includes any damage, whether material or moral, caused by the internationally wrongful act of a State'.[26] Thus, there must be a causal link between the internationally wrongful act and the injury for which reparation is claimed. If such a link exists, the responsible state is required to make 'full reparation' for the injury it has caused.

As the Draft Articles state, reparation for an injury caused by an internationally wrongful act 'shall take the form of restitution, compensation and satisfaction, either singly or in combination'.[27] In virtually all investor–state cases, claimants are seeking compensation for injuries they claim to have sustained as a result of a treaty breach. With respect to the meaning of 'full reparation' required by Article 31 quoted previously, Article 36 of the Draft Articles makes clear that

---

[23] See eg *Emilio Agustín Maffezini v The Kingdom of Spain*, ICSID Case No Arb/97/7 (Decision of the Tribunal on Objections to Jurisdiction) (25 January 2000) ¶ 78; *White Industries Australia Ltd v The Republic of India*, UNCITRAL (Final Award) (30 November 2011) ¶¶ 8.1.1–8.1.21; *Ioannis Kardassopoulos and Ron Fuchs v The Republic of Georgia*, ICSID Case No ARB/07/15 (Award) (3 March 2010) ¶¶ 532–34.

[24] Draft Articles, Art 4(1) provides: 'The conduct of any state organ shall be considered an act of that State under international law, whether the organ exercises legislative, executive, judicial, or any other functions, whatever position it holds in the organization of the state, and whatever its character as an organ of the central Government or of a territorial unit of the State.'

[25] Draft Articles, Commentary to Art 1(1).   [26] Draft Articles, Art 31(2).

[27] Draft Articles, Art 34.

'[t]he State responsible for an internationally wrongful act is under an obligation to compensate for the damage caused thereby, insofar as such damage is not made good by restitution' and that '[t]he compensation shall cover any financially assessable damage including lost profits insofar as it is established'. Thus the basic standard to be applied is that of full compensation (*restitutio in integrum*) for the loss incurred as a result of the internationally wrongful act. This statement represents the accepted standard in customary international law and is often supported by reference to the *Chorzów Factory Case* in which the Permanent Court of International Justice stated: '[I]t is a principle of international law, and even a general conception of law, that any breach of an engagement involves an obligation to make reparation.'[28] Also:

The essential principle contained in the actual notion of an illegal act—a principle which seems to be established by international practice and in particular by the decisions of arbitral tribunals—is that reparation must, so far as possible, wipe out all the consequences of the illegal act and reestablish the situation which would, in all probability, have existed if that act had not been committed.[29]

Customary law therefore requires a tribunal to award 'full compensation' to a claimant for the injuries to an investment caused by a state's treaty violations, to seek 'to wipe out all the consequences' of that state's illegal acts, and to place the claimants 'in the situation which would, in all probability, have existed' if that state had not committed its illegal acts. Moreover, it should be noted that in order to ensure full compensation to injured parties, customary international law authorizes the payment of interest on the principal sum due from the time the amount should have been paid until the date when the payment obligation is actually fulfilled.[30]

The application of the aforementioned customary international law principles on damages is in theory rather simple. It requires a tribunal to engage in a three-step process. First, it must determine the value of the investment in the hypothetical situation where the offending state did not take measures that violated its treaty obligations, a situation that may be called 'without measures'. Second, it must then determine the value of the investment as a result of the offending measures that the state actually took, a situation that may be called 'with measures'. Third, a tribunal must next subtract the second value from the first and then actualize that amount to present value by means of an appropriate rate of interest to arrive at the damages owing to the injured investors in order to

[28] *The Factory at Chorzów (Germany v Poland)* (Judgment) (13 September), 1928 PCIJ, Series A, No 17, at 29.
[29] ibid 47.
[30] Draft Articles, Art 38 provides:
  1. Interest on any principal sum due under this chapter shall be payable when necessary in order to ensure full reparation. The interest rate and mode of calculation shall be set so as to achieve that result.
  2. Interest runs from the date when the principal sum should have been paid until the date the obligation to pay is fulfilled.

put them in the financial position in which they would have been had the state not breached the applicable investment treaty.[31] One may embody this simple idea in the following equally simple formula, in which V is equal to the value of the investment in the two situations: **Damages = V without measures – V with measures**. In many instances of treaty violations, for example outright seizure of an investment by the state without compensation, the value of the investment in the second of the previously-described situations will be zero. In other situations, for example where a state through regulatory action fails to accord an investment 'fair and equitable treatment' or to grant it 'full protection and security', the injured investment may still have residual value of which a tribunal in determining damages must take account.

While the aforementioned theory and basic legal principles governing damages in investor–state conflicts may appear simple, in practice their application in actual cases is far more complicated. Specifically, it requires tribunals and counsel for claimants and governments to venture outside legal science into the usually unfamiliar domain of finance in order to determine the value in monetary terms of the allegedly injured investment in the two situations just described, one of which, the 'without measures situation', is hypothetical and requires tribunals, lawyers, and their experts to construct a scenario as to what would have happened to the value of the investment in question if the host state had not violated the applicable treaty. In order to determine the value of the loss to an injured investment, one must have recourse to valuation techniques drawn from the science of finance.

16.5 Valuation Techniques and Damages

(a) In general

It is often said that 'valuation is more art than science'. One of the reasons for this sentiment is that many diverse, seemingly scientific valuation methods can be applied in different ways to arrive at different results. This diversity of valuation methods is apparent in the calculation of investor compensation in cases of expropriation.[32] One of the reasons for this diversity of methods is that investment treaties do not provide guidance on the specific methodology to be applied in

---

[31] *AIG Capital Partners, Inc and CJSC Tema Real Estate Co v Republic of Kazakhstan*, ICSID Case No ARB/01/6 (Award) (7 October 2003) ¶ 12.1.1: 'The standard for compensation adopted in cases of expropriation of investments and enterprises has been the restoration of the Claimant to the position it would have enjoyed but for the taking: this has now ripened into and has been recognized as a principle of customary international law.'

[32] TW Wälde and B Sabhi, 'Compensation, Damages, and Valuation' in P Muchlinski et al (eds), *The Oxford Handbook of International Investment Law* (OUP, 2008) 1049, 1070–82; M Ball, 'Assessing Damages in Claims by Investors Against States' (2001) 16 ICSID Rev—FILJ 408; A Newcombe and L Paradell, *Law and Practice of Investment Treaties: Standards of Treatment* (Kluwer Law International, 2009) 385.

deciding on 'fair market value', 'real value', 'adequate compensation', or whatever compensation standard may be specified in the treaty.

Compensation for injury requires a standard for determining precisely what an injured party should receive as a result of a state's wrongful conduct. As noted in Chapter 3, before the development of investment treaties, considerable disagreement existed within the international community regarding what standard should be applied in cases of expropriation. One of the purposes of the investment treaty movement was to end that debate by agreeing to an international standard. In a reflection of the increasing convergence on the issue, many treaties have adopted some version of the 'Hull formula', which requires that compensation should be 'prompt, adequate and effective'.[33] The term 'prompt' generally means that payment should be made without undue delay. 'Effective' means that the payment should be made in realizable and readily transferable currency; accordingly, payment in forty-year bonds denominated in local currency, for example, would not be considered effective. 'Adequate' compensation has been much more difficult to define. In a real sense, in the contentious relationships between offending states and aggrieved investors, adequacy exists in the eye of the beholder. Treaties have therefore sought to give greater precision to the standard with respect to expropriation, although as noted earlier they usually provide no guidance whatsoever with respect to other treaty violations.

Rather than leave the interpretation of the standard of prompt, adequate, and effective compensation solely to the discretion of arbitrators, many investment treaties define the terms in detail and provide instruction for their application. For instance, it is common for investment treaties to specify that the investor shall be owed the 'market value' of the investment before the expropriatory act was taken or became known to the public. Moreover, treaties also authorize tribunals to award interest on the amount owing from the date of expropriation until the respondent state pays the injured investor. For example, Article 5(2) of the Korea–Congo BIT, while requiring compensation for expropriation to be 'prompt, adequate and effective', also provides that such compensation shall amount to:

the fair market value of the expropriated investments immediately before the expropriation took place or before the impending expropriation became public knowledge, whichever is the earlier, shall include interest at the applicable commercial rate from the date of expropriation until the date of payment, and shall be made without undue delay, be effectively realizable, and be freely transferable.[34]

Similarly, Article 1110.2 of NAFTA seeks to set down a standard for compensation with some degree of specificity:

Compensation shall be equivalent to the fair market value of the expropriated investment immediately before the expropriation took place ('date of expropriation'), and shall not

---

[33] UNCTAD, *Bilateral Investment Treaties in 1995–2006: Trends in Investment Rulemaking* (2007) 48; R Dolzer and C Schreuer, *Principles of International Investment Law* (OUP, 2008) 91.

[34] Agreement between the Government of the Republic of Korea and the Government of the Democratic Republic of Congo for the Promotion and Protection of Investments (17 March 2005).

reflect any change in value occurring because the intended expropriation had become known earlier. Valuation criteria shall include going concern value, asset value (including declared tax value of tangible property) and other criteria, as appropriate to determine fair market value.

Subsequent paragraphs of Article 1110 specify that compensation is to be paid without delay, that it shall include interest at commercial rates from the date of expropriation to the date of payment, and that upon payment the compensation will be freely transferable.

A few treaties are less specific in establishing standards of compensation. Instead of market value, they may require 'real value',[35] 'reasonable compensation',[36] or simply 'compensation'.[37] These formulations of a treaty's standard for compensation provide ample room for controversy as to their meaning and application in specific expropriation cases. Therefore, they may have the net effect of increasing investors' insecurity about their rights in cases of expropriation. For example, a standard of 'just compensation' would allow a state to offset environmental or other damage, while the 'market value' is less amenable to such an interpretation. Indeed, the concept of market value seems to be more concrete and so may be more easily applied than other options employed in international treaties.

Even a treaty's specific promise to pay market value for expropriated investments may be problematic in specific cases. For one thing, investment treaties rarely define in detail the specific meaning of 'market value' or 'effective compensation'. Consequently, the very content of the standard may become a subject of controversy between aggrieved investors and offending host states. Arbitral tribunals have defined the term by drawing on the notion of a market transaction between willing buyers and sellers. Thus, one useful definition of market value, elaborated by the Iran–US Claims Tribunal in *Starrett Housing Corporation v Iran*, is 'the price that a willing buyer would pay to a willing seller in circumstances in which each had good information, each desired to maximize his financial gain, and neither was under duress or threat, the willing buyer being a reasonable person'.[38]

---

[35] Agreement between the Government of the Kingdom of Thailand and the Government of the Hong Kong Special Administrative Region of the People's Republic of China for the Promotion and Protection of Investments (19 November 2005), Art 5(1).

[36] Agreement between the Government of Australia and the Government of the People's Republic of China on the Reciprocal Encouragement and Protection of Investments (11 July 1988), Art 8.1.

[37] Agreement on the Encouragement and Protection of Investments between the Government of Hong Kong and the Government of the Kingdom of the Netherlands (19 November 1992), Art 5(1).

[38] *Starrett Housing Corp v Iran*, 16 Iran–USCTR 112, 201 (Final Award). See also World Bank Guidelines on the Treatment of Foreign Direct Investment (1992), IV(5):

> In the absence of a determination on agreed by, or based on the agreement of, the parties, the fair market value will be acceptable if determined by the State according to reasonable criteria related to the market value of the investment, i.e., in an amount that a willing buyer would normally pay to a willing seller after taking into account the nature of the investment, the circumstances in which it would operate in the future and its specific characteristics, including the period in which it has been in existence, the proportion of tangible assets in the total investment and other relevant factors pertinent to the specific circumstances of each case.

The ultimate goal of any valuation process in an investor–state dispute is to determine the market value of a specific asset in two instances: (1) what a willing buyer would pay to a willing seller for the investment had the state respected its treaty commitments; and (2) what a willing buyer would pay to a willing seller for the investment that has sustained injury as a result of a treaty breach. Similarly, in compensating an investor for an injury sustained to an investment as a result of the breach of a treaty by a contracting state, the goal is also to determine the market value—what a willing buyer would pay a willing seller for what was lost just prior to the action taken by the state in violation of the treaty that caused the financial injury to the investor. The problem in applying this standard is that no market for the injured asset usually exists to which one can readily refer. So, while the definition of market value just quoted is helpful, neither it nor investment treaties employing it explain precisely how to apply the concept to injured assets in particular cases. Indeed, often the determination of what a willing buyer would pay a willing seller for an expropriated asset prior to the expropriation is a highly speculative exercise. In fact, in many cases no willing buyer or willing seller for such an asset exists to provide concrete data for such a determination.

As a result, tribunals and others concerned with the evaluation of injuries to investments must have recourse to a variety of techniques whose purpose is to arrive at an approximation of what that fair market value would be if a fair market existed.

The literature on valuation is extensive[39] and highly technical. The purpose of the final section of the chapter is merely to introduce the reader to the general approaches used by financial experts and tribunals in arriving at a monetary award that approximates the market value of an investment injured by a treaty breach.

(b) Three basic approaches to valuation

In the absence of such treaty-based guidance, parties and their experts have employed a variety of valuation techniques from the fields of finance and economics, none of which are specifically authorized by investment treaty provisions. Basically, these diverse techniques reflect three general approaches to valuation: (1) the market or sales comparison approach; (2) the income approach; and (3) asset-based or cost approach.[40] Each of these three approaches has numerous variations as to how they are applied.

---

[39] See generally, I Marboe, *Calculation of Compensation and Damages in International Investment Law* (OUP, 2009); S Ripinsky and K Williams, *Damages in International Investment Law* (British Institute of International and Comparative Law, 2008); M Kantor, *Valuation for Arbitration* (Kluwer Law International, 2008). Transnational Dispute Management has published a number of articles in the category 'Compensation and Damages in International Investment Arbitration', available at <http://www.transnational-dispute-management.com/journal-categories-articles.asp?cat=51> accessed 17 January 2015.

[40] For a full discussion of each of these approaches and the ways in which tribunals have used them, see Marboe (n 39 above) 185–315. See also Ripinsky and Williams (n 39 above).

(i) Market or sales comparison approaches

The market or sales comparison approach is based on two assumptions. First, if an active market exists for the asset subject to valuation, the best source for determining what a willing buyer would pay a willing seller for that asset is that market itself. Thus, if a tribunal is seeking to value a machine destroyed by government action or inaction, the best source of information for valuing that machine is the current market in which it is bought and sold. Second, if an active market for a specific asset does not currently exist, one may nonetheless arrive at a fair approximation of the market value of that asset by examining the purchases and sales of similar assets that have been transacted in the market. Thus, this approach makes a value determination by engaging in a process of making comparisons. The principal problem in applying this approach is finding an appropriate comparator.

Comparators that have been used include share prices, prior transactions, and comparable sales of the identical or similar assets.[41] Thus in the case of *American International Group v Iran*, a decision of the Iran–US Claims Tribunal, in valuing the claimant's investment lost as a result of the 1979 Iran revolution, the tribunal relied heavily on the prices of the shares before the expropriation of the claimant's stake by the new Iranian government.[42] On the other hand, the less the similarity between the comparator and the asset lost, the more it will be open to challenge by a respondent state.

(ii) Income capitalization approaches

Among financial experts, the prevailing view is that the value of an asset or business is best determined as a function of the benefits or the income that it will yield its owner. According to this view, the proper approach to valuing such asset or business is to calculate the total future financial benefits that the assets will provide and then to discount that amount to its present value. Various methodologies have developed using this income capitalization approach. One of the most used methods is discounted cash flow (DCF). This approach first requires a tribunal to calculate the total amount of income that will be derived from the asset or business in the future in the absence of any treaty violation, an exercise that is usually fraught with uncertainty since it necessitates a prediction about an uncertain future. The DCF method then requires a determination of the appropriate discount rate to be applied in the exercise, a rate that will need to take account of several variables, including the risk to be attached to that income stream and the prevailing cost of capital. Going-concern value or DCF is thus a forward-looking method that values the enterprise on the basis of its future expected cash flow and then, using a discount rate that takes account of the cost of capital and risk, discounts that estimated cash flow to arrive at a present value.

---

[41] See *Ioannis Kardassopoulos and Ron Fuchs v Georgia*, ICSID Case No ARB/07/15 (Award) (3 March 2010) ¶¶ 539–600.

[42] *American International Group v Iran* (1983) 4 Iran-US CTR 96, 106–9.

While financial experts are entirely comfortable in applying DCF and its variants to value an asset, tribunals have often viewed this methodology with scepticism, not because they doubt the soundness of the methodology but because they question the evidentiary validity of the estimates of income projections and the reliability of chosen discount rates. Many tribunals have been reluctant to adopt income capitalization in awarding damages in investor–state disputes because of what they considered the 'speculative' nature of the results of such a valuation, particularly where the business to be valued had not been in existence long enough to establish a reliable record of earnings on which the DCF or similar income methodology might be used.[43] While they recognize that income capitalization methods are common in business as a way of valuing businesses and asset transactions, they have argued that it would be inappropriate to compare the situation of an investor and a state in a dispute over the breach of investment treaty to buyers and sellers in the marketplace. As the tribunal stated in *CME v Czech Republic*:

there is no disagreement between the parties as to the fact that each of these methods are among '*the most common means by which buyers and sellers come to conclusions about company value*'. However, such '*conclusions about company value*' are generally not undertaken in the context of determining the extent to which one party may or may not be liable for damages. (emphasis in original)[44]

(iii) Asset-based or cost approaches

The asset-based or cost approaches look to the value of the components of an asset or business in order to determine its total value. In comparison to income approaches, asset-based or cost approaches have the advantage of not requiring tribunals to speculate about the future incomes to be derived from the asset or to arrive at complex calculations about an appropriate discount rate.[45] Asset-based

---

[43] See eg *Mr Franck Charles Arif v Republic of Moldova*, ICSID Case No ARB/11/23 (Award) (8 April 2013) ¶ 576; *Wena Hotels Ltd v Arab Republic of Egypt*, ICSID Case No ARB/98/4 (Award) (8 December 2000) ¶¶ 123–128; *Compañía de Aguas del Aconquija SA and Vivendi Universal SA v Argentine Republic*, ICSID Case No ARB/97/3 (Award) (20 August 2007) ¶¶ 8.3.1–8.3.13; *Mohammad Ammar Al-Bahloul v Republic of Tajikistan*, SCC Case No V064/2008 (Final Award) (8 June 2010) ¶¶ 71–99.

[44] *CME Czech Republic BV v Czech Republic*, UNCITRAL (Final Award) (14 March 2003) ¶ 359.

[45] The tribunal in *Vivendi v Argentina (II)* decided to turn to alternative means of valuation because future lost profits could not be relied on. The tribunal considered '"book value"—the net value of an enterprise's assets, "investment value"—the amount actually invested prior to the injurious acts, "replacement value"—the amount necessary to replace the investment prior to injurious acts, or "liquidation value"—the amount a willing buyer would pay a willing seller for the investment in a liquidation process', and ultimately selected 'investment value'. *Compañía de Aguas del Aconquija SA and Vivendi Universal SA v Argentine Republic*, ICSID Case No ARB/97/3 (Award) (20 August 2007) ¶¶ 8.3.11–8.3.13. See also *Metalclad Corp v United Mexican States*, ICSID Case No ARB(AF)/97/1 (Award) (30 August 2000) ¶¶ 121–122: 'The Tribunal agrees with Mexico that a discounted cash flow analysis is inappropriate in the present case because the landfill was never operative and any award based on future profits would be wholly speculative... the Tribunal agrees with the parties that fair market value is best arrived at in this case by reference to Metalclad's actual investment in the project.'

or cost approaches are focused largely on the past, not the future, and therefore risk depriving the claimant of the *current* value of the loss to an investment, that is, the value required by international law, for it is the current value that will place the investor in the position that it would have been in had the treaty violation not taken place.

Three methodological variations of asset-based or cost approaches are to be found in arbitral awards:

1. *book value*, which is based on the actual costs incurred to establish the investment as those costs are reflected on the books (ie the balance sheet) of the affected enterprise;

2. *replacement value*, which is the amount needed to acquire an asset of the same type as that which was expropriated or injured due to a treaty breach; and

3. *liquidation value*, which is what a willing buyer would pay for the assets of the expropriated enterprise in liquidation.

When applied to the same set of facts, each of these methods may result in a considerable variation in value. The choice of the appropriate method and how it should be applied is always the subject of significant dispute among the parties. While individual tribunals and negotiators usually arrive at a pragmatic answer, the law of investment treaties gives little guidance to them in choosing and using valuation methods.

Index